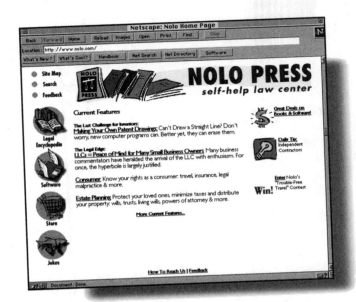

Fourth Edition

PLAN YOUR ESTATE

*A*bsolutely everything you
need to know to protect
your loved ones

by attorneys Denis Clifford & Cora Jordan

NOLO PRESS BERKELEY

YOUR RESPONSIBILITY WHEN USING A SELF-HELP LAW BOOK

We've done our best to give you useful and accurate information in this book. But laws and procedures change frequently and are subject to differing interpretations. If you want legal advice backed by a guarantee, see a lawyer. If you use this book, it's your responsibility to make sure that the facts and general advice contained in it are applicable to your situation.

KEEPING UP TO DATE

To keep its books up to date, Nolo Press issues new printings and new editions periodically. New printings reflect minor legal changes and technical corrections. New editions contain major legal changes, major text additions or major reorganizations. To find out if a later printing or edition of any Nolo book is available, call Nolo Press at 510-549-1976 or check the catalog in the *Nolo News,* our quarterly newspaper. You can also contact us on the Internet at www.nolo.com.

To stay current, follow the "Update" service in the *Nolo News.* You can get a free one-year subscription by sending us the registration card in the back of the book. In another effort to help you use Nolo's latest materials, we offer a 25% discount off the purchase of the new edition of your Nolo book when you turn in the cover of an earlier edition. (See the "Special Upgrade Offer" in the back of the book.)

This book was last revised in: **April 1998.**

FOURTH EDITION

Book Design	JACKIE MANCUSO
Cover Design	TONI IHARA
Illustrator	MARI STEIN
Production	STEPHANIE HAROLDE
Proofreader	ROBERT WELLS
Indexer	JANE MEYERHOFER
Printing	CONSOLIDATED PRINTERS, INC.

Clifford, Denis.
    Plan your estate / by Denis Clifford & Cora Jordan. -- 4th ed.
      p. cm.
    Includes index.
    ISBN 0-87337-390-1
    1. Estate planning--United States--Popular works. I. Jordan,
Cora, 1941-   . II. Title.
KF750.Z9C59 1997
346.7305'2--dc21

97-20516
CIP

Quantity sales: For information on bulk purchases or corporate premium sales, please contact the Special Sales department. For academic sales or textbook adoptions, ask for Academic Sales. 800-955-4775, Nolo Press, Inc., 950 Parker St., Berkeley, CA, 94710.

ACKNOWLEDGEMENTS

Even more than most Nolo books, this one would never have seen the light of day without the generous efforts and contributions of many fine people. So our thanks to all those friends who helped us with this book, both putting it together and with previous editions over the years:

Four friends at Nolo Press, without whose efforts this book wouldn't have existed: Jake Warner, as ever, a great editor, writer and critic; Mary Randolph, a uniquely gifted and great editor, writer and organizer extraordinaire; Barbara Kate Repa, another superb editor and writer; and Stephanie Harolde, who over many years read all of our editing scrawls and turned them into coherent pages, and also did much fine editing as she was preparing yet another draft of the manuscript.

Mark Peery of Greenbrae, California, a superb estate planning lawyer (and great friend).

All our other friends and colleagues at Nolo Press. In the past, we've listed everyone, but now we have 70 or more employees, plus more outside writers and an employee manual. Still, Nolo retains the relaxed, friendly atmosphere that makes it such a pleasant (as well as productive) place to work.

Dorcas Moulton, Amanda Cherrin and Naomi Puro, for their contributions to the cover painting on the original book.

Ken Fischer, Concord, California, a fine insurance agent; Bill Hudspeth, Austin Trust Co., Austin, Texas; Magdelen Gaynor, another fine estate planning attorney, White Plains, New York; Adalene Pettis of State Farm Insurance Co.; and James Wickett of the National Federation of Independent Businesses.

And our continued appreciation to other friends who also helped with other editions of this book: David Marcus; Paul Remack, R.G. Financial Service, San Francisco; Dave Brown, Peter Jan Honigsberg, Robert Wood of Athearn, Chandler & Hoffman, San Francisco; members of the Bay Area Funeral Society, Walter Warner; people who helped prepare the manuscript—Sandy Wieker, Christy Rigg, Cathy Cummings and Bethany Korwin-Pawloski; and Keija Kimura, Carol Pladsen and Linda Allison.

And finally, but certainly not leastly, Denis's heartfelt thanks to the many readers who have written to him with suggestions, comments, corrections and other thoughts for improving earlier editions of this book.

TABLE OF CONTENTS

INTRODUCTION: HOW TO USE THIS BOOK

A. How This Book Works I/3

B. Will You Need Professional Help? I/4

C. Other Nolo Resources I/5

PART I: SETTING YOUR GOALS

1

SELECTING YOUR ESTATE PLANNING GOALS

Part I: Setting Your Goals 1/2

Part II: Laying the Groundwork 1/2

Part III: Children 1/3

Part IV: Wills 1/4

Part V: Probate and How to Avoid It 1/4

Part VI: Understanding Estate and Gift Taxes 1/6

Part VII: Reducing or Eliminating Estate Taxes 1/7

Part VIII: Imposing Controls Over Property 1/8

Part IX: Taking Care of Personal Issues 1/9

Part X: Family Business Estate Planning 1/10

Part XI: Going Further 1/11

Part XII: Sample Estate Plans 1/11

2

PERSONAL CONCERNS AND ESTATE PLANNING

A. Avoiding Conflict 2/2

B. Leaving Unequal Amounts of Property to Children 2/5

C. Providing Care for Minor Children 2/7

D. Subsequent Marriages 2/8

E. Long-Term Care for a Child With Special Needs 2/9

F. Concerns of Unmarried Couples 2/10

G. Worries About the Effect of Inheriting Money 2/11

H. Disinheriting People, Including Children 2/12

I. Communicating Your Decisions to Family and Friends 2/13

PART II: LAYING THE GROUNDWORK

3

SPECIAL PROPERTY OWNERSHIP RULES FOR MARRIED PEOPLE

A. What You Need to Know 3/3

B. Marital Property in Community Property States 3/5

C. Marital Property in Common Law States 3/7

D. Moving to a Different State 3/9

4

INVENTORYING YOUR PROPERTY

A. Instructions for the Property Inventory Worksheet 4/2

B. Your Property Worksheet 4/8

5

YOUR BENEFICIARIES

A. Types of Beneficiaries 5/3

B. Primary Beneficiaries 5/3

C. Life Estate Beneficiaries and Final Beneficiaries 5/6

D. Alternate Beneficiaries 5/6

E. Residuary Beneficiaries 5/7

F. Gifts Shared by More Than One Beneficiary 5/7

G. Establishing a Survivorship Period 5/8

H. Explanations and Commentary Accompanying Gifts 5/8
I. Disinheritance 5/9
J. Simultaneous Death 5/10
K. Property You Give Away by Will or Trust That You No
   Longer Own at Your Death 5/11

Part III: Children

6

Children

A. Naming Someone to Take Custody of Your Minor Children 6/2
B. Naming an Adult to Manage Your Child's Property 6/5
C. How Your Children's Property Should Be Managed 6/6
D. Naming Children as Beneficiaries of Life Insurance 6/14
E. Leaving Property to Children Who Are Not Your Own 6/14
F. Disinheritance 6/15

Part IV: Wills

7

Wills

A. A Will as the Centerpiece of Your Estate Plan 7/2
B. A Back-Up Will With a Comprehensive Estate Plan 7/2
C. What Makes a Will Legal? 7/4
D. Types of Wills 7/5
E. What Property Cannot Be Transferred by Will? 7/7
F. Can My Will Be Successfully Challenged? 7/8
G. Keeping Your Will Up to Date 7/8

PART V: PROBATE AND HOW TO AVOID IT

8

PROBATE AND WHY YOU WANT TO AVOID IT

A. What Is Probate? 8/2

B. Probate Fees 8/3

C. Avoiding Probate 8/4

D. When You May Want Probate 8/8

E. Debts, Taxes and Probate Avoidance 8/8

F. Probate Reform 8/9

9

LIVING TRUSTS

A. Does Everyone Need a Living Trust? 9/2

B. Living Trusts Explained 9/4

C. Major Decisions in Creating a Living Trust 9/8

D. Creating a Valid Living Trust 9/12

E. Keeping Your Living Trust Up to Date 9/14

10

JOINT TENANCY AND TENANCY BY THE ENTIRETY

A. What Is Joint Tenancy? 10/2

B. Joint Tenancy Bank Accounts 10/3

C. Joint Tenancy Safe Deposit Boxes 10/4

D. Tenancy by the Entirety 10/4

E. Joint Tenancy in Community Property States 10/5

F. Tax Concerns Affecting Joint Tenancy 10/6

G. Drawbacks of Joint Tenancy 10/11

H. When Joint Tenancy Makes Sense 10/12

I. Creating a Joint Tenancy for Property With
    Documents of Title 10/13
J. Creating Joint Tenancy for Personal Property Without
    Documents of Title 10/15

11

PAY-ON-DEATH DESIGNATIONS

A. Choosing Beneficiaries 11/2
B. Pay-on-Death Bank Accounts 11/3
C. Naming a Pay-on-Death Beneficiary for Government Securities.... 11/5
D. Naming a Beneficiary for Stocks and Bonds 11/5
E. Car Registration 11/6

12

LIFE INSURANCE

A. Do You Need Life Insurance? 12/2
B. Types of Life Insurance 12/5
C. Life Insurance and Probate 12/10
D. Choosing Life Insurance Beneficiaries 12/10
E. Reducing Estate Taxes By Transferring Ownership of
    Life Insurance Policies 12/11

13

RETIREMENT BENEFITS

A. Social Security 13/2
B. Individual Retirement Programs 13/3
C. Pensions 13/5
D. Choosing Beneficiaries for Your Retirement Programs 13/7
E. Using Disclaimers for Retirement Accounts 13/9
F. Probate and Taxes 13/10

14

STATE LAW EXEMPTIONS FROM NORMAL PROBATE

A. Using Your State Laws in Estate Planning 14/2

B. State Law Probate Exemption Rules 14/3

C. Summary Chart of State Law Exceptions to Normal Probate 14/5

D. California Exemptions From Normal Probate 14/10

E. New York Exemptions From Normal Probate 14/12

F. Texas Exemptions From Normal Probate 14/12

G. Florida Exemptions From Normal Probate 14/13

PART VI: UNDERSTANDING ESTATE AND GIFT TAXES

15

ESTATE TAXES

A. Federal Estate Tax Exemptions 15/2

B. The Big Picture: Death Taxes and Gift Taxes 15/4

C. Will Your Estate Have to Pay Taxes? 15/5

D. Calculating and Paying Estate Taxes 15/9

E. Reducing Federal Estate Taxes 15/12

F. The Federal Income Tax Basis of Inherited Property 15/13

G. State Death Taxes 15/14

16

GIFTS AND GIFT TAXES

A. The Federal Gift Tax: An Overview 16/2

B. What Is a Gift? 16/3

C. How Federal Gift Tax Works 16/6

D. State Gift Tax Rules 16/8

E. Using Gifts to Reduce Estate Taxes 16/9

F.   When Not to Give Property Away: Tax Basis Rules 16/13

G.   Using Gifts to Reduce Income Taxes 16/15

PART VII: REDUCING OR ELIMINATING ESTATE TAXES

17

AN OVERVIEW OF ONGOING TRUSTS

A.   Trusts to Save on Estate Tax 17/3

B.   Ongoing Trusts Used to Control Property 17/4

C.   Ongoing Trusts and Avoiding Probate 17/4

D.   What Ongoing Trusts Can't Do 17/5

E.   How Ongoing Trusts Work 17/5

F.   The Trustee 17/7

G.   Taxation of Ongoing Trusts 17/10

18

ESTATE TAX-SAVING BYPASS TRUSTS

A.   Overview of Bypass Trusts 18/2

B.   IRS Restrictions on Bypass Trusts 18/3

C.   AB Trusts: Bypass Trusts for Couples 18/5

D.   Bypass Trusts for Unmarried Persons 18/16

19

OTHER ESTATE TAX-SAVING MARITAL TRUSTS

A.   QTIP Trusts 19/3

B.   Trusts for Non-Citizen Spouses: QDOTs 19/13

C.   Marital Deduction Trusts 19/15

D.   Widow's Election Trusts 19/17

20

CHARITABLE TRUSTS

A. An Overview of Charitable Trusts 20/2

B. The Income Tax Deduction 20/4

C. A Closer Look at Charitable Remainder Trusts 20/7

D. A Closer Look at Charitable Lead Trusts 20/11

E. Types of Charitable Trusts: A Comparison 20/14

21

OTHER ESTATE TAX-SAVING TRUSTS

A. Generation-Skipping Trusts (GSTT Trusts) 21/2

B. Irrevocable Life Insurance Trusts 21/7

C. Grantor-Retained Interest Trusts: GRATs, GRUTs and GRITs 21/10

22

DISCLAIMERS: AFTER-DEATH ESTATE TAX PLANNING

A. Advantages of Disclaimers 22/2

B. Couples and Disclaimers 22/4

C. IRS Rules for Disclaimers 22/6

D. Disclaimers and Living Trusts 22/9

23

COMBINING ESTATE TAX-SAVING TRUSTS

A. Combining Two Estate Tax-Saving Trusts 23/2

B. Combining a Charitable Trust With Other Estate
   Tax-Saving Trusts 23/4

C. Combining Three Different Estate Tax-Saving Trusts 23/5

D. Using Ongoing Trusts and Gift-Giving to Reduce Estate Tax 23/6

PART VIII: IMPOSING CONTROLS OVER PROPERTY

24

PROPERTY CONTROL TRUSTS FOR SECOND OR SUBSEQUENT MARRIAGES

A. How a Marital Property Control Trust Works 24/2
B. Restricting the Surviving Spouse's Rights Over Trust Property 24/3
C. The Role of the Trustee 24/6
D. Savings on Estate Taxes 24/7
E. Working With a Lawyer 24/8

25

TRUSTS AND OTHER DEVICES FOR IMPOSING CONTROLS OVER PROPERTY

A. Educational Trusts 25/3
B. Trusts for Persons With Special Needs 25/4
C. Spendthrift Trusts 25/6
D. Sprinkling Trusts 25/7
E. Trusts to Manage Your Own Property 25/10
F. Powers of Appointment 25/10
G. Combining a Property Control Trust With Estate Tax-Saving Trusts 25/13

PART IX: TAKING CARE OF PERSONAL ISSUES

26

INCAPACITY: HEALTH CARE AND FINANCIAL MANAGEMENT DIRECTIVES

A. Health Care Decisions 26/2
B. Financial Management Decisions 26/8
C. Guardianships and Conservatorships 26/9

27

BODY AND ORGAN DONATION, FUNERALS AND BURIALS

A. Making Your Own Choices 27/2

B. Leaving Written Instructions 27/3

C. Donating Your Body or Organs 27/4

D. Death Notices 27/4

E. Services and Ceremonies Following a Death 27/5

F. Funerals 27/6

G. Cremation 27/8

H. Burials 27/9

PART X: FAMILY BUSINESS ESTATE PLANNING

28

FAMILY BUSINESS ESTATE PLANNING

A. Operation of the Business 28/2

B. Reducing Estate Taxes 28/5

C. Avoiding Probate of a Family Business 28/9

PART XI: GOING FURTHER

29

USING LAWYERS

A. Hiring a Lawyer 29/2

B. Doing Your Own Research 29/6

30

AFTER YOUR ESTATE PLAN IS COMPLETED

A. Storing Your Estate Planning Documents 30/2

B. Revising Your Estate Plan 30/3

31

AFTER A DEATH OCCURS

A. Wills 31/2

B. Probate Avoidance Living Trusts 31/2

C. Ongoing Trusts for Estate Tax Savings or
    Property Management 31/4

D. Preparing and Filing Tax Returns 31/5

E. Trustee's Reports to Beneficiaries 31/6

F. Collecting the Proceeds of a Life Insurance Policy 31/6

G. Obtaining Title to Joint Tenancy Property 31/6

PART XII: SAMPLE ESTATE PLANS

32

SOME ESTATE PLANS

A. A Prosperous Couple in Their 60s and 70s 32/2

B. A Wealthy Couple in Their 70s 32/2

C. A Single Man in His 60s 32/3

D. A Younger Couple 32/4

E. A Widow in Her 80s 32/5

F. A Couple in Their 60s, in a Second Marriage 32/6

G. An Unmarried Couple in Their 40s 32/7

GLOSSARY

APPENDIX: STATE DEATH TAX RULES

INDEX

INTRODUCTION:

HOW TO USE THIS BOOK

A. How This Book Works I/3

B. Will You Need Professional Help? I/4

C. Other Nolo Resources I/5

With this book, you can learn how to sensibly plan for the transfer of your property to your loved ones after you die, with a minimum of fuss and waste. Depending on your situation, this process can be straightforward and simple, involving little more than preparing a will yourself, without ever visiting a lawyer. But if your estate is large or your family needs are complicated, you may need expert help with sophisticated estate tax planning or to create complex legal devices to control what happens to your property after your death. At either end of this spectrum, as well as in between, this book points you in the right direction.

 WARNING TO LOUISIANA RESIDENTS:

This book is designed for residents of all states except Louisiana, which has a legal system based on Napoleonic Code, different from the other states. If you live in Louisiana, please return this book to Nolo Press for a full refund.

Your "estate" is simply all the property you own, whatever it's worth. The "planning" required can be understood by normal, intelligent people—you don't have to be an astrophysicist or even an attorney. Indeed, with the aid of this book and other Nolo resources, you may decide that you can safely do much, or even all, of your estate planning yourself, without professional help.

The word "plan" can be misleading. It doesn't mean you'll have a document that looks like a map, or one that has lots of charts and graphs. And it doesn't have to mean you'll end up with a thick file of papers filled with obscure legalese. Your estate plan will simply consist of the methods and documents you've chosen to handle the matters that concern you.

Plan Your Estate is useful for people with estates of any amount, from relatively modest to many millions. Many of the methods this book covers are equally desirable for small estates as well as large ones. For instance, probate avoidance methods work equally well for estates worth thousands as for those worth millions. Similarly, planning for what happens if you become incapacitated involves substantially the same concerns no matter what the size of your estate. But it's also true that larger estates tend to require more complicated and more in-depth estate planning, particularly tax planning. So we provide thorough discussions of the major ways to save on estate taxes.

While this book focuses on legal and practical issues of estate planning, we want to acknowledge that, viewed from a larger perspective, these are often of minor concern in the face of the overwhelming emotional force and mystery of death. In Chapter 2 we discuss some of the human realities of estate planning, but this book doesn't attempt to deal with the larger meanings of death; they are appropriately left to philosophers, clergy, poets and—ultimately—to you. But it's important to recognize that thinking about estate planning touches (at least) on our own mortality—a difficult subject to think about, to talk about, and to plan for. The ancient Greeks believed the inevitability of death could best be faced by performing great deeds. Christian religions offer the promise of eternal life; preparing for death means preparing to "meet your maker." Other cultures have prepared for death in a wide variety of ways, often with elaborate ceremonies.

However you choose to emotionally and spiritually prepare for death—your own or someone you care for—there are also practical consequences that must be handled. In the U.S., if no planning has been done, often a host of highly paid professionals—from lawyers to CPAs, financial advisors, real estate agents and insurance brokers—consume many thousands of dollars that could have been saved. Estate taxes that might have been reduced or avoided can consume much more. This money, obviously, comes from the estate of the person who died—money that would otherwise be available for your family, friends or others to inherit. So, in the final analysis, preparing an estate plan is an act of love for your inheritors. Although you don't directly face the consequences of procrastination and avoidance, they will, unless you decide to act.

This book does not present pre-packaged estate plans for so-called "standard" situations. With that kind of approach, if a husband and wife have minor children and an estate of approximately $200,000, Plan A is proposed. But a husband and wife with no minor children and an estate over $200,000 should use Plan B. Then there's plans C, D and E, and who knows how many more.

The problem with off-the-shelf estate plans is that, as we all know, real life isn't standardized. There are too many variables in most people's situations to make a one-size-fits-many approach work well. A far better approach is for you to take stock of your own needs and desires, and determine what your personal estate planning goals are. Then, with the broad-based information we present here, you should be able to come up with a good idea of the estate plan you want—one that is geared to your personal situation.

A. How This Book Works

Plan Your Estate covers all major aspects of estate planning, from simple wills to complex estate tax-saving trusts. Estate planning can involve many different factors. Common concerns can include:

- worries about the care of minor children;
- writing a will and avoiding probate;
- saving on estate taxes;
- providing for all family members when there has been a second or subsequent marriage.

To prepare the plan that best suits you, you need to understand the different ways of accomplishing each of you particular estate planning goals, as well as how those goals can be connected. This book explains what choices you have, how they work, and the advantages and drawbacks of each.

Unlike many Nolo books, this is not a do-it-yourself law book, with legal forms you can tear out and complete. Rather, the book is divided into parts, each covering a major estate planning concern. Chapter 1 gives you an overview of each part, so you can select only those that concern you. We encourage you to use *Plan Your Estate* as a workbook. Feel free to underline and highlight text or make notes in the margin.

Estate planning is one of the more jargon-ridden areas of law (rather a feat). We've tried to keep use of this lawyer dialect to a minimum, but it isn't possible to eliminate it entirely. To make this material as comprehensible as possible, each important term is defined when it's first used in the text. Also, there's a glossary near the back of the book. Please use it as often as you need to be sure you really understand what you are reading.

LOOK FOR THESE ABBREVIATIONS AND ICONS

To aid you in comprehending the information presented, we use several icons to advise you of some special alert. These icons are:

A caution that there may be some serious risk, or danger, that can arise in this facet of your estate planning.

Indicates where we are definitely offering our own (best) advice, not merely "objective" information.

Lets you know when we believe you need the advice of an attorney, often an estate planning expert.

Refers you to helpful books or other resources.

We believe this book to be the most thorough estate planning manual written for the non-lawyer. But the book doesn't claim to present definitive advice on every aspect of the field. Many subjects covered, such as estate taxes, life insurance, irrevocable trusts or even wills can get very complicated for people with very large estates or complex family situations. This partially explains why there are volumes of books on each topic in any good-sized law library. Some other subjects are still more esoteric and complex, such as planning when you own property in several countries, or for valuable copyrights or patents.

Also, we do not cover what is often termed "elder law," or retirement issues, which include financial planning for old age, choosing nursing care home, and protecting assets. Elder law is a separate field from estate planning and this book is big enough. While we do not generally cover pensions or retirement plans, including IRAs or 401(k) plans, we do discuss how any funds left in these plans at your death can best be transferred to beneficiaries.

B. WILL YOU NEED PROFESSIONAL HELP?

Many people worry that estate planning, in reality, means handing thousands of dollars over to lawyers in exchange for mysterious documents. 'Tain't necessarily so. The good news is that you may well be able to accomplish all of your estate planning goals without any professional help. By the time you've finished this book you'll be able to make a sensible evaluation of whether or not you need to hire a lawyer or other expert. Make this judgment carefully, of course, but do remember that lawyers, accountants and other experts aren't magicians. The cost of hiring an expensive estate planner, if you have a moderate estate, is often greater than any savings or certainty you achieve from her.

For most people with moderate estates, the process of estate planning isn't nearly as forbidding as many professionals make it seem. It's our experience, working in this field for over 20 years, that most people who have estates worth less than the federal estate tax threshold and who have clear desires about their property, can safely prepare their own estate tax threshold and who have clear desires about their property, can safely prepare their own estate planning documents from other Nolo resources, listed in Section C, below.

In some situations, however, even people with modest estates need legal help to do the best estate planning. For example, if you want to provide long-term care for a disabled child, you should see a lawyer to be sure you've best protected any assets you leave for that child's benefit.

Many people with estates exceeding the federal estate tax threshold will conclude that they need the assistance of an experienced lawyer to complete their estate planning. If you do decide you need expert help, the knowledge you gain here should help keep your costs to a minimum. Since you already know the basics, you won't need to purchase this information at upwards of $200 per hour. Also, if you educate yourself and do much of your initial planning, you're more likely to end up with something that fully expresses your own desires. And you'll be able to better judge whether the attorney is giving you fair value for your money, or simply running up your bill—after all, he knows you have some money.

Finally, some advice about self-help estate planning. Don't back away from preparing your general plan, or even the documents you want, because of derisive comments of some lawyers. Certain members of the legal establishment have tried to frighten the public with horror stories of disasters that befell some benighted person who prepared her own estate plan. For example, a renowned lawyer once remarked sarcastically that anyone who can take out his own appendix can write his own will. This analogy is just plain false. A more accurate one is that if you can understand a standard tax form, you can determine your estate planning goals and, at least in general terms, choose the best legal methods desirable to accomplish them. The truth is that, with the aid of

Nolo resources, hundreds of thousands of people have successfully written their own wills.

C. OTHER NOLO RESOURCES

As Nolo Press authors we are, of course, in favor of do-it-yourself law and avoiding lawyers when that's feasible. Throughout *Plan Your Estate,* we alert you when a Nolo book or software program provides more detailed, and how-to-do-it, coverage of an aspect of estate planning than this book does. It may seem self-serving for us to recommend other Nolo products, so let us tell you why we do. Nolo pioneered self-help law, showing people how to safely do it themselves. Our materials have been created and updated with great (often excruciating) care over many years. Literally millions of people have successfully used a Nolo self-help resource. Quite frankly, we believe our resources are by far the best for self-help purposes.

Nolo's estate planning resources include:

* *WillMaker,* software that enables you to prepare a comprehensive will. It includes a basic trust for your minor children, allowing you to choose the age at which your children inherit property you leave them.

* *Nolo's Living Trust,* software that enables you to prepare a probate-avoidance living trust (but not an estate tax-saving trust).

* *Make Your Own Living Trust,* a complete explanation, including forms, of how to prepare a living trust. The book contains forms and information enabling a married couple with a combined estate over the federal estate tax threshold to prepare a tax-saving "AB" trust.

* *Nolo's Will Book,* an in-depth explanation of how to prepare a will that covers all normal needs, including simple trusts for your minor children.

Will forms are available as tear-outs or on a computer disk included with the book.

- *The Quick and Legal Will Book,* which enables you to prepare a basic will efficiently.

- *8 Ways to Avoid Probate,* a thorough discussion of all the major ways to transfer property at death outside of a will.

- *How to Probate an Estate* (California Edition), enables Californians to handle normal probate without an attorney.

- *The Deeds Book* (California Edition), explains how to use deeds to transfer California real estate for estate planning purposes.

- *Beat the Nursing Home Trap: A Consumer's Guide to Choosing and Financing Long-Term Care,* a practical guide that provides all the information you need to help make the best arrangements for long-term care. It shows how to protect assets, arrange home health care, find nursing and non-nursing home residences, evaluate nursing home insurance and understand Medicare, Medicaid and other benefit programs.

- *Social Security, Medicare and Pensions,* an invaluable guide through the current maze of rights and benefits for those 55 and over, including Medicare, Medicaid and Social Security retirement and disability benefits, and age discrimination protections.

You can order any of these books direct from Nolo Press. A complete catalog of Nolo books and software is at the back of this book. ■

1

SELECTING YOUR ESTATE PLANNING GOALS

Part I:	Setting Your Goals	1/2
Part II:	Laying the Groundwork	1/2
Part III:	Children	1/3
Part IV:	Wills	1/4
Part V:	Probate and How to Avoid It	1/4
Part VI:	Understanding Estate and Gift Taxes	1/6
Part VII:	Reducing or Eliminating Estate Taxes	1/7
Part VIII:	Imposing Controls Over Property	1/8
Part IX:	Taking Care of Personal Issues	1/9
Part X:	Family Business Estate Planning	1/10
Part XI:	Going Further	1/11
Part XII:	Sample Estate Plans	1/11

There are a number of ways to leave property to those you want to have it after your death. The peculiarities of our system of inheritance mean that substantial amounts of money and time can often be saved if property is labeled and transferred by certain legal methods rather than others. But to choose wisely among these methods, you must first clearly define your estate planning goals.

This book is divided into 12 parts; each one covers a different estate planning goal or purpose. This chapter gives you an overview of each goal, so you can select the ones that matter to you. It also presents a sample estate plan of a couple in their 50s, so you can get a feel for what kinds of decisions and documents you may end up with.

We urge you to read all chapters of every part that concerns you before you actually begin to formulate your own estate plan. Different aspects of estate planning are often intertwined. For example, it just doesn't make sense to decide what property should pass under your will—and so go through probate—until you understand whether some of it might be better left by other, probate-avoiding, methods. Similarly, if you have a good-sized estate, you'll need to understand how estate taxes work before you can determine the wisest ways to transfer property to your loved ones. The point is that you need a good overview of all the parts of estate planning that concern you before you begin to make your plan.

PART I: SETTING YOUR GOALS

Use Part I to focus on your estate planning goals. After reading this first chapter, you should be able to decide which parts of the book probably apply to your situation.

You should also take some time to mull over important human issues that can arise in estate planning—such as leaving unequal amounts of property to different children, or avoiding potential conflict. Chapter 2, Personal Concerns and Estate Planning, discusses some of these concerns. Unless you're very confident that your personal situation is clear and not conflicted, be sure to check it out.

PART II: LAYING THE GROUNDWORK

This part covers primary concerns of any estate plan: what you own and whom you want to leave it to.

Obviously, you'll need to be sure what you own. Also, sensible planning usually requires at least a rough idea what your property is worth. Chapter 4, Inventorying Your Property, contains a worksheet you can use to list all your major items of property or just use as a safety check, to make sure you haven't overlooked anything.

Your "estate" includes all the property you own, minus anything you owe (assets minus liabilities). You may find it useful to use the worksheet to make a rough estimate of the dollar value of your estate, which can be helpful both for general planning purposes and to predict whether or not your estate will likely be liable for estate taxes. Of course, your estate will very likely have a different worth when you die, so precise figures aren't necessary.

You can't leave what you don't own. Ownership rules for single people are simple. Except as limited by contract (such as a partnership agreement or other form of shared ownership), you can leave all property you own outright. For these purposes that fact that some institution has a claim on the property, such as a mortgage on a house or a loan lien on a car, isn't shared ownership.

Property ownership rules for a married person can be more complex. Read Chapter 3, Special Property Ownership Rules for Married People, before you start inventorying your property. Two areas of law may restrict your right to leave property. First are rules affecting ownership of property acquired during marriage. There are two basic systems; which one applies to you depends on which state you live in. The majority of states follow the "common law" system where, in general, the owner of property is the person whose name appears on the ownership document. The other system, applicable in eight states, mostly in the West, is "community property," where most property acquired during a marriage is owned equally by both spouses.

UNMARRIED COUPLES: WHO OWNS WHAT?

Unless an unmarried couple—gay, lesbian or heterosexual, it makes no difference—agrees to share ownership of specified property, each member of the couple owns only his or her own property. An agreement to own property jointly must often be in writing to be enforceable. In most states, an oral agreement is effective if it can be proved, but that can often be difficult. In short, it is best for unmarried couples to put any property-sharing agreement in writing.

If you're part of an unmarried couple where each person has kept all property separate (a written agreement to do this, listing the property of each person, is a good idea here as well), each of you is free to give your property to whomever you wish. However, if property ownership is shared, either under the terms of a written contract or in a tenancy in common or partnership, you're only free to dispose of your share, unless the contract or partnership agreement provides otherwise.

Property held by unmarried couples in joint tenancy goes to the survivor automatically.

For more information on property ownership problems of unmarried couples and sample property-sharing agreements, see either *The Living Together Kit*, by Ihara and Warner (Nolo Press), a detailed guide designed to help unmarried couples minimize their entanglements with the law, or *The Legal Guide for Lesbian and Gay Couples*, by Curry, Clifford and Leonard (Nolo Press).

In common law states, laws limit a spouse's right to disinherit the other spouse. As explained in Chapter 3, in these states a surviving spouse has the right to receive a certain portion of a deceased spouse's property, no matter what that spouse provided or intended. If you plan on leaving your spouse more than half your property, these laws can't affect you.

For most people, the heart of estate planning is deciding who gets what. You may have a very clear idea of whom you want to leave your property to. If so, fine. Still, there are a number of issues that you may want to consider, from naming alternate beneficiaries to leaving shared gifts to forgiving debts. Chapter 5, Your Beneficiaries, discusses these and other concerns about your inheritors.

PART III: CHILDREN

The word children can have two meanings. The first is minors, legally those under age 18. The second is one's offspring of any age. Parents, obviously, can have adult children. Chapter 6, Children, covers estate planning issues pertaining to children in either sense of the word.

The major focus of the chapter is minor children, because a number of special estate planning problems arise with them. Of course if you have minor children, you'll want to plan for what would happen in the unlikely event that you and the other parent (if there is one involved) both die before your children became legal adults. Most likely your first concern is who would raise the children if you couldn't. In your will, you can name someone to serve as the "personal guardian" for your children—the adult who would be responsible for raising them if neither parent could. Your nomination isn't automatically legally binding, but courts normally confirm the person you name if the other parent isn't available. Chapter 6 also discusses what you can do if you do not want the other parent to obtain custody.

The second big issue is who will manage any property you leave to your minor children. Minors cannot legally own property, above a minimal amount, without adult supervision. So leaving property to your minor children requires you to choose a method for adult management. Chapter 6 explains the four legal methods you can use to impose adult supervision over property you leave to minors, and the advantages and drawbacks of each.

PART IV: WILLS

Everyone should have a will, the most basic estate planning device. Chapter 7, Wills, explains why and shows you what you can accomplish in your will

In your will you name your "executor," the person with legal authority to administer the transfer of your will property. This chapter discusses the responsibilities of an executor, and presents some thoughts on selecting yours.

Wills do have one big drawback: Property left by a will must go through probate. So don't decide what property to transfer by your will until you've looked at transfer methods that avoid probate, which are discussed in Part V.

Whatever you decide about avoiding probate, you still need a will. At a minimum, a will is a backup device essential to transfer any property that somehow wasn't transferred by other methods, such as property you overlooked or is unexpectedly acquired after your probate avoidance devices were set up (a surprise inheritance, lottery winnings).

In most all states, a will is the only document you can use to name a personal guardian for your minor children. Also, a will is best for transferring some types of property, like a personal checking account or vehicle, that usually aren't convenient to transfer by any other method.

PART V: PROBATE AND HOW TO AVOID IT

Probate, to be precise, is the name given to the legal process by which a court oversees the distribution of property left by a will. The probate process is examined in detail in Chapter 8, Probate and Why You Want to Avoid It.

Probate proceedings are generally mere formalities, because there's rarely any dispute about a will, but they are nevertheless usually cumbersome and lengthy. During probate, your assets are identified, all debts and death taxes are paid, fees for lawyers, appraisers, accountants and for filing the case in court are paid, and the remaining property is finally distributed to your inheritors. The average probate proceeding drags on for at least a year before the estate is actually distributed.

The very word "probate" has acquired a notorious aura. Commonly, it's an institutionalized rip-off of a dead person's estate by lawyers, and sometimes other officials or executors, who get large fees for what in most cases is routine, albeit tedious, paperwork. For example, if a father leaves his estate equally among his three children, and no one contests the will, why should a lawyer be paid a hefty sum to shuffle papers through a bureaucratic maze?

Because probate lawyers are expensive, we've been asked many times by will beneficiaries if they can safely handle probate without an attorney. Unfortunately, except in California and Wisconsin, the answer is normally "no," at least not without considerable difficulty. (In California, probate can be done without an attorney by using *How to Probate an Estate,* by Julia Nissley (Nolo Press). Wisconsin has a simplified probate system, with court clerical assistance for completing the forms.) Legally, it's permissible in most states (but not, for example, in Florida) for the executor named in a will to act for the estate, appear in probate court and handle the proceedings without an attorney. But probate is a technical and tedious area of the law. Without good instructions, which are unfortunately non-existent outside of lawyer texts (except, to repeat, in California) the forms can seem very complicated to the uninitiated. Further, in some situations, there are court proceedings to attend. In short, learning how to do probate from scratch normally takes considerable time and risks continuing frustration. Worse, the courts and clerks can be unhelpful, or even hostile, to lay people.

A wiser choice is to reduce or eliminate probate fees by transferring property outside of probate. If you have a moderate estate, you can probably prepare probate-avoidance devices and documents yourself, without an attorney. The next six chapters explain the major probate-avoidance devices:

- Living trusts, which allow you to retain full control over trust property while you live; after your death, your living trust property is transferred quickly to your beneficiaries.

- Joint tenancy, a form of shared property ownership with the key element that the surviving owner(s) of joint tenancy property automatically inherit the share of a deceased owner. No probate is required.

- Pay-on-death designations, which let you name a beneficiary to quickly and easily receive, without probate, assets such as bank accounts or stocks when you die.

- Life insurance, the proceeds of which go directly to the policy beneficiary, without going through probate.

- Individual retirement programs, such as IRAs, profit-sharing plans or 401(k) plans, where you can leave any money remaining in the account to a named beneficiary. The money is transferred outside of probate.

- State law exemptions from normal probate, which allow smaller estates to go through a simplified probate procedure or avoid probate altogether. These rules apply to estates ranging from less than

$5,000 to $140,000, depending on the state. A list of each state's rules is in Chapter 14.

Reading about probate avoidance doesn't mean that you must decide to pursue it. Some people intelligently decide that all the estate planning they want, for now, is a will.

Although you may find it surprising, limiting estate planning to making a will can, in the right circumstances, make good sense. For example, many younger people in good health often sensibly decide to postpone detailed estate planning for later. A will naming a personal and property guardian for minor children and leaving their relatively modest amount of property to a spouse, partner and perhaps also a few close friends or relatives is all they want, and need, now. Since probate doesn't happen until death, a younger person should have plenty of time to plan to avoid it later in life.

In contrast, for older people with a reasonable amount of property, or people in ill health, it makes little sense to depend on a will alone. The amount of time and effort it takes to plan to avoid probate is just not that much—certainly far less than will be consumed going through it, not to mention the significant costs saved.

Aside from avoiding probate altogether, if you significantly reduce the value of property transferred by probate, you'll likely reduce the attorney's fee as well. A useful concept here is the "probate estate," the portion of your estate that must go through probate. Anything that is transferred by probate-avoiding methods is not part of the probate estate; it goes directly to inheritors without court proceedings. If you plan wisely, you can reduce considerably the size of your "probate estate" or even eliminate it entirely.

Some reasons for probate. In unusual situations, probate can be useful. If your estate will have many debts or claims by creditors, probate provides a forum for resolving those claims with relative speed and certainty. And if creditors who are notified of the probate do not file claims within a set period (usually, a few months), the claims are barred forever.

PROVIDING READY CASH

One goal of estate planning can be to provide ready cash for immediate family needs or, later on, to pay any death taxes or other debts. Particularly if you are your family's main provider, your survivors will need immediate cash for their living expenses, or for the "costs of dying"—hospitalization, funeral and burial expenses—and other debts and taxes that are due promptly.

If most of your property is transferred by will, your family won't get it while probate moves on. Immediate family members can ask the probate court to release limited amounts for necessities, but it's wiser to plan to have money available without going to court and paying attorneys' fees.

If most of your property will be transferred outside of probate, there is much less reason to worry about arranging for ready cash, since cash is usually accessible promptly. However, if most of your assets aren't "liquid"—that is, cannot easily be converted to cash—you may still need to provide a source of ready cash. For example, if your worth is in real estate and shares of a private corporation that can't readily be sold, your family might have trouble obtaining cash for daily expenses. Traditional sources of cash are life insurance policies, and money in a "pay-on-death" bank account.

PART VI: UNDERSTANDING ESTATE AND GIFT TAXES

Most people who engage in comprehensive estate planning want to know about estate taxes. Will your estate be liable for taxes? What can be done to reduce or avoid them? In Chapter 15, Estate Taxes, you'll learn how these death taxes work and whether or not your estate is likely to be subject to tax.

A "death tax" is one imposed on the property of someone who has died. Death taxes are called by various names. The federal government, which imposes the stiffest taxes, calls them "estate taxes." About half the states impose death taxes. Some states call them "inheritance taxes." In theory, these states tax the recipients of a deceased person's property rather than the property itself, but the reality is the same—the taxes are paid out of the deceased's estate.

You may learn that no death taxes will be assessed against your estate. Federal law exempts a certain amount of property from tax. This amount gradually increases from $625,000 in 1998 to $1 million in 2006. People with larger estates will probably face federal estate taxes.

If you're a member of a couple (married or not) with a combined estate exceeding the federal estate tax threshold, you should consider tax planning if each of you plans to leave most or all of your property to the other. Without planning, the survivor would wind up with an estate subject to tax after he or she dies. With sensible planning, this result can often be avoided or reduced. (See Part VII, Reducing or Eliminating Estate Taxes.)

Chapter 15 explains the other major federal estate tax exemptions. Most important is what's called the "marital deduction," which provides that all property left or given to a spouse is exempt from estate or gift tax. However, the marital deduction does not apply to property a citizen spouse gives or leaves to a non-citizen spouse.

Chapter 15 also covers the concept of tax "basis" and how that applies to inherited property. Very briefly, the "basis" of property is the dollar value put on your ownership interest when determining the profit or loss from sale. To simplify here, we can say that the basis of property you own is the purchase price. However, if you inherit property, your basis is not the cost to the person who left you the property, but the market value of the property when that person died. This is called a "stepped-up" basis. If you plan to leave property that has significantly increased in value since you purchased it, it's important to understand how this "stepped up basis" works, and can be used in estate planning.

To get a solid grasp of estate taxes, you also need to understand gift taxes, which are covered in Chapter 16. At first hearing, the phrase "gift taxes" sounds like something Scrooge came up with. How can you tax generosity? But if there were no gift taxes, estate taxes could be avoided simply by giving away property while you live instead of leaving it when you die. So the federal government, and a few states, impose tax on substantial gifts, currently above $10,000 to any person in one year.

DEFINITION OF A GIFT

A "gift" is property you transfer freely (not by sale or trade) to a person or institution. Throughout this book, "gift" is used both to describe property you give away during your lifetime and property you leave at your death. This saves us from having to use the legalese "bequest," "devise" or "legacy."

Separate taxes and probate. Don't confuse avoiding probate with estate tax or gift tax saving. Unfortunately, avoiding probate doesn't have any effect on estate or gift taxes.

PART VII: REDUCING OR ELIMINATING ESTATE TAXES

These chapters cover the major methods of estate tax reduction, aside from tax-free gifts. These methods require using some form of irrevocable trust, or, sometimes, a number of trusts. We call these "ongoing" trusts because they function as independent entities for an indefinite time. This is in contrast to a probate-avoidance living trust, which is normally operational only for a brief period, after the death of the person who set it up.

Because an irrevocable trust is an independent legal entity, it must obtain a federal taxpayer ID number. Separate trust financial records must be kept, and an annual trust income tax return filed, with any tax due paid. (See Chapter 17, An Overview of Ongoing Trusts.)

The most common estate tax saving trust is a bypass trust. And by far the most popular bypass trust is one for a couple, commonly called an "AB" trust.

An AB trust can be desirable for couples with a combined estate worth more than the federal estate tax threshold, if each person wants to leave everything (or almost everything) to the other. If the property were left outright, the surviving spouse would end up with an estate exceeding federal tax threshold. An AB trust can eliminate entirely, or, with wealthier estates, significantly reduce, these taxes.

AB trusts should be used only with full knowledge of their limits as well as their advantages.

(Chapter 18, Estate Tax-Saving Bypass Trusts, spells out the pros and cons.)

Other marital estate tax saving trusts are covered in Chapter 19. A "QTIP" trust enables a surviving spouse to postpone taxes otherwise due on property worth over the federal estate tax threshold left in an AB trust.

This chapter also explains what's called a "QDOT" trust, which can be very important if you are married to a non-citizen. As we've said, the marital deduction does not apply to property left to a non-citizen spouse. So normally any property over the federal estate tax threshold left by a citizen spouse to a non-citizen spouse is taxable when the citizen spouse dies. A QDOT trust enables the non-citizen spouse to postpone payment of any taxes due until after her or his death.

Whether you're married or not, if you're interested in making a large gift to a charity, and also getting a tax break, you may want to investigate charitable trusts, covered in Chapter 20. With these trusts, you can leave property to charities and simultaneously obtain income tax as well as estate tax benefits. A charitable trust makes sense, from an estate tax perspective, only if your estate exceeds the federal estate tax threshold. However Chapter 20, Charitable Trusts, also provides useful information about charitable gifts, no matter how large your estate.

Still other kinds of ongoing trusts can be used by anyone, married or not, to save on estate taxes. These trusts, covered in Chapter 21, include:

• Generation-skipping trusts, where you leave property in trust for grandchildren and avoid estate taxes on the trust property when your own children die.

• Irrevocable life insurance trusts, which can, in the right circumstances, save a bundle on estate taxes.

• Grantor retained interest trusts, which can yield income and estate tax benefits if you transfer your home to a trust for a set period.

One other strategy that can sometimes lower a family's overall estate tax burden is the use of a "disclaimer," which is akin to a trust. A disclaimer is simply a statement that you decline to accept property left to you—a legal way of saying "no thanks." (Chapter 22 explains shows how disclaimers are used.)

Finally, Some people use more than one kind of trust to achieve the most tax savings. (See Chapter 23, Combining Estate Tax Saving Trusts.)

PART VIII: IMPOSING CONTROLS OVER PROPERTY

For one or more reasons, you may want to impose controls over property you leave—in other words, to legally prevent the beneficiary from gaining unfettered ownership of the property. (Chapter 6 discusses controls you can use over property left to minors. This part covers restrictions on adult beneficiaries.) These types of controls require use of a trust.

You might want to impose such controls if you've remarried and want to balance the interests and needs of your current spouse with those of children from a former marriage Chapter 24, Property Control Trusts for Second or Subsequent Marriages, explains how you can create a trust that leaves the other spouse certain defined rights in the trust property for his or her life, but preserves the principal for your children, who receive the trust property when the surviving spouse dies.

Many issues can come up when trying to balance the rights of the spouse and the children. For example, can the life estate spouse sell trust property? What rights do the children have to see that the trust principal is being preserved? There is no generic solution to these questions. The answers must be worked out individually, fitting your specific desires and needs.

In a number of other situations, discussed in Chapter 25, you may want a property control trust, including:

- **You want to help pay for a child's college or other schooling costs.** Here you'll need to decide if you want to define what school costs include and what the criteria for being in school are or if you'll let the trustee make those decisions.

- **You want to establish a "special needs" trust for someone with a disability.** Common problems include who to select as trustee, and doing all that's legal to preserve the disabled person's eligibility for government assistance.

- **You want to restrict a beneficiary's access to his or her inheritance.** If you believe an adult beneficiary can't responsibly handle money, you may want to set up a "spendthrift trust." It controls the beneficiary's freedom to use trust property, including the ability to pledge it as a loan.

- **You want to create a trust allowing the trustee to decide how property is distributed to adult beneficiaries.** With what's called a "sprinkling trust," the trustee is authorized to distribute, within any limits set by the trust, unequal amounts of trust income or principal among the beneficiaries. (A "family pot trust" for minor children is a form of sprinkling trust. See Chapter 6, Children.)

- **You want someone else to decide what happens to some or all of your property after your death.** This is called a "power of appointment." The person you authorize can select your beneficiaries and decide how much of your property they receive, within any limits you've set.

PART IX: TAKING CARE OF PERSONAL ISSUES

When you're making plans for what happens to your property, don't overlook two important personal concerns that can affect what happens to *you*. First is making arrangements for handling your financial and medical affairs if you become incapacitated and are unable to make these decisions yourself. Second is what you want done with your body after you die. What are your choices, and how can you make your decisions binding?

To be sure your wishes are carried out if you become incapacitated, you need to prepare several documents. For healthcare, you can prepare a document authorizing someone you've chosen to make health care decisions for you. You can also make binding provisions for what you want done regarding specific healthcare issues. Many people specifically address the artificial prolonging of life by use of technology when death is imminent. If you prefer a "natural death," you can require that in your healthcare document.

Depending on your state, you'll need a "durable power of attorney," a "living will" or a "healthcare directive." These documents normally become effective only if you actually become incapacitated and can't communicate your wishes.

To handle money matters if you become incapacitated, you can prepare a document called a "durable power of attorney for finances." In this document, you appoint someone to handle your financial affairs and make financial decisions for you. You can include any limits or directions regarding your finances that you wish to.

Chapter 26, Incapacity: Health Care and Financial Management Directives, discusses these issues.

PROTECTING ASSETS IN CASE OF CATASTROPHIC ILLNESS

Many people are concerned that if they become seriously ill, all their savings—indeed, all their assets—will be consumed to pay for health care. This is far from an irrational concern. To address it, some people ask for a will clause, or a simple trust, or anything, that will prevent their assets from being used for expensive medical bills. Unfortunately, this is not an easy matter to handle. No simple clause or trust can safely accomplish this. About the best you can do is:

- Seek advice from an expert attorney in your state. The attorney must know applicable federal laws and regulations. He must also be up-to-date on your state's laws.

- If you're a member of a couple, research how you can best protect the assets of the person who doesn't become ill. Many states allow one spouse to shield his or her property from liability for medical bills of the other spouse. This is covered in depth in *Beat the Nursing Home Trap,* by Joseph L. Matthews (Nolo Press).

- Consider transferring some of your property to trusted family members before you become seriously ill. You need to be careful here, and work with an expert in the field. Recent federal law changes make it a crime to give away property and then apply for federal medical aid within 36 months of the transfer.

All this can be tricky and even dangerous. Both federal and state legal rules change rapidly. Nevertheless, a lawyer in your state experienced in elder law issues should be able to provide you with some measure of asset protection. This is likely to be less than you want, but the best you can do.

The options you have for disposing of your body after death are covered in Chapter 27. Subjects covered include death notices, donation of body parts for transplants, or entire body for medical research, funerals, cremation, burials, and how to leave binding

written instructions. Doing this kind of planning can be a great gift to your loved ones, freeing them from burdensome tasks immediately after your death and almost always saving significant amounts of money.

PART X: FAMILY BUSINESS ESTATE PLANNING

Small business owners have special estate planning concerns. Chapter 28, Family Business Estate Planning, covers some basic issues: operation of the business after an owner's death, planning to reduce or eliminate any possible estate taxes on the business, and avoiding probate of it. Business estate planning is a complex field, and we can delve into only the most central issues, but at a minimum this chapter should enable you to determine which areas you might want more help with.

FAMILY LIMITED PARTNERSHIPS

Some people believe that, somehow, creating a "family living partnership" can eliminate all estate taxes, no matter how large the estate and how flimsy the "business." The notion is that the parents can transfer their property into a partnership business entity, with their children, and possibly grandchildren, sharing ownership as limited partners. The parents hope that as a result, the partnership will be transferred to younger generations tax-free.

For such a plan to succeed, the IRS must be convinced that the limited partnership has a real business purpose. Calling your home or stock investments a business doesn't make them one. But if you own a real business, there can be estate tax advantages to creating a limited partnership for it, and transferring minority interests to future inheritors. The pros and cons of this are discussed in more depth in Chapter 28.

PART XI: GOING FURTHER

Once you've determined, at least in outline, what your estate planning goals are and how you want to address them, you may want to see a lawyer or other expert.

Chapter 29, Using Lawyers, discusses the different types of lawyers and other experts that may be helpful, or necessary, for you to pin down the specifics of your plan and prepare the documents you need. The chapter explores how to find a good lawyer, and how to work with one, including making fair and sensible fee arrangements. You may also decide to do some legal research on your own; this chapter introduces the basics of how to find the law you need.

After your planning is done and the documents you want have been prepared, you'll need to know what do with them. Chapter 30, After Your Estate Plan Is Completed, covers storing them, making copies, and when to revise your estate plan.

Doing conscientious estate planning while you're alive is a boon to your loved ones—but someone must still complete the process after your death. Chapter 31, After a Death Occurs, gives you an overview of how your property will be transferred, however that property is left—by will, living trust, joint tenancy, pay-on-death account or life insurance. It next discusses what happens if estate taxes are assessed and an estate tax return must be filed. The chapter also covers some important matters about ongoing trusts, including how they actually are put in gear, and the responsibility of the trustee to report to the trust beneficiaries.

PART XII: SAMPLE ESTATE PLANS

Now that you've read this first chapter, you should have some focus on a the major issues you want to address in your estate planning. Part XII provides several examples of estate plans, to aid your understanding of how different goals and components can be melded into one plan.

In the hope of giving you a clearer notion now of what the end product of your efforts may be, here's one sample estate plan.

Abel Rublestam and Lynn Montgomery are married and in their 50s—he's 58, she's 51. They live in a non-community property state. They have two children, Matt and Rebecca. Matt is married and has two young children. Rebecca is in graduate school.

Their property. The couple share ownership of all their property. Their estate consists of a home worth $350,000 ($280,000 equity), securities (stocks and bonds) worth $80,000, money-market saving of $36,000, life insurance on each spouse which pays $200,000 on death, and their one-third ownership of the R-S corporation, a family business. It's hard to determine the exact value for their business interest. As a rough guess, they decide it's worth at least $600,000. The current worth of each spouse's estate, in 1988, is $748,000.

Their estate planning goals. The couple want to avoid probate. They also realize that each one's estate is over the amount of the personal estate tax exemption for 1988. Also, their combined estate of $1,496,000 would be subject to estate tax no matter what year the second spouse dies in. So they want to eliminate any possible estate taxes.

They consider leaving more property to Matt, because of his family responsibilities. But they decide to leave equal amounts to both children. They don't want to seem to favor one child, or one lifestyle. Also, they don't want to have to revise their plan if some major family event happens to one of their children—such as Matt has a third child or gets divorced or Rebecca has a child.

Their plan. The couple prepare a living trust to avoid probate. In that trust, they create an AB trust to save on overall estate taxes. Each leaves the other all his or her property. Both name their children as two of the final beneficiaries of their AB trusts.

They carefully transfer title to their home, R-S stock and securities accounts into the living trust's name, having already checked that the bylaws of their co-op apartment association and the R-S corporation permit this.

They hold their money market funds in joint tenancy. The survivor will inherit all of the money in the account. This money will not become part of an AB trust, but because it's a relatively minor amount, that won't affect their estate tax situation.

Each spouse names the other spouse as beneficiary of their life insurance policy.

When they're older, if their assets increase significantly in value, the couple intend to make tax-free gifts of $10,000 per year each to their children, but decide that they are not ready to do this now.

Each prepares a basic will. Each also prepares a durable power of attorney for heath care authorizing the other spouse to make health care decisions if one becomes incapacitated. Each durable power of attorney specifically authorizes a spouse to terminate life support equipment if the other has a terminal illness. Each also prepares a durable power of attorney for finances, naming the other as his or her attorney-in-fact. ■

2

Personal Concerns and Estate Planning

A. Avoiding Conflict 2/2

B. Leaving Unequal Amounts of Property to Children 2/5

C. Providing Care for Minor Children 2/7

D. Subsequent Marriages 2/8

E. Long-Term Care for a Child With Special Needs 2/9

F. Concerns of Unmarried Couples 2/10

G. Worries About the Effect of Inheriting Money 2/11

H. Disinheriting People, Including Children 2/12

I. Communicating Your Decisions to Family and Friends 2/13

Underlying the creation of any estate plan are profound human concerns: a primal urge for order and the desire to pass on property to loved ones. A good estate plan is an accurate reflection of your deepest personal wishes. Although much of this book is about mechanics, methods and documents, it's important to remember that no matter how well you deal with the legal devices, your estate plan won't succeed unless you take human concerns into account, too.

We make no claim to being experts on the psyche. Indeed, we are wary of "experts" (or anyone) who claim precise understanding of something as complex and mysterious as human beings. Happily, you don't need an expert to cope with the human realities that can come up in your estate planning. You do need common sense and candor about the strengths, weaknesses and genuine needs of close family members, and perhaps friends as well. Legal aspects of estate planning are significant, of course (that's why we're here) but should never interfere with what you know in your heart needs to be done.

Many people face no serious personal problems in their estate planning. They know who they want to leave their property to. They do not foresee any possibility of conflict between their beneficiaries, nor threat of a lawsuit by someone claiming they were illegally denied their inheritance. On the human level, these people can, happily, focus on the satisfactions they expect their gifts to bring.

Other people's situations are not so clear and straightforward. They must deal with more difficult human dynamics, such as possibilities of family conflicts, or dividing property unequally between children, or providing care for minor children, or handling complexities arising from second or subsequent marriages.

Before beginning your legal planning, it's vital that you assess your personal circumstances and decide how you want to resolve any difficulties. If you're planning to leave all your property to your spouse or two compatible children, or are otherwise sure you don't face any human problems, wonderful. You can safely go on to the next chapter that concerns you. If, however, you think you might face complications—or if you're not sure what kinds of problems can come up—read this chapter, which discusses a number of human concerns drawn from Denis's estate planning practice.

A. AVOIDING CONFLICT

Estate planning involves money—cash or assets that can be sold for cash. Money, as most of us learn as we get older, is strange stuff—or, more accurately, people can do strange things because of the desire for money. (If the love of money isn't *the* root of all evil, it's certainly up there as a big one.) So the first step in creating an estate plan is to recognize that if you plan unwisely, your plan may lead to bitterness, strife and lawsuits rather than the happiness you surely intend. Avoiding conflict after your death to the extent reasonably possible should be a central goal of estate planning.

Start by asking yourself about the potential for conflict in your personal situation. If this potential exists, what can you do to eliminate or at least reduce it? One important thing to remember is that disputes are not always over property that is worth a lot of money. If different family members or other inheritors have deep emotional attachments to heirlooms, or what they stand for, or can't stand the idea of *that person* getting it, fighting can become fierce even if the heirlooms themselves won't make anyone rich.

John Gregory Dunne, in his autobiography *Harp* (Simon&Schuster), gives an excellent description of one family's fight over heirlooms. His Aunt Harriet failed to specifically state who got what of her many items of personal property. Dunne wrote:

In legal terms, Aunt Harriet became..."Estate of Harriet H. Burn," appraised and organized, room by room, into "8 carved Hepplewhite mahogany chairs" and "Coalport 'Kings Plate' china service for twelve" and "Repro. Victorian loveseat, blue brocade" and "Light blue upholstered settee, soiled." The house was sold, the belongings apportioned to the surviving children and grandchildren. There is something so metaphorical and final in the act of dividing up the possessions a family has accumulated over several lifetimes and more generations; for the first time I thought there might be a good argument for primogeniture. It was not that the furniture and china and crystal and silver and linens had great worth; it was just that each piece, each object had a private history, a special meaning for one or the other of us. For a family, the process of apportionment is like psychoanalysis or the confessional box; long-buried resentments surface, old hurts and forgotten slights. In the end, a lawyer drew up the order of selection; his ground rules were worthy of Solomon:

"The order of selection will be determined as follows: each of you is requested to pick a number from one to ninety-nine and advise me of it by return mail: the person whose number is closest to the first two numbers of the Connecticut Daily Lottery on Tuesday, October 7, will have first pick, and so forth.... If the first person who selects property picks an item in an amount worth $1,400, the second person will be entitled to pick as many items as he or she wishes up to $1,400 in value. The third person would then have the right to choose property in the amount equal to the value selected by the person who preceded him or her and so forth until all items have been selected. In this way, each family unit will have an opportunity to select property, in turn and essentially of equal value."

The Connecticut State Lottery: God, if there is one, must have a sense of humor.

With some wise planning, the conflicts among the Dunne family could have been forestalled. After all, well before Aunt Harriet died, a lawyer could have drawn up this distribution method, complete with the Connecticut State Lottery. So even if you can't, or don't want to, decide before your death exactly who gets what, you can still create a binding method for peaceful and fair distribution of your property after you die.

Let's explore general ways to avoid conflict by looking at three different family situations. Then, we will discuss ways to avoid conflict. But here at the beginning we do want to note that in some cases, conflict simply can't be avoided.

EXAMPLE 1: CHOOSING AN EXECUTOR

Patrick and Clara have five children. One, Sean, is a lawyer. Patrick and Clara admit to themselves, though they never reveal it to others, that Sean is their one grasping child, who has always wanted the most, materially, from his parents and the world. Indeed, by sheer persistence, Sean has already managed to acquire a substantial number of family heirlooms. Sean tells his parents he wants to supervise distribution of their property (after both die) as executor of their wills and successor trustee of their living trust, stating that he's obviously the most professionally qualified.

At first, Patrick and Clara aren't sure what to do. Their concern isn't that Sean will violate their wills and distribute their major items of property unequally. Rather, they worry that the personal possessions they have left to all their children won't be divided fairly. After considerable discussion, they decide they don't want Sean to have sole authority to supervise the distribution of their estate. Basically, they conclude that while they love him as they do their other children, they simply can't rely on him to be able to put his own desires aside and distribute their heirlooms impartially. They'd prefer to have their daughter Maude, the kindest and most level-headed of their kids, be both executor and successor trustee, which will allow her to preside over the division of the personal items. However, they're afraid of offending Sean, something they're determined not to do.

After much thought, they decide to have three executors and successor trustees—Sean, Maude and another daughter, Maeve. (Patrick, Jr. lives in Europe and isn't interested, and Polly is preoccupied with her medical career). A majority of executors can decide how the estate is handled. This solution his may be a little awkward, and it sets up the possibility that Maude and Maeve may have to combine forces to cope with Sean (as they've had to do for 30 years). But Patrick and Clara feel it has a good chance of success. They plan to talk, diplomatically to Maude, Maeve and Sean to try to achieve some common understanding of what they want. But even if Sean is dissatisfied, the couple believes there is far less risk of serious family strife than if Sean were named sole trustee and executor.

EXAMPLE 2: A CHILD FROM A PREVIOUS MARRIAGE

Sol and Bernice have two children in their late 20s, Abel and Alexis, and a combined estate worth about $730,000. Sol also has a 34-year-old daughter, Lilith, from his first marriage, who he's seen very rarely since his marriage to Bernice. Sol wants to leave Lilith $100,000. "That's absolutely ridiculous." Bernice exclaims. 'You're just trying to absolve yourself of the guilt you feel for being unable to see Lilith all these years." Sol retorts, "Isn't it my money?" Bernice points out that half of it is her money, because their property lists both their names as owners (see Chapter 3, Special Property Ownership Rules for Married People). Sol says, "Yes, but half of $630,000 is $315,000, so I can leave $100,000 to Lilith if I want to." But he soon admits that this "divide my estate" approach would mean he would be leaving Bernice $215,000, with nothing for his other two children. In short, Sol realizes that Bernice is right—his children from his present marriage would almost surely feel hurt.

Sol and Bernice decide to work through this problem together. After some lengthy talks, they decide that Sol will leave $40,000 to Lilith, and the rest to Bernice (assuming Bernice survives Sol). When Bernice dies, she will pass on everything that's left to Abel and Alexis. They then check with the two children to see if this seems fair to them as well. Happily, it does. Abel says, "Hey, it's your money, Pa." Their daughter adds, "So enjoy." Both convince Sol and Bernice that they think the gift to Lilith is fair.

they've worked out an agreement to divide some items of property and share others. Everyone is in good spirits. Al studies the agreement and secretly concludes that it's more complex than necessary, and in some small ways not completely fair. Still, his kids accept it, and that's what matters to him, so he includes it in his will.

B. LEAVING UNEQUAL AMOUNTS OF PROPERTY TO CHILDREN

Sometimes parents want to leave unequal amounts of property to their children, but don't want to give the impression that they favor the child who is given more. Here are some examples of how people have handled this matter.

EXAMPLE 1: A DISGRUNTLED CHILD

Jim's parents, Mort and Lisa, paid for his college and dental school education and helped him purchase his first house. Melinda, their other child, has always been an independent sort who, while a loving daughter, has prided herself on making it on her own. Now Mort and Lisa want to equalize their gifts by leaving considerably more to Melinda in their estate plan. Some hints of their thinking are enough to disturb Jim, and he argues that in balance, Melinda will wind up with more than half.

Mort and Lisa talk it over and decide they'll stick to their original plan. They think the dollar figures for each child are close to even overall, and that Jim is being a bit grasping. They also conclude that they won't discuss the subject with Jim again. But in their estate

EXAMPLE 3: FAMILY HEIRLOOMS

Al is a widower with three children. Although there's no problem dividing his big ticket items among his children equally—they all agree on that—all three children have expressed deep attachment to a number of relatively inexpensive family treasures. Al decides they have to talk it out. He gets all three children together and says "You're going to have to work it out among you. Come up with something you all agree on and I'll do it. But don't make me guess, and don't leave me worrying that you'll be fighting amongst yourselves when I'm gone."

A family retreat is planned and carried out. It takes longer than any of them anticipate, but the kids stick with it, and eventually, a few flashes of temper and some weary hours later, planning documents (a will and a living trust), they'll try to explain why and how they determined the distribution. They'll emphasize that they love both children equally and are determined to treat them equally. Mort and Lisa hope that being fair and firm with Jim will gain his respect in the end.

EXAMPLE 2: THE STRUGGLING MUSICIAN

Ayyad, a widower with a moderate estate, has four grown children. Three are well-established in conventional business careers with excellent future prospects. One is a serious, but impoverished, jazz musician. Because of his greater need, Ayyad considers leaving the musician most of his estate, but decides to confer with his children before finalizing that plan.

To Ayyad's surprise, he learns that two of his children don't agree with his plan. One has never much cared for his musician brother, thinking him irresponsible. (Besides, this child never liked his music, anyway.) Another child points out that she has two children and that, in today's market, neither her nor her husband's jobs are really secure. The musician, she reminds Ayyad, has provided him with no loving grandchildren. The daughter asks whether her children shouldn't receive some "rainy-day" funds from their grandfather.

Ayyad says he'll think this over. He decides he doesn't want to talk it over further with his kids. This is, after all, his decision. He's gotten their input, but it's up to him to decide.

Finally, he decides to divide his total estate by percentages: 50% will go to the musician (Ayyad admires his son and thinks he is sincere, not indulgent.) 12.5 % will go to each of his other two children with no children of their own, and 25% to the daughter with children. If any of his other children has a child, or if the musician gains a measure of financial success, Ayyad plans to revise these percentages.

In an effort to soothe feelings, Ayyad writes a detailed letter explaining his decision and expressing his love and good wishes for each child. He attaches the letter to his living trust, where it will be revealed to his children after his death.

EXAMPLE 3: UNEQUAL EARNINGS

Barbara and Barry have two grown children and a substantial estate. Their son is a doctor; their daughter is a part-time college student and environmental activist who wants a career helping make the world a better place, but isn't sure what that career is (or if it exists at all). Barbara and Barry consider leaving the bulk of their wealth to their daughter, figuring that their son is much more secure. But then, on reflection, they decide they don't want such an imbalance. Medicine, they reason, is surely changing, and may not be as lucrative in the future. Also, their son already has one child, with more hoped for. Who knows what his needs may become in the future. And anyway, they've been helping to support their daughter, and expect they may do so for several more years, until she's begun to carve out her niche.

Barbara and Barry decide, for the time being, to divide their estate equally between the two children. But they also agree to periodically review their plan, to see they now want to leave more property to one child.

C. PROVIDING CARE FOR MINOR CHILDREN

A prime concern of parents of minor children is who will take care of their children if the parents die. If both parents are involved in raising the child (together, or in the case of divorce or separation, with the participation of both), the principal worry is what happens if both parents die. Obviously, if there is only one parent, because the other is dead or has effectively abandoned the child, the sole parent is likely to be even more concerned that his children will be well cared for if he dies.

In either case, the primary issues are who will raise the child *and* who will be responsible for supervising property the parent(s) leave to the child. These issues are discussed in depth in Chapter 6, Children. Here we want only to indicate some of the emotional concerns that may be raised when trying to resolve them.

EXAMPLE 1: THE BEST CHOICE

A married couple, Taylor and Sondra, have two grade-school-age children. Taylor and Sondra discuss who will raise their children if they both die before the kids are adults. Taylor strongly promotes his sister, Beth, as the suitable guardian. Sondra thinks Beth is a snob and declares she doesn't want her children raised in that household. She suggests her older brother, Louis. Taylor retorts that Louis may be good with money, but he has a terrible temper and doesn't have the most stable marriage.

Fortunately, Taylor and Sondra are sensitive enough to realize they have to talk seriously to reach an agreement on who would make the best guardian. After considerable discussion, and a fairly successful effort to feel out the kids, they settle on Sondra's best friend, Hilda, who they both trust and respect, and who has children about the same age and is willing to accept the responsibility for raising the children.

But both Sondra and Taylor agree that Hilda is not very sensible with money. They worry that she couldn't sensibly manage the money they would leave for the children. Hilda isn't overjoyed to hear this, but she is good-hearted. She accepts Sondra and Taylor's solution—she will be the children's personal guardian, and Louis supervises the money left them until they're old enough to get it outright. Louis also agrees to this arrangement.

EXAMPLE 2: SOMEONE WHO'LL ACCEPT THE JOB

Marcie, a single parent, wants her best friend, Shoshana, to be the guardian of Katherine, Marcie's nine-year-old daughter, should Marcie die before Katherine is 18. To Marcie's surprise, Shoshana says she can't accept the responsibility. She has two kids of her own, and that's all she can handle. Marcie is hurt, and worries there's no one she trusts who will do the job. After some reflection and discussion with other friends, Marcie realizes that her brother Alex is willing to be guardian. Marcie is not overjoyed: Alex and she weren't really close as kids and still aren't. But she realizes that Alex is a trustworthy person and that Katherine would be well cared for with him. She concludes that her best estate plan is to stay alive until her daughter is an adult, but if she doesn't, she will rely on Alex.

D. SUBSEQUENT MARRIAGES

People who've married more than once may face problems reconciling their desires for their present spouse and family with their wishes for children from their prior marriages. Individual situations can vary greatly, often depending on whether marriages occurred relatively early or late in life and on how well family members get along. But one thing is obvious—if yours is a non-traditional family, you must carefully consider, and do your best to reconcile, needs that may be competing and conflicting. These issues are covered in more depth in Chapter 24, Property Control Trusts for Second or Subsequent Marriages.

EXAMPLE 1: HER KIDS, HIS KIDS

Katerina and Pavel get married when they are in their 50s. Katerina has a son from her prior marriage. Pavel has three children, two daughters and a son. Katerina and Pavel both work. Pavel has a slightly higher income, and savings of $400,000 to Katerina's $130,000. They buy a house, with each spouse contributing half the down payment, and equally sharing the monthly payments. Both spouses want to insure that, when the other dies, the survivor gets to live in the house for the rest of his or her life. When both spouses die, they want the house to be divided equally, with one share going to Katerina's son and the other share divided between Pavel's three children. Similarly, by use of a marital property control trust (see Chapter 24), each spouse's assets will be left for the "use" of the surviving spouse, with "use" defined to mean the right to receive income the property generates or literal use of some property (for example, a car). Neither spouse can invade the other's principal.

Katerina and Pavel consider the wisdom of discussing their plan with all their children.

Since they have chosen Eve, one of Pavel's daughters, to wind up their affairs after their death in the role of the successor trustee of their living trust, they have already discussed it with her. But because Katerina's son, Tad, has never accepted Pavel, and remains hostile to him, Katerina and Pavel sadly decide that talking their plan over with Tad will only provide an occasion for more rancor. So they simply don't tell him what they've agreed upon.

EXAMPLE 2: THE IMPOVERISHED HUSBAND

Angelina, in her 70s, is a wealthy widow with three grown children. She marries Arthur, also in his 70s. They live in Angelina's house. Arthur, who has very little property, has two children from a prior marriage who Angelina does not particularly care for. As she plans her estate, Angelina realizes she wants to allow Arthur to remain in the house if she dies before he does, but doesn't want him to be able to rent out the house, nor be able to sell it and buy another one. She discusses her concerns with him. He is bothered that she doesn't trust him fully. She explains frankly that her children, who are delighted she has married Arthur, are nevertheless concerned that his children might end up with what they see as their inheritance.

Angelina decides to leave much of her property outright to her children. She will create a trust for the house, and leave enough money in the trust to pay for mortgage and upkeep on the house, plus a little extra to supplement Arthur's Social Security and small pension. The trust will be managed by the most responsible of her children. Arthur will have the right to live in the house for the duration of his life and receive the income produced by the trust.

Arthur agrees with this arrangement, but asks what happens if he gets ill and must be hospitalized? Will he be thrown out of the house? His concern prompts Angelina to realize that there are aspects of the trust to pin down. She doesn't want to allow the possibility that Arthur can be thrown out of the house if he's in the hospital for a week. But also, if he moves permanently to a nursing home, she prefers that the house then be turned over to her children rather than remain in trust until Arthur dies. She discusses her concerns with Arthur. He's understanding but concerned, himself, about becoming ill and having to leave the house for a while and then not being able to return to it.

After considerable discussion, Angelina and Arthur agree that he will retain the right to live in, or return to, the house if he's lived away from it for up to eight consecutive months. If he's been away from it for a longer period than that, the house will come under management by the trustee, who can rent it out. But the trustee cannot sell it or live in it or allow other children to live in it while Arthur lives. Any income from the rental is added to the trust income available for Arthur.

Since Angelica is leaving much of her property outright to her children, outside this trust, she feels it is fair for them to wait to inherit the house until Arthur's death. He's in his 70s after all. Anyway, she may well outlive him, and she'll certainly keep the house herself until her death. Angelica then sees a good estate planning lawyer to prepare the trust she wants. With the lawyer's aid, Angelica pins down precisely how the trust will work.

E. LONG-TERM CARE FOR A CHILD WITH SPECIAL NEEDS

Parents of mentally and sometimes physically disabled children may need to provide care and support for those children whether they are minors or adults. Providing this care often requires the help of experts, particularly to coordinate the parents' contributions with rules on government benefits. Usually, a long-term trust must be created. This type of trust is discussed further in Chapter 25, Trusts and Other Devices for Imposing Controls Over Property, Section C. Also, it may well be that, in their estate planning, parents, like it or not, may need to concentrate most of their resources for their disabled child, leaving less for any other children.

EXAMPLE: WORKING IT OUT

The Balfour family has a disabled child Bob, age 15, who will need care all his life. They have two other children, both of whom are healthy. The Balfours' primary estate planning concern is doing all they can to arrange for Bob's care after they die. They realize this means leaving Bob most of their modest estate. They discuss this with their 19-year-old daughter, Rebecca, who says "that's fine." Their other son, Jeb, resents Bob a little and isn't so acquiescent. But the Balfours decide that protecting Bob remains their top priority. They hope that, as Jeb matures, he will understand the difficulties Bob faces and that his resentment that Bob got more than his share (as Jeb defines it) of parental attention will fade.

There are many questions the parents must resolve about Bob. Who will be responsible for Bob's personal care after they die? How can they best leave money for his use? How will any money they leave be treated when determining eligibility for government benefits? After all, it makes no sense to leave money to Bob if it means he will be ineligible for government help until it's all used up.

The Balfours must chose a personal guardian to be responsible for Bob until he becomes a legal adult, at age 18, and a financial guardian or manager to supervise any money they leave for Bob, as long as Bob lives.

The Balfours discuss these concerns themselves and then broaden their discussion to include Rebecca and other family members and close friends they are considering for these two tasks. Eventually, they choose Mrs. Balfour's younger sister to be Bob's personal guardian if needed. They name their closest friend, William, to be Bob's financial manager, until Rebecca turns 30. After that, she will become Bob's financial manager.

To understand how to dovetail money they leave Bob in trust with government benefits, the Balfours do some preliminary research. They decide to establish a "special needs" trust for Bob. They have this trust drafted by an expert who designs it to maintain Bob's eligibility for government assistance programs and to provide control for the trustee (the property manager) over trust property used for Bob's benefit.

F. CONCERNS OF UNMARRIED COUPLES

Unmarried couples have no right to inherit each other's property, unless each member of the couple makes a will or legally leaves property to the other. A central concern of most unmarried couples is to do just this. Happily, unmarried people—whether lesbian, gay or heterosexual—have the right to leave their property to whomever they want, as long as they're competent. (Even if one or both has been legally married in the past, they have no obligation to their ex-spouse, unless specific support is still required by the divorce decree.) In case of serious legal threat by hostile family members, a couple may take action to establish by clear proof that they were competent when they prepared their estate plan.

EXAMPLE: VIDEOTAPE EVIDENCE

Ernest and Linda have lived together for many years. Aside from a few small gifts to friends or family, each wants to leave all their property to the other after death. They're concerned with efficiency and economy, but above all they want to be sure that their estate plan can't be successfully attacked by several close relatives who have long been hostile to their lifestyle. Ernest and Linda each prepare a living trust leaving their property as they desire. They videotape their signing and the notarization of this document to provide additional proof they were both mentally competent and not under duress or undue influence when they signed.

G. WORRIES ABOUT THE EFFECT OF INHERITING MONEY

Sometimes people worry that someone they want to leave money or property to cannot handle it. In other words, they fear their gifts will have destructive results: the beneficiaries may be too young or too immature, for example. Resolving these concerns always requires a careful examination both of the strengths and weaknesses of the potential beneficiaries. Sometimes it also involves putting one's own worries and prejudices under as objective a personal microscope as possible.

EXAMPLE 1: THE SCHOOL OF HARD KNOCKS

Ely is quite wealthy, and worried about the effects of his wealth on his children and grandchildren. He grew up poor, worked hard all his life and made a small fortune. Shouldn't his kids, now in their 20s and 30s and just making their way in the world, be encouraged to continue to work hard, at least until they're old enough to keep a large inheritance in perspective? If Ely dies soon, and each child inherits over $1 million, will they lose their incentive to strive for goals they might strive for otherwise? Ely is not the type to question whether losing the incentive to strive might be a good thing. He had it, he wants his kids to have it. Ely wonders if his best estate plan wouldn't be to say, "Being of sound mind, I spent all I could and I give the rest to charity"? And what about his grandchildren? Should he give money only to those who join his business? (The fact that none of his children did still rankles.)

No matter how much Ely learns about the intricacies of tax planning and probate avoidance, he needs to do some serious thinking and reflecting on the subject of his money and his family before he can hope to make a sound estate plan. Or put another way, Ely needs to better understand the complicated nature of his own emotions and expectations pertaining to his money. Once over this hurdle, he should be better able to make up a plan to benefit his children and grandchildren.

For example, perhaps Ely will realize that his dedication to making it the hard way is perhaps a tad extreme, but does contain some truth. If so, he may leave (or even give) moderate amounts of property to his children outright to help them cope better with parenting their young children. Ely will leave the rest of his estate in trust for his children. Each child will receive a moderate amount of income for a number of years, only getting the bulk of the property at the age Ely has chosen. (For example, Joseph Kennedy, Sr., established trusts for each of his children that didn't release the trust property until that child became 50 years old.)

Ely decides he doesn't want to pressure, or hire, a grandchild into his business by promises of additional inheritance. Instead, he creates an education trust for each grandchild, leaving each $50,000 for college or other educational costs.

EXAMPLE 2: THE GRASSHOPPER AND THE ANT

Sylvia, a wealthy widow, has two children in their 30s: Yvonne, the sensible one, and Colleen, who's always been improvident and often more than a little self-destructive. Sylvia wants to leave her estate equally to her two daughters. She'll give Yvonne's half to her outright, but she's troubled by the thought of Colleen receiving several hundred thousand dollars. Sylvia decides it's sensible to leave

Colleen her money in what's called a "spend-thrift" trust, where a trustee, someone other than Colleen, controls the money (principal), and Colleen receives only the trust income. (See Chapter 25.) She can only draw on any of the trust principal if the trustee agrees she needs it for educational, medical or other essential needs.

Sylvia still faces three important problems: First, who is to be trustee of the trust? Second, should she tell Colleen what she's decided upon? Third, when should the trust end? Sylvia discusses both questions with Yvonne, who convinces her mother that, for reasons having to do with sibling rivalry, she—Yvonne—shouldn't be the trustee. Sylvia reluctantly agrees that, given the personalities involved, and the fact that Colleen will hate not to get the money outright, it's sure to be personally destructive if one sister controls the other's inheritance. So, Sylvia decides to appoint her younger brother as trustee. She also decides the trust will end when Colleen becomes 45, at which point she will get all the money outright. She hopes Colleen will be fully responsible by then. Finally, she decides to tell Colleen her plan, although she's not joyously anticipating that discussion. She softens the blow by also telling Colleen that if, over the coming years, she decides Colleen has matured and can handle money, she will change her estate plan and leave Colleen her money outright.

H. DISINHERITING PEOPLE, INCLUDING CHILDREN

Some parents want to disinherit a child, or children. Other people want to ensure that certain relations or ex-friends get none of their property. Legally, there is

no need to disinherit friends or relatives other than your spouse or children—they inherit nothing unless you expressly leave them some property. When it comes to your spouse, he or she normally has rights to a certain percentage of your property. (See Chapter 3, Special Property Ownership Rules for Married People.) It is legal to disinherit a child, however, if you take affirmative steps to do so. (See Chapter 6, Children, Section F.) But deciding to disinherit a child is often not easy to do, emotionally.

EXAMPLE 1: THE BAD SEED

Zorba and Kyria have three children—two daughters and a son—and a substantial estate. They are very close to the two daughters, but bitterly on the outs with their son, Nikos. Zorba and Kyria had originally intended to leave most of their property to each other, with some to the two daughters they're close to. Then, when the surviving spouse dies, the remaining property would be divided between the two daughters. But they have second thoughts. Do they really want to cut their son out entirely? This feels too harsh, too rejecting. And if they do cut Nikos out entirely, are they creating any real risk that he will be able to invalidate their estate plan? Although their lawyer tells them that since they are clearly competent, and can legally disinherit Nikos with little danger of him overturning their estate plan, they decide that both parental charity and prudence dictate the same decision. Each will leave Nikos $25,000 and include a "no-contest" clause in their wills. This clause states that if any beneficiary challenges a will, he gets nothing if his challenge is unsuccessful. The parents expect that Nikos will take the certain $50,000 he'll receive from both parents rather than the risk and the cost of a lawsuit he's almost sure to lose. Also, despite the bitterness they feel towards Nikos, both Zorba and Kyria are relieved that they haven't allowed it to cause them to completely disinherit one of their own children.

EXAMPLE 2: THE CHARITY

Peter has two grown children, both very prosperous. Peter decides he wants to leave most of his estate to his favorite charity—a cause he deeply believes in—and the rest to his children. He hints at this to them. One child is supportive; the other is very upset, arguing that property should stay in the family. Peter decides to stick to his plan, accepting whatever disapproval or conflicts it will cause. In his living trust, he states expressly why he has decided that the bulk of his property is best given to the charity, and that even though he has done this, he loves his children deeply.

I. COMMUNICATING YOUR DECISIONS TO FAMILY AND FRIENDS

Many of the examples we've just discussed demonstrate our belief that communication can usually, though certainly not invariably, resolve potential estate planning difficulties with family and friends. Happily, in many families, talking about the older generation's estate planning isn't difficult. Both the parents and the children want the planning to be out in the open, so there will be no surprises down the road. Of course, there are certainly families where raising the subject of the parents' (or grandparents') estate plan may bring up tension, or touch on old conflicts—and others where the response will not be easy to predict. Only you can decide whether, when

and how to talk about your plans, but here are some suggestions that may help with your thinking process:

- Whom do you want to talk to? Obviously, you need to talk to anyone you are naming to have responsibility for your minor children, or for supervising the distribution of your property after you die. But what about some, or all, of your beneficiaries?

- What should you talk about?

- Do you want to tell people what you've already decided and why, or ask for advice, or state that, within reason, you're open to suggestions? Or do you want to discuss the mechanics of how your estate plan will work with your inheritors? (You should, of course, with your executor and successor trustee.)

- Do you want to give your inheritors copies of your estate plan?

Talking, of course, is not a guarantee of clear sailing. There are occasions when someone doesn't want to hear or talk, or others when communication only reveals a deep and unbridgeable gulf. And from the older generation's point of view, there can be risks involved with communication: if they promise money to beneficiaries, they may feel guilty if a future medical necessity eats up some—or all—of that money. They may also worry that their revealing their plans will expose undesirable qualities like greed and hard-heartedness in those promised to inherit.

From the younger generation's viewpoint, it can be very difficult to open up estate planning discussions with parents. You certainly don't want to try to force a parent to talk about his or her property or plan. At the same time, you may need or want the reassurance that sensible planning has been done. We can suggest no magic formula to make this easier. All you can do is be tactful and genuinely concerned and see if that opens any doors.

But we do think it makes sense for all parents to at least indicate that planning has been carried out. If not, it's a good idea for communication to be initiated by a child, especially if that child knows or suspects her parent, or parents, have not taken care of even the basics. Saying this is easy, but of course, there can be many barriers to candor, such as:

- a general societal code that death is an unmentionable, especially with one's own parents

- fear that motives can be misunderstood. A parent may fear being seen as trying to manipulate a child by offering inherited money for demonstrations of love. A child, in turn, may fear that raising the subject will be seen as pushy or greedy

- the sense that honor lies in not caring about a parent's property, or that of any other loved one.

Still, the results of talking openly are usually positive. For example, we know of a situation in which a child who had done very well financially asked her parents to leave a disproportionate share of their estate to the other children. The children's discussion provided the impetus for their parents to do estate planning they'd intended to do for years. They were quite relieved to finally have it accomplished. Even where there are less dramatic results, we feel that communication, particularly among family members, about one's estate plan is a healthy process that can aid in preventing later conflicts. ■

3

SPECIAL PROPERTY OWNERSHIP RULES FOR MARRIED PEOPLE

A. What You Need to Know 3/3
B. Marital Property in Community Property States 3/5
    1. What Is Community Property? 3/5
    2. What Is Separate Property? 3/6
    3. Pensions 3/6
    4. Distinguishing Community and Separate Property 3/7
C. Marital Property in Common Law States 3/7
    1. Who Owns What 3/8
    2. Family Protection in Common Law States 3/8
D. Moving to a Different State 3/9
    1. Moving From a Common Law State to a Community
       Property State 3/10
    2. Moving From a Community Property State to a
       Common Law Property State 3/10

If you are married, special state property ownership laws may affect your estate planning. These laws determine what you own individually and what you own as a member of a couple, and may also give your spouse a right to claim a share of your property after your death.

If you and your spouse plan to leave all, or the lion's share, of your property to each other, it's not of much practical importance to understand who legally owns each item of property. After all, as long as the survivor will get all, or even most, of the property, it's not important how it's labeled. However, if you plan to make substantial gifts of property to someone other than your spouse (especially if your spouse might prefer that you didn't), it's essential that you understand both who owns the property and whether there are any rules in your state which give your spouse the right to at least a minimum portion of it at your death. Otherwise, your decision to give property to someone other than your spouse may occasion a nasty conflict after your death.

IF YOU'RE UNSURE OF YOUR MARITAL STATUS

Most people are quite certain of their marital status. If you're not, here's what you need to know.

The divorce decree. You're not divorced until you have a final decree of divorce (or dissolution, as it's called in some states) issued by a state court in the United States, or under limited circumstances by the legally empowered authorities of a foreign country. (See below.)

If you think you're divorced but never saw the final decree, contact the court clerk in the county where you think the divorce was granted. Give the clerk your name, your ex-spouse's name and the date, as close as you know it, of the divorce.

Legal separation. Even if a court has declared you and your spouse legally separated, and you plan to divorce, you are still married until you get the divorce decree.

Foreign divorces. Divorces issued to U.S. citizens by courts in Mexico, the Dominican Republic or another country may not be valid if challenged, especially if all the paperwork was handled by mail. In other words, if you or your spouse got a quickie foreign divorce, you may well be still married under the laws of your state. On the other hand, foreign divorces, where both spouses were present in person or through a representative, may be recognized as valid in the U.S. If you think that someone might make a claim to some of your property after your death based on the invalidity of a foreign divorce, see a lawyer.

Common law marriages. In some states, a couple can become legally married by living together, intending to be married and clearly presenting themselves to the world as a married couple. Even in states that allow such common law marriages, most couples who live together don't have common law marriages. Folk law notwithstanding, no magic number of years of living together automatically establishes a common law marriage. If you really do have a valid common law marriage, you must go to court and get a divorce to end it—there's no such thing as a common law divorce.

A. WHAT YOU NEED TO KNOW

In the U.S., there are two major types of marital property law systems. Eight states, mostly in the West, have "community property" law. (Louisiana which has a form of community property, originally from French law, isn't covered in this book.) The other 41 states and the District of Columbia follow the "common law" system.

COMMUNITY PROPERTY AND COMMON LAW STATES

COMMUNITY PROPERTY	COMMON LAW
Arizona	All other states and
California	the District of
Idaho	Columbia
New Mexico	
Nevada	
Texas	
Washington	
Wisconsin (called "marital property")	

In community property states, spouses typically share ownership of most property, even if only one spouse's name is on the title slip or deed. In these states, each spouse is free to leave his or her half of the property as desired, but has no control over the other spouse's half

In the "common law" states the spouse whose name appears in the ownership document owns that property. However, unlike community property states, these state provide that each spouse has a legal right to claim at least a minimum portion of the other's property at death, even if the deceased spouse left it all to someone else.

Marital property ownership can be confusing. This chapter discusses the basic rules that apply to marital property. It's impossible, short of a ten-volume treatise, to cover every complexity and nuance of marital property law for every state. If you have a question that isn't answered in these pages, you'll need to see a lawyer or research it yourself. (See Chapter 29, Using Lawyers.)

If you think marital property laws could affect your situation, you need to know:

1. Which state is your "domicile," the legalese term for where you permanently live, where you have your home.

You can have only one domicile. The state of your domicile governs your marital property—except real estate in another state or country. If you have homes in two or more states, it can be important which you choose as your legal domicile, both for property ownership and state inheritance tax purposes. Given a choice, it's usually best to opt for a state that imposes no, or low, property taxes. (See Chapter 15, Estate Taxes, Section G, for information on state death taxes.)

If you are unsure where you are domiciled. If you own two or more homes in the U.S. or live both in the U.S. and abroad, see a lawyer to discuss how this affects your estate planning. You must determine which state's or country's laws govern your marital property and what, if anything, you can do to change this if you so desire.

2. The property ownership laws of your home state, and of any other state or country where you own real estate. Real estate is controlled by the law of the state or country where it is located, no matter where you live.

Divorce means a new estate plan. If you get divorced, re-examine your estate plan and bring it up to date. In most states, divorce automatically revokes your will as to gifts left to your former spouse—but not in all states. Even in states where a divorce invalidates an earlier will's gifts to a divorced spouse, you still need to designate whom you now want to get that property. Also, in almost all states, divorce does not revoke a living trust, even if an ex-spouse benefits from it.

VARYING STATE PROPERTY OWNERSHIP LAWS BY CONTRACT

If you and your spouse don't like the way your state's law defines how the two of you share ownership of jointly owned property, you can normally agree to change it. To accomplish this, you need a valid contract between you and your spouse. For example, in most states you can agree to change the ownership status of property acquired prior to marriage, which would normally be owned as separate property by the acquiring spouse, to joint ownership. A written agreement to do this made before a marriage, where the couple set out the terms by which their property, before and after marriage, shall be owned, is called a "prenuptial contract" or "marital contract."

Prenuptial contracts must comply with your state's laws governing them. Generally, this means they must be in writing, voluntarily agreed to by both spouses, and have been agreed to after fair disclosure by both spouses of their property ownership and financial obligations. These agreements often explicitly cover inheritance, and property ownership, for estate planning purposes. Of course, valid agreements can also be made after a couple is married.

Marital contracts and inheritance rights can be a confusing combination. If you want to prepare, or already have, a marital property contract and are in doubt as to how its provisions affect your rights to leave property at death, see an attorney.

RESOLVING CONFLICTS OVER PROPERTY OWNERSHIP

It's not crucial to define which spouse owns what property if you and your spouse plan to leave all or most of your property to each other, or in a way the other approves of. However, if you and your spouse discover any conflict over your property ownership that will significantly affect your estate planning, you need to deal with it.

It's best, of course, if you are able to resolve any disagreements between yourselves. If that doesn't work, we urge (parental as we may sound) that you get professional help—from a mediator, lawyer, or a therapist. If a mutually agreeable compromise isn't reached prior to death, and one spouse tries to leave property the other believes he or she doesn't own, there is real danger of a nasty court fight. After resolving any problems, both spouses should sign an agreement setting forth their decisions

---

B. MARITAL PROPERTY IN COMMUNITY PROPERTY STATES

The basic rule of community property law is simple: During a marriage, all property earned or acquired by either spouse is owned in equal half shares by each spouse—except for property received as "separate property" by only one of them through gift or inheritance. This community property concept derives from the ancient marriage laws of some European peoples, including the Visigoths, which passed to Spain and then to many Western states through Spanish explorers and settlers. For estate planning purposes, there are no restrictions on how each spouse can leave his or her half of their community property. Neither is required to leave it to the surviving spouse, although, of course, many spouses do.

In community property states, "separate property" is property owned entirely by one spouse. Property owned by one spouse before a marriage remains separate property even after the marriage, as long as it's kept separate. Also, property one spouse is given or inherits is his or her separate property.

For many couples in long-term marriages, characterizing their property is relatively easy: it's all community property. Any property owned by either spouse before marriage is either long gone or so totally mixed with community property that it has long since lost its separate property status. Neither spouse has inherited or been given any substantial amount of separate property during the marriage, or if they have, it, too, has been mixed into the community pot. Still, even if you believe this to be your situation, read the next few pages to be sure.

1. What Is Community Property?

Unless the husband and wife agree to something different, the following is community property:

• all income received by either spouse from employment or by other means (except by gift or inheritance to one spouse) during the marriage. This generally refers only to the period when the couple is living together as husband and wife. From the time spouses permanently separate, most community property states consider newly acquired income and property as the separate property of the spouse receiving it.

• all property acquired with community property income during the marriage, and

• all separate property that is transformed into community property under state law. This transformation can occur in several ways, including when one spouse makes a gift of separate property to both of them. Generally, such a transfer must be done with a signed document.

Example: Ned Terrlin owned a home for five years before he married Sally. He then signed a new deed for the house, listing the new owners as "Ned and Sally Terrlin, as community property." Ned has given one-half ownership of the house to Sally.

Community property can also be transformed into separate property by gifts between spouses. The rules for how to do this differ somewhat from state to state. Normally, if real estate is given, the gift must be in writing. And even for other property, the strong trend is to require that the gift must be made in writing.

Another common example of transformation of separate property is when it gets so mixed together with community property that it's no longer possible to tell the difference between the two. Lawyers call this "commingling."

Example: When she got married, Felicity had a bank account with $14,000 in it, her separate property. During her marriage, now in its 27th year, she maintained this account, depositing money she or her husband earned and making frequent withdrawals. No money in the account is separate property. The original $14,000 has long since been "commingled" with community property funds.

Each spouse can keep his or her own income as separate property. All community property states except Washington allow spouses to treat income earned after marriage as separate property if they sign a written agreement to do so and then actually keep their income separate—for example, in separate bank accounts.

2. What Is Separate Property?

The following property qualifies as separate property:

- all property owned by either spouse prior to marriage
- all property received by one spouse after marriage by gift or inheritance, and
- all property earned or accumulated by one spouse after permanent separation.

As mentioned, separate property stays that way so long as it is not:

- hopelessly mixed (commingled) with community property, or
- transferred in writing to shared ownership by the separate property owner.

Income from separate property. Community property states have different rules for classifying certain types of income derived from separate property:

California, Arizona, Nevada, New Mexico and Washington: Any income from separate property during a marriage is also separate property.

Texas and Idaho: Income from separate property during a marriage is community property.

Wisconsin: Its law is unclear on this point; if it concerns you, see a lawyer.

3. Pensions

Generally, private pensions and military pensions are considered community property—at least the proportion of them attributable to earnings during the marriage. However, benefits from certain major federal pension programs, including Social Security and Railroad Retirement, aren't community property because federal law classifies them as the separate property of the employee.

4. Distinguishing Community and Separate Property

Most married couples have little difficulty determining what's community property and what is each one's separate property. However, these issues can get complicated. Divorce courts churn out a continual stream of decisions on the fine points of community versus separate property. Here are a few potential problem areas in estate planning.

Appreciated property. In most community property states, when the separate property of one spouse goes up in value, this appreciation is also separate property. However, sometimes one spouse owns separate property before a marriage, but both spouses contribute to the cost of maintaining or improving it during the marriage. The result can be that the property is part community, part separate. If the property substantially appreciates in value over the years, it can be difficult to determine what percentage of the current value of the property is separate property and what is community property.

A common example is a house that was originally owned by one spouse. Then for a length of time, say 10 or 20 years, both spouses pay, from community funds, for mortgage, insurance, and upkeep. If the value of the house grew during the marriage, the couple can determine what portion of the present value is community property by agreeing in writing on any arrangement they decide is fair.

Businesses. If a family-owned business was owned by one spouse in whole or part before marriage and grew later, difficult ownership questions can arise. As with home ownership, the basic problem is to figure out what proportion (if any) of the increased value is community property. Again, a married couple can agree on any arrangement they want to. If both spouses work in the business, one sensible approach is to consider all the increase in value from the date of marriage as community property. However, if only the spouse who originally owned the business works in it, resolving ownership percentages can be more difficult. If it's likely the business would have grown in value anyway, much of the increase could reasonably be regarded as separate property.

Monetary recovery for personal injuries. As a general matter, personal injury awards or settlements are the separate property of the spouse receiving them, but not always. In some community property states, this money is treated one way (community property) while the injured spouse is living and another way (separate property) upon his death. Also, the determination as to whether it's separate or community property can vary when the injury is caused by the other spouse. In short, there's no easy way to characterize this type of property. If this issue concerns you, see a lawyer.

Additional Resources

Good sources of information if you're interested in pursuing this community property law further are:

- *Community Property Law in the United States,* by W. S. McClanahan (Bancroft-Whitney)

- *Nolo's Pocket Guide to Family Law,* by Robin Leonard & Steve Elias (Nolo Press).

C. MARITAL PROPERTY IN COMMON LAW STATES

Common law states protect spouses and keep them from being left out in the (property) cold when the other spouse dies. But they do it in a very different way than community property states.

1. Who Owns What

In common law states, there's no rule that property acquired during a marriage is owned by both spouses. Common law principles are derived from English law, where in feudal times the husband owned all marital property; a wife had few property ownership rights and couldn't even leave any property by will. Still today, in the common law states, the spouse who earns money or acquires property owns it separately and solely, unless, of course, he or she transfers it into shared ownership.

In common law states, the property you own for estate planning purposes, whether you are married or not, consists of:

- everything held separately in your name if it has a title slip, deed or other legal ownership document (this always includes real estate, vehicles, securities and bank accounts, and your ownership interest in joint tenancy or other shared ownership property), and

- all other property you have purchased from your assets or income.

For example, if you earn or inherit money to buy a house, and title is taken in both your name and your spouse's, you both own it. But if your spouse earns the money to buy it, but somehow title is placed in your name alone, you own it. Similarly, no matter who puts up funds to buy a house, if title is in your spouse's name, he or she owns it.

Despite the general rule stated here, these states have rules that prevent a spouse from disinheriting the other.

2. Family Protection in Common Law States

Common law states give a surviving spouse legal rights to claim a certain portion—usually one-third to one-half—of the other's estate.

Suppose, for example, one spouse owns the family house, the car and bank accounts in his name alone and attempts to leave it all to a stranger (or, worse, a lover). Can the stranger kick the surviving spouse out of the house, empty the bank accounts, and so on? Of course, this rarely happens, but just in case, the common law property states prevent the surviving spouse from being completely, or even substantially, disinherited. While many of these protective laws are similar, they do differ in detail.

The methods that common law states use to protect families were developed hundreds of years ago by English courts, which were confronted with the same problem of a few people disinheriting their spouses. In response, they developed legal concepts called "dower" and "curtesy." "Dower" refers to the rights of a surviving wife; "curtesy" is the share received by a surviving husband. When the United States was settled, most states adopted these concepts. To this day, all common law states still retain some version of dower and curtesy, although many have dropped the old terminology and simply provide for "spousal inheritance rights" or some similar phrase.

In most common law property states, a spouse is entitled to one-third of the property left by the other. In a few, it's one-half. The exact amount of the spouse's minimum share often depends on whether or not the couple has minor children.

In some states, the surviving spouse must be left only a certain percentage of the property that is transferred by will. In other states, property transferred by other means, such as a living trust or joint tenancy, is included when calculating whether a spouse has received his or her minimum legal share of property. This is called the "augmented estate"

Example: Alice leaves her husband, Mike, $10,000 and her three daughters $90,000 each in her will. However, Alice also leaves real estate worth $500,000 to Mike by a living trust. The total Mike receives from this augmented estate, $510,000, is more than one-half of Alice's total property, so he has nothing to gain by insisting on his right to make a claim against her will property.

A surviving spouse does not automatically inherit that share that's guaranteed by law; he or she must go to court and ask for it. So if a person leaves nothing to a spouse or leaves less than the spouse is entitled to under state law, the surviving spouse has a choice of either taking what the will or other transfer document provides or rejecting the gift and instead claiming the minimum share allowed by state law. Taking the share permitted by law is called "taking against the will."

Example: Leonard's will leaves $50,000 to his second wife, June, and leaves the rest of his property, totaling $400,000, to his two children from his first marriage. June can take the $50,000 or elect to take against the will

and receive her statutory share of Leonard's estate. Depending on the state, this will about one-third to one-half of Leonard's total estate.

When a spouse decides to take against the will, the property which is taken must come out of what was left to others. In other words, somebody else is going to get less. In the above example, the children will receive much less than Leonard intended. So, if you don't provide your spouse with at least the statutory share under your state's laws, your gifts to others may be seriously reduced.

If you want to leave your spouse little or nothing, see a lawyer. Put bluntly, if you don't wish to leave your spouse at least one-half of your property, and you haven't gotten your spouse's unforced and written consent to your plan, your estate may be heading for a legal mess. See a lawyer.

D. MOVING TO A DIFFERENT STATE

A will or living trust valid in one state is, broadly speaking, valid in all. However, problems can develop when married people move from a community property state to a common law property state or vice versa. This is because the property each spouse owns (and is therefore free to leave or give away) may change. If spouses move from one state to another which follows the same property ownership system (for example, New York to Florida, or California to Texas), there is no need to worry about new marital property ownership rules.

Remember, technical property ownership rules are not a worry if spouses plan to leave all (or the lion's share) of their property to each other, or in a way the other spouse approves of.

1. Moving From a Common Law State to a Community Property State

What happens when a husband and wife acquire property in a non-community property state but then move to a community property state? California, Idaho and Washington (community property states) treat the earlier acquired property as if it had been acquired in a community property state. The legal jargon for this type of property is "quasi-community property." Thus, if you and your spouse moved from any non-community property state into California or Idaho, all of your property is treated according to community property rules. (See Section B, above.)

The other community property states don't recognize the quasi-community property concept for estate planning purposes and instead enforce the rules of the state where the property was acquired. So if you moved into any of the other community property states from a common law state, you'll need to assess your property according to the rules of the state where you used to live.

2. Moving From a Community Property State to a Common Law Property State

When spouses move from a community property state to a common law property one, each generally retains a one-half interest in the property accumulated during marriage while they lived in the community property state. However, the courts have not been entirely consistent in dealing with the problem in situations where the property is in one spouse's name.

Spousal disagreements. If you have moved from a community property state to a common law state, and you and your spouse have any disagreement or confusion as to who owns what, check with a lawyer. ■

4

INVENTORYING YOUR PROPERTY

A. Instructions for the Property Inventory Worksheet 4/2

    1. Section I: What You Own 4/2

    2. Section II: What You Owe 4/8

    3. Section III: Your Net Worth 4/8

B. Your Property Worksheet 4/8

Preparing a thorough written inventory of your property is a good idea for thorough estate planning, so you can:

- remind yourself of what you own

- determine what you owe

- estimate the current net value of your estate as an aid to estate tax planning

- pin down any shared ownership of property

- make a handy list to refer to when leaving gifts to beneficiaries in a will or living trust, and

- have your assets organized in case you later consult an estate planning lawyer.

This being said, it's still up to you to decide whether you want to itemize your property in detail or simply estimate its overall worth. For some people, as much precision as possible is an important part of the process—we wouldn't dare say fun—of planning their estate. For others, giving the subject just enough thought to arrive at a decent ballpark estimate suffices. For example:

- If you want to leave all your property to one person, perhaps your spouse, or to your spouse for his lifetime use and then equally to your children, there is far less need to itemize all major items of property than if you wanted to leave separate gifts to a good-sized list of people.

- If you are confident that your net estate is worth less than the federal estate tax threshold, and is likely to remain so, there's no reason to estimate the value of your estate for tax purposes. (See Chapter 15, Section A.)

Example: Jane wants to leave all of her woodworking tools and equipment to her friend Alice, her car to her friend Amy, and everything else she owns (stocks, jewelry, money market funds and personal & household possessions) to her longtime companion Mary. She knows her estate is worth no more than

$400,000, well under the federal estate tax threshold, that the state she lives in imposes no death taxes, and that she has no significant debts. Jane decides there's no need for her to list separately each item of property, since with two easy-to-remember exceptions, she's leaving it all to Mary.

One caveat here. If you're a member of a couple, and plan to leave most or all of your property outright to the other member, and your combined estates exceed the estate tax threshold, estate taxes will probably be assessed when the second spouse dies. So you may want to do some tax planning. (See Chapter 18, Section C.)

A. INSTRUCTIONS FOR THE PROPERTY INVENTORY WORKSHEET

Section B of this chapter contains a worksheet to help you inventory your property. As you'll see, you can record a wide range of property. Take a minute to get acquainted with its structure.

The following detailed description of the worksheet and the suggestions for completing it are for those who want or need to be thorough. It's up to you to decide how extensive and detailed your own listings need to be—or if you don't want to use the chart at all.

1. Section I: What You Own

In Section I of the chart, you list your assets—all the property you own. There are four kinds of information to give for each item of property:

- Column 1—a description of the item of property

- Column 2—if ownership of that item is shared, enter the type of shared ownership

- Column 3—the percentage of any shared owner-ship property you own
- Column 4—the net value of each item of property (or your share of it) you own.

Now let's take a minute to review the information that should be entered in each column.

You May Be Worth More Than You Think

We've been surprised to learn that quite a few people who have worked hard for years, and live a frugal life, find it difficult to admit that their assets could be worth more—sometimes substantially more—than the federal estate tax threshold.

This can occur with owners of appreciated real estate or a successful small business. When asked how much a residence or business is worth, the owner may think in terms of what was paid for it, plus some, relatively small, mark-up. We've seen situations where this estimate was hundreds of thousands of dollars off the mark. Or a person may have become so accustomed to the family furniture and paintings he doesn't consider the possibility that the heirlooms are now much sought-after antiques or valuable art.

This lack of fiscal up-to-dateness can mean that a person just doesn't want to admit that he has money. But indulging in denial at the cost of not planning one's estate carefully is no favor to one's beneficiaries, who most likely hope you'll take sensible steps to pass money to them, rather than giving a large amount to the government in taxes. So, be sure your estimates as to how much your property is worth are contemporary.

Column 1: Identify and Describe Your Property

Here you identify your property with sufficient detail so there can be no question what it includes. This worksheet divides your property into four groups:

A. Liquid assets, which include cash, savings, checking and money market accounts, and certificates of deposit.

EXAMPLES:

- Certificate of Deposit No. 10235, Lighthouse Savings and Loan Association, Ventura, CA
- My savings account at Bay Bank (if you have only one savings account)
- My savings account number 18-17411 at Bay Bank (if you have more than one savings account).

B. Other personal property, which includes all your property except liquid assets, business interests and real estate. This catch-all category includes stocks, mutual fund shares, other securities, bonds, automobiles, jewelry, furs, precious metals, artworks, antiques, tools, life insurance, collectibles, etc.

EXAMPLES:

- 50 shares Transpacific Corporation common stock
- $10,000 El Dorado Drainage and Water System, District of Alameda, 1980 bond series C, 10.5% due June 1, 2000
- 1986 Ford automobile, License # 123456
- All my fishing equipment
- Gold earrings with the small rubies in them purchased from Charles Shreve and Co. in 1971

- Daumier print captioned "Les beaux jours de la vie"
- Life insurance policy #A106004, You-Bet-Your-Life Insurance Co.
- All my carpenter's tools, including my power saws.

If you are like most people, you have all sorts of minor personal possessions you don't want to bother itemizing. To deal with these, you can group a number of items in one category: "all my tools," "all my dolls," or baseball cards, or records, or machines and equipment or household furniture—whatever. Of course, some items without large monetary value may have great emotional worth to you and your family: a photo album, an old music box, a treasured chair. List these individually as you desire.

As another alternative, you can conclude your list with one catch-all item such as "all my other personal possessions and furnishings."

C. Business personal property, including all business interests, except any real estate used in that business

EXAMPLES:

- My shares of stock in the Mo-To Corporation
- My business d/b/a Ace Stationery Store, Boca Raton, Florida
- My partnership interest in JTL Partnership Enterprises, Main Office, Detroit, Michigan
- All my copyrights and rights to royalties in the book with the following titles, currently published by Acme Press, Berkeley, California [titles listed]
- My membership interest in the Gaelic Basketball Lounge Limited Liability Company.

D. Real estate, including all business real estate, and all houses coops/condominiums, mobile homes attached to land, undeveloped or agricultural land. (The rules on when an attached mobile home becomes "real estate" vary from state to state. If this matters to you, see a lawyer.)

To describe real estate, simply list its address or location. This is normally the street address. If there's no post office address, as with undeveloped land, simply describe the real property in normal language like this: "my 120 acres in Lincoln County near the town of Douglas." You don't need to use the legal description from the deed.

EXAMPLES:

- 126 Oceanview Terrace, Mendocino, California
- My lot on Keeler Street, Middletown, Ohio
- 1001 Main Street (the Fullerton Hardware Building), Moose, New York.

Real property often contains items which are properly classified as personal property. For instance, farms are often sold with tools and animals. If you intend to keep both together (as one gift), indicate what this "together" consists of. It's best to specify the large ticket items (tractor, cattle) and refer generally to the rest of the items as "personal property."

EXAMPLES:

- My 240-acre truck farm in Whitman County with all tools, animals, machines and other personal property located there
- My fishing cabin on the Wild River in Maine with all the fishing gear, furniture,

tools and other personal property which
are found there

- My ownership of the mobile home
located at E-Z motor camp, and all
possessions and furnishings contained in
it.

Column 2: Type of Shared Ownership

You need to be concerned with Columns 2 and 3
only if you own some property with someone else. If
you are single and own all your property outright,
you can simply skip to the instructions for Column 4.
However, if you are married or have entered into
personal or business shared ownership transactions,
please read what follows carefully. Obviously, before
you can sensibly plan your estate, you must clearly
understand what you own and therefore have the
power to leave.

You probably know whether you own property
with others. However you may have to do some
investigating to be sure about just how you and the
other owner(s) hold title to the property. Never guess.
If you're not sure how you own an item of property,
take the time to find out. For example, you may have
to locate the deed to your house or your stock
ownership records to clarify whether you and your
spouse own them in joint tenancy. You can check real
estate records at the county property recorder's office.

If you live in a community property state, are
married, and you and your spouse own both separate
and community property, you may have some
difficulty determining exactly what you and your
spouse own. (We discuss this in Chapter 3.) For
example, if you are unsure whether a $23,000 bank
account is community property or your separate
property, bear in mind that you and your spouse can
resolve the confusion by jointly characterizing this
account in either ownership category. To do this
legally, however, it's important to put your conclu-
sion in writing, signed by both of you.

Below we give you a summary of the different
legal forms possible for shared ownership. Some of
these concepts may be new to you. If after reading
what follows you don't understand exactly what a
particular form of shared ownership means, you
needn't worry. They are explained in more depth in
later chapters. Simply note on your worksheet that

the property is held in some form of shared ownership and complete the "Shared Ownership" column later.

Here are the symbols you can use to record the major types of shared ownership:

- **Joint Tenancy (J.T.):** Property held with a written ownership document identifying the owners either as Joint Tenants or Joint Tenants With Right of Survivorship. Under these forms of ownership, each joint tenant owns an equal share of the property. The share of the first tenant to die must go to the survivors, even if there's a will or living trust to the contrary. (Joint tenancy is discussed in detail in Chapter 10.)

Joint tenancy must be created by a written document. If you own property using the phrase "Joint Tenancy With Right of Survivorship," there is no question what type of shared ownership you have. But what about writings that are less clear? For example, suppose your real estate deed says "Tenancy in Common With Right of Survivorship"? In Oregon, this has the same practical effect as joint tenancy; in some other states, it surely doesn't. The point is—don't guess. If you're not clear what kind of legal animal you've got, check it out by doing your own research or checking with a lawyer knowledgeable about real property law.

Similarly, suppose owners are listed simply with an "and" or an "or"? For example, two people own real estate with the title listed as held by "Smith and Jones." Two others own real estate with title listed as "Smith or Jones." Are either of these joint tenancy? The answer is that it depends on the state in which the property is located. Under most states' laws, neither by itself constitutes joint tenancy, but if you hold ownership with another person with "and" or "or" in the title document, you need to know the specific rules of your state.

- **Tenancy by the Entirety (T.E.):** This form of ownership, limited to married couples, is recognized in a minority of states. It is almost identical to joint tenancy and creates a right of survivorship between spouses. It must be created in writing. (See Chapter 10.)

- **Community Property (C.P.):** In the community property states (listed in Chapter 3, Section A), any property spouses earn or acquire during a marriage is shared community property. Even if only one spouse's name is on the title document, if the property was bought with money earned during the marriage, it's community property. There are a few "separate property" exceptions, discussed below.

Don't overlook the fact that you and your spouse may own partnership interests, corporate shares, or an interest in a tenancy in common which is also community property.

You can leave your one-half share of community property to whomever you want to have it. Since the other one-half of the community property belongs to your spouse, you obviously have no power to leave it by your will or living trust.

- **Community Property With Right of Survivorship:** A form of community property that means that the surviving spouse automatically inherits the property when the other spouse dies. In other words, community property that functions like joint tenancy property. Available in Arizona, Nevada, Texas and Wisconsin.

- **Separate Property:** In the eight community property states, all property that isn't community property is held separately. Property that is given to or inherited by one spouse is his or her separate property. Likewise, property owned by each spouse prior to marriage remains separate property, if it's kept distinct from community property.

In the common law states (listed in Chapter 3, Section A), separate property means all property that each spouse owns individually, including all property where one spouse's name appears on the title document, unless there is a written contract to the contrary.

- **Partnership (P.):** Property owned by business partners, regulated by a partnership agreement (including shares in a limited partnership). Partnership agreements often contain detailed rules as to what happens to a partner's share at death.

- **Corporate Shares (C.S.):** Shares of a small or closely held corporation (only a few owners) may be freely transferable at death. However, your freedom to transfer them may also be regulated by corporate bylaws or a separate shareholders' agreement.

- **Limited Liability Co. (LLC):** a type of business ownership allowing owners advantages of both the corporate and partnership forms. An LLC must be establish by formal documents under state law.

- **Tenancy in Common (T.C.):** Any property held in shared ownership which isn't in another type of ownership—in other words, all shared property not owned in joint tenancy, tenancy by the entirety, community property, partnership, corporation or LLC. Tenancy in common includes considerable property spouses own together in common law property states. You can own any percentage of tenancy in common property (.005%, 95%, etc.)—owners' shares don't have to be equal, as they must be for joint tenancy property. If the ownership deed doesn't specify the type of shared ownership, it's probably tenancy in common, although, as mentioned above, in some states the word "or" may indicate joint tenancy ownership. Unlike joint tenancy, where there is an automatic right of survivorship for joint tenants, you can leave your portion of property held as tenants in common as you choose, unless restricted by a contract.

Example: Natalie and Jeremy Engels live in North Carolina, a common law property state. They hold several securities, their house and a piece of land with both their names on the title documents, but no joint tenancy designation. They are presumed to own the property as tenants in common, with each owning a 50% share.

Column 3: Percentage of Shared Property You Own

In this column, list the percentage of each item of shared property you own. People who own property as tenants in common, or in partnership or corporation, should be particularly careful —you can own any percentage of the property. Especially with a partnership, you must check your partnership agreement to be sure. With a tenancy in common, co-owners normally own equal shares (33.3% if you are one of three), unless there is a written agreement to the contrary.

If you own an interest in a partnership or a small corporation, make sure you check your agreement or corporate documents to see if there are any restrictions on your rights to transfer your interest at death. Often other business owners have an option to purchase your shares. (See Chapter 28, Section A.)

Column 4: Current Net Value of Your Ownership

In this column, estimate the "net value" of each item listed. Net value means your equity in your share of the property. Equity is the market value of your share, less your share of any debts on it, such as a mortgage on a house or the loan amount due on a car.

Making estimates normally doesn't require that you burden yourself seeking exact figures or expert appraisals. After all, the value of your estate will surely change some by the time you die. Here you need only ballpark figures. For example, if you have a reasonable notion what's going on about market prices, and you believe that the net worth of your interest in your house, after you subtract the mortgage, is about $200,000, your car $5,000, and your stamp collection $35,000 if you put an ad in a philatelist's journal, use those numbers. Only with more complex types of property, in particular business interests, may expert help be desirable.

Example 1: Clay owns a house with a market value of $350,000 as a tenant in common with his sister Ava; each owns half. Clay computes the net value of his share by first subtracting the amount of mortgages, deeds of trust and liens from the market value to arrive at the total equity in the property

* Market value: $350,000
* Owed on mortgage: $110,000
* Lien against the property: $10,000
* Total equity ($350,000 minus $120,000): $230,000
* Net worth of Clay's share: $115,000

Example 2: Stacey is sole owner of the Maltese Falcon Restaurant, a successful business she has run for 23 years. She has only a vague notion of its market value since she has never been interested in selling it. To competently plan her estate, she needs a reasonable estimate of the worth of the business. This can be difficult to make, particularly since the market value of her restaurant includes the intangible of "good will." Stacey talks to an accountant to help her arrive at a sensible estimate of the worth of the restaurant.

The last step in Section I of the Property Worksheet is to add up the net value of all your assets, and list that sum in Part E.

2. Section II: What You Owe

In Section II, Liabilities, list any liabilities—debts—you haven't already taken into account in Section I. For example, in Section II, list any significant personal debts—the $10,000 loan from a friend or $5,000 unsecured advance on a line of credit. Also list all other liabilities, such as tax liens or court judgments. Remember, you have taken account of mortgages on your real estate and payments owed on your motor vehicle in Section I, so don't list them here.

Add up your estimate of all your liabilities and list that sum in Part D of Section II.

3. Section III: Your Net Worth

Finally, in Section III of the chart, estimate your current net worth. To get this figure, simply subtract your total liabilities listed in Section II from your total assets listed in Section I.

B. YOUR PROPERTY WORKSHEET

Remember, this chart is purely for your convenience. It can be as messy or as neat as you care to make it. Also, pencil is recommended (unless you're the type who does the *New York Times* crossword puzzle in ink).

PROPERTY WORK

I. ASSETS

Column 1 Description of Your Property	Column 2 Type of Shared Ownership	Column 3 Percentage You Own	Column 4 Net Value of Your Ownership

A. Liquid Assets

1. cash (dividends, etc.)

2. savings accounts

3. checking accounts

Column 1 Description of Your Property	Column 2 Type of Shared Ownership	Column 3 Percentage You Own	Column 4 Net Value of Your Ownership
4. money market accounts			
5. certificates of deposit			
6. mutual funds			

Column 1
Description of Your Property

B. Other Personal Property

(all your property except liquid assets, business interests and real estate: houses, buildings, apartments, etc.)

Column 2
Type of Shared Ownership

Column 3
Percentage You Own

Column 4
Net Value of Your Ownership

1. listed (private corporation) stocks and bonds

_____ _____ _____ _____ _____

_____ _____ _____ _____ _____

_____ _____ _____ _____ _____

_____ _____ _____ _____ _____

2. unlisted stocks and bonds

_____ _____ _____ _____ _____

_____ _____ _____ _____ _____

_____ _____ _____ _____ _____

3. government bonds

_____ _____ _____ _____ _____

_____ _____ _____ _____ _____

_____ _____ _____ _____ _____

Column 1 Description of Your Property	Column 2 Type of Shared Ownership	Column 3 Percentage You Own	Column 4 Net Value of Your Ownership
4. automobiles and other vehicles, including planes, boats and recreational vehicles			
_____	_____	_____	_____
_____	_____	_____	_____
_____	_____	_____	_____
5. precious metals			
_____	_____	_____	_____
_____	_____	_____	_____
_____	_____	_____	_____
6. household goods			
_____	_____	_____	_____
_____	_____	_____	_____
_____	_____	_____	_____
7. clothing			
_____	_____	_____	_____
_____	_____	_____	_____
_____	_____	_____	_____

Column 1 Description of Your Property	Column 2 Type of Shared Ownership	Column 3 Percentage You Own	Column 4 Net Value of Your Ownership
8. jewelry and furs			
	_____	_____	_____
	_____	_____	_____
	_____	_____	_____
9. art works, collectibles and antiques			
	_____	_____	_____
	_____	_____	_____
	_____	_____	_____
10. tools and equipment			
	_____	_____	_____
	_____	_____	_____
	_____	_____	_____
11. valuable livestock/animals			
	_____	_____	_____
	_____	_____	_____
	_____	_____	_____

Column 1 Description of Your Property	Column 2 Type of Shared Ownership	Column 3 Percentage You Own	Column 4 Net Value of Your Ownership
12. money owed you (personal loans, etc.)			
13. vested interest in profit sharing plan, stock options, etc.			
14. limited partnerships			
15. vested interest in retirement plans, IRAs, death benefits, annuities			

Column 1 Description of Your Property	Column 2 Type of Shared Ownership	Column 3 Percentage You Own	Column 4 Net Value of Your Ownership
16. life insurance			
17. miscellaneous (any personal property not listed above)			

C. Business Personal Property

1. patents, copyrights, trademarks and royalties

Column 1
Description of Your Property

Column 2
Type of
Shared
Ownership

Column 3
Percentage
You
Own

Column 4
Net Value
of Your
Ownership

2. business ownerships (partnerships, sole proprietorships, limited liability companies, corporations, etc.; list separately and use a separate sheet of paper if you need to elaborate)

name and type of business

_____   _____   _____   _____

_____   _____   _____   _____

_____   _____   _____   _____

3. miscellaneous receivables (mortgages, deeds of trust, or promissory notes held by you; any rents due from income property owned by you; and payments due for professional or personal services or property sold by you that are not fully paid by the purchaser)

_____   _____   _____   _____

_____   _____   _____   _____

_____   _____   _____   _____

_____   _____   _____   _____

Column 1 Description of Your Property	Column 2 Type of Shared Ownership	Column 3 Percentage You Own	Column 4 Net Value of Your Ownership

D. Real Estate

address

_____ | _____ | _____ | _____
_____ | _____ | _____ | _____
_____ | _____ | _____ | _____
_____ | _____ | _____ | _____

address

_____ | _____ | _____ | _____
_____ | _____ | _____ | _____
_____ | _____ | _____ | _____
_____ | _____ | _____ | _____

address

_____ | _____ | _____ | _____
_____ | _____ | _____ | _____
_____ | _____ | _____ | _____
_____ | _____ | _____ | _____

Column 1 Description of Your Property	Column 2 Type of Shared Ownership	Column 3 Percentage You Own	Column 4 Net Value of Your Ownership
address _____	_____	_____	_____
_____	_____	_____	_____
_____	_____	_____	_____
_____	_____	_____	_____
address _____	_____	_____	_____
_____	_____	_____	_____
_____	_____	_____	_____
_____	_____	_____	_____

E. TOTAL NET VALUE OF ALL YOUR ASSETS $ _____

II. LIABILITIES *(what you owe)*

Many of your liabilities will already have been accounted for because you listed the net value of your property in Part I of this chart. For example, to determine the net value of your interest in real estate, you deducted the amount of all mortgages and encumbrances on that real estate. Similarly the value of a small business is the value after business debts and other obligations are subtracted. For this reason, the only liabilities you need list here are those not previously covered. Don't bother with the small stuff (such as the phone bill, or what you owe on your credit card this month), which changes frequently. Just list all major liabilities not previously accounted for, so you can get a clearer picture of your net worth.

Column 1
To Whom Debt Is Owed

Column 2
Net Amount of
Debt You Owe

A. Personal Property Debts

1. personal loans (banks, major credit cards, etc.)

_____   _____

_____   _____

_____   _____

_____   _____

_____   _____

2. other personal debts

_____   _____

_____   _____

_____   _____

_____   _____

_____   _____

Column 1 To Whom Debt Is Owed	Column 2 Net Amount of Debt You Owe

B. Taxes

(include only taxes past and currently due. Do not include taxes due in the future or estimated estate taxes)

C. Any Other Liabilities

(legal judgments, accrued child support, etc.)

D. Total Liabilities

(excluding those liabilities already deducted in Section I)

III. YOUR NET WORTH

Total Net Value of All Your Assets (Section I. E.)
minus Total Liabilities (Section II. D.)

$ _____

5

Your Beneficiaries

A. Types of Beneficiaries 5/3

B. Primary Beneficiaries 5/3

    1. Simple Beneficiary Situations.. 5/3

    2. Minors as Primary Beneficiaries 5/4

    3. Forgiving Debts 5/4

    4. Restrictions on Beneficiaries 5/4

    5. Pets as Beneficiaries 5/5

C. Life Estate Beneficiaries and Final Beneficiaries 5/6

D. Alternate Beneficiaries 5/6

E. Residuary Beneficiaries 5/7

F. Gifts Shared by More Than One Beneficiary 5/7

G. Establishing a Survivorship Period 5/8

H. Explanations and Commentary Accompanying Gifts 5/8

I. Disinheritance 5/9

    1. Disinheriting a Spouse.. 5/9

    2. Disinheriting a Child 5/10

    3. No-Contest Clauses 5/10

J. Simultaneous Death.. 5/10

K. Property You Give Away by Will or Trust That You No
Longer Own at Your Death 5/11

Deciding which persons or organizations you want to receive your property—who will be your beneficiaries—is obviously a main focus of your estate plan. This chapter raises some important concerns about choosing and naming beneficiaries. Even if you are sure who you want to receive your property and are tempted to skip ahead, we urge you to read at least Sections A through F, which cover important information everyone should take into account. Read the rest of the sections only if the subjects concern you.

Most people know, quite clearly, when they begin their estate planning, who their major beneficiaries will be. You may want to write down the names of all your beneficiaries when you start actually preparing your estate planning documents, like a will or living trust, but that's not necessary now.

SOME THOUGHTS ABOUT GIFT GIVING

What is a gift? That question can be more complex, and interesting, than you might think at first.

In our predominantly commercial culture, gifts, whether they are made during life or at death, are special. They are free, voluntary transfers of property, made without any requirement of receiving anything in return. The essence of gift-giving is generosity, an open spirit. To say one makes gifts "with strings attached" is not a compliment.

Much of the satisfaction of estate planning comes from contemplating the positive effects your gifts will have on those you love. Sometimes, this satisfaction is quite focused—you know how much Judith has always liked your mahogany table, and now she'll get to enjoy it. Others are more general—your son can buy a house with the money you leave him, which you hope will relieve some of the financial and emotional pressures that have been weighing on him.

We mention the spirit of giving here because we've learned that it's easy to get entrapped by the details of estate planning and lose sight of your real purpose. So, if technicalities and legalities start to get to you, take a break and remember to whom you're giving your property and why.

If you wish to explore in profound depth what gift giving is, or can mean, read Lewis Hyde's *The Gift* (Vintage/Random House), a brilliant exploration of how gifts work in many cultures.

A. TYPES OF BENEFICIARIES

As you know, the word "beneficiaries" means people or institutions you leave property to. There are different types of beneficiaries; the major types discussed in this book are:

- **Primary beneficiaries.** Those you leave identified gifts of property to.

- **Alternate beneficiaries.** Those named to receive a gift if the primary beneficiary can't receive it.

- **Life estate beneficiaries.** People who receive what's called a "life estate" interest in property, which means some rights to receive income from or to use the property during their life, but who never become legal owners of the property. Life estate beneficiaries have no rights to leave this property when they die.

- **Final Beneficiaries.** Those named to inherit property after a life beneficiary for it dies.

- **Residuary beneficiaries.** Those named to receive property left under a will or trust that is not expressly left to other beneficiaries. Usually, an alternate residuary beneficiary is also named.

B. PRIMARY BENEFICIARIES

Primary beneficiaries are usually named to receive a specific item of property. For example, a will might state: "I leave my car to my sister Joanne Corbett." Some people name many primary beneficiaries for different items. And some name none at all, simply leaving all their property to their residuary beneficiaries.

1. Simple Beneficiary Situations

If you know you want to leave all your property to one or a few people—say your spouse or children—you still may face some additional complexities. Do you want to name an alternate beneficiary, in case the person you've originally named dies before you do? (See Section D, below.) Suppose you want to name two or more alternate beneficiaries. What happens if they wind up receiving your property? Does each one receive an equal share? If they inherit real estate, must it be sold unless all agree to keep it? In sum, even with a seemingly very simple beneficiary situation, you'll almost always need to go further than just naming one person to receive all you've got.

NAMING BENEFICIARIES IN YOUR ESTATE PLANNING DOCUMENTS DOESN'T REQUIRE A LAWYER

If you are considering preparing your estate planning documents yourself, don't be put off by fears you must hire a lawyer, or use tricky legalese, to identify beneficiaries. You can safely name them in simple, plain English, using the names by which your beneficiaries are normally known.

Even if a beneficiary later changes his or her last name, that's no reason for you to revise your will or trust. For example, if a daughter later marries or divorces and decides to change her last name, you don't need to change her name as listed in your living trust or will. She, and others concerned, will be clear about whom you meant.

2.   Minors as Primary Beneficiaries

Estate planning issues concerning children are discussed in Chapter 6. Here we briefly summarize the options available if you're considering naming a minor child as primary beneficiaries (or, indeed, as any type of beneficiaries).

Minor children can own only a small amount of property outright in their own names. This amount, which is set by state law, varies from about $2,500 to $5,000. Any property belonging to a minor above this amount must be legally controlled and supervised by an adult. So if you are contemplating leaving a substantial gift to a minor, you should choose an adult to be responsible for it. Your basic options are:

- A gift for your own children can be left outright to the other parent, who will use it for the children's benefit. If spouses—or even ex-spouses—get along and trust one another to manage money well, this is usually the simplest way to handle the matter.

- Leave the gift to the child, and name an adult to be responsible for supervising it. That adult can be one of the child's parents, but doesn't always have to be. When you have decided who the adult supervisor will be, your next step is to decide what legal form you want to use to make the gift. These issues are covered in Chapter 6.

3.   Forgiving Debts

One form of gift is to forgive a debt, essentially leaving a gift to your debtor. Any debt, written or oral, can be forgiven.

Example: Bud loaned his daughter Kathlyn and son-in-law Tyrone $30,000 for a down payment on a house, but doesn't want them to be obligated to repay his estate after he dies. So, in his will, Bud includes a provision stating

"I forgive the loan of $30,000 I made to Kathlyn and Tyrone Benson in 1988."

If you're married and forgiving a debt, be sure you have full power to do so. If the debt was incurred while you were married, you may only have the right to forgive half the debt (especially in community property states) unless your spouse agrees in writing to allow you to forgive his or her share of the debt as well.

4.   Restrictions on Beneficiaries

There are two possible types of restrictions on gifts to beneficiaries:

- restrictions you, the giver, want to impose, and
- restrictions imposed by law.

a.   Personal Restrictions

Most people simply leave their property outright to family, friends or charities. However, sometimes a person wants to make a gift with restrictions or conditions on it, something like "if such and such happens, then the gift shall go to..." Sometimes called "dead-hand control," the obvious risk is that circumstances are almost sure to change, so you must try to anticipate what is likely—or even possible—to occur in the future, and provide for it. For instance, suppose you left a gift "to John, if he quits smoking." Who could ever tell if John fully quit smoking? He can't be watched around the clock each day. And how long is "quit"? These kind of restrictions on gifts are probably unenforceable—but they surely can enrich lawyers.

Restrictions. If you're determined place restrictions on a gift, see a lawyer.

b. Legal Restrictions

With very few limits, you can leave your property to whoever you choose. While the few existing legal restrictions on beneficiaries rarely apply, let's be cautious and review them briefly.

- Some felons and anyone who unlawfully caused the death of the person who wrote the will (or living trust) cannot inherit under it.

- You cannot attempt to encourage or restrain some types of conduct of your beneficiaries. For example, you cannot make a gift contingent on the recipient's marriage, divorce or change of religion.

- You cannot validly leave money for an illegal purpose—for example, to establish the Institute to Encourage Minors to Smoke.

c. Charities as Beneficiaries

A few states (the District of Columbia, Florida, Georgia, Idaho, Mississippi, Montana and Ohio) have laws restricting your ability to leave large percentages of your property to charities. These laws, holdovers from centuries past, were enacted primarily to discourage churches and other charitable organizations from using unfair means, such as promising elderly people a place in heaven, to fill their own coffers at the expense of a surviving family.

Gifts to charities. If you're in one of these states, you should check with an attorney if you desire to leave a large part of your estate—certainly more than half—

to a charitable institution, especially if you believe your spouse or children might object. However if you're leaving a relatively small percentage of your estate to a charity, you needn't worry about these restrictions no matter where you live.

5. Pets as Beneficiaries

As a part of their estate planning, many pet owners arrange informally for a friend or relative to care for a pet. But what if the person you asked to provide care can't afford to keep an animal, or isn't available when needed? Usually, more formal arrangements are better. Here are a few tips:

- In most states, you can't leave money or property to a pet, either through a will or a trust. If you do, the property you tried to leave your pet will go, instead, to your residuary beneficiary. However, in the following states you can name a pet as a beneficiary of a trust:

Alaska	Montana
Arizona	New Mexico
California	New York
Colorado	North Carolina
Missouri	Tennessee

- You can use your will or living trust to leave your pets, and perhaps some money for expenses, to someone you trust to look out for them. Don't make the gift of an animal a surprise—make sure the people you've chosen are really willing and able to care for pets.

- Consider making arrangements for veterinary care for your animals. You can leave money to a vet (working out an amount with the vet in advance) or write out a life care contract with a vet. A vet may agree to provide lifetime care in exchange for a lump sum, or to use the money as a credit toward services.

These issues are discussed in detail in *Dog Law,* by Mary Randolph (Nolo Press).

C. LIFE ESTATE BENEFICIARIES AND FINAL BENEFICIARIES

As we've said, a life estate beneficiary receives only a limited interest in property. This interest ends when the beneficiary dies. The person who originally left the life estate property names another beneficiary or beneficiaries, usually called the "final beneficiary" to inherit the property outright when the life beneficiary dies.

> **Example:** Mac leaves his brother Sam a life estate interest in Mac's house. Mac names his daughter Gay as the final beneficiary. Mac dies. Sam inherits the life estate interest in the house. (If Mac outlived Sam, the life estate interest could never become effectual.) Sam can live in the house, or rent it, but never becomes the legal owner. When Sam dies, the house will go outright to Gay.

Life estates are usually created by a trust. The rights of the life estate beneficiary and the final beneficiaries must be carefully defined in the trust document. Life estate trusts are used for one or both of two purposes:

- to reduce or eliminate estate taxes. (See Chapter 18, Estate Tax-Saving Bypass Trusts.)
- to impose controls over property. For example someone in a second marriage may want to leave her mate a life estate interest in property, with that property then going to her children from a prior marriage when the mate dies. (See Chapter 24, Property Control Trusts for Second or Subsequent

Marriages.) Or a parent may want to leave property to a disabled child in a long term managerial trust. (See Chapter 25, Trusts and Other Devices for Imposing Controls Over Property.)

D. ALTERNATE BENEFICIARIES

Most people name alternate beneficiaries to inherit property if their first choices die before they do. This is especially appropriate if you leave some gifts to older people or people in poor health. Also, you simply might not have the time, or inclination, before your own death, to revise your estate plan if a beneficiary dies before you.

On the other hand, this is one of the many estate planning issues where there are no absolutes. Some people decide they don't want the morbid bother of worrying about their beneficiaries dying before they do. Often, they leave their property to people considerably younger than they are—for example, their children. If a beneficiary dies before they do, they'll probably be able to modify their will, trust or other document to name a new beneficiary. If they don't, the property will go to their residuary beneficiary (see below), who might, anyway, be the same person or persons they would name as their alternate.

There can be alternate alternates, and indeed, as many layers of alternates as you care to create. Creating a second, third or more layers of alternates can get quite complicated. There are many "Ifs" to work out—"If Joe dies and if Jane dies and if Jack and Jill die..." then what? Usually resolving how to clearly draft a will or trust with layers of alternates requires the assistance of a lawyer

E. RESIDUARY BENEFICIARIES

Whatever you decide about alternate beneficiaries, you should definitely name a residuary beneficiary or beneficiaries in your will, and your living trust if you use one. As we've said, a residuary beneficiary receives all property left under a document that isn't received by other beneficiaries, either because none was named to get the property, or they didn't survive to inherit it. Your residuary beneficiary is your back-up, to be sure your property goes to someone you've chosen

If you prepare a living trust, the residuary beneficiary you name there only receives any remaining trust property not received by other beneficiaries. The residuary beneficiary you name in your will receives all property not left other beneficiaries by any other.

Example: Esther receives a surprise inheritance of $23,000 three weeks before she dies. She did not revise her will or living trust to leave this money to a primary beneficiary. The money is inherited by the residuary beneficiary of Esther's will.

A residuary beneficiary doesn't have to serve solely as a back up. Some people leave all of their property to their residuary. Other leave most to the residuary, naming only a few primary beneficiaries for modest gifts.

It's wise, and standard, to name an alternate residuary beneficiary so you have another back-up in case your residuary beneficiary dies before you.

F. GIFTS SHARED BY MORE THAN ONE BENEFICIARY

Sometimes people want to leave shared gifts, particularly to their children. A shared gift is one left to two or more beneficiaries; each receives a portion of ownership of the property. This is different from leaving property with directions that it be sold and the profits divided between beneficiaries. With a shared gift, all the beneficiaries own the property itself.

Example: Virginia leaves her house to her three children—Alan, Patsy and Philip—in equal shares. Each owns an undivided one-third interest in the house.

If you're considering leaving a shared gift, you should resolve some important questions. First, what percentage of ownership does each beneficiary receive? You should spell out the percentages in your will or trust. If you don't, it's generally presumed that you intended equal shares, but this rule isn't ironclad. There's no good reason to be silent on this matter. If you want a gift shared equally, say so.

The next issue is control of the property. Generally, the beneficiaries must decide how to handle their shared ownership. They may all want to keep the property, or decide to sell it and split the proceeds. But if the beneficiaries can't agree how to use the property, they may end up in court. In most states, any co-owner can go to court and force a sale, with the net proceeds divided by percentage of ownership.

If you don't think the beneficiaries can resolve any problems that arise, a shared gift is a bad idea. There's little you can do to forestall serious conflicts.

You can try, by putting rules governing what the shared owners can do in your will or trust. For instance, you could specify that "The house cannot be sold unless all three of my children agree on it." But often other problems follow. If two kids want to sell the house, but one doesn't, who manages the house? Must it be rented at market value? Can the child who wants to keep the house live in it? If so, must that child pay the others rent? And what happens if one child dies? The difficulties of dealing with these types of complications mean it usually is rarely sensible to try to impose long-term control on shared gifts.

The final issue to consider is what happens if a beneficiary of a shared gift predeceases you. Here things can become quite complicated. To return once more to the house Virginia wants to leave to her three children, what are her options if she wants to name alternate beneficiaries?

- She can specify that a deceased beneficiary's share is to be divided between her surviving children.

- She can name three separate alternate beneficiaries, one for each child—for example, each of their spouses.

- She can provide that a deceased child's share is to be divided equally between that beneficiary's own children, or, if there are none between her surviving children.

- She can name another alternate beneficiary (a friend or other relative) to receive the interest of any child who dies before she does.

Juggling and resolving these types of contingencies can get confusing, especially if you want two or more layers of alternate beneficiaries. Still, many people want to work out having alternates for shared gifts, which, of course, is fine. If pinning down how it will work gets too tricky, see a lawyer—or consider making your alternate beneficiary plan for shared gifts less complicated.

G. ESTABLISHING A SURVIVORSHIP PERIOD

A survivorship period requires that a beneficiary must survive you by a specified time period to inherit. The purpose of a survivorship period is to ensure that if the beneficiary dies soon after you do, the property will go to the alternate you've selected, rather than to the people the beneficiary chose to inherit his property.

Survivorship periods are commonly used in wills. Since probate takes months, you're not tying up your property by imposing a short survivorship period— 45 to 60 days is common.

Using the same reasoning, establishing a survivorship period of more than a few weeks isn't usually desirable for property transferred by living trust, since a principal advantage of a living trust is that property can be transferred quickly to the new owners. (See Chapter 9, Living Trusts.) There's no sense in setting up a living trust to allow quick transfer of property and then frustrating that result by requiring beneficiaries wait many months to inherit.

H. EXPLANATIONS AND COMMENTARY ACCOMPANYING GIFTS

If you wish, you can provide a brief commentary when leaving a gift in a will or a living trust.

Example: I leave $40,000 to my business associate, Mildred Parker, who worked honestly and competently with me over the years, and cheerfully put up with my sporadic depressions and weirdnesses.

There are times, particularly in family situations, when an explanation of the reasons for your gifts can help avoid hurt feelings or family fights.

Example: I leave my house at 465 Merchant St., Miami, Florida, and all stocks and bonds I own as follows:

> 40% to my son Theodore Stein
>
> 40% to my daughter Sandra Stein Smith
>
> 20% to my son Howard Stein

I love all my children deeply and equally. I leave 20% to Howard because he received substantial family funds to go through medical school, so it's fair that my other two children receive more of my property now.

Another approach is to write a letter stating your views and feelings, and attach the letter to your will or living trust. If you have a lot to say, a letter can be a better way to go than trying to include it all in your will or living trust. Further, a will becomes a matter of public record and so would your comments. If you don't want to expose your sentiments anyone who chooses to look at a probate court file, a letter protects your privacy

Your letter isn't officially a part of a legal document, and has no legal effect. It is prudent for you to state in your letter that you understand this, to eliminate any possibility someone could claim you intended the letter to somehow modify the terms of your legal documents.

Short of libel, the scope of your remarks is limited only by your imagination. Some writers have expressed, at length and in their own chosen words, their love for a mate, children and friend. By contrast, Benjamin Franklin left his son William, who was sympathetic to England during our Revolution, only some land in Nova Scotia. Franklin's will stated, "The fact he acted against me in the late war, which is of public notoriety, will account for my leaving him no more of an estate than he endeavored to deprive me of." And the German poet Heine wrote a will leaving his property to his wife on the condition that she remarry, so that "there will be at least one man to regret my death." William Shakespeare cryptically left his wife his "second best bed," a bequest that has intrigued scholars for centuries.

I. DISINHERITANCE

You can disinherit most people simply by not leaving them property. Indeed, "disinheritance" isn't the apt word since no one except your wife (in common law states) and children (in some situations) have any legal claim on your property.

1. Disinheriting a Spouse

If you live in one of the 41 common law states or the District of Columbia, you cannot disinherit your spouse. (See Chapter 3, Special Property Ownership Rules for Married People, Section C.) These states allow a spouse to claim a significant portion of your estate despite your wishes, although many states do allow a spouse to waive these rights in a written marital property agreement.

By contrast, in community property states, a spouse has no legal rights to inherit any of the other spouse's property. Or, put another way, each spouse has the right to leave their one-half of the community property and all his or her separate property as he or she sees fit.

UNMARRIED COUPLES

Unmarried couples living together have no statutory rights to inherit any of each other's property. Each person can leave his or her property to anyone he or she wants to, which of course can include the other person. And if the couple has signed a valid contract which gives the other the specific right to inherit specific property, that contract will be enforced, even over will provisions to the contrary.

2. Disinheriting a Child

The rules for disinheriting a minor child are discussed in detail in Chapter 6, Children, Section F. Here we briefly summarize them.

In all states, you have the power to disinherit any or all of your children, if you do so expressly. However, if you fail to mention a child in your will, that child may have a legal right to claim part of your property. Some states laws protect only children born after the will was written. Other states protect any child not mentioned in the will.

The goal of these laws is to prevent children from being unintentionally overlooked. You don't have to leave your children property as primary beneficiaries. The point is to establish that you considered each child when leaving property. Many spouses validly leave all their property to the other spouse, naming their children as alternate beneficiaries. This shows that the children weren't overlooked.

If you want to disinherit a child, you must state that explicitly in your will. There is no legal requirement that you state a reason, but you can if you wish.

LEAVING PEOPLE A MINIMAL AMOUNT

You may have heard that some lawyers recommend leaving a minimal amount, usually one dollar, to certain close relations. This is not legally necessary and is a bad idea. Doing so burdens your executor with trying to track down these beneficiaries, and then get them to sign a receipt for one dollar. And all this when they had no rights to any of your property to begin with.

---

3. No-Contest Clauses

A "no-contest clause" in a will or living trust is a device used to discourage beneficiaries of your estate plan from suing to void the plan and claiming they are entitled to more than you left them. Under a no-contest clause, a beneficiary who unsuccessfully challenges a will or living trust forfeits all his or her inheritance under that document.

No-contest clauses can be sensible if there's a risk that a beneficiary might challenge your will or living trust, claiming that you were incompetent or unduly influenced. The risk of losing all property left to him may by itself deter a potential challenger from suing.

In most situations, a no-contest clause isn't necessary, since there no reasonable risk of lawsuit by a beneficiary. Also, you don't have to be "fair" when distributing your property. Absent fraud, duress or mental incompetence, you can leave it however you want to, with the exceptions for spouse or children noted above.

Potential will/living trust fights. See a lawyer if you fear a beneficiary might contest your will or living trust. There may be a number of things you can do to establish that you are competent to make your estate plan and to protect your estate from lawsuits, or at least increase the odds your side will prevail.

J. SIMULTANEOUS DEATH

Many couples, married or not, who leave their property to each other wonder what would happen to the property if they were to die at the same time. (Another common concern—what happens to children if both parents die simultaneously—is discussed in Chapter 6, Children, Section A.) If a survivorship period is imposed on beneficiaries, that includes a spouse, so the issue is taken care of.

Example: Hermancia's and Ed's wills leave their property to each other. Each one's will imposes a 45-day survivorship period on all beneficiaries. Hermancia names their daughter Raquel as alternate beneficiary. Ed names Hermancia and his brother Malachy as co-alternate beneficiaries, each to receive 50%.

Hermancia dies. Ed dies 25 days after she does. Because Ed did not survive 45 days after Hermancia, he never became owner of her property. It goes directly to Raquel. Malachy does not inherit any of the property originally owned by Hermancia. (He does, of course, inherit half the property owned by Ed.)

If no survivorship period is imposed, and you and your spouse die simultaneously, your property could pass to your spouse or mate, and then immediately to your spouse's inheritors. That might not be the result you want. To eliminate this possibility, you can use a "simultaneous death" clause, which provides that when it's difficult or impossible to tell which spouse died first, the property of each spouse or mate is disposed of as if he or she had survived the other.

How, you may ask, can simultaneous death clauses logically work? How can you be presumed to have outlived your spouse for your will's purposes and she also be presumed to have outlived you for her will's purpose? Yes, it is a logical paradox, but in the real world it works. Under the law, each estate is handled independently of the other. Each spouse's will is read as if the other spouse's will didn't exist. This allows both spouses to achieve the results each wants in the event of simultaneous death. As Oliver Wendell Holmes put it, "The life of the law has not been logic, it's been experience."

K. Property You Give Away by Will or Trust That You No Longer Own at Your Death

Before your estate can pay any cash gifts you leave, it must pay all your last debts and taxes, including death taxes. After that, if your estate doesn't have enough money available to pay your cash gifts, there's trouble. This necessitates what's called an "abatement" in legalese. An abatement means a reduction of gifts when there isn't enough to go around. Specific provisions in your will governing how a shortfall of cash is to be handled will be enforced. Otherwise, the matter is normally resolved by your executor.

There's an obvious way to avoid this sort of nasty post-death mess—don't leave more cash than you're confident you'll have. And if your cash resources go below this amount, revise your cash gifts. ■

6

CHILDREN

A. Naming Someone to Take Custody of Your Minor Children 6/2

    1. Choosing the Personal Guardian 6/3

    2. If You Don't Want the Other Parent
       to Become Personal Guardian 6/4

B. Naming an Adult to Manage Your Child's Property 6/5

    1. Leaving Property to Your Spouse for the Benefit
       of Your Children 6/5

    2. Choosing Your Child's Property Manager 6/6

    3. Selecting Different Property Managers for Different
       Minor Children 6/6

C. How Your Children's Property Should Be Managed 6/6

    1. The Uniform Transfers to Minors Act 6/7

    2. Trusts for Children 6/9

    3. Which is Better for You, the UTMA or a Child's Trust ? 6/10

    4. Naming a Property Guardian 6/11

    5. Comparison of the Four Major Ways to Leave a Child or
       Young Adult Property 6/12

D. Naming Children as Beneficiaries of Life Insurance 6/14

E. Leaving Property to Children Who Are Not Your Own 6/14

F. Disinheritance 6/15

When you're working on your estate plan, the word "children" can have two meanings. The first is "minors"—people who are not yet 18. The second meaning is offspring of any age; parents who live long enough can have "children" who are in their 40s, 50s or even older. This chapter focuses primarily on minor children because of the special problems inherent in planning for them. We also discuss ways to leave property to a young adult child, when you're concerned that the child may not be sufficiently mature to handle money responsibly.

Most parents of minor children are extremely concerned about what will happen to their children if disaster strikes and the parents die unexpectedly. If both parents are raising the children, the major concern is usually simultaneous death of the parents. If you're a single parent and the other parent is deceased, has abandoned the child or is unavailable for some other reason, you'll want to arrange for someone else to care for, and quite possibly, help and support the child if you die while the child is a minor.

Providing for your minor children if you die involves two distinct concerns:

1. Who will raise the children if you can't—that is, who will be each child's personal guardian?

2. How can you best provide financial support for your children? What money or property will be available? Who will handle and supervise it for the child's benefit? And what legal method is best for managing it?

These concerns are addressed in depth in this chapter.

This chapter does not deal with adult "children" in as much depth because you don't need to appoint a personal guardian for them, nor is a property guardian legally required. However, you may not want to allow your children to receive substantial amounts of property outright while they're still in their 20s or even early 30s. This chapter explains how you can impose mature adult supervision over gifts you leave to young adult children.

Finally, if you want to disinherit a child—not common, but it does happen—there are special rules you must follow, which are covered in this chapter.

REVISE YOUR ESTATE PLAN WHEN A CHILD IS BORN OR DIES

If, after preparing your estate plan, you have an additional child, revise that plan by providing for the new child. If you don't, that child has a legal right to inherit a portion of your property. (The exact percentage depends on state law.) You should also, of course, make sure that all property left to a deceased child is redirected to other beneficiaries.

A. NAMING SOMEONE TO TAKE CUSTODY OF YOUR MINOR CHILDREN

If two biological or adoptive parents are willing and able to care for a minor child, and one dies, normally the other has the legal right to assume sole custody. If the parents are married, or even if they are divorced, as long as both parents are cooperating to raise their children, this rule presents no problem. But what happens if both parents die? Or a sole parent dies?

If no parent is available, some other adult must be legally responsible for raising the child. This adult is called the child's "personal guardian." No personal guardian is required if the child is "emancipated," which means the child has achieved the legal status of an adult; normal grounds are marriage, military service or factual independence validated by court order.

A child's personal guardian must be named in a will. Except in a couple of states, you cannot use a living trust, or any other document, for this purpose. If you have minor children, this is an obvious reason why a will is essential.

It's important to understand that the person you name as a minor's personal guardian in a will doesn't actually become the legal guardian until approved by a court after your death. The judge has the authority to name someone else if the judge is convinced it is in the best interests of the child. In short, children are not property, and naming a personal guardian in a will doesn't have the same automatically binding effect as a provision leaving a lamp to someone. However, if, as usual, no one contests your choice for your child's personal guardian, a court will almost certainly confirm this person. In practice, a court will reject an unopposed nominee only if there are obvious grave and provable reasons, such as alcoholism, a serious criminal background or provable child abuse. As a responsible parent, we presume you wouldn't select a guardian with such problems.

1. Choosing the Personal Guardian

You may well know whom you want to name as your child's personal guardian. But this isn't always an easy question. We know people who've struggled hard to decide on the best choice. Keep in mind the obvious: You can't draft someone to parent your kids. Be sure any person you plan to name is ready, willing and able to do the job.

You should always name an alternate personal guardian as well, just in case your first choice is unable or unwilling to serve.

Where two parents are involved in raising their kids, they should agree on whom they want to appoint—naming different people could result in a nasty conflict, if both parents died simultaneously.

It's best not to name a couple as joint guardians, even if they will likely function that way. Doing this raises many potential problems, including what happens if the couple splits up. Better to simply name the member of the couple you rely on the most.

In many families today, children don't all share the same two biological parents, and you may want to name different guardians for different children. Naming different personal guardians for different children is certainly legal. A court would likely follow this arrangement, unless there's persuasive proof that it would be harmful to a child.

Example: Irene is a single parent with two sons, aged 14 and 15, from her first marriage, and a daughter, Bo, age four, from her second. Her first husband has never taken any interest in the children. Her second ex is a decent, though from Irene's view, well below superb, father to Bo, and has also tried to be a decent father to the boys. Irene's brother, Biff, is close to her sons, and she and they feel he would be the best personal guardian for them. But Biff isn't wild about raising a young child. Also, Irene recognizes that if she named Biff as guardian of Bo, and she died while Bo was a minor, the result would probably be a court fight with Bo's father, who would likely prevail. So Irene names her second ex as personal guardian of Bo, and Biff as guardian of her boys. She attaches a statement to her will explaining why she believes this is best for the children.

Choosing a personal guardian does not automatically mean you're also selecting that person to manage any money you leave for your children. Selection of an adult to manage a minor's property is discussed below in Section B. Here we simply want to note that if you're worried that the person you name as personal guardian isn't good with money, you can name someone else for that latter job. There are obvious risks of conflict in having one person have legal authority to raise a child and another to manage money used to support and educate the child. If you decide to divide authority between two persons, be sure that both people you want to name are willing to accept their roles. If the two potential guardians do really accept this, your major problem is solved.

2. If You Don't Want the Other Parent to Become Personal Guardian

A parent raising a child may not want the other parent to get custody, for any of a number of reasons. Here are a couple of examples:

- I don't want my ex-husband, who I believe is dangerously mentally unstable, to get custody of my children if I die. How can I prevent him from becoming personal guardian? Choose another guardian?

- I have legal custody of my daughter and I've remarried. My wife is a far better mother to my daughter than my ex-wife, who mostly ignores her, and is occasional mean to her. What can I do to try to make sure my present wife gets custody if I die?

There is no definitive answer to these types of questions. Assuming a contested case was presented to a court, a judge's decision would very likely turn on both the facts of each situation and the judge's own beliefs. One generally adhered to rule is that one parent cannot succeed in appointing someone other than the other natural parent to be personal guardian, unless the second parent:

- has legally abandoned the child, or

- is unfit as a parent.

If the other parent seeks custody after your death, it's usually quite difficult to prove that the parent is unfit, absent serious problems such as alcohol abuse, a history of child molestation or violence or mental illness. Your negative opinion of the other parent is never enough, by itself, to deny custody. If you want to name someone other than the other parent as personal guardian for your children, be sure that person knows that this may lead to a custody fight.

It's unlikely that anyone except the child's other parent would win custody against your wishes. For instance, if you name your best friend Betty to raise your children if you can't and Betty can be proved to be a caring adult, it's unlikely that someone else, such as the child's grandmother, or uncle, could gain custody over your choice.

It can be a good idea to attach a letter to your will explaining your choice for personal guardian. Here's an example of such a letter:

SAMPLE LETTER EXPLAINING YOUR CHOICE FOR GUARDIAN

I have nominated my companion, Peter N., to be the personal guardian of my daughter, Melissa, because I know he would be the best guardian for her. For the past six years, Peter has functioned as Melissa's parent, living with me and her, helping to provide and care for her, and loving her. She loves him and regards him as her father. She hardly knows her actual father, Tom D. She has not seen him for four years. He has rarely contributed to her support or taken any interest in her.

Date: January 15, 1998

[Signed by:]   Juanita R.

It is also possible to explain your choice of guardian in your will.

Potential custody fights. If you don't want the other biological parent to gain custody, it's wise to discuss the details of your situation with a lawyer who specializes in family law. If there's a disputed custody proceeding after your death, a judge has wide discretion in deciding how much weight, if any, to give to a written statement about your child's custody you made before you died. A good lawyer should help guide you to prepare the most persuasive case you can. This might include preparing your best statement of why the other parent shouldn't get custody, and identifying people who will back up your statement by their court testimony, if necessary.

depending on the method you select for leaving property to your child. (See Section C, below.) For now, let's simply call this adult your child's "property manager." If you have minor children, a vital part of your estate plan is selecting their property manager.

In addition, you may wish to choose an adult to manage any property you leave your younger adult children. You, like many parents, may not want property to be turned over to children when they become legal adults at age 18. If you wish, you can have that property supervised by a more mature person until the children become 25, or even 35 or older, and are (presumably) more responsible.

TAXATION OF A CHILD'S INCOME

Income received by a minor child age 14 or over is taxed at the normal income tax rate for that child. But income to a child 13 or under is taxed differently. Under the "kiddie tax," all income over $1,300 per year received by a child 13 or under is taxed at the higher of the two parents' tax rate. This kiddie tax has eliminated income tax incentives for parents, or others, to transfer income-producing property from themselves, and their own high tax brackets, to a minor under age 14.

B. NAMING AN ADULT TO MANAGE YOUR CHILD'S PROPERTY

Minor children cannot own property outright, free of adult control, beyond a minimal amount—usually in the $1,000 to $5,000 range, depending on the state. This means there must be an adult legally responsible for all property owned by a child. This person may be called a "custodian," "trustee" or "property guardian,"

1. Leaving Property to Your Spouse for the Benefit of Your Children

One alternative for parents of minor or young adult children is for each to leave property outright to the other spouse to be used for their child's benefit. This approach makes sense if the parents trust each other, but obviously isn't a good choice if the other parent is not available or financially imprudent. Even if you leave all property to your spouse, it's always wise to name a backup child's property manager. This takes care of the remote possibility that you and your spouse might die simultaneously.

2. Choosing Your Child's Property Manager

When deciding whom to name as your minor child's property manager, here's a sensible rule: Name the same person you choose to have custody of the children (their personal guardian) unless there are compelling reasons to name someone else. For example, choose a different person if you're concerned that the personal guardian doesn't have sufficient financial or practical experience to manage property prudently.

You should also name an alternate property manager in case your first choice can't serve. Again, name the same person you designated as the child's alternate personal guardian unless there are strong reasons to choose someone else.

The duty of the property manager is to manage the property you leave for your children honestly and in their best interests. This means using it to pay for normal living expenses and health and education needs. If you pick someone with integrity and common sense, your child's property will probably be in good hands. If substantial funds are involved, the property manager can pay for help to handle the more technical aspects of financial management. For instance, it's routine for a property manager to turn complicated tax and accounting matters over to an accountant.

Obviously, it's important to name a property manager who is sincerely willing to do a job that may, depending on the ages of your children, last for many years. It's also wise to choose someone the other members of your family respect and accept. You want your children to inherit money, not family arguments.

Except as a last resort, don't name a bank or other financial institution to be property manager. Most banks won't manage accounts they consider too small to be worth the bother; as a rough rule, this means accounts worth less than $250,000. And even for larger estates, they charge hefty fees for every little act. In addition, it's our experience that banks are simply too impersonal to properly meet your own child's needs. Far better, we think, to name a human being you trust than a bureaucracy. But if you can't find any adult who's willing and competent to be your child's property manager, normally it's better to name a financial institution than to make no choice at all, which amounts to leaving the matter up to a court. You'll need to check around with different banks and private trust companies to see which ones will accept the job and seem most likely to do it for reasonable fees.

3. Selecting Different Property Managers for Different Minor Children

In some situations, you may want to name different property managers for different minor children. Doing this is legal. And unlike naming a personal guardian, it doesn't require court approval.

C. How Your Children's Property Should Be Managed

Your next task is to choose which legal method you want to use to leave property to your minor or young adult children. There are four basic options for leaving property to minor children:

- a custodianship, under the Uniform Transfers to Minors Act
- a child's trust
- a family pot trust

- a property guardianship.

For young adults over 18 to 21, your only choice is a child's trust.

1. The Uniform Transfers to Minors Act

You can leave gifts to your child (or to any minor) in your will or living trust under what is called "the Uniform Transfers to Minors Act" (UTMA), a law that has been adopted by every state except Michigan, South Carolina and Vermont. Here your child's property manager is called a "custodian." The custodian's management ends when the minor reaches age 18 to 25, depending on state law.

Here's how leaving a gift using the Uniform Transfers to Minors Act works. In either your will or living trust, you identify the property and the minor you are leaving it to. You then appoint the adult custodian to be responsible for supervising the property until the age the child must receive the property (see chart below). You provide that the custodian is to act "under the [your state's] Uniform Transfers to Minors Act." You can also name a "successor custodian" in case your first choice can't do the job.

The custodian has great discretion to control and use the property in the child's interest. Among the specific powers the UTMA gives the custodian are the right, without court approval, "to collect, hold, manage, invest and reinvest" the property, and to spend as much of it "as the custodian considers advisable for the use and benefit of the minor." The custodian must also keep records so that tax returns can be filed on behalf of the minor and must otherwise act as a prudent person would when in control of another's property. A custodian does not, however, need to file a separate income tax return. The custodian is entitled to be paid reasonable compensation from the gift property. No court supervision of the custodian is required.

Each gift under the Uniform Transfers to Minors Act can be made to only one minor, with only one person named as custodian. A child who reaches the age the Act specifies for termination gets the remaining balance of the gift. The custodian must also furnish an accounting of all funds distributed.

A limitation of the UTMA is that, in most states, custodianships end at age 21, and even at 18 in others. Particularly if your children are already teenagers and your estate is substantial, you may want property management to last longer. If so, you may wish to use child's trusts, which allow you to designate an older age at which property management ends. (See Subsection 2, below).

STATES THAT HAVE ADOPTED THE UNIFORM TRANSFERS TO MINORS ACT

State	Gift Must Be Released When Minor Reaches Age:	
Alabama	21	
Alaska	18	(can be extended up to 25)
Arizona	21	
Arkansas	21	(can be reduced to no lower than 18)
California	18	(can be extended up to 25)
Colorado	21	
Connecticut	21	
Delaware	21	
District of Columbia	18	
Florida	21	
Georgia	21	
Hawaii	21	
Idaho	21	
Illinois	21	
Indiana	21	
Iowa	21	
Kansas	21	
Kentucky	18	
Maine	18	(can be extended up to 21)
Maryland	21	
Massachusetts	21	
Minnesota	21	
Mississippi	21	
Missouri	21	
Montana	21	
Nebraska	21	
Nevada	18	(can be extended up to 25)
New Hampshire	21	
New Jersey	21	(can be reduced to no lower than 18)

State	Gift Must Be Released When Minor Reaches Age:	
New Mexico	21	
New York	21	
North Carolina	21	(can be reduced to no lower than 18)
North Dakota	21	
Ohio	21	
Oklahoma	18	
Oregon	21	
Pennsylvania	21	
Rhode Island	18	
South Dakota	18	
Tennessee	21	
Texas	21	
Utah	21	
Virginia	18	(can be extended to 21)
Washington	21	
West Virginia	21	
Wisconsin	21	
Wyoming	21	

STATES THAT HAVE NOT ADOPTED THE UTMA

At present, the UTMA has not been adopted in Michigan, South Carolina or Vermont.

Even if you live in one of these states, it is theoretically possible for you to use the UTMA in your will, if the minor or custodian or gift property itself resides in an UTMA state when you die. But for most parents, all these are and will likely remain in the state where they live. Even if one of them is now in an UTMA state, you don't know where it will be when you die. Committing yourself to this kind of updating is an unnecessary burden, since you can easily use a child's trust instead.

2. Trusts for Children

There are two major types of trusts you can use to provide property management for property you leave to your children: a "child's trust" or a "family pot trust." (Other, more sophisticated trusts, such as a "special needs" trust for a disabled child, or a "spend-thrift" trust for a child who simply can't handle money sensibly, are discussed in Chapter 25.) With a child's trust, you leave specified property to one child; that property is held separately from any property you leave for other children. If you have more than one child, you can create a child's trust for each child. With a family pot trust, you leave property collectively for two or more children in one common fund; any amount of trust property can be spent for any child.

A trust is a legal entity under which an adult, called a "trustee," has the responsibility of handling money or property for someone else—in this case, your child or children. So if you create a trust, your child's property manager is called the "trustee" or "successor trustee." The trust document sets out the trustee's responsibilities and the beneficiary's rights.

A child's trust or family pot trust can be established either by will or living trust. If one is established as part of a living trust, the property placed in trust avoids probate. If you use your will, the property must go through probate before it's turned over to the trust.

Both a child's trust and a family pot trust are legal in all states. All property you leave to a beneficiary for whom a trust is established will be managed under the terms of the trust document. If you create either type of trust, any property inherited by a minor beneficiary will be managed by the trustee until the beneficiary reaches the age when he or she is entitled to receive the trust property outright.

The trustee's powers are specified in the trust document. Normally, the trustee may use trust assets for the education, medical needs and living expenses of the beneficiary or, with a pot trust, beneficiaries. With a family pot trust, the trustee doesn't have to spend the same amount on each beneficiary; this flexibility is one of the pot trust's main advantages.

With a child's trust, you can select the age the beneficiary must reach before trust property is turned over to him or her. So child's trusts are commonly used when a large amount of money is left for a child, and the giver doesn't want that child to inherit the property outright before a mature age, perhaps 30 or 35. A child's trust can also be used for property you leave to minors or young adults who aren't your children—your grandchildren, for example.

A child's trust shouldn't last a lifetime. If you want a child's trust to last beyond age 30 or 35, you need to face the likelihood that their problem goes deeper than their youth, and they may never be able to manage their own finances. You may need a more complicated trust. (See Chapter 25.)

Most family pot trusts last until the youngest beneficiary becomes 18. By that age, with all beneficiaries legal adults, it makes less sense to treat them all as one family unit. But you could have a pot trust last until the youngest beneficiary becomes 21, or even older, if you're sure that you want to keep your children's property lumped together this long. Also, some pot trusts are drafted so that they convert to individual trusts when the youngest child reaches 18.

A pot trust is most often used by parents with younger children. These parents want to keep family money together, capable of being spent on any child as needs require. The trustee, like a parent, decides how much money shall be spent on each child. If one child has a serious illness or other extraordinary needs, the maximum family resources possible is there for him or her.

Although family pot trusts clearly have the appeal of flexibility, they can make the trustee's job tougher as compared with a child's trust, where each child's property is legally separate from the trust property of other children. With a pot trust, the trustee may literally be called on to choose between one child's need for expensive orthodonture and another's desire to go to a pricey college.

If there is a wide age gap between children, a pot trust is less desirable. If one child is 16 and another is two, and the trust ends when the youngest becomes 18, the oldest must wait until age 32 to receive any property outright, which may not be what the parents want. Further, it's likely to be harder to balance needs between children of widely varying ages. How much of the pot should be spent for the eldest's college needs? How much retained for the youngest? When children are closer together in age, these types of troubling differences are less likely to arise.

Some parents whose children are young and close in age decide a pot trust is best for the children now. Then, when a child grows older—say the eldest reaches 16—the parents may decide to pull property for that child out of the pot trust and put it in an individual trust or UTMA custodianship.

IF A CHILD NEVER INHERITS PROPERTY OR RECEIVES IT WHEN OLDER

If you arrange for property management for a minor or young adult, but that person never inherits the property, no damage is done. Likewise, if the beneficiary has already passed the age at which management was slated to end, the management provisions for that beneficiary are simply ignored. For instance, suppose you identify a favorite niece to take property as an alternate beneficiary, and create a child's trust for that property until the niece turns 30. If the niece never inherits the property because your primary beneficiary survives you, no child's trust will ever be established for her. Similarly, if the niece does inherit the property, but is 31 when you die, she will receive the property outright, and the trust provisions will never take effect.

---

3. Which is Better for You, the UTMA or a Child's Trust?

We've already discussed some key factors in deciding which method is most appropriate for your family. But because this issue can be so important, let's examine it in more detail.

As a general rule, the less valuable the property involved and the more mature the child, the more appropriate the UTMA is because it is simpler and often cheaper, from a tax point of view, than a trust. There are a several reasons for this.

• Because the UTMA is built into state law, financial institutions know about it and should make it easy for the custodian to carry out property management duties. In states where the UTMA allows for property management until 21 or 25, setting up an UTMA custodianship can be particularly sensible if you leave property worth less than $50,000 to $100,000 to your child. Normally, amounts of this size will be fairly rapidly expended for the child's education and living needs, and are simply not large enough to tie up beyond age 21.

- Another factor can be the age of the child at the time you create your will or living trust. If your daughter is now two years old, it will obviously take far more money to support her until adulthood than if she is currently 17. For instance, $100,000 left to a two-year-old will likely be used up before she gets to college, but $100,000 left to a 17-year-old should at least last through college or whatever else she plans in the next four years.

- Using the UTMA can also be desirable because trust income tax rates are now higher than individual rates. (See Chapter 17, An Overview of Ongoing Trusts, Section G.) Annual income above $1,500 retained in a child's trust at the close of its tax year is taxed at higher rates than is property subject to the UTMA, which is taxed at the child's individual tax rate. Any trust income spent for the child's benefit during the year will be taxed at the child's rate, not the trust rate. But for income held in the trust, a higher tax rate applies.

- A child's trust is desirable when you want to extend the age at which a beneficiary receives property to well beyond when that child becomes a legal adult. As a rough cut-off point, if you're leaving more than $100,000 to a child, a child's trust is desirable.

Unlike UTMA custodianships, with a child's trust no age limit is imposed by state law. With a family pot trust any termination age is theoretically possible, but as we've discussed, they usually end when the youngest child turns 18, so they also aren't suitable for imposing longer age limits on beneficiaries. By contrast, child's trusts can be, and often are, established for young adults already over age 18 or 21, when a parent (or other older adult) believes the child is not a good bet now for responsibly handling property they might inherit.

Example: Marilyn, a single parent, creates a living trust leaving her estate, worth $720,000, equally to her two children, Todd, age 25, and Carolyn, age 27. Carolyn has always been frugal, if not parsimonious, with money. She has been saving money from the time of her first allowance. Todd is the flip side of the coin. He runs through whatever cash he has at the blink of an eye and, from Marilyn's perspective, often goes beyond generosity to recklessness with money. So in her living trust, Marilyn leaves Carolyn her half of Marilyn's estate outright. However, Todd's half is left in a "child's trust," with Marilyn's brother—a stable type if ever there was one—as trustee. Todd will not receive any trust property outright until he becomes 35. By that age, Marilyn hopes he will have become sensible enough to manage a large amount of money.

4. Naming a Property Guardian

It is rarely wise to leave property to your children to be supervised by the property guardian. There are several reasons:

- The property must go through your will, which means it will go through probate.

- Property guardians are often subject to court review, reporting requirements and strict rules as to how they can expend funds. All this usually requires hiring a lawyer and paying significant fees, but in our view does little to guarantee that the property manager will do a good job. And those lawyer fees, of course, come out of the property left to benefit the minor.

- Property guardianship must end at age 18.

All this said, your will should still name a property guardian to serve as a back-up to handle any property which for some reason isn't covered by a trust or custodianship.

Specifically, naming a property guardian in your will provides a supervision mechanism in case:

- Your minor children earn substantial money after you die, or receive a large gift or inheritance that doesn't, itself, name a property manager.

- You and your spouse leave property to each other to use for your children, naming the children as alternative or residuary beneficiaries without bothering to add an UTMA designation or establish a child's trust or pot trust. If both spouses die simultaneously, the property will be managed by the property guardian.

- You failed to include in an UTMA custodianship, child's trust or pot trust some property you want your children to inherit. This can occur because of oversight or, more likely, because you didn't yet own the property when you established your will or living trust and didn't amend that document later.

Creating a child's trust, pot trust or a custodianship under your state's UTMA is really quite simple to do, so normally the children's property guardian should be used only for the back-up purposes listed above. However, if you want to postpone estate planning or keep it to the bare minimum, it is far wiser to name a property guardian than ignore the issue altogether. Having your minor child's property supervised by a property guardian you name in your will is certainly preferable to having a judge appoint someone for the job. So, for example, a young couple, both healthy and unlikely to die for decades, may not want to deal with other supervision methods now. But if they do both die, they don't want a court deciding who'll manage the property they leave for their children. So, they create wills, where each names a property guardian to manage property for their children's benefit if both die simultaneously.

5. Comparison of the Four Major Ways to Leave a Child or Young Adult Property

Below is a chart that summarizes the rules for and reasons to use each of the four major methods for leaving gifts to your minor or young adult children:

LEAVING GIFTS TO YOUR MINOR OR YOUNG ADULT CHILDREN

	Gift Under UTMA	Child's Trust	Property Guardian	Family Pot Trust
Availability	All states but MI, SC and VT	All states	All states	All states
Amount of Property	If maximum age for release of gift is 18 in your state, then use is often best for mature children or for smaller gifts under $50,000 (depending on current age of child). If age for release is 21 or 25, sensible for gifts for $50,000 to $100,000 or more, especially to make sure money will be managed to last through college	Often good for gifts of any amount if UTMA age for release of gift in your state is 18, or if UTMA isn't applicable in your state. Often good for gifts in excess of $100,000 if UTMA applies in your state and age for release of gift is 21 or perhaps even 25	Last resort no matter what the amount	Any amount
Paperwork	No trust tax returns required, but minor must file a yearly return based on money actually received. Custodian must give accounting when property turned over to child	Trustee must file yearly income tax returns for trust. Retained trust income over $1,500 taxed at higher rate than child's individual rate	Usually substantial because reports must be presented to court	Trustee must file yearly income tax return for trust. Trust income over $1,500 kept in trust is taxed at higher rate than any child's individual rate
Court Supervision	None	None	Guardian must make regular reports to court	None
Termination	In most states, custodian must turn over property to child at age specified or by statute, usually 18-21 (25 in CA, AK, NV)	You specify the age at which the minor gets control of the trust property	Guardian must turn property over to child at age 18	Usually, when youngest child reaches age 18 or 21
Uses of Property	Custodian has broad statutory power to use property for child's living expenses, health needs and education	Trustee normally has power to use any of child's trust property for minor's needs for living expenses, health needs and education	Heavily limited and regulated by state law	Trustee can spend any trust property for any beneficiary

D. NAMING CHILDREN AS BENEFICIARIES OF LIFE INSURANCE

Some may think we've put the legal cart before the financial horse here—all this discussion about how to leave property to your children before any talk of how to acquire some valuable property to begin with. Well, this is a book on how to dispose of an estate, not about how to acquire one. Indeed, if we were masters of that, maybe we wouldn't have bothered writing the book. So all we can offer here is some general advice.

If you don't have the luxury of putting significant amounts aside, the best way to be sure cash will be available for the children if you die is to purchase some term life insurance. Term is the cheapest form of life insurance. Younger parents can obtain a significant amount of coverage for relatively low cost, for the obvious reason that statistically they are unlikely to die soon, so the risk to the insurance company is low. (Life insurance is discussed in depth in Chapter 12.)

If you name your children as beneficiaries, or alternate beneficiaries, of your policy, and you die while the children are minors, the insurance company cannot legally turn over the proceeds directly to them. If you haven't arranged for another method of adult supervision over the proceeds, court proceedings will be needed to confirm the children's property guardian. This means this property guardian can become enmeshed in the time-consuming court reporting requirements state laws typically impose. It also means the property guardian can only spend money under the terms of state law.

Here are your options for avoiding problems:

- Name the children as policy beneficiaries and name a custodian under the UTMA. Most insurance companies permit this, and have forms for it. Essentially, you fill out a separate form for each minor, providing the usual UTMA information—

the beneficiary's and the custodian's name, state, and age of termination, if you get to choose. If you want the proceeds to go to more than one child, you'll need to specify the percentage each one receives.

- Leave the proceeds to your child or children using a child's trust or a pot trust as part of a living trust. You name the living trust (or the trustee, if that's what the insurance company prefers) as the policy beneficiary in the living trust. You name minor(s) as beneficiaries of any insurance proceeds that trust receives and create the child's or pot trust to handle those proceeds. You'll need to give a copy of your living trust to the insurance company.

It may not be possible to leave insurance proceeds to a child's trust or minor's trust created by a will. Some insurance companies balk at this, on the grounds the trust won't come into existence until you die, and the policy beneficiary must be in existence when named. Rather than try to persuade an insurance company that this can be done, better to use the UTMA or create a living trust to achieve your goals.

E. LEAVING PROPERTY TO CHILDREN WHO ARE NOT YOUR OWN

If you want to leave property to minor or young adult children who aren't your own, you have the following choices:

- Leave the gift outright to the child's parent or legal guardian, and rely on the parent to use the gift for the benefit of the child.
- Leave the gift in your will or living trust through the Uniform Transfers to Minors Act. (The Act is discussed in Section C, above.) This is best suited for gifts under $50,000 to $100,000.
- Leave the gift through your living trust or will, by creating a child's trust for that gift. You can create a child's trust for any young adult beneficiary who

you believe is not presently capable of managing property wisely. You name the trustee of this child's trust, to manage all property in it. Doing this makes sense for large gifts—roughly, above $50,000 to $100,000. This plan can make good sense for gifts to grandchildren, particularly if the trustee is the child's parent and will supervise that child's trust.

Example: John, an elderly widower, wants to leave some antique furniture from his living trust to his 13-year-old grandniece Sally. He decides to make the gift using his state's Uniform Transfers to Minors Act. He names Sally's mother, Mary, to be the custodian. Her husband Fred is the alternate custodian. In his living trust, John makes the following gift: "Sally Earners shall be given the following furniture: my Hoosier cabinet, my two oriental rugs and my three stained glass lamps; Mary Earners is to be custodian under the Minnesota Uniform Transfers to Minors Act. If Mary Earners is unable to serve, or continue serving, as custodian, the successor custodian shall be Fred Earners."

• The least desirable method is to leave the gift in your will. If the child is a minor when you die, court proceedings will be necessary to appoint a property guardian to supervise the gift. And since you are not the child's parent, you can't even appoint or suggest a property guardian for him or her in your will.

F. DISINHERITANCE

To an outsider, it may seem sad that a parent would want to disinherit a child, but it's surely been known to happen. Whatever the reasons, it's legal for a parent to do so.

At the same time, legal rules protect children, and children of a deceased child, from being accidentally disinherited. The legalese for accidentally overlooked children is "pretermitted heirs." In most states, your children have a statutory right to inherit from you if you leave them out of your will or fail to make one. Grandchildren do not have any statutory right to inherit if their parent (your child) is still alive, so there is no need to disinherit them if you don't want them to inherit. However, children of a deceased child (your grandchildren) may have the same inheritance rights as that child.

Special rule for Floridians. The Florida Constitution (Art. 10, § 4) prohibits the head of a family from leaving his residence in his will, to someone other than spouse or child, if either exist.

Most states require that you mention each of your children in your will. You can name a child and then expressly disinherit him, or functionally disinherit him by leaving him nothing, or a very small gift. Even if you transfer all your property by a living trust, to be safe, you must use a will to disinherit a child or the children of a deceased child. The reason is simple: some state laws require disinheritance to be accomplished by will, and only by a will.

The laws of each state protect your children who are born after your will is made ("afterborn children") by entitling them to a share of your estate. Similarly, many states also provide that if you don't mention a child (or the children of a deceased child) in your will, that omitted child, or the children of a child who has died before you, are entitled to some of your property. How much a child gets depends on whether you leave a spouse and how many other children you have.

What if you provide for your children outside your will—by leaving them property from your living trust, for example—but didn't mention them in your will? They could, at least in theory, claim to be accidentally overlooked heirs and demand additional shares of your estate. In defining whether a child is overlooked, and therefore entitled to receive a share of your estate, some state's laws specifically refer to omitting a child from a "will." Read literally, these statutes don't allow property left to a child by a living trust (or other method) to be considered to determine if a child has been overlooked. Of course, given the purpose of the preterminated heir statutes—to protect children from being accidentally disinherited—it's senseless to read the statute so literally. But who says the law can't be senseless?

So, to be absolutely safe, even if you generously provide for your children outside of your will, you should list the names of all your children (and children of a deceased child) in your will and make some provision for them.

Remember, for the "preterminated heir" issue to become a problem, a child must file a lawsuit contesting your will and estate plan. If you trust that your children aren't going to sue, you don't have to worry about this. ∎

7

Wills

A. A Will as the Centerpiece of Your Estate Plan 7/2
B. A Back-Up Will With a Comprehensive Estate Plan 7/2
C. What Makes a Will Legal? 7/4
D. Types of Wills 7/5
    1. Handwritten Wills 7/5
    2. Pour-Over Wills 7/5
    3. Statutory Wills 7/6
    4. Other Types of Wills 7/6
E. What Property Cannot Be Transferred by Will? 7/7
F. Can My Will Be Successfully Challenged? 7/8
G. Keeping Your Will Up to Date 7/8
    1. Does Divorce Automatically Revoke a Will? 7/8
    2. What Happens If I Have a Child or Marry After I
        Make a Will? 7/9
    3. Is My Will Valid If I Move to a New State? 7/9

A will is what many people think of when they first consider estate planning. This makes sense. Everyone should have a will, whether or not they engage in more extensive estate planning. And quite a number of people decide that a will is all the planning they need, at least for the time being.

As you undoubtedly know, a will specifies who gets property covered by that document when you die. A will can also serve other vital purposes, such as appointing a personal guardian to raise your minor children if you and the other parent aren't available.

Property left by a will must normally go through probate. As we've mentioned, probate is usually costly and burdensome. So a substantial portion of this book is devoted to explaining how to avoid this process. (Probate is discussed on more detail in Chapter 8.) However, despite the downside of probate, every estate plan should at least include a "back-up" will to cover things that probate-avoidance devices don't take care of.

A. A WILL AS THE CENTERPIECE OF YOUR ESTATE PLAN

Many people reasonably decide to make a will the centerpiece—or even, in some cases, the only piece—of their estate plan. They decide that, for the foreseeable future, a will accomplishes their estate planning goals. They can sensibly postpone more complicated, and perhaps more costly, estate planning work. You may be this kind of person if:

• No matter what your age or health, you simply don't want the bother of more extensive estate planning. Quite a few people say, "Yes, I guess I should probably do full-scale estate planning, but I never get around to it, so I'd better at least make a will now and think about the full-scale plan later." After all, a will achieves their basic goal of distributing their property as they see fit, with as little

disturbance to themselves as possible. Sure, a will is likely to lead to probate, but the goal of probate avoidance, as sensible as it is, should never obscure the more important goal of seeing to it that your property goes to the people and organizations you want to receive it.

• You're healthy and, statistically, unlikely to die for decades. If you just want to be certain your basic wishes for your property are carried out in the very unlikely event you die unexpectedly, a will achieves this goal with considerably less paperwork than a living trust. And as you acquire property, and people close to you are born and die, it can be a lot easier to make a new will than to amend a living trust.

• Your primary estate planning goal is to ensure, to the best of your abilities, that if you die, your minor children are well provided for and cared for. A will allows you to name a personal guardian (something that, in most all states, can't be done by any other document), while also allowing you to create a method for adult supervision of any property you leave to your children. Years later, of course, if you accumulate considerable property, you may want to engage in more thorough estate planning.

B. A BACK-UP WILL WITH A COMPREHENSIVE ESTATE PLAN

If you prepare a thorough estate plan and arrange to avoid probate for all your property do you still need a will? Yes. It's always desirable to have at least a simple will, which we call a "back-up" will, as part of your estate plan for one or probably more of the following reasons:

• **To dispose of suddenly acquired property.** Anyone may end up acquiring valuable property at or shortly before death, such as a sudden gift or inheritance, or even a lottery prize. Of course, it's sensible to promptly revise your estate plan to name a specific beneficiary to inherit this property. But what if you don't get around to it before you die? If you have a will, that property will go to your residuary beneficiary, who, by definition, takes "the rest of your property"—that is, everything that isn't left to some specific named beneficiary. Unfortunately, there's no easy way to leave left-over property through a living trust, because property must be formally added to the trust for it to be subject to the trust provisions.

- **To dispose of property not transferred by a probate avoidance device.** If you buy property but don't get around to planning probate avoidance for it (by placing it in your living trust, for example), a will is a valuable back-up device, ensuring that the property will go to whomever you want to have it (your residuary beneficiary), and not pass under state law. Similarly, if somehow you've failed to transfer some of your existing property to a probate avoidance device, for example, because you didn't properly complete transfers of title, a will directs that property to your residuary beneficiary.

- **To name a personal guardian for your minor children.** If you have minor children, you need a will to achieve the vital goal of naming a personal guardian for them. You can't use any other device for this purpose (except a living trust in a couple of states). Also, in your will you can appoint a property guardian for your children, to manage any of their property not otherwise legally supervised by an adult. (See Chapter 6, Children.)

- **To leave property you've inherited but is still in probate.** If someone has left you property by will, and that property is still enmeshed in probate when you die, you can't arrange to transfer it by a probate avoidance device such as a living trust, since you don't have title to the property. But

under your will, that property goes to your residuary beneficiary.

- **To disinherit a child or spouse.** You can expressly disinherit a child in your will. (See Chapter 6, Children, Section F.) You can disinherit a spouse in your will only if you live in a community property state. (See Chapter 3, Sections B and C.)

- **To name your executor.** In your will, you name your executor, the person with legal authority to supervise distribution of property left by your will, and to represent your estate. It can be a good idea to have an executor even if you have also set up a living trust and named a successor trustee to manage it when you die, because banks and other financial institutions can be reassured to know an executor exists. The successor trustee and executor are often the same person.

CHOOSING YOUR EXECUTOR

Your executor should be the person you trust the most and who's willing to do the job. If you plan to prepare a living trust, it's generally best that your executor be the same person you chose to be the successor trustee of your trust. If possible, it's best to name an executor who lives in your state, or near it. A few states require an executor to live in-state.

It's simpler to name just one executor, but you can name co-executors, or even several executors, if you have good reason for it. There can be compelling reasons—family harmony is one common example—for selecting more than one trustee.

Some conservative estate planners recommend selecting a bank to be your executor We strongly recommend against this, unless you have no other option. Your executor is your link to the future, in charge of distributing your property after your death. You want someone human, with genuine concern, not an impersonal institution that charges fees for every small act. If your most trusted friend is your banker name him as executor, but not the bank itself.

- **In case probate is not required.** Some states don't require probate, or greatly simplify probate, for small or modest estates. (See Chapter 14, State Law Exemptions From Normal Probate.) If your estate qualifies for simplified treatment, there's no need to use a series of probate avoidance devices—a will is all you need. And in some states, even larger estates can make use of simplified probate. For example, California allows personal property worth up to $100,000 to be transferred by a will without any probate. Property transferred by probate avoidance methods doesn't count toward

this $100,000 limit. So, in California (and in some other states), a will can be a handy method for making small gifts—that treasured antique clock to a niece, or $3,000 to a fondly remembered employee—once you have arranged to transfer the bulk of your estate outside of probate.

C. WHAT MAKES A WILL LEGAL?

Drafting a legal will isn't nearly as complicated as most people fear. The requirements are:

- You must be at least 18 years old in all states, except Wyoming, where you must be at least 19 to make a valid will.

- You must be of "sound mind." The fact that you're reading and understanding this book is, as a practical matter, sufficient evidence that you meet this test.

- The will must be typewritten or printed on a computer printer. (See Section D, below, for a discussion of handwritten wills.)

- The will must have at least one substantive provision. The most common one leaves some, or all, of your property to whomever you want to have it.

- You must appoint at least one executor.

- You must date the will.

- You must sign the will in front of two witnesses (three in Vermont). Witnesses need only be:

  - Adults (usually over 18) and of sound mind.

  - People who won't inherit under the will. Will beneficiaries cannot be witnesses.

Witnesses watch you sign your will and then sign it themselves. They must be told that it's your will they are signing, but they don't have to read it or be told what it contains.

There's no requirement that a will be recorded or filed with any governmental agency. Nor need a will be notarized.

Still you may want to use a notary when singing your will and having it witnessed. In most states, having the witnesses sign a brief statement called a "self-proving" affidavit, which is then notarized, can eliminate any need for a witness to testify at subsequent probate proceedings.

WHAT A WILL LOOKS LIKE

Years ago, when Denis was a partner in a small law firm, he learned that some clients were disappointed that their wills didn't look more impressive; a few sheets of typed paper seemed lacking in "gravitas." So he began stapling each will in a blue cover-binder, and attaching a red ribbon and red wax seal. Some clients appreciated these touches—although they were certainly not legally required. If you want extras like these, you can purchase what you need at most stationery stores, for far less than if you buy them from a lawyer.

D. TYPES OF WILLS

There are various types of wills. To help clear up any confusion, we briefly cover the main ones here.

1. Handwritten Wills

A handwritten will (called "holographic" in legalese) must be written, dated and signed entirely in the handwriting of the person making the will. It does not have to be witnessed. Handwritten wills are recognized by about 25 states. We definitely don't recommend them, even in the states where they're legal.

Handwritten wills aren't recommended because probate courts traditionally have been very strict when examining them after the death of the writer. Since a handwritten will isn't normally witnessed, judges sometimes fear that it might have been forged. Also, a judge may require proof that the will was actually and voluntarily written by the deceased person, which sometimes isn't easy to do. In short, given the tiny bit of extra trouble it takes to prepare a typed will and have it witnessed, it's reckless not to do it.

2. Pour-Over Wills

A "pour-over" will is one that directs that the property subject to it goes to (be "poured over" into) a trust. For example, sometimes people make their living trusts the beneficiaries of their wills. When the will property is poured over to the trust, the trust document controls who receives that property.

a. When a Pour-Over Will Is Undesirable

Pour-over wills are rarely a good idea to use with a basic probate-avoidance living trust. Pour-over wills do not avoid probate. All property that is left through a will—any kind of will—must go through probate, unless the amount left is small enough to qualify for exemption from normal probate laws. Probate is most definitely not avoided simply because the beneficiary of a will is a living trust.

It's generally better to simply use a standard back-up will to take care of your left-over (non-living trust) property. In the back-up will, you can name the people you want to get the property, and skip the unnecessary extra step of pouring the property through the living trust after your death.

When used as a back-up will, a pour-over will actually has a disadvantage that standard wills don't: It forces the living trust to go on for months after your death, because the property left through the pour-over will must go through probate before it can be transferred to the trust. Usually, the property left in a living trust can be distributed to the beneficiaries, and the trust ended, within a few weeks after the person's death.

b. When You May Want a Pour-Over Will

There are, however, two situations in which you might want to use a pour-over will. The first is if you set up an AB living trust to save on estate taxes. With this device, the spouses want up to the maximum amount of property allowed under the federal estate tax exemption to eventually wind up in the trust of the deceased spouse. (See Chapter 18, Estate Tax-Saving Bypass Trusts, Section C.) So each spouse writes a pour-over will, leaving his will property to the AB trust. (After one spouse dies, the other spouse should amend her or his will or prepare a new one.)

Also, if you set up, as part of your living trust, a child's trust to provide management for property left to a young beneficiary, you may want any property that child inherits through your will to pour over into that trust. Otherwise, you would create two trusts for the child: one in the will and one in your living trust.

3. Statutory Wills

A statutory will is a pre-printed, fill-in-the-blanks, check-the-boxes will form authorized by state law. California, Maine, Michigan and Wisconsin have statutory wills. In theory, statutory wills are an excellent idea—inexpensive, easy to complete and reliable. Unfortunately, in practice, statutory wills are so limited in scope they aren't useful for most people.

The choices provided in the statutory forms are quite narrow and cannot legally be changed—that is, you can't customize them to fit your situation or, indeed, change them at all. For example, the Michigan form allows you to make only two cash gifts (aside from household property); everything else must go to your spouse or children.

Normally, statutory wills are useful only if you are married and want all or the bulk of your property to go to your spouse (or, if she predeceases you, in trust for your minor children). Because of the limitations of statutory wills, the movement to introduce them in other states has stalled. No state has adopted a statutory will since the late 1980s.

4. Other Types of Wills

You will almost surely want a formal, witnessed will, either as your primary estate planning device or as a back-up to a living trust. But you may also have questions about other types of wills. Here are some wills we have been asked about:

- **Oral wills.** Oral wills (also called "nuncupative" wills) are valid in a minority of states and, even where valid, are acceptable only if made under special circumstances, such as the will maker's perception of imminent death on the battlefield or in some other highly unusual circumstance. Clearly, they are not to be relied on as a serious estate planning device.

- **Video or film wills.** Video or film wills are not valid under any state's law. But films of a person reciting will provisions, such as to whom they are leaving property, can be useful evidence if a will is challenged, to demonstrate that the will maker was of sound mind and didn't appear crazy or under undue influence.

Avoiding lawsuits over your will. If you truly fear a will contest based on your lack of sound mind or the undue influence of a beneficiary, ask a lawyer about using videos or films to help establish that you were thinking clearly when your will was signed.

- **Joint wills.** A joint will is one document made by two people, usually a married couple. Each leaves everything to the other, and then the will goes on to specify what happens to the property when the second person dies. In effect, a joint will can prevent the surviving person from changing his mind regarding what should happen to the survivor's property. We don't recommend joint wills. Even if circumstances change radically, the survivor is prevented from revising or revoking any part of the will. If you want to impose controls over property you leave to your spouse, the sensible way to do it is through a trust. (See Chapter 24, Property Control Trusts for Second or Subsequent Marriages.)

- **Contracts to make a will.** A contract to make a will—that is, an agreement to leave certain property to the other person who signs the contract—can be valid, but is usually not wise. The usual case in which such contracts are made is where someone provides services—care, or live-in nursing—in return for an agreement that the person receiving the care will leave property to the person providing the care. Tying up your property like this so you cannot change your will, even if circumstances change, isn't desirable for many reasons. Most lawyers prefer to establish a trust in these situations.

Making promises binding. If you face a situation in which you want to guarantee now that someone will receive money from your estate, see a lawyer.

- **Living wills.** A living will (sometimes called a "Directive to Physicians") has no relation to a conventional will at all. Essentially, a living will is a document in which you state that you want a natural death and don't want your life artificially prolonged by use of life support equipment. Depending on state law, other issues related to health care can also be covered. They are discussed in Chapter 26, Incapacity: Health Care and Financial Management Directives.

E. WHAT PROPERTY CANNOT BE TRANSFERRED BY WILL?

Property that is transferred by a binding probate avoidance device can't also be transferred by will. In other words, once you place property in one of the following forms of ownership, listing that property in your will has no effect:

- Property in a living trust—it goes to the beneficiaries named in the trust document

- Joint tenancy property—at your death, your share automatically goes to the surviving joint tenants (but if all joint tenants die simultaneously, you can leave your share by will)

- Money in informal bank account trusts or pay-on-death accounts. The person you designate as beneficiary on the account document inherits

- Life insurance proceeds payable to a named beneficiary or beneficiaries—they go to the beneficiaries

- Funds remaining in retirement plans, including pensions, IRAs and profit-sharing plans, payable to named beneficiaries—the beneficiaries in these programs get these assets no matter what your will says

- Property that is promised to someone in a living together contract, partnership agreement, corporate shareholder agreement or other contract.

F. CAN MY WILL BE SUCCESSFULLY CHALLENGED?

The fact that many people worry about the possibility of lawsuits over their wills shows how fear-ridden estate planning has become. Fortunately, the reality is that will challenges, let alone successful ones, are rare. The legal grounds for contesting a will are limited to extreme circumstances. Basically, your will can be invalidated only if you were under age when you made it, or were clearly mentally incompetent (not of "sound mind"), or the will was procured by fraud, duress or undue influence.

A person must be pretty far gone before a court will rule that she lacked the capacity to make a valid will. For example, forgetfulness or even the inability to recognize friends don't by themselves establish incapacity. It's important to remember that courts presume that the will writer was of sound mind; a challenger must prove incapacity. Similarly, a will is rarely declared invalid on grounds it was procured by fraud, duress or undue influence; this requires proof that some evildoer manipulated a person in a confused or weakened mental or emotional state to leave his property in a way the person otherwise wouldn't have.

If you fear a lawsuit. If you think someone might contest your will, it's best to prepare in advance how to prevail against any lawsuit. Or if there are special circumstances, such as a seriously debilitating illness, that you believe might raise questions about your competency and the validity of your will, it's also prudent to see a lawyer. This can mean having the lawyer come to see and perhaps even physically help you. For example, in many states, if you're too ill to sign your own name, you can direct that a witness or an attorney sign it for you. In any unusual physical or mental circumstances, it's prudent to have a lawyer's assistance, especially if substantial amounts of property are involved. It could always be claimed that if you were too ill to sign your name, you weren't mentally competent. In any subsequent court challenge to the will, the lawyer's testimony that you appeared to be in full possession of your faculties could be very important.

G. KEEPING YOUR WILL UP TO DATE

If important circumstances change, you may need to revise your will.

1. Does Divorce Automatically Revoke a Will?

In some states, if you get divorced after making a will, the provisions that left property to your former spouse are automatically revoked. But that's not true in all states. In any case, you should always revise your will and bring your estate plan up to date after a divorce. (See Chapter 30, After Your Estate Plan Is Completed.)

2. What Happens If I Have a Child or Marry After I Make a Will?

If you have a child or get married after you make your will, you must revise your will, and your estate plan, to reflect your new situation. If you don't, your estate may become entangled in laws designed to protect "afterborn children" and spouses. (See Chapter 6, Children.) In any case, you'll probably want to revise your estate plan to provide for the new child or spouse.

3. Is My Will Valid If I Move to a New State?

A will signed in one state remains valid if you move to another state. However, it's often advisable to draft a new will after a permanent move. If you're married and move from a common law property state to a community property state or vice versa, the marital property ownership laws of your new state may affect your will. (See Chapter 3, Section D.) Or your new state may have a different form for a "self-proving" will affidavit than your old one did. Or you may want, or be required to, appoint one executor who lives in your new state. ■

8

PROBATE AND WHY YOU WANT TO AVOID IT

A. What Is Probate? 8/2
B. Probate Fees 8/3
C. Avoiding Probate 8/4
    1. Informal Probate Avoidance 8/7
    2. Planning to Avoid Probate 8/7
D. When You May Want Probate 8/8
E. Debts, Taxes and Probate Avoidance 8/8
F. Probate Reform 8/9

Many people aren't sure what probate actually is, except that it involves lawyers and courts in transferring property after one's death. One thing they do know is they want to avoid it. That's a sound instinct. In most instances probate is a costly and time-consuming business, providing no benefits except to attorneys.

A. WHAT IS PROBATE?

Probate is the legal process that includes:

- Filing the deceased person's will with a local court (depending on the state, the court may be called the "probate," "surrogate" or "chancery" court).
- Identifying and inventorying the deceased person's property.
- Having that property appraised.
- Paying off debts, including death tax.
- Having the will "proved" valid to the court. (This is almost always a routine matter; indeed, it's so routine that it's done without a formal hearing in many states, unless there is a contest, which is extremely rare.)
- Eventually, distributing what's left as the will directs.

If the deceased person didn't leave a will, or the will isn't valid and the deceased didn't leave the property in any other way, such as through a living trust or joint tenancy, the estate will still go through probate. The property is distributed to immediate family members as state law (called "intestate succession" law) dictates.

People who defend the probate system (mostly lawyers, which is surely no surprise) assert that probate prevents fraud in transferring a deceased person's property. In addition, they claim it protects inheritors by promptly resolving claims creditors have

against a deceased person's property. In truth, however, most property is transferred within a close circle of family and friends, and few, if any, estates face creditors' claims. Whatever bills the deceased had—often not many—are readily paid out of the property left. (According to a study by the American Association of Retired People (AARP), the great majority of creditors' claims are filed by the funeral industry, who have learned to use probate as a collection device.) In short, most people have no need of probate's so-called benefits. The system usually amounts to a lot of time-wasting, expensive mumbo-jumbo of use to no one but the lawyers involved.

The actual probate functions are essentially clerical and administrative. In the vast majority of probate cases, there's no conflict, no contesting parties, none of the normal reasons for court proceedings. Likewise, probate doesn't usually call for legal research, drafting or lawyers' adversarial skills. Instead, in the normal, uneventful probate proceeding, the family or other inheritors of the dead person provide a copy of the deceased person's will and other needed financial information. The attorney's secretary then fills in a small mound of forms and keeps track of filing deadlines and other procedural technicalities. In some states, the attorney makes a couple of routine court appearances; in others, the whole procedure is normally handled by mail.

There is so much money in the probate business that some lawyers hire probate form preparation services to do all the real work. In most instances, the existence of these freelance paralegal services is not disclosed to clients, who assume that lawyers' offices at least do the paperwork they are paid so well for.

A typical probate takes up to a year or more, often much more. Denis once worked in a law office that was profitably entering its seventh year of handling a probate estate—and a very wealthy estate it was. By contrast, property transfers by other legal means, such as a living trust, can usually be completed in a matter of weeks.

Probate usually requires both an "executor" and someone familiar with probate procedures, normally a probate attorney. The executor, appointed in the will, is responsible for making sure that the will is followed. The executor, who is usually a spouse or friend of the deceased, hires a probate lawyer to do the paperwork. Then the executor does little more than sign where the lawyer directs, while wondering why the whole business is taking so long.

B. PROBATE FEES

For their services, the lawyer and the executor are each entitled to a hefty fee from the probate estate. However, many executors don't accept a fee, especially if they inherit much of the property anyway.

A recent report by the American Association of Retired People estimated that probate attorneys annually receive fees of $1.5 billion. In many states, the fees are what a court approves as "reasonable." In a few states, the fees are a percentage of the estate subject to probate. Either way, probate attorney fees for an uncomplicated estate with a value of $400,000 (these days, often little more than a home, some savings and a car) can amount to $10,000 or more. And, in addition, there are court costs, appraiser's fees and other possible expenses. Moreover, if there

are any "extraordinary" services performed for the estate, the attorney or executor can often ask the court for additional fees. Some lawyers even persuade (or dupe) clients into naming them as executors, enabling the lawyers to hire themselves as probate attorneys and collect two fees—one as executor, one as probate attorney.

Is a probate lawyer really necessary? One obvious way to reduce probate fees would be for your executor to appear in court without an attorney ("in pro per") as the representative of your estate. Unfortunately, a few states don't permit the executor to act without a lawyer. And some judges make things difficult for an executor who tries to go it alone. The only states in which it's a reasonable choice for most people are California (see *How to Probate an Estate,* by Julia Nissley (Nolo Press), an excellent self-help book designed for, and used by, thousands of non-lawyers), and Wisconsin, which has an established pro per procedure. (See Chapter 14, State Law Exemptions from Normal Probate, Section B.) In other states where in pro per action is theoretically possible, there are no comprehensive published materials, nor is other help available to non-lawyers. Without help, learning to complete the forms, understanding the intricacies of court petitions, estate inventories, "proof of service" declarations, and so on, is likely to be very difficult. And to make matters worse, court clerks and judges are likely to be unsympathetic (to put it mildly), so any mistake is likely to cause delay, and possibly embarrassment. Still, handling a probate without a lawyer is not impossible. Legal secretaries and paralegals typically copy necessary forms and follow procedures set out in lawyer practice manuals. These are usually available at public law libraries, and many people have successfully used them.

In all states (including California and Wisconsin), rather than trying to save money by having your estate probated without an attorney, it generally makes more sense to see if you can avoid probate at least for the bulk of your property. This approach involves transferring the big ticket items of your property—for example, your house and stock portfolio—outside of probate, leaving only less valuable items to be passed by your will. (As you know, we recommend that you always have a least a back-up will. See Chapter 7, Section B.)

If the value of the property transferred by your will is relatively low, probate may not be required. Most states except small will estates from probate. The limits vary from state to state. (See Chapter 14.)

Finally, if some of your estate will be subject to probate, you can try to reach an agreement with an attorney to do your probate for less than the conventional fees. If the probate of your estate is routine, it will be sufficiently profitable even at a fee lower than the conventional rate. If you do arrange a reduced fee, put something in writing, even if it's only a letter confirming this arrangement. However, you cannot bind your attorney to handle the probate of your estate for a reduced fee. In fact, you don't have the power to select the attorney at all. The law gives this authority to the executor.

EXCESSIVE PROBATE FEES

Marilyn Monroe's estate offers an extreme example of how outrageous probate fees can be. She died in debt in 1962, but over the next 18 years, her estate received income, mostly from movie royalties, in excess of $1,600,000. When her estate was settled in 1980, her executor announced that debts of $372,136 had been paid, and $101,229 was left as the final assets of the estate, for distribution to inheritors. Well over a million dollars of Monroe's estate was consumed by probate fees.

C. AVOIDING PROBATE

In response to the manifest waste perpetrated by the probate system, a number of legal methods have been developed to avoid probate entirely. Because leaving property in a will usually results in probate, probate avoidance methods involve arranging, prior to death, to transfer property by other legal means. The major probate avoidance methods are:

- revocable living trusts (Chapter 9)
- joint tenancy (Chapter 10)
- "pay-on-death" designations, most often used for bank accounts, but also available for securities (stocks and bonds) and vehicles in two states (Chapter 11)
- life insurance (Chapter 12)
- Retirement accounts that go to a designated beneficiary (Chapter 13)
- state laws that exempt from probate certain amounts of property left by will (Chapter 14), and
- gifts you make while you're still alive (Chapter 16).

Below is a summary chart of the pluses and minuses of each method. Deciding which method, or combination of methods, is best for you is a major part of estate planning. So please read all the chapters on probate avoidance methods before you make final choices.

TRANSFER DEVICE	AVOIDS PROBATE?	MAJOR ADVANTAGES	DRAWBACKS
Will	No, except in limited circumstances for small estates. (See Chapter 14.)	Simple and easy to prepare; can serve other purposes, such as naming guardian for minor children. Often a good interim device to use until later in life.	Normally puts property in probate where inheritors face attorney's fees and other costs and time delays.
Living Trust		Complete control over property while alive; flexibility in providing for beneficiaries. Allows for property management in case of incapacity.	More trouble to establish than a will. Initial attorney's fees can be higher. More trouble to maintain than a will.
Joint Tenancy	Yes.	Can be simplest probate avoidance device to create.	Fine for long-term couples owning property together, but usually not a good substitute for a living trust later in life, because each joint tenant can normally sell their interest. There may be gift taxes involved in creating joint tenancy and putting property in joint tenancy. May mean partial loss of stepped up tax basis.
Tenancy by the Entirety	Yes.	Easy to create.	Available only in some states; limited to married couples. Can be a problem if one spouse becomes incapacitated.
Pay-on-Death Bank Accounts	Yes.	Very easy to create; no additional costs.	Limited to bank accounts and some government securities. Not a good idea when small children may inherit, since a property guardian will have to be appointed. (See Chapter 6.)

TRANSFER DEVICE	AVOIDS PROBATE?	MAJOR ADVANTAGES	DRAWBACKS
Transfer on Death Car Registration	Yes.	(If available) can be easy to create, and simplest way to transfer car.	Available only in California and Missouri.
Transfer on Death Registration for Securities	Yes.	Easy to do. Name inheritor on securities' registration form.	Not available in all states.
Naming Beneficiary to Pension Plan or Retirement Account	Yes.	Generally easy to do.	Can be limits imposed by specific policy, program, plan.
Life Insurance	Yes.	Good way to provide quick cash for beneficiaries or to pay estate taxes. Proceeds don't go through probate.	If family members will not need immediate cash (or if they don't rely on you for support), the expense of policy may not be justified.
State Law Exemptions to Normal Probate	Yes.	Can work well if state allows this method to be combined with other probate avoidance methods.	Only relatively small amounts of property qualify. Rules vary for each state. (See Chapter 14.) You have to understand your state's laws; research or hiring an attorney may be required.
Dying Intestate, Without Creating any Property Transfer Method	No.	No effort required.	Usually a terrible choice. Property will be distributed according to state law, which is likely not to be exactly as you wish. Your executor (administrator) will be appointed by judge. Guardian for your minor children selected by a judge.

1. Informal Probate Avoidance

Some people ask, "Why not just divide up a deceased relative's or friend's property as the will directs, and ignore the laws requiring probate?" Indeed, some small estates are undoubtedly disposed of this way, directly and informally by family members.

For example, say an older man lives his last few years in a nursing home. After his death, his children meet and divide the personal items their father had kept over the years. What little savings he has have long since been put into a joint account with the children anyway, so there's no need for court proceedings there. If the father owned no other property, the children have, in effect, "probated" his estate.

For this type of informal procedure to work, the family must be able to gain possession of all of the deceased's property, agree on how to distribute it, and pay all the creditors. Gaining possession of property isn't difficult if there's nothing but personal effects and household items. However, if real estate, securities, bank accounts or other property bearing legal title papers, such as cars and boats, are involved, informal family property distribution can't work. Title to a house, for example, can't be changed on the say-so of the next of kin; someone with legal authority must prepare, sign and record a deed transferring title to the house to the inheritors.

One good rule is that whenever outsiders are involved with a deceased's property, do-it-yourself distribution by inheritors is not feasible. For instance, creditors can be an obstacle. A creditor concerned about being paid can usually file a court action to compel a probate proceeding.

Another stumbling block can be getting family members to agree on how to divide the deceased's possessions. If there's a will, it may not be a problem, since the will acts as a legal blueprint for distribution. If there is no will, things can be trickier. One alternative is for the family to look up and agree to abide by the state intestate succession rules, which specifically cover situations in which there is no will. Or, in either case, the family may simply adopt their own, mutually agreed-on settlement. For example, if, despite a will provision to the contrary, one sibling wants the furniture and the other wants the tools, they can simply trade. All inheritors must agree to the estate distribution if probate procedures are bypassed. Any inheritor who is unhappy with the estate distribution can, like creditors, file for a formal probate.

In sum, informal probate avoidance, even for a small estate, isn't something one can count on. Realistically, probate avoidance must be planned in advance.

2. Planning to Avoid Probate

Because probate has justifiably come to be viewed as an unnecessary device designed to fill lawyers' coffers, some have concluded that probate must be avoided for every last bit of one's property. In our view, this is too rigid. True, most people who take the time to plan their own estate decide they want to avoid probate, at least for the major items of property they own. As we've said, this is fine, but prepare a back-up will as well.

But do you want to plan to avoid probate now? Many younger people sensibly elect to put off planning to avoid probate until they are at least in middle age. For example, a younger couple may decide that making wills accomplishes their principal needs, which are to leave most or all property to each other, and to provide money and a guardian for their children if they should die at the same time. They understand that using probate avoidance methods will require some paperwork now, and perhaps some legal fees. Since it's highly unlikely they will die soon and suddenly (should they become ill, they'll normally have time to plan), and because they haven't yet accumulated a great deal of property, they decide to wait a few decades before engaging in probate avoidance planning.

D. WHEN YOU MAY WANT PROBATE

If your estate owes a lot of debts, probate may be a good idea. Most estates don't involve complex creditor problems. Most deceased persons leave little more than conventional household debts: mortgages, utilities, magazine subscriptions, auto loans, credit cards. Probate is not necessary to handle these debts. But if there's a significant risk that many creditors, especially those owed large sums, will make claims against your estate, probate can be advisable, especially if your executor will contest one or more of these claims.

If you own a failing business, or are involved in complicated financial transactions, or complex litigation, probate can provide benefits because it provides a ready-made court procedure for resolving creditors' claims faster than by normal lawsuit. Creditors who are notified of the probate proceeding must file their claims promptly with the probate court, often within four or six months after probate begins, or they needn't be paid. This is a much shorter deadline than would otherwise apply and can allow beneficiaries to take their property (or what's left) free of anxiety about future creditors' claims.

If you believe someone may challenge your estate plan in court, probate can be the most efficient way to resolve the conflict. Any estate planning device, whether it be a will, living trust, or any combination of legal methods, can be attacked by a lawsuit after your death. Fortunately, the legal grounds for attack are quite limited. The challenger must prove the estate plan is a result of someone's illegal act, such as fraud, duress or undue influence over the deceased person, or the challenger must establish that the deceased person was mentally incompetent when the documents were signed. These legal theories are hard to prove, although easy to allege. If you believe there's a risk that your estate may be subject to legal attack, even by someone who has little chance of success, probate may be advisable as part of your plan to defeat that attack. Under probate law, only a brief time is allowed for attacking a will, and the people who witnessed the signing of the will should be able to testify that you were of sound mind.

Lawsuit fears. If you're worried about a lawsuit, you should discuss your estate planning with an attorney. Together, you can decide what your best course of action is.

E. DEBTS, TAXES AND PROBATE AVOIDANCE

What about debts? If an estate is probated, debts and taxes are paid before property is distributed to inheritors. If duly notified creditors don't make their claims within the allotted time, they're simply cut off. But if there's no probate, obviously, a probate court can't ensure that debts get paid. However, there's no indication that judicial policing is needed. Many people leave no significant debts, and even if some do, they normally leave sufficient assets to pay them. It's important to realize that the primary financial obligations most people do have—mortgages on real estate, or loans on cars—don't need to be paid off promptly after the owner dies. Normally, the person who inherits the asset becomes liable for the mortgage or loan. In other words, mortgages or car loans pass with the property and don't need to be paid off separately.

If no probate occurs to cut off creditors' claims, all the deceased's property remains liable for debts, including any death tax. This is true even after the property is transferred to inheritors. If only one person will inherit from you, that person will be responsible for paying your debts and any death tax from the inherited property. If there are several inheritors, the responsibility for paying debts and taxes can, theoretically, become more confusing, but this confusion can be eliminated in advance by earmarking money in your estate plan to pay debts. One way to do this is to allocate, in a living trust, specific assets (a bank account, or a particular stock) to pay debts and taxes. If you don't have a suitable asset available to do this, consider purchasing insurance to provide cash.

If you're concerned about death taxes, read Chapter 15, Estate Taxes, to learn whether any federal or state tax will likely be due at your death. If death taxes seem unlikely, this is, obviously, one less thing to worry about. If death taxes seem likely, plan to leave enough cash or property that can easily be sold, to cover them.

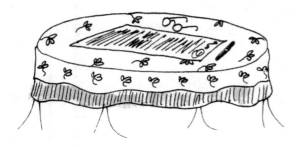

F. PROBATE REFORM

Why is probate so time-consuming and expensive? Why is probate court approval required for so many routine actions when there's normally no conflict whatsoever? Aside from the mystique of professionalism and good old greed, the history of probate supplies most of the answer. Probate became legal business through a quirk of English history. In medieval England, wealth and power resided almost exclusively in the ownership of land. It passed, by feudal law, to the eldest son. Inheritance of land was a political matter of direct concern to the king, so land transfers after a death were done through the king's courts.

The proceedings were technical, formal and costly. Personal property (everything except real estate) was transferred by much simpler ways. When the United States became independent, it followed the traditional British legal system for land inheritance. But instead of distinguishing between land and personal property, our new nation tossed everything into the new "probate" court. Over 200 years later, all types of property can still be transferred through these formal judicial proceedings.

Over the years, there have been countless efforts to reform probate by making it easier or cheaper, or to simply do away with it. But because a complicated probate system means substantial fees for lawyers, the legal profession continues to fiercely defend it.

Lawyers' assurances that probate is necessary sound increasingly hollow. Even the British eliminated tedious, expensive probate proceedings over half a century ago. In 1926, England reformed its probate system to provide that the person named in the will as the executor (normally a nonlawyer) simply files an accounting of the estate's assets and liabilities with the tax authorities, who appraise the inventory and assess any death tax due. If the papers are in order, as they should be in all routine probates, a "grant of probate" is issued in as little as seven days. Without any further court proceedings, the executor then handles all the estate's problems—paying the bills, collecting assets and distributing gifts to inheritors. Only if there's a problem, such as a will contest or a contested debt claim, is the matter referred to the Principal Registry, the functional equivalent of our probate courts.

In most countries in Western Europe, probate is even simpler. Wills are presented to a notary when signed. A notary, under this system, is a quasi-judicial official who's responsible for ensuring the validity of documents. Upon death, the deceased person's successor named in the will performs the probate functions without any judicial supervision. If there are disputes such as contests of the will or disputed creditors' claims, they are handled like any other legal conflict.

Will our probate system be reformed soon? Any improvement is likely to be slow and grudging. True, most people favor probate reform, in a vague way. And there's some real pressure on a number of state legislatures to adopt genuine probate reform, on the order of the simplified estate distribution system used in England or other countries. HALT (Help Abolish Legal Tyranny), a Washington, D.C.-based law reform organization, is one leader in this movement. Unfortunately, though, probate reform isn't a hot, glamorous issue that deeply moves many voters; without lots more public pressure, politicians (many of whom are lawyers, or sensitive to the lobbying of lawyer groups) are unlikely to become seriously interested in it.

Much of what passes currently for probate reform merely simplifies probate procedures for lawyers, but keeps the overall system, particularly the fees, intact. For example, under names like "Independent Administration of Estate Act," or "Unsupervised Administration Law," a number of states have passed laws simplifying probate procedures. But because these laws don't improve nonlawyer access, the result is that lawyers have continued to do the vast majority of probates, charging their same high fees while doing less work.

There's more at work to prevent probate reform than lawyer greed, however. Ours is a society professing devotion to equality, but also to freedom, and that leaves us a little confused about money, especially inherited wealth. We don't have any blood aristocracy, but the grandchildren of wealthy people like Rockefeller, Vanderbilt or Kennedy and thousands of others inherit money taxed at a much lower rate than any English lord or French duke can.

It's not an exaggeration to say that a principal role for American lawyers is to legitimate wealth. Corporate lawyers are the clergy of money, and present themselves accordingly. They dress in dull garb, display grave demeanors and occupy somber offices. Wherever the millions originally came from—whether hard, honest toil or robber baron's thievery—lawyers will be standing by. Even if money is filthy to start with, after a couple of generations of lawyers get through with it, it becomes more respectable and, when a few suitable charities are involved, almost holy. And the inheritors receive the money in clear conscience. After all, they didn't have anything to do with any earlier shenanigans.

Probate has been an essential part of this sanctification process. The idea seems to be that if you make the legal process surrounding the transfer of money on death complex and formal, it keeps attention off who decided what the rules are for inherited money anyway.

But despite inertia and greed, there is one real incentive to probate reform, and that's the fact that many middle-class people are learning to avoid the system. An endearing trait of Americans is that they are as good at avoiding rules as they are at inventing them. As we'll discuss in more detail in later chapters, the living trust is currently the most popular of a small flock of safe, easy probate-avoidance schemes—so popular, indeed, that unless lawyers make probate simpler, cheaper and fairer, Americans may succeed in killing it through almost universal avoidance. ∎

9

LIVING TRUSTS

A. Does Everyone Need a Living Trust? 9/2

B. Living Trusts Explained 9/4

    1. What Is a Living Trust? 9/4

    2. How a Living Trust Works 9/5

    3. Living Trusts and Income Taxes 9/6

    4. Living Trusts and Death Taxes 9/6

    5. Living Trusts and Minor Children 9/7

    6. Living Trusts for Couples 9/7

    7. Living Trusts and Your Debts 9/8

C. Major Decisions in Creating a Living Trust 9/8

    1. Choosing Property to Put in the Living Trust 9/9

    2. Choosing the Trustees of Your Living Trust 9/10

    3. Naming Trust Beneficiaries 9/12

    4. Arranging for Debts and Taxes to Be Paid 9/12

D. Creating a Valid Living Trust 9/12

    1. Preparing Your Living Trust Document 9/13

    2. Transferring Trust Property Into the Trustee's Name 9/13

E. Keeping Your Living Trust Up to Date 9/14

    1. If You Move to Another State 9/15

    2. Amending Your Trust 9/15

    3. Adding Property to Your Trust 9/15

    4. Selling or Refinancing Trust Property 9/15

    5. Revoking Your Living Trust 9/15

A living trust is an efficient and effective way to transfer property at your death—without probate. Essentially, a living trust is a legal document (a few pieces of paper) that controls the transfer of any property you have placed in the trust; when you die, beneficiaries you've named receive trust property. If this sounds a lot like a will, you're right. A living trust allows you to do the same basic job as a will, with the huge plus of avoiding probate.

One big advantage of living trusts is that they are extremely flexible: You can transfer all your property by living trust, or, if appropriate, use a living trust to transfer only some assets, transferring the rest by other methods. Also, living trusts normally are not made public at your death. Wills, on the other hand, become part of the public record during the probate process.

Living trusts are called "living" (or sometimes "inter vivos," which is Latin for "among the living") because they're created while you're alive. They're also called "revocable" because you can revoke or change them at any time, for any reason, before you die. While you live (as long as you are mentally competent), you still effectively own all property you've transferred to your living trust and can do what you want with that property, including selling it, spending it or giving it away.

Aside from some paperwork necessary to establish a probate avoidance living trust and transfer property to it, there are no serious drawbacks or risks involved in creating or maintaining the trust. You don't need to maintain separate trust tax records or obtain a taxpayer ID number for the trust. All transactions which are technically made by the trust are reported on your personal income tax return.

A basic probate avoidance living trust can also be combined with other types of trusts. For example, you can create a living trust that first avoids probate and then continues for years after your death to save on estate taxes, control property left to someone with special needs, or provide for your spouse and chil-

dren from a previous marriage. (Ongoing trusts to save on estate tax or control property are discussed in detail in Chapters 17 through 25.)

For many people of moderate means, whose estates won't have to pay federal estate taxes, the job is simply to avoid probate. Here's a summary of how a living trust works to accomplish that.

First, you create the living trust document. In it, you name yourself as trustee to manage the trust property, and a successor trustee (usually a family member or close friend), to distribute the property when you die. You also name the trust beneficiaries, who receive the property when you die. You then formally transfer property into the trust's name. When you die, the successor trustee simply obtains the property from whoever holds it, and transfers it to the named beneficiaries. No probate or other court proceeding is required.

A. DOES EVERYONE NEED A LIVING TRUST?

Most people who plan their estates eventually turn to a living trust to transfer some, and often the bulk, of their property. If you want to arrange to avoid probate now, because you're elderly, seriously ill or own lots of valuable property and don't want to risk it going through probate, a living trust is probably the best probate avoidance device.

But despite our enthusiasm for living trusts, not everyone needs one. The reason is twofold. First, some people don't really need to plan to avoid probate now. Second, other probate avoidance methods may fit a particular estate planning situation better. Good estate planning can't be reduced to one universal formula. To make sensible decisions, you need to understand what a living trust can and cannot do and how it can be used with other estate planning methods in devising your overall plan. Norman Dacey, in his pioneering work *How to Avoid Probate!* (Crown), essentially asserts that living trusts should be used by all people in all situations. A number of lawyers now make the same claim in advertisements and seminars. These claims are much too broad.

You may not need a living trust, at least not right now, if you're in one of these categories:

- **You are young, healthy and unlikely to die for a long time.** People in their 30s, 40s, and sometimes older, usually have the primary goals of seeing that their property will be distributed as they want in the highly unlikely event they die suddenly, and to see that young children are cared for. A will, perhaps coupled with life insurance, often achieves these goals more easily than a living trust does. A will is simpler to prepare and easier to revise than a living trust. While using a will normally means property goes through probate, this only occurs after death. As long as a person is alive, the fact that probate will be avoided is of no benefit. Because very few younger, healthy people die without any warning, it can make good sense now to make and revise a will for a number of years. Later in life, when the prospect of death is more imminent, and the person has (hopefully) accumulated more property, a living trust can be established to avoid probate.

- **You can more sensibly transfer assets by other probate avoidance devices.** Living trusts aren't the only game in town; joint tenancy, "pay-on-death" bank accounts and life insurance are among the other methods you can use to leave property outside of probate. And, as we've said, the laws in some states allow certain amounts or types of property (and occasionally property left to certain classes of beneficiaries, such as a surviving spouse) to be transferred without probate even if a will is used. (See Chapter 14.) None of these methods has the breadth of a living trust, which can be used to transfer virtually all types of assets. However, each can be easier to use, and equally efficient, in particular circumstances. For example,

adding a pay-on-death designation to a bank account is very simple, and it costs nothing. At your death, the money in the account will go to the person you named, without probate.

- **You have, or may have, complex debt problems.** If you have many creditors, probate provides an absolute cut-off time for notified creditors to file claims. If they don't do so in the time permitted, your inheritors can take your property free of concern that these creditors will surface later and claim a share. A living trust doesn't create any such cut-off period, which means your property could be subject to creditors' claims for a much longer time.

- **There's no one you trust to oversee your trust after your death.** One crucial element in having a living trust work effectively is someone you fully trust who serves as your successor trustee. No court or government agency makes sure your successor trustee complies with the terms of your living trust. So, if you don't have a spouse, child, other relative, friend or someone else you believe is truly trustworthy to name as successor trustee, a living trust isn't for you.

- **You own little property.** If you don't own much of monetary value, probate fees won't amount to that much anyway. There isn't much point in bothering with a living trust and probate avoidance.

- **You don't currently have title to property but expect to receive it.** A living trust only works to transfer property you currently own. If you've been left property by someone's will that is still in probate, or you expect to get money from a lawsuit settlement, only a will can be used to transfer that property. Of course, no one knows what property they might receive shortly before death, which is one reason it is always wise to back up a living trust with a will.

<table>
</table>

**BE WARY OF "FREE" LIVING TRUST
SEMINARS OR HIGH-PRESSURE SALESPEOPLE**

There are lots of ads these days for free seminars on living trusts. Usually, these events are nothing more than elaborate pitches for paying a lawyer (or some non-lawyer entity or service) $1,000 or more to write a living trust. Sometimes salespeople contact prospective customers by phone and pressure them to make an appointment to buy a living trust. Is it worth it? Usually not.

Seminar sponsors try to sell the idea that much of your estate is likely to be gobbled up by estate tax and probate unless you set up trusts now to avoid some of the tax and buy life insurance to pay the rest. In truth, most people don't have estates large enough to owe estate tax. Further, there are many ways to avoid probate, and you should evaluate them all before deciding what's best for you.

The sponsors won't tell you this, but instead hustle:

• lots of life insurance, to pay for supposed estate tax, and

• a fill-in-the-blanks trust that they claim will avoid probate while reducing estate tax—a version of what we call an AB trust.

Be sure you need these alleged benefits before paying a substantial amount for them. Do you really need to avoid probate now? Is your estate likely to be liable for estate tax? If so, and you are married, what type—if any—of AB trust makes sense? Is your situation too complex for a standard form? Buying a trust from a seminar is a bit like buying aluminum siding from a door-to-door salesperson. If you really need exactly what the person is selling, you can satisfy yourself by checking references and making certain that the company provides a quality product, and that the price is fair. But that takes a lot of work, and there are better ways to find legal help. (See Chapter 29, Using Lawyers.)

B. LIVING TRUSTS EXPLAINED

Don't let the word "trust" scare you. True, the word can have an impressive, slightly ominous sound. Historically, monopolists used trusts to dominate entire industries (for example, the Standard Oil Trust in the era of Teddy Roosevelt's "trust-busting"). And while many people don't know exactly how a trust works, they do know, vaguely, that trusts have traditionally been used by the very wealthy to preserve their riches from generation to generation. (Indeed, isn't one version of the American dream to be the beneficiary of your very own trust fund?) Trusts may even appear to some as a particularly obnoxious form of lawyers' black magic, somehow enabling people to escape tax or other financial obligations. The reality is—as it tends to be—more mundane.

1. What Is a Living Trust?

Living trusts are, in basic concept, simple. You create a legal entity called a trust, and transfer something of value to it. You keep control over it while you're alive, and at your death, it goes to the person you've named to inherit it.

To create a trust, you must sign a document that specifies:

1. The "trustee," who has the authority to manage the trust property. You name yourself as the trustee.

2. The "successor trustee," who turns the trust property over to the beneficiaries after your death.

3. The property that is subject to the trust.

4. The "beneficiary" or beneficiaries of the trust, who receive the trust property at your death.

5. Other terms of the trust, including the fact that you can amend or revoke it at any time.

A MINI-GLOSSARY OF LIVING TRUST TERMS

The person who sets up a living trust (that's you) is called the **grantor, trustor** or **settlor.** These terms mean the same thing and can be used interchangeably. You can also set up a trust with your spouse; in that case, you are both grantors.

The grantor creates a written **trust document** or instrument, containing all the terms and provisions of the trust.

All the property you own at death, whether in your living trust or owned in some other form, is your **estate.**

The property you transfer to the trustee, acting for the trust, is called, collectively, the **trust property, trust principal** or **trust estate.** (And, of course, there's a Latin version: the trust corpus.)

The person who has power over the trust property is called the **trustee.**

The person the grantor names to take over as trustee after the grantor's death (or, with a trust made jointly by a couple, after the death of both spouses) is called the **successor trustee.**

The people or organizations who get the trust property when a grantor dies are called the **beneficiaries** of the trust. (While a grantor is alive, technically he or she is the beneficiary of the trust.)

you're mentally competent. You appoint yourself as the initial trustee, to control and use the trust property as you see fit. If you become mentally incapacitated, your successor trustee steps in and manages the trust property for your benefit, as long as you live. If you regain your mental capacity, you regain the authority to manage your living trust property.

And now for the legal magic of the living trust device. Although a living trust is really only a legal fiction during your life, it assumes a very real presence for a brief period after death. When you die, the living trust can no longer be revoked or altered. And because property held in a living trust does not need to be probated, the successor trustee can immediately transfer it to the trust beneficiaries.

Some paperwork is necessary to complete transfer of the trust property to the beneficiaries, such as preparing new ownership documents. Still, these matters can normally be handled (without a lawyer) in no more than a few weeks. Once the trust property is legally received by the beneficiaries, the trust ceases to exist.

2. How a Living Trust Works

The key to a living trust established to avoid probate is that you, the grantor, aren't locked into anything. You can revise, amend or revoke the trust for any (or no) reason, any time before your death, as long as

Example: Travis intends to leave his painting collection and his house to his daughter, Bianca, but he wants to have complete control over the house and the collection until he dies, including the right to sell any painting in the collection if he chooses. At the same time, he doesn't want the $300,000 value of this house and the $250,000 value of the collection to be subject to probate. Travis reasons that it's pretty silly to pay thousands of dollars in probate fees just to have his own house and paintings turned over to his daughter.

So Travis establishes a living trust, with the house and paintings as the trust's assets. He names himself as trustee, with full power to control the trust property. Bianca is named as the successor trustee, to take over after he dies. He also names Bianca as the trust beneficiary.

When Travis dies, Bianca, acting as successor trustee, turns the paintings over to the beneficiary, herself, as directed by the terms of the trust. And, as trustee, she prepares and records a deed transferring the house from the trust to herself. The trust then ceases to exist. All probate proceedings, delays and costs are avoided. And because the estate is worth less than the federal estate tax threshold, no federal estate tax is assessed. (See Chapter 15, Estate Taxes, Section A.)

3. Living Trusts and Income Taxes

As we've said, during your life, a living trust doesn't exist for income tax purposes. The IRS treats the trust property as it does any other property you own. So, you don't have to maintain separate books, records or bank accounts for your living trust. And because, while you live, the trust isn't functionally distinct from you, your living trust can't be used to lower your income tax.

SELLING YOUR HOME FROM A TRUST: TAX BREAKS

Many people put their homes—their most expensive asset—into their living trusts. If you do, you won't lose any tax benefits:

• You can still deduct mortgage interest.

• You can sell your principal home once every two years and exclude $250,000 of capital gains from income taxation. A couple can exclude $500,000.

---

4. Living Trusts and Death Taxes

Let us say it loud, clear and in big type: LIVING TRUSTS DESIGNED TO AVOID PROBATE DON'T SAVE ON DEATH TAXES. We emphasize this because when some people hear the word "trust," they feel it must mean "tax savings."

A living trust designed to avoid probate can, however, be combined with a second trust designed to save on death tax. A common example of this is when a spouse uses a living trust to first avoid probate and then to establish a trust to pay income to the surviving spouse for his or her life, with the property in the trust going to the children or grandchildren when that spouse dies. This popular estate tax saving device is called an "AB" trust. (See Chapter 18, Estate Tax-Saving Bypass Trusts, Section C.)

5. Living Trusts and Minor Children

You can leave property to minors using a living trust. Many married people name their spouse as beneficiary of their trust, and their minor children as alternate beneficiaries. If you leave minors property in your trust as any type of beneficiary, you impose adult management over that property in the trust document. The different methods of adult management are discussed in Chapter 6, Children.

6. Living Trusts for Couples

A living trust can work as effectively for a couple as for a single person. And any couple, married or not, can use one living trust to handle both their shared property and any either owns individually. Because most couples who use living trusts are married, the discussion that follows is cast in terms of "spouses" and "marital property." However, the concepts discussed apply equally to unmarried couples.

The fact that a couple can create a shared living trust to cover the property of both doesn't mean they must. In some circumstances, it may make sense for each spouse to make a separate living trust. For example, if each spouse owns mostly separate property, a combined living trust may make little sense. But if spouses share ownership of much or all of their property, as is usually the case, it's generally preferable that they use one living trust for their property.

If you live in a community property state, in which spouses equally own most property acquired after marriage, you and your spouse almost certainly own property together. Even in the other (common law) states, where one spouse may legally be the sole owner of much property, spouses who have been married for many years typically regard most or all property as owned by both. (See Chapter 3 for a list of common law and community property states and an explanation of both systems of property ownership.) Unmarried couples can also share ownership of property, if they choose, and register any ownership/title document in both their names as co-owners.

Setting up two separate living trusts for shared property owned by a couple is generally undesirable because ownership of the shared property must be divided. That's a lot of trouble. Worse, it can lead to unfair and undesired imbalances—for example, one spouse's stocks might go up in value while the other's declined.

Fortunately, there is no need for spouses to divide property this way. Instead, a couple can create one trust and transfer the shared property to it. (You can also put individually owned property into the trust.) Each spouse has full power to name the beneficiaries of his or her portion of the property put in trust.

When the first spouse dies, the trust is split in two. One trust contains all property of the deceased spouse. The other contains all property of the surviving spouse. The deceased spouse's property is transferred to the beneficiaries he or she named in the trust document. One beneficiary is commonly the surviving spouse, but children, friends and charities may also inherit property.

The diagram below shows how this type of marital living trust works. In this example, the husband and wife transfer their shared ownership property into one living trust. The husband is the first spouse to die, the "deceased spouse." The wife is the "surviving spouse."

HOW A SHARED LIVING TRUST WORKS

1. Husband and wife transfer shared property to trust. (Each spouse can also transfer individually owned property)

2. Husband dies. Shared trust property is divided in half.

3. Husband's one-half ownership of shared property, and any individually owned property, goes to his beneficiaries. All property owned by wife, including her half of shared property, remains in her trust.

4. Wife's property stays in living trust.

```
        ┌─────────────────────────┐
        │  REVOCABLE LIVING TRUST  │
        │    Husband and wife's    │
        │      shared property     │
        └─────────────────────────┘
            ↙               ↘
    ┌───────────┐       ┌───────────┐
    │ Husband's │       │  Wife's   │
    └───────────┘       └───────────┘
          │         to spouse
          │              │
          ↓              ↓   ↓
    ┌──────────┐   ┌──────────────────┐
    │  Other   │   │    REVOCABLE     │
    │beneficiaries│ │  LIVING TRUST    │
    └──────────┘   │  Wife's property │
                   └──────────────────┘
                            │
                            ↓
        ┌─────────────────────────────┐
        │   REVOCABLE LIVING TRUST     │
        │ Wife's property (including   │
        │ property received from       │
        │ husband)                     │
        └─────────────────────────────┘
```

7. Living Trusts and Your Debts

Property in a revocable living trust is not immune from attack by your creditors while you're alive. You have complete and exclusive power over the trust property, so a judge is not going to let you use the living trust (which you can revoke at any time) to evade creditors.

On the other hand, if property is put in a trust that you can't revoke or change (called an "irrevo-

cable trust"), it's a different legal matter. (See Chapter 17.) Property transferred to a bona fide irrevocable trust cannot be reached by your creditors. The key words here are "bona fide." If an irrevocable trust is set up only to defraud creditors, it's not bona fide.

IF IT SOUNDS TOO GOOD TO BE TRUE...

Some "authorities" have inaccurately stated that property in a revocable living trust can't be grabbed by your creditors during your life. They argue that, for collection purposes, a revocable living trust is legally distinct from its creator. We know of no law or case that supports this position.

Shielding property. If you're concerned about protecting your assets from creditors, see a lawyer.

C. MAJOR DECISIONS IN CREATING A LIVING TRUST

Let's look a little deeper into the key decisions you'll need to make if you want to create a living trust, whether you do it yourself or get help from a lawyer.

Initially, you must make four major decisions:

1. What property will be in the trust?

2. Who will be the successor trustee? (You, or you and your spouse, are the initial trustee or trustees.)

3. Who will be your beneficiaries?

4. If you transfer most or much of the value of your estate by living trust, how will any debts and taxes outstanding at your death be paid?

1. Choosing Property to Put in the Living Trust

You can place all your property in your living trust, or transfer some, or even most, of it by other means, such as a will or joint tenancy. In general, if you decide to use a living trust to avoid probate, it's sensible to transfer all your big-ticket items to it, unless they are covered by another probate avoidance technique. Thus, if you and your spouse already own your house in joint tenancy, you've already arranged to avoid probate of the house.

Example: Mr. and Mrs. Tramsey share ownership of a house with an equity of $150,000, held in joint tenancy, personal possessions worth $20,000, U.S. Government bonds worth $40,000, stock worth $100,000 and a savings account with $60,000 in it. Each wants to leave his or her half of the house, personal possessions, cars and stocks and bonds to the other. Because the house is already in joint tenancy, the survivor will become the sole owner free of probate. (See Chapter 10.) To take care of the personal possessions, stocks and bonds, the Tramseys decide to create a revocable living trust.

However, when it comes to their savings account, they both decide that, at death, each will leave his or her half directly to their son, not to the surviving spouse. They learn that the simplest way to transfer bank accounts outside of probate is by using a pay-on-death account. (See Chapter 11, Pay-on-Death Designations, Section A.) So, the Tramseys divide the money in their savings account in half, and each spouse then creates a separate pay-on-death account, naming their son as beneficiary, to receive the money in that account when he or she dies.

Many people do put real estate into their living trust. A couple of special issues come up when real estate is involved:

- **Property taxes.** In some states, transferring real estate sales to a new owner can result in property being immediately reappraised for property tax purposes. By contrast, if the property is not transferred to new owners, it usually won't be reappraised for a set period of years, or (in a few states) at all. Because you and your living trust are considered the same basic entity while you're alive, there's no real change in ownership and therefore no reappraisal. If you want to be absolutely sure that this is true in your state and county, check with your local property tax collector.

- **Homestead protection.** State homestead protections, which typically protect your equity interest in a home from creditors up to a designated amount, should not be lost because real estate is transferred to a living trust. If you are not seriously in debt, there is no need to worry about this one. However, if you're in debt and concerned that a creditor may try to force a sale of your house, check your state's homestead rules carefully.

2. Choosing the Trustees of Your Living Trust

You must make two choices when it comes to naming a trustee to manage the trust property: who will be the initial trustee, and who will take over as the successor trustee when the first trustee dies or becomes incapacitated.

a. Your Initial Trustee

As discussed, the initial trustee of your living trust is usually you, the person who set it up. Serving as trustee is how you continue to absolutely control your trust property.

If you and your spouse (or significant other) set up a trust together, you'll both be co-trustees. When one spouse dies, the other continues as sole trustee.

One spouse as trustee. It's possible, but very unusual, to have only one spouse be the original trustee of a shared living trust. If you're interested, see a lawyer.

Naming someone else as initial trustee. If you want to name someone besides yourself to be your initial trustee because you don't want to, or cannot, continue to manage your own assets, it greatly complicates matters. You'll probably need much more detailed controls on the trustee's powers. In addition, under IRS rules, if you aren't a trustee of your own living trust, separate trust records must be maintained, and a trust tax return filed. However, completing this return need not be particularly onerous; all the IRS requires is filing the face page of the fiduciary return (Form 1041) and a summary listing of items of trust income and expense. These items are actually reported on the trust creator's regular Form 1040 income tax return.

Naming co-trustees. You can name two people (or even more) to serve as initial trustees. This can be desirable if you want or need someone else to manage the trust property for you while you live but you don't want the IRS complications that come with a separate trustee. You name yourself and someone else as trustees and authorize either to act for the trust. Since you are, legally, one of the trustees, the IRS does not require that separate trust records be kept or trust tax returns filed.

b. Your Successor Trustee

It's also essential that you name at least one successor trustee. Your successor is the person who makes your trust work after you die, by distributing its assets to your beneficiaries. With a shared marital trust, the successor trustee takes over after both spouses die. Also, the successor trustee is normally authorized to take over management of the trust if you (or you and your spouse, with a shared marital trust) become unable to handle it yourself.

When you decide on your successor trustee, your job isn't done. You should also name an alternate successor trustee, in case the successor trustee dies before you do or for any other reason can't serve.

c. The Job of the Successor Trustee

The primary job of the successor trustee is to turn trust property over to the beneficiaries you have named. No court's approval is required, and normally this task is not difficult if the property and beneficiaries are clearly identified. Still, some effort is required.

The successor trustee obtains several certified copies of the death certificate of the grantor and presents one, with a copy of the living trust document and proof of her own identity, to financial institutions, brokers and other organizations that have possession of trust assets. Institutions that deal with financial assets—from title companies to stockbrokers—are familiar with living trusts and how they work. They should not balk at accepting the authority of the successor trustee.

If any documents of title must be prepared to transfer trust property to the beneficiaries, the successor trustee prepares them. For example, to transfer real estate to the beneficiaries, the successor trustee prepares, signs and records (in the local land records office) the following documents:

1. A deed showing the beneficiaries as the new owners, and

2. A short statement (declaration) stating that the original trustee (the grantor) has died and the successor trustee has taken over.

In addition to dealing with property subject to formal ownership (title) documents, the trustee supervises the distribution of all other trust assets—household furnishings, jewelry, heirlooms, collectibles—to the appropriate beneficiaries. The trust ends when all beneficiaries have actually received the trust property left to them in the trust document.

d. Choosing Your Successor Trustee

Your successor trustee should be the person you feel is most trustworthy to do the job and who's willing and able to do it. Often a principal beneficiary, such as a spouse or adult child, is named as successor trustee. However, if you believe the beneficiary (much as you love him or her) will be troubled by the practical details and paperwork, it is preferable to name someone else.

When you prepare a back-up will, name your successor trustee to serve as executor, too. If a different person fulfilled each function, conflicts could arise.

e. Choosing Co-Successor Trustees

Legally, you can name as many successor co-trustees as you want, with power divided between them as you specify. However, because of coordination problems and possible conflicts among multiple trustees, it's generally best to name a single successor trustee. This isn't invariably true, however. For example, you might name two or more children as successor co-trustees, to avoid being seen as favoring one child over others. This can be especially appropriate if the children are equal beneficiaries of the trust. And if the children all get along, doing this rarely causes a problem. However, if the children are prone to conflict, you do none of them a favor by having them share power as trustees. It's better just to name the most reliable one and let the chips fall as they will.

f. Choosing a Bank as Successor Trustee

In our experience, it is usually a bad idea to name a bank or financial institution as successor trustee. There are plenty of horror stories involving the indifference or downright rapaciousness of banks acting as trustees of family living trusts. Think of it this way: Your successor trustee is your link with the ongoing life of your loved ones. You want that link to be a human being you trust, not a corporation dedicated to the enhancement of its bottom line. However, if there is no human being you believe will act honestly and competently as your successor trustee, and after reviewing the other probate avoidance devices discussed in this book, you are still determined to establish a living trust, you'll need to select some financial institution to do the job. Probably the best choice here is a private trust company. These companies generally offer more humane and personal attention to a trust than a bank and can be more reasonable about fees.

3. Naming Trust Beneficiaries

Beneficiaries, of course, are simply the people or organizations you choose to inherit your trust property. You can select anyone you want to be beneficiaries of your living trust. And generally, you can leave each beneficiary whatever trust property you want.

Certain trusts require you to name certain types of beneficiaries. For example, if you set up a probate avoidance trust combined with an AB estate tax saving trust, you must name a life beneficiary (your spouse) and final beneficiaries, who receive property after the death of the second spouse. Each spouse can name his or her own final beneficiaries. Commonly, both spouses name the same final beneficiaries—their children—but that's not mandatory. Spouses in second or subsequent marriages often name their children from prior relationships.

If you create a shared living trust with your spouse, each of you can name your own beneficiaries. Commonly, each spouse names the other as the sole beneficiary, with their children as alternate beneficiaries. In other situations, people may wish to divide their property between their spouse and children. And, of course, you can choose other beneficiaries: relatives, friends or charities.

> **Example:** Malcolm and Ursula create a shared living trust. They have been married for 30 years; neither was previously married. They have one child, Suzanne. Each spouse leaves the bulk of their property to the other. Each also leaves some smaller gifts to relatives, friends and charities. Both name Suzanne as their alternate beneficiary and residuary beneficiary. They both name Suzanne's husband, Tom, as alternate residuary beneficiary.

4. Arranging for Debts and Taxes to Be Paid

Many people don't leave any substantial debts or income or death tax obligations when they die. (Leaving a house with a mortgage isn't a concern here; the mortgage simply passes with the house.) If you fit into this category, you can go on to other concerns.

When you die, your successor trustee will pay whatever bills you owe, either from property you earmarked in your trust document for this purpose, or from trust property generally. Either way, no beneficiary will suffer a substantial loss.

However, if you transfer the bulk of your property by living trust and will likely have significant debts, including death taxes, it's best to identify trust assets that you want used to pay off these obligations. First, of course, you'll need to make a realistic appraisal (or at least a decent guess) of what you'll owe, for both regular debts and taxes, at your death. (See Chapter 15).

D. CREATING A VALID LIVING TRUST

Some people have a lawyer prepare their living trust. If your estate plan calls for combining a living trust with one or more sophisticated ongoing trusts designed to minimize taxes, it's likely you'll need a lawyer to prepare these trusts for you. But other people can safely prepare living trusts themselves, using a good self-help book or software package. In fact even if you fully intend to pay a lawyer to draft documents, it's still a good idea to educate yourself about living trusts and even to prepare a draft trust.

Make Your Own Living Trust, by Denis Clifford (Nolo Press). This book contains all the forms and instructions you need to make two kinds of trust: a simple probate-avoidance trust, or a tax-saving trust for couples, called an AB trust.

Nolo's *Living Trust Maker* software (Nolo Press) allows you use your computer to generate a probate-avoidance trust. It does not create a tax-saving AB trust.

However you decide to proceed, there are two crucial steps in creating a valid living trust:

1. Preparing the living trust document.

2. Transferring title to property into the name of your trustee (that is, you) as trustee of your living trust.

We'll look briefly at each step, to give you an idea what creating a living trust involves.

1. Preparing Your Living Trust Document

No law specifies the form a living trust must take. As a result, there is no such thing as a standard living trust. Indeed, there are a bewildering variety of living trust forms, including some attorney-created forms that contain vast piles of verbiage that serve little real-world purpose, except to generate attorney fees.

Something simpler is all you need. Your living trust document must define all the terms of the trust. It names the trustee and successor trustee and your beneficiaries, and lists the trust property. You list the trust property on one or more "schedules" attached to the main trust document. You need only identify each item of property in a way that your successor trustee and beneficiaries unambiguously know what's referred to. No legal rules require property to be listed in any particular form.

You should sign the trust document in front of a notary public. Unlike wills, no witnesses are required.

2. Transferring Trust Property Into the Trustee's Name

An essential step in making your trust effective is to transfer ownership (title) of property to the trustee. If you don't, your successor trustee won't be able to transfer it to your beneficiaries. To achieve this, you register title to trust property, if the item has a title document, in the trustee's name, as "Ellen Yurok, as trustee for the Ellen Yurok Trust."

Many estate planning lawyers insist on doing this work. They don't necessarily do it to raise their fees (though that is one result) but because they believe that clients can't be relied upon to do the job right. We think that with clear instructional materials, you can do this work yourself. But even if you decide to let a lawyer do it, you'll benefit from gaining a basic understanding of what's involved.

NAMING THE TRUST AS BENEFICIARY

If you simply name your living trust itself as the beneficiary to receive specified property after you die, you do not have to re-register title to that property. For example, if you want your living trust to receive the proceeds of your life insurance, designate your successor trustee as the policy beneficiary. But do not transfer ownership of the policy or account into the trustee's name. While you live, you, not the trust, are the legal owner of the policy. The trust is simply who you've named to receive benefits payable on your death.

For purposes of transferring title into the trustee's name, there are two types of property: those with ownership (title) documents and those without.

a. Property Without Ownership (Title) Documents

Many types of property don't have title documents, including all kinds of household possessions and furnishings, clothing, jewelry, furs, tools, most farm equipment, antiques, electronic and computer equipment, art works, bearer bonds, cash, precious metals and collectibles. You transfer these items to the trust simply by listing them on a trust schedule. In addition, you can use a "Notice of Assignment" form, a simple document that states that the property listed on it has been transferred to the trustee's name.

b. Property With Ownership (Title) Documents

It is vital that all items of trust property that have ownership documents (title papers) be registered in the trustee's name. Your living trust won't affect any property with an ownership document that is not re-registered in the trustee's name.

Property with title documents includes:

- real estate, including condominiums and coopera-tives
- bank accounts
- stocks and stock accounts
- most bonds, including U.S. government securities
- corporations, limited partnerships and partner-ships
- money market accounts
- mutual funds
- safe deposit boxes

- vehicles, including cars, most boats, motor homes and planes.

Usually, it costs nothing or very little to make these transfers. A very few localities, however do impose hefty transfer and recordation tax. Also, there may be special local forms that must be completed for the transfer to be recorded. For example, in Califor-nia, transfers of real estate must be reported on a "Preliminary Change of Ownership" form, available at County Recorders' offices. No fee or tax is required to file this form.

GIFT TAX WORRIES

Because your living trust can be revoked at any time before you die, you don't make a gift simply by transferring property to the trust. Therefore, no federal or state gift tax can be assessed. (See Chapter 16 for a discussion of gift taxes.)

E. KEEPING YOUR LIVING TRUST UP TO DATE

You need to keep your living trust up to date by making appropriate changes if you acquire or dispose of major items of property or find that, for one reason or another, you want to change your beneficiaries or successor trustees. You can do this kind of work yourself, or you can have a lawyer do it for you. But because a lawyer may not know of changes in your personal life that would result in your wanting or needing to amend your living trust—changes such as divorce, marriage, having a child, selling a major trust asset—it's up to you to keep your trust updated.

You can amend or revoke your living trust at any time. However, often a shared living trust document can be amended only by both spouses. This prevents one spouse from pulling a fast one with trust property in the event of a dispute or divorce. When one spouse dies, his or her portion of the trust becomes binding and irrevocable, and the successor trustee distributes the property according to the trust's terms. The surviving spouse can now amend or revoke his or her own portion of the trust, like any other single person.

1. If You Move to Another State

Your living trust remains legal and valid if you move to a different state after establishing it. Revocable living trusts are valid and used in every state.

However, if you're married, and you move from a community property state to a common law state, or vice versa, you may want to check the marital property ownership laws of your new state to make sure that the property you believe is yours really is. (See Chapter 3, Section D.)

2. Amending Your Trust

You must amend your living trust by a signed document and have it notarized. Amendments are usually for simple, clear changes—such as adding a new beneficiary, deleting a beneficiary, changing a successor trustee, or deleting property from the trust. Amendments are not appropriate for making major revisions or wholesale changes in your living trust. In that case, revoke the old trust and prepare a new one.

3. Adding Property to Your Trust

Many living trust forms specifically give you the right to add property to your trust. You can do so simply by listing the new property on the appropriate schedule and transferring title to it (if it has a title document) to the trustee's name.

Just because property has been added to your trust does not mean you've provided for who will receive it after your death. So you may need to amend your trust to name the beneficiary for newly added property.

4. Selling or Refinancing Trust Property

If you decide to sell or refinance property owned by your trust, you can either:

- sell or refinance it directly out of the trust. Acting in your capacity as trustee, you sign the title document or otherwise authorize the sale by completing a bill of sale, sales contract or other document; or

- in your capacity as trustee of the living trust, first transfer title of the trust property back to yourself as an individual (from yourself as trustee), and then sell or refinance the property in your own name.

Use whichever way is most convenient. If real estate is involved, what is most convenient is generally what the title company requests.

Be sure you amend your trust document if you remove property from it, so that the trust document doesn't appear to give away property that's no longer in the trust.

5. Revoking Your Living Trust

You can revoke your living trust at any time, for any reason. Revocation must be done in a signed document. A basic shared trust or AB living trust can usually be revoked by either spouse any time. The reason either spouse can revoke a living trust, but it takes both to amend it, is that revocation simply returns both spouses to the status quo. ■

10

JOINT TENANCY AND TENANCY BY THE ENTIRETY

A. What Is Joint Tenancy? 10/2
B. Joint Tenancy Bank Accounts 10/3
C. Joint Tenancy Safe Deposit Boxes 10/4
D. Tenancy by the Entirety 10/4
E. Joint Tenancy in Community Property States 10/5
F. Tax Concerns Affecting Joint Tenancy 10/6
    1. Federal Estate Taxes 10/6
    2. Joint Tenancy as a Taxable Gift 10/7
    3. Joint Tenancy and Federal Income Tax Basis Rules 10/8
    4. State Income Tax Basis Rules 10/10
    5. Local Property Taxes 10/11
G. Drawbacks of Joint Tenancy 10/11
    1. Any Joint Tenant Can End the Joint Tenancy 10/11
    2. Creditors and Joint Tenancy 10/12
    3. Incapacity 10/12
H. When Joint Tenancy Makes Sense 10/12
    1. Couples Buying a House 10/12
    2. Transfers Into Joint Tenancy When Death Is Imminent 10/13
I. Creating a Joint Tenancy for Property With Documents of Title 10/13
    1. The Language Required 10/13
    2. Real Estate 10/14
J. Creating Joint Tenancy for Personal Property Without
Documents of Title 10/15

This chapter explains what joint tenancy is and how it works, and explores the advantages and drawbacks of using joint tenancy to avoid probate. The chapter also explains the workings of tenancy by the entirety, which is similar to joint tenancy and available in most, but not all, states for married couples only.

The purpose of joint tenancy is to avoid probate. To simplify and generalize, joint tenancy can be desirable for people, usually a couple, who want to share ownership of property. By contrast, it is rarely sensible for a sole owner to transfer property into joint tenancy with another owner to avoid probate.

A. WHAT IS JOINT TENANCY?

Joint tenancy is one way co-owners, called "joint tenants," can own property together. Under some circumstances, it is a useful probate avoidance tool, because all property held in joint tenancy carries with it the "right of survivorship." This means that when one joint tenant dies, his or her ownership share of the joint tenancy property is "automatically" transferred to, and becomes owned by, the surviving joint tenant(s), without the need for probate.

> **Example:** Ron and Linda own their house and a stock account in joint tenancy. At Ron's death, ownership of his half share of the house and stock account automatically goes to Linda, who becomes 100% owner of this property, without probate.

The automatic right of a surviving joint tenant or tenants to inherit is basic to this form of ownership. You cannot leave your interest in joint tenancy property to anyone but the other joint tenant(s). If you leave it in your will to someone else, that provision has no effect. However, in most all states, you can easily terminate a joint tenancy ownership while you and all the other joint tenant owners are alive, changing your share into a form of property called "tenancy in common." You can then transfer or leave you share to whomever you wish.

Other forms of shared ownership, such as tenancy in common or partnership property or community property, don't create a right of survivorship, and you can leave your share of it by will or living trust.

SIMULTANEOUS DEATH OF JOINT TENANTS

Many joint tenants, as well as married tenants by the entirety, are concerned about what will happen to their property if they die simultaneously. After all, if there's no surviving owner, the right of survivorship that's central to joint tenancy has no meaning. To deal with this highly unlikely but still potentially worrisome possibility, in your will you can name a beneficiary to inherit your share of the property in the event of simultaneous death. Or, if you don't, the property would still pass under your will, to your residuary beneficiary.

Any number of people can own property together in joint tenancy, but they must all own equal shares (except in Ohio). The owners share equally in all income, profits and losses from their property. If an ownership document specifies different percentages or shares of ownership, it's a tenancy in common, not a joint tenancy, and there's no right of survivorship for the co-owners.

UNEQUAL OWNERSHIP OF PROPERTY

If you want to own property in unequal shares, you must do it as tenants in common. For example, two people living together may decide to own property in unequal shares because one person initially has more money to invest in the property than does the other. (Contracts and forms to create a tenancy in common are contained in the *Living Together Kit* and the *Legal Guide for Lesbian and Gay Couples*, both published by Nolo Press.) Property held in tenancy in common does not avoid probate automatically. To avoid probate, each owner can put his or her interest in the property into a living trust. (See Chapter 9, Living Trusts.)

It's common that real estate is owned in joint tenancy, but any type of property can be owned in this manner and avoid probate. Bank accounts, automobiles, boats and mobile homes are all routinely held in joint tenancy for just this reason.

STATE RESTRICTIONS ON JOINT TENANCY

Alaska	No joint tenancy in real estate, except for husband and wife, who may own as tenants by the entirety.
Texas	To establish joint tenancy, owners must sign a joint tenancy agreement.

B. JOINT TENANCY BANK ACCOUNTS

A joint tenancy bank account can be a useful means of avoiding probate, especially when two people are already a family unit and are sharing income and expenses. Most banks have standard joint tenancy account forms, and all common types of bank accounts, including checking, savings and certificates of deposit, may be owned in joint tenancy. To open such an account, all people involved sign the account papers as "joint tenants with right of survivorship." (Some banks abbreviate this "JTWROS.") When one joint tenant dies, the other can obtain all the money in the account, with no need to go through probate.

In most joint tenancy bank accounts, any owner can withdraw any or all of the money in the account at any time. If the purpose of the account is for shared expenses—as the family account of a husband and wife—this isn't normally a problem. If it may raise difficulties, inquire if a bank will let you require two signatures for withdrawals on a joint tenancy account. Many will.

A joint tenancy bank account is generally not a good idea if your only purpose is to leave your own money at death to someone else. By changing the ownership document for the account to list the other person as a joint owner, you give that person complete legal access to the account now. The other person can remove all the money in the account at any time while you're alive. As just mentioned, you could try to protect yourself by requiring that both of you must sign to validly withdraw money, but this means you'll have to get someone else's signature each time you want to withdraw your own money from the account.

There's a better way to do it. If your goal is to avoid probate for money in your own account, a pay-on-death account allows you to retain full and exclusive control over your money while you live and still have the account avoid probate. (See Chapter 11, Section A)

If you're considering creating a joint bank account by adding someone's name to your individual account, you may wonder if you have to concern yourself with gift tax. Happily, no legal gift is made by creating a joint bank account or depositing money in it. However, a gift is made by the depositor if the other person takes money out of the account. Under current IRS rules, the other person could remove up to $10,000 per year, without there being any gift tax liability. (The rules for gifts and gift taxes are discussed in Chapter 16.)

C. JOINT TENANCY SAFE DEPOSIT BOXES

A joint tenancy safe deposit box can be a sensible place to keep important papers—wills, funeral instructions, burial or body donation, directions and documents relating to veteran, union or company pensions or benefits, or individual retirement programs, such as IRAs. This is true because either joint tenant can normally obtain instant access to the documents when they are needed.

If you decide to get a joint tenancy safe deposit box, be sure to specify on the bank account cards whether or not the co-owners share ownership of all contents of the box. This can be particularly important if you keep valuable objects, such as jewelry, in the box. In some states, joint tenancy rental of a safe deposit box gives both joint tenants access to the box, but doesn't necessarily create ownership rights to that box's contents unless it's clearly spelled out. So if you don't want the other person with access to the box to own certain property in it, be sure it's clear that the joint tenancy in the safe deposit box is for access only. And of course, you would also want to leave the property in the box by your living trust or will.

Don't store estate planning documents in a safe deposit box that may be sealed after an owner's death. In some states with state death tax, safe deposit boxes are sealed by a bank as soon as it is notified of the death of an owner. The contents

cannot be released until the box is inventoried by a government official. So if your state has a death tax (see Chapter 15, Section G), check with your bank's officials to see whether the safe deposit box will be sealed upon death of a joint tenant, and how one gets the box unsealed. Usually this can be done reasonably quickly and easily. If not, however, a safe deposit box isn't a good place to store documents that you want to be readily available at your death, including your living trust and will.

D. TENANCY BY THE ENTIRETY

"Tenancy by the entirety" is a form of property ownership that is similar to joint tenancy, but is limited to married couples. It has almost the same advantages and disadvantages of joint tenancy, and is most useful when a couple acquire property together. If you do not live in a state which specifically allows, by statute, tenancy by the entirety, you cannot use it.

STATES WHICH PERMIT TENANCY BY THE ENTIRETY

Alaska	Maryland	Oklahoma
Arkansas	Massachusetts	Oregon*
Delaware	Michigan*	Pennsylvania
District of Columbia	Mississippi	Rhode Island
Florida	Missouri	Tennessee
Hawaii	New Jersey	Vermont
Illinois*	New York*	Virginia
Indiana*	North Carolina*	Wyoming
Kentucky*	Ohio**	

*Allowed only for real estate.

**Only if created before 4/4/85.

Like joint tenancy, property owned in tenancy by the entirety does not go through probate when one spouse dies; it automatically goes to the surviving spouse.

If property is held in tenancy by the entirety, neither spouse can transfer her or his half of the property alone, either while alive or by will or trust. It must go to the surviving spouse. Also, in general, tenancy by the entirety property is better protected than joint tenancy property from creditors of just one spouse. If someone sues one spouse and wins a court judgment, in most states the creditor can't seize and sell the tenancy by the entirety property to pay off the debt. And if one spouse files for bankruptcy, creditors cannot reach or sever the property held in tenancy by the entirety.

E. JOINT TENANCY IN COMMUNITY PROPERTY STATES

This section is of interest only to married people who live in or own real estate in a community property state: Arizona, California, Idaho, Nevada, New Mexico, Texas, Washington or Wisconsin.

Most property accumulated by either spouse during a marriage is the community property of both. (See Chapter 3, Special Property Ownership Rules for Married People, Section B, for a discussion of the rules.) Spouses can, and commonly do, hold their community property in joint tenancy with each other to avoid probate when the first spouse dies. Doing this can make good sense. However, for certain important income tax reasons (explained in Section F3, below), it's important to be able to show the IRS that community property held in joint tenancy for probate avoidance purposes is still community property.

In Arizona, Nevada, Texas and Wisconsin, state law expressly permits spouses to hold property "as

community property with right of survivorship." In other words, you can, with proper wording in the title document, obtain joint tenancy benefits for community property.

In the other community property states, there's no statutory authorization for holding community property in joint tenancy. In these states, a standard method of achieving this goal is to hold title in joint tenancy and prepare a separate document, signed by both spouses, declaring that identified property "retains its character as community property, despite our holding title to this property in joint tenancy, which we do solely for convenience, to avoid probate." Why this rigmarole? Because some title companies refuse to permit transfers of real estate into "community property held in joint tenancy," maintaining the two legal forms are inconsistent. Since, in the real estate world, it's often sadly true that the law is whatever the title companies say it is, it's safer in these states to go the two-document route: hold title in joint tenancy, and have a separate document stating the property remains community property. Interestingly, neither title companies nor the IRS have any objection to this. It's the all-too-frequent legal story: What you cannot do directly, because of institutions, courts or misapplication of legal technicalities, you can do indirectly—if you know how.

Although the vast majority of spouses in community property states who hold property in joint tenancy do so with one another, one spouse might wish to place property into joint tenancy with someone else. If the property is the separate property of the transferring spouse, there's no ownership problem, since it's her property to do with as she wishes. (But see Section F, below, for possible tax disadvantages.) However, if the property is community property, serious ownership problems can develop between the surviving spouse and the surviving joint tenant. The reason for this is simple: Each spouse automatically owns one-half of all community property, whether or not his or her name appears on property ownership documents. Thus, the surviving spouse can successfully contend that you have authority to transfer only half of the community property into joint tenancy with someone else. If you do more, you've giving away your spouse's property.

> **Example:** Mrs. Abruzzi, who has one daughter, owns a house as her separate property. She marries Mr. Mykenas. For several years, they use their community property income to pay mortgage payments on the house. Mrs. Abruzzi decides to transfer the house into joint tenancy with her daughter to avoid probate at her death. When Mrs. Abruzzi dies, Mr. Mykenas could claim that part of the house was community property because community funds were used for mortgage payments. Half of the community property portion of the house is his. Mrs. Abruzzi has no legal right to transfer his portion to her daughter.

F. Tax Concerns Affecting Joint Tenancy

Before deciding whether you want to use joint tenancy in your estate planning, you should understand the possible tax implications. The major concerns are estate taxes, gift taxes, income tax "basis" rules and property tax reappraisals. We know wading through this probably sounds dreary, but hang in there—you can make it through. And you do need to know this material before you can sensibly resolve whether or not you want to use joint tenancy.

1. Federal Estate Taxes

Owning property as a joint tenant or tenant by the entirety doesn't affect your taxable estate for federal estate tax purposes. The federal government includes the value of the deceased's jointly owned property in the taxable estate. How that value is determined depends on whether the joint tenancy owners were married or not.

a. If You're Married

The tax rule for marital joint tenancies is simple. When a husband and wife own property as joint tenants or tenants by the entirety, one-half of the market value of the property, as of the date of death of the joint tenant, is included in the federal taxable estate of the first spouse to die. It doesn't matter what amount of money either spouse actually put up to buy the property.

> **Example:** Lou and Isabelle are married and live in New York. During their marriage they purchased real estate as tenants by the entirety. Isabelle actually paid the entire down payment for the property from her savings. Mortgage payments were shared more or less equally by both spouses. Isabelle dies. The IRS rules provide that 50% of the market value of the property on the date of her death is included in her taxable estate. This is true even if she in fact put up more than 50% of the total cost of the property.

Either spouse may transfer separately owned property into joint tenancy with the other spouse without any liability for gift taxes. No gift taxes are assessed against any gift made between a husband and wife, no matter how much it is worth.

b. Unmarried Joint Tenancies

The IRS rules defining the worth of a non-married joint tenant's share in joint tenancy property are more tricky than for married couples. Under the IRS rules, if you own joint tenancy property with someone who isn't your spouse, the value of your interest is based on how much you contributed for the costs of the jointly owned property. If the deceased put up all the money to purchase a piece of joint property, the full market value of the property (at death) is included in the taxable estate. If the you paid half the cost of acquiring the property, 50% of its worth is included in your taxable estate.

But here's where matters get sticky. The IRS presumes that the first joint tenant to die contributed all of the money for the purchase of jointly owned property, "less any part that is shown to have originally belonged to ... (another) person." (IRC Section 2040.) The IRS also presumes that the first joint tenant to die paid for all capital improvements, if any. The surviving joint tenant(s) can overturn these presumptions by proving that the survivors made cash or other contributions toward buying or maintaining the property. To the extent the surviving tenants can prove that they put up part of the purchase price, mortgage payments or other expenses, the value of the joint tenancy property interest included in the deceased's taxable estate will be reduced proportionately. Therefore, one risk for unmarried people of holding property in joint tenancy is that, unless good records are kept, the full value of the jointly owned property will be subject to death taxes twice: When the first joint tenant dies and then again when the survivor dies.

Example: Decades ago, Phil and his sister Patsy bought a house as joint tenants. They each contributed half the purchase price and paid off the mortgage equally, but any records that can prove that have long since vanished. Patsy dies in 1998. The full 1998 market value of the house is included in her taxable estate, since the IRS presumes she contributed all the purchase price and Phil has no proof to rebut this presumption. Phil, the surviving joint

tenant, owns the entire house until he dies in 2002. The full 2002 market value of the house is included in his taxable estate, because he now owns all the property. Had Phil and Patsy kept records, only half the value of the house would have been included in Patsy's taxable estate.

2. Joint Tenancy as a Taxable Gift

If you create a joint tenancy, you may be making a taxable gift (except between married couples). To understand the basics of how gift taxes can affect joint tenancy, all you need to know is that the federal government currently assesses taxes against any gift over $10,000 made to any person, other than one's spouse, in a calendar year. (See Chapter 16, Gifts and Gift Taxes.)

Gift taxes can affect joint tenancy because the IRS takes the position that, except for joint bank accounts (discussed below), a taxable gift is made when joint tenancy is created if the owners don't pay equally for the property. So if you put up all the money to purchase property, but list another person as a joint tenant, you've made a legal gift of half-ownership of the property. If the value of that gift exceeds $10,000, you must file a gift tax return and gift taxes are assessed. In other words, if a sole owner of property worth more than $20,000 transfers ownership into joint tenancy with another person, a taxable gift has been made, because the half given away is worth more than $10,000.

Example: Martha transfers her house, worth $300,000 (all equity), into joint tenancy with her son Richard solely to avoid probate. The IRS position is that she has made a taxable gift of one-half the value of the house (less the $10,000 exempt amount).

However, to remind you, if a bank account is opened in joint tenancy, with one person actually making all or most of the deposit, there's no taxable gift. Only if a new co-owner actually withdraws money is there a legal gift. This exception also applies to buying a savings bond in joint tenancy. Only when a person takes possession of more than his original contribution (by withdrawing money from the bank account, or selling an interest in the bond) is there a taxable gift.

Normally, no gift taxes must actually be paid when a gift of joint tenancy is made. Any tax assessed is deducted from the giver's estate/gift tax credit. (See Chapter 16, Section C.) In other words, cash will not have to be spent, out-of-pocket, to pay any gift tax assessed, but a gift tax return must still be prepared and filed, a hassle to many people.

3. Joint Tenancy and Federal Income Tax Basis Rules

In most cases, someone who inherits joint tenancy property gets a break on income taxes if she eventually sells the property. To understand this, you need to understand the tax concept called "stepped-up" basis. (The tax basis rules and their application to estate planning generally are discussed generally in Chapter 15, Section F.)

TAX BASIS OF PROPERTY

Put simply, the "basis" of property is the overall dollar cost to you of your interest in that property. To determine the profit or loss if you sell the property, deduct your basis from the selling price. For example, Gus buys stock for $50,000, which is his tax basis for the stock. Two years later Gus sells the stock for $70,000. His taxable profit is sale price ($70,000) less basis ($50,000), leaving $20,000 profit.

The basis is not always simply equal to the owner's original purchase price. For example, the basis of real estate can be its purchase price plus the cost of any capital improvements,.

Example: Ardmore buys a house for $200,000 and puts $37,000 into capital improvements. Thus the property's basis is $237,000. If Ardmore sells the house for $350,000, his taxable profit (sales price minus basis) is $113,000.

Under federal law, the basis of inherited property is changed to its market value on the date the deceased owner dies. If the market value has increased from the price the deceased owner paid for the property, the basis to the inheritor is "stepped up" to the higher death-date value. In other words, if B inherits property from A, B's basis in the property is its market value when A died, *not* its basis to A.

Example: Grant's basis in his house was $120,000. Grant dies and leaves the house to Serena under Grant's will. The market value of the house when Grant died was $350,000. When Serena inherits the house, her tax basis for it is stepped up to that market value of $350,000. If Serena sells the house for that amount, she has no taxable gain.

If the market value of property has risen substantially above the original owner's basis, it's clearly desirable for an inheritor of that property to receive a stepped up basis to the value as of the date of the owner's death. In the above example, if Serena had only received Grant's basis in the house of $120,000 and she then sold the house for the market value of $350,000, she would have a taxable profit (or capital gain) of $230,000. Instead, because of the stepped-up basis, she has no taxable profit.

Okay, now to apply this to joint tenancy. The general IRS rule for joint tenancy is that a surviving joint tenant gets a stepped-up basis only for one-half the value of the property, the half owned by the deceased owner. The half owned all along by the surviving joint tenant retains its original tax basis. (A different rule applies to couples in community property states. See Subsection a, below.)

Example: Ellen and Julie buy an investment property (a rental house) for $100,000 and hold it in joint tenancy. Each contributes the same amount to the down payment and operating expenses. When Ellen dies, the property is worth $200,000. The basis of Ellen's half of the property is "stepped up" to $100,000. The basis of Julie's half remains at $50,000, her share of the original purchase price. So Julie's new total net basis becomes $150,000.

This rule does not create any special problem when expenses of buying the joint tenancy were shared equally, or it was created between spouses. But, as we've discussed, if one of the owners did not contribute an equal share to the purchase price (except for spouses), federal tax law includes in the estate of the first joint tenant to die the full market value of the property, less any part the surviving owner can prove he paid for. So if someone transfers solely owned property into joint tenancy as a gift, the entire value of that property will be included in the giver's taxable estate. And because the entire value is included in that estate, all of the property will receive a stepped-up basis.

Example: Mary transfers her house, worth $250,000 (all equity), into joint tenancy with her son, Ed, who pays nothing for his share (it's a gift). When Mary dies, the house is worth $340,000. The full value of the house—$340,000—is included in her taxable estate, because Ed didn't contribute any cash for the property. And because the full value of the house is included in Mary's taxable estate, all of that property receives a stepped-up basis. So Ed's basis is now $340,000.

Sharp-eyed readers may have noticed a problem here. Wasn't Mary supposed to file a gift tax return when she originally transferred the house into joint tenancy with Ed? Yes, that's what the law requires. Since gift tax was assessed, doesn't Ed become the full legal owner of half the property, so that only half of its value is included in Mary's estate, and only half of it receives a stepped-up basis? The answer is no. Despite Mary's filing the gift tax return, the IRS includes all the value of the property in her estate and all the property receives a stepped-up basis. Mary's estate does receive a credit for the gift tax previously assessed.

a. Community Property Held in Joint Tenancy

The stepped-up tax basis rules are different for married couples who live in the eight community property states. In these states, both shares of community property held in joint tenancy are entitled to a stepped-up basis upon the death of a spouse, no matter what contributions were made to the initial purchase. Thus, if a husband and wife own community property real estate in joint tenancy purchase for

$200,000 and worth $2 million at the husband's death, the both the husband's and wife's share get a stepped-up basis of $1 million.

But to get the full stepped-up basis, you must be able to prove to the IRS that the joint tenancy property is community property. Otherwise, only the half of the deceased spouse gets the stepped-up basis. So if you're married and hold any community property in joint tenancy, be sure you can prove it retained its character as community property. (See Section B, above.)

b.   Joint Tenancy Property Acquired Before 1977 in Common Law States

If you live in a non-community property state and you acquired joint tenancy property before 1977, the tax basis rules were and remain different. Prior to 1977, the full value of joint ownership property is included in the value of the estate of the first owner to die. So the surviving spouse received a stepped-up basis for the whole property. (This rule applied to all joint tenants, not only married couples.)

In some circumstances, this can result is significant income tax savings for the surviving joint owner, if subsequently the property is sold.

Example: Rob and Sue bought a farm for $30,000 in 1955, as tenants by the entirety in Iowa. Rob died in 1993. Under the pre-1977 tax law, the full current value of the property, $3,400,000, is included in Rob's taxable estate. However, no estate taxes must be paid because all Rob's interest in the farm goes to his wife, under the rules of tenancy by the entirety, and all property left to a surviving spouse is free of estate tax.

Because the full value of the farm was included in Rob's taxable estate, all of it receives a stepped-up basis to its value at Rob's death. So Sue's basis in the farm is now $3,400,000. If she immediately sold the property for the market value, she should have no taxable gains. By contrast, if Rob and Sue had bought the farm after 1977, and the same figures applied, only Rob's half of the property would get a stepped-up basis, in this case, $1,700,000. Sue's half would retain her share of the original basis, which is one-half of $30,000, or $15,000. So Sue's total basis would be $1,715,000. If she immediately sold the property, her taxable gain would be $1,685,000

The moral: Anyone who bought property in joint tenancy before 1977 has a big tax incentive to keep that form of ownership, rather than transferring the property to a different form of ownership, such as placing it in a living trust.

4.   State Income Tax Basis Rules

State tax basis rules can also be quite complicated. However, in general, there's little need to worry about these rules. State income taxes take small enough bites that, in our opinion, they aren't worth bothering about when you're doing estate planning. Also, joint tenancy applies most often to real estate, and land obviously can't be moved from a high-tax state to low- or no-tax one.

More legal worries. If you have a large estate and want to be extremely cautious and review the impact of your state's basis rules on your estate plan, see a tax lawyer or other tax expert.

5. Local Property Taxes

In some areas of the country, real estate is reassessed for local property tax purposes every time it changes hands. This usually means that taxes go up, sometimes a lot if your property hasn't been reassessed recently.

In general, creating a joint tenancy interest in real property isn't a "change of ownership" if the original owner is one of the new joint tenants. In California, for example, there is no property tax reappraisal if you transfer your property into joint tenancy with yourself and others. However, as a general rule, if the original owner isn't one of the new joint tenants, then any creation of a joint tenancy interest is a change of ownership, and the property will be reassessed. Before relying on this advice, however, contact your local property tax assessor and determine the specific rules for what types of transfers trigger the reassessment of property.

Example 1: Mrs. Jefferson owns two pieces of real estate. She transfers title to the first to herself and her husband, Raymond, as "joint tenants with right of survivorship." She transfers title to the second to herself and her daughter, Lila, also as "joint tenants with right of survivorship." There has been no change of ownership in either of these transfers for reassessment purposes in most all states.

Also, when Mrs. Jefferson dies, there may be a reappraisal, depending on state property tax rules.

Example 2: Mrs. Jefferson gives a third lot to her son and his wife "Raymond Jefferson and Jane Jefferson, as joint tenants with right of survivorship." There has been a "change of ownership," since the original owner, Mrs. Jefferson, isn't one of the new joint tenants. This is likely to trigger a property tax reassessment.

G. DRAWBACKS OF JOINT TENANCY

We've already discussed the advantageous fact that joint tenancy property avoids probate, and the tax basis rules applicable to joint tenancy. In addition, as part of deciding whether to use joint tenancy, there are certain possible risks you should consider.

1. Any Joint Tenant Can End the Joint Tenancy

As long as all joint tenants are alive, any of them can terminate the joint tenancy, whether or not the other owners consent to it. (But, to repeat, this is not true for tenancy by the entirety property.) Some states require a joint tenant who wants to end the joint tenancy to go to court and get formal court partition (division) of the property. In other states, any joint tenant has the power to end it without court rigmarole, and can retain his interest, now held as a tenant in common, to do with as he wishes. In either case, if there's a sale, the new owner takes his interest as a tenant in common with the remaining original owners. If the new and old owners can't resolve a conflict, either can ask a court to partition the property into equal halves. If that isn't feasible, the court will order a sale with the proceeds divided in equal shares.

The risk that a co-owner may sell her share of the property may not be serious for couples or close friends who purchase property together with money they each contribute. In this situation, if a divorce, separation or other reason to end the joint tenancy occurs, each joint tenant simply gets her or his fair share. However, if solely owned property is transferred into joint tenancy by an older person in the form of a gift, the situation is quite different. The older person has given up ownership of half the property. And unlike putting property into a living trust, he can't change his mind later and take it back.

Example: Sid transfers his house into joint tenancy with his nephew Joe. Then the two have a bitter fight. Sid wants to regain sole ownership of the house. Joe says, "Nothing doing. I'm half owner, legally, and there's nothing you can do about it." And there isn't.

So, one question to answer before you transfer property into joint tenancy is: Do you absolutely trust that your joint-tenant-to-be won't sell the property or do anything with the ownership interest that's adverse to you? If you have any doubts, joint tenancy isn't for you.

A living trust may be a better way to transfer property ownership. To eliminate the risk of giving property to someone in joint tenancy who could then sell his interest in the property, or turn into someone whom you later don't get along with, we advise people in Sid's situation to create a living trust. Then name whomever you want as beneficiary for the house. If you have a falling out later, you can simply amend the trust and change beneficiaries.

2. Creditors and Joint Tenancy

Creditors of any joint tenant may go after (legally "attach" or "foreclose") that tenant's individual interest, but not the other joint tenants' interests. But a court may order the whole property sold to reach the debtor's share.

Generally, upon the death of one owner, the surviving owner takes the property free of any responsibility for the deceased's debts. But, in a number of states, a creditor of the deceased owner can go after the property if:

- the deceased person had pledged his interest in the property as security for a loan

- the creditor sued, got a judgment and initiated legal steps to collect the money before the deceased died, or

- the creditor can show that the joint tenancy arrangement was a scheme set up solely to defraud creditors.

3. Incapacity

Any form of shared ownership can become difficult if one owner becomes incapacitated. The other owner(s) may need someone with legal authority to act for the incapacitated owner, particularly to sell the property or refinance it.

The best way to authorize someone to act for you if you become incapacitated is by use of a durable power of attorney for finances (discussed in Chapter 26, Incapacity: Health Care and Financial Management Directives). To be secure, owners of joint tenancy property should be sure each has prepared a durable power of attorney. Otherwise, there's a risk a court proceeding will be required if one owner becomes incapacitated.

H. WHEN JOINT TENANCY MAKES SENSE

Don't interpret our comments about the risks of joint tenancy as a damning indictment against using it under all circumstances. In some situations, owning property in joint tenancy certainly does make sense. For people who value simplicity (joint tenancy is easy to create), and whose situations don't involve the drawbacks and risks we've discussed, joint tenancy can work fine.

1. Couples Buying a House

A married couple, or any couple, buying a house can sensibly use tenancy by the entirety or joint tenancy if each person wants the other to receive his or her interest in the house on death. Indeed, buying a house in joint tenancy or tenancy by the entirety is probably the most common way this form of ownership is used.

2. Transfers Into Joint Tenancy When Death Is Imminent

If a sole owner of property is likely to die soon, transferring that property into joint tenancy can be a useful last-minute probate avoidance device if no previous estate planning has been done.

> **Example:** Avram, who is old and in rapidly declining health, lives in a co-op apartment in Manhattan. Avram wants the apartment to go to his daughter, Molly, whom he trusts totally—and he wants to avoid probate. He also loathes paperwork and wants the transfer accomplished as simply as possible. Avram can simply transfer ownership of the property into joint tenancy with his daughter. It requires less paperwork than a living trust. He doesn't worry about filing a gift tax return, since by the time it's due, there will probably be an estate tax return instead. And since Molly didn't contribute any cash for the purchase of the co-op, it will all receive a stepped-up basis to the market value at Avram's death.

Transfers of solely owned property into joint tenancy are less desirable if the original owner is likely to live an appreciable time. In this situation, a gift tax return must actually be filed (well, it's supposed to be); then there's more paperwork, and possible subsequent estate tax credit calculations when the original owner dies. For long-term planning with solely owned property, a living trust remains a better method.

I. CREATING A JOINT TENANCY FOR PROPERTY WITH DOCUMENTS OF TITLE

Joint tenancy is commonly used for many types of property with documents of title, including real estate, stocks, vehicles, bank accounts and safe deposit boxes. There are two ways property with documents of title can be placed in joint tenancy:

- Two or more people buy or acquire property and take title in joint tenancy.
- A person who owns property can transfer title into joint tenancy with another person or people.

1. The Language Required

To create a joint tenancy, the title document must contain words that clearly demonstrate the owners' intention. In most states, joint tenancy may be created by putting the phrase "in joint tenancy" or "as joint tenants" in the ownership document. In some states, it's traditional or required to use the phrase "joint tenants, with right of survivorship," or "in joint tenancy with right of survivorship." This is sometimes abbreviated "JTWROS." Sometimes, the following is used: "Joint tenancy, not as tenants in common, and with right of survivorship." Simply listing the owners' names joined by "and" or "or" is not normally adequate to create a joint tenancy, although a few states allow it.

You may not remember how you took title to a piece of real estate, or your car, or your bank account. To see if shared ownership property is held in joint tenancy, look on the deed (for real estate) or the title slip (for other kinds of property, such as cars). If it doesn't say the co-owners own the property "as joint tenants" or "with right of survivorship" or similar language, the property isn't held in joint tenancy.

If you decide to transfer some of your existing property into joint tenancy, you must learn your state's law to learn the exact wording needed. If you're transferring real estate, any reliable title company or lawyer can tell you. You'll find that a few states have special requirements governing how a joint tenancy is created. For example, in Florida, a joint tenancy can be created only in an instrument of transfer—a deed made when property is sold or given away. In South Carolina, a joint tenancy for real estate must use the words "with right of survivorship." And in Oregon, the functional equivalent of joint tenancy

is created by using the phrase "tenancy in common with right of survivorship."

2. Real Estate

To demonstrate how simple creating joint tenancy can be, here is a deed used to transfer solely owned real estate into joint tenancy. In this deed, Alfred Smyth has created a joint tenancy in real estate between himself and his son Anthony.

INDIVIDUAL GRANT DEED

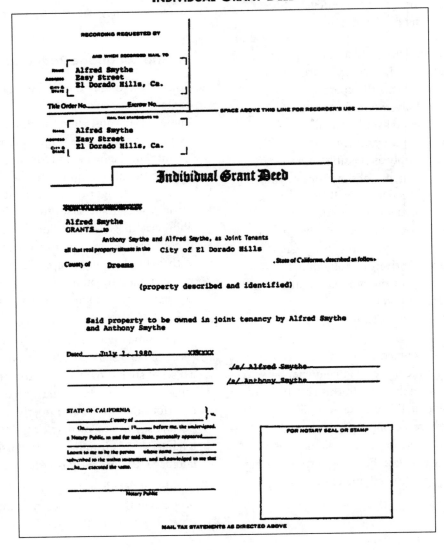

J. CREATING JOINT TENANCY FOR PERSONAL PROPERTY WITHOUT DOCUMENTS OF TITLE

You can also create joint tenancies for property without documents of title, such as valuable paintings, jewelry or even for your shoes. All you and the other co-owners have to do is declare in a signed document that you all own the property "in joint tenancy" or "as joint tenants." The document doesn't need to be filed with the county land records office, unlike deeds putting real property in joint tenancy. However you should have your signatures notarized.

Example: Guy and Danielle have been together for years. They have acquired a considerable amount of household furnishings, including appliances, furniture and glassware. Each wants the other to receive all their property when one of them dies. They want to avoid probate and the possibility that a member of either one's family could claim any of their property. So, Guy and Danielle write up and sign a joint ownership document, stating that all the household furnishings listed in it are their joint tenancy property. ■

11

Pay-on-Death Designations:

Bank Accounts, U.S. Government Securities, Stocks and Bonds, Motor Vehicles

A. Choosing Beneficiaries 11/2
    1. Multiple Beneficiaries 11/2
    2. Alternate Beneficiaries 11/2
    3. Children as Beneficiaries 11/2
B. Pay-on-Death Bank Accounts.. 11/3
    1. Advantages of P.O.D. Bank Accounts 11/3
    2. Opening a P.O.D. Account 11/4
    3. Estate Taxes 11/4
    4. Before You Open a P.O.D. Account 11/4
C. Naming a Pay-on-Death Beneficiary for Government Securities 11/5
D. Naming a Beneficiary for Stocks and Bonds 11/5
E. Car Registration 11/6

With a pay-on-death or transfer-on-death designation to the title document of certain property, you formally name another person, or persons, to receive that property, or whatever is left of it, when you die. Property left with a pay-on-death ("P.O.D.") designation avoids probate. When you die, the property goes directly to the named beneficiary.

Pay-on-death designations have become widely used, particularly for bank accounts and government securities. More recently, many states have adopted laws allowing the use of transfer-on-death registration for securities—stocks, bonds or stock brokerage accounts. A couple of states, California and Missouri, also allow transfer-on-death registration for motor vehicles. Finally, individual retirement programs, such as IRAs, allow you to name someone to receive any funds left in the account at your death; this use of a P.O.D. designation is discussed in Chapter 13, Retirement Benefits.

Pay-on-death accounts avoid probate with a minimum of paperwork. Normally, an institution, such as a bank or the U.S. Treasury Department, provides you with one simple form on which you designate the beneficiary, and that's it. The beneficiary, of course, has no rights to any of the property until your death.

A. CHOOSING BENEFICIARIES

There are few restrictions on whom you can name as a P.O.D. beneficiary (sometimes called a "payee"). But there are some issues that may concern you.

1. Multiple Beneficiaries

You can name more than one beneficiary for a P.O.D. account, except with government securities. (See Section C, below.) You simply list all beneficiaries on the account form. Each will inherit an equal share of the money in the account unless you specify differently.

Be careful when leaving unequal shares. In a very few states—for example, Florida—you cannot change the equal shares rule. If you're concerned about this issue, check your state's laws or open a separate account for each beneficiary.

2. Alternate Beneficiaries

With a P.O.D. account, you cannot name alternate beneficiaries. If you name one beneficiary and he doesn't outlive you, the P.O.D. designation doesn't work, and the funds in the account will pass to the residuary beneficiary of your will. If you name more than one P.O.D. beneficiary, and one dies before you, all money left in the account goes to the surviving beneficiaries. The lesson here is clear: if you're concerned about what happens if a P.O.D. beneficiary doesn't survive you, a P.O.D. account isn't for you, unless you're prepared (and able) to create a new account if a beneficiary does predecease you.

3. Children as Beneficiaries

It's fine to name a minor—a child under 18—as a P.O.D. beneficiary. However, as we've discussed in Chapter 6, Children, if you do this you should consider what might happen if that child is still a minor at your death. Depending on your state's laws, you can choose between the following options:

• You can name an adult "custodian" for the property, under the Uniform Transfers to Minors Act (valid in every state except Michigan, South

Carolina and Vermont). All you need do is name the custodian as the P.O.D. payee of the account. This custodian then has the legal responsibility to manage and use the money on behalf of the child. Then, when the child reaches the age required or permitted under your state's UTMA, the property is tuned over to the child. (See Chapter 6, Section C.)

Example: Mary-Kate wants to make her grandson, Mike, the P.O.D. payee of a bank account. Mike is six years old. So Mary-Kate names Mike's father, Claude, as custodian of the money in the account. On the bank's form, Mary-Kate puts, in the space for the P.O.D. payee, "Claude du Monde, as custodian for Mike du Monde under the Florida Uniform Transfers to Minors Act."

If Mike is not yet 21 when his grandmother dies, Claude will be legally in charge of the money until Mike's 21st birthday.

• If state law allows it, money left to a minor can simply be turned over to the beneficiary's parents. The parents hold the money for the benefit of the child until the child reaches age 18. Unfortunately, at present only five states follow this sensible approach:

Delaware

Michigan (up to $5,000)

New Jersey

New York (up to $10,000)

West Virginia.

• You can leave the money directly to the child. But if the child is a minor when you die, the parents will have to go to court and ask to be appointed guardians of the money. So, as we discussed in Chapter 6, this is almost never a desirable choice.

B. Pay-on-Death Bank Accounts

Here we look deeper into how pay-on-death bank accounts work. This type of account is called by various names by different banks in different parts of the country. Common names, aside from "P.O.D." account, include "informal trust," "bank trust account," and a "Totten trust" (perhaps from an old New York case, *Re Totten,* although some commentators have suggested the name is derived from the German "Tod," meaning death).

Whatever it's called, it works the same way. You open an account in your name, as depositor, and name the beneficiary—whomever you want to receive whatever money is in the account when you die. Sometimes you list yourself as trustee for the benefit of your beneficiary. As long as you live, the beneficiary has no rights to any money in the account. You can spend it freely—indeed, spend it all, if you want to or need to. After your death, the beneficiary can promptly obtain whatever money remains in the account simply by presenting the bank with proof of identity and a certified copy of the death certificate.

Example: Ray Jones wants to leave cash, probate-free, to his two daughters. He simply opens a pay-on-death trust certificate of deposit account as "Ray Jones, depositor, as trustee for Michelle and Mary Jones, equal beneficiaries." After he dies, his daughters go to the bank, present a copy of his death certificate and proof of their identities to bank officials, and then withdraw and divide equally all money in the account.

1. Advantages of P.O.D. Bank Accounts

There are normally no risks in creating a P.O.D. bank account. Unlike joint tenancy bank accounts, there's no danger that the beneficiary will withdraw any money from the account while you're alive. In addition, you can close the account any time and can change the beneficiary at any time. You can deposit or withdraw any amount desired (subject, of course, to any penalties the bank applies on early withdrawal, if you have a C.D. account).

Because you retain complete control over the account until death, establishing a pay-on-death account isn't a gift, and therefore doesn't involve gift tax concerns. Only when the beneficiary gets the money at your death does legal ownership of that money change.

2. Opening a P.O.D. Account

An appealing aspect of a P.O.D. account is that it's so easy to open. Most banks, including most credit unions, have standard forms for opening this kind of account; they will do the paperwork for you. A P.O.D. account may either be a newly opened account or an existing account to which you add a beneficiary designation. Banks don't normally charge extra fees for holding your money in a P.O.D. account.

Generally, any regular bank account, including checking, savings or certificates of deposit accounts, may be used as a P.O.D. account. In practice, these accounts are usually savings accounts, since it's more likely there will be substantial funds in a savings account at the depositor's death than in a checking account. And because most checking accounts don't pay interest, they aren't suitable places to keep substantial sums.

3. Estate Taxes

The money in a P.O.D. account is included in the taxable estate of the depositor. (See Chapter 15, Estate Taxes, Section A.) So a P.O.D. account only works as a probate avoidance device, and will not save on federal or state death tax, assuming your estate is large enough to have to pay them.

4. Before You Open a P.O.D. Account

If you decide to open a P.O.D. account, there are a few concerns you should be aware of and ask about at your bank:

- **Early withdrawal penalties.** If the type of bank account you choose for a P.O.D. account requires holding a deposit for a set term, or paying a substantial penalty for early withdrawal—as would be the case, for example, for a six-month certificate of deposit—the penalty is usually waived if the depositor dies before that term expires and the beneficiary claims the funds.

- **Spouse's share of estate.** If you try to disinherit your spouse, the person you name as P.O.D. payee may not get the money in your account. The reason is simple. In many states, if your spouse goes to court and claims a share of your estate, funds deposited in a P.O.D. account may be paid to the spouse. (See Chapter 3, Section C.)

- **State death tax.** If your state has a state death tax (see Chapter 15, Estate Taxes, Section G), death tax liens (legal claims) may be imposed on P.O.D.

accounts. The liens must be removed before the funds can be transferred to the beneficiaries. This is normally done by demonstrating to the tax authority that the estate has ample funds to pay tax, and is routine for most estates.

C. NAMING A PAY-ON-DEATH BENEFICIARY FOR GOVERNMENT SECURITIES

You can hold U.S. Treasury Department securities (T-bills) in a pay-on-death account form. The Treasury Department, or your investment advisor (if you have one), can provide you with the correct form. In that form, you register ownership of your securities in your (the purchaser's) name, followed by "payable on death to [whomever you name as beneficiary]." If a minor (or incompetent adult) is beneficiary, that status must be stated on the registration.

There can only be one primary owner and one beneficiary for a government security. So a P.O.D. account will not work for government securities if you want the money divided between different beneficiaries.

D. NAMING A BENEFICIARY FOR STOCKS AND BONDS

In many states, you can add a transfer-on-death designation to brokerage accounts, or to individual securities (stocks and bonds) under the Uniform Transfers-on-Death Securities Registration Act.

STATES THAT ALLOW TRANSFER-ON-DEATH REGISTRATION OF SECURITIES		
Alabama	Maryland	Oklahoma
Alaska	Minnesota	Oregon
Arizona	Mississippi	Pennsylvania
Arkansas	Missouri	South Dakota
Colorado	Montana	Tennessee
Connecticut	Nebraska	Texas
Delaware	Nevada	Utah
Florida	New Hampshire	Virginia
Idaho	New Jersey	Washington
Illinois	New Mexico	West Virginia
Iowa	North Dakota	Wisconsin
Kansas	Ohio	Wyoming

In these states, if you register your stocks, bonds, securities accounts or mutual funds in a transfer-on-death form, the beneficiary or beneficiaries you designate will receive these securities promptly after your death. No probate will be necessary. If you live in one of these states, your broker can provide the forms you'll need to name a beneficiary for your securities or security account.

Your broker isn't required to cooperate. Although most stockbrokers and corporate transfer agents offer transfer-on-death registration (where legally permitted), the law doesn't require them to do so; it simply allows them that option. Of course, if they don't offer you that option, you can threaten to switch brokers, or sell your shares, which may well overcome resistance.

Even if you don't live in one of these states, you can use a transfer-on-death registration for securities if any of the following is true:

- The stockbroker's principal office is in a state which has adopted the law.

- The issuer of the stock or the stockbroker is incorporated in a state which has adopted the law.

- The transfer agent's office is located in a state which has adopted the law.

- The office making the registration is in a state that has adopted the law.

If you want to avoid probate but can't use a transfer-on-death designation for your securities, it's usually better to use a living trust rather than joint tenancy. With a living trust:

- the beneficiary of the living trust has no right to the securities while you live; and

- you can change the beneficiary or end the living trust if you wish.

With joint tenancy, you cannot decide to remove the joint tenant as co-owner, and that person is legal co-owner of half of the stock/securities.

E. CAR REGISTRATION

Presently, only two states allow vehicles to be registered in a transfer-on-death form. Missouri pioneered using car registration as a probate avoidance device and California adopted a similar law. (Over two years after it was adopted, however, some local California

DMV offices have not heard of it and have no forms for it. The California law, in case you need to convince a skeptical clerk at the DMV, is Section 4150.7 of the Vehicle Code.)

Under the Missouri law, a car owner can designate on the vehicle title document a person or persons to receive ownership of the car when the present owner dies. The new owners obtain title to the car (and the car itself) without any court proceedings. California law is similar, except that California allows this method only for one owner (not for co-owned cars) and you can name only one beneficiary.

AVOIDING PROBATE FOR SMALL BOATS

In California, transfer-on-death registration is also available for small boats, called "undocumented vessels," which include the myriad of small pleasure boats that aren't required to have a valid marine document from the U.S. Bureau of Customs. Only one owner and one beneficiary may be listed (California Vehicle Code Section 9852.7).

Other states are currently considering legislation similar to Missouri's and California's. Hopefully, this type of transfer-on-death car registration will soon become a widely used method of probate avoidance for the cars that are part of nearly every estate. ■

12

Life Insurance

A. Do You Need Life Insurance? 12/2
    1. Long-Term Needs 12/2
    2. Short-Term Needs 12/3

B. Types of Life Insurance 12/5
    1. Term Insurance 12/6
    2. Permanent Insurance 12/6
    3. Single-Premium Life Insurance 12/8
    4. Survivorship Life Insurance 12/8
    5. "First to Die" Life Insurance 12/9
    6. Annuities 12/9

C. Life Insurance and Probate 12/10

D. Choosing Life Insurance Beneficiaries 12/10
    1. Special Rules or Community Property States 12/10
    2. Minor Children as Beneficiaries 12/10

E. Reducing Estate Taxes By Transferring Ownership of
Life Insurance Policies 12/11
    1. Transferring Ownership to Other People 12/12
    2. Gift Tax Concerns 12/12
    3. How to Transfer Ownership of Your Policy 12/13
    4. Life Insurance Trusts 12/13

L ife insurance has long been a part of much
estate planning in the United States. Indeed,
one fear a number of people have of the
phrase "estate planning" is that it's a cover for hard-
sell visits by life insurance agents. Although life
insurance certainly does not need to be a part of every
person's estate plan, it can be very useful, especially
for parents of young children and those who support
a spouse or a disabled adult or child. It can also
provide cash to pay debts and (especially) estate
taxes.

A. DO YOU NEED LIFE INSURANCE?

In addition to helping to support dependents, life
insurance can help solve several other common estate
planning problems. These include:

- **Providing immediate cash at death.** Insurance
  proceeds are a handy source of cash to pay the
  deceased's debts, funeral expenses, and income or
  death taxes. (Federal estate taxes are due nine
  months after death, so cash to pay them doesn't
  have to be raised immediately.)

- **Probate avoidance.** Normally, the proceeds of a
  life insurance policy avoid probate because you
  name your beneficiary in the policy instead of in
  your will. This means that the proceeds can be
  transferred quickly to survivors with little red tape,
  cost or delay (see Section C, below).

- **Death tax reduction.** When an insurance policy
  is not legally owned by the person who is the
  insured (as explained in Section E), the proceeds
  are excluded from the insured's taxable estate. This
  can significantly reduce death tax liability of the
  insured's estate. Obviously, though, this is only a
  benefit for people whose estates are large enough
  to face death tax liability in the first place.

Having indicated some of the reasons life insurance can be desirable, let us again emphasize that
simply buying some is not an adequate way to plan
an estate. Many, if not most, people who have no
minor children or financially strapped dependents
simply don't need life insurance. Those who decide to
purchase insurance should know exactly why they are
buying it, the best type of policy for their needs, and
of course, should buy no more than they need. As a
group, Americans certainly believe in life insurance,
holding over two trillion dollars worth—far more, per
capita, than any other country.

Here are some questions to ask yourself to help
evaluate your life insurance needs.

1. Long-Term Needs

To determine whether it makes sense for you to
purchase insurance to provide financial help for
family members over the long term, consider these
factors:

- How many people are really dependent on your
  current earning capacity over the long term? If the
  answer is "no one," it's doubtful that you need life
  insurance.

- How much money would your dependents really
  need, and for how long, if you died suddenly?

- When you determine how much money your
  dependents will need, subtract the worth of
  property you leave them and any amounts that will
  be available from public and any private insurance
  plans that already provide coverage. Social Security and dependents' benefits will probably be
  available, and you may also be covered by union
  or management pensions or a group life insurance
  plan.

• And don't forget to subtract any other likely sources of income, such as the help reasonably affluent grandparents would assuredly provide for your children in case of disaster. Also, remember that bright kids may get at least partial scholarships, and dependent spouses caring for young children can usually return to work at some point.

2. Short-Term Needs

Now, assess whether you need life insurance for short-term needs.

• How long is it likely to be, after you die, before your property is turned over to your inheritors? If your property will avoid probate, there's usually little need for insurance for short-term expenses, unless you have no bank accounts, securities or other cash assets. By contrast, if the bulk of your property is transferred by will, and therefore will be tied up in probate for months, your family and other inheritors may need the ready cash insurance can provide. While a probate court will usually promptly authorize a family allowance or otherwise allow a spouse or other inheritor access to estate funds, it can still be nice to have insurance proceeds available.

• What assets would be available to take care of immediate financial needs? Aside from buying insurance, there are other, cheaper, ways of providing ready cash, such as leaving some money in joint or pay-on-death bank accounts, or placing marketable stocks and other securities in joint tenancy.

• Will your estate owe substantial debts and taxes after your death?

Lawyers and financial advisors call cash and assets that can quickly be converted to cash "liquid." If your estate has almost all "non-liquid" assets (real estate, collectibles, a share in a small business,

jewelry) there may be a major loss if these assets must be sold quickly to raise cash to pay bills, as opposed to what they could be sold for later if there had been enough liquid money from insurance or other sources to meet all pressing bills. Obviously, if your estate has significant funds in bank accounts or marketable securities, you won't need to purchase insurance for this purpose.

Example: Alicia's estate consists of several valuable pieces of real estate and one-half interest in a profitable antique store, but includes very little cash and no life insurance. When she dies, she owes debts of $90,000 (aside from mortgages) and death taxes of $120,000. To raise this money, her beneficiaries (technically, her executor) must sell some of her real estate or her interest in the store. Unfortunately, the country is suffering a recession, and the market value of both antiques and real estate is down. To make matters worse, canny real estate people spread the word that this is a "distress sale" to raise money for estate obligations. As a result the price the beneficiaries receive when they sell one of the pieces of real estate is far below what they would have received if they had the flexibility to choose when to sell the property. Had Alicia purchased an insurance policy with a pay-off at death of $210,000 or more, the need to sell the real estate would have been eliminated.

• If you are sole owner of a business, how much cash would it need on your death? Do you want, and expect, that some of your inheritors will continue the business? If so, do you think there will be a sufficient cash flow so the new owners can successfully maintain the business? How much is your death likely to reduce cash flow? How much will it affect the value of the business, if it

must be sold? Do you need insurance proceeds to cover any cash flow shortage of the business? (Chapter 28 discusses estate planning for business in more detail.)

If you don't plan to have your inheritors continue the business, the questions are simpler. Will there be enough cash so the business can continue to stay live until it is sold? Is there really anything to sell? For many personal service businesses, the answer is no—the business ends when the person providing the service dies.

BUYING INSURANCE

If you don't own life insurance and think you want it, you need to talk to an insurance salesperson or broker. Normally, a salesperson sells for one company only, while a broker can place your policy with one of several. In theory, this would seem to be a reason to prefer a broker, but in practice, the integrity of the person you are dealing with is far more important than is the legal relationship to an insurance company or companies.

If you do contact an insurance salesperson, look for a person who will function as an ally, offering additional information and proposing alternatives—not forcing you. If you get too much quick-sell pressure, contact someone else. And here's one more tip: some salespeople don't recommend that you buy term insurance, or try to talk you out of it, for no other reason than they get a much higher commission from selling you whole life or universal. (See Section B, below, for an analysis of the pros and cons of various types of life insurance.)

Before you contact anyone who sells insurance, you should have a good idea of what kind of policy you need and how much it should cost. The cost of the same insurance can vary considerably from company to company. Often, relatively small mutual companies charge lower rates than some of

the giants of TV advertising, and some brokers charge lower "discount" commissions.

Resources: There are some books that explain the ins and outs of life insurance, including buying life insurance. A couple of the better life insurance books are:

- *How to Insure Your Life,* by Reg Wilson & the Merritt Editors (Merritt)

- *Your Life Insurance Options,* by Alan Lavine (John Wiley and Sons, Inc.)

You can also contact a free life insurance rate-shopping service, which will provide information on the costs of different companies' policies. These resources include:

- Select Quote, 800-343-1985

- Insurance Quote, 800-972-1104

These organizations often make money if you buy a "product" (life insurance) they recommend, so use any information they give you as a starting point. Also, a rate shopping service may offer quotes for only one type of insurance product; generally, you should look at various types in order to make an informed decision. Still, these companies can provide useful information, even if they have some self-interest in promoting a product.

B. TYPES OF LIFE INSURANCE

If you are interested in life insurance, any salesperson will be delighted to explain the bewildering array of policies available to you. But unless you educate yourself first, it's all too easy to get mesmerized by insurance policy lingo and end up paying too much for a policy that may not even meet your needs. Basically, for estate planning purposes, there are two main types of life insurance: term, which provides insurance only for a set period, and some form of "permanent" insurance, which the company can never cancel as long as the premiums are paid. Over time, permanent issuance will build a cash value which produces returns for the policyholder. However, although permanent insurance policies do function as one type of investment, maximizing your investment return is not the purpose of insurance. If that's what you want, look elsewhere.

Permanent insurance includes whole life, universal life and variable life (discussed below). Any of these types of life insurance can be purchased with one lump sum, called a "single-premium payment," which can be a useful estate planning device if you have sufficient funds and want to lock in your life insurance now. We explain each in the sections which follow.

HOW SAFE IS YOUR INSURANCE COMPANY?

As some surprised and angry insurance policy owners have learned to their dismay, insurance companies can encounter serious financial trouble, and even go broke. For instance, a few insurance companies invested heavily in junk bonds and "go-go" real estate deals during the '80s, and paid the price of insolvency when glimmers of fiscal (and societal) sanity returned to these economic areas in the '90s.

There is no national or federal insurance guarantee fund for life insurance companies similar to FDIC insurance for bank depositors. In 47 states, there is some sort of industry-sponsored state guarantee fund. (Colorado, Louisiana, New Jersey and Washington, D.C., have no such funds.) While these funds offer most policyholders the reasonable hope that they won't lose everything they invested if their insurer goes broke, you still certainly don't want to have to wait for state regulators to take charge of an insolvent company, investigate and finally—and it can take a while—determine how much money you get back.

To avoid this sad scenario, check the reliability of the insurer you plan to buy a policy from. Several major companies rate the financial stability of insurance companies. It's prudent to check your insurance agency against one—and even better, two—of these rating systems, to be sure the company you're interested in got top grades.

The names of the major rating companies are:

- Weiss Research (the most rigorous of the bunch)
- A.M. Best (Best Insurance Reports) (ambest.com)
- Duff & Phelps
- Moody's Investors Service
- Standard and Poor's.

You should be able to locate the reports of these companies at a large public library and perhaps online. If not, your insurance agent should be able to assist you with locating their business offices and phone numbers. Each company has a slightly different code for its rating—for instance, Weiss Research's top rating is "A+" whereas Standard and Poor's top rating is "AAA." Each company will provide you its rating code system.

A trustworthy insurance agent is a must. There are a bewildering number of variations of life insurance policies. Without writing an entire book on the subject, it's impossible to explain the names of every possible option to you here. We can tell you about the basic forms, and offer two pieces of advice: First, many of the variations are of the "bells and whistles" type, minor differences that don't mean nearly as much as some insurance agents may claim. Second, when it comes to selecting a policy, or fine-tuning your needs, your choice of an insurance agent is crucial. Unless you are prepared to do an immense amount of research yourself, you'll have to rely somewhat on the advice of your agent. So you surely need one you trust. We're fortunate to have fine insurance agents (now friends) and can attest to the value of working with someone you trust and like.

1. Term Insurance

Term insurance provides a pre-set amount of cash if you die while the policy is in force. For example, a five-year $130,000 term policy pays off if you die within five years—and that's it. If you live beyond the end of the term, you get nothing (except, of course, the continued joys and sorrows of life itself). With term insurance, you pay only for life insurance coverage. The policy does not develop reserves.

Term insurance is the cheapest form of coverage over a limited number of years As a candid life insurance man once said, "It provides the most bang for the buck, no question—over the short term." There are many types of term insurance, such as policies that have an automatic right to renew for an additional term, but these options don't change the basic fact that term insurance pays off if you die

during the policy time period and doesn't pay anything if you live beyond that period.

Term life insurance is particularly suitable for younger people with families, who want substantial insurance coverage at low cost. Since the risk of dying in your 20s, 30s or 40s is quite low, the cost of term insurance during these years is as reasonable as life insurance prices get. Also, if you need insurance only for a short time, say to qualify for a business loan, term is your best bet. However, the older you are, the more expensive term insurance becomes when you compare how much you have to pay in premiums to the pay-off value of the policy. This, of course, is understandable, as the older you are, the greater the chance you will die during the policy term.

As mentioned above, term policies offered by different companies have all sorts of differences, some fairly significant. For example, some policies are automatically renewable at the end of the term without a medical examination, often for higher premiums, and some are not. Some have premiums set for a period of years, but others guarantee a premium rate only for the first year. After that, the rate can go up. Some can also be converted from a term to whole life or "universal" policy during the term, again without needing to requalify. But as we've said, with term insurance you never lock in the right to maintain the policy no matter how old you become. If you want ensure that insurance will continue in force your entire life, term isn't for you.

2. Permanent Insurance

Permanent insurance is automatically renewable without a new physical examination of the insured. With a permanent policy, your premium payments for the first few (or more than a few) years cover more than the actuarial cost of the risk of death. The excess money goes into a reserve account, which is invested by the insurance company. Unless the company is disastrously managed, these investments yield returns—interest or dividends. A proportion of these are passed along to you. These returns can be used to add to your policy reserves or borrowed against, after a set time. And if you decide to end the policy, you can cash it in for the "surrender value."

Returns that accumulate are not taxable, unless the money is actually distributed to you. Certain partial withdrawals can even be made without paying tax. By contrast, the interest on bank accounts is subject to tax in the year it is paid, even if left untouched in the account.

a. Whole Life Insurance

Whole life (sometimes called "straight life") insurance provides a set dollar amount of coverage which can never be canceled, in exchange for fixed, uniform payments. Because the payments are the same throughout your life, the premiums are comparatively high (versus your statistical risk of death) in the early years of the policy (this is why reserves are built up). Assuming you live a long while after the policy was issued, your payments become low, compared to your risk of death. In other words, insurance companies take in substantially more money on whole life policies during their first few years than they pay out on those policies. The insurance company invests the surplus. Some of the surplus becomes your cash reserve, which grows over time. The cash reserve earns dividends, paid by the insurance company. After a set time, usually several years, you have the right to borrow against the cash reserve. You can also, of course, cancel the policy and receive its cash surrender value.

Whole life often is not desirable for younger people with small children who don't have adequate savings to cope should a main income-provider die. People in this group usually can't afford initially expensive permanent policies.

b. Universal Life Insurance

Universal life combines some of the desirable features of both term and whole life insurance, and offers other advantages. Over time, the net cost usually is lower than whole life insurance. With universal life, you build up a cash reserve, as with whole life. But you can also vary premium payments, amount of coverage, or both, from year to year. In contrast, whole life requires one set payment amount, which cannot be varied, for the life of the policy. Also, universal life policies normally provide you with more consumer information. For example, you are told how much of your policy payments goes for company overhead expenses, reserves and policy proceed payments, and how much is retained for your savings. This information isn't usually provided with whole life policies

There can be other significant advantages to universal life; an insurance agent will be glad to explain them to you.

c. Variable Life Insurance

Variable life, sometimes called "variable universal life insurance," refers to policies in which cash reserves are invested in securities, stocks and bonds. In a sense, these policies combine an insurance feature with a mutual fund. Since over the past decade, overall prices on the stock market have risen dramatically, variable life policies have usually produced the best returns. But of course, there's a potential downside to this also. These policies are almost sure to bring unpleasant surprises when financial markets decline.

3. Single-Premium Life Insurance

With single-premium life, you pay, up-front, all premiums due for the full duration of the policy. Normally, any policy with a savings feature can be purchased with a single premium. Obviously, this requires the expenditure of a large amount of cash—$5,000, $10,000 or often much more, depending on your age and the dollar amount of the policy.

A reason to commit so much cash to buying an insurance policy is that it enables you to give the fully-paid-for policy to new owners. As explained in Section E of this chapter, there can be major estate tax savings if someone other than the insured owns the policy. That way the gift tax obligation is computed on the current—not future—value of the policy. And because there are no more payments to make, a gift of a single-premium policy doesn't involve risks that the new owners will fail to make payments and cause the policy to be canceled.

4. Survivorship Life Insurance

Survivorship life insurance (also called "second to die" or "joint" insurance) is a relatively new type of insurance. It provides a single policy that insures two lives, usually spouses. When the first spouse dies, no proceeds are paid. Indeed, the policy remains in force, and premiums must continue to be paid, as long as a spouse lives. The policy only pays off on the death of the second spouse.

Why would any couple want such a policy? Mainly for use as part of an estate plan for wealthier couples who expect that substantial estate taxes will be assessed on the death of the second spouse. (See Chapter 15, Estate Taxes.) None of this is of interest to people with moderate-sized estates or smaller, so if you are in this category, you don't need to read this section.

This type of insurance can be particularly desirable when a major family asset is a valuable family business, or real estate interests—assets that aren't liquid, and which the survivors may not want to sell. Or suppose two children inherit a family business, but one doesn't want to keep it going. The other could use her share of the insurance proceeds as an initial buy-out payment, so she could retain ownership of the business.

This kind of insurance can also be desirable if one member of a couple is in less than good health. If the other spouse is in reasonably good health, the couple can usually obtain survivorship life insurance.

Because two lives are insured, premiums for survivorship life policies are comparatively low compared to policies on one person's life. It's those old insurance companies' actuarial tables again: The odds on two people dying in X time period are less than on one. But, of course, cost also depends the age and the health of the insured couple.

The federal tax statute governing survivorship life insurance is somewhat ambiguous. Because this is a new and complex area, you need to check with a good estate planning lawyer with current knowledge of the tax rulings on this type of policies. Also, discuss this issue with your insurance agent to ensure your survivorship policy will have the effect you intend. It may be best to have the policy owned by a life insurance trust. (See Section E, below, and Chapter 21, Section B.)

5. "First to Die" Life Insurance

"First to die" life insurance is, as the name indicates, the reverse of survivorship insurance. With a first to die policy, two (or occasionally more) people, usually business partners or co-owners, are insured under one policy. Because these policies are usually maintained as a part of a business buy-out agreement, usually the company or partnership itself buys and maintains the policy. When the first insured dies, the policy pays off, with the funds typically paid to the company or partnership. Effectively, this means payments go to the other owners of the business.

A first to die policy is significantly cheaper than individual policies for two, or several, business owners. Obviously, insuring against only one death exposes an insurance company to lower risks, and lesser proceed payments, than if several people are separately insured for the same amount.

When one business owner dies, the proceeds of a first to die policy can be used to pay off the worth of the deceased owner's interest, under a buy-out clause. Or, if the deceased owner's beneficiaries wish to, and are allowed to, participate in the business, the funds can be used for the costs of whatever adjustments and problems the business faces because of the death of an owner.

Example: Paul, Gabe and Liz are equal partners in a video rental store. Their partnership agreement provides that if a partner dies, the two surviving partners can buy out that partner's interest according to a set valuation formula. The business does not have a great deal of ready cash. Almost all the available cash the partners had was consumed by opening the business, acquiring inventory and operational costs.

So the partnership buys a "first to die" policy covering the lives of the three partners. The partners have made a rough guess of how much the business is worth now, and paid for a policy that pays off about half this value. In theory, they need coverage for only one-third of the value, but they hope and expect their business will increase, so want to include some allowance for increased value of a deceased partner's interest.

If a partner dies, the life insurance pays the proceeds to the partnership. The value of the deceased partner's interest is determined from the formula. The two surviving partners pay this amount to the deceased partner's inheritors. If there are any insurance proceeds left over, the partners can use them however they agree upon. And when everything is wound up, the two surviving partners now own the business 50-50.

6. Annuities

Basically, an annuity is a policy in which an insurance company contracts to pay the policy beneficiary a certain cash amount each year, or month, instead of one lump sum upon death. There are all sorts of annuity policies and combinations of annuity payment plans with cash-value life insurance policies. Some people who don't trust their own ability to hold onto money even purchase an annuity policy when times are good, naming themselves as beneficiary. They thus provide themselves with a set income for life, beginning at a specified age.

An estate planning advantage of an annuity is that you can buy one that will provide periodic payments to someone you believe is unable (too young, or too much of a wastrel) to handle one large lump sum insurance payment. In this sense, annuities work somewhat like a trust.

However, even if you want to arrange for periodic payments to a beneficiary, you should consider other alternatives, including establishing a trust. (See Chapter 17, An Overview of Ongoing Trusts.) Annuity policies tend to be a relatively expensive way to meet your objective. Also, they are not flexible. For example, if special needs of the beneficiary arise, such as an extended illness, the payments often cannot be increased, as they often can be with a well-designed trust. In short, it's usually wiser to buy a more prosaic type of insurance and have the benefits put in trust should you die, to be administered by a trusted friend or family member who can vary pay-outs to meet the needs of the trust beneficiary.

C. LIFE INSURANCE AND PROBATE

The proceeds of a life insurance policy are not subject to probate unless you name your estate as the beneficiary of your policy. If anyone else, including a trust, is the beneficiary of the policy, the proceeds are not included in the probate estate, and the proceeds are paid to the beneficiary without the cost or delay of probate. Except when your estate will have no ready cash to pay anticipated debts and taxes, there is no sound reason for naming your estate, rather than a person or persons as the beneficiary or beneficiaries of an insurance policy.

Think again before naming your estate as a life insurance beneficiary. In our experience, the problem of a deceased person having substantial debts and no liquid assets is rare. In most instances, estates contain enough cash, or other assets that can be sold for cash, to pay debts and taxes. Unless life insurance proceeds are used for estate costs, they will be distributed to someone, eventually. So it seems foolhardy to reduce the amount inheritors receive from your life insurance because of probate costs—or

add to the time your inheritors must wait before they get this money.

D. CHOOSING LIFE INSURANCE BENEFICIARIES

As you know, when you buy life insurance, you name the policy's beneficiaries—those who will receive the proceeds when you die. As long as you own the policy, you can change beneficiaries, as long as you are mentally competent. You can't, however, change an insurance beneficiary by naming someone else in your will or living trust. If one person is named as a beneficiary of a life insurance policy, but another person is named as the beneficiary of the policy in the insured's will or living trust, the first person remains the legal beneficiary. If you want to change a beneficiary, contact your insurance agent, or company, and complete the appropriate form.

1. Special Rules or Community Property States

If you live in a community property state (see Chapter 3, Section A, for a list) and buy a policy with community property funds, one-half of the proceeds are owned by the surviving spouse, no matter who the policy names as the beneficiary. This result can be varied by a written agreement between the spouses, in which one spouse transfers all interest in a particular insurance policy to the other spouse. Again, contact your insurance company for the proper form.

2. Minor Children as Beneficiaries

If you want your minor children to be the beneficiaries of your life insurance policy, you need to arrange some legal means for the proceeds to be managed and supervised by a competent adult. If you don't, and your children are not legal adults at your death, the insurance company would require that a court appoint a property guardian for the children before releasing the proceeds. As discussed in Chapter 6, Children, this is not desirable, since it necessitates attorney's fees, court proceedings and court supervision of life insurance proceeds left to benefit your children—costs and hassles the children surely won't benefit from. There are several ways to prevent this.

Grandparents or other friends or relatives who name minors as beneficiaries of their life insurance policies can also use these methods.

- Rethink your plan to name minors as beneficiaries of your life insurance policy. Instead, name a trusted adult beneficiary who you are confident will use the money for the children's benefit.

- Name your living trust (or successor trustee, depending on which the insurance company prefers) as the beneficiary of the policy. In the trust document, you name the minor children as beneficiaries of any money the trust receives from the insurance policy. You also establish within the trust a method to impose adult management over the proceeds, which can be either a child's trust or an UTMA custodianship

- Leave the proceeds directly under your state's UTMA, by naming as policy beneficiary an adult "custodian" for the minor child.

E. REDUCING ESTATE TAXES BY TRANSFERRING OWNERSHIP OF LIFE INSURANCE POLICIES

This section is important only if your estate will likely have to pay federal estate taxes. (See Chapter 15.)

Whether or not life insurance proceeds are included in the deceased's taxable estate, and so subject to federal death taxes, depends on who owns the policy when the insured dies. If the deceased

owned the policy, the full amount of the proceeds are included in the federal taxable estate; if someone else owned the policy, the proceeds are not included.

Example: Melissa purchases and owns an insurance policy covering her life, with a face value of $200,000, payable to her son, Jeff, as beneficiary. Melissa's business partner, Juanita, owns a second policy, covering Melissa's life for $400,000, payable to Juanita. She will use these proceeds to pay Jeff, Melissa's sole inheritor, the worth of Melissa's interest in the business. Melissa dies. All the proceeds of Melissa's policy, $200,000, are included in her federal taxable estate. However, none of the $400,000 from the policy Juanita owns is part of Melissa's federal taxable estate, because Melissa did not own the policy.

There are two ways you can transfer ownership of a life insurance policy. First, you can simply give the policy to another person or persons. Second, you can create an irrevocable life insurance trust, and transfer ownership to that entity. Here we'll primarily focus on the first method. The second we discuss briefly here, and in more depth in Chapter 21, Section B.

If you choose to transfer a life insurance policy, you must do it with the knowledge of, and with forms approved by, the issuing company. The transfer won't be legally effective if the insurance company has no record of it.

You have the right to assign or give ownership of your life insurance policy to any other adult, including the policy beneficiary. (The only exceptions are some group policies, which many people participate in through work, and which don't allow you to transfer ownership.)

1. Transferring Ownership to Other People

Transferring ownership of your policy to another person or persons involves a trade-off: Once the policy is transferred, you've lost all your power over it, forever. You cannot cancel it or change the beneficiary. To make this point bluntly, suppose you transfer ownership of your policy to your spouse, and later get divorced. You cannot cancel the policy or recover it from your now ex-spouse. Nevertheless, in many situations, the trade-off is worth it, as, for example, when you transfer policy ownership to a child (or children) you have a close and loving relationship with.

The IRS has some special rules about determining who owns a life insurance policy when the insured dies. *Gifts of life insurance policies made within three years of death are disallowed for federal estate tax purposes (and often for state death tax purposes, too).* This means that the full amount of the proceeds are included in your estate as if you had remained owner of the policy.

> **Example:** Louise gives her term life insurance, with proceeds of $300,000, payable on death, to her friend, Leon, in 1995. She dies two years later. For federal estate tax purposes, the gift is disallowed, and all the proceeds,

$300,000, are included in Louise's taxable estate. If Louise had transferred the life insurance policy more than three years before her death, none of the proceeds would have been included in her taxable estate.

The message here is obvious: If you want to give away a life insurance policy to reduce estate taxes, give the policy away as soon as feasible. (And don't die for at least three years.)

Another IRS regulation provides that a deceased person who retained any "incidents of ownership" of a life insurance policy is considered the owner. The term "incidents of ownership" is simply legalese for keeping any significant power over the transferred insurance policy. Specifically, the proceeds of the policy will be included in your taxable estate if you have the legal right to do any one of the following,

- change or name beneficiaries of the policy
- borrow against the policy, pledge any cash reserve it has or cash it in
- surrender, convert or cancel the policy
- select a payment option—decide if payments to the beneficiary can be a lump sum or in installments.

2. Gift Tax Concerns

When a life insurance policy is transferred from the original insured owner to a beneficiary, the transaction is regarded as a gift by the tax authorities. So, under current gift tax rules, if a policy with a present value of more than $10,000 is transferred to one person, gift taxes will be assessed. (See Chapter 16.) Even so, the amount of gift tax assessed will be far less than the tax cost of leaving the policy in your estate. This is because the proceeds payable under a policy when the insured dies are always considerably more than the worth of the policy while the insured lives.

Example: In 1998, Eugene transfers owner-ship of his universal life insurance policy to his son, David. The cash surrender value of the policy when he transfers it is $22,000. Under IRS rules, $12,000 worth of this value is subject to gift tax. Eugene dies four years after giving his son the insurance policy, which pays $300,000. None of this $300,000 is included in Eugene's federal taxable estate. (Nor are the proceeds considered income to David, for federal income tax purposes.)

HOW MUCH IS A LIFE INSURANCE POLICY WORTH FOR GIFT TAX PURPOSES?

If you're considering giving away an insurance policy, you'll want to know the present worth of that policy. If it's over the amount of the annual gift tax exclusion, gift tax will be assessed on the transaction. Under IRS rules, the value of a gift of a life insurance policy for gift tax purposes is its cost (what it would cost to buy a similar policy), not the cash surrender value. For fully paid-up policies, this value is easy to determine, but where further payments will be made, the value of the gift is harder to figure out. Under IRS rules, "all relevant facts and elements of value shall be considered." The IRS regulations use phrases like, "the interpolated terminated reserve as of the date of the gift, plus any prepaid premiums," as a method for determining value. (IRS Reg. 25.2512-1.) Yes, these words are bizarre. All you need do with them, however, is repeat them slowly to your insurance company. They will then give you the dollar value, for gift tax purposes, of your policy.

Fortunately, most insurance companies will provide, on request, an informal estimate of the gift tax value of a policy before you make the actual gift. They will also provide the appropriate forms (usually Treasury Department Form 938) for submission with the gift tax return, if need be.

---

3. How to Transfer Ownership of Your Policy

You can give away ownership of your life insurance policy by signing a simple document, called an "assignment" or a "transfer." To do this, notify the insurance company, and use its assignment or trans-fer form. There's normally no charge to make the change. Also, the policy itself will usually have to be changed to specify that the insured is no longer the owner.

After the policy is transferred, the new owner should make all premium payments, unless of course the policy is fully paid up. If the previous owner makes payments, the IRS might contend that the previous owner was keeping an "incident of owner-ship," so the proceeds of the policy must be included in the deceased owner's federally taxable estate—precisely what you're trying to avoid. If the new owner doesn't have sufficient funds to make the payments, you can give her money to be used for these payments.

If you give a paid-for single-premium policy to a new owner, there's no question about who makes future payments. There aren't any. Because it's paid for in full once it's purchased, single-premium life can be a particularly convenient type of policy to give to a new owner in order to reduce the giver's estate taxes. However, there can be a drawback here, too. The value of the policy, at the time of the gift, may exceed the amount that can be given free of gift tax (cur-rently, $10,000 or less). If so, gift tax will be assessed on all value over the gift tax exempt amount. By contrast, if the giver gives a policy not subject to gift tax, and then every year gives the new owner no more than the gift tax exempt amount to pay for annual premiums, no gift tax will be assessed.

4. Life Insurance Trusts

An irrevocable life insurance trust is a legal entity you create while you live for the purpose of owning life insurance you previously owned. An irrevocable trust is, like a corporation, simply a legal entity, distinct from any human being. (These trusts are covered in more depth in Chapter 21, Section B.)

Once you transfer ownership of life insurance to the trust, it owns the policy, not you. So the proceeds aren't part of your estate.

Why create a life insurance trust, rather than simply transfer a life insurance policy to someone else? One reason can be that there's no one you want to give your policy to. In other words, you want to get the proceeds out of your taxable estate, but you want to exert legal control over the policy and avoid the risks of having an insurance policy on your life owned by someone else—perhaps a spouse or child you don't trust to pay policy premiums. For example, the trust could specify that the policy must be kept in effect while you live, eliminating the risk that a new owner of the policy could decide to cash it in.

Example: Marcie is the divorced mother of two children, in their 20s, who will be her beneficiaries. Neither is sensible with money. Marcie has an estate of $400,000, plus universal life insurance which will pay $500,000 at her death. She want to be sure her estate will not be liable for estate taxes, and so desires to transfer ownership of her policy. However, there's no one Marcie trusts enough to give her policy to outright. With the controls she can impose through a trust, however, she decides it's safe to allow her sister, the person she's closest to, to be the trustee of a life insurance trust for the policy. She creates a formal trust, and transfers ownership of the life insurance policy to that trust. After Marcie's death, her sister will handle the money for the children under the terms of the trust document.

There are strict requirements governing life insurance trusts. If you want to gain the estate tax savings:

- The life insurance trust must be irrevocable. If you retain the right to revoke the trust, you will be considered the owner of the policy, and the proceeds will be taxed in your estate upon death.

- You cannot be the trustee.

- You must establish the trust at least three years before your death. If the trust has not existed for at least three years when you die, the trust is disregarded, for estate tax purposes, and the proceeds are included in your taxable estate.

Get legal help for a life insurance trust. If you want to explore using a life insurance trust, you'll need to see a lawyer. Tax complexities must be considered: How will future premium payments be made? If the person establishing the trust makes the payments directly, or even indirectly, how will that affect estate taxes? Personal concerns also have to be carefully evaluated. Crucially, who will be the trustee? Or, suppose you have a child after the trust becomes operational? Or a child gets divorced? Or marries or remarries? There aren't any standard answers to these questions. You have to carefully work out what you want. ■

13

RETIREMENT BENEFITS

A. Social Security 13/2
B. Individual Retirement Programs 13/3
    1. Traditional Individual Retirement Programs 13/3
    2. Roth IRAs 13/4
    3. 401(k) Accounts 13/4
C. Pensions 13/5
    1. Regular Payments Upon Retirement 13/6
    2. Lump Sum Payment 13/6
    3. Rolling Pension Funds Into an IRA or
       Another Pension Plan 13/6
D. Choosing Beneficiaries for Your Retirement Programs 13/7
    1. Naming Your Spouse 13/7
    2. Naming Others as Beneficiaries 13/8
    3. Naming Your Living Trust as Beneficiary 13/9
    4. Naming an Irrevocable Trust as Beneficiary 13/9
E. Using Disclaimers for Retirement Accounts 13/9
F. Probate and Taxes 13/10
    1. Probate 13/10
    2. Estate Tax 13/10
    3. Income Tax 13/11

When they retire, most people are entitled to payments from one or more retirement programs, such as Social Security payments, military benefits, private or public employee pensions, union pension plans or an individual retirement program.

Obviously, when you do your estate planning, you need to take into account any retirement benefits you or other family members will have coming. For example, a married couple should consider each spouse's retirement income. If a surviving spouse can expect generous monthly pension checks that will cover living expenses, with a little left over, the other spouse may understandably decide to leave at least some money and property directly to children or friends. Similarly, buying a life insurance policy on the life of a breadwinner makes great sense if there will be little continuing income should he or she die, and much less if a generous pension is in the offing.

If you don't already know, be sure you learn what to expect on that magic day when you retire—and what your family can expect after your death. We know of people who have discovered they were never covered by a pension plan at all. And when someone has divorced, the former spouse may have a legal interest in retirement funds that can greatly complicate any distributions.

Planning for a financially comfortable retirement can be complicated, and we don't get into that subject here. This chapter covers the basics of retirement plans as estate planning devices: how common kinds of retirement benefits—Social Security, individual retirement programs and pensions—are transferred after death, and the impact of choosing beneficiaries to inherit these benefits.

Beat the Nursing Home Trap, by Joseph Matthews (Nolo Press).

Tax Savvy for Small Business, by Frederick W. Daily (Nolo Press).

A. SOCIAL SECURITY

The most extensive retirement program in the United States is the federal Social Security system. Despite periodic anxieties that the program will run out of money, it has always managed to make regular payments to millions and continues to do so. Payments usually begin at age 65 (although it's possible to elect to receive smaller payments at age 55, or even younger if you become blind or disabled).

Social Security also provides payments to many surviving relatives of covered wage-earners, even if these people are not entitled to payments based on their own earnings record.

These people usually receive some benefits based on a deceased wage-earner's record:

- **Surviving spouses.** A widower or widow who is 65 or older receives, for life, 100% of the deceased spouse's Social Security benefits if the deceased spouse was over 65 at death. A surviving spouse who is between 60 and 65 gets a smaller amount. Remarriage after age 60 doesn't terminate benefits. A surviving spouse cannot receive double benefits, both on the basis of the deceased spouse and because of his own Social Security contribution. However, the surviving spouse can choose to receive whichever payment is larger.

- **Former spouses.** If the marriage lasted at least ten years, a divorced ex-spouse of the deceased person, who does not remarry before age 60, receives payment for life. It's possible for both a surviving spouse and an ex-spouse to collect Social Security based on the same deceased wage-earner. A divorced ex-spouse can receive full benefits at age 65, and reduced benefits from age 60.

- **Unmarried children.** Children up to 18 (or 19, if attending high school full time) receive benefits.

- **Children disabled before age 22.** These children can get benefits for as long as they're disabled. This program is of particular interest to parents with a mentally or physically disadvantaged child who will need lifetime care. It means they can create an ongoing "special needs" trust (see Chapter 25, Trusts and Other Devices for Imposing Controls Over Property, Section B) to supplement Social Security income; they don't have to start from scratch.

- **Other dependents.** Under certain circumstances, grandchildren, great-grandchildren, and dependent parents age 62 or older may be eligible for payments.

In addition, Social Security pays one lump-sum death payment of $255 to the surviving spouse or child eligible for benefits.

People under 70 who receive Social Security payments—their own or as the survivor of a deceased worker—may have the payments reduced if they work. If earnings exceed "exempt amounts" set by law, payments are cut. Anyone over 70, however, can earn an unlimited amount without any reduction in payment.

Social Security, Medicare and Pensions, by Joseph Matthews (Nolo Press), explains how to find out what you and your family members can expect to receive in the way of Social Security payments.

B. INDIVIDUAL RETIREMENT PROGRAMS

In addition to depending on Social Security and savings and investments, many people contribute regularly to one or more individual retirement programs to provide them with assets when they get older. These programs are not designed to be estate planning devices. There may be nothing left in a program account when the owner/beneficiary dies. However, often there is money left, sometimes large amounts, so it's important that you consider the possible effects of your individual retirement programs on your estate planning.

1. Traditional Individual Retirement Programs

As you doubtless know, individual retirement programs, such as profit-sharing plans (formerly called Keogh plans), regular IRAs (Individual Retirement Accounts), and SEP-IRAs are retirement plans you fund yourself. The money you contribute is tax-deductible (within limits); you don't pay tax on the earnings, either, until you withdraw them after retirement. You are in charge of how the money is invested.

A profit-sharing plan is for the self-employed, as is usually a SEP-IRA. By contrast, any income earner can create a regular IRA by making annual contributions. Currently, annual contributions of up to $2,000 are tax-deductible if you aren't covered by a company retirement plan (this deduction is phased out for high earners). You can contribute more, but you can't take the tax deduction.

If you withdraw money early—usually before age 59-1/2—a penalty is imposed, unless you are disabled or the money is used for educational expenses or for first-time home buying (this amount has a limit).

You must begin to take money from your account when you reach age 70-1/2. Then the percentage of the total that you must withdraw each year is determined by your statistical life expectancy, or your life expectancy and that of the beneficiary you've named to inherit any remaining funds at your death. (If the beneficiary is more than ten years younger than you, the IRS treats the beneficiary as only ten years younger, for calculating required withdrawal amounts.) In theory, this means that all of the funds in the program will be used up by the time you and the beneficiary have both died. And, of course, you can withdraw more than the minimum required amount if you decide to, and deplete the account that way.

All money remaining in an individual retirement program (if there is any) at the death of the owner goes to a named beneficiary or beneficiaries free of probate. You simply specify the beneficiary or beneficiaries on the account documents. The money can be paid in a lump sum or in installments. (See Section D, below.)

2. Roth IRAs

A new kind of individual retirement account became available in 1998. Named after Senator William Roth, the Roth IRA differs from the traditional IRAs just discussed.

You fund a Roth IRA with money that has already been taxed. As in a regular IRA, the money is allowed to grow tax-free until it is withdrawn. But when you do withdraw it, no further tax is due as long as the money was in the account at least five years.

The biggest difference, for estate planning purposes, between regular IRAs (and most retirement plans) and a Roth IRA is that you don't have to start withdrawing money from a Roth IRA when you reach age 70-1/2. In fact, you can still contribute to it after that age and leave the money intact for your heirs.

The tax penalty for withdrawing funds before age 59-1/2, however, does apply to a Roth IRA, with several exceptions. Again, there is no penalty if you are disabled. There is also no penalty if funds are paid to a beneficiary upon the death of the individual. And you may take money out penalty-free to buy a first-time house, not only for yourself, but also for a child, grandchild or parent.

Annual contributions are currently limited to $2,000 a year. Individuals who earn over a certain amount are limited to lesser amounts.

Roth IRAs are so new that many particular situations have not yet been addressed by the IRS. For instance, it is possible to convert a regular IRA into a Roth IRA upon payment of all income tax due to date on the account. If this sounds appealing to you, see an accountant for the latest word from the IRS.

- IRS Publication 590 provides detailed (and complex) information on personal retirement arrangements, such as IRAs.

- IRS Publication 560 covers retirement plans for the self-employed, such as profit-sharing plans.

3. 401(k) Accounts

Many employers now offer employees what are called 401(k) plans or 403(b) plans. (The 401(k) is for businesses, the 403(b) for nonprofit corporations and government workers.) Employees defer a portion of their wages, having them paid instead into the retirement plan. Many employers match these funds or at least make some contribution to the account. It's up to the employees whether or not to participate.

Money in your account is invested, according to your direction, in investments offered by the plan administrator. That money grows (at least you hope it grows) tax-free over the years until you withdraw it. In some cases, you can retire at age 55 and take money out without penalty. You must begin withdrawing it at age 70-1/2. At your death, the beneficiary you named receives whatever funds are left in the account. If you are married, the beneficiary must be your surviving spouse unless your spouse signed an agreement giving up this right. (See Section D below.)

If the money contributed to the plan was never taxed, every withdrawal is subject to income tax. If part of the contribution consisted of money that was taxed previously, a formula will be used to figure out what portion of the withdrawal is subject to income tax. The interest that has been accruing in the account tax-free is also subject to income tax.

C. PENSIONS

A pension, unlike an individual retirement program, is not under your control. Your company sets up a pension plan, and determines what rights you receive. You may acquire the right to receive payments— perhaps generous ones—and this right may extend to your surviving spouse or perhaps other beneficiaries, depending on the pension program. But you don't have any say over how the money in a pension fund is invested, and you have only limited say (at most) over how and when you receive benefits.

SPECIFIC PENSION PROGRAMS

There are many types of pensions: military, railroad, union, and so on. The benefits these programs may provide depend on the specifics of each program. Check the rules of each program that applies to you.

No law requires an employer to offer a pension plan. And there's no legal requirement that a pension plan pay benefits to a surviving spouse or anyone else. Some are generous, some are miserly, and some don't even bother to say "tough luck, friend."

PENSION PLAN LAWS

ERISA, the federal law covering pensions, requires that every pension plan spell out who is eligible for coverage. Plans do not have to include all workers, but they cannot legally be structured to benefit only top executives or otherwise discriminate—for example, by excluding older workers.

If you are eligible to participate in your employer's pension program, you are entitled to several documents:

- **A summary plan description.** Explains the basics of how your plan operates. ERISA requires that you be given it within 90 days after you begin participating in a pension plan, and that you must be given any updates to it.

  This document will tell you the formula for vesting in the plan, if it is a plan that includes vesting. A vesting plan means that you must work for a certain required period to be eligible for benefits. A formula is used to determine your benefits and the contributions that your employer will make to the plan. The summary will also tell you whether or not your pension is insured.

- **A summary annual report.** A yearly accounting of your pension plan's financial condition and operations.

- **Survivor coverage data.** A statement of how much your plan would pay to a surviving spouse or beneficiary should you die. Your plan administrator is also required to give you a detailed, individual statement of the pension benefits you have earned if you request it in writing or are going to stop participating in the plan because, for example, you change employers. You have the right to one such statement per year.

When you are ready to retire, you are indeed fortunate if your pension plan office provides tax assistance. For instance, money contributed during certain years may be taxed at different rates. It is truly necessary to get the tax help you need. A one-time visit to a good accountant will pay off in the long run.

1. Regular Payments Upon Retirement

Upon retirement, many people, if they have the choice, opt to draw a monthly sum from their pension plans. The amount of the payments depends on many factors, as defined by the plan, including: how long you worked, what your salary was, how much was contributed, your age and the age of the beneficiary you have named to receive payments upon your death. The payments will continue for your lifetime. If you have named a beneficiary, such as a spouse, to also receive payments, the amount of the monthly payment will be slightly adjusted to account for the beneficiary's age.

> **Example:** Jon retires at age 65. His wife, Sita, is six years younger than he is. Their monthly payment from Jon's pension plan is slightly less than if he had been the sole beneficiary of the plan, to account for the extra years of life expectancy for Sita.

2. Lump Sum Payment

Some pension plans allow employees to take the entire amount in their retirement accounts (based on age and amount contributed, plus interest and account earnings) in one lump sum. A number of people choose to do this, believing that they can

invest the money and get a greater return than regular payments would bring. Or some may just want the money to buy their dream ship to sail around the world.

Whatever the reason, if you wish to take a lump sum and the plan allows it, you must get tax advice. Again, part of the amount may be taxable, part not and another part at different rates. In some cases, you are allowed to average the income tax on the amount withdrawn (although it is still due unless you "roll it over" into an IRA—see below).

3. Rolling Pension Funds Into an IRA or Another Pension Plan

One option available for taking pension funds, if your plan allows it and if you are not yet 70-1/2, the age when distributions must begin, is to roll the money over. You put your pension funds directly into an IRA and defer income tax until later. The money will continue to grow tax-free until it is distributed to you.

> **Example:** Lars takes early retirement at age 62 from Acme Plastics. He has a healthy income from real estate he has bought over the years. He requests the pension plan administrator to directly roll (distribute) his entire pension fund to his IRA at the Able Investment Bank.

You can also roll over money in a company retirement fund if the company discontinues the plan, and you have what's called a "vested interest" in the plan. In other words, you have the right to obtain the money set aside for you in the plan if the company goes broke, or just decides to discontinue the retirement plan, for whatever reason. When you receive your money, you have 60 days to put it into (roll it over) a new (or existing) IRA in your name. If the money is not rolled over into an IRA within 60 days, the money is then treated as having been distributed to you. You will owe income tax on the money, plus a 10% penalty charge for a premature distribution of retirement funds if you are under 59-1/2 years old.

What if you simply change jobs? Depending on the companies involved, you may have the option of leaving your benefits in the old plan where they will continue to grow tax-free. Or you may take them and roll them into your IRA. Or, if both companies allow it, you may roll the old benefits directly into a new pension plan.

Example: Maude has worked for Sunshine Graphics for 15 years. She is offered a position at a higher salary in another city. She checks with both pension plans and discovers that she can have her old benefits distributed directly into her new pension plan with no tax due until she retires and starts withdrawing money.

Publications on Pension Plans. IRS Publication 575 discusses the rules for many pension plans, but it's not easy reading.

A number of brochures on pensions, which are easier to understand, are available from The American Association of Retired Persons (AARP), 601 E Street NW, Washington, DC 20049, 202-434-2277, and The Pension Rights Center, 918 16th Street, NW; Suite 704, Washington, DC 20006, 202-296-3778.

If you want help understanding the details of your pension or retirement plan and can't get what you want on your own, you'll need to see a pension-plan expert, or a lawyer knowledgeable in this specialized field.

D. CHOOSING BENEFICIARIES FOR YOUR RETIREMENT PROGRAMS

Retirement accounts often contain money when the account owner dies. Sometimes, they are a significant part of an estate. Choosing who will inherit these retirement funds may be one of the most important estate planning decisions you make.

You can (and should) always name a beneficiary for an individual retirement program: an IRA, profit-sharing or 401(k) account. If you have vested rights in a pension, you may also be able to name a beneficiary to inherit your vested rights.

1. Naming Your Spouse

Many married people name their spouse as the beneficiary of their retirement funds. They want to support their spouses, and in larger estates, defer estate tax. Leaving assets to the surviving spouse postpones tax, under the marital deduction, until the death of the surviving spouse.

If you have a 401(k) plan, you must name your spouse as the beneficiary unless the spouse signs a waiver. Most pension plans follow the same rule, imposed by federal law. Different laws apply to individual retirement programs like IRAs or profit-sharing plans; you can name anyone you choose as beneficiary. However, in community property states, the spouse has a legal interest in money the other spouse has earned unless that spouse signs a document giving up the interest. This can affect both individual retirement programs and pension funds.

Spouses, as retirement program beneficiaries, get several breaks that other beneficiaries don't. A surviving spouse who inherits the money as beneficiary of an individual retirement program account can have the money paid out over the same period of time she would have had if she had created the plan herself. Another advantage given only to a surviving spouse is the choice of rolling retirement funds over. For example, a spouse can take pension fund money in a lump sum and roll it into his or her own retirement plan. This defers income tax for the surviving spouse and allows the money to continue to grow tax-free until the spouse reaches mandatory withdrawal age.

With personal retirement programs like IRAs, if the beneficiary is the surviving spouse, the spouse can elect to treat the IRA as her own.

Example: Oho names his spouse Kia as the beneficiary for his IRA. When Oho dies, Kia is only 55 years old. She converts the IRA into one of her own, and it continues to grow tax-free until she reaches the required age for distribution.

If your estate is large enough to face estate tax, you can still leave any funds remaining in your retirement accounts to your spouse. Your personal estate tax exemption can be applied to property left to other beneficiaries.

Example: Randolph dies in 2006, with an estate of $2 million, including $300,000 in a profit sharing plan. His spouse, Rose, is the beneficiary of these funds, so they will not be subject to estate tax because of the marital deduction. Randolph had placed his other assets in an AB trust, with income to go to Rose. Since the amount of these assets is over the personal exemption of $1 million for 2006, some estate tax is due when he dies. (See Chapter 15.) But at Rose's death, those trust assets—including any growth in value—will pass tax-free to their children.

2. Naming Others as Beneficiaries

For one reason or another, some people name a child or other person as beneficiary. These beneficiaries may have some options regarding how they receive the money over time. In fact, fairly complicated rules can apply to the beneficiary's choice.

In some cases, the beneficiary can elect to take the money remaining in the account in lump sums, sometimes distributed over several years.

Other beneficiaries may receive installment payments based on life expectancy. These options are a complex matter, and it's usually wise to consult a tax expert.

If you are attempting to equalize gifts you leave to your children (as many folks do), and retirement funds seem likely to be part of your estate, remember the income tax consequences. The beneficiary of a retirement program (except funds in a Roth IRA) will have to pay income tax on any money received.

Example: Trish wants to be completely fair and equal to her two children. She leaves her house, worth $300,000, to her son. She designates her daughter as the beneficiary of her SEP-IRA, also worth $300,000 now. The daughter's inheritance is not equal to her brother's even if the SEP-IRA is still worth $300,000 at Trish's death, because it is reduced by the income tax she will pay.

3. Naming Your Living Trust as Beneficiary

Should you name your living trust (assuming you have one) as the beneficiary of your retirement programs? Usually it's not a good idea. Here's why.

- Because no probate is needed to transfer funds in a retirement account to the named beneficiary in the first place, there is no need to name your living trust as beneficiary in an effort to avoid probate.

- When you name a person as a beneficiary, minimum withdrawals will be based on estimates of how long both you and the beneficiary, such as your spouse or mate, will live. By contrast, if you name a living trust, minimum withdrawals are based only on your own life expectancy. So if you name the trust as beneficiary, a higher amount of money must be withdrawn each year (assuming a human beneficiary is younger than you are). This increases the likelihood that little or no money will be left in the account at your death.

- At your death, all money remaining in the account must be distributed within five years. Longer distribution periods are available if you name an individual to be beneficiary.

4. Naming an Irrevocable Trust as Beneficiary

Sometimes designating an irrevocable trust to receive what's left in your individual retirement accounts at your death can make sense. You can accomplish this by naming the trustee of the trust as the beneficiary.

One good reason for wanting to do this is when the beneficiaries are minors and need their money managed by a trustee. The same is true if the beneficiary is incapable—for whatever reason—of managing money. If the trust is properly structured and irrevocable, payments can be received based on the life expectancy of the oldest beneficiary.

Retirement benefits and AB trusts. It is possible to leave retirement funds directly to the trustee of Trust A of your AB trust, and to obtain lifetime distributions for the beneficiary of the trust. This kind of retirement planning is complicated, and expert help is a must. The trust that will receive retirement funds must be irrevocable when it receives the money, and the trustee's powers have to meet strict IRS rules. Usually, the retirement plan administrator must have a copy of the document. Whether you have already retired also affects how the trust is drawn. A good estate lawyer can prepare this kind of trust plan to take effect at your death.

E. USING DISCLAIMERS FOR RETIREMENT ACCOUNTS

Disclaimers are explained at length in Chapter 22. Basically, an inheritor can refuse (disclaim) property left to him or her, causing the property to go to someone else. Disclaimers can save on estate tax for people with large estates and substantial sums left in retirement programs.

This is one way it can be done. You set up a formula AB trust that will hold the amount of your personal exemption in the year you die. (See Chapter 18, Section C.) You also designate your spouse as the primary beneficiary of your retirement programs. But you designate the trustee of the trust (usually your spouse) as the alternate beneficiary for these programs. At your death, if the amount in the AB trust isn't enough to take advantage of the entire personal tax exemption, your spouse can disclaim some or all of the retirement benefits and direct them to Trust A. Your spouse, of course, will be entitled to the benefits of the trust.

Example: Lola drafts an AB trust that will pay the income to her husband Riki for his life. She names Riki as the beneficiary of her individual retirement program. She names the trustee of the AB trust (also Riki) as the alternate beneficiary for these programs. Lola dies in the year 2002, when the personal estate tax exemption is $700,000. The retirement program contains $300,000, and her other assets are worth $600,000. Riki disclaims $100,000 of the benefits, so they go into the trust with her other $600,000 of assets. The total in the trust is now $700,000, the full exempt amount.

A spousal disclaimer can also send retirement benefits into a trust for the benefit of children or simply outright to others.

Example: Ron and Didi have a combined estate worth $1.6 million. They have left everything to each other with their children as alternate beneficiaries. Didi is the primary beneficiary of Ron's 401(k) program, and their children are the alternate beneficiaries. When Ron dies in 2002, Didi disclaims enough of Ron's property, including what remains in his IRA, to equal $700,000, the amount of the

personal exemption for that year. All of the disclaimed property goes to the children, and Ron has made full use of his personal estate tax exemption.

F. PROBATE AND TAXES

No matter what the assets in your estate are, you want to avoid probate and minimize any taxes that may be owed to the government when you die. Funds left in your retirement programs at your death are no exception.

1. Probate

Money in an individual retirement program (such as a IRA, Roth IRA or 401(k) account) that is left to a named beneficiary at the owner's death does not go through probate. The plan administrator pays the funds directly to the named beneficiary.

If a surviving spouse or other beneficiary is entitled to receive pension payments under the terms of a pension earned by a deceased worker, those don't go through probate either. Again, they're paid directly to the recipient.

2. Estate Tax

The money you leave in an individual retirement program—for example, the remaining balance in an IRA, profit-sharing account, 401(k) plan or pension—is subject to federal estate tax. It doesn't matter how the funds are paid out, whether in a lump sum or over time. The value in the program at your death is part of your estate for estate tax purposes.

If the value of your estate exceeds the amount of the personal estate tax exemption, estate taxes will be assessed. Of course, if a surviving spouse inherits the retirement benefits, this money is not taxable, because of the unlimited marital deduction.

In rare instances, pension funds for a few people who retired before 1984 are wholly or partially exempt from estate tax. Changes in the law which now include these funds in the taxable estate are not retroactive to a small group. If you think you may be in this group, see a lawyer or accountant.

3. Income Tax

Generally, no income tax is due on inherited money. For example, if you leave a bank account to your son, he won't have to report it as income. Rules are different for some tax-advantaged retirement programs, however. Someone who inherits the funds in an individual retirement program, such as a traditional IRA account or 401(k) account, must pay income tax on the money. That's because when the money was socked away in the account over (usually) many years, the contributions were tax-deductible, and the income accumulated without being taxed.

The money in one of the new "Roth IRAs," however, is not taxed when the beneficiary inherits it. That's because contributions to the Roth IRA are not tax-deductible when made. Income from contributions that have been in the account for at least five years is not taxed when it's withdrawn, either before or after the death of the account owner. ∎

14

STATE LAW EXEMPTIONS FROM NORMAL PROBATE

A. Using Your State Laws in Estate Planning 14/2

B. State Law Probate Exemption Rules 14/3

    1. Reading the State Law Probate Exemption Chart 14/3

C. Summary Chart of State Law Exceptions to Normal Probate 14/5

D. California Exemptions From Normal Probate 14/10

    1. The Community Property Petition 14/10

    2. The Affidavit of Right 14/10

E. New York Exemptions From Normal Probate 14/12

F. Texas Exemptions From Normal Probate 14/12

    1. The Affidavit 14/12

    2. Summary Probate 14/13

G. Florida Exemptions From Normal Probate 14/13

    1. Simplified Family Probate 14/13

    2. Summary Probate 14/14

    3. No Probate Required 14/14

As a general rule, property left in a will must go through probate. However, there are exceptions; a number of states' laws allow a certain amount of property to be left by will, either free of probate or subject only to a very simplified probate process. (Aside from the laws discussed in this chapter, some states have very specialized methods to avoid probate in specific circumstances, such as property owned by a military veteran who dies in a state veterans' home, or permitting payment of small amounts of wages. Since these statutes almost always involve small amounts of property in narrow circumstances, and aren't germane to planning an estate, they're not covered here.)

It's important to understand that there are two basic types of state law exemptions to normal probate. Some states have adopted one type, some the other, some both, and some neither. A summary of each state's laws is provided in Section C.

The first type eliminates probate altogether for lower amounts of property, ranging from $5,000 to $100,000, depending on the state. Where this type of law is in effect, a qualifying inheritor can collect property left to her simply by completing an affidavit (a statement signed under oath), and presenting it to the person or institution holding the property, plus whatever additional proof state law requires—such as a copy of the will, a certified copy of the death certificate, or personal identification. The property is then turned over to the inheritor.

The second type of state law exemption to probate provides a summary court procedure far simpler—and normally faster and cheaper—than conventional probate. Again, the size of estates which can use this procedure varies greatly by state. How simplified the procedure is, and what types of property it applies to, also varies by state. Some summary procedures are easy enough to do without a lawyer. Others still require a lawyer, so they result in at least some attorney's fees, court costs and delays.

A. USING YOUR STATE LAWS IN ESTATE PLANNING

How can you use your state's probate exemption laws in your estate planning? Generally, by combining a will that qualifies for probate exemption or simplified probate under state law with other probate avoidance techniques for the rest of your property.

Few, if any, readers of this book will be able to totally avoid probate solely by using their state's probate exemptions laws. Most estates are worth far more than the amount of property that can normally be transferred completely free of probate. And even when it comes to planning to use simplified probate procedures (in the states where they are available), most people will find that only a small part of their property qualifies.

Fortunately, in California, New York and in some other states, the probate-exemption law can still be valuable, even if you have a larger estate than the exempted amount. This is because you can combine this method with other probate avoidance devices, such as living trusts and joint tenancy. For instance, in California, property worth up to $100,000 can be transferred by affidavit probate-free, with the rest of a larger estate transferred by other probate avoidance devices, such as a living trust. Similarly, in New York, property worth up to $10,000 can be left probate-free by will, and the rest of the estate transferred by other probate avoidance devices.

Unfortunately, many states' probate exemption laws don't allow this method to be combined with other probate avoidance devices. In these states, it is the total amount of property in the entire estate, not just the property subject to the will, which determines if the dollar limits of the probate exemption law has been exceeded.

B. STATE LAW PROBATE EXEMPTION RULES

Each state's probate exemption law is different. Section C, below, contains a chart summarizing each state's law. This chart provides three categories of information for each state:

1. the amount of property that can be transferred by will free of probate

2. the amount of property that can be transferred by will through summary (simplified) probate

3. the citation to the state's probate exemption statute.

The summary chart is designed to give you sufficient information to decide whether you want to investigate the usefulness of your state law for your estate planning. The chart does not set forth the operational details of your state's laws, which would require a book in itself.

The chart does not tell you whether you can combine your state law's exemptions from normal probate (if any) with other probate avoidance methods. This is because, oddly, state laws often ignore this issue; what is permitted is, in many states, determined by accepted custom and practice in the legal community. If you learn from the chart that your state has a probate exemption law you might want to use in your estate planning by preparing a will that qualifies for the exemptions, you should take one or more of the following steps to determine your state's precise requirements and accepted legal practice:

• Read the statute yourself. In Chapter 29, Using Lawyers, Section B, you'll find a discussion of how to research legal statutes.

• Contact the clerk of the court that handles probate matters to see if they provide any consumer information or will answer your questions.

• Consult a lawyer who knows about the accepted practices. Since you're asking for limited and specific information, the fee should be reasonable.

The probate exemption rules and legal customs of the four largest states—California, New York, Texas and Florida—are examined in detail in Sections D, E, F and G. In California and New York, the accepted legal practice is that you can combine a will qualifying for probate exemption laws with other probate avoidance methods.

The chart in Section C also does not define how each state's law calculates its dollar limit to determine the value of exempted property—that is, whether the dollar limit is defined as your gross estate (the market value of everything you own with no deduction for debts), net estate (market value less debts and encumbrances) or net probate estate (net value only of property left by will). Obviously this can make a big difference. A car worth $10,000 on which you owe $8,500 might be valued at $10,000 in one state and $1,500 in another. Again, the statutes are normally not clear on this. How the value of property that can be transferred free of probate is calculated in each state is usually a matter of custom in the legal community, so you will need to check further if this is relevant to your situation.

1. Reading the State Law Probate Exemption Chart

As an example of how to read the probate exemption law chart in Section C, let's look at Illinois. The chart provides:

ILLINOIS

Category 1: Affidavit Procedure Instead of Probate: $50,000, personal property; also, if all beneficiaries agree, and are Illinois residents, and no death taxes due.

Category 2: Summary Probate: $50,000

Category 3: Statutes: Illinois Comp. Statutes, Ch. 755, 5/25-1, 5/9-8+.

**NOTE FOR CALIFORNIA
AND WISCONSIN READERS**

Residents of these states are fortunate. In California, Nolo Press publishes a detailed book, *How to Probate an Estate*, by Julia Nissley, which explains step-by-step how California's probate exemption law works and provides all forms necessary to handle a probate proceeding without a lawyer.

In Wisconsin, there's a state-mandated procedure for probating a deceased's solely owned property informally without an attorney. An interested person applies to the Probate Registrar, who will assist with the informal probate.

Category 1: Affidavit Procedure

This category tells you whether the state has a law allowing any property left by a will to be transferred by affidavit, free of normal probate. If there's a "no" in this category, the state doesn't have this kind of law.

Using an affidavit procedure means the inheritor(s) state, on a notarized document, that the will of the deceased left them certain specified property. To obtain this property, the inheritor simply presents the affidavit, personal ID, and a copy of the deceased's will to whoever holds that property. No actual court proceedings (notice of hearings, hearings before a judge, formal pleadings) are required. Some states still require a relatively simple affidavit to be filed with a court or court clerk. Others don't require any judicial filing at all.

If a dollar figure is listed in this first category, it means the state has a law allowing property up to that dollar amount to be transferred by this affidavit method. Next, any restrictions on the type of property that can be transferred are listed; many states

allow only personal property, not real estate, to be transferred. In any case, real estate is normally so valuable these days that it's unlikely that an interest in real estate would fall below the dollar limits, unless that ownership is a small percentage of the property. Finally, any restrictions on who the beneficiaries can be are summarized ("only to spouse and children").

The chart doesn't set forth the precise information which must be in an affidavit if one is required. To determine this, you'll need to research your state's law.

To return to our Illinois example, Category 1 states "$50,000, personal property." This means personal property worth up to $50,000 can be transferred by affidavit, free of probate, in Illinois. Then this category states "also, if all beneficiaries agree, and are Illinois residents, and no state inheritance or federal estate taxes are due." This means there is another type of affidavit transfer, free from normal probate in Illinois, if the specified requirements are met—all beneficiaries must be Illinois residents and agree to the transfer outside of probate, and no death taxes can be owed.

Category 2: Summary Probate

This category provides the same kind of information as Category 1 for those state laws that offer a simplified version of probate for certain amounts of property. Many states, such as Illinois, have both an affidavit procedure and a separate summary probate procedure. The actual operation of these laws varies widely from state to state. Most importantly, the statutes themselves usually don't specify that probate attorney fees must be reduced from those charged for normal probate.

To return again to our Illinois example, Category 2 reads: "$50,000," without any other restrictions. This means property worth up to $50,000—either personal property or real estate—can be transferred by summary probate.

Category 3: Statutes

This category gives you the legal citation to your state's probate exemption statute.

If your state has two statutes, one for an affidavit procedure and another for simplified probate, both citations are given. In such cases, the first citation given is to the affidavit procedure statute. The citations are to the first section of the relevant statute. The + symbol after the statutory cite means that other pertinent sections follow the first section that is noted.

The Illinois example states: "Illinois Comp. Statutes, Ch. 755, Sections 25-1, 9-8+." This means the statute for the $50,000 affidavit procedure is found in Section 25-1. The statute for the $50,000 summary probate procedure is found in Section 9-8 and those immediately following.

C. SUMMARY CHART OF STATE LAW EXCEPTIONS TO NORMAL PROBATE

ALABAMA

Affidavit Procedure Instead of Probate: No

Summary Probate: $3,000, personal property only

Statute: Code of Alabama, Title 43, Ch. 2, Section 690+

ALASKA

Affidavit Procedure Instead of Probate: $15,000 less liens and encumbrances, personal property only

Summary Probate: Up to value of homestead allowance, exempt property, family allowance, expenses of death and last illness

Statute: Alaska Statutes Title 13, Ch. 6, Sections 13.16.080, 690, 695

ARIZONA

Affidavit Procedure Instead of Probate: $30,000 personal property and $50,000 real property

Summary Probate: No (except for certain types of family property)

Statute: Arizona Revised Statutes, Sections 14-3971+; 14-1973+

ARKANSAS

Affidavit Procedure Instead of Probate: $50,000

Summary Probate: Limited amounts only for surviving spouse or dependents

Statute: Arkansas Statutes Annotated, Sections 28-41-101+

CALIFORNIA

Affidavit Procedure Instead of Probate: $100,000 with real estate interest no more than $10,000, plus any vehicles owned by the deceased (cars, mobile homes, trucks), up to $5,000 of back pay.

Summary Probate: To surviving spouse, community property petition, no dollar limit

Statute: California Probate Code, Sections 13050, 13100+,13200+, 13500+

COLORADO

Affidavit Procedure Instead of Probate: Net estate, $27,000

Summary Probate: Limited to amount set by several other statutes

Statute: Colorado Revised Statutes, Sections 15-12-1201+

CONNECTICUT

Affidavit Procedure Instead of Probate: $20,000 personal property only

Summary Probate: No

Statute: Connecticut General Statutes Annotated Sections 45a-273+

DELAWARE

Affidavit Procedure Instead of Probate: $20,000, personal property only. Beneficiaries can only be spouse, grandparents, children or other specified relations, trustee or funeral director

Summary Probate: No

Statute: Delaware Code Annotated, Title 12, Sections 2306+

DISTRICT OF COLUMBIA

Affidavit Procedure Instead of Probate: No (except if entire estate is no more than two cars, and all debts and taxes are paid)

Summary Probate: $15,000

Statute: District of Columbia Code, Title 20, Sections 351+

FLORIDA

Affidavit Procedure Instead of Probate: No (except for very small estates with less than specified exceptions)

Summary Probate: $25,000, property in Florida subject to probate; $60,000 for estate left primarily to family members

Statute: Florida Statutes Annotated, Sections 735.301+; 735.201+, 735.101+

GEORGIA

Affidavit Procedure Instead of Probate: No

Summary Probate: No

Statute: No applicable statute

HAWAII

Affidavit Procedure Instead of Probate: $60,000 personal property

Summary Probate: $20,000 property in Hawaii

Statute: Hawaii Revised Statutes, Sections 560:3-1201; 560: 3-1205

IDAHO

Affidavit Procedure Instead of Probate: $50,000 personal property

Summary Probate: No dollar limit (Statute provides useful do-it-yourself instructions)

Statute: Idaho Code, Sections 15-3-1201+

ILLINOIS

Affidavit Procedure Instead of Probate: $50,000, personal property; also if all beneficiaries agree and are Illinois residents and no death taxes due

Summary Probate: $50,000 and no U.S. taxes due

Statute: Illinois Comp. Statutes, Ch. 755, 5/25-1, 5/9-8+

INDIANA

Affidavit Procedure Instead of Probate: $15,000, personal property only

Summary Probate: No dollar limit (if all heirs agree)

Statute: Indiana Statutes Annotated, Sections 29-1-8-1+; 29-1-7.5 1+

IOWA

Affidavit Procedure Instead of Probate: $10,000 personal property

Summary Probate: $50,000 total value of probate and non-probate Iowa property only to surviving spouse or child; $15,000 to parent or grandchild; $10,000 to relatives

Statute: Iowa Code Annotated, Sections 635.1+

KANSAS

Affidavit Procedure Instead of Probate: $10,000 personal property

Summary Probate: No dollar limit on some estates if court and heirs agree

Statute: Kansas Statutes Annotated, Sections 59-3201+; 3301+

KENTUCKY

Affidavit Procedure Instead of Probate: No

Summary Probate: By agreement of all beneficiaries; when spouse receives probate estate under $7,500 (intestate only, or where renunciation of will by spouse)

Statute: Kentucky Revised Statutes, Sections 391.030+, 395.450+

LOUISIANA

This book is not applicable in the state of Louisiana.

MAINE

Affidavit Procedure Instead of Probate: $10,000

Summary Probate: Limited to amounts set by several other statutes

Statute: Maine Revised Statutes Annotated, Title 18A, Sections 3-1201+

MARYLAND

Affidavit Procedure Instead of Probate: No

Summary Probate: Up to $20,000 of Maryland probate property

Statute: Annotated Code of Maryland, Estates and Trusts Law, Sections 5-601+

MASSACHUSETTS

Affidavit Procedure Instead of Probate: No

Summary Probate: $15,000, personal property; for close family only

Statute: Massachusetts General Laws Annotated, Ch. 195, Sections 16, 16A

MICHIGAN

Affidavit Procedure Instead of Probate: No

Summary Probate: $15,000

Statute: Michigan Compiled Laws Annotated, Section 700.102

MINNESOTA

Affidavit Procedure Instead of Probate: $20,000 personal property

Summary Probate: Court can order if certain conditions met

Statute: Minnesota Statutes Annotated, Sections 524.3-120

MISSISSIPPI

Affidavit Procedure Instead of Probate: No

Summary Probate: $500 or less

Statute: Not applicable

MISSOURI

Affidavit Procedure Instead of Probate: No

Summary Probate: $40,000

Statute: Annotated Missouri Statutes, Trusts & Estates, Section 473.097

MONTANA

Affidavit Procedure Instead of Probate: $7,500

Summary Probate: Limited to amounts set by several other statutes

Statute: Montana Code Annotated, Title 72-3-1103+, 72-2-412+

NEBRASKA

Affidavit Procedure Instead of Probate: $25,000 personal property

Summary Probate: Limited to amounts set by several other statutes

Statute: Revised Statutes of Nebraska, Sections 30-24, 125+

NEVADA

Affidavit Procedure Instead of Probate: $20,000 personal property if no real estate owned in Nevada

Summary Probate: $200,000 with court approval

Statute: Nevada Revised Statutes, Sections 145.010+, 146.070+

NEW HAMPSHIRE

Affidavit Procedure Instead of Probate: No

Summary Probate: $10,000 personal property

Statute: New Hampshire Revised Statutes Annotated, Ch. 553: 31+

NEW JERSEY

Affidavit Procedure Instead of Probate: No (only if no valid will, then $10,000 to spouse, or $5,000 to others)

Summary Probate: No

Statute: New Jersey Statutes Annotated, 3B-10-3; 3B-10-4

NEW MEXICO

Affidavit Procedure Instead of Probate: $30,000

Summary Probate: Limited to amounts set by several other statutes

Statute: New Mexico Statutes, 45-3-1202, 45-3-1204

NEW YORK

Affidavit Procedure Instead of Probate: $10,000 personal property (plus certain types of exempt property, to specified dollar limits)

Summary Probate: $10,000 personal property

Statute: Consolidated Laws of New York Annotated, Surrogates' Court Procedure Act, Sections 1301+

NORTH CAROLINA

Affidavit Procedure Instead of Probate: No

Summary Probate: No (if no valid will $10,000, personal property only; $20,000 for surviving spouse)

Statute: General Statutes of North Carolina, Ch. 28A, Sections 25-1.1

NORTH DAKOTA

Affidavit Procedure Instead of Probate: $15,000 personal property

Summary Probate: Up to amounts of family allowances plus costs of death

Statute: North Dakota Code, Sections 30.1-23-01+, 30.1-23-01+

OHIO

Affidavit Procedure Instead of Probate: No

Summary Probate: $35,000; $85,000 if to spouse

Statute: Ohio Revised Code Annotated, Section 2113.03

OKLAHOMA

Affidavit Procedure Instead of Probate: No

Summary Probate: $60,000

Statute: Oklahoma Statutes Annotated, Title 58 Sections 241+

OREGON

Affidavit Procedure Instead of Probate: No

Summary Probate: $140,000; personal property $50,000, real estate $90,000

Statute: Oregon Revised Statutes, Sections 114.505+

PENNSYLVANIA

Affidavit Procedure Instead of Probate: No

Summary Probate: $25,000 personal property

Statute: Pennsylvania Statutes Annotated, Title 20, Sections 3102+

RHODE ISLAND

Affidavit Procedure Instead of Probate: No (except person(s) who paid funeral costs, last bills, etc., up to $10,000)

Summary Probate: No

Statute: No applicable statute

SOUTH CAROLINA

Affidavit Procedure Instead of Probate: $10,000 (but affidavit must be approved and signed by a judge)

Summary Probate: $10,000

Statute: Code of Laws of South Carolina, Sections 62, 3-1201; 3-1203+

SOUTH DAKOTA

Affidavit Procedure Instead of Probate: $25,000

Summary Probate: No limit

Statute: South Dakota Codified Laws, Sections 29A-3-1201+

TENNESSEE

Affidavit Procedure Instead of Probate: $25,000

Summary Probate: No

Statute: Tennessee Code Annotated, Title 30, Ch. 4, Sections 101+

TEXAS

Affidavit Procedure Instead of Probate: $50,000

Summary Probate: No dollar limit if will writer provides for "independent administration" and that no other action shall be had in county court, other than the probating and recording of the will and the return of an inventory; also, if all beneficiaries agree

Statute: Texas Probate Code, Sections 137+, 145+

UTAH

Affidavit Procedure Instead of Probate: $25,000 personal property

Summary Probate: Limited to amounts set by several other statutes

Statute: Utah Code, Title 75, Section 3-1201+

VERMONT

Affidavit Procedure Instead of Probate: No

Summary Probate: Limited to amounts set by several other statutes

Statute: Vermont Statutes Annotated, Title 14, Sections 1901+

VIRGINIA

Affidavit Procedure Instead of Probate: $10,000 personal property

Summary Probate: Benefits, wages up to $10,000

Statute: Code of Virginia, Sections 64.1-132.1+, 64.1-123.1+

WASHINGTON

Affidavit Procedure Instead of Probate: $60,000 personal property

Summary Probate: Executor may ask court for "nonintervention powers," regardless of size of estate

Statute: Revised Code of Washington Annotated, Title 11, Sections 62.010+; Title 11, Sections 68.010+

WEST VIRGINIA

Affidavit Procedure Instead of Probate: $100,000

Summary Probate: No

Statute: West Virginia Code, Ch. 44-3A-1+

WISCONSIN

Affidavit Procedure Instead of Probate: $10,000 personal property

Summary Probate: $30,000, and all to surviving spouse or child, plus Wisconsin has an "informal" probate procedure that doesn't require a lawyer and has no dollar limit

Statute: Wisconsin Statues Annotated: Sections 867.01+

WYOMING

Affidavit Procedure Instead of Probate: $70,000 personal property

Summary Probate: $70,000

Statute: Wyoming Statutes Annotated, Sections 2-1-201; 2-1-205+.

D. CALIFORNIA EXEMPTIONS FROM NORMAL PROBATE

California has two simplified probate procedures:

1. The "community property petition" allowing all property left to a surviving spouse to be transferred by summary probate.

2. What is commonly called the "Affidavit of Right" allowing property worth less than $100,000 (with no interest in real estate in excess of $10,000) to be transferred by affidavit entirely outside of probate.

1. The Community Property Petition

By using a community property petition, a surviving spouse can readily obtain the portion of the deceased spouse's property left to him or her. It makes no difference if it's jointly owned community property or the deceased's separately owned property. There's also no dollar limit either on the total amount of the estate or the amount of the property that can be transferred to the surviving spouse by this method. Even if some of the deceased's share of the community property is left to others, the spouse can still obtain his or her portion of it left through a will, without the expense of probate.

The community property petition is a simple one-page, two-sided form that can be prepared by a surviving spouse who is entitled to property of a deceased spouse, either from a will (or by intestate succession if there was no will). The petition is filed with the local probate court, which sets a hearing date. Notice of the hearing must be given to certain people, including all beneficiaries named in the will. Then the hearing is held, and the property ordered transferred to the surviving spouse unless someone contests the petition, which is very rare. Most surviving spouses should be able to handle the process without a lawyer. The steps needed to file a community property petition, and to get court approval, are explained in detail, including sample forms, in *How to Probate an Estate,* by Julia Nissley (Nolo Press).

2. The Affidavit of Right

If a deceased left, by will or intestate, property worth less than $100,000 (net), and no interest in real estate worth more than $10,000, the inheritors can obtain that estate by filing a simple form, called an "Affidavit of Right," with the people or organizations holding the deceased's property. In addition, the inheritors can also collect all of the following under the Affidavit of Right: all vehicles owned by the deceased, no matter how much they are worth, and up to $5,000 owed in back pay.

The purpose of the Affidavit of Right is to enable beneficiaries of a deceased who left a small estate to obtain the cash and other assets they inherit immediately without a lot of red tape. The Affidavit can be prepared and filed by the inheritors who are entitled to the deceased's estate, either by will or, if there's no will, by the laws of intestate inheritance. If there's more than one beneficiary under a will (or the intestacy laws if there's no will), all the beneficiaries must sign the Affidavit of Right. A copy of the Affidavit is then presented to persons or organizations holding the property left by the will; they must promptly release the assets to the beneficiaries. Sample forms and instructions are contained in *How to Probate an Estate*.

An Affidavit of Right doesn't have to be filed with any state agency. No court or other probate proceeding is required. There's no procedure to verify the inheritor's declaration that the deceased's net estate in California is worth less than $100,000. In this one instance, the law appears to go by the honor system.

Example: Harry Billings dies in Los Angeles, California. Under Harry's will, his sole beneficiary is his adult daughter, Myra. Harry owned no real estate. His estate is worth $108,500: bank accounts and a CD worth $83,000; personal property (stereo, household furniture, two valuable cameras, some rare books) worth $15,000; a car (owned outright by Harry) with a market value of $6,000, and back wages owed Harry (unused vacation pay) of $2,500. Even though Harry's estate, left by his will, exceeds $100,000, all of the property may be collected by Myra by Affidavit of Right. His bank CD and personal possessions are worth a total of $98,000, under the $100,000 limit. Separate exemptions allow his car and back wages to be claimed by Affidavit of Right.

Myra simply completes the Affidavit of Right and attaches one copy each of the will and death certificate. She then gives one set of the documents, plus her own ID, to Harry's bank, a second set to the holder of the personal property—in this case, Harry's landlord—a third set to the DMV, and a fourth set to the company that owes Harry the back vacation pay. The bank and the holder of Harry's personal property must release it to her promptly. The Department of Motor Vehicles will re-register the car in Myra's name, and the company will turn over Harry's unused vacation pay to her.

The affidavit must state, under oath, that the total value of the deceased's estate in California is less than $100,000. However, as we've explained, certain items, such as vehicles, no matter how much they are worth, don't count towards the $100,000 limit.

What about property transferred by a living trust or a P.O.D account? The California Affidavit of Right statute isn't clear, but as previously mentioned, standard California legal practice has long assumed that property in a living trust or informal bank trust account isn't counted toward the $100,000 limit. Thus, savvy Californians with good-sized estates can use other probate avoidance methods to pass their valuable items of property and rely on the Affidavit of Right procedure to avoid probate on the rest, which they leave by will.

Example: Teresa has an estate consisting of a house in Los Angeles, with equity of $620,000; a summer cottage at Stinson Beach, with equity $220,000; the furnishings of her two houses worth $40,000; a bank account of $60,000; life insurance with total proceeds of $300,000; and various heirlooms worth a total of $45,000. At her death, she wants her children to receive all her property, except for the heirlooms, which she intends to give to cousins and other relatives. Teresa doesn't think of herself as wealthy; she acquired her houses years ago, when "a dollar was a dollar" and prices low. But, in fact, her taxable estate now amounts to $1,285,000. Rather than have all this property subject to regular probate:

1. She transfers the houses and furnishings into a living trust, naming her children as beneficiaries;

2. She creates a pay-on-death bank account for her savings, naming her children as beneficiaries;

3. She assigns ownership of her life insurance policies outright to their beneficiaries, and gives up all ownership of them.

Now, only the heirlooms, worth less than the $100,000 limit, remain in Teresa's probate estate. She can distribute these by her will, and her inheritors can claim them simply and speedily by using an Affidavit of Right.

E. NEW YORK EXEMPTIONS FROM NORMAL PROBATE

New York law provides a simple affidavit procedure for estates of personal property (no real estate) worth less than $10,000. Also, New York exempts entirely certain property of a deceased spouse which is set aside for the surviving spouse, or the deceased's minor children if there is no spouse. The total amount of property that can be set aside for family use is $26,150. All property set aside for family use isn't counted as part of the $10,000 that can be exempted from probate. Thus, in theory, an estate totaling $36,150 could be eligible for New York's affidavit procedure if the maximum amount of exempt property was left to a surviving spouse or minor children.

Under the affidavit procedure, the deceased's executor acts as a "voluntary administrator," preparing an affidavit listing the property and beneficiaries and filing it with the probate court (called "surrogate court") clerk. The executor then has authority to collect the deceased's personal property and distribute it to the beneficiaries according to the will or the intestacy laws.

Although the statute isn't clear about whether the affidavit procedure can be combined with other probate avoidance devices, accepted New York legal practice is that it can be. Thus, if someone transfers big-ticket items like houses and stocks by living trust, she could then transfer small personal gifts, with a total value less than $10,000, by her will free from normal probate.

F. TEXAS EXEMPTIONS FROM NORMAL PROBATE

Texas has two simplified probate procedures:

1. An affidavit allowing summary transfer of estates worth less than $50,000, and

2. A summary probate with no dollar limit.

Also, Texas probate is normally quite easy. An uncontested estate can be heard by a judge within ten days of filing a petition for probate.

1. The Affidavit

Under Texas law, certain small estates can be transformed by use of an affidavit filed with the clerk of the county court. The affidavit procedure is available only if the estate has a value, excluding homestead and exempt property, of less than $50,000. Exempt property is certain community property that can be "set aside" for the deceased's family—including an automobile, household furnishings, clothing, food and last wages. Homestead property is community real estate protected under Texas law.

All people receiving part of the estate must sign and swear to the affidavit. The affidavit can be filed by any beneficiaries only if 30 days have passed since the deceased has died and no one has filed for formal probate. The affidavit must list the estate's assets and liabilities, the names and addresses of all people receiving part of the estate, and whether they take that property under a will or by intestacy. If there's a will, it usually is filed with the affidavit, although this isn't required by statute.

After the affidavit is filed with the county court clerk, the clerk issues a certified copy of the affidavit to the beneficiaries. The affidavit entitles them to collect debts owed the deceased, collect and receive estate property, and to have title to automobiles, bank accounts, stocks or real estate transferred. Anyone releasing or transferring property to someone on the authority of such an affidavit is discharged from any further liability on that property. The responsibility for properly disposing of the property falls on the person collecting the property with the affidavit.

A creditor can prevent collection by affidavit by filing for formal probate within 30 days of the deceased's death. And, even if collection by affidavit occurs, those who collect the deceased's property remain liable to the estate creditors.

Since all those with rights to an estate must sign it, the affidavit is practical only if there are no disputes about who should receive what property. Although title can be transferred under the authority of the affidavit, others can dispute it later. (Where title may be disputed, the summary probate procedure described in Subsection 2 below may be more desirable.)

The $50,000 ceiling on the value of estates collectable by affidavit limits the use of the process. Most estates containing real property will exceed that limit. However, since the value of homestead property is excluded from the $50,000 calculation, the statute may have broader use with small estates where a spouse survives the deceased. This is because the family home, often the principal estate asset, would be excluded from the $50,000 calculation. Therefore, where there's a surviving spouse, a moderate-sized estate, including the family house, might be collected and distributed by the affidavit process. However, where there's no surviving spouse, the affidavit process will be limited to small estates.

2. Summary Probate

The Texas summary probate has no dollar limitations. Under this procedure, the executor files an application to probate the will, exactly as in traditional probate. A hearing is then held on the validity of the will. If the will is proved valid, and it's shown that the estate has no outstanding debts or other problems, the court orders summary probate, dispensing with many of the tedious steps of normal probate. (The Texas statute is silent, however, on whether summary probate means reduced attorney's fees, which means that it's up to your inheritors to negotiate.)

The court order admitting the will to probate serves the same function as the small estate's affidavit: it authorizes transfer of the deceased's property to those entitled to it under the will. Furthermore, since the will has been proved in court, title to the property transferred in this way isn't open to challenge. This avoids a problem that sometimes occurs with the small estates affidavit. However, Texas summary probate does normally require an attorney, so the major drawback of normal probate is still involved and it isn't therefore a satisfactory alternative to probate avoidance techniques.

G. FLORIDA EXEMPTIONS FROM NORMAL PROBATE

Florida law provides three different types of simplified probate. However, all three are quite restrictive, and therefore of no use to most Florida readers who wish to plan their estate to avoid probate.

1. Simplified Family Probate

Family members can petition a probate court for a simplified form of probate (called "Family administration") if there's a will and:

- The primary beneficiaries are the surviving spouse and/or "lineal descendants" (children, grandchildren) and/or "lineal ascendants" (parents, grandparents, etc.) and any specific or general gift to others is a minor part of the estate; and

- The value of the gross estate, for federal estate tax purposes, is less than $60,000; and

- The entire estate consists of personal property.

Thus a family, or any member, can petition for simplified probate only if the total net value of the estate is less than $60,000, and none of it is real estate. This net value includes all property transferred by a living trust or joint tenancy, since the worth of this property is included in the federal taxable estate. Most Florida readers' estates will be well in excess of the relatively modest amount of $60,000.

2. Summary Probate

Florida law also permits summary probate (called "summary administration") if 1) there's a will and 2) the value of the entire estate subject to probate in Florida, less the value of property exempt from creditors, is less than $25,000. Property exempt from creditors, under Florida law, includes:

- Homestead property (basically, a house) exempted under the state constitution

- A "family allowance," specified by statute, for the support of the deceased's family

- Certain property of a deceased—household furniture, furnishings and appliances (up to a net value of $10,000), cars, personal effects not disposed of by will (up to a net value of $1,000)—which can be claimed by the deceased's surviving spouse or minor children.

Again, this summary probate procedure is too restrictive for most people to use. The amount left by will can't exceed $25,000. The wording of the statute indicates that you can't combine summary Florida probate with probate avoidance devices. For example, suppose you transfer all your property by living trust, except for personal items worth $15,000 which you leave to a friend by a will. Can your friend obtain this property by "summary" probate? Probably not.

3. No Probate Required

For certain very small estates, Florida doesn't require probate. These estates can consist only of personal property, not real estate, that is:

- exempt from creditors under Florida law or the state constitution, and

- not worth more than "the amount of preferred funeral expenses and reasonable and necessary medical and hospital expenses of the last 60 days of the last illness." ■

15

ESTATE TAXES

A. Federal Estate Tax Exemptions 15/2

B. The Big Picture: Death Taxes and Gift Taxes 15/4

C. Will Your Estate Have to Pay Taxes? 15/5

    1. Estimating Your Net Worth 15/5

    2. Property Left to Your Spouse 15/6

    3. Special Rules for Non-Citizen Spouses 15/7

    4. Gifts to Charities 15/8

    5. Other Estate Tax Exemptions 15/8

D. Calculating and Paying Estate Taxes 15/9

    1. Filing a Federal Estate Tax Return 15/9

    2. Property Valuation 15/9

    3. How to Calculate Federal Estate Taxes 15/10

    4. Planning for Payment of Estate Tax 15/12

E. Reducing Federal Estate Taxes 15/12

    1. Give Away Property While You Live 15/13

    2. Create an Estate Tax-Saving Trust 15/13

F. The Federal Income Tax Basis of Inherited Property 15/13

G. State Death Taxes 15/14

    1. Your Residence for State Death Tax Purposes 15/15

    2. Estate Planning for State Death Taxes 15/15

    3. Summary of State Death Tax Rules 15/15

All U.S. citizens, and all others owning property in the U.S., are subject to federal death taxes, called "estate taxes." All property you own, whatever the form of ownership, and whether or not it goes through probate after your death, is subject to federal estate taxes.

Most people, however, don't have to worry about estate taxes—their estates aren't large enough to be taxed. Basically, no estate taxes are required if the net value of the "taxable estate" transferred at a person's death is less than $625,000 to $1 million, depending on the year of death. However, an estate where 50% or more of the total value is a family business or farm isn't subject to tax unless the total net estate exceeds $1.3 million.

If an estate is over the taxable amount, however, federal estate taxes can take a large bite. The tax rate is determined by the size of the taxable estate; the more you own, the higher the rate. The tax rate starts at 37% and rises to 55% for estates over $3 million.

In addition, a minority of states impose death taxes on property of a deceased who lived or owned real estate in that state.

When estate planners talk about estate or death taxes, the focus is almost always on federal taxes, which can devour much more of an estate than can state taxes.

A. FEDERAL ESTATE TAX EXEMPTIONS

Before worrying about federal estate taxes, obviously you'll want to assess whether you're likely to owe them. Several federal tax law exemptions and deductions allow you to leave substantial amounts of property free of estate taxes. The most important of these are:

- **The personal estate tax exemption** which allows a set dollar amount of property to pass tax-free, no matter whom it is left to (IRC Section 2010).

LEGAL CITATION: THE INTERNAL REVENUE CODE

You'll see a number of references in this and other chapters to the "IRC," which is the conventional abbreviation for a set of tax laws known as the Internal Revenue Code. The Internal Revenue Code can be found in Volume 26 of the United States Code, the collection of all federal statutes.

THE PERSONAL ESTATE TAX EXEMPTION

Year of Death	Amount of Personal Exemption
1998	$625,000
1999	$650,000
2000	$675,000
2001	$675,000
2002	$700,000
2003	$700,000
2004	$850,000
2005	$950,000
2006	$1,000,000
and after	$1,000,000

We use the term "estate tax threshold" to mean the amounts of the personal exemption in any and all years. Thus "estate tax threshold" refers to the existence of the exemption and the range of exempt amounts, from $625,000 to $1 million.

If your estate is over the amount of the personal exemption for the year of your death, taxes will be assessed unless other exemptions or deductions apply.

If you have made taxable gifts during your life, the amount of the personal exemption will be reduced. Currently, you can give property worth up to $10,000 per recipient in a calendar year free of gift tax. (See Chapter 16, Gifts and Gift Taxes.)

- **The marital deduction,** which exempts from estate tax *all* property left to a surviving spouse. (IRC Section 2056(a).) The marital deduction is not allowed for property left to non-citizen spouses. But the personal estate tax exemption can be used for property left to non-citizen spouses. (See Section C3, below, for more on leaving property to a non-citizen spouse.)

- **The charitable deduction,** which exempts all property left to a tax-exempt charity. (IRC Section 2055(a).)

- **The small business exemption,** this special exemption of up to $1.3 million, is discussed in Chapter 28, Family Business Estate Planning, Section B.

DEATH TAXES ON PROPERTY OUTSIDE THE UNITED STATES

If you own property or earn income in another country, your estate may well be subject to death taxes in that country. But also, if you earn income in another country, and are a U.S. citizen or resident, some or all of the property taxed by the other country may be taxed by the United States as well.

International estate death tax planning requires a lawyer. If you own property or earn income in another country, you'll definitely need legal help with your planning.

If your estate is likely to be subject to federal estate tax, you'll want to resolve several important questions, including:

- How can you eliminate, or at least reduce, those taxes and achieve your other estate planning goals?

- What source of funds will be used to pay estate taxes?

- Do you want to try to estimate now how much the tax is likely to be?

NO INCOME TAXES ON INHERITED PROPERTY

Because quite a number people worry about this, we want to state directly that someone who inherits property does not have to pay income taxes on the worth of inherited property. However, after a person inherits property, any income subsequently received from the property is regular income, and so subject to income tax.

Special rules for capital gain taxes on the sale of inherited property are discussed in Section F, below.

B. The Big Picture: Death Taxes and Gift Taxes

Before we get into the details of federal and state death taxes, let's pull back and look at the underlying reasons for these taxes.

Whether or not to tax property transferred at death is a decision that every society with private property makes for itself. In the days of "survival of the fittest" capitalism in 19th century America (oozing back currently), there were no federal estate taxes. By contrast, in some European countries today, death taxes take a very significant portion of larger estates. Modern America is somewhere in-between.

Trying to reduce death taxes to a minimum through estate planning is sometimes thought of as a form of lawyer's magic, by which taxes can be avoided completely no matter how large the estate. It's certainly true there is some gimmickry in some schemes of the very rich to avoid death taxes.

Indeed, avoiding or minimizing taxation at death has been criticized. Doubters maintain that it is a game for the rich, and that society would be better off if people couldn't pass immense sums from one generation to the next. Perhaps. Since neither of us stands to inherit big money, we're not zealous to protect estates of billionaires. Still, we've noticed that even many progressives seem to prefer to leave whatever wealth they've acquired to family, friends or worthy causes rather than have it turned over to the government.

Federal estate taxes are an attempt to balance two conflicting principles: First, everyone should be able to pass on property they've acquired; and second, this is not a land of aristocracy—some of the wealth of the rich should be returned at death to the public for the general welfare. To achieve this balance, estate tax policy attempts to distinguish between property of the middle class, which is exempt, and property of the wealthy. Overall, estate taxes achieve this balance. Particularly with the ongoing increases in estate tax exemptions that began in 1998, few estates will be subject to tax.

Under federal estate tax law, both taxable gifts made during one's life and the estate transferred at death are taxed at the same rate. The gift tax prevents wealthy people from giving away much or all of their property before they die and thus avoiding estate tax. Since the tax imposed on a taxable gift made during one's life is identical to the estate tax imposed on the same value of property left on death, there is no tax incentive to give large amounts of property away.

Example 1: Marcus makes taxable gifts totaling $245,000 during his life. This amount is deducted from his personal estate tax exemption. When he dies in 1999, his net estate is worth $555,000.

To determine the tax owed, first calculate the available exemption.

The personal exemption for 1999:	$650,000
Subtract taxable gifts:	$245,000
Remaining exemption	$405,000

Then determine the taxable amount

Net estate	$555,000
Subtract remaining exemption	$405,000
Taxable amount	$150,000

The tax rate is 37% for a tax of $55,500.

Example 2: Mathew, Marcus's twin, makes no taxable gifts. He dies in 1999 with a net estate worth $800,000. Again, the personal exemption is $650,000, so $150,000 is subject to tax, at the same rate Marcus's estate paid, 37%. Mathew's estate also pays a total of $55,500 in taxes.

C. WILL YOUR ESTATE HAVE TO PAY TAXES?

Whether or not your estate will owe federal estate tax depends on several factors: the size of your estate, whom you leave it to and when you die.

1. Estimating Your Net Worth

You can't, of course, know what the value of your estate will be at your death. The best you can do is make a sensible estimate of your current net worth (assets minus liabilities). This should be sufficient for estate tax planning purposes.

If you completed the property worksheets in Chapter 4, Inventorying Your Property, Section B, you should have a ballpark estimate of your current net worth. If you didn't complete the property worksheet, you'll need to make some estimate, now, of your present net worth—unless you know it is well below the estate tax threshold. In that case, don't worry about estate taxes for the time being. If you later strike it rich, or semi-rich, that will be the time for you to learn about estate taxes and ways to reduce them.

Under federal estate tax law, most property is valued at its market value as of the date of the owner's death, less any debts on the property. However, a few types of property can be valued at less than their market value. Family farmland can be valued for its (continued) use as a farm, not at its highest possible market value. So can real estate used in a family business. So even if farmland would be worth more if sold to a developer to build an apartment complex or a shopping center, you don't have to use that higher value. (The specific tax rules on this are discussed in Chapter 28, Section B.)

Also, it may be hard to determine the value of some types of property, such as royalty rights or stock in a closely held corporation. Make your best guess—or pay for an expert's opinion.

2. Property Left to Your Spouse

As we stated earlier, all property left to your spouse at death is not subject to federal gift or estate taxes, no matter how much the property is worth. This is called the "marital deduction."

Example: Pedro leaves his wife Rebecca $5,770,000. No estate tax is assessed.

No marital deduction for property left to non-citizen spouse. If your spouse is not a U.S. citizen, property you leave her or him is not eligible for the marital deduction. The special estate tax rules that apply to non-citizen spouses are discussed below, in Section 3.

a. How the Marital Deduction Works

To stress the most important point about the marital deduction: It makes no difference how much money or property is given during life or passed at death to the surviving spouse. Whether it's a $500,000 house, $1.2 million in emeralds or a $500 million collection of Impressionist paintings, it's all exempt from estate tax. It makes no difference what legal form the property left to the surviving spouse is in—whether it's community property, joint tenancy property, "quasi-community" property or separate property.

The marital deduction is in addition to all other allowable estate tax deductions.

Example: Sue has an estate valued at $6.6 million. She leaves $600,000 to her children and $6 million to her husband. All Sue's property is exempt from federal estate taxes—the $6 million because of the marital deduction and the $600,000 because it is below the estate tax threshold.

b. How the Marital Deduction Can Be a Tax Trap

The fact that no federal estate tax is assessed when property is left to the surviving spouse can mislead people into thinking that leaving everything to a spouse must be the best thing to do. It often is not. The marital deduction can have a downside if members of a couple together own assets worth more than the amount of the personal estate tax exemption. That amount, as you know, ranges from $625,000 to $1 million, depending on the year of death. Increasing the size of the surviving spouse's estate can eventually result either in estate tax being assessed, when there otherwise would be none, or in higher estate taxes.

Example: Barbara and Tim are married; each has an estate of $600,000. If Tim leaves all his property to anyone but Barbara (or a tax-exempt charity), no tax will be owed because his property is under the estate tax threshold. If Tim leaves it all to Barbara, no tax will be due because of the marital deduction. However, if she dies with an estate of $1.2 million (her $600,000 plus her inheritance of $600,000), tax must be paid. Somewhere between $625,000 and $1 million of her property will be exempt, depending on the year of death, but at a minimum $200,000 will be subject to tax. If Barbara only owned her half of the original estate, no estate tax at all would be due.

This tax trap is particularly dangerous when both spouses are elderly. The survivor isn't likely to live long enough to really benefit from legally owning the deceased spouse's property.

It is often wiser, from an estate tax viewpoint, to use the personal exemptions of both members of the couple, rather than only one, as can occur if the marital deduction is used. The standard, and popular, way to avoid this tax trap is to create what's called an "AB" trust, which allows the surviving spouse to have income from and use of the deceased spouse's property, but never become the legal owner of it. Doing this allows the personal estate tax exemption to be used for each spouse's property. (See Chapter 18, Estate Tax-Saving Bypass Trusts, Section C, for an explanation of how these trusts work.) Another alternative is for each spouse to leave property directly to children or other beneficiaries. However, this leaves the surviving spouse without income or use of the deceased spouse's property, which many married couples don't want.

3. Special Rules for Non-Citizen Spouses

As we've said, no marital deduction is allowed for property one spouse leaves to the other if the surviving spouse is not a citizen of the United States. It doesn't matter that a non-citizen spouse was married to a U.S. citizen or is a legal resident of the U.S. The surviving spouse must be a U.S. citizen to be eligible for the marital deduction.

In contrast, property a non-citizen spouse leaves to a citizen spouse is eligible for the marital deduction. Congress seems to have feared that non-citizen spouses would leave the U.S. after the death of their spouses, whisking away their wealth to foreign lands, so it would never be subject to U.S. tax. Presumably, Congress thought that citizen spouses will remain here.

Even without the marital deduction, a U.S. citizen can leave a non-citizen spouse a good deal of property free of estate tax. The personal estate tax exemption can be used for property left to anyone, including a non-citizen spouse. So property worth between $625,000 and $1 million (to say it again, depending on the year of death) can be left tax-free to a non-citizen spouse.

Example: Lucy leaves all her property to her husband Devi, a non-citizen. When she prepares her estate plan, her estate is worth $500,000. Whatever the year of her death, this amount will be under the estate tax threshold. However, in 1999 Lucy unexpectedly inherits $300,000 and shortly thereafter dies. Her total estate is $800,000. The personal estate tax exemption for 1999 is $650,000. Because Devi is not a citizen, $150,000 of Lucy's estate is subject to tax.

There are two ways, however, that a spouse can give or leave property to a non-citizen spouse and obtain additional estate tax benefits. First, U.S. gift tax law provides that a citizen spouse can give the other, non-citizen, spouse up to $100,000 per year free of gift tax. (IRC Section 2525(i)(2).) Thus, a citizen spouse with an estate exceeding $900,000 could be sure that no estate tax could be owed by giving the non-citizen spouse $100,000 in each of three years, then leaving him the remaining $600,000 at death.

Second, all property left by one spouse to a non-citizen spouse in what's called a "Qualified Domestic Trust" (QDOT) is not subject to estate tax until the non-citizen spouse dies. (See Chapter 19, Section B.)

Tax planning for non-citizen spouses. These special rules mean that if you're married to a non-citizen and have an estate worth more than $625,000, you should see a lawyer.

If a non-citizen spouse becomes a naturalized U.S. citizen before the deceased spouse's estate tax return must be filed (nine months after death), the surviving spouse is then entitled to the full marital deduction. For a prosperous couple residing in the U.S., and who are not both U.S. citizens, obtaining the estate tax advantage of the marital deduction can be one good reason for becoming U.S. citizens.

4. Gifts to Charities

All gifts you make while you live or leave at your death to tax-exempt charitable organizations are exempt from federal estate and gift taxes. If you plan to make large charitable gifts, be sure you've checked out whether the organizations are in fact tax-exempt. The most common way an organization establishes that it's a tax-exempt charity is by obtaining a ruling from the IRS, under Internal Revenue Code Section 501(c)(3). (These organizations are referred to, in tax lingo, as "501(c)(3) corporations.") Many charitable institutions, particularly colleges and universities, provide extensive information about tax-exempt gift-giving and offer a variety of gift plans.

Making substantial gifts to charities through trusts is discussed in Chapter 20, Charitable Trusts.

5. Other Estate Tax Exemptions

There are also federal estate tax deductions for:

- funeral expenses, which can range from minimal to many thousands of dollars
- estate expenses, such as probate fees; again, a wide variety is possible here, up to tens of thousands of dollars or even more, depending on the worth of the probate estate and state probate fee rules
- any claims against the estate, and
- state death tax paid, and death tax imposed by foreign countries on property the deceased owned there.

For most people, these exemptions are relatively minor. It's rarely necessary to estimate them to see whether or not your estate is likely to be liable for estate taxes. If you're close enough to the tax threshold so that these deductions may matter, you're close enough to consider estate tax planning.

D. CALCULATING AND PAYING ESTATE TAXES

Here we discuss when an estate tax return must be filed, property valuation for estate tax purposes, how to calculate the amount of taxes owed, and when the taxes must be paid.

1. Filing a Federal Estate Tax Return

A tax return, IRS Form 706, must be filed for an estate with a gross value exceeding the amount of the personal exemption for the year of death. That's *gross*, not net. This means that, for purposes of deciding whether a return must be filed, you don't subtract the amount a deceased owed from what he owned. An estate tax return may have to be filed even though no taxes are actually due.

> **Example:** Dan's estate consists of cash (money market funds) of $200,000, household goods, a car and other personal property worth $50,000 and two houses, both heavily mortgaged.
>
> Here are the gross and net estate figures:

Gross Estate	Net Estate
$200,000 cash	$200,000 cash
$50,000 personal property	$50,000 personal property
$400,000 house	$100,000 equity in house
$200,000 house	$100,000 equity in house
$850,000 total	$450,000 total

Dan dies in 1999, when the personal estate tax exemption is $650,000. Because Dan's gross estate exceeds this amount, an estate tax return must be filed. But because his net estate is well under this amount, no tax will be due.

If an estate tax return must be filed, it's due within nine months of the death of the deceased, but extensions can be granted.

The executor of the deceased's will is the person legally responsible for filing an estate tax return, if due. If there is no will, but there is a living trust, the job falls to the successor trustee named in the trust.

In perhaps the most common situation, a person creates both a will and living trust and names the same person to serve as executor and successor trustee. If the executor and successor trustee are not the same person, both must cooperate so the executor has sufficient financial information to determine if an estate tax return need be filed, and what the right figures are if one is required.

Filing a return. If a federal estate tax return does need to be filed, a tax expert must be hired to prepare the Form 706. It is not an easy form to complete, and there are no good self-help materials available.

2. Property Valuation

Under federal law, a deceased's property can be valued as of the date of death, or six months afterwards (referred to in tax lingo as the "alternate valuation date"). Which valuation date is desirable for your estate is a matter your successor trustee and executor of your will must decide with a lawyer, and perhaps a tax adviser as well.

Example: Ellen dies on March 1, 1998. She owned real estate with a net worth of $1 million on that date. There's a sudden crash of real estate values in her area. Six months after her death, her real estate is valued at $824,000. Her executor takes advantage of the alternate valuation date to value her real estate at the lower amount, and so removes $176,000 from her taxable estate.

There are special valuation rules for family farms or real estate used in a family business. See Chapter 28, Section B.

3. How to Calculate Federal Estate Taxes

Most people don't need to bother with trying to estimate the amount of taxes their estates may have to pay. For them, the important issue is whether tax will likely be owed, not trying to guess the exact dollar amount of that tax. After all, they don't even have precise valuations of their property now, and they know those values will surely change by the time they die. However, if you want to try to make an estimate, or if you simply want to understand how estate taxes actually work, read on.

Technically, the personal estate tax exemption works by use of something called the "unified credit." The credit is called "unified" because the same tax rate applies to taxable lifetime gifts as to property left on death. The credit is the amount of tax that would otherwise be due on the exempt amount for the year of death, as shown below.

Unified Gift/Estate Tax Credit

Year of Death	Personal Exemption Credit	Estate Tax
1998	$625,000	$202,050
1999	$650,000	$211,300
2000	$675,000	$220,550
2001	$675,000	$220,550
2002	$700,000	$229,800
2003	$700,000	$229,800
2004	$850,000	$287,300
2005	$950,000	$326,300
2006	$1,000,000	$345,800
and after	$1,000,000	$345,800

The unified credit begins to be phased out for estates worth over $10 million and ends for estates worth over $21,040,000. (Still, we imagine that inheritors of such large estates will manage somehow.) The amount of the unified credit available at death is reduced if you made taxable gifts during your lifetime. (See Chapter 16.)

Here's how you use the estate tax credit to calculate the amount of tax owed.

- First, determine the amount of the net taxable estate, by subtracting all allowable deductions.

- Next, compute the "tentative tax" from the estate tax table below. This is the tax that would be due on the net estate if there were no unified credit (that is, no personal estate tax exemption).

- Finally, subtract the amount of the unified credit for the year of death from the tentative tax. The result is the tax actually owed.

What does all this translate to in reality? It means that if tax is owed, the rates start high. The lowest rate is a hefty 37% to 41%, depending on the year of death. If you die with an estate worth $750,000 in 1999, when the personal exemption is $650,000, the amount subject to tax is $100,000. However, the tax rate applied is not the rate for $100,000, but the rate for $750,000, or 37%. The tax owed is $37,000.

The tax rate increases to a maximum of 55% for estates over $3 million. Clearly this is a tax worth avoiding or minimizing to the extent you can legally do so.

Example 1: Bernie dies in 1999 and leaves his net estate of $3 million to his children. The tentative tax on $3 million, from Column C of the Unified Federal Estate and Gift Tax Rates chart, is $1,290,800. From this amount subtract the unified tax credit for 1999 of $211,300. The tax due is $1,079,500.

UNIFIED FEDERAL ESTATE AND GIFT TAX RATES

Column A net taxable estate over	Column B net taxable estate not over	Column C tax on amount in column A	Column D rate of tax on excess over amount in column A
$ 0	$10,000	$ 0	18%
10,000	20,000	1,800	20
20,000	40,000	3,800	22
40,000	60,000	8,200	24
60,000	80,000	13,000	26
80,000	100,000	18,200	28
100,000	150,000	23,800	30
150,000	250,000	38,800	32
250,000	500,000	70,800	34
500,000	750,000	155,800	37
750,000	1,000,000	248,300	39
1,000,000	1,250,000	345,800	41
1,250,000	1,500,000	448,300	43
1,500,000	2,000,000	555,800	45
2,000,000	2,500,000	780,800	49
2,500,000	3,000,000	1,025,800	53
3,000,000	infinity	1,290,800	55

Example 2: Todd dies in 2000 with a net estate worth $925,000, which he leaves equally to his friend Zeke and his sister Flo. Here is how Flo, the executor of Todd's estate, determines the tax due.

To begin, she uses the Tax Rate chart to figure the tentative tax due on $925,000. This is a three-part calculation.

- First, she looks at Column A and Column B and finds that $925,000 falls between $750,000 in Column A and $1 million in Column B. Column C lists the tentative tax on $750,000 as $248,300.

- Next, she calculates the tentative tax on the remaining $175,000 by multiplying this amount by the tax rate of 39% (Column D). The result is $68,250.

- Finally, she adds these two amounts together to get the total tentative tax.

Now that she's got the tentative tax figured, she can subtract the tax credit Todd's estate is entitled to. For deaths in the year 2000, the unified gift/estate tax credit is $220,550.

MORE INFORMATION ON FEDERAL ESTATE TAX LAWS

More detailed information about federal estate and gift taxes can be found in "Federal and Estate Gift Taxes," IRS Publication 448. It's available free at many IRS offices or online at www.irs.ustreas.gov.

You can also read the relevant federal tax statutes, if you dare to plunge into this morass of legalese. It is dense, even for tax professionals. Federal estate tax laws are found in the Internal Revenue Code, Volume 26 of the United States Code, the official collection of all federal statutes.

---

4. Planning for Payment of Estate Tax

Unless a will or living trust directs otherwise, IRS rules prorate estate taxes among the assets that go to people (except your spouse and non-charitable organizations). This means that those receiving a larger proportion of the estate pay a larger proportion of the taxes. If you want to vary this by having certain assets used to pay your estate taxes, you'll need to state that specifically in your will or living trust.

Be careful, however, if you make such arrangements. Sometimes payment of estate tax can become a real problem or even destroy an estate plan. Suppose, for example, you leave your house to your son and your stock and cash to your daughter. Any remaining assets pass to your husband. You want your son to receive the house free and clear of estate taxes, so you provide that estate taxes are to be paid out of your daughter's inheritance. To make sure your daughter isn't short-changed, you leave her what you think will be enough extra to pay the estate taxes on the house.

Over the years, the house more than doubles in value, but you've spent quite a bit of your cash and sold some of your stock. Come estate tax time, much of your daughter's inheritance goes to pay the estate taxes on the house. The result that is your son gets your house, which is worth twice what you figured on, and your daughter gets significantly less than you planned on. So, to point out the obvious, keep your estate planning in tune with your current financial situation, especially if you're using the payment of estate taxes to balance inheritances.

E. REDUCING FEDERAL ESTATE TAXES

What can you do to reduce federal estate taxes if you think your estate will be liable for them? Not as much as you might think, although for the very wealthy, high-priced experts do come up with ingenious, pushing-the-edge tax dodges. For the rest of us, aside from making use of the estate tax exemptions and deductions discussed above, there are only a few major ways you can lower estate taxes.

1. Give Away Property While You Live

While you're alive, you can give a certain amount of property each year free of estate/gift tax. Currently, you can give property worth $10,000 or less per person per year. A couple can give $20,000 a year tax-free to one person. Tax-exempt gift giving works well for people who can afford it, and can be particularly advantageous for those who have several children, grandchildren or other objects of their affection. (See Chapter 16, Gifts and Gift Taxes, Section E.)

Making gifts of portions of a family business or other business assets like stock options, can, in the right circumstances, significantly reduce or eliminate estate taxes. This use of gift-giving is discussed in Chapter 28, Section B.

2. Create an Estate Tax-Saving Trust

A number of different types of trusts can be used to save on overall estate taxes, depending on your circumstances and desires. We discuss these trusts in detail in Chapters 18 through 23. If you individually, or you and your spouse together, have an estate exceeding $625,000 to $1 million, be sure to check out those chapters carefully to determine if you might be able to use one or more of these trusts. Your final decision should be made only after consultation with an experienced estate planning lawyer.

F. The Federal Income Tax Basis of Inherited Property

Though it's not strictly speaking an estate tax matter, the question of what inherited property is valued at, for the purpose of calculating gain or loss from subsequent sale is, to many people, closely related. It is a tax question, and it can apply to property you leave. Because this issue matters to so many people, we discuss it here.

Let's start with a definition. The word "basis" means the value assigned to property from which taxable gain or loss on sale is determined. The concept of a property's basis is a tricky one, not made any easier by the fact that "basis" is not defined in the tax laws. When property is purchased, its basis is generally its cost. In fact, basis is often referred to as "cost basis." If you buy a painting for $5,000, for example, it has a basis equal to its cost—$5,000. If you sell the painting two months later for $16,000 (lucky you), your taxable profit is $11,000.

sale price	$16,000
minus basis	$5,000
gain	$11,000

The original cost basis can be adjusted up, for certain types of improvements to property, or down, for reasons like depreciation. If you make what's called a "capital improvement" to a house, such as putting in a new foundation, the cost of the improvement is added to the basis of the property. Capital improvements, very roughly, last more than a year.

Example: Green Is Good, Inc., bought an old barn to in which to design and make bicycles. The barn cost the company $270,000, so the company has a cost basis in it of $270,000. Over the next year, Green Is Good spent $230,000 for capital improvements to the barn, installing a new fire control system and a new roof.

Here's how the company determines the "adjusted basis"

original cost	$270,000
capital improvements	+$230,000
adjusted basis	$500,000

The company takes depreciation deductions for the barn on its income taxes of $30,000 over two years. The property's adjusted basis now becomes $470,000, since the deduction for depreciation lowers the adjusted basis of the property.

The barn is sold to T. Donald Bump (who plans to use the barn for a weekend getaway) for $600,000.

Green Is Good, Inc., determines its profit this way

Sale price	$600,000:
Subtract basis	-$470,000
Profit	$130,000

T. Donald's cost basis in the barn is $600,000.

Now to move to the tax basis of inherited property. *Under federal tax law, the basis of inherited property is "stepped up" to its fair market value at the date of the decedent's death.* Actually, this is a simplification of the rule, which is that the basis of inherited property is adjusted *up or down* to the market value as of the date of death. However, the assumption that prices of property rise over time is so ingrained in our economic life, whatever the short- or medium-term fluctuations, that the term commonly used is "stepped-up" basis. And in practice, for property owned for any long period of time, the inheritor's basis—the net value of the property at death of the original owner—is almost always higher than that of the original owner.

Example: During the two years that T. Donald owned the barn until his death in 1999, he made no capital improvements to the barn. At the time of his death, when the barn was inherited by T. Donald Jr., it had appreciated in value to $800,000.

T. Donald Jr.'s basis in the barn is stepped up to:	$800,000
T. Donald Jr. sells the barn three months later for:	$750,000
Subtract basis	-$800,000
T. Donald Jr.'s loss:	($50,000)

The fact that the basis of property is stepped up at the owner's death to its fair market value means that it's almost always desirable to hold on to highly appreciated property until it can pass at death. That way, your inheritors obtain the advantage of the stepped-up basis rule. Thus, if T. Donald sold the barn a year before he died, when it was worth $780,000, he would have had to pay federal taxes (and possibly state income taxes) on $180,000 ($780,000 sale price minus his $600,000 basis).

If T. Donald gave the barn to T. Donald Jr. during his lifetime, T. Donald Jr. would have had the same basis in the barn as T. Donald had—$600,000. Gifts made during life are not entitled to a stepped-up basis. Only transfers at death qualify for this desirable tax treatment.

G. STATE DEATH TAXES

Twenty-seven states and the District of Columbia have effectively abolished state death taxes. The rest impose death taxes on:

- all real estate owned in the state, no matter where the deceased lived; and

- the personal property (everything but real estate) of residents of the state.

1. Your Residence for State Death Tax Purposes

Technically, states that impose death taxes on residents do so on all persons "domiciled in the state." "Domicile" is a legal term of art. It means the state where you have your permanent residence, where you intend to make your home. Generally, it's clear where your domicile is. It's the state where you live most of the time, work, own a home and vote.

Sometimes, however, it's not so clear. If you have homes in different states, there may be no decisive evidence of which state is your domicile. For example, several states, eager for tax revenue, claimed that Howard Hughes was domiciled there. A less dramatic and more common example is a person who divides his time between homes in two states. In some circumstances, it's quite possible that more than one state would assert the person was domiciled there.

Example: Rita retired and moved from Michigan to North Carolina. However, she returns often to Michigan to visit her children, keeps several bank and brokerage accounts in Michigan, and never bothers to register to vote in North Carolina. Michigan might claim, on her death, that Rita remained domiciled there and never transferred her domicile to North Carolina.

If you do divide your residence between two or more states, make sure you make it clear which state you are domiciled in. Normally, this means being sure that you maintain all your major personal business contacts and vote in the state you claim as your domicile. Obviously, if one state doesn't have death taxes and the other is a high death tax state, you might want to establish your domicile in the no-tax state.

2. Estate Planning for State Death Taxes

If you live or own real estate in a state that has death taxes, it's sensible to consider the impact of those taxes. In many instances, the bite taken from estates by state death taxes is annoying, but relatively minor. However, in some states, larger bites can be taken, especially for property left to non-relatives. For example, Nebraska imposes a 15% death tax rate if $25,000 is left to a friend, but only 1% if it's left to your child. Also, in many states with inheritance taxes, there is no tax on property left to a surviving spouse. (See the Appendix, Chart I.) It's probably rare that someone would change the amount of property left to a beneficiary because of state death taxes, but you should at least evaluate the issue if it applies.

If your state has death taxes, it may have other laws that affect your estate planning as well. For example, some states with death taxes require a deceased's bank accounts or safe deposit boxes to be "sealed" until a release is obtained from tax officials. It's normally fairly quick and easy to do this, as long as the officials are convinced the estate has enough assets to pay the taxes.

3. Summary of State Death Tax Rules

Following is a summary of each state's death tax rules. You can look up the specifics of those death tax rules in the Appendix.

a. States That Have No Death Taxes

Nevada is the only state that has no death taxes at all.

b. States That Effectively Impose No Death Taxes

In many states, there's no reason to concern yourself with state death taxes when you plan your estate. These states do, technically, impose death taxes on estates that are subject to federal estate tax. In those instances, a state death tax return must be filed. However, the state tax is taken out of what is owed the IRS. In other words, part of the tax that would otherwise be included with the federal estate tax return is paid to state tax authorities instead. Your estate pays no additional taxes. This is commonly called a "pick-up" death tax.

The important point is that in these states, state death taxes are matters for accountants and estate tax preparers. They have no real impact on the amount of your estate that's left for your beneficiaries.

c. States That Impose Inheritance Taxes

"Inheritance" taxes are imposed on the receiver of inherited property, not the estate. Typically, state inheritance tax statutes divide receivers into different classes, such as "Class A, Husband or Wife," "Class B, immediate family— children, parents, etc.," "Class C, brothers, sisters, cousins, etc.," "Class D, all others." Each class receives different death tax exemptions and is taxed at a different rate. The general rule is that the highest exemption and lowest rate applies to spouses, or "Class A."

d. States That Impose Estate Taxes

Some states impose a tax, like the federal government's, on the taxable estate itself, without regard to who the beneficiaries are. For state estate tax purposes, the taxable estate is all real estate in the state, and all personal property of a person who was domiciled in the state, except personal property having a specific, real location in another state.

SUMMARY OF STATE DEATH TAX RULES

STATE	INHERITANCE TAXES?	ESTATE TAXES?	STATE	INHERITANCE TAXES?	ESTATE TAXES?
Alabama	effectively, no	effectively, no	Missouri	effectively, no	effectively, no
Alaska	effectively, no	effectively, no	Montana	yes	no
Arizona	effectively, no	effectively, no	Nebraska	yes	no
Arkansas	effectively, no	effectively, no	Nevada	no	no
California	effectively, no	effectively, no	New Hampshire	yes	no
Colorado	effectively, no	effectively, no	New Jersey	yes	no
Connecticut	yes	no	New Mexico	effectively, no	effectively, no
Delaware	yes	no	New York	no	yes
District of Columbia	effectively, no	effectively, no	North Carolina	yes	no
Florida	effectively, no	effectively, no	North Dakota	effectively, no	effectively, no
Georgia	effectively, no	effectively, no	Ohio	no	yes
Hawaii	effectively, no	effectively, no	Oklahoma	yes	no
Idaho	effectively, no	effectively, no	Oregon	effectively, no	effectively, no
Illinois	effectively, no	effectively, no	Pennsylvania	yes	no
Indiana	yes	no	Rhode Island	effectively, no	effectively, no
Iowa	yes	no	South Carolina	effectively, no	effectively, no
Kansas	yes	no	South Dakota	yes	no
Kentucky	yes	no	Tennessee	yes	no
Louisiana	yes	no	Texas	effectively, no	effectively, no
Maine	effectively, no	effectively, no	Utah	effectively, no	effectively, no
Maryland	yes	no	Vermont	effectively, no	effectively, no
Massachusetts	no	yes	Virginia	effectively, no	effectively, no
Michigan	yes	no	West Virginia	effectively, no	effectively, no
Minnesota	effectively, no	effectively, no	Washington	effectively, no	effectively, no
Mississippi	no	yes	Wisconsin	effectively, no	effectively, no
			Wyoming	effectively, no	effectively, no ■

16

Gifts and Gift Taxes

A. The Federal Gift Tax: An Overview 16/2
    1. The Annual Exclusion 16/2
    2. Other Exemptions 16/3
    3. When Gift Taxes Are Paid 16/3
B. What Is a Gift? 16/3
    1. The Giver's Intent 16/4
    2. The Recipient's Control Over the Gift 16/4
    3. Common Kinds of Gifts 16/5
C. How Federal Gift Tax Works 16/6
    1. Gift Tax Payment and Rates 16/6
    2. Gifts of Life Insurance Made Near Death 16/7
    3. The "Present Interest" Rule 16/7
    4. Gifts to Minors and the "Present Interest" Rule 16/7
    5. "Crummey" Trusts and the Present Interest Rule 16/8
    6. The Federal Gift Tax Return 16/8
D. State Gift Tax Rules 16/8
E. Using Gifts to Reduce Estate Taxes 16/9
    1. Using the Annual Exemption Repeatedly 16/10
    2. Giving Property That Is Likely to Appreciate 16/11
    3. Gifts of Life Insurance 16/12
    4. Gifts of a Family Business 16/12
    5. Gifts to Minors 16/12
F. When Not to Give Property Away: Tax Basis Rules 16/13
    1. Special Rules for Community Property 16/14
    2. State Basis Rules 16/15
G. Using Gifts to Reduce Income Taxes 16/15

W e're used to thinking of gifts as a personal matter, not as an aspect of financial or estate planning. Up to a point, this is accurate; birthday or holiday presents don't normally have tax consequences. However, for a gift worth a substantial amount of money, the rules change. Currently, if you give more than $10,000 to one recipient in one year, the excess is subject to gift tax, unless the recipient is your spouse or another exemption applies.

Here we'll explore the federal gift tax rules, and the major ways gifts can be used to save on or eliminate gift taxes. To remind you, the federal gift tax rate is the same as the estate tax rate. The idea is to tax property the same way whether you give it away during your life or leave it at your death. Another way of saying this is that taxable gifts reduce amount of your personal estate exemption. (See Chapter 15, Estate Taxes, Section A.)

OTHER REASONS TO MAKE GIFTS

This chapter focuses on the gift tax and making tax-exempt gifts, but we're aware that many people, including those with estates over the estate tax threshold, are reluctant or unwilling to make big gifts simply to reduce their taxable estate. For them, the tax savings alone aren't worth the loss of the property given away. Making a large gift often involves many factors, with tax consequences being only one, often a relatively small one. Our focus on gift taxes and tax-saving doesn't mean we're suggesting that these matters should be central to your decisions regarding making substantial gifts. Still, even if your primary motive in making a substantial gift isn't to save on taxes, why not take full advantage of the gift tax rules?

A. THE FEDERAL GIFT TAX: AN OVERVIEW

Gift tax is assessed against the giver of a gift. The recipient of a gift is not liable for federal gift tax, unless the giver failed to pay any tax actually due. Only in that case will the IRS go after the recipient for any gift tax liability.

1. The Annual Exclusion

Currently, federal law exempts from gift tax the first $10,000 you give to any person or non-charitable institution in a calendar year. Lawyers often call this "the annual exclusion." (Internal Revenue Code Section 2503(b).). Starting in 1998, the $10,000 figure is indexed to the cost of living, rounded down to the closest thousand dollars. This means the cumulative increases in the cost of living must total over $1,000 before the amount of the annual exclusion is increased to $11,000.

So if you give someone $25,000, the first $10,000 of that gift is exempt from gift tax, while the remaining $15,000 is not. Married couples can combine their annual exclusions, which means that they can currently give away $20,000 of property tax-free, per year, per recipient.

The annual exclusion can be extremely important. You can use it repeatedly over a number of years to reduce the size of your estate and hence your ultimate estate tax bill. Here are some examples of how the annual exclusion works:

- You give $8,000 to a cousin in one year: There are no federal gift tax consequences.
- You give $16,000 to the cousin in one year: $6,000 is subject to gift tax.
- You give $8,000 each to two cousins: None of the $16,000 is subject to gift tax.

• You give $7,000 each to two cousins, three years in a row; none of this $42,000 is subject to gift tax.

2. Other Exemptions

Some types of gifts are completely exempt from federal gift tax:

• **All property one spouse gives the other, no matter how much it's worth.** (IRC Section 2523(a).) However, there's a different rule if the spouse receiving the gift is not a U.S. citizen. A U.S. citizen can give his or her non-citizen spouse up to $100,000 worth of property per year free of gift tax.

• **All property given to a tax-exempt charity.** (IRC Section 2522.)

• **Gifts spent directly for someone's medical bills or school tuition.** (IRC Section 2503(e).)

This final exemption has a couple of twists. First, the money must be paid directly to the provider of the medical service or the school. If you give the money to an ill person or student, who then pays the bill, the gift is not tax-exempt. Nor can you reimburse someone who has already paid a medical or tuition bill and have this be a tax-exempt gift. Finally, you cannot pay for a student's other educational expenses, such as room and board, and have this treated as a tax-exempt gift.

Example: Victor gives $6,000 outright to his son, $50,000 to his wife, $20,000 to CARE (a tax-exempt charity), pays $12,000 for his grandson's tuition at college and also pays $21,000 for a daughter's medical bills. All these gifts are completely exempt from federal gift tax.

3. When Gift Taxes Are Paid

Gift taxes that are assessed against you, as giver of a gift, are not payable until and unless your total taxable gifts exceed the amount of the personal exemption for the current year. Instead, any tax imposed on the gifts you make eats up some of your personal estate tax exemption and thus reduces the amount that can later pass tax-free. So people with estates worth under the estate tax threshold don't have to worry about actually paying gift tax. However, a federal gift tax return must be filed for any gift over the amount of the annual exclusion (to repeat it again, currently $10,000) to a person per year (IRS Forms 709 or 709-A). And if you have a substantial estate, having made taxable gifts may cut into what you can leave free of estate tax.

Example: In the last ten years of her life, Sheila gives her two children a total of $300,000 over and above the $10,000 annual exemptions. These taxable gifts use up a portion of her personal estate tax exemption. Sheila dies in 1999 with an estate valued at $500,000. The amount of the personal exemption is $650,000.

To determine if Sheila's estate owes tax:

Size of estate	$500,000
Add taxable gifts	$300,000
Total taxable	$800,000
Subtract personal exemption	$650,000
Amount taxable	$150,000

B. WHAT IS A GIFT?

Before exploring more about gifts and estate planning, let's be sure you know what a gift is, legally.

Some transactions simply can't, by law, count as taxable gifts. For instance, you can perform services—

from dispensing medical treatment to repairing a trombone—freely, without being held by the IRS to have made a taxable gift of the market value of your services. Similarly, you can lend property to someone, even for an extended period of time, and there's no legal gift.

Example: Grandpa Elijah has an old Rolls Royce that he lets his grandson Jacob drive. Indeed, Elijah has basically turned the car over to Jacob, although Elijah still pays for the car insurance. There is no gift—and would not be even if Jacob paid for the insurance, since Elijah remains the car's legal owner.

1. The Giver's Intent

In common understanding, a gift is the voluntary transfer of property made without receiving anything of value in exchange. (In legalese, anything of value is called "consideration.") In other words, a gift is a permanent transfer of property that isn't commercial in spirit.

From the point of view of the IRS, the crucial element in determining whether or not a gift is made is the giver's intent, which can be distinctly murky. For example, say you obtain a valuable painting from Frank. Did Frank intend to give you that painting, or lend it to you? Or was he hoping to sell it to you and wanted you to have it for a while before he mentioned the price?

If someone's intent may not be obvious (now or in the future), it is an excellent idea to accompany a gift with a written statement explaining that it's a gift, so that the status of the transaction is clear. If there is no clear written evidence, the IRS doesn't know when you transfer something for less than its market value whether you intend to make a gift or you're just a poor businessperson. So, it does the only thing it can do—it looks at the "objective evidence" and demands

gift tax if the transaction doesn't appear reasonable from a commercial (economic) point of view.

Example: Linda paid $15,000 to her niece for an office lamp and deducted the $15,000 as an expense of her small business. If the IRS questions this transaction and contends it was really a gift, Linda must convince the IRS that this was a bona fide commercial transaction (for example, that the lamp was a valuable antique), not a gift disguised as a purchase.

LOOKING DEEPER INTO GIFTS

For a fascinating discussion of the varied meanings of giving, read *The Gift: Imagination and the Erotic Life of Property*, by Lewis Hyde (Random House). The book brilliantly explores the spirit involved in giving and receiving a gift, from a Christmas present to creating a work of art, and how the giving spirit interacts with commercial culture.

---

2. The Recipient's Control Over the Gift

For a transaction to be a legal gift, the property must be delivered to and accepted by the recipient.

Example: Matt puts $10,000 into a drawer for Nina. There's no legal gift until Nina removes the money.

The giver must release all control over the property. If the giver retains any interest in the gift property, there is no legal gift.

Example: Sonya gives stocks she owns to her daughter, Misha, transferring the account into Misha's name. But Sonya continues to receive directly all of the dividends from the stocks. Legally, Sonya has not made a valid gift.

Gifts of real estate can be tricky. Some parents want to give a valuable house (aren't they all?) to a child, and structure the gift so that no gift tax is assessed. For example, a parent may take a mortgage on the property, with payments of $10,000 a year, and then forgive each year's payment when it becomes due. The IRS has disallowed schemes like this on the grounds that no legitimate mortgage existed. If you want to make a gift of real estate free of gift tax, see a lawyer.

Also, a gift of real estate will be disallowed, for tax purposes, by the IRS if the giver held onto some important right over the property—for example, the right to receive rents from a small apartment building. To avoid this problem, you must comply with all applicable IRS rules.

If you give a tangible item (cash, an heirloom, pictures), the relinquishment of control necessary to establish a gift is usually easy to prove—the recipient gains unrestricted possession over the property. In other situations, the question of control may be more difficult to ascertain. For example, if a gift is contingent on a future event, that event must be determinable by some objective standard. "To Desiree, when she becomes 21," or "When she travels to Paris" is objective; "When she's happily married" is not.

Property you place in a revocable living trust isn't a gift because you retain full control over the property and can revoke the trust if you wish. The beneficiaries you name in the trust document have no current right to the trust property. Likewise, if you establish an irrevocable trust and retain the power to change who will benefit from it, even if you, yourself, are specifically excluded as a possible beneficiary, there's no gift.

Example: Roger, a wealthy older man, puts money in an irrevocable trust for his grand-niece Olivia, to be used for her eventual college and possible graduate school costs. He appoints a trustee and gives her authority to alter the purposes for which the trust money can be spent. Roger also retains the right to substitute a new trustee. Because Roger still has so much control over the trust property, there has been no gift for gift tax purposes.

3. Common Kinds of Gifts

Here are some types of transactions that are legal gifts:

- Making an interest-free loan. Really? Yes. Federal law provides that an interest-free or artificially low-interest loan is a gift by the lender of the interest not charged. An "artificially low" interest rate is any rate below market interest rates when the loan was made. So, if you lend a friend $30,000 interest-free, you are making a taxable gift of the interest you didn't charge. But because of the $10,000 annual gift tax exclusion discussed above, gifts of interest on most loans don't have gift tax consequences. For example, at a 10% simple interest rate, a single person can make an interest-free loan of $100,000 to a person without gift tax liability. A married couple could lend a person up to $200,000 interest-free before the annual interest would exceed $20,000, the couple's combined annual gift tax exclusion.

- Handing someone cash, a check or any tangible item, with the intention of making a gift.

- Transferring title to real estate, stocks or a motor vehicle into another's name, without receiving anything of value in exchange. Remember that if you reserve the right to receive any income from the property, such as rent or dividends, no valid gift of the entire property is made.

- Transferring property to an irrevocable trust you create to benefit another person. The trust must have an objective standard of when property is to be given to the beneficiary, as mentioned above. An irrevocable trust means you can't change your mind and alter or terminate the trust once it is created. (By contrast, as we've mentioned, since a living trust is almost always revocable, naming someone as a beneficiary doesn't guarantee they will receive the property, so no gift is made.)

- Withdrawing funds someone else deposited in a joint (not community property) bank account.

- Irrevocably assigning a life insurance policy to another. (See Chapter 12.)

- Forgiving a debt.

- Assigning a mortgage or court judgment to someone without receiving fair compensation in return.

- Making a non-commercial transfer of your property into joint tenancy with another person. (Except for joint bank accounts; in that case, the rule is that a gift is made only when one depositor withdraws money deposited by the other.)

Partial gifts. Federal law authorizes "partial gifts." (IRC Section 2512(g).) These are gifts where you receive something of value back, but the gift is worth far more than what you received. Making a partial gift is a complex tax matter and you'll need to see a lawyer.

C. How Federal Gift Tax Works

Before you can sensibly evaluate whether you want to use gifts as part of your estate plan, you need to thoroughly understand how the federal gift tax actually works. We touched on this above; now we present a more thorough treatment of this important subject.

Gift tax applies to all gifts made by U.S. citizens and residents, and also to gifts of property by non-resident aliens if the gift property is physically located in the U.S. The most obvious example is real estate in the U.S.

Here are the basics.

1. Gift Tax Payment and Rates

As we've discussed, currently if you give a gift worth more than $10,000, you must file a gift tax return, (unless the gift is exempt from tax) and the IRS will assess a gift tax against you.

The IRS requires that the amount of the gift tax be used to reduce the amount of your personal estate/gift tax exemption. You cannot choose to pay gift tax now and "save" all of your personal exemption for later use.

> **Example:** Amber gives Beatrice an expensive car, worth $55,000; $10,000 worth of the gift is exempt from tax, so tax will be assessed on $45,000. Amber cannot simply pay the amount of the tax now and preserve the full amount of her personal estate/gift tax exemption until her death. Rather, the IRS requires that she use up $45,000 of her personal exemption.

The estate/gift tax rates are graduated, so the higher the taxable value of the gift, the higher the gift tax rate that applies to it. Also, the tax rate is cumulative. This means that in determining the gift tax rate applied to a current gift, the value of all taxable gifts given (since January 1, 1977) must be added. Otherwise, large estates could be transferred at lower tax rates by piecemeal giving.

Example: Carol gives her niece $20,000 two years in a row. Each year, $10,000 of the gift is exempt from tax. Here are the gift tax consequences:

	Year 1	Year 2
Amount given	$20,000	$20,000
Amount taxed	$10,000	$10,000
Tax rate based on	$10,000	$20,000
Tax rate	18%	20%
Tax assessed	$1,800	$2,000

2. Gifts of Life Insurance Made Near Death

Almost all gifts can be made up to the moment you die and qualify as legal gifts under the IRS rules. However, a few types of gifts must be made at least three years before the giver's death, or the gifts are disallowed for estate tax purposes. A gift of a life insurance policy is the significant one in this category. If a life insurance policy is given away within three years of death, the IRS acts as if the gift were never made, and includes the full amount of the proceeds in the giver's taxable estate. (If gift tax has already been paid, that amount will be credited towards any estate tax due. IRC Section 2012(a).) This is for estate tax purposes only; it doesn't affect ownership of the policy, which remains with the recipient.

Disallowance of a gift of life insurance can result in a substantial increase in the size of the giver's taxable estate. The proceeds paid on the death of the insured are always worth much more than the value of the same policy given away before the insured dies.

For example, a whole life policy that pays $300,000 on an insured's death might have a cash surrender value of $50,000 two years or two days before the owner dies. (Gifts of life insurance are discussed in more detail in Section E3, below, and Chapter 12, Section E.)

3. The "Present Interest" Rule

Under IRS rules, the annual gift tax exclusion only applies to gifts of what is called a "present interest." This means that the person or institution who receives the gift has the right to use it immediately. For the great majority of gifts, this is no problem. The receiver obtains full control when the gift is made. By contrast, gifts that someone can use only in the future, not when the gift was made, do not qualify for the annual exclusion. These are called gifts of a "future interest."

Example: Kim gives $10,000 outright to her friend Gayle and places another $10,000 in an irrevocable trust to benefit her friend Madeleine. Madeleine, age 32, can use principal from the trust only when she turns 35. The gift to Gayle is a gift of a present interest, because Gayle gets the money now. The gift to the trust for Madeleine is a gift of a future interest, because she has no right to the money when Kim gives it. So gift tax is assessed against the $10,000 Kim gives to the trust.

4. Gifts to Minors and the "Present Interest" Rule

Gifts to minors can qualify for the annual exclusion, even though the minor isn't given (indeed, by law, cannot be given) full present access to or control of the gift property. Federal law (IRC Section 2503(c)) provides that in order to make a gift to a minor that qualifies for the annual exemption, three conditions must be met:

1. The gift, and any income it produces, must be used or retained in trust, or an UTMA account, for the minor's benefit.

2. The remainder of the gift must go outright to the child when she or he reaches age 21. The gift can go outright to the child when she or he becomes 18 or older, up to 21.

3. If the child dies before reaching the age to receive the gift outright, the remainder of the gift must be paid to his or her estate.

5. "Crummey" Trusts and the Present Interest Rule

To get around the present interest rule for gifts to adults, lawyers invented a crafty device called a "Crummey trust" (so called because it was judicially approved in the case of *Crummey v. Commissioner*, 397 F.2d 82, 1968). For one of a number of reasons, a giver may not want an adult recipient to become owner of a gift, but still wants to get the annual exclusion for the gift. The common case is a gift to an irrevocable trust to pay for trust-owned life insurance on the giver's life. A gift to a trust is not generally a gift of a "present interest." So in order to obtain the annual exclusion, beneficiaries of the trust are given the right, for a limited time—as little as a few days—to accept (in legalese, to "withdraw") the gift. But they don't withdraw the gift, so it lapses and the gift becomes owned by the trust. Because the beneficiaries had the legal right to take the gift, it now qualifies as a gift of a "present interest" and gets the $10,000 exclusion.

Crummey trusts are tricky. If Crummey trusts seem fuzzy to you, don't feel alone. They are used only with more complicated estates where there's a need for something like a life insurance trust. Crummey trusts must be created by a lawyer.

6. The Federal Gift Tax Return

You must file an IRS gift tax return when your regular income tax return is filed (normally, April 15) if you:

- have made non-exempt gifts over the amount of the annual exclusion to any person or organization during the previous taxable year, or

- have made gifts over the amount of the annual exclusion to a tax-exempt organization during the previous taxable year. No tax is assessed for such tax-exempt gifts obviously, but the IRS still requires a return to be filed. Who knows why?

The IRS does not require a gift tax return to be filed for gifts between spouses (unless the recipient is not a U.S. citizen and the gift exceeds $100,000) or for gifts for educational or medical expenses, no matter how large the gift.

D. STATE GIFT TAX RULES

Most states have no gift tax. Generally, when they exist, state gift tax rules and rates are the same as that state's death tax rules and rates.

For most people, state gift tax is a minor matter, and doesn't enter into their estate planning. An exception can be people with large estates who live in states that levy relatively high gift and death taxes. In this situation, some people consider whether it's worthwhile to move their home from a state that imposes gift and death taxes to one that doesn't. This can be especially sensible for those who already own homes in two states, one of which doesn't levy these taxes. (See Chapter 15, Estate Taxes, Section G, for more on this issue.)

E. USING GIFTS TO REDUCE ESTATE TAXES

For people with larger estates, making tax-exempt gifts while living, either to individuals or charities, can be a significant part of their estate plan.

SOME THOUGHTS ON GIFT-GIVING AND TAXES

Estate planners have developed a number of ways to use gifts to reduce, or even eliminate, estate tax for many people who would otherwise face a tax bill. Before plunging into this subject (game might be a better word), take stock of what you really feel about making gifts now. Will giving property to your children or grandchildren enhance their lives? Or are they not yet ready to handle or appreciate your generosity? For example, helping a 21-year-old get an education or the head of a new family buy a house may be a truly great gift. By contrast, you may not want your money spent by a young person on a two-week vacation in Las Vegas or an expensive car. (But then, doesn't every kid merit a convertible?)

Many people make substantial gifts primarily for personal reasons, but with the awareness that they're obtaining estate/gift tax benefits, as well. Using gifts to reduce the size of your estate when you die can be desirable if:

- Your estate will probably owe estate tax (see Chapter 15); and

- The property you want to give has not greatly appreciated in value since you acquired it (if it has, it's better, for tax reasons, to transfer it at death. See Section F, below); and

- You don't need all of your assets and income to live on.

This last concern, of course, requires an evaluation of how much money and property you think you'll need (or want) now and in the future, as well as what your resources are, including income from retirement plans, Social Security, savings and investments. Some people, who may not want to use up any of their principal for gifts, may decide to use some of their income for gifts.

Example: Mr. and Mrs. Tureba, in their 70s, have four children. The Turebas have an estate totaling $1,140,000: a house worth $275,000 (all equity), stocks currently valued at $120,000, savings of $340,000, and business investments of $405,000. At first, the Turebas don't feel comfortable with the thought of giving away any of this property. However, their incomes are substantially more than they need to live on. The figures are:

Retirement plan income	$32,000
Social Security	$12,000
Mrs. Tureba's part-time job	$8,000
Returns from investments	$56,000
Total Annual Income	$108,000

After completing a detailed budget (what fun), the Turebas figure they spend about $35,000 a year, and taxes claim another $30,000. In short, in addition to all the money and property they have already put aside, they're saving over $40,000 per year. Looking at the reality that this is likely to be more than they will ever need, the Turebas decide to give away $10,000 a year to each of their four children, rather than increase their savings. Over ten years this will result in their giving $400,000 to their children, all gift tax free.

THE TIMING OF GIFTS

For wealthy people who engage in extensive tax-saving gift giving, the timing of making gifts can be important. To briefly summarize what can fast become complicated, if the cumulative gifts made are over the estate tax threshold, it's advantageous to make taxable gifts near the beginning of the tax year. Although the gift tax is the same, no matter when the gift is made during the year, if you make a taxable gift in January, you do not have to pay the gift tax until April of the following year. In the meantime, the income from the gift goes to the recipient rather than increasing your taxable estate.

By contrast, charitable gifts are often given at the end of the tax year, so the giver can receive the income from the asset for most of the year, while obtaining the charitable tax deduction for that same year.

1. Using the Annual Exemption Repeatedly

Although the annual gift tax exclusion (to repeat, currently $10,000) may not seem like an immense sum, it can often be used over time to achieve substantial estate tax savings. The key is using this $10,000 exemption as fully as possible. It's a simple matter of multiplication. If you use the $10,000 annual exemption for gifts to one person for five years, you've given away five times as much ($50,000) tax-free as you would if you gave the same $50,000 to the same person in one year and qualified for only one $10,000 exemption. If you make $10,000 gifts to five recipients in one year, you've also given away $50,000 tax-free. And obviously, it follows that if you make five $10,000 gifts to five people for five years, you've given $250,000 away tax-free. (And since spouses can each make $10,000 gifts, giving as a couple multiplies your gift tax exemption by two.)

Example: Patti owns a successful small business, with an estimated net worth of $2 million. Her other assets are worth roughly $475,000. Patti intends to leave her business to her four children. To reduce the value of her eventual estate, she incorporates her business and starts giving her children stock. She can give each of her children stock worth $10,000 per year gift tax-free—a yearly total of $40,000. For ten years she gives each child $10,000 worth of stock, transferring a total of $400,000 tax-free.

This example assumes the worth of the company remained the same for ten years, unlikely in the real world. In practice, Patti would have to review the worth of her company yearly.

2. Giving Property That Is Likely to Appreciate

If you're prosperous and your estate will be subject to estate tax, it can make particularly good sense to give away property that you believe will appreciate substantially in the future, especially if it hasn't gone up in value much already. At first, this may seem a little complicated, but if you read what follows carefully, you'll see it really isn't.

Here is the basic idea. If property you own seems reasonably likely to go up in value substantially in the future, giving it away now not only excludes its present worth from your estate but also eliminates the value of its likely future appreciation from your estate.

Example: Brook, in her 60s, recently purchased some vacant land for $160,000 cash. The property is located in an area she believes will be ripe for development in a few years. She intends to leave this land to her niece, Laura, when she dies. If she waits to transfer the property until her death, then the market value of the property when she dies will be included in her taxable estate. But if Brook gives the land to Laura soon after buying it in 1997, all of its appreciation in value, as well as its current worth, won't be included in Brook's taxable estate.

The gift will be subject to gift tax. So $10,000 will be exempt from gift tax, but $150,000 won't be. Still, if Brook is right about the land increasing in value, the gift tax assessed will be far less than estate tax imposed on the appreciated property would be at Brook's death, for the obvious reason that the appreciated property will be worth more, and therefore taxed at a higher rate.

By contrast, it usually doesn't make sense to give away property that has already gone up in value, especially if you may not live long. The reason, as more fully explained in Section F, is that the recipient of a gift has the same tax basis in the property as the giver did (which is, very roughly, usually what the giver paid for the property). On the other hand, an inheritor obtains a basis that is stepped up to the fair market value of the property at the time of death. (The concepts of "basis" and "stepped-up basis" are discussed in depth in Chapter 15, Section F.)

Example: Bill bought 1,000 shares of stock at $5 a share. It's now worth $30 a share and is still going up. If he gives it now to his daughter Betsy, her cost basis will be $5 per share. If he leaves it to Betsy upon his death, her stepped-up basis in the stock will probably be

$30 a share or higher, depending on its market price when he dies.

This difference will be vitally important when Betsy sells the stock. If its cost basis is $5 a share and she sells it for $30 a share, she will have to pay capital gain tax on the $25 per share profit. By contrast, if the basis is stepped up to $30 because the transfer is made at death, and she sells the stock at $30 a share, she won't owe any capital gain tax.

3. Gifts of Life Insurance

In some situations, making a gift of life insurance can substantially reduce or eliminate federal estate tax. In fact, from a gift tax standpoint, giving life insurance can often be the most advantageous way to transfer a large sum out of your estate, since the gift normally has a low value for gift tax purposes. But because gifts of insurance policies can be such a good tax deal for the giver, special rules apply. The most important one is that the gift must be made more than three years before you die to be effective for estate tax purposes.

Gifts of life insurance are discussed in Chapter 12, Section E. As we've discussed above, the value of the gift of an insurance policy is always much lower than the proceeds paid in the event of the insured's death.

4. Gifts of a Family Business

Gifts of minority interests in a family business can result in significant estate tax savings. Currently, sophisticated estate tax planners play some very fancy games here. See Chapter 28, Family Business Estate Planning, Section B.

5. Gifts to Minors

You can make a gift to a minor (a child under 18) during your life, as well as leave a minor property when you die. A minor cannot legally control any substantial amount of property in his or her own name. An adult must have that responsibility. If, while you are alive, you make a gift directly to a child, rather than to his or her parents or guardians, you have two choices.

Your options are to:

1. Give the money in a trust. If you, while living, make a gift to a minor using a properly drafted child's trust, you obtain the annual gift tax exclusion in the year the gift is made. (See Section C4, above.)

2. Appoint a "custodian" for the gift, under your state's Uniform Transfers to Minors Act (UTMA) or Uniform Gifts to Minors Act (UGMA). [UTMA, UGMA, Let's Call the Whole Thing Off.] The UTMA applies in all states but Michigan, South Carolina and Vermont, where the UGMA applies. The UGMA only provides a device for making gifts to minors while you live, not for leaving property to them when you die.

Using either Act, you can, while you live, make a gift to a minor by naming an adult custodian for the gift property. (See Chapter 6, Children, Section C.)

In most states, the custodianship must end when the child turns 21 or 18. Obviously, that satisfies the IRS age requirement that the minor must receive the gift outright by age 21. In Alaska and Nevada, however, you must be sure to provide that the recipient will receive the gift at some age between 18 to 21. These states' laws are unclear and could be interpreted as extending the custodianship past age 21, if you don't provide otherwise.

Gifts to minors made while one is alive are often given primarily for personal reasons, not for gift tax savings. Your personal motives may override maximizing gift tax savings, or those motives may work harmoniously with gift tax rules.

Example 1: Oksana, who is quite prosperous, wants to be certain her grandson Viktor and granddaughter Marya will have enough money to attend college. Viktor is 12 and Marya is ten. Oksana wants to make the gift now, so she can take pleasure in knowing that her grandchildren know their educational future is secure. She creates an educational child's trust for each, to last until the child is 30, naming their father as trustee. Oksana realizes that by doing this, she will not obtain the annual gift tax exclusion for any money she gives the trust, because, as we explained, federal tax law requires the child to receive the money outright by age 21 for the exclusion to apply. But Oksana wants adult supervision of the trust until the children are 30, because she doubts that any 21-year-old is likely to be able to handle large amounts of money responsibly. Her concern over this issue overrides any consideration of tax savings.

Example 2: In 1998, Biff decides to give an expensive thoroughbred horse worth $50,000 to his niece Brenda, age 16, who has loved horses since she was small. Biff makes the gift under his state's UTMA, which requires the horse to be legally turned over to Brenda when she becomes 21—which is fine with Biff. Biff names Brenda's mother, Josette, as custodian for the gift. They all know this is only technical, since Brenda will be, and wants to be, responsible for the horse.

Biff is not assessed gift tax on $10,000 of his gift. He is assessed gift tax on the remaining value of $40,000.

F. WHEN NOT TO GIVE PROPERTY AWAY: TAX BASIS RULES

Much of this chapter has discussed why it is often advantageous, from an estate/gift tax point of view, to give away property before you die. But this isn't always the case. It's usually unwise to give away an asset (as opposed to leaving it at death) that has substantially appreciated in value since you purchased it, especially if you are older and likely to die before decades pass.

In order to understand why it is often better for the recipient to inherit appreciated property than to receive it during the giver's lifetime, you need to understand the tax concept of "basis." While we've discussed this concept in Chapter 15, Estate Taxes, Section F, it's so important that here we focus on how this applies to gifts.

The tax basis of property is the value (dollar figure) from which gain or loss on sale is determined. When property is purchased, its basis is generally its cost. In fact, basis is often referred to as cost basis. If you make major (capital) improvements to property—for example, adding a deck to your house—the cost of the improvement is added to the basis of the property.

The recipient of a gift takes the same basis in the property as the giver had. This is called the "carry-over" basis, in tax jargon.

Example: Lewella's basis in her house is $100,000 (net purchase price plus capital improvements). The house now has a market value of $320,000. Lewella gives her house to Megan. Megan's (carry-over) basis in the house is $100,000. If Megan then sells the house for $320,000, her taxable profit is $220,000 ($320,000 minus her basis of $100,000).

The basis rules for inherited property differ from those applicable to gifts. The tax basis for property a person inherits is the fair market value at the date of the original owner's death. So if the value of the property has gone up since the owner acquired it, the tax basis is increased (in taxese, "stepped up") from the deceased's basis to the value of the property at death.

Example: If Lewella dies and leaves her house to Megan, Megan's basis in the house is increased to its market value at Lewella's death, which is $320,000.

This stepped up basis rule means there are major (capital gain) tax savings for the recipient if an asset that has appreciated in value is transferred at death instead of given to that recipient while the giver is still alive.

Example: Edward owns a Redon pastel painting, which he bought as an astute art student for $20,000. Sixty years later, an appraiser informs him it's worth $1.5 million. If Edward were to sell the painting, his taxable gain would be $1.5 million less his basis of $20,000. If he gives the painting away and the recipient sells it, the tax situation is the same—only now it's the recipient who owes capital gain tax on the profit.

By contrast, if Edward dies and leaves the painting to the same recipient in his living trust, his beneficiary's stepped up basis in the painting is $1.5 million. If the beneficiary promptly sells the painting, there's no taxable gain.

1. Special Rules for Community Property

If you're married and own community property (see Chapter 3, Special Property Ownership Rules for Married People, Section B, for a discussion of community property and a list of the eight community property states), another federal tax basis rule can be significant for any gift planning you consider. On the death of one spouse, the basis of each spouse's half of the community property is stepped up to the property's fair market value at the time of the spouse's death.

Example: Felicia and Max are residents of California, a community property state. They own a grand house in Malibu they bought decades ago for $100,000. The basis of each spouse's interest is $50,000, one-half the purchase price. When Felicia dies, the market value of the house is $8,000,000. Because of the stepped-up basis rule for community property, the federal tax basis of each spouse's half-interest in the house steps up to $4,000,000. If Max sells the house for $8 million shortly after Felicia's death, he will not owe any capital gain tax. The sale price equals the stepped-up basis of the house. In contrast, if the house had been sold before Felicia died, their profit would have been $7.9 million. Under capital gains tax law, $500,000 of the amount would be exempt because the profit is from sale by a couple of a home. So capital gains tax would be assessed on $7.4 million.

Again, what all this means is that there may be a considerable federal tax advantage for inheritors if a couple retains, until one of them dies, community property that has substantially increased in value since they purchased it.

2. State Basis Rules

Estate planning decisions are rarely affected by state basis rules. In general, the impact of state tax basis rules on gifts or inherited property is minor, because the tax rates involved are relatively low in those states that impose gift and death taxes. If you want to explore your state's rules, you can either research that issue yourself (see Chapter 29, Using Lawyers, Section B) or consult an accountant or tax attorney.

G. Using Gifts to Reduce Income Taxes

If you are prosperous and are willing to give income-producing property to someone in a lower tax bracket while you are still alive, you can achieve some overall income tax savings in addition to the possible federal estate and gift tax savings discussed earlier in this chapter. With the current maximum income tax rate close to 40%, a gift to a person in a lower tax bracket, especially someone in the 15% bracket, will obviously result in less income tax being paid on income received from the property. Of course, you will not see the tax savings yourself, because you no longer own the property.

Be wary of giving property to children under 14. You may well not obtain an income tax benefit for a gift to a child under age 14. The reason is that all income over $1,300 a year received by minors under 14 years, from any gift (whether from their parents or otherwise), is taxed, for federal income tax purposes, at the highest tax rate of their parents. So if the parents are not in a lower bracket than you are, income tax advantages is eliminated. ∎

17

AN OVERVIEW OF ONGOING TRUSTS

A. Trusts to Save on Estate Tax 17/3

B. Ongoing Trusts Used to Control Property.. 17/4

C. Ongoing Trusts and Avoiding Probate 17/4

D. What Ongoing Trusts Can't Do 17/5

E. How Ongoing Trusts Work 17/5

    1. When an Ongoing Trust Takes Effect 17/5

    2. Tax Status of Ongoing Trusts 17/6

    3. How Long an Ongoing Trust Lasts 17/6

F. The Trustee 17/7

    1. The Trustee's Duties 17/7

    2. Choosing the Trustee 17/8

    3. Naming More Than One Trustee 17/9

    4. Trust Companies and Banks as Trustees 17/9

    5. Choosing a Successor Trustee.. 17/10

G. Taxation of Ongoing Trusts 17/10

An "ongoing" trust is a trust that is intended to operate as an independent legal entity for a long time, usually years or even decades, after the death of the person who establishes it (the grantor). Often, but not in all cases, an ongoing trust begins to operate as a separate legal entity only at the death of the grantor. An ongoing trust can be created in a will or in a living trust, or by a document making the trust operational while the trust grantor is alive. Once operational, these ongoing trusts are irrevocable.

The two basic functions of ongoing trusts are to:

1. Save on estate taxes

2. Impose long-term controls on the management of trust property.

Some ongoing trusts serve both purposes, some only one.

Many people need only a simple probate-avoidance living trust, not an ongoing trust. By our terms, a living trust is not ongoing, because it functions as a separate entity only for a brief time after the grantor's death. By the end of this chapter, you should have a pretty clear idea of whether or not you need some type of ongoing trust.

This chapter explores basic features common to all ongoing trusts. Other chapters delve into some specific types of ongoing trusts, including:

- Estate tax-saving "bypass" trusts, including the commonly used AB trust (Chapter 18).

- Other estate tax-saving marital trusts, including a "QTIP" trust to postpone payment of estate taxes (Chapter 19).

- Charitable trusts (Chapter 20).

- Other estate-tax saving trusts, including generation-skipping trusts, irrevocable life insurance trusts and grantor-retained interest trusts (Chapter 21).

- Using disclaimers (declining inherited gifts) for estate tax purposes (Chapter 22).

- Combining ongoing estate tax savings trusts (Chapter 23).

- Trusts useful to people with children from a prior marriage (Chapter 24).

- A trust to impose controls over property (Chapter 25).

- A basic child's trust or family pot trust, to control property inherited by a minor or young adult (Chapter 6).

ONGOING TRUSTS AND MEDICAL BILLS

Many people would like to include a "catastrophic illness" clause or provision in any ongoing trust they create, to prevent trust assets from being used to pay medical bills if a trust beneficiary suffers a catastrophic illness. Couples often are particularly concerned with preserving their trust assets from claims by medical providers or government agencies. At the very least, the couple doesn't want both members' assets used to pay for one's catastrophic illness.

Unfortunately, no simple trust clause applicable in all states will achieve this desired result. A provision properly geared to current federal laws and regulations and your specific state's laws and your situation may provide some protection. But such provisions rarely, if ever, consist of a single clause or paragraph; indeed, they often go on for pages and require sophisticated knowledge of all applicable laws and regulations. Such provisions must be prepared by an expert. It's absolutely essential to be up-to-date here.

A. Trusts to Save on Estate Tax

One goal of many ongoing trusts is to save on estate taxes. Most estates don't owe estate tax, but if you expect that yours will, there's good reason to want to cut the tax bill. Federal estate taxes are substantial. As you know by now (we hope), taxes kick in when a person dies owning property worth more than the personal estate tax exemption for the year of death. The exemption is $625,000 in 1998, and rises over the next eight years until it tops out at $1 million in 2006 and thereafter. Rates start at 37% to 41% and reach 55% for estates over $3 million. (See Chapter 15, Estate Taxes, Section A, for a discussion of the estate tax laws and a table listing the personal exemption amount for each year.)

Any individual with an estate over the estate tax threshold should explore tax-saving trusts. A couple with a combined estate large enough likely to be subject to estate tax can use an ongoing AB trust that becomes operational after one member dies to achieve significant estate tax savings.

If you are afraid you might be overwhelmed by reading about tax-saving trusts, don't give up. You don't need to master the complexities of actually preparing most of these types of trusts. This book contains no forms for preparing your own estate tax-saving trusts. Except for AB trusts (see Chapter 18, Estate Tax-Saving Bypass Trusts, Section C), these trusts are always complex and technical, and must be prepared by a lawyer.

Don't assume that estate tax-saving trusts aid only a handful of millionaires, or that they are somehow fraudulent (or at least sleazy). That's simply not true. Many prosperous folks can take advantage of what these trusts offer, and they are perfectly legal.

If you still have any doubts about the value of investigating estate tax-saving trusts, consider the following analogy: When you sit down each year to fill out your income tax forms, would it ever occur to you to just skip personal exemptions and deductions you are entitled to and cheerfully send that money to the government? Well, that's exactly that you're doing if you prepare an estate plan that ignores exemptions and deductions available through the use of estate tax-saving trusts.

Let's look at what really happens to a hard-earned dollar (at least, we presume it was hard-earned) when it is subject to estate tax. You could call this the case of the disappearing dollar. Your original dollar, when you earned it, was subject to income tax, probably at roughly 30%, at a minimum (and quite possibly higher, particularly if you paid state income or Social Security taxes). So now you've got, at most, 70 cents left. If the 70 cents is subject to estate tax at the minimum rate of 37%, there's only 44 cents left. And for very large estates, the estate tax goes up to 55%, which leaves less than 35 cents. (And you can take another nickel away if the estate went through probate.)

We want to offer you sufficient information about major types of estate tax-saving trusts so you can decide whether it's worth your time and money to hire a lawyer to create one or more for you. Also, by reading the next six chapters, you should be able to discern if a lawyer is providing helpful, accurate information and advice about estate tax-saving trusts or is primarily concerned with running up your bill.

B. ONGOING TRUSTS USED TO CONTROL PROPERTY

In addition to saving on estate taxes, ongoing trusts can also be used to provide for the management and control of property you don't want to leave outright to someone. Property control trusts are particularly common when spouses have children from prior marriages. Often, each spouse wants to leave the other spouse well-provided for. At the same time, each spouse doesn't want to leave everything outright to the other spouse, because each wants the bulk of his or her property to eventually go to his or her children. An ongoing trust can be used to achieve both these goals. (See Chapter 24, Property Control Trusts for Second or Subsequent Marriages.)

An ongoing trust to control property is also desirable or essential in other circumstances, including situations in which:

- You leave property to minors (or persons who have been declared legally incompetent) who are not legally permitted to own substantial amounts of property outright.

- You believe the beneficiary can't handle money responsibly.

- The beneficiary needs what's called a "special needs trust" to provide long-term support but not interfere with the beneficiary's eligibility for federal or state assistance.

- You decide you no longer want the burdens of administering your own property and want to turn that task over to someone else. For instance, someone who is old and ill may know that it's sensible to arrange for others to handle her finances. There are various methods to arrange for this, including preparing a durable power of attorney for finances. (See Chapter 26.) Sometimes people prefer a trust, however, because it is a more traditional legal form, and the trust property will avoid probate on the grantor's death.

Property control trusts for each of these situations are discussed in Chapter 25.

C. ONGOING TRUSTS AND AVOIDING PROBATE

Property left in ongoing trusts doesn't automatically avoid probate. Most ongoing trusts become operational only when the grantor dies. So to avoid probate of property left in these trusts, ongoing trusts are usually incorporated as a part (a big part) of a living trust. By using a living trust, the property avoids probate after the person's death and goes straight into the now-operational ongoing trust.

Example: Pilar wants to establish an ongoing trust to manage the property she intends to leave to her kid brother, Juan, who is 20 years her junior. She wants to create an ongoing trust because Juan, age 28, has always squandered whatever money he's acquired and shows no signs of change. Within her revocable living trust, Pilar creates an ongoing trust in which the trustee controls how and when money is given to Juan from the trust. This trust will become operational only after Pilar dies. Under the terms of the living trust, the property left to Juan will be transferred to the ongoing trust without probate.

As long as Pilar lives, the living trust, and the ongoing trust contained in the living trust, are revocable. When Pilar dies, the ongoing trust becomes irrevocable and cannot be changed by anyone, including Juan.

All of the ongoing trusts discussed in the next chapters can be made part of a living trust, except ongoing trusts that become operational before the grantor dies. To say this metaphorically, just because an ongoing trust and a probate-avoidance living trust are technically different legal animals doesn't mean they can't drink at the same pond. We stress this here because it's important to understand you don't need to risk probate by creating an ongoing trust. We don't repeat this for each ongoing trust we discuss. These discussions are already complex enough.

D. WHAT ONGOING TRUSTS CAN'T DO

Expert estate planning lawyers can sometimes come up with truly ingenious plans to fit a family's particular needs and save on estate taxes. But some lawyers and financial planners push the line of what's legally safe. It's up to you to decide how safe or aggressive you want to be. But before betting a big estate on the cutting-edge theories of any estate planner—lawyer or not—it's wise to get a second, perhaps more conservative, opinion.

Those who believe trusts are truly lawyers' magic may seek or fall victim to what we call the "daydream" trust. In a daydream trust, the grantor wants to use an ongoing trust to:

• Avoid all income taxes,

• Shield the property from all creditors, and

• Retain complete control over trust property or, at the very least, have full access to it in times of need.

It should come as no surprise that the daydream trust is just that—a fantasy. Tax rules do not allow people to escape legal responsibilities simply by use of a trust. You can't use a trust to escape responsibility for legal debts and obligations, including child support, alimony, court-ordered judgments or any other legal debt.

Likewise, if you retain any control over your trust or benefit from it, the IRS will not allow the trust to be used to lower your income taxes. For example, some tout trusts designed to save big money on income and estate taxes, while at the same time giving the grantor great powers over trust assets. The IRS looks askance at this.

E. HOW ONGOING TRUSTS WORK

Once an ongoing trust becomes operational, it is a legal entity separate from any person or organization. It is also, as we've stressed, irrevocable—that is, the terms of the trust cannot be changed. Before the trust takes effect, however, it can be revoked or changed at any time. You're not bound by its terms. Most people don't want an ongoing trust to become irrevocable while they are alive. Understandably, they don't want to be locked into having given away some of their property during their life.

1. When an Ongoing Trust Takes Effect

A trust becomes operational when it actually becomes effective in the real world as a legally distinct entity. As we've said, most often this happens at the death of the trust creator. Once an ongoing trust becomes operational, the trustee must obtain a taxpayer ID number for the trust, keep accurate trust financial records and file an annual federal trust income tax return and any state trust tax returns required.

> **Example:** Alma, age 73, creates a living trust to avoid probate. As one component of this living trust, she creates an ongoing trust for her disabled daughter, with Alma's niece Maureen as trustee. Only when Alma dies does this ongoing trust for her daughter become operational and irrevocable. Then Maureen must handle the trust property and accompanying paperwork.

Occasionally, however, people want an ongoing trust to become operational and irrevocable during their lifetime. For example, charitable trusts are often set up this way. Such irrevocable trusts are operational as soon as the trust documents are signed and notarized. Trust property is promptly given to the charity, and the grantor retains certain rights to receive income from it. (See Chapter 20, Charitable Trusts.)

There can be other reasons to make an ongoing trust operational during your lifetime, rather than at your death. For example, an irrevocable life insurance trust must be operational at least three years before the grantor's death to obtain estate tax savings. (See Chapter 21, Other Estate Tax-Saving Trusts, Section B.)

2.   Tax Status of Ongoing Trusts

If an ongoing trust takes effect while you are alive, the property placed in the trust is a gift, subject to gift tax, unless the beneficiary is a tax-exempt charity. (See Chapter 16, Gifts and Gift Taxes, Section A.) If the ongoing trust is created in a will or living trust and takes effect when you die, the property in the trust is part of your taxable estate; whether or not

your estate will actually owe estate tax depends on its size, the year of death and possibly other factors. (See Chapter 15, Estate Taxes, Section A.) In some states, it is also subject to state death tax.

3.   How Long an Ongoing Trust Lasts

How long an ongoing trust lasts is defined in the trust document. While some trusts last for a set number of years, usually termination of the trust is triggered by a certain event. The trust may, for example, last until a surviving spouse dies; when that happens, trust property is distributed to the couple's children, and the trust ends. A trust for grandchildren may last until the youngest reaches age 30 or 35, or whatever age the grantor chooses, at which point the grandchildren receive all remaining trust property.

A legal rule called "the rule against perpetuities" requires a trust to have a set ending time, or set ending event. This rule prevents someone from tying up property for generations without that property ever being owned outright by anyone. For example, you can't leave property "first to my daughter, then equally to her children, then equally to their grandchildren," and so on. Society has decided that there should be a finite period during which the instructions of a deceased person can control the disposition of property. At some time, some person has to own the property outright and be free to sell it or give it away.

The intricacies of the rule against perpetuities have baffled law students for generations. For practical purposes, the rule means you can legally tie up property only for people who are alive when you die. That means you can leave trust property for your grown children to use during their lives and specify that, at their deaths, the property goes outright to their children. But if you try to impose controls on their grandchildren's freedom to use or dispose of the property, you risk running afoul of the rule against perpetuities.

If you want to impose controls on property for more than one generation, you'll definitely need an expert estate planning lawyer's advice to determine if what you want is legally possible.

F. The Trustee

The trustee of an ongoing trust has serious responsibilities, and choosing a reliable trustee is a crucial part of creating an ongoing trust.

1. The Trustee's Duties

For any type of ongoing trust, the trustee must manage the trust property prudently and comply with any specific management instructions in the trust document.

Terminology Note: When an ongoing trust is created as a component of a living trust, you are the original trustee. When you die, a person you've named as trustee for the ongoing trust manages it. Often, but not always, this person is the same as the successor trustee of your living trust. We refer to the person who manages an ongoing trust that becomes operational at your death simply as the "trustee."

The trustee's powers are usually set out in detail (sometimes many pages of detail) in the trust document. For example, the trustee may be given the specific power to sell trust real estate, or to buy or lease new real estate.

General legal rules also govern the trustee. Legally, the trustee is a "fiduciary," which means she is held to the standard of highest good faith and scrupulous honesty when handling trust business (unless the trust document itself declares a lesser legal standard). For example, unless it's specifically authorized in the trust document, the trustee may not personally profit from any financial transaction involving the trust.

The trustee of an ongoing trust will most likely engage in various business or financial transactions on behalf of the trust. For instance, the trustee will probably deal with banks or other financial institutions. The trustee may well be involved in other trust financial matters, from leasing trust property to dealing with the IRS. The trustee may also have to make investment decisions, or buy or sell trust property.

Sometimes, the trustee's actual financial responsibilities can be rather simple. For example, if the trust primarily consists of a valuable house, the trustee has to be sure the house is properly maintained, and perhaps decide to sell it. But often the trustee's work is more difficult. If much of the trust money is invested, the trustee must decide if the investments are reasonable ones—neither absurdly cautious nor too risky. If the trust property includes a business or a complex investment portfolio, managing the property can be quite a task. For this reason, it's normally permissible for a trustee to hire financial or investment advisors and pay for their advice from trust assets.

The trustee of an ongoing trust must also distribute trust income (or principal) to the beneficiaries as the trust document directs or permits. Sometimes this, too, is far from simple. If the trust document allows the trustee some discretion in whether or not to distribute trust income or principal on behalf of a certain beneficiary, it may not be easy for the trustee to decide what to do.

The trustee of an ongoing trust that becomes operational at the grantor's death is responsible for handling all trust paperwork—for example, getting the taxpayer ID number from the IRS and keeping accurate trust financial records. Professional help can be used here if, in the trustee's judgment, it's necessary. The trustee is also responsible for having the annual trust income tax return (IRS Form 1041) filed. If any federal tax is owed, the trustee must pay it from trust funds. Finally, the trustee must handle any required state income tax return.

Eventually, when the trust ends, the trustee must distribute any remaining trust property to whomever was named as the final trust beneficiary or beneficiaries.

Because of these responsibilities, most trustees of ongoing trusts are paid. The trust document often allows the trustees to pay themselves "reasonable compensation" or a set amount per hour from trust property. Of course, you can expressly prohibit pay for your trustee, but it's not wise. Are you sure you can rely on a person to do the work required of a trustee without compensation? And even if someone would do it, do you really think it's fair? After all, the trustee will be spending time on work you created by establishing your ongoing trust.

2. Choosing the Trustee

Obviously, if you create an ongoing trust, you must give serious thought to who will serve as the trustee. The two most important criteria your trustee should meet are that you completely trust the person and that he or she wants to do the job.

The trustee should also have some financial common sense. You may decide, in fact, that you want your trustee to have considerable financial expertise. For instance, you may want a trustee who understands the difference between a balanced, fairly conservative investment portfolio (a mix of income-oriented stock and bond funds, for example) and

much riskier investment in someone's great idea for a new business or speculation in real estate.

If you can find all this in one person, fine, but remember—your trustee can always hire investment advisors. Someone you trust, and who is willing to do the job of trustee, can't be purchased.

Making this choice may also raise sensitive personal issues. For one thing, your trustee will have an ongoing relationship with the trust beneficiaries.

Example: Malik has three children from his former marriage. He wants to leave the income from his estate to his wife, Libby, during her life, and on her death, have his estate divided equally among his children. Who should be trustee of the ongoing trust he creates to achieve these goals?

Malik must carefully evaluate a number of factors:

- What is the relationship between Libby and his children?

- If Libby is the sole trustee, will she truly guard the trust principal for his children?

- If one of his children is the trustee, will he be fair to Libby—or will he try to retain in the trust as much of the money as he can, regardless of what Libby needs?

- If Libby and one of Malik's children are co-trustees, can they get along?

- What will happen if they can't?

Different types of ongoing trusts raise different concerns about your choice of trustee. These issues are discussed in subsequent chapters, which cover various types of ongoing trusts.

3. Naming More Than One Trustee

Legally, you can name two, or even several, persons to serve as co-trustees. But before you do, make sure you have some compelling reason. Having two or more people serve as trustees for a trust that may last a long time, can lead to serious conflict or confusion.

If you do decide to appoint co-successor trustees, you must decide how they will share authority—whether each can act separately for the trust or all must agree in writing to act for the trust. But even more important, you must have complete confidence that all your trustees will get along. Do be cautious here. Sharing power and property can lead to unexpected results. If the co-trustees are prone to conflict, you may well create serious problems, and will be doing none of them a favor by having them share power.

If co-trustees can't agree, say, on how to manage trust property, the situation can get very messy. Your trustees could wind up in court. Not only would this probably waste trust money, but the end result might be much worse, and generate more animosity than if you had just picked one person to be trustee in the first place and let the chips fall where they may.

4. Trust Companies and Banks as Trustees

Would you and your beneficiaries be better served if a professional trustee (from a bank or private trust company) were named as a trustee? Generally, we believe not. Indeed, our strong preference is for you to select a person you know and trust to serve as trustee. A trustee should have good money sense and be reasonably knowledgeable about the financial world, but in most cases does not need to be an expert.

Banks can be very impersonal, perhaps paying little attention to trusts worth less than (many) millions, or treating a beneficiary as a nuisance. In addition, they charge overall management fees, and often additional fees for each tiny act, which can cost a bundle.

But if there is no person you trust who is willing to serve as trustee, and you want to create an ongoing trust, you'll have to select a financial institution as your trustee. Also, with certain complicated types of property, such as oil and gas interests, beneficiaries can benefit from professional management. Your best bet is probably to use a private trust company, a business that specializes in trust management. They tend to be smaller and less impersonal than banks, and more focused on trust management. If you're extremely cautious, you might even want to name another institution as an alternate trustee, just in case your first choice goes out of business or decides not to handle smaller trusts. But doing this means you have to make arrangements with two private trust companies—which means extra work.

A possible compromise is to name co-trustees—an individual you trust and a financial institution. The hope is to get a measure of investment savvy but still have a real person in the mix. The reality may be less inviting. Many institutions won't accept a co-trustee arrangement in the first place. And anytime you appoint co-trustees, potential problems abound. (See Section 3, above.) Unless there's a financial institution you really feel comfortable with, a better bet is just to name an individual trustee, who can hire good financial advisors if needed.

5. Choosing a Successor Trustee

Since your ongoing trust will likely last a while, somewhere down the line, your first choice may become unable to perform the job. So it's a good idea to give some thought to arranging for a successor trustee. You can simply name one or more successor trustees in your trust document. You can also authorize an acting trustee to name, in writing, additional successor trustees. The trustee would do this if—and only if—the trustee and any successor trustees you named are unable to serve. This should ensure that the position of trustee never becomes vacant. (If it did, there would have to be a court proceeding to name a new trustee.) Also, this ensures that any trustee will at least have been chosen by someone you trust.

> **Example:** Shannon's living trust creates an ongoing trust for her two young grandchildren, to last until they reach age 35. She names the children's mother, Carolyn (her daughter), as the trustee and Carolyn's husband, Bill, as the successor trustee. She also includes in the trust document a provision allowing any trustee to name, in writing, additional successor trustees.
>
> Carolyn dies a few years after the trust becomes operational, and Bill becomes trustee. He writes a document naming his brother Al, then Al's wife, Jane, to serve as trustees if he can't. Before either child is 35, Bill is killed in a car crash. Al then becomes the trustee.

G. TAXATION OF ONGOING TRUSTS

It is rarely desirable, at least from an income tax standpoint, to have an ongoing trust retain for over a year income generated by trust property. Trust income tax rates are now higher than individual income tax rates. An ongoing trust is taxed on all income over $100 that it retains at the close of the tax year. If the trust distributes income earned in that year to a beneficiary, that income is taxed at the beneficiary's rate, not the trust's.

If a beneficiary's income tax rate will be lower than the trust's rate, the rule is simple: trusts that retain income (over a year) pay more in income tax, and thus ultimately have less to distribute to the beneficiaries. So, in most cases, the trustee must feel that, for some non-income tax reason, it's vitally important that the trust accumulate income, assuming the trust authorizes it.

Current trust tax rates begin at 15% for retained trust income and reach a top rate of 39.6% for retained trust income over $7,500.

TRUST INCOME RATES	
Retained Trust Income	**Income Tax Rate**
$100–$1,500	15%
$1,500–$3,500	$225 plus 28% of the excess over $1,500
$3,500–$5,500	$785 plus 31% of the excess over $3,500
$5,500–$7,500	$1,405 plus 36% of the excess over $5,500
Over $7,500	$2,125 plus 39.6% of the excess over $7,500 ■

18

ESTATE TAX-SAVING BYPASS TRUSTS

A. Overview of Bypass Trusts 18/2

B. IRS Restrictions on Bypass Trusts 18/3

    1. Right to Spend Trust Principal 18/3

    2. The "5 and 5" Power 18/5

C. AB Trusts: Bypass Trusts for Couples 18/5

    1. How an AB Trust Reduces Estate Tax 18/6

    2. Is an AB Trust Best for You? 18/8

    3. How an AB Trust Is Created 18/10

    4. Choosing the Trustee 18/11

    5. The Rights of the Life Beneficiary 18/11

    6. How Much Property to Place in an AB Trust 18/12

D. Bypass Trusts for Unmarried Persons 18/16

    1. Unmarried Couples 18/16

    2. Single Persons 18/18

A "bypass" trust is an ongoing trust designed to lessen or eliminate overall estate taxes. The most popular form of this trust, commonly called an "AB" trust, is used by couples with a combined estate exceeding the estate tax threshold. It sometimes goes by other names, such as a "marital life estate trust," a "credit shelter trust" or an "exemption trust."

Bypass trusts can also be used to impose restrictions over a beneficiary's rights to trust property. This type of trust is discussed in Chapter 24, Property Control Trusts for Second or Subsequent Marriages, and in Chapter 25.

A. OVERVIEW OF BYPASS TRUSTS

Here are the basics of how a bypass trust works. You create an ongoing trust, either by will or within a living trust, that will take effect at your death. You name a beneficiary, usually your spouse, who has certain rights to use of that trust property during his or her life.

The property in the trust is part of your taxable estate. Usually, no estate tax will be due. (We discuss this later.) The main benefit comes when the surviving spouse dies. The key is that your spouse never legally owned the trust property. This is true even if he or she had the rights to receive all income generated by the property, or to use it (a house, for example). Because the surviving spouse never legally owned the property, it isn't counted as part of his or her estate, for estate tax purposes, when he or she dies.

When your spouse dies, the trust property goes to the final beneficiaries you specified in the trust document, usually your children. No estate tax is taken out of the trust property when the second spouse dies. By contrast, if you had left your property to your spouse outright, it would have been included as part of her taxable estate when she died.

The person you name to receive rights in the trust property during his or her life is called, fittingly, the "life beneficiary." The life beneficiary has only those rights to the trust property specified in the trust document. These rights can include receiving all trust income, using trust property (for example, living in the family home) or certain limited rights to spend trust principal for specific needs (for example, medical care and support).

Technically, it is the trustee who decides whether or not to spend trust principal for authorized needs of the life beneficiary. But in most tax-saving bypass trusts, the trustee and the life beneficiary are the same person. Still, the life beneficiary is never the legal owner of the trust property. She has no power to decide who receives it after her death.

Both couples (married or not) and individuals can create a bypass trust.

Example 1: Cecilia has been married to Lou for over 40 years. They have one grown child, Marietta, who is 37. Cecilia creates a bypass trust to become effective at her death. The trust will hold all her major items of property, both what's hers alone and her half of the assets she and Lou own together. She names Lou as life beneficiary. At Cecilia's death, he will have the right to receive all the income the trust property generates and to use the trust principal for basic needs like medical care for the rest of his life. When he dies, the trust property will pass outright to the final beneficiary, Marietta.

Example 2: Jefferson creates a bypass trust, naming his best friend, Isaac, as the life beneficiary. Isaac has the right to receive trust income, and also to live in the house the trust owns. Jefferson's trust document specifies that when Isaac dies, the property will be divided equally between Jefferson's children, the final beneficiaries.

To understand how bypass trusts actually save on estate taxes, obviously you need to know how those taxes work. (They are discussed in detail in Chapter 15, Estate Taxes.) Here we repeat three basic federal estate tax rules:

- Every person can leave a total at death, tax-free, equal to the amount of the personal exemption. This amount is $625,000 in 1998 and will rise until the year 2006 when it becomes $1 million. (See Chapter 15 for the exact exemption amounts for each year.) The personal exemption is available whether assets are left to one beneficiary or divided among many. The amount you can leave tax-free is reduced if you made taxable gifts during life. (See Chapter 16, Gifts and Gift Taxes.)

- Married people can leave any amount tax-free to a spouse who is a U.S. citizen. (See Chapter 15, Section A.) In tax lingo, this is called the "marital deduction."

- If you leave property worth more than the amount of your personal exemption in the year of your death outright to someone other than your spouse (say your brother), and a few years later he dies owning property worth more than his own exemption, estate tax will be levied twice on your property—once when you die and once when your brother dies.

Enter the bypass trust, where property is left for the use of a life beneficiary and then goes to a final beneficiary. Because under U.S. tax law and IRS rules, the life beneficiary never becomes the legal owner of the trust assets, property in the trust is subject to estate tax when the grantor dies, but is not taxed again when the life beneficiary dies—hence the name "bypass" trust.

Example: Continuing with Cecilia and Lou, from the above example, let's say Cecilia has property worth $700,000 when she dies in 2002. Lou's estate is also worth $700,000 when Cecilia dies.

If Cecilia had left her property outright to Lou, his total estate would be $1.4 million. If he were to die a year later, his personal exemption would also be $700,000. So $700,000 would be subject to estate tax. The amount of the tax would be $280,000. But because Cecilia used a bypass trust, no estate tax will be due on either's death. Cecilia's $700,000 is the exempt amount in 2002, so no tax is due. And since Lou is never the legal owner of Cecilia's trust property, his estate remains at $700,000 and so will not be subject to estate tax when he dies.

B. IRS Restrictions on Bypass Trusts

All bypass trusts must comply with applicable IRS regulations. If yours doesn't, the estate tax savings you're after will be lost.

1. Right to Spend Trust Principal

The trustee cannot be given complete freedom to spend trust principal for the life beneficiary. If the trustee has such unlimited rights, the IRS will regard the life beneficiary as the legal owner of the trust property, and impose estate tax on it when the life beneficiary dies.

The IRS does, however, allow the trustee to spend (invade) the trust principal for the life beneficiary's "health care, education, support and maintenance ... in accord with his or her accustomed standard of living." (IRS Regulation 320.2041-1(c)(2).) Spending trust principal for these purposes is allowed because, according to the IRS, the need for these expenditures can be judged against an "ascertainable standard."

Example 1: Arlo leaves his property in a bypass trust with his wife Sirpa as the life beneficiary. Sirpa is the trustee and she has the right to invade trust principal for her health care, education, support and maintenance. As trustee, she may sell trust property, invest it or exchange it. For instance, if the trust includes a home, she could ordinarily sell it and buy a retirement condo with the proceeds.

By contrast, if the trust document says that trust assets can be spent for, say, the "comfort" or "well-being" of the life beneficiary, the IRS considers this an "unascertainable" standard. In that case, the trust assets will be regarded as legally owned by the life beneficiary and taxed at his death, even if no trust money was in fact ever spent for these purposes.

Example 2: Let's assume Arlo's trust gave Sirpa the right to spend principal for her comfort. Even if she never spends any of the principal for any purpose, the IRS will consider her as the owner of the trust property and it will be subject to estate tax at her death.

This right to be able to spend trust principal for basic needs of the life beneficiary is crucially important to many couples. They want to conserve as much of their estate as possible for their children or other final beneficiaries, but they don't want the surviving spouse to risk running out of money for vital needs, such as health care or normal living expenses. A bypass trust document that is properly drafted—using the language acceptable to the IRS—eliminates this risk. The surviving spouse will have the right to use any amount of principal necessary for basic expenses, including medical care.

Example: Walter and Marjorie, a working couple in their late fifties, own shared property worth $1.2 million. They each draft a bypass trust for their half of the property, specifying that the income goes to the other spouse for life, with the assets then going to their children. Each includes in their trust language "powers," (in legal lingo) that give the survivor (as trustee) the right to spend trust principal for his or her health care, support and maintenance.

Each spouse has taken advantage of their personal exemption instead of leaving all property to the survivor and wasting the exemption of the first spouse to die. No estate tax will be due when the first spouse dies. They will avoid any federal estate tax on the trust money when the second spouse dies. If their financial situation remains stable (or their wealth increases), the survivor may never need to spend trust principal. However, they have provided a security back-up that allows the survivor to use all of the assets they both own if necessary.

You don't have to give the trustee the broad powers to spend principal that the law allows. In some situations, particularly second or subsequent marriages, one or both spouses may not want to give a surviving spouse the right to spend trust principal for support, and may even want to further restrict use of trust property. Normally, this is because a spouse wants to be sure trust property remains intact for her own children or other final beneficiaries. Indeed, you can forbid spending any of the trust principal at all. (See Chapter 24.)

2. The "5 and 5" Power

Another IRS rule allows you to give the trustee of a bypass trust what is called a "5 and 5" power. This authorizes the trustee to invade the trust principal annually for a beneficiary, for any reason whatsoever, up to a maximum of 5% of the trust principal or $5,000, whichever is greater. The trustee can be given authority to exercise this right for the life beneficiary, the final beneficiaries, or both. The trust document must specifically state which beneficiaries are eligible to receive trust property under the 5 and 5 power.

The 5 and 5 power is not in favor with many sophisticated estate planning lawyers these days. They reason that it's better to rely solely on a provision allowing the trustee to invade principal for the life beneficiary's "health care, education, support and maintenance," which protects the life beneficiary in case of real need. The risk of the 5 and 5 power is that it can allow the life beneficiary to use up, over the years, much or even all of the trust principal for any reason whatsoever.

One advantage of a 5 and 5 power, however, is that a final beneficiary, not just the life beneficiary, can benefit from it. If you think that one or more of the final beneficiaries (such as a child or children) may need money from the trust while the life beneficiary is alive, you can specify that the trustee can use the 5 and 5 power to benefit some or all of the final beneficiaries. (A "sprinkling trust" can also be used to benefit several beneficiaries. See Chapter 25, Trusts and Other Devices Imposing Controls Over Property, Section D.) For instance, if the trust document authorized it, a trustee might use the 5 and 5 power to spend some trust principal for the education of a needy final beneficiary, particularly if the life beneficiary would remain financially comfortable even after that money was spent.

The trustee does not have to exercise the 5 and 5 power. Each year it is up to the trustee to decide whether or not an eligible beneficiary should be given trust principal under this power. Normally there are no adverse tax consequences if the 5 and 5 power isn't exercised.

C. AB TRUSTS: BYPASS TRUSTS FOR COUPLES

For many couples who think their combined estate may be subject to estate tax, the ideal result can be simply stated: You want the surviving spouse to have access to the deceased spouse's property, if he or she needs it, but you don't want the surviving spouse to become the legal owner of that property, because then hefty estate tax will be due when the second spouse dies. You can achieve these goals with an AB trust, which is simply a bypass trust for married couples.

To summarize what we discussed in Section A, above, here's how it works. Each spouse creates an AB trust. (Usually, it's added onto a basic probate-avoidance living trust.) Instead of leaving his or her share of property outright to the survivor, each spouse leaves all, or at least the bulk, of his or her property to Trust A. When one spouse dies, the survivor gets only a "life estate" interest in all property of the deceased spouse that goes into the Trust A. The surviving spouse continues to have his or her separate revocable living trust, Trust B.

Each spouse names his or her final beneficiaries for his or her Trust A, who receive this trust's property when the surviving spouse dies. Most commonly, the final beneficiaries for both spouses are their children.

AB trusts involve some complexities and drawbacks, but they do work very well for many couples and families. Indeed, they are a standard component of most estate plans prepared by lawyers for couples with larger estates. For many older couples, the drawbacks amount to no more than relatively minor accounting and recordkeeping hassles after one spouse dies, which they feel are well worth it to conserve up to hundreds of thousands of dollars worth of their property for their children or other final beneficiaries.

DO YOU NEED A LAWYER?

You may wonder whether or not it's wise to prepare an AB trust yourself, without the aid of an attorney. If you and your spouse have a combined estate worth between $625,000 and $1,250,000, quite possibly you can go it alone. Forms and complete instructions for preparing an AB trust for couples in this situation can be found in *Make Your Own Living Trust,* by Denis Clifford (Nolo Press). The AB trust in that book is designed for couples who want to allow the surviving spouse the maximum legal rights over the trust property, while still gaining the estate tax-saving advantages of this type of trust.

You should consult a lawyer and should not use the trust in that book if:

• You and your spouse expect to have a combined estate exceeding twice the estate tax threshold. Consult a good estate planning lawyer to explore more sophisticated options to reduce estate tax.

• You want to impose limits on the rights of the surviving spouse to use trust property. This includes many couples in second or subsequent marriages, who want to be sure the bulk of their property is preserved for children from prior marriages.

• You need a more complicated type of ongoing trust, such as a special needs trust for a disadvantaged child or a spendthrift trust for a child who can't properly manage money.

---

1. How an AB Trust Reduces Estate Tax

You may wonder why a married couple needs an AB trust. After all, because of the marital deduction, one spouse can leave the other an unlimited amount of money free of federal estate tax. But what happens when the second spouse dies? For couples with a combined estate exceeding the estate tax threshold, the result is often an estate tax trap.

For example, if spouses with a combined shared estate of $1.2 million (that is, each owns $600,000) leave their portion to each other, the surviving spouse will wind up with $1.2 million. Say the first spouse dies in 1999 and the second in 2000 when the estate tax exemption is $675,000. When the second spouse dies, $525,000 will be subject to estate tax (the $1.2 million minus the exemption). The tax is a whopping $207,250.

Using an AB trust provides tax savings because the property in Trust A (the deceased spouse's share) is subject to estate tax only when the first spouse dies. If there is less than the personal exemption amount in that spouse's trust, no federal estate tax is due. And the Trust A property isn't subject to estate tax when the second spouse dies, because, as we've stressed, the second spouse never legally owned it.

Example: Arnold and Maggie share ownership of $1.6 million worth of property. (For the ease of both the authors and the readers, we will assume they both die after 2005, when the personal exemption becomes $1 million.) Maggie dies first, and Arnold a year later. If each leaves his or her property to the other, and the survivor leaves all their property to their two children, here are the tax consequences:

Without an AB Trust

On Maggie's Death:

Gross estate (1/2 shared property)	$800,000
Final bills, burial costs, etc.	($10,000)
Net taxable estate	$790,000
Estate tax due (Because of the marital deduction.)	$-0-

On Arnold's Death:

Gross estate (his $800,000 and $790,000 inherited from wife)	$1,590,000
Final bills, burial costs, etc.	($10,000)
Net taxable estate	$1,580,000
Tax assessed	$591,800
Credit for personal exemption (after 2005)	$345,800
Estate tax due	$146,000

Now let's look at what happens if Maggie and Arnold each create an AB trust, where each leaves his or her property in the A trust for the benefit of the surviving spouse for his or her life. When the second spouse dies, the trust property will be distributed to their children.

With an AB Trust

On Maggie's Death:

Gross estate (1/2 shared property)	$800,000
Final bills, burial costs, etc.	($10,000)
Net taxable estate	$790,000
Estate tax due	-0-

(because of Maggie's $1 million exemption)

On Arnold's Death:

Gross estate	$800,000
Final bills, burial costs, etc.	($10,000)

Net taxable estate $790,000

Estate tax due	-0-

(because of Arnold's $1 million exemption)

Neat, isn't it? By using an AB trust, no estate tax at all is paid. By contrast, without the trust, $146,000 must be handed over to the government in estate tax, instead of going to the children. What's more, owing tax also saddles the husband's executor (probably one of the children) with the hassle of having to file a federal estate tax return. And other costs may be involved if estate tax must be paid, such as appraisal fees. (However, if an AB trust is used, similar appraisal costs may also have to be paid at the first spouse's death in order to divide the property between the now irrevocable Trust A and the surviving spouse's continuing, revocable Trust B.) Finally, because estate tax must be paid when Arnold dies, his assets may be tied up for nine months after his death (that's when the estate tax return is due) before what's left can be transferred to the children.

You can place whatever property you want in your AB trust. You can place all your separate property and all your half of shared property, or any portion of either, in your trust.

If the Trust A assets appreciate substantially by the time the life beneficiary dies, this appreciation is not subject to any estate tax. The Trust A assets are subject to tax once, and only once—when the grantor dies.

Example: Isabel and Simon own shared assets totaling $1.4 million. They each draft an AB trust for their $700,000 shares, with their children as the final beneficiaries. Isabel dies first, and Simon lives for another 20 years without spending any of the Trust A principal. At Simon's death, the Trust A property is worth $1.5 million. No estate tax is assessed against the Trust A property when Simon dies. The full $1.5 million is now distributed to the children with no estate tax ever paid on these assets.

2. Is an AB Trust Best for You?

AB trusts aren't for everyone. Before deciding to use an AB trust, you and your spouse should understand what you're getting into. Once one spouse dies, that spouse's Trust A becomes irrevocable; it imposes limits and burdens on the survivor's use of the deceased spouse's property that cannot be changed. There are other important considerations as well. Here are some guidelines.

a. Size of Your Estate

If you and your spouse expect to have a combined estate worth less than the estate tax threshold when the second spouse dies, there's no reason to bother with an AB trust. Even if the first spouse to die leaves everything outright to the other, the surviving spouse's estate will still be under the federal estate tax threshold. (Remember that this figure is $625,000 in 1998 and will rise until the year 2006, when it levels off at $1 million. See Chapter 15.) Of course, if during your lives your combined estate grows significantly, you can then revise your plan and create an AB trust.

b. Your Intended Beneficiaries

If you don't want to leave the bulk of your property for use of your surviving spouse, but want instead to leave substantial amounts of property directly to other beneficiaries, an AB trust won't accomplish your goals.

c. Restrictions on the Surviving Spouse

Couples under 45 rarely create an AB trust. Younger couples usually don't want to risk tying up one spouse's assets in a Trust A. If one spouse dies prematurely, the surviving spouse may well live for decades, and would likely be far better off inheriting the deceased spouse's property outright. The survivor will inherit everything estate tax-free, no matter what the amount, because of the marital deduction. That surviving spouse will probably have years to use the money—and to arrange for other methods of reducing any eventual estate tax.

Similarly, couples where one spouse is considerably younger than the other and presumably will live much longer may not want an AB trust. Generally there's no need to burden the younger spouse with a trust designed to save estate tax when he or she is likely to live for many years.

Commonly, it's only as a couple reaches their 50s or 60s that they create an AB trust. But we've seen couples in their late 30s prepare AB trusts, because they want to be sure that they've done all they can to reduce estate tax. They've considered and accepted the possibility that one spouse's property may be tied up in trust for decades of the surviving spouse's life.

d. Difficulty Dividing the Property

At the death of the first spouse, the couple's shared property must be divided into two legally separate entities. One share is owned by the surviving spouse's revocable living Trust B and is under the surviving spouse's complete control. The other share is placed in the deceased's Trust A.

When the first spouse dies, an estate lawyer or accountant will be needed to determine how to best divide the couple's assets between the now-irrevocable Trust A and the continuing Trust B of the surviving spouse. Each item of the couple's shared property does not have to be divided 50/50 between the two trusts, but the total value of shared property in each trust must be equal. This means there is considerable flexibility in allocating assets between the two trusts. It takes an expert to decide on the best division, because different allocations have different tax consequences.

For example, what should be done with the family home? If full ownership of the house were placed in the Trust A, the house would be valued, for estate tax purposes, at its value on the death of the first spouse. By contrast, if the house were allocated to the surviving spouse, and she survives for many more years, the house would probably be worth more (given inflation) by the date of her death. Its increased value might result in the value of the

survivor's estate exceeding the personal exemption amount or, if her estate were already well over that, in extra tax being paid because of the increased worth of the house.

But there can also be drawbacks to including the full value of a house in Trust A. If the trust owns a house, certain tax advantages are lost. For example, an individual has the right to sell a house and retain up to $250,000 profit (capital gain) without tax. An irrevocable trust has no such right. So if the house may be sold in the future, it can be costly, income tax-wise, to place it in Trust A. This just scratches the surface of the complexity of dividing a couple's property between the two trusts on the death of a spouse. Of course, not every case is complex, but the surviving spouse should at least check the matter out with an expert before actually dividing up the couple's shared property.

e. Duty to File Trust Tax Returns

The trustee of Trust A must obtain a taxpayer ID number for the trust. The trustee must file an annual trust income tax return for that trust. This usually isn't a big deal, but like any tax return, it requires some work.

f. Complicated Recordkeeping

After the first spouse dies, the surviving spouse must keep two sets of books and records, one for her own property, including property in Trust B, and one for Trust A property.

g. Potential Family Strife

No matter what age you are, an AB trust works best when all involved—both spouses and all final beneficiaries—understand and agree on the purposes of the trust. Again, these goals are to save on overall estate tax and at the same time give the surviving spouse the maximum allowable rights to use trust income, and principal if necessary. Without this agreement, serious conflicts between the surviving spouse and the final beneficiaries may develop. This can be particularly true when there are children from a prior marriage.

If there is any potential for conflict between the surviving spouse and the final beneficiaries of the trust, an AB trust may well provoke or aggravate it. After all, in theory at least, there is an inherent conflict of interest between the life estate beneficiary and the final beneficiaries. The final beneficiaries may want all the trust principal conserved, no matter what the surviving spouse needs. On the other hand, the surviving spouse may want or need to use up most or even all of the trust principal for health care, education or maintenance.

Another conflict can arise if the surviving spouse becomes ill and can no longer serve as trustee. If a child who stands to eventually receive trust assets takes over as successor trustee, it's possible the child might be more concerned with preserving principal than with a parent's medical or other needs. We've heard of such situations, where it seemed to other family members and friends that a child disregarded his parent's basic needs and instead protected the trust principal for himself.

Conflicts can also occur if the final beneficiaries believe the surviving spouse, as trustee, is not managing the trust property sensibly—for example, by investing in very speculative stocks or risky real estate deals. If this situation arises, there can be real trouble, possibly even a lawsuit.

An AB trust is less likely to create strife down the road if:

- Family members trust each other, are reasonably close and are able to work out any conflicts that might arise.

- The final beneficiaries understand that taking the trouble to create an AB trust is a generous act; after all, the trust benefits the children, not the people who create the trust. The final beneficiaries receive much more of the couple's estate than they would have if the spouses had left property outright to the other.

- If Trust A allows the surviving spouse, as trustee, to spend trust principal for his "support, health, education and maintenance," the final beneficiaries can be trusted to support the surviving spouse if he decides to spend trust principal for any authorized reason.

FINAL BENEFICIARIES IN SECOND MARRIAGES

Couples in a second or subsequent marriage often want to name different final beneficiaries for each spouse's property. Each often wants children from a prior marriage as final beneficiaries. Fortunately, each spouse creates his or her own separate AB trust, so each has the right to choose the final beneficiaries for his or her own trust property. (This issue is discussed further in Chapter 24.)

---

3. How an AB Trust Is Created

Normally, an AB trust is combined with a living trust. (See Chapter 17, An Overview of Ongoing Trusts.) That way, when one spouse dies, the trust property first avoids probate, and then the irrevocable Trust A becomes operational.

Each spouse owns his or her distinct portion of the living trust property, which includes half of any community or co-owned property, and all that spouse's separate property. When one spouse dies, that spouse's Trust A, containing whatever portion of his or her property was designated for the Trust, becomes irrevocable. The surviving spouse, normally also the trustee, takes over management of the trust's property and must comply with all terms of the trust.

Meanwhile, the surviving spouse's Trust B (that is, her portion of the couple's original living trust) continues to be revocable, as long as she lives. The surviving spouse can amend her living trust to create whatever new provisions and beneficiary clauses seem appropriate. Or, she can leave her trust as it is. When she dies, the property in Trust B will go directly to whomever she named as the final beneficiaries in her living trust. The Trust A property will be distributed according to the original terms of the document.

4. Choosing the Trustee

We discussed how to select the trustee of a bypass trust in Chapter 17, Section F. There are, however, some special considerations when you're choosing the trustee for an AB trust.

Most couples want the surviving spouse to serve as initial trustee of Trust A, which becomes operational when the first spouse dies. To do that, the trust document simply makes both spouses initial trustees of the AB trust. Because Trust A doesn't become operational until one spouse dies, only the surviving spouse will actually serve as trustee.

Example: Mark and Vera have three grown children and a combined estate worth approximately $1.4 million. In their shared living trust document, each creates an AB trust. Each specifies that all his or her property is to go into his or her Trust A at his or her death. The document names both spouses as co-trustees of the trusts.

Mark dies first. His property goes into Trust A, which is now operational. Vera is the sole trustee and will manage the property in Trust A. She also remains trustee for Trust B, a revocable living trust, which holds her own property.

Living trust documents normally also name a successor trustee for Trust A to take over management of the trust property if the surviving spouse becomes incapacitated. You may also want to name an alternate successor trustee.

If you don't want your surviving spouse to be trustee of your Trust A, you can name someone else. For example, your spouse may be infirm, not sensible about financial affairs or simply uninterested.

If you wish, you can name more than one person to serve as co-successor trustees. For example, you might want to name your two adult children, or your spouse and one adult child, as co-trustees. (The potential pitfalls of naming co-trustees are discussed in Chapter 17, Section F.)

When selecting the successor and alternate successor trustees for an AB trust, ask several questions about your choices:

- Does the person or persons want to serve?
- Is the person capable of handling the trustee's duties?
- Would trust management duties create an undue burden on that person?
- Will the trustee be paid?
- Do you completely trust the person to manage the property as you would wish?

5. The Rights of the Life Beneficiary

Many couples want to make sure the surviving spouse has the broadest possible power over the trust property. As discussed in Section B, the trustee can be given all of the following rights:

- the right to distribute all trust income to the surviving spouse (and remember, the trustee and the surviving spouse are usually the same person)
- the right to control the trust property (use it, as with a house, or buy or sell, as long as principal is conserved)
- the right to spend trust principal in any amount needed for the surviving spouse's "health, education, support or maintenance, in his or her accustomed manner of living," and
- the 5 and 5 power (Section B, above).

However, you can place all kinds of restrictions on the rights of the life beneficiary to Trust A property. The only possible complication is that a surviving spouse in non-community property states has the right to claim a certain portion (usually about one third) of the deceased spouse's estate. As long as the surviving spouse has been left a substantial portion of your estate or is content with what she's inherited, there will be no problem. Even with these considerations, the rights to trust property can be fairly narrow.

Example: Sam is in his 60s and is married to Diane. He has two adult daughters by his former marriage. Diane does not have children of her own. Sam's estate is worth $700,000, consisting mainly of a residence and a stock portfolio. He also has a life insurance policy that will pay $400,000 to Diane at his death. Diane has only around $50,000 in assets. Sam wants to support Diane, preserve as much as possible for his daughters, use his personal estate tax exemption, and take advantage of the benefit of an AB trust.

Sam prepares an AB trust for all his assets. When Sam dies, the income from property in Trust A will go to Diane for life; the principal will go to his daughters after Diane's death. Sam worries, though, that if he dies, Diane may

remarry someone who'll push her to get at the trust principal. On the other hand, he doesn't want Diane to go without medical care she might need but can't pay for herself. So he names a daughter he trusts, not Diane, to be the successor trustee of Trust A. He also includes a provision in his trust that allows the successor trustee to invade the principal for Diane's health care only if all of her other assets are exhausted and the income from the trust is not sufficient. He feels that this is the best he can do for everybody, and hopes that his wife and children will agree.

Other still more restrictive provisions can be imposed if you wish. For example, the surviving spouse can be denied the right to invade Trust A principal for any reason. Or use of Trust A property can be strictly controlled—for instance, the surviving spouse can be given the right only to live in a house owned by the trust, not to sell it. Also, it's legal to provide that a spouse's benefits end if he remarries. If he remarries, the Trust A property is promptly turned over to the final trust beneficiaries. All these types of restrictions are discussed in depth in Chapter 24.

6. How Much Property to Place in an AB Trust

In 1998, each spouse can leave up to $625,000 in an AB trust without any estate tax liability. As we've said, this amount goes up steadily until the year 2006, when it levels at $1 million. If a couple has a combined estate that will be subject to estate tax, they'll want to take advantage of both of their personal estate tax exemptions by creating an AB trust and each leaving their own property in the trust. Doing this won't, however, necessarily eliminate all estate tax on the death of the first spouse. For example, if a couple has shared property worth $3 million, each one's share is worth $1.5 million. If a spouse's entire $1.5 million is placed in a Trust A, part of it will be subject to estate tax, no matter what the year of death. So to reduce estate taxes further, each spouse may want to limit the amount in their Trust A to the personal exemption amount in the year of death, and leave the remainder outright to the surviving spouse or in another trust which will defer estate tax until the death of the second spouse. (See Chapter 19, Other Marital Estate Tax-Saving Trusts, Section A.)

a. Using a Formula Clause

Many estate planners advise you not to leave all your property to your Trust A. Similarly, they recommend that you do not specify a dollar amount of property to be put in your Trust A. Instead, they recommend putting what's called a "formula" clause in the trust document. Essentially, the formula provides (in heavy legalese) that the worth of assets put in the A trust is to equal the amount of the personal estate tax exemption for the year of death. Any property of the deceased above this amount is handled by other tax-avoidance methods.

A formula AB trust is useful for people whose estates are likely to be over the estate tax threshold. If your estate is well under this threshold, you don't need a formula clause. If your estate is over the estate tax threshold, a formula clause ensures that you don't have to amend your AB trust as the amount of the personal exemption increases, or as your assets increase. As the exemption amount goes up over the next few years, a formula clause trust will always be current. This will also be so if Congress decides to change the exemption amounts in the future.

Example: Monica and Tony have a combined estate of $1.6 million, owned equally. They each create an AB trust, using a formula clause that provides that Trust A will contain that

amount that results in no estate tax when the first spouse dies. The remaining assets go outright to the surviving spouse. Monica and Tony don't have to worry about relatively minor changes in the estate tax law, and the survivor doesn't have to worry about paying any estate tax when the first spouse dies. If one of them dies in the year 2000, Trust A will hold $675,000, the amount exempt for that year. If the death is in 2003, the amount will be $700,000 and so on. If the death occurs after 2005, when the exempt amount reaches $1 million, unless their finances have grown enormously (or Congress changes the law again), the trust will hold all of the assets of the first to die.

If you want to place more or less than the exempt amount in your Trust A, a formula clause is obviously not desirable. This is sometimes done with large estates to balance overall estate taxes. (See Subsection b, below.) A formula clause if useful only if you decide that the best course is to place exactly the current exempt amount in your Trust A at your death.

Wealthy couples often combine a formula AB trust with other tax deferral methods and defer estate tax until later. Many couples simply do not want to pay any estate tax until they must—after the second spouse's death. They can accomplish this by each leaving no more than the exemption amount for the year of death in the Trust A, and all the rest to the surviving spouse. This property can be left to the surviving spouse outright or in another trust like a QTIP which qualifies for the marital deduction and defers tax until the second death. (See Chapter 19, Section A, for more on QTIPS.)

Example: Theo and Rita have an estate of $3 million, owned equally. They prepare a formula AB trust. Rita dies in 1999. Under the formula, $650,000 is placed in her Trust A. The balance of her estate—$850,000—goes outright to Theo, and is exempt from estate tax under the marital deduction.

If Rita died in 2006, $1 million would have been placed in her Trust A, and $500,000 would have gone outright to Theo. And if Congress raised the estate tax exemption to $1.5 million in 2010, and Rita died in that year, all of her estate would be put in her Trust A.

Using a formula AB trust can be desirable, no matter how much money the couple has, when it's likely that one spouse will long outlive the other. The deceased spouse leaves all property over the exemption amount to the surviving spouse free of estate tax. The surviving spouse will, hopefully, have many years, even decades, to use that money. The income and potential growth in value of the assets the spouse receives can far exceed any additional estate tax that eventually has to be paid. Also, the surviving spouse can take other actions to lower eventual estate tax, such as making regular tax-free gifts. (See Chapter 16, Gifts and Gift Taxes, Section E.)

Finally, there can be other reasons to postpone estate taxes that may outweigh any higher overall tax costs. For instance, if an estate consists of property that is not liquid, such as a family-owned business or a valuable residence, it may be worth waiting and paying extra tax dollars at the second death to prevent having to sell assets to get cash for tax at the first death.

b. Placing More Than the Exempt Amount for the Year of Death in an AB Trust

In larger estates—and especially for older couples— sometimes it's sensible for each spouse to place assets worth more than the tax-exempt amount in an AB trust. The reason is those old graduated estate tax rates, which start at 37% and go to 55% for estates over $3 million. The larger the estate when it is taxed, the higher the percentage that will be lost to estate tax. This means for couples with substantial estates, overall estate tax can be lowered if some of their property is taxed when the first spouse dies.

Example: Carl and Sophia have a combined estate of shared property worth $4 million. They each draft an AB trust, specifying that property equal to the amount of the personal exemption be put in the A trust when the first spouse dies. They leave all other property outright to the other. Carl dies first. They both die after 2005. The personal exemption is $1 million. If Carl's A trust contains $1 million, and his final bills are $25,000, $975,000 is left to Sophia. No estate tax is due when Carl dies.

Carl's gross estate	$2,000,000
Final bills, costs, etc.	($25,000)
Net taxable estate	$1,975,000
Property in A trust	$1,000,000
Property left to Sophia	$975,000
Estate tax due (because of the personal estate tax exemption and the marital deduction)	-0-

Sophia's estate is now worth $2,975,000. If her estate remains the same and she dies several years later, here's the tax picture:

Sophia's gross estate	$2,975,000
Final bills, costs, etc.	($25,000)
Net taxable estate	$2,950,000
Estate tax at 53%	$1,264,300
Estate tax credit for the $1 million personal exemption	($345,800)
Estate tax due	$918,500

Now let's suppose that Carl's A trust contains all of his assets, $2 million, not just $1 million. Income to Sophia from that amount during her life should suffice for her needs; after all, she also owns $2 million outright. All of Carl's property is subject to estate tax when he dies; none is left outright to Sophia, so none qualifies for the marital deduction.

Here's the estate tax picture when Carl dies:

Carl's gross estate	$2,000,000
Costs, etc.	($25,000)
Net taxable estate	$1,975,000
Estate tax at 45%	$769,550
Estate tax credit for the $1 million personal exemption	($345,800)
Estate tax due	$423,750

And at Sophia's death:

Sophia's gross estate	$2,000,000
Costs, etc.	($25,000)
Net estate	$1,975,000
Estate tax at 45%	$769,550
Estate tax credit for the $1 million personal exemption	($345,800)
Estate tax due	$423,750

By increasing the value of the property in the Trust A when the first spouse dies, Carl's and Sophia's estates have paid a total of $847,500 in estate tax. Compared to the $918,500 in tax if $1 million had been put in the trust, they have saved $71,000 for their inheritors.

If Carl had used no A trust at all and had just left everything to Sophia, her taxable estate would have been $3,950,000. After her personal $1 million tax exemption, her estate would pay $1,467,500 in tax.

c. Spouses Who Own Different Amounts of Property

Spouses who don't own equal amounts of property need to take that difference into account when setting up an AB trust. Even if the total value of the couple's property is worth less than their combined personal exemptions, if the value of one spouse's separate property plus her interest in shared property adds up to an amount large enough to owe estate tax, that spouse has estate planning decisions to make. Does she want to place all her property in her Trust A when she dies, and have some estate tax paid on her estate? Or does she want to leave anything over the exempt amount to her husband, free of tax under the marital deduction?

To save money on estate tax, wealthy couples with different-sized estates can create AB trusts designed to equalize the worth of the two estates. This way, the wealthier spouse's estate tax rate is lowered, because the estate tax rate goes up as the value of the estate increases. Overall, the estate tax paid will be less.

Example: Joe has a $2 million estate; his wife, Nelda, has $800,000 in assets. Joe's estate plan places $1.4 million in his Trust A and leaves the remaining $600,000 outright to Nelda. No estate tax is due on this $600,000 because of the marital deduction. If Joe dies first, his taxable estate is $1.4 million. The estate tax rate on this amount is 43%. Nelda receives the $600,000, making her estate worth $1.4 million. The taxable estates of the two spouses have been equalized, and overall estate tax has been lowered.

D. Bypass Trusts for Unmarried Persons

Anyone, whether married or not, can use a life estate bypass trust. In either case, the trust document names a life beneficiary to receive specified rights to the trust property, and final beneficiaries to receive the trust property when the life beneficiary dies.

You may want to consider a bypass trust if:

- You want to leave property to someone only for his or her life, then outright to others.

- You trust the life beneficiary or someone else to serve as the successor trustee of the trust after you die, while the life beneficiary lives. This trustee

must protect the rights of both the life beneficiary and the final beneficiaries.

1. Unmarried Couples

An unmarried couple can achieve the same overall estate tax savings with a bypass trust as can a married couple. The terminology is different; the trust isn't usually called an AB trust, the term applied to a married couple's trust. Instead, the trust is sometimes simply called a bypass trust or a "life estate trust."

Of course, the marital deduction is not available for unmarried couples. Any amount one of them owns in excess of his personal exemption will be subject to tax when he dies, unless it's simply left to charity or another estate tax-saving trust, such as a charitable remainder trust, is used. (See Chapter 20, Charitable Trusts.) Still, the estate tax savings an unmarried couple can achieve by using bypass trusts can be substantial.

Example 1: Ira and Selma, an unmarried couple, have no children. They've been together for over 30 years, and all of their combined estate of $900,000 is held in shared ownership. Ira has a much younger brother to whom he's very close. Selma is equally close to two nieces. Ira and Selma each leave the other his or her property in a bypass trust, rather than outright, and names his or her own relatives as final beneficiaries of each one's life estate trust. As a result, they avoid estate tax, and each ensures that his or her property will eventually go to the desired final beneficiaries.

Example 2: Antonio and Gina are an unmarried couple with two children. Their combined estates total $1.2 million. They wish to provide support for each other for life and then leave their assets to their children. If the first to die leaves a $600,000 share outright to the other, then on the survivor's death, some estate tax will be due, no matter what the year of death. However, if each of them creates a bypass trust with the other as the life beneficiary, the children will eventually inherit all the property tax-free. This is because by establishing a bypass trust, both Gina's and Antonio's personal estate tax exemptions are used.

Example 3: Shizue and Takanori each own property worth $1 million. After one of them dies, they want the other to have the use of and the income from the deceased partner's property. But each also wants to preserve the bulk of their estate for other beneficiaries. Each creates a bypass trust consisting of all his or her property, with income from the trust going to the other for his or her life. Also, each authorizes the other to use any amount of trust principal for health care or basic maintenance. At the second death, remaining assets in the trust will go to their respective relatives.

Shizue dies first, in 2007 (her exemption is $1 million) and Takanori ten years later. Assuming the property values remain the same, let's look at the tax picture.

On Shizue's death:

Gross estate	$1,000,000
Federal estate tax due (because of personal exemption)	-0-

On Takanori's death:

Gross estate	$1,000,000
Federal estate tax due (because of his personal exemption)	-0-

Takanori never owned the $1 million left by Shizue in her life estate trust, so it bypassed his estate for tax purposes. At his death, those assets pass tax-free to the relatives Shizue named in her trust document.

Now, let's look at what would have happened without a trust, if each had just left everything to the other. On Shizue's death, no estate taxes are due because of her personal exemption.

On Takanori's death, however, you can see how not using a bypass trust costs their inheritors several hundred thousand dollars:

Gross estate	$2,000,000
Federal estate tax (Estate tax credit)	$780,800
for his personal exemption	($345,800)
Estate tax due	$435,000

The $435,000 saved by using the bypass trust will go, eventually, to their final beneficiaries.

The savings would be even greater if the value of the property went up before Takanori's death. For example, if Takanori lived 15 more years, the value of Shizue's bypass trust property might rise to $1.5 million or more. That appreciation would pass to the final beneficiaries without further tax, because the property was already taxed when Shizue died.

2. Single Persons

A single person, not a member of a couple, usually isn't concerned with providing for another person for her or his life, then having property go to other final beneficiaries. And there usually isn't any reason to look for tax savings through a trust, since there is no one other person the single person might combine his estate with, as there often is with a couple. Still, a life estate bypass trust can prove every bit as effective in saving on eventual taxes for final beneficiaries as it is for a couple.

Example: Gustav, a bachelor, leaves all of his property, worth $700,000, in a bypass trust with his brother Ludwig as the life beneficiary. At Ludwig's death, the assets are to go to Gustav's favorite two nephews, Ludwig's sons.

As you can see from the table in Chapter 15, if Gustav dies before the year 2002, a small amount of estate tax will be due at his death. For instance, if he dies in 2000, $25,000 would be subject to estate tax. But the personal exemption from estate tax increases until 2006, when it becomes $1 million. And by the year 2002, the exemption is already at $700,000, which would cover all of Gustav's property, so no tax would be due on his death after that. But the real tax savings comes at Ludwig's death.

When Ludwig dies, the property in Gustav's trust (no matter how much it is worth at the time) passes tax-free to his sons. This is true even if that property has increased greatly in value, because the trust assets have bypassed Ludwig's estate. Now let's look at what would have happened without the bypass trust, if Gustav just left his property outright to Ludwig.

Nothing changes at Gustav's death; if federal estate tax is due, it will be paid. But when Ludwig dies, Gustav's property will be added to all other property Ludwig owns, for estate tax purposes. If Ludwig's estate, when he dies, was worth $1.5 million (including the amount he received from Gustav), here are the tax figures.

Ludwig's gross estate	$1,500,000
Federal estate tax	$555,800
Estate tax credit if he dies after 2005 for $1 million personal exemption	($345,800)
Estate tax due	$210,000

In sum, single people who want to support another person for life, then have their property benefit other younger beneficiaries, can sensibly use a bypass trust. ∎

19

OTHER ESTATE TAX-SAVING MARITAL TRUSTS

A. QTIP Trusts 19/3
    1. How QTIP Trusts Work 19/3
    2. Long-Term Tax Consequences of QTIP Trusts 19/4
    3. Who Can Benefit From a QTIP Trust 19/5
    4. The Surviving Spouse's Rights 19/6
    5. Powers That May Be Given to the Surviving Spouse 19/8
    6. The "QTIP Election" 19/10
    7. The Reverse QTIP Election 19/12
    8. Planning for a QTIP 19/13
B. Trusts for Non-Citizen Spouses: QDOTs 19/13
C. Marital Deduction Trusts 19/15
    1. Power of Appointment Trusts 19/16
    2. Estate Trusts 19/17
D. Widow's Election Trusts 19/17

Because estate tax laws treat the married and unmarried differently, we do too. This chapter covers tax-saving trusts available only to the legally married. Unmarried people—whether couples or single—can skip this chapter.

Married couples can take advantage of several kinds of trusts, other than the AB trusts discussed in Chapter 18, to save on estate tax. This chapter covers some of the most popular and useful kinds, including:

• **QTIP Trusts.** A QTIP trust allows a married person to name the surviving spouse as the life beneficiary of trust property. When the second spouse dies, the property passes to final beneficiaries named by the first spouse. This type of trust is labeled a Qualified Terminable Interest Property trust in federal tax law. Usually, this obtuse jargon is shortened to "QTIP." So far, a QTIP trust sounds just like a marital AB trust, right? However, unlike an AB trust, with a QTIP, when the first spouse dies all the property in the trust is exempt from estate tax, no matter how much it's worth. This is because under IRS rules, property in the QTIP trust qualifies for the unlimited marital deduction.

However, property remaining in the QTIP trust when the second spouse dies is included in that spouse's estate, for estate tax purposes. So taxes are postponed, not eliminated. The principal reason to use a QTIP is to avoid paying any estate tax when the first spouse dies, which makes more money available to the survivor.

QTIPs are useful only if you and your spouse have a combined estate exceeding the estate tax threshold. The personal estate tax exemption is $625,000 in 1998 and will grow until $1 million by 2006. (See Chapter 15, Section A.)

Generally, QTIPs aren't used unless a couple's combined estate exceeds their combined exemptions. Couples with estates worth less than this

amount—$2 million after 2005—generally need use only an AB trust.

• **QDOT Trusts.** If you're married to a non-citizen and have an estate worth over the estate tax threshold that you want to leave to your spouse, consider a QDOT trust. (Section B.) This trust lets you defer estate tax until the death of the second spouse.

• **Marital Deduction Trusts.** These types of trusts have been largely replaced by QTIP trusts. The marital deduction trusts provide the estate tax postponement of a QTIP, but unlike a QTIP, permit the surviving spouse to name the final beneficiaries, make gifts of principal and accumulate income. (Section C.)

• **Widow's Election Trusts.** This rarely used trust enables the first spouse to die to name final beneficiaries for both spouses' estates. (Section D.)

A. QTIP TRUSTS

The four basic purposes of a QTIP trust are to:

1. Postpone estate tax on the estate of the first spouse to die until the second spouse dies.

2. Leave money and property for the use (but not outright ownership) of the surviving spouse.

3. Name final beneficiaries (often, children or grandchildren, including those from a prior marriage) to receive the trust property at the death of the surviving spouse.

4. Allow for some after-death (lawyers call it "post-mortem") flexibility. As we discuss below, your executor (the person in charge of carrying out the terms of your will) can evaluate the estate tax situation and choose whether or not a QTIP you've created should actually become operational.

Find a knowledgeable lawyer. To prepare a QTIP trust, you need an expert estate planning lawyer. Many complex issues can arise when actually preparing the trust, and a mistake can be fatal, estate tax-wise. The IRS regularly refuses to grant trusts QTIP status because they didn't conform to all applicable federal regulations. If that happens, estate tax isn't postponed, and the major benefit of a QTIP is wasted. (For tips on finding a good lawyer, see Chapter 29, Using Lawyers, Section A.)

1. How QTIP Trusts Work

As we've said, a QTIP trust is similar in many aspects to an AB trust. In each case, a spouse is the grantor (the person wh creates the trust). Each spouse can create a separate QTIP trust for his or her property, whether it's separate property, half of shared prop-

erty, or both. In both QTIPs and AB trusts, the surviving spouse is the life beneficiary. The original grantor gets to name the final trust beneficiaries—normally, his or her children—to receive his or her trust property when the surviving spouse dies.

The big difference between these two types of trusts is that with a QTIP, no federal estate tax is assessed against trust property when the first spouse dies—no matter how much that property is worth. With a regular AB trust, property above the amount of the personal exemption for the year of death is subject to estate tax when the grantor dies.

You can use both an AB trust and a QTIP trust together. Indeed, using these two trusts for each spouse is the foundation of the estate plans of some wealthier people. When the first spouse dies, property worth up to the amount of the personal exemption for that year is placed in a formula AB trust and is exempt from estate tax. All that spouse's remaining property goes into the QTIP trust, which is also exempt from tax. (Combining these two types of trusts in an estate plan is discussed further in Chapter 23, Combining Estate Tax-Saving Trusts, Section A.)

Example 1: Li-shan leaves $700,000 in an AB trust and $900,000 in a QTIP trust, with her husband as life beneficiary of both trusts. When she dies in 2003, no federal estate tax is due. Property in the QTIP trust is exempt because it qualifies for the unlimited marital deduction. (Any property left in the trust will be taxed when Li-shan's husband dies.) The $700,000 in the AB trust is exempt because Li-shan's personal estate tax exemption for 2003 is $700,000. By contrast, if Li-shan had left $900,000 in the AB trust and $700,000 in the QTIP trust, with her husband as life beneficiary, $200,000 of the AB trust would have been subject to estate tax when Li-shan died.

Example 2: Bernice, who is married to George, has an estate worth $2.6 million. She creates both a formula AB trust (see Chapter 18, Section C, on formula clauses) and a QTIP trust for her remaining assets. Using both trusts, she is able to use her personal estate tax exemption and postpone all taxes. If she left the entire $2.6 million in a QTIP trust, no estate tax would be due when she died, but the whole amount would be taxed at her husband's death. She would never use her personal exemption, and the estate tax savings the exemption offers would be lost.

QTIPs AT A GLANCE

- A QTIP trust creates a life estate for the surviving spouse, who is entitled to:

  * use trust assets, such as a residence, for her lifetime,

  * receive trust income regularly, and

  * spend trust principal to the extent allowed by the trust document.

- In the trust document, the grantor names final beneficiaries, who will inherit the QTIP trust assets when the surviving spouse dies.

- No estate tax is assessed when the grantor dies.

- When the surviving spouse dies, the full net value of the property in the QTIP (as of that date) is included in her taxable estate.

- The QTIP assets do not go through probate after the death of the surviving spouse.

---

2. Long-Term Tax Consequences of QTIP Trusts

It's vital to understand that estate tax on QTIP trust property is not eliminated. When the second spouse dies, tax must be paid on all property in that spouse's estate. Under tax law, this includes the full net worth of all property in the QTIP, valued as of the date of the surviving spouse's death.

Example: Sheila leaves property worth $2 million in a QTIP, with Atah, her husband, as life beneficiary. No tax is due at her death. Atah has an estate of $1 million of his own and his total estate, now including property in the QTIP, is $3 million. He dies in 2006 when his personal exemption is $1 million. The $2 million in the QTIP (or whatever the amount is at the time) will be taxed.

Because all of the value of QTIP property is included in the taxable estate of the second spouse to die, the tax rate will almost always be higher than if the first spouse had left that property by other methods, including making use of her own personal exemption.

Example: Gregor leaves $500,000 in an AB trust and creates a QTIP trust for his wife, Natalie, with his children as final beneficiaries. When Gregor dies $1.5 million is placed in the QTIP. Natalie's separate estate is worth $1 million, and now her total estate will be $1 million + $1.5 million = $2.5 million. The tax rate on this sum will be higher than the rate that would have been applied to Gregor's total estate of $2 million.

If the property in the QTIP trust increases in value during the surviving spouse's life, that increase is subject to estate tax when that spouse dies. Again, this is not true for property in an AB trust. With an

AB trust, the value of the trust property for tax purposes is determined only once, at the date of death of the grantor spouse.

Example: Ivan creates a QTIP trust with property that is worth $1.1 million when he dies. By the time his wife, Olga, dies 12 years later, the value of the trust property has risen to $5.6 million. This total $5.6 million is included in Olga's taxable estate.

3. Who Can Benefit From a QTIP Trust

QTIPs are popular with some estate planners. But why, given the possible tax drawbacks just discussed? Most importantly, because some wealthier couples decide that postponing tax payment until the second spouse dies is worth any eventual tax cost. They strongly do not want to have any of their estate eaten up by tax when the first spouse dies, even if more taxes are paid in the long run. Moreover, it's far from clear, usually, that it will cost more in the long run. With a QTIP, a surviving spouse who outlives the other by a significant period of time—say a few years or more—will receive income from all the deceased spouse's property, without having had any taken out to pay estate tax. This money the surviving spouse receives from the trust property may exceed any additional tax paid on that spouse's death.

But why use a QTIP instead of leaving property outright to the surviving spouse? Because one spouse or both prefers the control a QTIP provides—the power of the original grantor to name the final beneficiaries for the trust. A unique advantage of a QTIP trust is that it allows you to have the trust property treated, tax-wise, as if the surviving spouse inherited it outright (i.e., use the marital deduction) and simultaneously allows you to impose controls over this property and specify who eventually inherits your share.

Finally, because each member of a couple can create separate AB trusts and QTIPs, neither spouse must sacrifice his or her personal estate tax exemption. Rather, the usual plan, as we've said, is for each spouse to create a formula AB trust to use his or her personal estate tax exception, and a QTIP trust to postpone payment of estate tax on any additional property.

QTIPs are commonly used when one spouse in a second marriage is older and more affluent than the other. Typically, the wealthy spouse wants to provide adequate financial resources during the other spouse's life, but also wants the trust property to go to kids from an earlier marriage after the surviving spouse's death. An AB trust alone won't work well here, because it depends on each spouse owning a significant part of the couple's property (as is usually the case in long-term marriages). But a QTIP does the job nicely. A full 100% of the wealthier spouse's property is available for the surviving spouse's use, as life beneficiary, because no estate tax is levied when the first spouse dies.

Example: Sam, who is in his late 70s, has assets worth $1.3 million when he marries Angela, his second wife. She has very little property of her own. If Sam dies before Angela does, he wants to be sure she is provided for, but he also wants to ensure that his children from his previous marriage are the final beneficiaries of his property.

Sam feels that Angela may need all the income his $1.3 million could provide. For this reason, he does not want to create just a normal AB trust for his estate, part of which would be taxed on his death. Also, Sam does not want to leave Angela money outright (which he could do, tax-free, because of the marital deduction). He wants to preserve his principal, to the extent possible, for his children.

So Sam creates a QTIP trust, containing all of his assets, which will become effective at his death. Angela is the life beneficiary. Sam designates his children as the trust's final beneficiaries, to receive all that's left when Angela dies. No tax will be due at Sam's death (if Angela is still alive) because all property in a QTIP trust takes advantage of the unlimited marital deduction. Income from the trust property will go to Angela for her life. Also, if he chooses, Sam can specify that trust principal can be used for Angela's "support, education, health or maintenance" in any amount. Or, at the other extreme, he can greatly restrict invasion of the principal, to try to best ensure that it's conserved for his children. (See Section 4, below.)

If you are in a second or subsequent marriage, you must try to balance the interests and needs of your current spouse and your children from a former marriage. (See Chapter 24, Property Control Trusts for Second or Subsequent Marriages.) Exactly how these needs are balanced depends on each situation— there is no one right way for how to use a QTIP trust in estate plans.

Example: Sol is married to Rosalie and has two children from a previous marriage. His estate is worth $1.7 million. He creates a QTIP trust of $1 million to take effect at his death. All of the income from the trust will be paid to Rosalie for her lifetime, and at her death the assets of the trust will go to his children.

Sol also leaves $350,000 outright to each child. No estate tax will be due on this $700,000 (after 2001) because of Sol's personal estate tax exemption.

Thanks to the marital deduction, at Sol's death no tax is due on the $1 million in the QTIP trust. At Rosalie's death, estate tax on the trust principal will be counted as part of her taxable estate.

4. The Surviving Spouse's Rights

The surviving spouse must be given the sole right to all income from property in the QTIP trust. Also, the surviving spouse must have the right to require that the trustee sell non-income-producing property and invest the sale proceeds in income-producing property. If the spouse doesn't have these rights, the IRS will rule that the QTIP property doesn't qualify for the marital deduction.

a. The Right to Receive All Trust Income

The surviving spouse must receive all of the income from an operational QTIP trust. There are no exceptions to this rule. The trustee (who is usually the surviving spouse) must distribute all income periodically (at least annually) to the spouse, and cannot accumulate income in the trust. If the surviving spouse becomes incapacitated, the trustee must spend the income for the spouse's benefit.

As long as the surviving spouse lives, the trustee of a QTIP trust cannot spend any of the principal or income from the trust for the benefit of anyone else. In general, this rule protects both the surviving spouse, who receives a continuing income, and the final beneficiaries, who are to later receive the trust principal.

But occasionally it can be troublesome. For example, suppose the surviving spouse remarries or earns a very large amount of money and no longer really needs the trust income. The spouse might want to end the trust and have its principal distributed to the final beneficiaries. Can't be done. A QTIP trust cannot end until the second spouse dies.

Or suppose that one of the final beneficiaries really needs some money from the trust, and the surviving spouse wants to give it. Officially, the trust's income, as well as the principal, cannot be spent directly on anyone else during the surviving spouse's lifetime. If the surviving spouse wants to help out, she must do so indirectly. Since all trust income is hers to do with as she wishes, once she receives some income, she can give it to the needy final beneficiary. But this is a legal gift, subject to gift taxes. Also, she won't be able to channel any of the principal to the final beneficiary.

Example: Alice directs that a QTIP trust be created at her death, with the income going to her husband, Mark. He has no rights to spend trust principal. At Mark's death, the assets of the trust will pass to her five children from two previous marriages.

Mark has a substantial estate himself, and several years after Alice dies, he remarries a very wealthy woman. But the income from the trust must continue to go to him.

Meanwhile, Alice's oldest son, Edward, has business trouble and desperately needs money to keep afloat. Because the trustee cannot obtain some of the principal of the QTIP trust for the son's benefit, even though Mark wants this, the business fails. This is hardly what Alice would have wanted. (Of course, Mark can give the income from the trust, once he receives it, to the son, or his own money, but he cannot touch trust principal.)

b. The Right to Demand That Trust Property Produce Income

You can put any kind of property into a QTIP—a house, furniture, money, stock, even a business—but the surviving spouse has the right to demand that any non-income-producing property be converted into a form of property that does produce income. So if the trust includes a safe deposit box full of gold coins or a collection of valuable antique chairs, the surviving spouse can demand they be sold and the profits invested in income-producing property.

Example: Gretchen creates a QTIP trust and names her husband, Lloyd, as the life beneficiary. The trust assets consist of stocks, bonds, a residence and a vacation home. After Gretchen's death, Lloyd decides that the income is not enough for him to live on in the manner he's used to. Using his authority as trustee, he sells the vacation home and invests the proceeds in property that yields income, such as bonds.

SUMMARY: IRS REQUIREMENTS FOR A VALID QTIP TRUST

In order to qualify as a valid QTIP trust under federal law (IRC Section 2056(b)(7)), the trust document must specify all of the following:

1. All income from the trust must be distributed to the surviving spouse at least annually.

2. The spouse can demand that the trust property be converted to income-producing property.

3. No one, not even the surviving spouse, may spend principal for the benefit of anybody but the spouse.

4. The executor of the deceased spouse's estate must elect, on the deceased's federal estate tax return, to have the trust be treated as a QTIP.

---

5. Powers That May Be Given to the Surviving Spouse

Now we move on to powers a grantor is allowed by the IRS to include in a QTIP, but are not mandatory.

a. The Power to Spend Trust Principal

As we've stated, a surviving spouse must receive all the income from property in a QTIP trust. There is no flexibility here. But when it comes to permitting principal to be spent (invaded), it's a different story—you have great flexibility.

Because the surviving spouse is considered, for estate tax purposes, the owner of all property in the QTIP, she can be given the right to invade trust principal for her benefit for any reason she wants, for any amount she wants. (This is another way in which a QTIP trust differs from an AB trust.) However, it's unusual to grant such broad power to spend trust principal. After all, this, in effect, leaves the property outright to the surviving spouse. If that's what you want, just do it directly, and no estate tax will be imposed at your death because of the marital deduction. Most QTIP trust grantors want to impose some restrictions on the surviving spouse, to protect the principal for the final beneficiaries.

Sometimes, the surviving spouse is given no right to spend trust principal, period. In other situations, the right to invade principal is defined very specifically and narrowly, such as for emergency health care only. Or the trust document may limit the right to spend trust principal to the IRS "objective need" standard, allowing invasion only when necessary for the surviving spouse's "education, health care, support or maintenance." (IRS Reg. 20.2041-1(c)(2).)

If the surviving spouse has the right to spend trust principal, there's an inherent risk of conflict between the spouse and the final beneficiaries, so the trust document creating the trust should be very specific about the spouse's rights. The last thing you want is a fight over what assets can and cannot be used, or what standard the spouse must meet to justify spending principal.

The surviving spouse frequently serves as trustee of a QTIP trust. If, however, broad invasion powers are granted, you may want to name a disinterested party as trustee or co-trustee, to avoid or at least reduce the chances of hostility and conflict between the beneficiaries.

b. The "5 and 5" Power

The "5 and 5" power is a distinct right, allowing the spouse the right to get $5,000 or 5% of the trust principal, whichever is greater, each year. There are no restrictions on how the surviving spouse can spend this money.

The surviving spouse does not have to use this 5 and 5 right in any one year. But if it is not used in one year, that year's right is lost. In other words, the right is not cumulative, year to year.

Example: Isabelle is the trustee and life beneficiary of a QTIP trust established by her late husband. The trust document includes a 5 and 5 power. If she doesn't exercise this right this year, she cannot take an extra 5% or $5,000 out of the trust principal next year.

The 5 and 5 power is not currently used much by sophisticated estate planners, because more controlled methods of allowing the surviving spouse access to the trust principal are usually preferable. (This is discussed in Chapter 18, Estate Tax-Saving Bypass Trusts, Section B.)

c. The Power to Distribute Trust Property Among Beneficiaries

One of the most important features of a QTIP trust is the power of the original grantor to control who gets the trust assets when the surviving spouse dies. Often, a grantor specifies that the assets go to his or her children. But a trusted spouse who survives many years after the other spouse's death may be in a far better position to know just which of a group of final beneficiaries designated by the grantor needs more than others, or which ones don't really need an inheritance at all. With a QTIP trust, the grantor can choose the group of possible final beneficiaries, but let the surviving spouse decide how much each one

actually inherits. The surviving spouse formally makes this decision in her living trust or will. In legal terms, this is called giving the spouse "a limited power of appointment" over the assets in the trust.

Example: Sara is married to Emmanuel, nine years younger than she is. Sara fully trusts Emmanuel and is confident he loves her family. Sara has two children, Alison and Lori, from a prior marriage. When Sara prepares her QTIP, Alison has two young children (and wants more) and Lori is single. Sara wants to provide for her own children but also leave direct gifts to her grandchildren.

She specifies that her children and grandchildren will be the final beneficiaries of her QTIP trust. She provides that each daughter will receive 30% of the trust property, and that the remaining 40% shall be divided among all her grandchildren when final distribution of the trust assets is made. She doesn't want to specify the precise divisions now because there may be (she hopes) additional grandchildren. And if Emmanuel survives her by a considerable time, she believes he will be in a far better position to decide how much money shall be given to each grandchild. So she gives Emmanuel authority to make the decision regarding actual distribution to the grandchildren.

Allowing the spouse to make such a decision can produce a fair and just distribution—one that may not have been foreseeable when the trust was created. One child may have completely dedicated himself to the family business, another may have special needs, and one child may have amassed such wealth that he needs less than the others. However, granting this power to the spouse is not very common in QTIPs. Most grantors want absolute control over who the final beneficiaries are. But if you have complete confidence in your spouse's judgment, granting this power can be sensible, especially when some desired beneficiaries are very young (or even not yet alive) when the trust is prepared.

6. The "QTIP Election"

A unique aspect of QTIPs is that the executor you name in your will must elect, on your federal estate tax return, to place property you left in a QTIP into that trust. Your executor has the final say here. You cannot require that he elect QTIP tax treatment for your property. If the QTIP election isn't properly made by the executor, no valid QTIP trust exists, period.

The QTIP election itself amounts to marking the correct box on the estate tax return and then listing the property that is to go into the trust. Seems simple, but it has surely been done wrong. In one case, an executor hurriedly filed an estate tax return, forgot to mark the box and then sought IRS permission to file an amended return electing a QTIP. Nope, said the IRS, which sometimes seems to take special delight in denying proposed QTIP trusts eligibility for the marital deduction.

Deciding how and whether to make the QTIP election can be difficult. The executor has several choices:

- not to elect the QTIP

- elect that all property the deceased left in the (possible) QTIP trust actually be treated as QTIP property, or

- elect to have only a portion of the trust property treated as a QTIP. For example, the executor can elect to have 60% of the trust property treated as a QTIP and 40% not. That 40% may be subject to estate tax now, depending on who it goes to.

These options make possible a great deal of strategic after-death tax planning. Key tax decisions can be made in light of current circumstances rather than being frozen years before. But in some family situations, it can require the wisdom of Solomon (not to mention high-quality tax advice) to decide which election option to take.

In larger estates, this QTIP election is sometimes used to equalize the value of each spouse's estate. For example, sometimes it makes estate tax sense to choose not to elect a QTIP and allow the deceased spouse's possible QTIP trust property to be included in the taxable estate. If electing the QTIP would result in the surviving spouse's estate being much larger than that of the first spouse to die, higher overall estate tax would be paid. So in such a case, after the first spouse's death, the executor might elect to go ahead and pay any estate tax assessed against that deceased spouse's property, because the tax rate is lower on this amount of property than it would be if this property were combined, for estate tax purposes, with the surviving spouse's.

This means the surviving spouse must accept tax payments now in exchange for overall tax savings later. Usually, the surviving spouse is the executor and is in charge of making this decision. But if the surviving spouse isn't the executor, and the two disagree, there can be a real power struggle.

Another option is for the executor to elect to have only a percentage of the deceased spouse's property receive QTIP treatment. This is called a partial QTIP election. This, too, can be used to lower overall estate tax. Any percentage of the trust property not elected to receive QTIP treatment still must, under IRS rules, be used for the surviving spouse's benefit. Nothing changes except the tax treatment. Estate tax is not deferred on the portion not elected. This portion can technically be left in the trust, but does not receive QTIP estate tax treatment. Two separate financial records must be kept—one for the trust property receiving QTIP treatment and one for the trust property that does not receive QTIP treatment.

The percentage of the property that does not receive QTIP treatment cannot go to someone else or to a trust benefiting someone else. The terms of the overall QTIP trust still govern both portions. The only effect is that tax is not deferred on the part not elected. But making a partial QTIP election, instead of a full one, can make a big difference, tax-wise.

Example: Ben has an estate worth $2 million. He is married to Gloria and has children from a first marriage. Gloria has her own property worth $2 million. Ben leaves his $2 million in a QTIP for Gloria, with the income to go to her and the assets to go later to the children from his first marriage. Ben dies in 2006, when the personal exemption is $1 million. At Ben's death, if the executor elects the full QTIP, these are the tax consequences:

Ben's gross estate	$2,000,000
Marital deduction for QTIP property	($2,000,000)
Estate tax due	$-0-

At Gloria's death:

Gloria's gross estate	$4, 000,000
Estate tax at 55%	$1,840,800
Personal $1 million tax exemption	($345,800)
Estate tax due	$1,495,000

Now suppose that the executor elects to have only 50% of Ben's property qualify for QTIP trust treatment.

At Ben's death:

Ben's gross estate	$2,000,000

Property given marital deduction for half of QTIP treatment	($1,000,000)
Taxable estate	$1,000,000
Estate tax	$345,800
Personal $1 million tax exemption	($345,800)
Estate tax due	-0-

At Gloria's death:

Gloria's gross estate	$3,000,000
Estate tax	$1,275,800
Personal $1 million tax exemption	($345,800)
Estate tax due	$930,000

By electing to have only half of the trust property qualify for the QTIP, $565,000 in eventual estate tax is saved for the final beneficiaries. The savings is possible because of the graduated estate tax. Electing a full QTIP would cause the second estate to be taxed at 55%. But with half of it taxed at Ben's death, both estates fall into a lower bracket, only 41%. (Chapter 15, Estate Tax, Section D, contains an estate tax rate chart.)

A number of issues can contribute to the decision your executor makes regarding the QTIP election. One factor is simply that circumstances may have changed (indeed, they always do, according to Buddha and Heraclitus) since you prepared the QTIP trust. Your original estate plan may not be the most financially desirable one after your death.

Example: Steve has an estate worth about $1 million. He drafts a QTIP trust for $900,000 of his assets and an AB trust for the remaining $100,000. His wife, Esther, has property of her own worth about $200,000. She will get the income from both trusts, and the principal from both will go to Steve's son, Zack, upon Esther's death.

Several years later, Esther inherits property worth $450,000, making her own estate now worth $650,000. Steve neglects to revise his estate plan. When Steve dies, if the QTIP trust goes into effect, Esther's estate will now be worth over $1.5 million for tax purposes—well over the amount of the personal exemption, no matter what the year of her death.

Let's assume Steve dies after 2005 so his personal exemption is $1 million. His executor looks at the whole picture and decides not to make a QTIP election that would postpone taxes. This means that $900,000 will still go into trust subject to the exact terms of the QTIP. But tax will not be deferred. The property will be subject to estate tax immediately, but no tax is due because of Steve's personal exemption. Esther will still get the income from both trusts, and Zack will still inherit the principal when she dies.

Making a partial QTIP election has significant drawbacks, however. An executor can make a partial QTIP election only in terms of a percentage or fraction of the total property originally left for the QTIP. For example, a trustee can elect to have 40% or 63% or one-third of the total property originally left for the QTIP actually qualify for QTIP tax treatment. What the executor cannot do is specify that certain specific assets be included in or excluded from the QTIP. The IRS simply doesn't allow that kind of maneuvering.

The real world consequences of a partial QTIP election can be difficult. For example, there can be much paperwork if two-thirds of your house is owned by a QTIP trust and one-third owned by another trust. Also, it can complicate matters like real estate tax or refinancing. Because of the complexities involved, partial QTIP election is not often recommended by many sophisticated estate planners.

7. The Reverse QTIP Election

A "reverse QTIP election" is a special legal procedure designed to avoid losing the million-dollar exemption from another tax imposed on gifts and bequests that skip generations. (See Chapter 21, Other Estate Tax-Saving Trusts, Section A.) Without a reverse QTIP election, all assets that are left by a grandparent to a grandchild (skipping the middle generation) or in other generation-skipping plans are subject to an extra tax, called the Generation-Skipping Transfer Tax or GSTT.

Sometimes a QTIP trust leaves the trust principal, at the death of the surviving spouse, to the grantor's grandchildren or other beneficiaries more than one generation away. When this happens, the law considers the surviving spouse (the life beneficiary) the one transferring the property for GSTT purposes. This means up to $1 million can go to the grandchildren GSTT-free, because there is a $1 million standard exemption from the GSTT. However, when the first spouse's executor makes a reverse QTIP election, the first spouse who died is legally the person who makes the eventual transfer to the grandchildren. This preserves that first spouse's $1 million GSTT exemption and allows the second spouse to transfer another million to grandchildren free of the Generation-Skipping Transfer Tax.

This reverse QTIP election is concerned only with generation-skipping trusts and the Generation-Skipping Transfer Tax. It is an entirely separate matter from the basic QTIP election, where the executor decides whether or not to use a QTIP, and if so, how much property to actually place in the QTIP trust.

8. Planning for a QTIP

You must plan for and create a QTIP trust document before you die. No one has any authority to create one for you, and obtain its estate-tax postponing advantages, after you die.

A vital issue you must decide is who will be the trustee, or trustees, of your QTIP trust. The trustee usually is your surviving spouse, but a grown child or someone else entirely can serve. Above all, choose the person you trust the most—and, of course, one who is willing to serve.

If you plan to choose your spouse, ask yourself a few questions. Do you fully trust your spouse to protect the trust principal, your final beneficiaries' inheritance? Do your final beneficiaries feel the same way? If the answer is "no," or you're not positive, perhaps a child should serve as co-trustee. Or, if you believe one of your children (and not your spouse) has the wisdom to best balance the needs of the surviving spouse against the final beneficiaries' rights to their eventual inheritance, you may want to name the child as sole trustee.

Obviously, there's no one-size-fits-all answer when it comes to choosing the trustee. A good lawyer may be able to help, by focusing your attention on your personal situation, but the final decision is definitely yours. (Choosing a trustee is discussed in Chapter 17, An Overview of Ongoing Trusts, Section E.)

Remember also that the executor of your will has the authority to decide whether or not property in the trust should actually receive QTIP treatment. So it's common to have your QTIP trustee be the same person as your executor.

Since by law you cannot deny the executor the power to decide whether or not to elect QTIP tax treatment for property you include in your QTIP trust, it's obviously vital that you have an executor you trust completely to make the best judgment in light of the interests of all trust beneficiaries—life beneficiary and final beneficiary.

B. Trusts for Non-Citizen Spouses: QDOTs

If you are married to someone who is not a citizen of the United States, property you leave to that spouse is not entitled to the unlimited marital deduction. In plain English, you cannot leave your non-citizen spouse an unlimited amount of money free of federal estate tax. The rule applies even if the non-citizen spouse is a legal resident of this country. Congress wanted to prevent non-citizen spouses from inheriting large amounts of money and then leaving the country, with the result that no U.S. estate tax would ever be paid on this money.

What can you do if you want to leave a large estate to a non-citizen spouse? First, it may make excellent sense to have the non-citizen spouse become a U.S. citizen. Usually this is possible, given some time. If, for whatever reason, a spouse doesn't obtain U.S. citizenship, there is one very important estate tax exemption that can be used by a citizen spouse for property left to a non-citizen spouse.

The personal estate tax exemption is available to each spouse, no matter who inherits the property. (See Chapter 15, Estate Taxes, Section A, for a table listing the amounts for each year.) So a citizen can leave her non-citizen spouse property worth up to the amount of her personal tax exemption in the year of death free of federal estate tax. Any amount over that left outright by a U.S. spouse to a non-citizen spouse is subject to estate tax.

If your estate is over the estate tax threshold, there is still one way to leave property to a non-citizen spouse and defer estate tax. All property, no matter how much it's worth, left by one spouse to a non-citizen spouse in what's called a "Qualified Domestic Trust" (QDOT) is allowed the marital deduction. (IRC Section 2056(A).) The federal estate tax that would otherwise be assessed on property in a QDOT is deferred until the non-citizen spouse dies. QDOTs are used only by spouses with an estate exceeding the estate tax threshold, because only these estates must pay federal estate tax.

The rules governing QDOTs, estate tax and non-citizen spouses are special and complicated. The IRS regulations here are new and may well change. Also, the U.S. has estate tax treaties with some countries which allow you to choose between the provisions of the treaty or the provisions discussed here. If you're married to a non-citizen and have an estate worth more than the estate tax threshold, you must get expert help for planning your estate.

Strict federal laws govern QDOT trusts. For example, if any trust principal is distributed to the non-citizen spouse during her life, estate tax is assessed on the amount distributed. So if the trust pays $150,000 from principal for a spouse's new boat, that amount is immediately subject to estate tax. There is a special exemption from estate tax for QDOT principal distributions to the non-citizen surviving spouse in cases of "hardship." The IRS defines hardship as an immediate need relating to health, maintenance, education or support that cannot be met with other reasonable means.

Example: If $150,000 were paid to the spouse from the QDOT for medical care (instead of a boat), the full amount would be exempt from estate tax if no other reasonable means of paying for this care were available. This is decided on a case-by-case basis. It's pretty awful to have the IRS so intimately involved in your daily living, but QDOTs can lead to such a situation.

Income the non-citizen spouse receives from the QDOT trust is taxable as regular income. Of course, this is true for any person, whether a U.S. citizen or not, for income received from any ongoing trust.

When the surviving non-citizen spouse dies, the QDOT trust assets are subject to estate tax. The tax is based on the value of the assets in the trust when the non-citizen spouse dies. Any increase in value in the trust property during the life of the surviving spouse is subject to estate tax on that spouse's death, unlike property in an AB trust.

GIFTS TO NON-CITIZEN SPOUSES

Under a special gift tax regulation, a citizen spouse can give up to $100,000 per year, free of gift tax, to a non-citizen spouse while both are living. (IRS Reg. 2523(i)(2).) By contrast, if both spouses were citizens of the U.S., they could give any amount to each other, free of gift tax. (See Chapter 16, Gifts and Gift Taxes, Section A.) While the annual $100,000 exemption allowed for gifts to non-citizen spouses is more limited than for gifts to citizen spouses, it is still a substantial amount. A U.S. citizen with an estate that's likely to owe estate tax should consider making large annual gifts to the non-citizen spouse.

A valid QDOT trust must meet all of the requirements of any trust that qualifies for the marital deduction, including:

- The surviving spouse must be entitled to receive all income from the trust.

- The QDOT trust must be "elected" by the executor of the grantor's estate on the estate tax return.

In addition, the QDOT must also meet the following special requirements:

- At least one of the trustees of the trust must be either a U.S. citizen or a U.S. corporation. Thus, the surviving spouse cannot be the sole trustee.

- The trust must comply with applicable IRS regulations. These regulations impose special security requirements (such as posting a bond or providing a letter of credit when the trustee is an individual) on QDOTs in excess of $2 million.

Example: Juan, a U.S. citizen, has an estate worth $2 million. He is married to Maria, who is a legal resident of the United States but not a citizen. Juan's estate plan includes an outright bequest to Maria of the amount that is exempt from federal estate tax because of Juan's personal exemption. The remaining assets will go into a QDOT trust for Maria's benefit during her life, and will be distributed, at her death, to their children. Juan appoints his brother Ricardo, who is a U.S. citizen, to serve as co-trustee with Maria of the QDOT trust. (Juan could also use a U.S. bank or other institution as a co-trustee.)

At Juan's death, his executor makes the election for the QDOT trust on Juan's federal estate tax return. No estate tax is due at this time because of the personal tax exemption and the QDOT trust. Maria will receive all of the income from the trust for her life and may receive necessary principal for her support. If she receives principal, it will be subject to estate tax upon distribution. At Maria's death, the assets remaining in the trust will be taxed.

The QDOT rules have one opening that is an incentive to a non-citizen spouse to become a U.S. citizen. If the spouse becomes a citizen before the deceased spouse's estate tax return is filed (generally, nine months after the death) or before any distribution of principal is made to the non-citizen spouse, property in the trust will receive the full marital deduction, and assets may be invaded during the spouse's lifetime without paying estate tax. The trust is no longer a QDOT, and the remaining assets will be subject to tax only when the surviving spouse dies.

A unique and extremely helpful aspect of a QDOT trust is that it doesn't necessarily have to be created before the grantor's death. If someone who is married to a non-citizen prepared a trust before the federal QDOT law went into effect in 1988, or just didn't know about the law, the surviving non-citizen spouse can request of the IRS that the estate plan be "reformed" to meet the guidelines of a QDOT trust. For example, if a citizen simply left all property outright to a non-citizen spouse, the spouse can request the creation of a QDOT trust and obtain an estate tax deferment for the property.

C. MARITAL DEDUCTION TRUSTS

Before 1981, when the IRS authorized the use of QTIP trusts, a marital deduction trust (IRC Section 2056(b)(5)) was the mainstay of estate plans for many couples. These trusts are similar to a QTIP trust in that taxes on trust property can be postponed until the death of the surviving spouse, and the surviving spouse is the life beneficiary of the trust. Before QTIP trusts, they were the only way to obtain the full marital deduction and retain control of the property during the life of the surviving spouse. In the past, these trusts were especially used to manage business affairs of the husband when the wife had no knowledge or interest in them.

Today, the QTIP trust has replaced these other trusts in popularity, but marital deduction trusts are still very useful in situations where one of their special features is desired.

You may want to create a marital deduction trust if:

- You want your spouse to be able to give away trust principal to someone else (such as a child) during the spouse's lifetime.

- You want your spouse to choose who will inherit trust property after the spouse's death.

- You want the trust to hold property that is non-income producing. In one type of trust, the spouse cannot demand that the property be sold to produce income (as the spouse can in a QTIP trust).

- The trust will hold property such as a business and will need to reinvest the income, rather than pay it regularly to the surviving spouse.

Marital deduction trusts are quite technical and must comply with applicable tax law and IRS rules. These trusts must be drafted by experts experienced with this type of trust.

Like a QTIP, one spouse creates a trust, naming the other spouse the life beneficiary. Trust property qualifies for the marital deduction, so no estate tax on property in the trust is paid when the first spouse dies. The trust property that remains when the second spouse dies is included in the taxable estate of the surviving spouse.

There are two types of marital deduction trusts. Let's look at each.

1. Power of Appointment Trusts

A "power of appointment" trust names the spouse as the lifetime beneficiary. As in a QTIP trust, the spouse is entitled to receive trust income and can require that trust property be converted to income-producing property. But to use this type of trust, you must give your surviving spouse either the right to invade the trust principal for any reason or to name those (including the spouse's own estate) to receive the trust property at your spouse's death or during his or her life. This is called a "power of appointment." (See also Chapter 25, Trusts and Other Devices for Imposing Controls Over Property, Section G.) This is in direct contrast to a QTIP trust, where you can, and normally do, limit the right to invade principal and you name the final beneficiaries.

The flexibility of invading principal and giving gifts of principal can be very attractive. When you prepare your trust, it may not be at all clear whether your surviving spouse will need access to the trust principal. Perhaps one or more of the final beneficiaries will genuinely need some of the trust principal while the surviving spouse is alive. One way to handle these uncertainties is to create a power of appointment trust and give the spouse power to make gifts of principal.

Example: Peter drafts a power of appointment trust for his wife, Lisa. Lisa will receive all income from the trust and can choose who will inherit the assets at her death. During her life, Lisa is authorized to give trust principal to each of their two children.

After Peter dies, Lisa is quite well off from other sources, but one of their children loses his job, and he and his family are threatened with eviction from their recently purchased home. Lisa decides to distribute $30,000 of trust principal to the child, bailing him out of this crisis.

This gift is a taxable event for estate tax purposes. Since the trust property will be part of Lisa's taxable estate, she will use part of her personal estate/gift tax exemption by making this distribution. (See Chapter 16, Gifts and Gift Taxes, Section A, for an explanation of the unified gift and estate tax system.)

The spouse doesn't have to have both an unlimited power to invade principal and a power to name other beneficiaries. Just one of the powers, such as the power to choose who inherits trust property (including her own estate) is all that is required.

If you give your spouse the right to name final beneficiaries of the trust property, you can then limit any powers to invade principal. For instance, the document could name only certain persons (like the children) who could receive principal. Or, you can choose not to grant power to invade principal to anyone, including the spouse.

The surviving spouse does not have to use the powers granted by the trust document. For example, you can designate the final beneficiaries, and if your spouse does nothing to change them, the property will pass to those you have chosen.

2. Estate Trusts

An "estate" trust is a special type of marital deduction trust requiring that when the surviving spouse dies, all remaining trust principal must go into his or her estate. (IRC Section 2056 (b)(1); IRS Reg. 20.2056(3)—2(b)(iii).) This means that the surviving spouse gets to choose the final beneficiaries, such as by will or within a living trust. Also, the estate trust property will go through probate on the death of the surviving spouse. What makes this trust special is that the trust property can be, and remain, non-income-producing. In all of the other trusts that defer taxes because of the marital deduction (including QTIP trusts), this is not possible.

Example: Suzanne's property holdings include several acres of woodland and a small house by a river. Suzanne grew up spending much happy time on this land (and in the river) and she wants to be sure the land is preserved for her children, if possible. As it is now, the land is not income-producing, and the house has no electricity and only rudimentary plumbing. Suzanne doesn't want the property improved or sold, so she leaves the land in a marital deduction estate trust. Specific directions in the trust document state that the land may not be sold while the trust lasts.

The other feature of this type of trust is that when the trust property does produce income, it does not have to be paid out to the spouse. At the trustee's option, the income can be accumulated, increasing the amount of the trust principal. If this occurs, income is taxed at the trust's higher tax rate. But for some purposes, this disadvantage may well be offset by allowing for business growth or other investment purposes.

Example: Arturo owns a large auto repair business with his brother, Sol. He leaves his share in an estate trust with his wife, Gilda, as life beneficiary. No tax is due because of the marital deduction. Sol will serve as trustee and manage the firm, reinvest income and guide the business growth. Gilda directs by her will that at her death, the trust property will go to their children.

D. WIDOW'S ELECTION TRUSTS

This rather peculiar trust with the unfortunate name is not confined to the benefit of just a wife. Either spouse can create a widow's election trust for the other.

Widow's election trusts are not common, and with good reason. Only if one spouse wants to control the disposition of both spouses' property, and the other spouse agrees to this, are they useful. These trusts are basically a relic from the time when men presumed it was best for them to control the disposition of family money, including property owned by their wives—and their wives accepted this view. Often, in the past, everything was in the husband's name and he could dispose of it as he wished.

This type of trust is a hybrid designed to use the personal estate tax exemption and take advantage of the unlimited marital deduction. In a sense, it does some of the same things you can accomplish by establishing a QTIP trust and backing it up with an AB trust. (See Section A, above.)

Among other problems, the tax rules governing widow's election trusts are so complicated that just reading about them can bring about a case of fatigue. However, bear with us, and we will outline the main tenets involved, so you will have at least a basic understanding of how these trusts work. Then, if you wish to pursue one as part of your estate plan, get out your checkbook and proceed to the most experienced trust attorney you can find.

Good advice is essential. These trusts are so rare and complicated that few estate planning lawyers really understand how they actually work. If you want to consider one, locate an expert lawyer who is knowledgeable about widow's election trusts.

With a widow's election trust, one spouse, traditionally the husband, leaves property to the other in trust, on the condition that the surviving spouse will "elect" to place her own property in the trust. The husband names the final beneficiary for this trust. Usually, the surviving spouse (presumed to be the wife) receives only the income, for her life, from the combined assets of both spouses. When the surviving spouse dies, all trust assets go to the final beneficiaries. By using this trust plan, the grantor can control both spouses' property, designate the final beneficiaries and avoid probate at the death of the surviving spouse. But the surviving spouse loses the right to name the beneficiaries for her own estate.

Example: Leon and Petra have a combined estate worth $3 million. Leon drafts a widow's election trust for his $1.5 million share. He names his children from a prior marriage as final beneficiaries. He leaves these assets to Petra only if she elects at his death to transfer her own $1.5 million share into the same trust. She will then receive the income from all of the assets for life, and on her death, the trustee will distribute the assets to Leon's children. Petra has no children of her own, so she does not object to this plan.

Why would anyone use a widow's election trust? Most of all, simply for the desire for control—the need of some people to keep all of both spouses' property together for management (or ego) purposes.

One very difficult aspect of these trusts is figuring out the estate tax applied to the trust property of the first spouse to die. This involves using actuarial tables and formulas, looking at the age of the surviving spouse and how much income the spouse can expect to be paid. Determining the tax is exceedingly tricky, and too complex to explain in detail here. Again, you'll need top-notch professional advice. ■

20

CHARITABLE TRUSTS

A. An Overview of Charitable Trusts 20/2
    1. The Basics of Charitable Remainder Trusts 20/2
    2. The Basics of Charitable Lead Trusts 20/3
    3. Selecting a Trustee for a Charitable Trust 20/3
B. The Income Tax Deduction 20/4
    1. Determining the Value of a Gift to a Charitable
        Remainder Trust 20/5
    2. Giving Appreciated Property to a Charitable Trust 20/6
C. A Closer Look at Charitable Remainder Trusts 20/7
    1. Charitable Remainder Annuity Trusts 20/7
    2. Charitable Remainder Unitrusts 20/8
    3. Pooled Income Trusts 20/10
D. A Closer Look at Charitable Lead Trusts 20/11
E. Types of Charitable Trusts: A Comparison 20/14

If you want to make a gift, especially a substantial one, to a charity, using a charitable trust may allow you to do it in a way that gives you significant tax benefits. As you'll see, there are several charitable trusts to choose from, and all can offer real financial advantages.

By contrast, if your basic estate planning goals are to pass on your property to family or friends, leave a few minor charitable gifts and pay less estate tax, then a charitable trust is probably not for you. The income tax and estate tax breaks charitable trusts can offer probably won't make up for the amount of property that is given to a charity instead of your family.

A. AN OVERVIEW OF CHARITABLE TRUSTS

There are two basic types of charitable trusts, each with its own obtuse name:

- charitable remainder trusts, including popular pooled charitable trusts (IRC Section 664), and
- charitable lead trusts (IRC Sections 664, 671).

These trusts have certain features in common:

They can become operational while you are alive. To gain the maximum tax advantages, most people create charitable trusts during life, in their highest income-producing years. A basic purpose of these charitable trusts is not simply to make a gift to a charity, but also to provide some income (or other benefits) to you or to someone else you choose.

They are irrevocable. Once you create a charitable trust and it becomes operational, it is irrevocable. You cannot change your mind and regain legal control of the property you have given to the trust.

Only tax-exempt charities are eligible. In order to obtain the tax benefits, you must make your gift to a charity that is approved by the IRS. Normally, this means a charity that has gained tax-exempt status under Section 501(c)(3) of the Internal Revenue Code. The IRS maintains a long list of acceptable public charities, which include educational institutions, research organizations and well-known organizations like United Way or CARE. Usually, the easiest way to determine if the charity you want to make a gift to is an approved charity is to contact the IRS and see whether it appears on their public charities list.

You get an income tax break. The value of the charitable gift is deductible from your income tax. (See Section B, below.)

Now let's take a quick look at the two kinds of trusts.

1. The Basics of Charitable Remainder Trusts

With a charitable remainder trust, you give property to an irrevocable trust and name an income beneficiary and a final beneficiary. The final beneficiary is always the charity.

The income beneficiary can be (and often is) yourself, but it can be your spouse, mate, child or anyone else. There can be more than one income beneficiary. This person (or persons) receives a set payment from the trust or a set percentage of the worth of trust property for the term defined in the trust. For example, the income beneficiary might receive 7% of the value of the trust per year, or a fixed sum of $8,000 per year. However, you cannot give the income beneficiary the right to receive all trust income, except in certain situations if the income beneficiary is your spouse.

You state, in the trust document, how long the income beneficiary will receive income from the trust property. This payment period can be a set number of years, or until the income beneficiary dies. At most, the income beneficiaries can have only the right to receive trust income during their lives. They never legally own the trust property, and it can never be included in their taxable estates.

The charity itself is usually the trustee of the trust property. As trustee, the charity is responsible for making proper payments to the income beneficiary. Usually, the charity converts any non-income producing property, such as raw land or artworks, into income-producing property.

Money received by the income beneficiary may be subject to gift tax. If an income beneficiary is anyone other than you or your spouse, the payments from the trust are considered a taxable gift from you to that person. Currently, if more than $10,000 in income is received per year, you will be assessed gift tax on the excess over $10,000 and will have to file a federal gift tax return.

Establishing a charitable trust can give your inheritors an estate tax break. When the trust assets become solely owned by the charity—that is, when the income beneficiary's interest ends—they are no longer part of your taxable estate.

Charitable remainder trusts are discussed in more detail in Section C, below.

2. The Basics of Charitable Lead Trusts

With a charitable lead trust, the charity receives income from the trust property for a set period of time. Then the trust property goes back to you or someone else you named to receive it. In other words, the process is the reverse of that used with charitable remainder trusts.

Charitable lead trusts are not as widely used as charitable remainder trusts. They are discussed further in Section D, below.

3. Selecting a Trustee for a Charitable Trust

You can serve as trustee of your own charitable trust, or you can choose someone else. Most people choose the charity itself to serve as trustee. In fact, most large public charities insist on serving as trustee. They want to manage all gifts made to them, including yours. Large charities have experienced investment staffs, and many people prefer to turn management and investment of trust property over to them.

A larger charity can also offer you other services. It may assist you in preparing the trust document. It may administer the trust free of any charge for the trustee's services. Finally, while you probably can't impose investment decisions over the charity serving as trustee, you can direct where you want the trust property to go after the income beneficiary's interest ends. For instance, if the trust will benefit a school, you could probably require that the property be used only for scholarship purposes in a certain field.

Matters can be different if you're making a gift to a smaller, less-established charity. Its cause may be noble, and its staff dedicated, but that's far from a guarantee of experience and sophistication regarding investments. So with a small or new charity, you may decide that it's wisest to name yourself as trustee, to better manage your property. But check to be sure the charity will allow it; even some small charities insist on serving as trustee of a charitable trust.

KNOW YOUR CHARITY

Many people make gifts to charities they know well, whether from publicity or personal experience. If you don't know the charity so well, investigate it thoroughly, including its history, current management and its annual financial reports.

You can check out particular charities on the Internet. You can find analyses of more than 600,000 charitable organizations at http://www.guidestar.org.

Books that evaluate charities and list what percentage of their funds actually go for charitable services include:

- *The Giver's Charity Rating Guide* ($3), American Institute of Philanthropy, 4579 Ladede Ave., Suite E17, St. Louis, MO 63103, and

- *The Wise Giving Guide* (free), National Charities Information Bureau, 19 Union Square West, Dept. 326, New York, NY 10003.

Before you agree to let the charity serve as trustee, do two things:

1. Work with a lawyer knowledgeable in charitable trusts. An experienced lawyer should be able to help you clarify what your income requirements are and what, if any, risk you might take on if the charity is trustee. You need to know whether the charity you have chosen has a good investment record—one that will protect your income interest. The lawyer should also be able to suggest other possible trustees, aside from yourself—perhaps a corporate trustee, like a private trust company.

2. Investigate the charity's management style and investment staff. If the charity is the trustee, you can't control what the trust assets are invested in, so it's vital that you have confidence in the charity's investment personnel. Who in the charity will actually be doing the trustee work? Does that person seem open and easy to talk to? Do you feel confidence in her judgment and human sympathies? How sophisticated is the potential trustee, and her staff, in money and investment management?

Don't choose the charity to be the trustee unless you are confident that the organization, and the people in it who will actually manage your trust and

its property, will protect the income beneficiary's interests. Any trustee, including a charitable organization, has what's called a "fiduciary duty" to do what's best for all the trust beneficiaries. But you want to rely on real people you actually trust, not abstract legal duties.

NAMING A BACK-UP CHARITY

To protect the income tax savings of a charitable trust, consider naming another tax-exempt charity as a back-up beneficiary, or provide in the trust document that the trustee can choose another charity if this need arises. In the unlikely event that the chosen charity becomes defunct or loses its IRS tax-exempt standing, this ensures that there can be no (retroactive) loss of any income tax deduction. It also ensures that the charitable gift can never be subject to estate tax, because there will always be some valid, IRS tax-exempt charity entitled to receive the trust property when the income beneficiary's term ends.

B. THE INCOME TAX DEDUCTION

You may get substantial income tax advantages by creating a charitable trust. That's because over time, you can deduct the full value of the gift to the charity from your income tax. The fact that a charitable remainder trust makes payments to you or some other beneficiary for many years doesn't change this basic rule.

Where things get tricky, though, is in determining the actual value of the gift to the charity for income tax deduction purposes. The value of your gift to charity is not simply the value of the property when you give it to the trust. With a charitable remainder trust, the IRS deducts from this value the estimated value of the income beneficiary's right to receive payments from the trust property.

Things are reversed in a charitable lead trust. The income tax deduction is the estimated value of the income the charity will receive. (See Section 1, below.)

Once the IRS determines the worth of a gift to a charitable trust, you are entitled to deduct 100% of this amount. But this deduction cannot be taken in a single year. Rather, you can deduct a certain percentage of the amount in the year the gift is made, and deduct the rest over the next five years.

The amount of the first year's deduction depends on how the IRS classifies the charity and on your annual income. The most you can possibly deduct is 50% of your adjusted gross income for the first year. For a gift to a charity to be eligible for the 50% deduction, that charity must be classified by the IRS as a "public" charity. Most widely known charities meet this requirement, such as schools, churches, the Salvation Army, the American Cancer Society and many environmental organizations.

Many private foundations, however, do not meet this public charity requirement. If your gift is made to one of these charities, you can take an income tax deduction of only up to 30% of your adjusted gross income the first year, and the rest over the next five years. To determine whether your charity makes you eligible for the 50% or 30% deduction, contact the IRS.

Example: Christopher creates a charitable remainder trust, with the charity CARE as the final beneficiary. He names himself as the income beneficiary. The IRS will determine the worth of his gift, for income tax purposes, by subtracting the value of his retained interest in the income from the trust principal. If the value of the gift is less than 50% of his income

for the year, he may deduct the entire gift that year.

If, instead, Christopher had given the money to a tax-exempt foundation not in the IRS 50% category, he would have been able to deduct only up to 30% of the amount of his income on that year's tax return. In either case, he can deduct the rest of his gift over the next five years. And in either situation, the deductions save enormously on income taxes.

REPLACING THE DONATED MONEY FOR YOUR INHERITORS

If you want to donate large sums to charity but are afraid that your inheritors might need the money, you are in luck if you are in good health. Many people take the money saved by the income tax deduction and purchase life insurance to cover the money "lost" by gift to the charity. You can then remove the life insurance from your estate for estate tax purposes. (See Chapter 12, Section E, and Chapter 21, Section B.)

---

1. Determining the Value of a Gift to a Charitable Remainder Trust

If you make an outright gift to charity, the income tax deduction permitted by the IRS is the gift's value at the time you make it. For example, if you write a $100,000 check to the Audubon Society, you're entitled to a $100,000 income tax deduction.

By contrast, if you make a gift to a charitable remainder trust while you are alive, determining the amount of your tax deduction is more complicated. The IRS determines the value of the charitable trust gift from tables that estimate your life expectancy (or that of whomever is the income beneficiary), current interest rates and what the charity is expected to receive (that is, how much principal will be left) when the income beneficiary's interest ends. The more the charity is expected to get, the bigger the tax deduction; the larger the expected return to the income beneficiary, the lower the deduction.

Example: Zola, who is 80 years old, creates a charitable remainder trust. She gives $800,000 in trust to her favorite charity, Save the Children, and retains the right to receive income equal to 6% of the trust principal annually for her life. After her death, the charity will receive all remaining trust property outright.

Curt, who is 40 years old, creates the same kind of trust, with the same amount of property and the same retained income rights. Under IRS rules, the value of Zola's gift to the charity is worth substantially more than Curt's, which means she can take a larger tax deduction. The reason is that Curt, who is just 40, will (under life expectancy tables) live much longer than 80-year-old Zola, so the trust will pay out much more money to Curt than Zola.

Because IRS calculations are influenced by prevailing interest rates, the precise worth of a gift to a charitable remainder trust depends on when the gift is made. To determine the actual amount, you need to see an expert who has the most current IRS tables. You could dig up the tables yourself, but figuring out how to use them, interweaving estimated interest rates, your life expectancy, and the value of the charity's interest is definitely not easy; indeed, for the uninitiated, it's close to impossible.

2. Giving Appreciated Property to a Charitable Trust

One of the most useful features of a charitable trust is that it provides a method to turn highly appreciated assets into cash without paying any capital gain tax. If you donate a non-income-producing asset in a charitable trust, the charity can convert it into an income-producing one. Though a charity isn't legally required to do so, it surely will if the asset—say an appreciated house or painting—isn't producing any, or much, current income. And whatever the profit from such a sale, no capital gain tax is assessed; charities are simply not liable for capital gain tax.

Here's how it works. You donate an appreciated asset to the charity, using a charitable remainder trust. The charity sells it for its current market value. The charity retains all the money received, without any subtraction for capital gain tax. As the grantor, you benefit in two ways. First, you get a tax deduction based on the sale price (the current value) of the asset. Also, the income you receive from the trust property will be based on this amount—which will obviously be higher than if capital gain tax had to be paid out of the sale's profits.

Example: Toni owns stock currently worth $300,000, which she paid $20,000 for 20 years ago. She creates a charitable remainder trust, naming the Red Cross as the charity-beneficiary. She funds her charitable trust with her stock. The Red Cross sells the stock for $300,000 and invests the money in a safe mutual fund. No taxes are paid. Toni, as the income beneficiary, will receive income from this $300,000 for her life.

Technically, there is a capital gain (profit) of $280,000 on the stock sale—that is, the sale price less Toni's original $20,000 purchase price. Had Toni sold the stock herself, she would have had to pay the capital gain tax.

Toni's trust document specifies that her annual income from the charitable trust will be 7% of the value of the trust property (currently $300,000). The IRS calculation of Toni's income tax deduction will also start from a gift worth $300,000.

C. A Closer Look at Charitable Remainder Trusts

There are different types of charitable remainder trusts. Each one offers different advantages and drawbacks. The three main types are:

- Annuity trusts, which pay the income beneficiary a fixed amount each year.

- Unitrusts, which pay the income beneficiary an amount equal to a percentage of the trust assets each year.

- Pooled income trusts, which let you contribute to an existing charitable trust and receive income for a set time.

1. Charitable Remainder Annuity Trusts

This type of trust provides a fixed dollar amount of income every year (an annuity) to the trust's income beneficiary, regardless of the value of the trust assets. When creating the trust document, you name the income beneficiary—often yourself—and the term of the annuity period—often your lifetime. You also state the precise dollar amount of annual income that the life beneficiary must receive throughout this period.

Once you have established the set yearly payment, and the trust is operational, you can't change that figure. For instance, if you create a trust worth $250,000 and specify that the charity pay you $13,000 a year for the rest of your life, you can't subsequently say, "Oops, I forgot about inflation. How about $18,000 a year?"

Since January 1, 1998, you can, theoretically, make the payments as high as 50% of the value of the trust. However, the law requires that the charity must actually receive at least 10% of the original gift at the end of the term. If the payment is set too high, it would require spending principal, possibly using up much of the gift before the payment term is over. Obviously, this defeats your desire to make a gift to the charity. And there are practical limits. First, the higher the set payments, the lower your income tax deduction. Second, a charity is unlikely to accept a gift, particularly if it must serve as trustee, where it is likely, or even possible, that much of the trust property will be consumed before the charity gets a gift.

The advantage of this type of trust is that if the trust somehow has lower-than-expected income—for example, during a period when interest rates are extremely low—the income beneficiary still receives the same annual income. The trustee must invade the trust principal, if necessary, to make the payments. This can't be done with other types of charitable remainder trusts.

If you create a charitable remainder annuity trust, you don't obtain a hedge against inflation. Payments from an annuity trust remain the same, even if there's significant inflation or the trust assets significantly increase in value.

You cannot give additional assets to a charitable remainder annuity trust after it's operational. (IRS Reg. 1.664-2(b).) Once the trust is created and funded, that's it. Of course, you could create a new, second trust, and many people do, but this is a fair amount of bother, especially with subsequent recordkeeping. So you should carefully decide, before creating a charitable remainder annuity trust, how much money you want to put in it and how large an annuity you want.

There are income tax advantages to using an annuity trust. The same property contributed to an annuity trust has a higher value for income tax deduction purposes than if placed in a charitable remainder unitrust. (See Section 2, below.) If you are not concerned about inflation and wish to reduce your estate tax and income tax, an annuity trust is often a better choice than a unitrust.

CHARITABLE REMAINDER ANNUITY TRUSTS AT A GLANCE

1. You fund the trust with appreciated (if possible) trust assets.

2. You take an income tax deduction, the amount of which is calculated according to IRS rules.

3. The trustee (usually, the charity) converts all assets into income-producing ones. No capital gain tax is due on the sale profits.

4. The trustee pays a set amount to the income beneficiary for the annuity period.

5. At the end of the annuity period, trust assets go outright to the charity. The value of these assets is not subject to federal estate tax.

---

2. Charitable Remainder Unitrusts

With this popular form of a charitable remainder trust, the trustee pays income each year from the trust to an income beneficiary—again, usually the grantor. But instead of a fixed amount, the income beneficiary gets a percentage of the current value of the trust property. For example, the trust document could specify that the income beneficiary receives 7% of the value of the trust assets yearly. Each year, the trust assets must be reappraised to obtain a current worth figure. If the value of the trust assets increases because of wise investment decisions by the trustee (or simple good luck), the payments received by the income beneficiary also increase. It is in the charity's interest to have the principal grow as much as possible so it will receive more at the end of the term.

Similarly, because the income beneficiary receives a fixed percentage, not a flat dollar amount, if inflation pushes up the dollar value of the assets, the payments to the income beneficiary go up accordingly. So a charitable remainder unitrust can serve as a hedge against inflation, in contrast to an annuity trust, where payments remain fixed no matter how rampant inflation becomes.

The payment to the trust income beneficiary must, under IRS rules, be at least 5% of the value of the trust assets each year and not over 50%. But here again, practical considerations, such as the grantor's desire to make a gift to charity, and the charity's willingness to accept and manage the trust property, mandate that the percentage be reasonable. It cannot be excessive enough to consume all the trust property during the income beneficiary's period of payment. The IRS requires that a minimum gift of 10% of the original assets go to the charity.

In certain situations, the trust document can direct that the income beneficiary be given all the income from the trust:

- if the spouse of the grantor is the income beneficiary, or

- if the trust property is the grantor's residence or family farm.

If you create a charitable remainder unitrust, you can, later on, transfer more property to the trust, if the power to make additional gifts was expressly provided for in the original trust document. (IRS Reg. 1664-3(b).)

Here's an example of how a charitable remainder unitrust can provide income tax relief, reduce estate tax and provide other benefits:

Example: Felix, age 60, earns a very comfortable salary and owns assets worth $3 million. Much of his property consists of his home and stock that he bought years ago. The stock has appreciated substantially in value; it cost $600,000 and is now worth $1.6 million. It currently pays little in dividends.

If Felix sells the stock and buys income-producing assets, he'll be obligated to pay capital gain tax on his profit from the sale. Setting up a charitable remainder unitrust offers one way to avoid this tax and guarantee income later, when Felix retires. Felix establishes a charitable remainder trust with himself as the income beneficiary for life and his alma mater, his state's university, as the final beneficiary. Felix funds the trust with the stock.

For income tax purposes, his donation to the charity is the full market value of the stock, less the IRS deduction based on his retained interest, age and current interest rates.

The $1 million profit on the sale of the stock is not taxed. The trustee reinvests the entire $1.6 million into well-paying investments. The trust document requires income to be paid to Felix at 6% of the trust value annually for life. This figure will be $96,000 the first year; it will change each year as (if) the value of trust assets changes. Obviously, if the value of the investment increases, Felix will receive more money. And equally obviously, it's desirable that the charity make wise investments to increase the odds that the trust principal will increase.

So far, Felix has avoided paying capital gain tax while turning an asset that paid little income into one that pays him much more. His income tax deduction will be almost $400,000, more than enough to buy life insurance to replace the gift amount for his inheritors, if he is healthy. He can then remove those proceeds from his taxable estate. (See Chapter 12, Section E, and Chapter 21, Section B.)

But there is even more good news. Felix has also reduced his estate to a level where much less estate tax will be due at his death. Felix has given money to the school for its eventual use instead of giving it to Uncle Sam. And he has a guaranteed income for life.

If Felix lives for 15 years while receiving income from this trust, the trust should pay him at least $96,000 x 15, or $1,440,000. If the trustee invests the original $1.6 million wisely, that principal amount should also increase significantly in 20 years. If the principal increases, Felix will obviously receive more than $96,000 a year.

3. Pooled Income Trusts

A popular type of charitable remainder trust is a pooled income trust, which allows people of more modest means to take advantage of charitable income tax deductions, donate to their favorite charity and receive an income for a set period. You don't set up your own pooled income trust; the charity does it. You simply donate to the charity. It pools your donation with other money it's been given, and manages all the money in one big trust.

Not every charity offers pooled income trusts, but most large ones do. Many universities and museums have established them for their loyal supporters. If a pooled fund is available, the charity will surely be delighted to discuss it with you, and help set up the paperwork.

Pooled income trusts operate very much like mutual funds. You contribute money, bonds or stocks to the charity. (Highly appreciated stock is desirable because, as we've discussed, the charity can sell it for its present market value and pay no capital gain tax.) The charity pools a number of individuals' donations, invests the money and pays interest to the donors according to its earnings. You can specify that your earnings be retained until you reach a certain age, such as retirement age of 65 or 70, with payments to start then. The charity receives what remains of your gift after your death. If invested wisely, chances are the charity's share will have appreciated in value significantly by them.

You cannot give tangible property—from real estate to jewelry—to a pooled trust. It's not permitted under federal law. This is not true for other types of charitable trusts.

In a pooled charitable trust, the charity is always the trustee—you have no option here. If you don't think that a charity will manage your gift well, its pooled income charitable trust is simply not for you.

Pooled income trusts can be attractive for many reasons. The charity does all of the work of setting up the trust and managing the assets. Also, unlike other charitable remainder trusts, you can easily add amounts to the trust after the initial contribution. So if you don't have a large portfolio or cash to donate at one time, you can still build a nice retirement income and at the same time benefit a good cause, by donating smaller amounts over years.

A deduction from your income tax is allowed every time you make a donation. The amount of the deduction is figured by using the IRS tables to value the charity's remainder interest. (See Section B1, above.)

Example: Yuki is a businesswoman in her 40s with a salary of $80,000 a year. She is not married and has no children. She wants to support her favorite museum and also plan for her retirement. Yuki contributes $10,000 to a charitable pooled fund managed by the museum and takes her income tax deduction, the exact amount of which is determined by the IRS tables. A year later she does the same thing.

She keeps this up for 20 years, adding more in high-income years and less in years when she has unexpected expenses. By age 65, when she needs the income, her pooled shares, having been well-managed by the fund, are worth around $400,000. She will receive whatever income this amount generates.

Yuki has accomplished both of her goals—giving a substantial amount to charity and providing a retirement fund for herself.

CHARITABLE POOLED INCOME TRUSTS AT A GLANCE

1. You contribute assets to a charity that has established a pooled trust.

2. You take an income tax deduction.

3. The charity combines your assets with other contributions in a fund.

4. The fund pays income to you, based on the fund's income on all pooled gifts.

5. You can make additional gifts. If so, you take further income tax deductions.

6. The fund keeps paying you for life, based on your total contributions.

7. At your death, the assets you contributed go outright to the charity.

Checking out a pooled charitable trust. The pool must meet strict federal requirements in order for your contributions to be tax-deductible. (IRC Sections 170(f)(2)(A), and 642(c)(5).) The rules dictate who can serve as trustees and how contributions are combined and invested. If you are dealing with a "brand name" charitable pool, you should be safe. If not, and your own investigations have not reassured you that the charitable pooled trust you're considering fully complies with federal law (and this may not be easy to determine), it is sensible to take all the information you can gather about the trust to a good tax advisor.

D. A Closer Look at Charitable Lead Trusts

A charitable lead trust works in reverse fashion from any form of charitable remainder trust. In a charitable lead trust, the charity initially receives a set amount of income from the trust for a set period, usually a number of years. If the charity's income from the trust property drops below the set level, the charity can invade the trust principal to pay itself the set amount. At the end of the period, the trust principal goes to the final beneficiaries named by the grantor. Usually, the final beneficiaries are the grantor's surviving spouse or children.

Charitable lead trusts do not offer all the tax advantages as charitable remainder trusts. But they do offer some of the same income tax advantages. For instance, if you donate appreciated property to a charitable lead trust, and the charity then sells it, no capital gain tax is assessed. Also, tax law allows you an income tax deduction of the amount that the charity is expected to receive, based on IRS tables.

Charitable lead trusts that become operational while the grantor lives are used rarely, because they involve a significant income tax drawback: Income from the trust paid to the charity (during the set payment period) is taxed to the grantor, because the assets will revert back to him or his inheritors later. So the grantor must pay income tax on income the charity, not he, receives. This can effectively cancel out the original tax deduction. Not a highly desirable state of affairs. Still, these types of trusts are occasionally used, mainly by the very wealthy. They can make sense if you have highly appreciated assets that you want to ultimately remain in the family, not be given to charity.

Example: Clark, a wealthy industrialist in his early 50s, wants to take advantage of every tax break he can find. He and his wife have many assets that will let them continue to live very well when they retire.

With the help of his lawyer, Clark creates a charitable lead trust, funded with real estate that he long ago paid $100,000 for and which is now worth $2 million. He chooses as the income beneficiary a research institute for the cure of Parkinson's disease and sets the income payments to the institute at 8% of the trust assets a year. At Clark's death, the trust assets are to go to his children.

The trustee sells the real estate and invests the proceeds in mutual stock funds. Clark avoids a large capital gain tax that would have been assessed if he personally sold the property, because the charity isn't taxed on the sale. Clark takes an immediate income tax deduction of the charity's projected income from these assets, based on the IRS tables that consider his life expectancy and interest rates. He knows he will have to pay tax on the income the charity obtains from these assets, but he hopes the gain

he's achieved from avoiding capital gain tax will cancel out this drawback.

Even more important to him, Clark is able to leave the trust property to his children. Also, he feels satisfaction that he has contributed to the possible cure of a horrible disease.

It's impossible to say exactly how much income tax Clark will pay on what the trust earns during his life, because it depends on how long he lives and on income tax rates. Let's say Clark lives for 25 more years. If the trust earns 8% a year, that's $80,000. At current top rates, income tax the first year would be $24,800. If the value of the trust keeps going up, the tax savings will be eaten away.

When the final beneficiaries don't need their inheritance right away, a charitable lead trust created upon the death of the grantor can occasionally be useful. It can let you save on estate tax, give to charity and still (eventually) benefit your family or other beneficiaries. If a charitable lead trust becomes operational on the grantor's death, any negative income tax consequence to the grantor is avoided. He won't be earning any more income. (Death solves that concern.) The purpose of the trust becomes the reduction of estate tax. The value of the charity's income interest for the period of years is not included in the taxable estate.

Example: Rachel directs in her living trust that upon her death, a charitable lead trust of $1 million be established for a period of 15 years. During those years, income payments of $80,000 annually will go to her favorite charity. At the end of the period, the remainder will go to her niece. The charity's interest in the trust is calculated using the IRS tables. In this case, it will probably be around $800,000. This $800,000 is deducted from the taxable value of Rachel's estate. If Rachel's property is in the 55% estate tax bracket, her estate saves about $440,000 in estate tax.

NAMING A CHILD'S TRUST AS THE FINAL BENEFICIARY OF A CHARITABLE LEAD TRUST

When children or young adults are the final beneficiaries of a charitable lead trust, it can be a good idea to create a children's trust to receive the trust principal, in case the children are not old enough or responsible enough to handle the money when the charitable term ends. (Children's trusts are discussed in Chapter 6, Children, Section C.) If children are the final beneficiaries, one child may need more money than the others, so a "family pot" trust may be advisable. Professional help here is a must.

CHARITABLE LEAD TRUSTS AT A GLANCE

1. You create and fund the trust, with appreciated assets if possible.

2. You take an income tax deduction.

3. The trustee converts all trust assets into income-producing assets.

4. Income goes to the charity for the set period.

5. You pay income tax on trust income paid to the charity.

6. At the end of the set period, all trust property, including appreciation, goes to the beneficiaries you chose.

There are two basic types of charitable lead trusts:

- Unitrusts, where a set percentage of the trust's net worth is paid to the charity for a period of years. The actual amount paid can vary over the years, as the trust assets are reappraised each year.

- Annuity trusts, where the grantor provides that a set dollar amount is to be paid to the charity each year.

E. TYPES OF CHARITABLE TRUSTS: A COMPARISON

TYPES OF CHARITABLE TRUSTS

	Charitable Remainder Unitrust	Charitable Remainder Annuity Trust	Pooled Income Trust	Charitable Lead Trust
Primary goals	Income tax and estate tax savings; hedge against inflation	Income tax and estate tax savings; fixed income for life	Income tax and estate tax savings; income (possibly for retirement)	Income tax and estate tax savings (though they can cause significant tax disadvantages); preservation of trust assets for final beneficiaries
Property you can transfer to trust	Money or tangible property	Money or tangible property	Money and stocks	Money or tangible property
Transfer additional property later?	Yes	No	Yes	Yes, if permitted in original trust document
Income tax deduction available to you	Smaller than with annuity trust, because IRS values the charity's share as less	Larger than with unitrust, because IRS values the charity's share higher	Yes	The value of charity's income interest for set period
Trustee	Anyone you choose, including yourself or the charity	Anyone you choose, including yourself or the charity	The charity only	Anyone you choose, including yourself or the charity as trustee
Income beneficiary	You or anyone else you name	You or anyone else you name	You or anyone else you name	The charity
Final beneficiary	The charity	The charity	The charity	You or beneficiaries you name
Income paid to income beneficiary	Fixed percentage of trust assets each year	Fixed dollar amount each year, even if trust principal must be used	Interest earned from donor's contribution to the pool	Fixed dollar amount or percentage of trust assets, whichever you specify in trust document ■

21

OTHER ESTATE TAX-SAVING TRUSTS

A. Generation-Skipping Trusts (GSTT Trusts) 21/2

    1. Is a Generation-Skipping Trust for You? 21/3

    2. Creating Two Generation-Skipping Trusts 21/4

    3. How the GSTT Works 21/5

    4. Options With Generation-Skipping Trusts 21/6

B. Irrevocable Life Insurance Trusts 21/7

    1. IRS Requirements 21/8

    2. Paying Insurance Policy Premiums 21/9

    3. When Circumstances Change 21/10

C. Grantor-Retained Interest Trusts: GRATs, GRUTs and GRITs 21/10

    1. Overview of GRATs, GRUTs and GRITs 21/10

    2. Grantor-Retained Annuity Trusts (GRATs) 21/12

    3. Grantor-Retained Unitrusts (GRUTs) 21/15

    4. Drawbacks of GRATs and GRUTs 21/16

    5. Grantor-Retained Income Trusts (GRITs) 21/17

    6. Questions to Ask About a Grantor-Retained
       Interest Trust 21/21

Individuals or couples with estates large enough to face federal estate tax can use a number of different types of trusts to save on overall estate taxes. For this chapter's purposes, "large enough" means, for a couple, that even if they use an AB trust, one or both of their estates will be over the estate tax threshold. The tax-saving trusts described in this chapter can be used by anyone, whether married, in an unmarried couple or single.

These trusts, however, are complicated. You'll need a lawyer to prepare the trust documents.

A. GENERATION-SKIPPING TRUSTS (GSTT TRUSTS)

A generation-skipping trust provides income to one generation of beneficiaries (called the middle or second generation) and then leaves the trust property outright to the next, or third, generation. One of the income beneficiaries—such as a child—usually serves as trustee. The benefit of a generation-skipping trust is that up to $1 million ($2 million for a couple) will avoid further estate tax when the second generation dies. In the right situation, these trusts can save a family a bundle on overall estate taxes.

There are no estate tax savings when the person from the older generation dies. All property in the trust is subject to estate tax at that point. But this type of trust works to transfer up to $1 million (plus any cost of living adjustments) tax-free when the middle generation dies. This middle generation never legally owns the trust property. That means the property in the generation-skipping trust isn't subject to tax when the trust property is turned over to the third generation.

Example: Alex, a grandparent, establishes a generation-skipping trust of $1 million to take effect at his death. His children, the middle generation, receive the income generated by the trust property while they are alive. They're called the income beneficiaries. When Alex's children die, no estate tax is assessed against the trust principal. The entire amount is turned over to his grandchildren, who are termed the final beneficiaries.

Use of a generation-skipping trust is not limited to your direct descendants. It can be used anytime you have beneficiaries in two subsequent generations and, of course, a sizable amount of money you're willing to tie up for a generation.

Example: Monroe, who has a lot of money, decides to leave $1 million to his niece and her three children in a generation-skipping trust. His niece, the "middle generation," receives trust income for her life. When she dies, the trust ends and the property is distributed equally among her three children (the "third generation"). No estate tax is assessed at her death, because she didn't legally own the trust property.

This tax break has a limit, however: any money placed in this type of trust exceeding $1 million is subject to an extra tax, called the "generation-skipping transfer tax" (GSTT), when the middle generation dies. Members of a couple can each transfer $1 million free of GSTT.

The $1 million amount that Congress has established as exempt from the GSTT will be indexed for cost of living increases after 1998. This increase in the exempt amount will be slight, but eventually may become a consideration when deciding whether or not you want one of these trusts.

Be warned—using a GSTT trust is complicated, and we provide only an overview of the subject. If you decide a generation-skipping trust is desirable, you absolutely need an expert in the field.

Congress created the GSTT because it wanted to put an end to one of the favorite estate-tax loopholes used by the very rich. Under the GSTT, every dollar over $1 million, plus cost of living adjustments, put in a generation-skipping trust is subject to the highest existing estate tax rate at the time the GSTT tax is applied, when the middle generation dies. This rate is 55%. This 55% GSTT tax is in addition to whatever estate tax was paid on the trust property at the death of the original grantor (the older generation). The tax is defined in IRC Section 2611, which refers to several other IRC sections as well.

Fussy actuarial rules apply if you create a trust to benefit your "non-lineal" descendants—that is, anyone except children, grandchildren and so on—to determine which generation they are in. Basically, the rules provide that a "generation" occurs every 25 years, except the "child" generation starts when a beneficiary is over 12-1/2 years younger than the grantor.

Example: Shanto leaves money in a trust that will pay income for life to his friend Lolly, who is 15 years younger than he is. At her death, the principal will go to Lolly's children. This is a generation-skipping trust, and Lolly will be considered a member of the "child" category.

ONE WAY THE RICH STAYED RICH

Before the adoption of the generation-skipping transfer tax, when Congress put a limit on the right to pass money to one's grandchildren free of estate tax in the middle generation, people with many, many millions (even billions) of dollars would leave the bulk, or perhaps all, of their property in generation-skipping trusts. Estate taxes were, of course, due when the trust grantor died, but no taxes at all would be assessed when the middle generation died. These types of trusts enabled the very wealthy to escape all estate tax in every other generation. And the income from a trust of many millions normally proved quite sufficient for the middle generation to live an affluent lifestyle. (Couldn't you survive well on the income from, say, $200 million?) Since Congress created the GSTT in the 1980s, there is no tax advantage in creating a generation-skipping trust worth more than $1 million.

1. Is a Generation-Skipping Trust for You?

You must have a substantial estate—usually at least a couple of million dollars (individually)—before a generation-skipping trust could make sense. With a generation-skipping trust, the middle generation can have the right to receive all trust income, but only restricted rights to spend principal. So you want to be sure that your immediate family will be well provided for at your death before you create a generation-skipping trust that will benefit the second generation down, usually your grandchildren.

Example: Abigail is a widow with two children and four grandchildren. Each of her children is established in a successful career and is quite prosperous. Abigail has an estate of $2.5 million. She decides to leave $750,000 outright to each of her children and create a generation-skipping trust for the remaining $1 million. This trust will become operational on Abigail's death. The trust will pay all income to Abigail's children, equally, during their lifetimes. When one child dies, all trust income will go to the surviving child. When the surviving child dies, the trust assets will be divided equally among Abigail's grandchildren, with no additional estate tax due. No GSTT tax will ever be due because of her GSTT exemption.

a. Will Your Spouse Need Your Property?

Trusts paying income to children and then leaving assets to grandchildren are sensible only if your spouse is already fully provided for—from his own property, other property you leave for his benefit, or both. Your spouse could also receive income from the trust, and have a limited right to invade principal, but if spousal need is a real concern, a GSTT is probably not what you need.

However, when the financial picture is quite secure, a generation-skipping trust can certainly save on overall estate taxes.

Example: Roberta and Byron own shared property worth $3.2 million. Neither has any separately owned property. Thus, each one's estate is worth $1.6 million, half the total. Each spouse creates the same estate plan: $625,000 is left in an AB trust, with the surviving spouse having maximum powers to spend trust principal for health care or other needs. They select $625,000 for their AB trusts because this way, they are assured none of this amount can be subject to estate tax, no matter what the year of death.

Each spouse feels that with their own $1.6 million, and the income generated by it, as well as possible use of principal in the AB trust for

basic needs, they are sufficiently protected economically. So each spouse leaves the balance of his or her estate in a generation-skipping trust for their children and grandchildren.

b. Will Your Children Need Your Property?

If you establish a generation-skipping trust, your children (the second generation) will not have outright ownership of any of the trust property (principal). They can serve as trustees and receive trust income. And, if expressly allowed by the trust document, they can spend trust principal deemed necessary by the trustee for their "health, education or maintenance." (This is the IRS "objective" standard for invasion of trust principal by life beneficiaries. See Chapter 18, Estate Tax-Saving Bypass Trusts, Section B.)

What this amounts to is that, for most people, a generation-skipping trust makes sense only if you're sure your children (the middle generation) will be financially comfortable without unrestricted access to the assets in the trust. If this isn't the case, you'll probably want to simply leave them the property outright. Also, if members of the middle generation are reasonably young and may survive you by decades, you may not feel secure tying up a lot of money in such a way that they can reach it only in limited circumstances.

2. Creating Two Generation-Skipping Trusts

Each member of a couple (married or not) can transfer $1 million in a generation-skipping trust free of GSTT. Thus, a wealthy couple can create two generation-skipping trusts for their children and grandchildren, placing a total of $2 million plus any cost of living adjustment in the trusts.

In second or subsequent marriages, each spouse may want to create a generation-skipping trust for her or his own children from a prior marriage, and for their children's children.

3. How the GSTT Works

Any gift of trust property to a beneficiary two generations down, no matter how it is made, is subject to the GSTT. As we've said, the GSTT tax rate is the highest rate on the federal estate tax scale, currently 55%.

If the amount in the original trust or gift exceeds $1 million plus any cost of living adjustment, the GSTT applies when any property or money is actually distributed to the third generation beneficiary.

a. When the GSTT Is Assessed

The GSTT, if applicable, is assessed when the final beneficiaries of a generation-skipping trust receive their property. Usually, this happens only after the middle generation dies. Two other types of transfers are also subject to the GSTT.

A "direct skip" is an outright gift to someone two (or more) generations down. For instance, if you leave $2 million outright to a grandchild, $1 million of that gift is exempt from the GSTT. The other $1 million is taxed at 55%. Also, the entire $2 million is included in your taxable estate, and so is subject to estate tax at your death. So the property is taxed twice.

Sometimes, a generation-skipping trust directs or permits payment to a beneficiary two generations removed from the grantor, while the middle generation is still alive. This is a "taxable distribution" and any such payments will be taxed under the GSTT, if the amount in the trust originally exceeded $1 million.

b. How the GSTT Is Assessed

As just discussed, the generation-skipping transfer tax will be due when the income (middle generation) beneficiary dies and the trust property goes to the final beneficiaries. In tax lingo, this event is called a "taxable termination."

However, whether or not a generation-skipping trust is subject to the GSTT is determined earlier, when the grantor dies—that is, when the trust becomes operational. If the amount in the trust at the time the grantor dies is less than $1 million, then all property in the trust is exempt from the GSTT tax. The tax will not apply when the trust assets are eventually distributed to the grandchildren, even if the worth of the those trust assets has increased significantly by that time.

Example: Frank is a widower with two children and four grandchildren. His total estate is worth $1.9 million. He sets up a generation-skipping trust of $1 million to take effect at his death. This $1 million is included in Frank's taxable estate when he dies. Frank has directed that all estate tax due on his death be paid from his other assets, not from property in the generation-skipping trust. So the full $1 million goes into the trust.

The trust will pay the income to his children for their lifetimes. When they die, the principal goes to the grandchildren. When the children die, the property in the trust is worth $3.5 million. No GSTT is assessed, because the amount in the trust when Frank died did not exceed $1 million and was therefore exempt.

The amount of money in the trust, for GSTT purposes, is determined after any estate tax assessed on, and payable from, the amount left in trust has actually been paid.

Example: Abigail funds her generation-skipping trust with her entire estate of $1.2 million. The income will go to her children for their lives, and when they die the assets will go to her grandchildren. She dies in the year 2001 when the personal exemption is $675,000. Estate tax of $207,250 will be due at Abigail's death. So after the tax is paid, the amount of her property left to go into the generation-skipping trusts will be under $1 million.

Determining in advance the exact tax rate that will be applied to property placed in a generation-skipping trust is not easy, especially when some of this property will be used to pay some portion of the grantor's estate tax. To really understand how this works means deciphering tax concepts like "inclusion ratios" and "applicable fractions." (The intrepid may

wish to study IRC Sections 2601, 2602.) For regular affluent folks, a certified public accountant (CPA) or lawyer with estate tax experience is essential here.

4. Options With Generation-Skipping Trusts

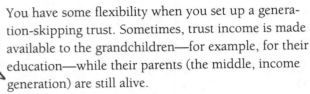

You have some flexibility when you set up a generation-skipping trust. Sometimes, trust income is made available to the grandchildren—for example, for their education—while their parents (the middle, income generation) are still alive.

In addition, other estate planing devices can be useful in combination with a generation-skipping trust. Most common is use of a bypass trust, usually an AB trust, with a generation-skipping trust. (See Chapter 18, Estate Tax-Saving Bypass Trusts, Section C.) Sometimes, the generation-skipping trust is combined with leaving property outright to a surviving spouse or a marital deduction trust such as a QTIP trust. (See Chapter 19, Section A.)

If you are married and wealthy, care must be taken to take advantage of each spouse's $1 million GSTT exemption. A couple could simply leave their money outright to each other and lose one GSTT exemption, as well as one personal estate tax exemption.

Example: Arto doesn't want his spouse, Riki, to have to worry about estate tax or trust documents at his death, so he puts off taxes by leaving everything outright to her under the marital deduction. They both want their waterfront home (which they own together) to eventually go to their favorite granddaughter, Allie.

When Riki dies several years after Arto, the home is worth $2 million. If she leaves it to Allie, the GSTT will rear its 55% head on $1 million. Arto didn't use his $1 million GSTT exemption. If Arto had put his share in a GSTT trust for Allie, no GSTT tax would ever be due.

Even when using an AB trust plan, when grandchildren are final beneficiaries, you can lose part of the GSTT exemption.

Example: Oscar and Gertie each leave the exact amount of the personal exemption in an AB trust that will eventually go to grandchildren. They do this by using a formula clause that will fund the trust with the amount of the exemption in the year of their death. (See Chapter 18, Section C.) They leave the remainder of their estates outright to each other. Oscar dies first in 2002, when the personal exemption is $700,000. He has used only $700,000 of his $1 million GSTT exemption.

This situation can be avoided by using a QTIP trust (see Chapter 19 for details on QTIP trusts). When property is left to a spouse in a QTIP trust, for estate tax purposes, the surviving spouse is the owner of the property. But for GSTT purposes, the law allows the executor to make what is called a reverse QTIP election. This is simply a request to make the first spouse the owner of property (or part of the property) for GSTT purposes that will go to grandchildren. The executor can make a partial election that will make sure each spouse uses their personal GSTT exemptions. (See Chapter 19, Section A6.)

Example: Oscar leaves $700,00 in the year 2002 in an AB trust with income to Gertie and assets to his grandchildren upon his death. He leaves a remaining $2 million in a QTIP with income to Gertie and the assets to be divided at Gertie's death among his children and grandchildren. The QTIP assets are considered Gertie's property for estate tax purposes. But his executor makes a reverse QTIP election for $300,000 of the QTIP property.

Although this portion will still be part of Gertie's property for estate tax, Oscar is considered the one eventually transferring the property to the grandchildren for GSTT purposes and it will be exempt from the GSTT tax. And another full $1 million can now pass to grandchildren from the surviving spouse from the QTIP trust that will not be subject to the GSTT tax. Both spouses have used their $1 million GSTT exemptions.

B. IRREVOCABLE LIFE INSURANCE TRUSTS

After your death, all the insurance proceeds paid from a policy you owned are included in your taxable estate. (See Chapter 12, Life Insurance.) If the payout is large, it may push the value of your estate over the federal estate tax threshold. So finding a way to remove life insurance proceeds from your taxable estate can save your inheritors a bundle in estate tax.

One way to remove life insurance proceeds from your estate is to use an irrevocable life insurance trust. This trust is a legal entity you create that becomes operational while you are alive. The trust becomes the owner of life insurance you previously owned as an individual or of a new policy purchased in the trust's name. Because the policy is owned by this legally independent trust, you are not the legal owner of the insurance proceeds, which therefore are not included in your taxable estate. Normally, the beneficiaries of the policy remain the same as they were before you set up the trust.

Irrevocable life insurance trusts aren't for everyone who faces estate tax, or even most of them. Indeed, simply giving the policy to someone is normally a better approach, if there's someone you trust to give the policy to. (See Chapter 12, Section E, for a discussion of the advantages and drawbacks of giving away your life insurance policy.) Life insurance trusts are for those who don't want the risks involved in giving their policy outright to another person. For instance, when the beneficiary of the life insurance isn't yet mature enough to be trusted with ownership, an irrevocable life insurance trust can be very desirable.

Get help. If you want to create or explore using a life insurance trust, see an experienced lawyer before you trundle off to your insurance company. In addition to the complexities of any irrevocable trust, there are also problems unique to a life insurance trust.

1. IRS Requirements

Strict IRS requirements govern irrevocable life insurance trusts. To gain the estate tax savings this type of trust can offer, you must conform to these rules.

a. The Trust Must Be Irrevocable

The life insurance trust must be absolutely irrevocable. If you retain any right to revoke or amend the trust, or affect the insurance policy in any way (such as naming a new beneficiary), the IRS will consider you to be the legal owner of the policy. That means the proceeds will be included in your taxable estate.

b. You Cannot Be the Trustee

Remember that the purpose of this trust is to remove the life insurance from your estate. You cannot control the trust, so you cannot be trustee. If you try to retain any rights which a trustee must have, the IRS will say you still own the policy.

Your spouse can be trustee, but you must be careful with this arrangement. You'll need expert legal help to make sure that the spouse is not given certain powers or too much power which might make him or her the legal owner of the policy. You want to keep the proceeds out of both of your estates, not just your own.

You can name your grown child, brother, a friend or even an institution to serve as trustee. No matter who you choose, you'll have more control over the trustee than you would over someone to whom you gave an insurance policy outright, because you create the trust document that establishes the trustee's powers.

Example: Pilar is the divorced mother of two children, in their 20s, whom she has named as beneficiaries of her universal life insurance policy. It will pay $400,000 at her death. In addition to the insurance policy, Pilar has an estate of $700,000. She wants to remove the proceeds of the policy from her estate. If she doesn't, her total estate of $1.1 million will be subject to federal estate tax.

But Pilar has a problem. Although she loves her kids dearly, neither child is sensible with money, and she doesn't trust them enough to give her policy to them outright. She fears they might fail to make the premium payments, or possibly even cash in the policy in a time of financial desperation. She wants to be sure the policy is kept in force until her death, so that all the proceeds—far more than the cash-in value of the policy—will be distributed to her children on her death.

Pilar decides to create an irrevocable life insurance trust for the policy and to name her sister, Julianna, the person she's closest to, to be the trustee.

Even aside from the crucial fact that Pilar trusts Julianna, there's no sensible reason for Pilar to worry about Julianna cashing in the policy. If Julianna did that, she wouldn't receive the cash surrender value herself; the trust, not Julianna owns the property. The cash-in money would remain in the trust until Pilar's death.

c. The Trust Must Exist for at Least Three Years Before Your Death

You must establish the operational trust at least three years before your death. If the trust has not functioned for at least three years when you die, the trust is disregarded for estate tax purposes, and the insurance proceeds are included in your taxable estate.

This three-year rule is obviously crucial. It means that if you want to establish an irrevocable life insurance trust, you should do so promptly. Clearly, it'd be unfortunate to create an irrevocable life insurance trust and die before the end of the three-year period, negating all estate tax savings the trust offered.

The reason for this three-year rule is that the estate tax savings offered by an irrevocable life insurance trust (or any transfer of life insurance ownership) can be so substantial that the IRS wants to prohibit last-minute transfers of life insurance, in anticipation of death. Three years seems like a pretty long "last minute," but sensible or not, the rule exists. If you want to create an irrevocable life insurance trust, do it soon. There are no benefits from waiting.

2. Paying Insurance Policy Premiums

One major concern when creating an irrevocable life insurance trust is how future premium payments to the insurance company will be made. If you set up

the trust, you cannot directly make the payments through the trust, or the IRS will consider you to have retained some control or interest in the policy. This means, as we've warned before, that all the proceeds payable on your death will be included in your taxable estate.

At least two payment options are available to you. First, you can give money to the beneficiaries each year so that they can make the payments themselves. Of course, you'll have to trust the beneficiaries to spend that cash on policy premiums. Second, you can include what are called "Crummey" trust provisions (so named because someone named Crummey was the first to have this type of trust validated) in your irrevocable life insurance trust.

Here's how Crummey trust provisions work. The trust document provides that each year, each trust beneficiary has the right to receive up to $10,000 from the trust property ($10,000 is currently the maximum that can be given to a beneficiary, per year, free of gift tax). Usually, the beneficiaries have a deadline, say January 15, to claim their money for the year.

Each year, you give up to $10,000 per person to the trust. Now things get tricky. Each year the beneficiaries decline to accept this money. By doing this, the gift is converted from a "future interest" (not eligible for the annual gift tax exemption) into a gift of a "present interest"—which means it qualifies for this exemption. (This distinction is discussed in Chapter 16, Gifts and Gift Taxes, Section C.) The trustee uses this declined money to pay that year's insurance premium. Any balance left over after the year's premiums have been paid is saved in the trust for future premium payments.

You should be aware that the IRS has made no secret of its distaste for Crummey trust provisions. So far, the Crummey method has remained legal, but the IRS may well find a new avenue of attack in the future. If the Crummey provision fails down the line, the gifts to the beneficiaries will be taxable, and not subject to the annual exemption. Even so, gifts for the amount of a premium are small when compared to the eventual proceeds.

If neither of these methods provides enough cash to pay the yearly insurance premium, or you consider the Crummey provisions too complicated and risky, what can you, the grantor, do? Perhaps you could purchase a single-premium policy, so there's no worry about future payments. Another approach is simply to give money to the trust and be assessed gift tax on it.

3. When Circumstances Change

Sometimes tricky personal concerns arise preparing or living with an irrevocable life insurance trust. For example:

- What happens if you get married, divorced or you have a child after setting up an irrevocable trust? Legally, it's up to the trustee to decide who the beneficiaries of the policy should be. Of course, a trustee who cares for you will probably revise the insurance beneficiaries as you want. For example, the trustee could add your new child as a beneficiary.

- Suppose you get divorced, and your ex-spouse is one of the beneficiaries of the life insurance policy and also of Crummey trust provisions you created to pay the premiums? Here's where matters can get very touchy. If the trustee simply removes the ex-spouse as a beneficiary of the policy, the ex-spouse could claim the trustee was really acting under your control. This could cause the entire trust to fail for estate tax purposes. With personal complexities like these, you must see a lawyer.

C. GRANTOR-RETAINED INTEREST TRUSTS: GRATs, GRUTs AND GRITs

Names to the contrary, this section is not about lifting weights or Southern cooking. Here we discuss three types of irrevocable estate tax-saving trusts. Their common feature is that you keep either income from trust property, or use of that property, for a period of years. Then the trust ends, and the property goes to the final beneficiaries you've named. These trusts can let you make a gift to people you love, save on gift taxes and save again on estate taxes. A good deal.

These types of trusts are called:

- Grantor-Retained Annuity Trusts (GRATs)
- Grantor-Retained Unitrusts (GRUTs), and
- Grantor-Retained Income Trusts (GRITs).

These trusts are for people who have enough wealth to feel comfortable giving away a substantial hunk of property. If you believe you'll want or need full control over all your property until you die, they are not for you.

1. Overview of GRATs, GRUTs and GRITs

GRATs, GRUTs and GRITs vary in some important aspects—such as how payment to the grantor is determined—but all have much in common. Here is how these trusts work to save on gift and estate tax.

First, you place property in one of these trusts. You can be, and usually are, the initial trustee of your trust. You also retain some interest in that property for a set period. The retained interest can be income generated from the trust property, or the right to use that property—such as living in a trust-owned house. You name final beneficiaries, who will receive the trust property when this period ends or at your death, whichever comes first.

Once established, the trust is irrevocable—you can't change your mind and take back any property from the trust. No matter how much you may need that property, it can never again be yours outright.

For gift tax purposes, the value of the gift you make to the trust is determined when the trust is established. This value never changes. You hope that while you have a retained interest in the trust property, the value of that property will increase significantly. If you outlive that period, and the property is turned over to the final beneficiaries before your death, this increase in value will never be subject to gift tax or estate tax.

Because you have retained an interest in the property—such as receiving income from the trust—the value of the gift, for gift tax purposes, is reduced; it is less than the property's market value. The gift tax is assessed on the value of the gift to the final beneficiaries, according to complex IRS tables.

see tables?

The annual gift tax exemption is not available, because the gift is not one for present use by any beneficiary but rather for use in the future. However, when you make your gift to the irrevocable trust, no gift tax must actually be paid, unless you have already used up your personal estate tax exemption by making previous taxable gifts. (See Chapter 16, Gifts and Gift Taxes, Section A.)

If you survive the set period, the property is transferred outright to the final beneficiaries. No new gift or estate taxes are assessed then. The only taxes ever assessed on this transaction are the gift taxes when the property is first placed in the trust. And because you no longer own the property at your death, the entire amount is excluded from your taxable estate.

As you'll see, the trick here is for you to outlive the set time (set by you in the trust document), so that the trust property is turned over to the final beneficiaries during your lifetime. If you do, the remaining value of the trust property will not be counted in your taxable estate. If you don't, the trust assets, complete with all appreciation in value, are included in your taxable estate. You gain nothing, estate tax-wise, and the money and time spent drafting the trust and administering it will have been wasted. Your estate will, however, get credit for any gift tax paid when the trust was created.

Both married and single folks can use a grantor-retained interest trust. Because estate tax breaks for single people are few and far between, a grantor-retained interest trust can be an attractive tax-avoidance technique for a wealthy single person.

Here's a rough example to show you how these trusts work. We'll get into more precise details soon enough.

Example: Phyllis, age 65, creates a GRIT (that's a grantor-retained income trust). She funds it with her house, worth $400,000, and retains the right to live in the house for 15 years. She names her son as the final beneficiary. The value of the gift (her house) to the trust is determined when she creates the trust. Her right to live in the house for 15 years is her income value, what it would cost someone to occupy the premises for that period. This is subtracted from the $400,000 gift for tax purposes.

house to Marsha?

Phyllis outlives the 15-year period she set. When she becomes 80, the house, now worth $725,000, is legally turned over to her son. Because gift tax was assessed on the $400,000 value of the house at the time the trust was created minus her retained interest, Phyllis has avoided paying gift tax on more than $325,000. Moreover, she has removed the house from her taxable estate, for the obvious reason that she's no longer the owner of it.

As you've probably already suspected, this trust sounds so terrific that it must have risks. When she turns 80, Phyllis will no longer own her house. If her son doesn't charge her rent, the IRS will consider him to have made a gift of the rent to his mother. If the reasonable rental value totals more than the annual gift tax exemption (currently $10,000), the son will have to file a gift tax return. (See Chapter 16, Gifts and Gift Taxes, Sections C and E.) Worse, her son could decide to sell the house, leaving Phyllis out on the street. And, as we discussed above, if Phyllis does not survive the time period she set in the trust document, the whole gamble collapses, and nothing is achieved, tax-wise.

2. Grantor-Retained Annuity Trusts (GRATs)

Another method for saving on gift and estate tax is a Grantor Retained Annuity Trust—a GRAT. Again, the grantor passes property—usually money or stock—to a child or favorite person, pays a reduced gift tax and removes the assets from the estate.

a. How GRATs Work

To establish a GRAT, you transfer some valuable asset, from cash to real estate to stocks to any property with significant value, to the trust. Under the terms of the trust document, the trustee (usually yourself) pays you, from the trust, an annual fixed sum (an annuity) for a set term of years. At the end of this term, the remaining trust assets go to the final beneficiary, perhaps your child, as the trust document directs. (IRC Section 2702.)

The benefit of a GRAT results from the fact that the IRS values the gift to the final beneficiaries only when the trust is established, not when the remaining trust property is later distributed, as long as you outlive the set period. Your retained interest greatly reduces the value of the gift for gift tax purposes,

even though the final beneficiary will normally receive (at a minimum) the full amount given.

The IRS tables used to determine the gift tax value of a gift to a GRAT are nearly impenetrable to all but real experts. They take into account the term period, life expectancy and the interest rates when the GRAT is created. Rather than bore, and quite possibly confuse you with a detailed explanation of how they work, we'll simply say they are one big reason you must see an expert if you want to set up one of these trusts.

Example: Hattie, a widow 60 years old, has assets worth $2 million. She sets up a GRAT with $1 million. The trust will last for 15 years and will pay Hattie $40,000 a year during the term. At the end of the term, or when Hattie dies, whichever happens first, the remaining trust assets will go equally to her three children. The value of the gift to the trust for gift tax purposes is set by an IRS formula that first subtracts Hattie's annuity interest ($40,000 times 15 years, or $600,000) and then considers Hattie's life expectancy and the amount in the trust ($1 million).

After subtracting the $600,000 value of Hattie's retained interest, the gift is initially worth $400,000. But now the IRS tables take into account Hattie's life expectancy and the interest rates when the trust is created. As a result, the value of the gift for gift tax purposes will be less than $400,000.

GRATs AT A GLANCE

1. You create and fund the trust, establishing the dollar amount of the annuity you will receive each year for the set period.

2. The value of the gift, for gift tax purposes, is determined when you fund the trust.

3. The trustee pays you an annuity annually.

4. When the annuity term ends, trust assets go to the final beneficiary.

Now let's continue the above example, to see in more depth how a GRAT works.

Example: The value of the gift to Hattie's children, for gift tax purposes, is determined at the time the trust is created. If Hattie has not used any of her gift and estate tax exemption by making other taxable gifts, no tax payment will actually be due at that time, because the gift is valued under the estate tax threshold. Instead, the value of the gift is deducted from Hattie's personal estate tax exemption.

Over time, the assets in the trust may well appreciate in value. This increase in value is not subject to tax. So, the real gift to her children will be much more than the taxable value of the gift.

Suppose Hattie's $1 million trust yields an actual annual return of 7%. That means income of $70,000 for the trust during the first year. After Hattie receives her $40,000 annuity, the extra $30,000 of income increases the amount of money in the trust. If this goes on year after year, with the trust assets increasing in worth each year, the same 7% return obviously yields more than the initial year's $70,000. For instance, the second year the income will be

7% of $1,030,000. And so it goes. The $1 million not only stays intact for the children, but gradually increases without tax consequences.

The more benefit you retain from the trust property, the less the property is worth for gift tax purposes. It follows then that the younger you are, and the longer the term during which you will benefit from the gift, the lower the taxable value of the gift. Likewise, the higher the annuity payments to you, the lower the taxable value of the gift.

Example: Sudata funds a GRAT with $1 million, retaining an annuity of $40,000 annually. But this GRAT is for a period of only ten years, rather than 15.

Her total benefit is $40,000 x 10, or $400,000, rather than $600,000 for a 15-year period. The gift tax value of the gift to the final beneficiary increases to closer to $600,000. (As we've said, the exact figure will be different, because of the IRS calculation tables.) That means a higher gift tax assessment.

If the value of the gift to the final beneficiaries exceeds the current estate tax exempt amount, you will have to pay gift tax when the trust is funded.

Example: In 1999, Max places $1 million in a GRAT and reserves a $20,000 annuity for himself for ten years. This results in a total benefit to him of $200,000 and a gift (to the final beneficiary) worth roughly $800,000. (Again, the IRS tables must be used to determine the precise taxable value of the gift.) Because the value of the gift exceeds Max's estate tax exemption, which is $650,000 in 1999, Max will have to pay gift tax on the roughly $150,000.

b. Increasing the Tax Savings From a GRAT

A GRAT is an irrevocable trust, which means that usually it functions as a separate taxable entity. However, it can be constructed in such a way that all income and capital gain from the trust are taxed to you, the grantor. This is called making the GRAT a "grantor trust." This way, more money is eventually given to the final beneficiaries.

Example: Theo funds a ten-year GRAT with a stock portfolio. Language in the trust document makes it a grantor trust. During the ten-year period, income from the trust is taxed to him and not to the trust. Also, during the trust term, as trustee, he sells part of the stock and makes a hefty profit. But Theo, not the trust, personally pays the capital gains tax due. This allows the trust assets to grow in value, and at the same time, further reduces Theo's estate.

A GRAT set up as a grantor trust can yield another potentially valuable tax saving if the assets you contribute to the trust go up substantially in value. Normally, if trust assets appreciate, the final beneficiaries of the GRAT would have to pay capital gain tax on the appreciation. To grasp what this means, a little review of cost basis rules is in order. (Basic rules are covered in more detail in Chapter 15, Estate Taxes.)

When you make a gift of property (land, stocks, jewelry or whatever) to someone other than a spouse during your life, the recipient receives and owns the property with your original cost basis. For example, if you give your son stock that you paid $40,000 for and is now worth $200,000, his tax basis will be $40,000. If he then sells the stock for $200,000, he will owe capital gain tax on $160,000. In contrast, if he inherited your stock at your death, his cost basis would automatically increase to the actual market value as of the date of your death. If he sold it for that

amount, no capital gain tax would be owed. This is why many people, especially elderly people, sensibly postpone making outright gifts of appreciated property until their deaths.

Fortunately, if you use a GRAT, the final beneficiaries don't have to receive the gift at your original basis. Instead, you can legally change the basis of low-basis property in a GRAT, so that when the final beneficiaries receive it, their cost basis is equal to the current market value of that property. The beneficiaries can sell the property when they receive it, without any capital gain tax being assessed. You can accomplish this bit of tax code magic by purchasing low-basis assets from the trust just before the set term ends, and replacing them with recently purchased assets.

Example: Joanne funds her GRAT with a combination of cash and stocks and makes it a grantor trust. This means she personally, not the trust, pays the tax on any income the trust makes, and also pays any capital gain tax if the trust sells any stock for a profit. Just before her set annuity term ends, she purchases all stock in the trust that has appreciated in value since it was placed in the trust. She replaces the stock with stocks of similar market value, recently purchased. When her annuity term ends, the children receive stock which has a basis at, or close to, its current market value, not stock with a low cost basis. If they had received low-cost basis stock, it would result in a big capital gain tax when they eventually sold the stock.

3. Grantor-Retained Unitrusts (GRUTs)

Don't you just love the jargon? Yes, it's bizarre, but you can comprehend it sufficiently so you can make an informed choice of whether you want to hire an expert for this. A grantor-retained unitrust, or GRUT, is very similar to a GRAT with this important difference: The income payment to you (the grantor) is not a fixed amount annually. Instead, the amount is equal to a percentage of the value of the trust assets for that particular year.

Each year, the new current value of the trust assets must be determined. Assuming a decent economy, in a well-managed trust, the worth of the assets should gradually increase over the years. In that case, the annual payments you receive would also get larger.

If the percentage payment is larger than the trust's earnings—for example, you're entitled to 8% of the trust's net worth, but the trust property earned only 5% this year—the rest comes out of the principal. Any trust income above the percentage set for you is added to the trust assets.

Just as with a GRAT, the gift tax value of the gift to the final beneficiary is established when the trust is created. The taxable value of a GRUT gift, for gift tax purposes, is determined by a complex IRS formula. The formula considers how much you can expect to receive over the set period, your age and life expectancy, and how long the trust is supposed to last. The older you are, the more valuable the gift; the longer the term of the trust, the lower the gift value.

Because your annual payment is based on the value of the trust property, a GRUT can give you some hedge against inflation. For example, say you have $1 million in a GRUT and get 7% of the value of the trust assets per year. If suddenly there's 20% annual inflation, the dollar value of the trust assets will, presumably, also increase by roughly 20%, to $1.2 million. Obviously, 7% of $1.2 million is a higher number than 7% of $1 million. But all you are

really doing is keeping up with inflation. In real dollar terms, you receive the same amount, although you receive more (inflated) dollars. No such hedge against inflation is available to grantors of a GRAT. They receive a set dollar amount every year, period.

Example: Ravi, aged 60, has an estate worth $900,000. He creates a GRUT of $300,000 that will last for ten years. Then the trust assets go to his friend Monica. The trust specifies that during the ten-year period, Ravi will receive, annually, 8% of the trust's net worth.

The first year, the trust pays out $24,000 to Ravi—8% of $300,000. If Ravi outlives the ten-year period, Monica will likely receive more than $300,000, and surely far more than the value the IRS assigned the gift when the trust was created. In addition, Ravi will have removed the $300,000 from his taxable estate.

GRUTs AT A GLANCE

1. You create and fund the trust, establishing the percentage return you will get each year for however many years you want the trust to last.

2. The value of the gift, for gift tax purposes, is determined when you fund the trust.

3. The Trustee pays you the established percentage of assets each year.

4. Trust assets are appraised annually.

5. When the term ends, the trust is terminated. Trust assets go to the final beneficiary.

4. Drawbacks of GRATs and GRUTs

The potential benefits of a GRUT or GRAT are rarely worth the risks involved unless you are very wealthy. If you have $10 million, putting $2 million in a GRUT or GRAT makes more sense than putting $500,000 in one if you have $2 million. Also, an expert must set up the trust, which is complicated and expensive.

Whether or not the drawbacks are likely to affect you depends on your family and tax situation. You should be aware of these drawbacks and evaluate how they could affect you and your beneficiaries before you create one of these trusts.

a. You Lose Control Over Trust Assets

As we've already stressed, once a GRAT or GRUT is established and operational, you lose legal ownership of the trust property. You can't later on turn around and decide that the income you receive from the trust isn't enough, and insist on higher payments. Nor can you get the trust assets turned back to you personally. Further, you cannot add to, or subtract from, the trust principal. Under the IRS rules, the amount put in the trust must stay there, period. Practically speaking, this means that if you or someone in your family suffers a financial disaster, the trust property isn't available to help out.

Further, if you do outlive the set term, you lose all benefit from the trust assets because they go to the final beneficiary at the end of the set term. Suppose you live for another ten years after the trust ends. You may well have become accustomed to the payments from the trust—or worse, may need them for expenses, such as medical costs. But anything you receive from the trust property (after the trust ends) will have to be a gift to you from the final beneficiaries—if they choose to make it.

b. Estate Tax Savings Are Not Guaranteed

Usually the biggest concern involved in deciding whether to use a GRAT or GRUT is the possibility that you won't outlive the period you've set to receive income from the trust. If you die before the set period has ended, all the trust property is legally part of your estate. All your possible estate tax savings are lost.

If you are married, you can plan to defer taxes in such circumstances by having the trust assets go to your spouse. All property left to your spouse (if he or she is a U.S. citizen) can pass estate tax-free under the marital deduction. If the surviving spouse is young and healthy, that spouse can make or revise her own estate plan to try to soften the estate tax blow when she dies.

But if the surviving spouse is elderly or in poor health and may not live long, or if you are single, your untimely death and the resulting addition of the trust property to your estate could mean higher estate taxes. In hindsight, another form of estate plan, such as a program of direct gift-giving, would have been preferable.

c. The Final Beneficiary May Have to Pay Capital Gain Tax

Stocks and bonds, as well as other property, are often used to fund GRATs and GRUTs. Over time, these assets are likely to go up in value. If they do, and unless you buy them back from the trust (usually near the end of the set term; see Section C2b, above), the cost basis of this property when the final beneficiaries receive it will be lower than its market value. The difference may be substantial. If it is, the final beneficiaries will have to pay a hefty capital gain tax if they sell the property.

Example: Mona funds a 15-year GRAT with stock currently worth $300,000 that she bought for $100,000. At the end of the term, the stock will go to her friend Kim. During the 15-year period, the value of the stock climbs to over $700,000. Mona cannot afford to repurchase the stock before the term ends because she doesn't have a spare $700,000. At the end of the 15-year period, Kim receives the stock, now worth $720,000. Her cost basis in the property is $100,000, Mona's original basis. If she sells the stock, she will owe capital gain tax on $620,000.

If the final beneficiary must pay capital gain tax, this of course reduces the real value of the gift. This loss must be balanced against any estate tax savings your inheritors gain because the property is removed from your taxable estate. By contrast, if you choose to keep the property until death and not create a GRAT or GRUT, the property's basis will be stepped up to its market value as of your death. In that case, if your inheritors promptly sell the property, no capital gain tax will be assessed.

Example: Mona simply leaves her stock outright to Kim, using a living trust. When she dies, the stock is worth $720,000. Kim's cost basis for the stock will be the full $720,000. If she promptly sells the stock for $720,000, she has obtained no taxable profit on the sale, so she will not owe any capital gain tax.

You should carefully review all available options, preferably with expert help. Each person's situation is so individual that there are no blanket rules for everyone.

5. Grantor-Retained Income Trusts (GRITs)

If you set up a GRIT, you receive all income from the trust assets for a set period. The assets go to the final beneficiary when you die or the term ends. GRITs were enormously popular before 1990. In that year, Congress took away any tax savings if the trust assets eventually benefit your family. "Family" includes your spouse, lineal descendants, ancestors, siblings and spouses of any of these family members.

The law left one exception. The one remaining form of GRIT that can save on taxes and be used for family members is called a "residence GRIT."

a. Qualified Residence GRITs

You may still successfully use a GRIT that will ultimately benefit family members, if it is funded only with your personal residence and nothing else. (IRC Section 2702.) This personal residence may be either your primary residence or a vacation home. You can do this for both, but you will need two separate trusts, one for each house. If the vacation home is sometimes rented by others, to qualify for a GRIT, you must actually use it each year for the greater of 14 days, or 10% of the time it is rented. So, if it is rented for 180 days a year, you must personally use it for at least 18 days, 10% of 180 days.

Here's how the residence GRIT works. You put your residence into a trust for a set period, usually about ten years. Your retained "income interest" during the term is the right to occupy the residence. At the end of the set period, the property goes to the final beneficiary you named in the original trust document.

Again, in order to obtain your goal, the trick is to outlive the term of the trust. If you don't survive the term, the full current value of the house is included in your taxable estate and your attempt at a reduced value gift fails. But your estate will get credit for any gift tax previously paid.

Couples who own homes together must create two residence GRITs, one for each person's share. The relevant federal statutes do not authorize a couple to set up a single residence GRIT for both of their interests in a shared home. A GRIT is an individual trust and gift. The value of the grantor's retained interest is determined, in part, by his or her individual life expectancy.

If you set up a residence GRIT, you are usually the trustee. The trust document gives you full control over management of the house—it's almost like retaining actual home ownership. Among other things, this means that you can still take an income tax deduction for mortgage interest and real estate taxes on the house.

When carefully drafted, the trust document creating your GRIT can allow you to make additional payments to the trust for mortgage payments, taxes, insurance and improvements. The document should also give you freedom to sell the property and reinvest the proceeds in another home.

Possibly more important, you can also retain the right, under IRS rules, to sell a principal residence and reinvest sale proceeds of $250,000 without capital gain tax. You may be able to take the proceeds and convert the GRIT into a GRAT.

The taxable value of the gift to the residence GRIT—the residence—is based on an IRS formula that considers the term of years of the trust, your age and current interest rates.

Example: Lucille, 60 years old, funds her GRIT with her primary residence, worth $1 million. The term of the trust is for 15 years, after which the residence will go to her son. The gift tax value of the gift to her son is figured by IRS formulas. In this case, Lucille's retained interest is worth about $750,000. So for gift tax purposes, the gift to the son is worth about $250,000.

If Lucille survives the 15-year term, her son will receive the house. Since the house will not be part of Lucille's taxable estate, the only tax assessed was on the $250,000 gift, when the trust was funded. (No tax would actually be paid, as long as Lucille hadn't already used up her personal estate/gift tax exemption.)

b. "Reversionary Interests" in a GRIT

One of the major reasons for the popularity of house GRITs is that the grantor can retain certain reversionary interests. Many estate planners suggest that married couples include a specific type of reversionary interest clause in a residence GRIT. This clause directs that if one spouse dies before the end of the term, the house is to be returned to the spouse's estate and given to the surviving spouse, so the unlimited estate tax marital deduction can be used.

Example: Celeste puts her summer cottage in a GRIT that will last 15 years; at the end of that period, the cottage will go to her daughter, Anna. But Celeste keeps a reversionary interest in the cottage so that if she dies during the term of the trust, the cottage reverts to her estate instead of going to her daughter. This would result in the property actually passing to Celeste's husband, so no estate tax will have to be paid if Celeste dies during the term.

In the past, you could structure a GRIT so that you had the right to purchase back the property from the trust before the term ends. Because the IRS viewed you as the property's owner until the set period ended, you had no taxable gain or loss on this purchase. This technique has been widely used to give the final beneficiaries a cost basis in the residence of current market value.

The IRS, however, was extremely critical of this procedure, and in 1996 it issued new proposed regulations prohibiting the sale of the residence back to the grantor or the grantor's spouse. (See Prop. Treas. Reg. 25.2702-5.) As of this writing, this regulation has not become final law, and estate planners are heatedly arguing against it. For now, though, the action by the IRS has effectively stopped this practice.

You will need expert help in drafting any kind of residence GRIT. You need someone who not only knows how to draft these GRITs, but also someone who is current on relevant law.

c. Drawbacks of Residence GRITs

As with all grantor-retained interest trusts, the flip side of the potentially big tax advantages of a residence GRIT are potentially big disadvantages. The drawbacks of a GRIT are essentially the same as for a GRAT or GRUT, covered above in Section C4. One drawback unique to a residence GRIT is that at the end of the set term, you no longer own your home. If you want to stay, you will owe fair rent to the final beneficiaries. For the wealthy, paying rent is often just another good way to pass on money to their children without gift tax and also to reduce their estate, and consequently its tax. But for people with less means, it could surely be a burden.

RESIDENCE GRITS AT A GLANCE

1. You create the trust and fund it with your house. You retain the right to live in the house, or sell it and buy a new one.

2. The value of the gift for gift tax purposes is determined when you transfer the house to the trust. It is reduced by your retained interest of living in the house.

3. When the term ends, the trust is terminated and the final beneficiary receives the trust assets.

REMEMBER KING LEAR

In a perfect world, a parent might create a residence GRIT for the benefit of a child or grandchild, who will lovingly allow the parent to continue to reside in the house until death. The child or grandchild would then, at the death of the parent, move in or sell the house.

Sadly, this is not always what happens. (Surprise—there's need and even greed in some families.) When several children are the final beneficiaries, they may decide to sell the property as soon as they become its legal owners. If they need the money and don't care what happens to the parent (the grantor), that parent could find herself losing a place to live.

Even if the parent is wealthy and could afford another house, a GRIT might make it easier for a well-meaning child to pack a parent off to a nursing home. After all, the child could rationalize, it's not even the parent's house any more.

Making another trust the final beneficiary of a residence GRIT can sometimes alleviate these potential problems, if you select a trustee who'll treat you honorably. Still, the trustee has a legal obligation to the final beneficiaries to produce the most income possible from the trust, which might necessitate selling the house. And if you can't trust your own kids, how can you be confident a separate trustee will be more reliable?

d. "Regular" GRITs

You establish a regular GRIT by giving property—any kind, such as stock, money or land—and retain the right to the income from the property for a set term. Congress eliminated the advantages of regular GRITs for direct family members, but not for other beneficiaries. In fact, nieces, nephews and cousins, as well as friends, can still be final beneficiaries for GRITs funded with property other than a personal residence. This is one strategy unmarried couples can use—and indeed, come out ahead on—because they are not legally "family."

In a regular GRIT, you receive all of the income for a set term from the trust property. The gift tax value of the gift consists of what the final beneficiary is expected to receive at the end of the set term. As with all of the other grantor-retained interest trusts, the IRS values the gift property for tax purposes when the trust is established, and does not revalue it again when the property is distributed to the final beneficiaries. Your income interest is subtracted from the total worth of the property to determine the value of the gift. The IRS tables used for this calculation take into account current interest rates, your age and the length of the term. The actual gift is usually substantially discounted for gift tax purposes.

Example: Joseph creates a ten-year GRIT for the benefit of his long-time companion, Al. He funds it with a stock portfolio worth $1 million. Because he will receive all of the income for ten years, the gift to Al in the GRIT is valued at much less than what Al will receive. For estate and gift tax purposes, the gift retains its original gift tax value no matter what the stock is worth ten years later, when Al becomes the owner (assuming Joseph is still alive). If Joseph doesn't survive the term, the full value of the trust assets as of the date of his death will be included in his taxable estate, just as if he had done nothing.

Like the other trusts discussed above, the shorter the term, the larger the taxable gift to the final beneficiary. But if you are in good health, and especially if you are single, regular GRITS still offer an attractive method of giving gifts, reducing the size of an estate and saving on taxes at the same time.

"REGULAR" GRITs AT A GLANCE

1. You create and fund the trust, specifying how long it is to last.

2. The value of the gift for gift tax purposes is determined when you fund the trust.

3. The trustee pays you all income annually.

4. When the term ends, the trust is terminated, and trust assets go to the final beneficiary.

---

6. Questions to Ask About a Grantor-Retained Interest Trust

If a GRAT, GRUT or GRIT sounds appealing, you need to sit down with an estate planning expert and carefully assess your situation. An expert should compare using any of these trusts with other possible estate planning alternatives. Make sure you get the answers to these questions:

- How do the tax savings from this type of trust compare with simply giving the gift directly (with any gift tax assessed), or making the gift over a period of years, using the annual gift tax exclusion repeatedly and allowing the beneficiary to invest the money you give?

- What are the likely savings overall, taking into consideration possible capital gain tax paid by the final beneficiary if he sells the trust property?

- What are the chances you will buy back appreciated property near the end of the set term if you retain a reversionary interest in trust property?

- Given your age, health and financial situation, and your feelings about money and security, can you risk parting with these assets irrevocably?

- Are you confident that present feelings about who you name as your final beneficiaries will remain the same for years?

- Is it better to create a grantor-retained interest trust and pay gift tax now (if necessary) on the gift property? Or is it wiser to hang on to the property and let your estate pay any estate tax due on this property after your death?

- Is a grantor-retained interest trust really desirable, considering your overall financial picture and the possible alternatives, including:

  * the personal estate tax exemption, which will increase to $1 million by the year 2007

  * a program of tax-exempt gifts over a number of years

  * using an AB trust so both spouses' personal estate tax exemptions are used

  * QTIP trusts

  * charitable trusts

  * life insurance policies owned by others on your life.

Answering these questions, and other personal ones that will surely come up, is time-consuming and requires a high level of expertise in estate planning. And remember that regulations concerning these discounted gifts change frequently, particularly the IRS interest tables. If your expert can't address all of your questions or thinks that you should leave all these decisions up to him, quickly find another expert, a genuine and simpatico one. ■

22

DISCLAIMERS: AFTER-DEATH ESTATE TAX PLANNING

A. Advantages of Disclaimers 22/2

    1. Estate Gift Tax Savings 22/2

    2. Fine-Tuning Gifts 22/3

    3. Adjusting for Unforeseen Circumstances 22/4

B. Couples and Disclaimers 22/4

C. IRS Rules for Disclaimers 22/6

    1. Putting the Disclaimer in Writing 22/6

    2. The Nine-Month Deadline 22/6

    3. The Person Disclaiming Property May Not Benefit
       From Disclaimed Property 22/7

    4. Special Rules for Surviving Spouses 22/8

D. Disclaimers and Living Trusts 22/9

    1. Planning For Disclaimers 22/9

    2. Problems With Trustees Directing Disclaimed Property 22/10

It may sound strange, but after you die, one or more of your beneficiaries may decide to decline to accept part or all of the property you left them. Refusing to take a gift is called "disclaiming" it. A beneficiary has the legal right under federal law (IRC Section 2518) to disclaim or refuse all, or any part, of a gift. If a beneficiary disclaims any property, it goes to whomever you specified in your trust or will to receive it if the primary beneficiary cannot or does not take it. The person who winds up with the gift is the alternate beneficiary for that gift, or, if you didn't name an alternate beneficiary, your residuary beneficiary.

You may wonder why anyone in our materially oriented society would be so unworldly as to refuse even some of an inheritance. It's not because the people who disclaim are noble or saintly. (They may be, but that's not what disclaimers are about.) The most common reason people disclaim gifts is to lighten their individual or their family's overall estate tax burden. Also, some people simply want property they could inherit to go instead to needier relations, without having to give it to them and being subject to gift tax.

A. ADVANTAGES OF DISCLAIMERS

Disclaimers can be an effective way for a beneficiary who already has plenty of property to pass a gift along to another person (usually a family member) who has less, and by doing so, save on estate and gift taxes.

1. Estate Gift Tax Savings

Once an estate reaches a certain size, estate tax kicks in and the tax is hefty. (See Chapter 15.) But under federal tax law, any property disclaimed by a beneficiary is never legally owned by that person. That means it cannot be included in that beneficiary's taxable estate at death. In addition, no gift tax is assessed against the person who disclaims a gift (in effect, giving it to someone else), again because the person never owned it.

Disclaimers can be particularly useful when the primary beneficiary already has a large estate and receiving the gift would add significantly to his eventual estate tax. If the alternate beneficiary has much less wealth, then overall estate tax can be reduced.

Example: Roger, an elderly widower, has an estate worth $540,000. He leaves it equally to his two children, George and Carlotta, and provides that if one of them cannot or does not take his or her half, it will go to the other. When Roger dies, his middle-aged children are in very different financial shape. Carlotta is a prosperous graphic designer, with an estate of roughly $900,000. Her husband has a similar-sized estate. George hasn't fared so well financially. His real estate business (his latest enterprise) was marginal from the start five years ago, and has been in a serious slump over the past year. George has almost no savings or other assets and a child with special educational needs.

Carlotta and George are close. Carlotta decides to disclaim her half of her father's estate ($270,000), so the entire $540,000 goes to George.

Carlotta disclaims the gift not primarily to save on estate tax, but because she felt George needed it and she didn't. But a pleasant side benefit is that there will be a significant estate tax savings. If Carlotta had accepted her half, her total estate would have grown to $1,170,000, increasing her eventual estate tax liability. As of now, George's estate is about $540,000—his inheritance. So his estate will not be subject to estate tax unless, of course, it increases significantly in value before his death.

Disclaimers can also be desirable if the primary beneficiary is older and may not live long, and the alternate beneficiary is younger.

Example: Barton dies in 2001 and leaves his estate of $500,000 to his sister Elizabeth, who is in her late 70s and has, herself, an estate of $800,000. The alternate beneficiaries for Barton's estate are Elizabeth's two children, both in their 30s, with very little property.

If Elizabeth accepted the gift, her estate would total $1.3 million. If she were to die in the year 2001 when the estate tax exemption will be $675,000, $625,000 would be taxed. The tax is $249,250. If Elizabeth instead disclaimed the gift, it would be divided between her two children. And if Elizabeth then dies the same year (assuming she still has $800,000), her estate tax would be only $47,250.

Clearly, disclaiming property can result in substantial estate tax advantages. But unlike a bypass trust (see Chapter 18, Estate Tax-Saving Bypass Trusts, Section A), which is established in advance to save on estate taxes, it's solely up to the beneficiary to make the decision to disclaim a gift or not. A beneficiary who is insecure, needy or even a tad greedy may choose not to disclaim property, even though disclaiming might be the wisest choice in light of "objective" personal need and overall estate tax consequences. But after all, the gift was left to that beneficiary. Disclaiming may make sense from the entire family's point of view, but it's hard to see it as a moral obligation.

2. Fine-Tuning Gifts

Disclaimers can allow beneficiaries to make adjustments regarding who gets what. This can be done to equalize beneficiaries' financial positions. The power

to disclaim can also help beneficiaries avoid problems of owning something together, having to come up with the money to buy out co-owners, or having to sell property that one of them loves.

Example: Tony, a bachelor, leaves his entire estate to his two nephews, Phil and Angelo, in equal shares. Each is the alternate beneficiary for the other's gift.

Among the assets at Tony's death is an ocean beachfront vacation home. Phil, with a sizable estate of his own, doesn't care about the ocean and spends his summers in the mountains, by freshwater lakes and rivers. Angelo, on the other hand, is not as well-off financially and has vacationed every summer of his life at the beach cottage. Phil disclaims his one-half interest in the beach property, keeping it out of his already large estate (and paying no gift tax whatever) when it then goes to Angelo.

Disclaimers can also be used when a person wants the property to go to the next in line for the gift.

Example: Babette leaves her house to her three children, in equal shares. Her living trust provides that the alternate beneficiaries for each child's share are his or her children. When Babette dies, all three of her children are quite well off. Two intend to accept their share of the house. One child, Fritz, disclaims his share, because he decides it's wiser to let it pass to his children, who are in their early 20s and starting their careers (or, at least, starting to earn money). Fritz knows his children will find much security in the financial nest egg his disclaimer provides for each.

If Babette had specified that the alternate beneficiaries for the house were her other children, Fritz would not have disclaimed his share. He would not have wanted that share divided between his brother and sister, bringing no benefit to his children.

3. Adjusting for Unforeseen Circumstances

Disclaimers can also be a lifesaver under pressing circumstances. For instance, a person may be over-generous or over-optimistic regarding his finances in his estate plan, and his financial situation at death may turn out to be worse than he anticipated. Beneficiaries can use disclaimers to achieve fair results—results the person would surely have wanted if he'd known how his finances would turn out.

> **Example:** Sven, who's doing well in business, prepares a living trust that leaves $200,000 each to his three children and the rest of his estate to his spouse. Later, after some business setbacks and an extended illness, his wealth has dwindled. When Sven dies, there will be almost nothing left for his widow after the $600,000 is given to his children. The children generously disclaim their inheritance so the money will go to their mother for her support.

This sounds good—indeed, ideal—but there is, of course, an obvious risk if a disclaimer is needed for this purpose. A child or any beneficiary may be unwilling to give up an inheritance, no matter what hardship that creates for someone else, even a parent. It would have been wiser for Sven to rewrite his living trust after his business reversals, simply leaving all his property to his wife.

B. COUPLES AND DISCLAIMERS

Couples, whether married or not, can sometimes cut their tax bills significantly by using disclaimers. It's common for each member of a couple to leave everything to the other, with the children named as alternate beneficiaries. The surviving mate, they hope, will pass the deceased person's property on to their children. Especially when spouses or mates are relatively young and don't have a big estate, this makes sense. Why tie up property in a trust when a surviving spouse may need that property for decades?

But a couple who had modest property holdings when they prepared their estate plan may turn out to be quite prosperous by the time one spouse dies decades later. In situations like this, the surviving spouse's ability to disclaim part of the deceased spouse's estate, and have it go directly to their children, can achieve substantial overall estate tax savings. (A surviving spouse can also disclaim property and have it go into a trust that benefits that spouse. See Section C4, below.)

> **Example:** While in their mid-50s, Boris and his wife Natasha created their estate plan, leaving all of their property to each other. Each named their three children as alternate beneficiaries. By their late 70s, together they own assets worth $900,000.
>
> Boris dies first in the year 2002, leaving his $450,000 share to Natasha. Natasha is not in good health. Natasha disclaims $200,000 of her inheritance, which means it will go directly to their children. She does this for two reasons. First, there's a possibility that Natasha may end up in a nursing home or need major health care. If so, her entire estate could be gobbled up with distressing speed. But the $200,000 she has disclaimed cannot be subject to claims from any of her health care providers.

The second reason for her disclaimer concerns estate taxes. As the chart below shows, in the year 2002, this would allow her to receive the maximum amount possible from Boris and still not have her estate subject to estate tax when she dies.

	Without Disclaimer	With $200,000 Disclaimer by Natasha
Value of Boris's estate	$450,000	$450,000
Estate tax due	-0- (because of the marital deduction)	-0- (because of Boris's personal exemption)
Value of Natasha's estate	$900,000	$700,000
Estate tax (because of Natasha's personal exemption for 2002)	$77,000	-0-

Now suppose Boris and Natasha had the same size estate, but Boris died suddenly in his late 50s. Natasha might well decide not to disclaim any of Boris's estate. It could be ten, 20 or many more years before her death, and she may well want or need all the $900,000 during her lifetime.

When a surviving spouse wants to disclaim an interest in property the spouses own together, that spouse can disclaim only that portion that was left to her by the deceased spouse. The other half of the property is and remains owned by the surviving spouse; obviously, no disclaimer of that portion is possible.

Example: Yaphet and Malika together own property worth $850,000. Yaphet also has well over $1 million in separate property. They each leave their half of the shared property to each other, with their three children as alternate beneficiaries. After Malika dies, Yaphet wants to disclaim all he can, so it will go to his children. He can disclaim only Malika's one-half share of their shared property, a total of $425,000. He cannot disclaim his own one-half share of that property (or, of course, his separate property), because that wasn't left to him by Malika—he owned it all along.

C. IRS RULES FOR DISCLAIMERS

Federal law requires that a beneficiary's disclaimer must be "qualified." This means that it must meet certain rules set out in IRC Section 2518. If these rules aren't complied with, the person disclaiming will not avoid legal ownership of the property for estate tax purposes, and the major purpose of the disclaimer will be lost. The IRS requirements are:

- The disclaimer must be in writing.

- A disclaimer by an adult must be completed within nine months of the death of the person leaving the property.

- A minor who has been left property must disclaim within nine months after reaching age 18.

- The person who disclaims property may not accept any benefit from the property before disclaiming it. (An exception exists for a surviving spouse—see Section 4, below).

- The person refusing the property may not direct where it then goes. The original will or trust document determines who receives the disclaimed property.

1. Putting the Disclaimer in Writing

A beneficiary who wants to disclaim inherited property—for whatever reason and whatever the type of property—is responsible for putting the disclaimer in writing. The beneficiary must deliver the written disclaimer to whomever is in control of the property at that time. This is usually the successor trustee of a living trust or the executor (personal representative) of a will.

Example: In her living trust, Carla leaves a money market account to her son, Francisco, and another of roughly equal value to her daughter, Eva. The trust provides that if either child dies before Carla does, the money goes to the other. She names Francisco as successor trustee of her trust.

At Carla's death, Eva is financially comfortable, but Francisco is struggling. Eva is also aware of the fact that her mother spent a large amount on her college and graduate education, while Francisco chose not to go to college. She wishes to disclaim so he can receive the money directly from Eva's estate without it being a taxable gift from her.

As successor trustee, Francisco is bound by law to follow the directions in his mother's trust. If Eva calls him up and tells him to take her money, he can't legally do it. He needs the written disclaimer so he can follow the trust instructions and satisfy IRS regulations. Only when armed with the signed disclaimer from Eva will he have the power to change his mother's primary instructions and take the money himself. (See Section D, below, covering complexities that can arise when a trustee of a living trust disclaims trust property or receives it by disclaimer.)

2. The Nine-Month Deadline

IRS rules require that a disclaimer must be made by adults within nine months of the death of the original giver—that is, the trust grantor or will writer.

DISCLAIMERS BY MINORS

A minor can disclaim a gift within nine months of becoming age 21. This raises some odd questions, such as who manages the property until the minor turns 21? What can be done with it? Who may benefit from the property during this time? The answers depend on state law. It's a very complicated legal matter. If you are the parent or guardian of a minor who has been left property and think it's possible the minor would want to disclaim that property at age 21, seek some good professional advice.

The nine-month period allows enough time, hopefully, for the adult survivors to begin getting back on their feet emotionally and to get the information they need to make wise financial decisions.

Example: Makoto dies suddenly in 2002, leaving a wife, Hanako, in her 60s and two adult children. His will leaves everything to Hanako or, if she doesn't survive him, to the children. Makoto's elder son, Keiji, who is executor of the will, sees immediately that the estate is worth about $1.5 million, more than Hanako, who has substantial assets of her own, needs. When Keiji hires a lawyer to probate the will, the lawyer advises changing things around for tax purposes. But no one in the family wants to think about these issues shortly after Makoto's death.

The nine-month period gives the attorney time to draft a tax-savings plan and explain it to the family. Also, the family has a chance to look at the situation and assess who needs what, and when.

In the end, Hanako decides to disclaim $700,000, the amount of the personal exemption in 2002. This allows Makoto's estate to use

its entire personal estate tax exemption of $700,000, which now goes to the children as alternates. Now Hanako inherits only $800,000. Her total estate is smaller than if she'd inherited the $1.5 million, so the estate tax that will be due at her death will be lower. But it's not only tax savings that motivate Hanako. She believes her children need this money now, when they are working hard and trying to raise their own children. With the disclaimer, they get it, with no taxable gift having been made by Hanako.

3. The Person Disclaiming Property May Not Benefit From Disclaimed Property

With one important exception, discussed below in Section 4, a beneficiary who wants to disclaim property cannot use or accept any benefit from the property, however brief the use or slight the benefit. One danger here is when a beneficiary takes a small benefit from a large gift. For example, if a you receive rent from gift real estate for a short time and then decide you want to disclaim the entire gift, it's too late. The disclaimer will not be valid for estate tax purposes.

Also, a beneficiary who will receive any benefit from the property after the disclaimer cannot disclaim the property. For example, a beneficiary cannot disclaim property that then goes into a trust that pays, or even could pay, the beneficiary any income. For instance, if a you were to disclaim a gift that goes into a family pot trust with 15 potential beneficiaries, including you, the disclaimer is not valid. The property still goes to the next beneficiary in line, but the transaction is considered, legally, a simple gift, and you may be assessed gift tax if the property is valuable enough.

4. Special Rules for Surviving Spouses

There's one exception to the general rule that a beneficiary can't receive any benefit from disclaimed property. A surviving spouse who disclaims a gift can still receive some benefits from it. This makes possible some flexible estate planning.

One strategy is to arrange things so that a surviving spouse can disclaim money inherited from the other. If the property is disclaimed, it goes into an AB trust, with the surviving spouse as life beneficiary. That spouse can be given rights to receive income from the trust, invade the principal for health care and other basic needs and use the trust property. When the second spouse dies, the trust assets go to the couple's children (or other beneficiary they chose). The IRS never considers the second spouse to die the legal owner of the disclaimed property, even though he may have benefited from that property.

Example: Benjamin and Esther, in their 40s, own shared property worth $800,000. Each has an estate worth $400,000. In their estate plan, each leaves their property outright to the other.

However, they worry about what will happen if they acquire considerably more valuable property but don't get around to revising their plan. Then there would be substantial federal estate taxes when the surviving spouse died, and an AB trust might be desirable. (See Chapter 18, Estate Tax-Saving Bypass Trusts, Section C.) On the other hand, the surviving spouse may need or want the entire estate, not just the right to get trust income or limited rights to invade principal, as an AB would provide. How can Benjamin and Esther decide now what's wisest? The answer is, they don't have to.

Suppose their total estate is worth $2 million when Esther dies after 2005. Esther leaves her $1 million to Benjamin, subject to his right to disclaim. Any amount disclaimed would go into an AB trust. Benjamin could disclaim the entire amount. In other words, Benjamin could decide that his own estate of $1 million plus the income from Esther's trust is enough for him. And after 2005, the personal exemption is $1 million so no tax will be due on Esther's death or on his. By using the disclaimer, Esther's estate and Benjamin's estate each take advantage of their personal estate tax exemptions, saving a significant amount in estate taxes and leaving more, eventually, to the children.

When the estates of the spouses are unequal, disclaimers can be used similarly, placing property where it's wisest for estate tax purposes. The goal is to equalize the value of both spouses' estates, or at least make them closer in size. The reason for this is that old graduated estate tax and the personal estate tax exemption. If one spouse has an estate of $4 million, and the other has nothing, they will pay more estate tax than if each spouse owned property worth $2 million.

Disclaimers used to equalize, or balance, spouses' estates are often used in combination with other estate tax saving devices, such as marital life estate trusts or QTIP trusts. (See Chapter 18, Estate Tax-Saving Bypass Trusts, Section C, and Chapter 19, Other Estate Tax-Saving Marital Trusts, Section A.)

Example: Guido, 60 years old, is married for the second time, to Sophia. Guido's assets total $4 million, and Sophia's financial worth is negligible. Guido wants to ensure that Sophia is taken care of in the case of his death, but he wants his estate to eventually pass to the children of his first marriage.

He creates a plan that will pay income to Sophia for her support from two trusts, one a formula AB trust worth the amount of his personal exemption in the year of death (see Chapter 18, Sec. C), and the other a QTIP trust consisting of his other assets. (Tax on property in a QTIP trust is deferred until the second spouse dies. See Chapter 19.) Guido directs that the income and then the principal of the QTIP trust be used up, if necessary, before paying Sophia income from the AB trust. At Sophia's death, the assets remaining in both trusts will go to Guido's children

If Sophia disclaims any amount of the QTIP trust property, it will go into the AB trust. She remains entitled to receive the income from that trust if she needs it. However, the amount in the AB trust is subject to tax at Guido's death, instead of at Sophia's death, when the property in the QTIP trust will be subject to estate tax.

Here's a chart of estate tax consequences if Sophia accepts all Guido's property or disclaims $1 million of it.

	Without Disclaimer	*With $1,000,000 Disclaimer by Sophia*
Value of Guido's estate	$4 million	$4 million
Estate tax due	-0-	$435,000

Without the disclaimer, there is no tax at Guido's death because of his $1 million exemption and the marital deduction for the QTIP assets. With the disclaimer, Guido's taxable estate is increased by $1 million, and subject to tax.

Value of Sophia's estate when she dies	$3 million	$2 million
Estate tax due paid by both	$945,000	$435,000

The estate tax saving of $75,000 is not the only benefit of this kind of strategy; much greater savings are lurking in the wings. A wise and creative trustee can fund the AB trust with high-growth assets (he hopes). If these assets do grow significantly in value during the surviving spouse's life, they will not be taxed at her death. This increase in value passes to the children free of estate tax.

At the same time, the property in the marital QTIP trust can be converted to high-yield assets, providing comfortable support for the surviving spouse. If she lives for 15 years, this trust may be spent down for her support, so the estate tax due at her death may actually be even lower than in the example above.

D. DISCLAIMERS AND LIVING TRUSTS

It could aid your inheritors if you directly incorporate your wishes concerning disclaimed gifts into your estate plan.

1. Planning For Disclaimers

Even though disclaimers are expressly authorized by federal law, incorporating a specific disclaimer provision in your living trust or will can create a helpful guide for your beneficiaries. A clause permitting beneficiaries to disclaim gifts you leave tells them that you know about disclaimers and personally authorize them. A beneficiary who wants to make a disclaimer doesn't have to worry about going against your desires. Also, not all beneficiaries (or successor trustees or executors) know about disclaimers, so specifically authorizing them can be a good means of alerting your beneficiaries that they exist.

You can also specify who is to receive property that one of your beneficiaries disclaims. This would be desirable only if you don't want a disclaimed gift to go the alternate beneficiary. This might be the case if the alternate beneficiary is likely to be in the same financial position as the primary beneficiary, as can be the case with husband and wife.

Example: Chang, a widower, leaves his $300,000 estate to his son Tai, with Tai's wife, Claudia, as the alternate beneficiary. But Chang also provides in his living trust document that should Tai disclaim any property, it then goes to Chang's favorite nephew. When Chang dies, Tai's and Claudia's assets are quite large; neither needs the inheritance. By contrast, the nephew, who is just starting out in business, really needs the money. Tai disclaims the gift, and the $300,000 goes directly to the nephew.

Because Tai never owns the property, his own estate is not increased for estate tax purposes. Nor has he made a taxable gift by disclaiming the gift and letting it go to Chang's nephew.

If Tai had accepted the gift, he could remove it from his estate by subsequently giving it to the nephew. But this would mean Tai would be assessed gift tax on $290,000, the taxable portion of the gift.

2. Problems With Trustees Directing Disclaimed Property

Many living trusts do not allow the trustee to determine who receives any trust income or property. The beneficiaries and their shares are all specified in the trust document. But if a beneficiary is considering disclaiming property that will then go into a trust, and the beneficiary has any powers at all over the

trust assets, expert advice is really needed. A legal power to direct who gets the disclaimed assets may not be readily apparent, but may be discovered upon a closer review. Even a power by the trustee to allocate income and principal might cause a disclaimer to fail.

Someone who both serves as the successor trustee of a living trust and inherits trust property may run into complications disclaiming property. The basic rule is that if you have any authority to direct where any of the disclaimed property will go, you can't disclaim it. The property can go to the person you choose, but for gift and estate tax purposes, it is considered your own property. You must resign as trustee or decline also the authority to direct distribution of trust property.

Example: Tsultrim and her husband, Yeshe, each create a living trust, providing that on a spouse's death, $625,000 of that spouse's property goes directly into a trust for their children. (This is the amount of the personal exemption in 1998.) Any remaining property goes outright to the surviving spouse. The surviving spouse will serve as trustee of the children's trust and have broad trustee powers, including the authority to distribute trust principal and income to the children if they need it.

Yeshe dies first. The couple's estate turns out to be larger than expected, so it would be desirable, from the overall estate tax viewpoint, for Tsultrim to disclaim the property Yeshe left to him and let it go into the children's trust. Estate taxes would be lower in the long run if some tax were paid on part of Yeshe's property at her death.

But as long as he serves as trustee of the trust for the children, Tsultrim can't disclaim any of the property Yeshe left him. That's because, as trustee, he has the authority to direct the distribution of property to the trust beneficiaries. To have a valid disclaimer, he will have to also disclaim this authority or resign as trustee altogether.

If you anticipate that a disclaimer may make sense, you can include a brief letter or note in the envelope with your will or living trust alerting the executor or successor trustee so beneficiaries can be told. You can suggest that it may be wise to make no distributions whatsoever until all concerned have consulted a tax advisor.

When you're preparing a living trust, be sure to discuss disclaimer possibilities with your attorney, and be sure the trust document is drafted so that potential problems are eliminated, to the extent possible.

You might want to work out potential problems in advance, when you prepare your estate plan, rather than leaving them unresolved until your death. For example, if your successor trustee would have to resign to make her disclaimer valid, obviously it's important who the alternate successor trustee will be. ■

23

Combining Estate Tax-Saving Trusts

A. Combining Two Estate Tax-Saving Trusts 23/2

B. Combining a Charitable Trust With Other Estate
Tax-Saving Trusts 23/4

C. Combining Three Different Estate Tax-Saving Trusts 23/5

D. Using Ongoing Trusts and Gift-Giving to Reduce Estate Tax 23/6

If you have a large estate, you may want to use more than one tax-saving trust in your estate plan. There are no legal rules or even fixed customs regarding how to combine trusts. This chapter can give you a sense of the possibilities offered. Your individual situation and desires will determine what combination, if any, is right for you.

Combining estate tax-saving trusts requires a lawyer. Combining estate tax-saving trusts involves sophisticated, technical legal work. So it should come as no surprise that you must have a lawyer do the work. Indeed, to understand precisely how different options could work for you, you'll need to carefully discuss your situation with a lawyer. Your legal bill will probably be substantial. But after all, you must have considerable wealth before it's worth combining different trusts, and doing so can (presumably) save you and your inheritors a bundle. A good lawyer's cost is probably well worth it.

A. COMBINING TWO ESTATE TAX-SAVING TRUSTS

One or both members of a couple, especially in second or subsequent marriages may want to combine a "formula" AB trust with a QTIP trust. (See Chapter 18, Estate Tax-Saving Bypass Trusts, Section C, on AB trusts and Chapter 19, Other Estate Tax-Saving Marital Trusts, Section A, on QTIP trusts.) The spouse who creates the trusts names the other as life beneficiary of each trust. Each trust's final beneficiaries, also named by the spouse who creates these trusts, receives that trust property when the life beneficiary dies. If the spouse who created these trusts survives the other, all his or her property goes, via the trusts, directly to the final beneficiaries.

By combining these two trusts, you can achieve several desirable goals:

- You make use of your personal estate tax exemption with the AB trust.

- If your spouse survives you, all of your property over the amount of the personal exemption in the year of your death is placed in the QTIP trust and qualifies for the unlimited marital deduction. So no federal estate tax at all is paid on your death.

- Your surviving spouse, as life beneficiary must be restricted in rights to spend principal of Trust A. Restrictions are also normally imposed on the rights of the surviving spouse to spend principal of the QTIP trust. Under IRS rules, the surviving spouse must be given unrestricted rights to all trust income generated from assets in the QTIP trust.

- You determine who will ultimately receive all property in your AB and QTIP trusts, after your surviving spouse dies.

Example 1: Malcolm, age 61, has been married to Sadie, age 47, for four years. He has three children from a former marriage. Sadie has a small estate of her own, consisting of savings worth $50,000. Malcolm, on the other hand, owns his house and various investments worth a total of $1,230,000. He also owns a life insurance policy that will pay $200,000 to Sadie at his death.

Although his children seem to accept Sadie, Malcolm senses uneasiness among them about whether they'll actually receive the inheritance they've been expecting from him. What might happen if Sadie survives Malcolm by 20 or 30 years: A remarriage? A sudden urge to seek thrills and bet fortunes at the race track?

Wanting to take care of everybody, if possible, and also to create no hard feelings, Malcolm creates the following plan.

If Sadie survives him, upon his death his property will be divided into a formula AB trust, which will contain property worth the amount of the personal exemption at the year of his death and a QTIP trust for the rest of his property. Sadie is the life beneficiary of both trusts, to receive all trust income. She has no rights to spend either trust principal. When Sadie dies, the property in both trusts will go to Malcolm's three children in equal shares.

Malcolm names Sadie and his daughter Hilda, the most level-headed of his children and the one who gets along with Sadie the best, to be co-trustees of both trusts.

Example 2: Carla has assets worth $950,000; her husband Peter's property totals $200,000. Carla is 73, Peter is 66. Carla has two children by a previous marriage. She wants to be sure her estate will avoid estate tax no matter what year she dies in. She also wants to both preserve her estate for her children and help Peter to live a comfortable life, if he survives her.

Carla creates a formula AB trust and a QTIP trust. Peter is the life beneficiary of both trusts, and her children are the final beneficiaries. Carla dies in 1999, when the personal estate tax exemption is $650,00. That amount of her property is placed in the AB trust. The balance of $300,000 goes into the QTIP trust.

The property in the AB trust is tax-free under the personal exemption. The amount in the QTIP is tax-free under the marital deduction when Carla dies. When Peter dies, this amount (let's assume it stays at $300,000) is part of his estate, for estate tax purposes. Peter's own estate is $200,000. The combined total, $500,000, is well under the estate tax threshold.

LEAVING ALL PROPERTY OVER THE EXEMPT AMOUNT OUTRIGHT TO THE SURVIVING SPOUSE

Many couples, particularly in first marriages, have no need for a QTIP trust. Commonly, these couples share ownership of most or all of their property and want the same people, usually their children, to eventually inherit their property. These couples have no desire for the primary purpose of a QTIP trust, to guarantee that a spouse controls final disposition of her or his property. Rather, a spouse simply leaves all property over the exempt amount outright to the other spouse, trusting that spouse will do what's best both for everyone.

Example: Miles and Suno, in their early 50s, have been married over 25 years. They have two children and substantial assets (all co-owned) worth over $4 million. Their estate plan consists of preparing a living trust in which each creates a formula AB trust, and a direction that any property above the formula be left outright to the surviving spouse.

No estate tax will be paid when the first spouse dies. The amount in the AB trust is tax-free under the personal exemption. The balance left to the surviving spouse is tax-free under the marital deduction.

While both Miles and Suno want their children to eventually inherit their property, neither wants or feels the need to impose on the other the restrictions of a QTIP trust. If one spouse dies prematurely, the other may survive for decades. Why limit this spouse's right over the deceased spouse's property?

B. COMBINING A CHARITABLE TRUST WITH OTHER ESTATE TAX SAVING TRUSTS

If you want to leave some of your property to causes you care deeply about, you may be eligible for some tax breaks. For example, gifts made to tax-exempt charities through a charitable trust are exempt from estate tax. (See Chapter 20, Charitable Trusts.) The other potential benefits from using a charitable trust are that you take an income tax deduction on the worth of the property to charity, and also avoid paying capital gain tax, if the charity sells appreciated assets you gave it.

Unless you are extremely wealthy or don't want to leave anything to family or friends, however, you may understandably be reluctant to give or leave significant assets to a charity. Fortunately, you can make a charitable gift, but do it in such a way that the value of the property donated is replaced in your estate. That way your other beneficiaries receive almost as much as they would have without the charitable trust.

How can you make this magic happen? In the right circumstances, by creating both a charitable trust and an irrevocable life insurance, trust. (Irrevocable life insurance trusts are discussed in Chapter 21, Section B.) You buy a policy payable to your other beneficiaries, and transfer that policy to the trust. The proceeds of the life insurance policy will be roughly equal to the amount your individual beneficiaries would have inherited from you if you hadn't made the charitable gift. And because you've established the life insurance trust, the proceeds from the policy won't be included in your taxable estate.

Here's a summary of how you could use a life insurance trust to replace money "lost" to individual beneficiaries because of a charitable gift:

1. First, you make a gift to charity through a charitable trust.

2. You create the life insurance trust. You fund it, for the purpose of making premium payments, with the income tax-savings you obtained by making the charitable gift. This means there is no significant actual cost to you to create and fund the trust. You choose a life insurance policy that will pay out, at your death, more or less the same amount that you gave the charity.

3. You include "Crummey provisions" in your life insurance trust document. These clauses allow gifts you make to the trust to qualify for the annual gift tax exclusion, currently $10,000 per person per year. (See Chapter 21, Section B.) Otherwise, if you gave money directly to the trust, it wouldn't qualify for the exclusion.

4. Your gift money remains in the insurance trust until the trustee spends it on insurance premiums. The net effect is that you have indirectly paid the insurance proceeds (you can get in trouble with the IRS if you pay them directly.)

Example: Aldo has four children and an estate worth $2 million. He funds a charitable trust with land currently worth $400,000. He bought the land for $170,000. The charity sells the land and buys stock that will provide payments to him for life. The charity will take what remains of the trust assets at his death.

When he creates the trust, Aldo obtains a significant income tax deduction. Also, by giving the land to charity, he avoids capital gain tax on the increase in value of $230,000 when the land is sold and converted to income-producing assets. And by removing $400,000 from his estate, he saves on estate tax, lowering his taxable estate to $1.6 million.

The property Aldo has given to charity would have gone to his children. But if he had kept the property, it would have been subject to estate tax.

Aldo creates an irrevocable life insurance trust. He buys and transfers to the trust a life insurance policy for $250,000—very roughly, the net amount (after estate taxes) "lost" to his children because of his charitable gift. He includes "Crummey" provisions in the life insurance trust, so he can give, free of gift tax, up to $40,000 a year to the trust—$10,000 for each of the life insurance trust's beneficiaries, his children. The trustee can use these funds to pay the premiums of the life insurance policy.

If you are in reasonably good health (and especially if you're young), replacing the donated assets by life insurance is usually the preferred choice. If you are elderly, in poor health, or not insurable for any reason, you can try other replacement methods.

Example: After Aldo establishes his charitable trust, he discovers that he is ill and that insurance on his life would be too costly, if available at all. He still sets up an irrevocable trust for his children and donates money to it. He will be subject to gift tax on the money he donates to the trust, but the trustee purchases assets he and Aldo hope will greatly appreciate in value. (Easier hoped for than accomplished, of course—not hard in a rising market, but otherwise, often difficult indeed.) Depending on the expertise of the trustee and some luck, the $50,000 each child would have received but for the charitable gift may eventually be recouped.

C. COMBINING THREE DIFFERENT ESTATE TAX-SAVING TRUSTS

In larger estates, you may even want to make use of several different estate tax-saving trusts. For instance, you could use a formula AB trust for property worth up to the exempt amount at death with a generation-skipping trust and a charitable trust.

Example: Guillermo and Maria, a couple in their late 70s, have an estate of $12 million owned equally. They want to leave their property to their children and to some friends and charities.

Each creates a formula AB trust, leaving property to the surviving spouse for life, and then to various final beneficiaries. Also, each creates a generation-skipping trust, leaving a $1 million in each's trust for their grandchildren. (See Chapter 21, Section A, on generation-skipping trusts.) Each also creates a charitable trust, funding it with $900,000. All property of the first spouse to die, after all these gifts are made, goes outright to the surviving spouse.

Guillermo dies in 1998. At Guillermo's death, $625,000, the amount of the personal exemption for 1998, is placed in his AB trust and $1 million goes into his generation-skipping trust. The charitable trust receives $900,000, with Maria receiving 6% income from this trust property for her life. Guillermo's remaining wealth, $3,475,000 goes outright to Maria. She might want to do some new estate planning, to minimize estate taxes on her death.

D. USING ONGOING TRUSTS AND GIFT-GIVING TO REDUCE ESTATE TAX

Ongoing trusts can be combined in a number of ways to reduce estate tax for the wealthy. You can leave gifts to your spouse, children, grandchildren and to charities, all by using different trusts. Here's an example of combining a generation-skipping trust, a charitable remainder unitrust, an irrevocable life insurance trust, an AB trust and a QTIP trust, all in one estate plan.

Example: Doris is 65 and married to Ted, her second husband. She has two children from her first marriage, both of whom are financially comfortable, and six grandchildren. Doris's estate is worth $7 million; Ted has a much smaller estate of $160,000.

If she dies first, Doris wants Ted to continue to live in the affluent style they've enjoyed, but she also wants most of her assets to go eventually to her children and grandchildren. She also wishes to contribute a sizable portion of her estate to charity. First, she sets up a charitable remainder unitrust of $1 million. (See Chapter 20, Charitable Trusts, Section C.) Ted and Doris will receive income from the trust annually. Next, she takes an income tax deduction based on the value of her gift to the charitable trust. Using the money saved on income tax, she purchases life insurance and funds an irrevocable life insurance trust. The beneficiaries of the life insurance are her children; they will receive an amount roughly equal to the amount she gave to charity. Proceeds from the life insurance trust will not be included in her estate for estate tax purposes.

Doris also establishes a formula AB trust, with Ted as the life beneficiary. When Ted dies, this trust's assets will be shared by her children.

Next, she establishes a generation-skipping trust of $1 million, with income paid to her children during their lives. This trust will be subject to federal estate tax when Doris dies, but not when the middle generation (her children) dies. When they die, this trust's assets will be distributed to the grandchildren. No estate tax will be paid on these assets when middle generation dies.

The remaining property in Doris's estate will go into a QTIP trust, with all income to Ted for life, and the assets to her children at his death. The trustee, one of Doris's children, can use the principal of this trust for Ted's medical care or basic support if the trustee decides it is needed.

Finally, during Doris's life, she also adopts a plan of giving gifts from her present income to keep her estate from increasing and eventu-ally resulting in more estate tax. She gives $10,000 annually, gift tax-free, to each of her two children, their spouses and the six grand-children. This is a total of ten people, so $100,000 a year is given away tax-free. (See Chapter 16, Gifts and Gift Taxes, Section E, for more on gift-giving programs.) ■

24

PROPERTY CONTROL TRUSTS FOR SECOND OR SUBSEQUENT MARRIAGES

A. How a Marital Property Control Trust Works 24/2

B. Restricting the Surviving Spouse's Rights Over Trust Property 24/3

C. The Role of the Trustee 24/6

    1. Heading Off Family Conflict 24/6

    2. Naming Co-Trustees 24/7

    3. Naming a Financial Institution as Trustee 24/7

D. Savings on Estate Taxes 24/7

E. Working With a Lawyer 24/8

In many second or subsequent marriages, one or both spouses may feel truly conflicted about estate planning. On one hand, a surviving spouse may well need use of or income from the deceased spouse's property, or may even need to spend some of that property, to live comfortably. On the other hand, children from a former marriage may believe they are entitled to all that property immediately after their parent dies. Even if the children aren't insistent, they may have financial needs their parent wants to help with. Even if children freely accept waiting for their inheritance until both spouses have died, the children may still be understandably concerned that their inheritance be preserved, not consumed by a surviving spouse. These kinds of problems—which can be dicey at the best of times—become even more complicated if your current spouse and children from a former marriage are estranged from each other.

This chapter discusses how you can use a trust, which we call a "marital property control trust," to try to balance the interests and needs of all concerned. This type of trust imposes controls over your property after your death, so that the surviving spouse has some use of it, or income from it, but never owns it outright. The property goes to your children when the surviving spouse dies. By placing restrictions on the surviving spouse's rights to trust property, you can feel confident that most or all of the trust principal should remain intact for your children. Marital property control trusts are, of course, no guarantee that family conflicts and tensions will be eliminated or even reduced. But they can achieve at least some control over your assets, and give you the comfort that you've done your best to provide for your spouse and your children.

Marital property control trusts can also be used to save on estate tax. (See Section D, below.)

This chapter focuses exclusively on concerns of spouses in second or subsequent marriages, because for many people this is a central concern of their estate planning. But trusts imposing property controls can be useful in many situations, not just those involving second or subsequent marriages. (See Chapter 25, Trusts and Other Devices for Imposing Controls Over Property.)

UNMARRIED COUPLES

This chapter talks in terms of subsequent marriages and surviving spouses, because most people who do this type of estate planning are married. But the principles apply equally to unmarried couples with children from previous relationships.

A. HOW A MARITAL PROPERTY CONTROL TRUST WORKS

A marital property control trust is in some ways similar to an AB trust (discussed in Chapter 18, Section C) but there are also important differences. The surviving spouse is the life beneficiary of the marital property control trust, which means he receives some benefits from the trust as long as he lives. However, his rights to use trust property, to receive trust income, and spend trust principal, are as limited as you decide upon.

With an AB trust that is intended only to save on estate tax, the surviving spouse is usually granted the maximum rights to use or spend trust property allowed under IRS rules. In marked contrast, with a marital property control trust, specific restrictions, expressly set out in the trust document, are imposed on the surviving spouse. The purpose of restricting the surviving spouse's rights is to protect the trust principal, so that it remains intact (or at least close to intact) until the surviving spouse dies, or, perhaps, remarries. Then the trust property goes outright to the grantor's children from a prior marriage, or other final beneficiaries the grantor named.

Example: Lisi and Greg get married in their late 30s. Lisi has a child from a prior marriage; Greg has two children from his prior marriages. Lisi and Greg have a child together, Dory. Lisi and Greg are now in their early 50s, and decide it's time to prepare their estate plan

Lisi owns separate property worth $400,000, and Greg owns separate property worth $310,000. Together they own a house that cost $320,000. Each contributed half the down payment for the house, and they share mortgage payments equally. Also, they own other shared assets worth a total of $275,000.

Each spouse creates a marital property control trust. The other spouse, as life beneficiary, has these rights in the trust property:

1. To remain in the house for life

2. To receive the income from any trust property

3. To spend trust principal only for medical costs that can't be paid for from other resources.

Each spouse names the final beneficiaries for his or her trust. Lisi decides that her final beneficiaries are Dory and her daughter from her prior marriage, who will share her trust's principal 50/50. Greg, who is not close to his children from his prior marriage, names them and Dory as his final beneficiaries. Dory will receive 70% of his trust property and the other two children will equally share the remaining 30%.

Because the purpose of a marital control trust is to preserve assets for your final beneficiaries, it's immaterial whether or not those assets will be subject to estate tax. You may want to create this type of trust although your estate is well under the estate tax threshold.

Example: Benny and Belle, each in their late 50s, marry. Benny has two children, ages 26 and 24, one each from two prior marriages. Belle has one child, age 19, from her prior marriage. Benny has an estate worth roughly $375,000; Belle's is worth $230,000. Neither estate is at all near the estate tax threshold

Because neither spouse has enough property to be securely self-sufficient should the other die first, each creates a marital property control trust, allowing the other spouse income for life from the trust but absolutely no right to invade trust principal. This way, they've each ensured that their estate will remain intact, to be received by their child or children after the surviving spouse dies.

How to Set Up a Property Control Trust

A marital property control trust usually is combined with a living trust to avoid probate. In that case, the marital property control trust remains revocable, as a component of the living trust, as long as you live and are mentally competent. After your death, your living trust property is transferred to your martial property control trust, without probate proceedings. At that point, your marital property control trust becomes irrevocable.

B. Restricting the Surviving Spouse's Rights Over Trust Property

You may impose a wide variety of restrictions on your surviving spouse's rights over the property in your marital property control trust. For instance, the surviving spouse may be given the right to receive income from the trust, but no right whatsoever to spend trust principal. Or you can name someone else, not the surviving spouse, to be the trustee of the trust. This, obviously keeps one source of real-world power from the surviving spouse. If someone else is the trustee, presumably there's less chance that the surviving spouse will get more than the trust document allows.

Example: Leticia, in her 70s, marries Ben, also in his 70s. Leticia has been married twice before, and has one grown child from each marriage, a daughter, Lindsay, and a son, Kevin. Her estate consists of her house, worth $275,000 (all equity), and savings of $580,000. Ben owns much less, about $40,000 in savings and stocks. He also receives a modest pension plus Social Security.

Leticia wants her property to eventually go to her two children, equally—but if she predeceases Ben, she doesn't want him thrown out on the street. She places her house and savings in a marital property control trust. She appoints Lindsay as trustee.

The trust document gives Ben the right to remain in the house, with all its current furnishings, for his life. If he leaves it for more than four consecutive months, whether to move to some tropical paradise or a nursing home, the house and furnishings can be sold or rented if the trustee decides that's desirable. Thus, Leticia leaves it up to Lindsay to decide what should happen to the house if Ben vacates it for more than four months. Leticia doesn't want to require that the house be turned over to her children in these circumstances. She just wants to protect her children, and not have the house empty, or rented out by Ben, for a long time. Leticia fully trusts Lindsay to make a wise decision if this matter comes up.

Ben also is to receive $5,000 per year from the income generated by the money in the trust. If the trust's annual income is lower than $5,000, Ben receives that lesser amount. If the income exceeds $5,000, Ben can be given any portion of the additional income if Lindsay, the trustee, determines he needs it for basic needs, such as health care or everyday expenses.

Each marital property control trust involves the unique circumstances of the couple and final beneficiaries involved. There are no set rules dictating what's right. You must try to foresee the future needs of your spouse and balance those needs with your desire to protect most, if not all, of the principal for your children or other final beneficiaries.

Here is a non-exclusive list of the controls that can be placed over the surviving spouse's right to trust property:

- The survivor is not named as trustee.

- The survivor can live in a house owned (or partially owned) by the trust, but has no right to sell it.

- The survivor can live in a house and can sell it, but only for the purpose of buying another residence, and then only with the approval of all trust beneficiaries.

- The survivor can live in a house but cannot sell it or rent it. And if the survivor moves into a nursing facility and remains there for more than a set time, the house must be turned over to the trust's final beneficiaries.

- The survivor (who is not the trustee) will be paid trust income only as the trustee determines is necessary for medical care or other basic needs.

- The survivor may drive a valuable car owned by the trust, but can sell it only with consent of at least one final beneficiary.

- The survivor must follow specific directions set out in the trust document, down to how he can use many items of trust property and care for valuable items such as antiques.

- If the surviving spouse remarries, the trust ends and the trust property goes to the final beneficiaries.

If your spouse and children don't get along, you may need to face the possibility that you will not be able to create a trust that will make all of them happy. In this case, you simply have to arrive at a resolution that seems the most wise and fair to you.

Example: Dottie and Sam have been living together for six years. Dottie is in her 50s and is the sole owner of a prospering women's clothing company. She owns, free and clear, a house worth $290,000, which she bought over 25 years ago. Her business is worth perhaps $500,000. (It's usually fairly hard to determine the market value of a small business, because often there is no actual market for it.) Her other assets total $130,000, so her total estate is worth $920,000. Sam owns property worth $200,000 and receives a small Social Security allotment.

Dottie has no children. She wants to leave her estate, eventually, to her niece, Betsy, who works with her in her business. Sam wants his property to go to his two children.

Dottie decides that Sam could need income, beyond his Social Security income and whatever his $200,000 may generate, to continue to live in the comfortable style they've enjoyed together. Also, she wants to keep her business intact—most of all, so that Betsy can eventually inherit it, but also so it can produce income for Sam. So Dottie creates a marital property control trust, with Sam as the life beneficiary. She names Betsy as trustee, because Betsy will

manage the business, owned by the trust. Sam is entitled to:

1. Live in their house for the duration of his life

2. Sell it and buy another place, if Betsy consents

3. Receive 25% of any profits from the clothing company (leaving the rest so the business can expand or maintain itself), or any income from other assets in the trust. When Sam dies, all the trust property goes to Betsy. Although Dottie's estate totals $920,000 now, it is unlikely that any estate taxes will be assessed when Dottie dies, because of the special $1.3 million dollar exemption for a family business. (See Chapter 28, Section B.) However, being cautious, Dottie specifies that if any estate tax must be paid, the money shall not come from the business or the house, so she can preserve these two assets for Sam, and then Betsy.

Sam also creates a marital property control trust that allows Dottie the income from his assets for her life but prohibits her from spending principal. When Dottie dies, Sam's property will be transferred between his children.

Sam's children do not get along well with Dottie, so he's reluctant to appoint one of his children as trustee of his trust. He feels confident that Dottie would not abuse the position of trustee. So he names her to be trustee, with the provision that she must give both children copies of the trust's annual income tax return, so they can see that the principal is not being spent.

C. THE ROLE OF THE TRUSTEE

Obviously, choosing the right trustee for a marital property control trust is vital. The trustee will have authority to manage the trust property and to make authorized payments to the surviving spouse. Also, the trustee may have some enforcement—or at least checking-up—responsibilities, to be sure that the surviving spouse's use of trust property complies with trust requirements. These duties can require diplomacy or tough decision making.

1. Heading Off Family Conflict

Choosing the trustee can be a difficult task, requiring some serious thought. If your current spouse and your children are on good terms or, better yet, really trust each other, you may not face much of a problem. Still, even when the nicest of people are involved, you should understand that there's an inherent potential for conflict between the surviving spouse and the final beneficiaries. The surviving spouse may want or believe she or he needs to spend trust property, including principal. The final beneficiaries clearly have an interest in preserving as much of the trust principal as possible. As you may have observed, even usually nice people can at times act in self-interested, and even mean-spirited, ways.

Whatever rules and restrictions you place over the surviving spouse's rights to trust property, it will be the trustee who must enforce them. So it's best if both you and all the beneficiaries have complete confidence in this trustee. If your surviving spouse or one of your children fits that bill, you're fortunate. But certainly it's not unheard of that children from a prior marriage don't really trust one's current spouse sufficiently to want him to be sole successor trustee. Similarly, the spouse will not want his rights—including, perhaps, such basic rights as where he can live—to be supervised by a child with whom he has a hostile relationship.

If you find yourself facing this situation, it should be no surprise that there's no magic solution that will please everyone. The best you can do is think long and hard about who is most likely to be fair to all involved, and to be seen by all as fair. If your spouse and children trust another family member—a sister, perhaps—choosing her to serve as trustee, assuming she's willing, may be the best solution. If the potential for conflict and mistrust between the surviving spouse and the final beneficiaries is severe, you may need to look for a more unconventional solution.

Example: Alberto is married to Miranda. Alberto also has a son, Francesco, age 23, from a prior marriage. To put it bluntly, Francesco and Miranda can't stand each other. What's worse, Alberto thinks neither of them is a particularly good money manager. Alberto discusses the trustee issue with Miranda and Francesco (separately) and they all agree that a trusted friend, Benito, should serve as trustee. Francesco has known Benito for many years, likes him and is relieved that Benito, not Miranda, will be the trustee. Since Benito is Alberto's age and may predecease Miranda, Alberto puts a provision in his trust that allows Benito to appoint another trustee if he can't do the job. Benito promptly names his wife, Carla, to step in if necessary.

Another possibility is simply to name whomever you feel will be fairest, even if that person is your spouse or a child mistrusted by others involved, and let the chips (and sparks) fall as they may.

2. Naming Co-Trustees

It's rarely a good idea to name co-trustees for a marital property control trust. You may hope to reduce potential conflict by naming your spouse and one of your children to serve as co-trustees, but if they don't get along, it could well make matters worse. The result could be a case of trustee gridlock, where each person's vote cancels out the other. Even a simple matter like payment of trust income could wind up in a court battle, if the trustees don't agree what "income" is. And if your spouse and your child or children get along, why bother with co-trustees?

Instead, consider requiring that the trustee provide annual trust income tax returns to all trust beneficiaries, or even copies of all monthly trust bank account statements. This allows non-trustee beneficiaries to check up on the trust without risking co-trustee power struggles.

3. Naming a Financial Institution as Trustee

If you can't find any family member or friend you think would be a suitable trustee, you have a serious problem. Your last resort is to name a financial institution, such as a private trust company, to serve as trustee. As we've discussed, there can be real drawbacks to this. (See Chapter 17, Section F.)

Many financial institutions will not handle trusts with property worth less than $250,000 or even $500,000. This eliminates many marital property control trusts altogether. Also, financial institutions usually charge hefty fees for serving as trustees. Finally, these institutions can be quite bureaucratic and impersonal, especially when handling trusts that seem like small potatoes to them. So if you must name one as trustee, try to establish a personal relationship with someone you can trust in the institution first.

D. Savings on Estate Taxes

For couples in second marriages with combined estates exceeding the estate tax threshold, a marital property control trust can be used for dual purposes: both to impose controls over the surviving spouse's rights to trust property and to save on overall estate taxes.

Example: In 1999, Khosro and Maheen, a couple in their late 70s, have a combined estate worth $1.3 million, with each owning half. Their home and personal belongings are valued at $400,000, and savings and stocks total $900,000. Khosro has a child from his previous marriage and Maheen has two from hers. They have no children from their marriage.

Each spouse creates a marital property control trust for all of his or her property. The trust documents provide that trust income will go to the surviving spouse, who also will have use of the home. The principal will be maintained for their respective children. The surviving spouse is not given the right to spend trust principal, even for health needs. The surviving spouse will receive income from the deceased spouse's share of their stocks and savings, which is $450,000. If interest rates average 6%, this property will generate income of approximately $27,000 a year for the surviving spouse. Khosro and Maheen both feel that when combined with the surviving spouse's own assets plus Social Security and retirement benefits, this amount of income will be sufficient.

Khosro and Maheen are also delighted that no estate tax will be due on either of their deaths, because each will make use of their personal estate tax exemptions. For 1999, the exempt amount is $650,000, and, as you know, it increases to a maximum of $1 million by 2006. So no matter what year each dies in, their entire $1.3 million estate will pass tax-free and intact to their children.

There is nothing particularly tricky about using a marital property control trust to achieve estate tax savings. Basically, you—or, more accurately, your lawyer—prepare the trust document, imposing whatever controls you want to over the surviving spouse's rights to trust property. The trust property is subject to estate tax when you die. If your estate is under the amount of the personal exemption for the year of death, all the trust property is exempt from tax. And because that property is never legally owned by your surviving spouse, it will not be subject to tax when he or she dies.

OTHER APPROACHES

What do you do if you are considering using a marital property control trust both for control and tax savings, and anticipate conflict between beneficiaries? First, you should realize that there are no fixed rules here. You really do have to come up with your own individual solutions. For instance, instead of a marital control trust, you could buy an annuity or insurance policy with the proceeds going to the survivor and leave all other property to the children. Or, particularly if you have a substantial estate, you could leave your children a hefty chunk outright and leave the rest in trust with your spouse as the life beneficiary and grant him, as trustee, fairly generous powers to spend trust principal. The principal may never be touched, but even if it is gobbled up, at least the children have already gotten something.

E. WORKING WITH A LAWYER

If you decide you want a marital property control trust, you'll need to have the trust document prepared by a good estate planning lawyer. There are too many options and possibilities for you to safely prepare one yourself. Also, there are no reliable self-help materials available. A good estate planning lawyer will have had experience with other people in second or subsequent marriages, and may be able to offer helpful suggestions for resolving your particular problems. She can also draft trust language that clearly and unambiguously expresses what you want. With this type of trust, it's especially important to avoid any possibly unclear or ambiguous phrases in the trust document. You don't want to leave any opening for beneficiaries to fight over what you intended.

PROPERTY CONTROL TRUSTS FOR SECOND OR SUBSEQUENT MARRIAGES

Although you will need a lawyer, you can still do much of essential work yourself. (See Chapter 29, Using Lawyers, Section A.) After all, it's best not to wander into a lawyer's office and start discussing your situation at $200 or more per hour. Try to work out a tentative plan of what you want before your first visit.

The principal issues with a marital property control trust are practical, human ones: working out what's fair (as best you can) and deciding who will be best able to carry out your decisions as successor trustee of your trust. These concerns may be easy to state but, in real life, they can be quite difficult to resolve. The best advice we can give is to be candid with yourself. Try to face family and domestic realities, even if they're not all rosy and romantic. Once you've carefully thought about your situation, needs and desires, write down your specific concerns and what, if any, special problems you anticipate. This should mean less time spent with a lawyer, thus reducing your fee—which likely will still be enough to make you blink. ■

25

TRUSTS AND OTHER DEVICES FOR IMPOSING CONTROLS OVER PROPERTY

A. Educational Trusts 25/3
B. Trusts for Persons With Special Needs 25/4
    1. Choosing the Trustee 25/4
    2. Eligibility for Government Assistance 25/4
C. Spendthrift Trusts 25/6
D. Sprinkling Trusts 25/7
    1. Adding Sprinkling Powers to an AB Trust 25/8
    2. Other Uses of Sprinkling Trust Provisions 25/9
    3. Choosing an Independent Trustee 25/9
E. Trusts to Manage Your Own Property 25/10
F. Powers of Appointment 25/10
    1. Kinds of Powers of Appointment 25/11
    2. Limited Power of Appointment in QTIP Trusts 25/12
G. Combining a Property Control Trust With Estate
Tax-Saving Trusts 25/13

In a number of situations, sensible estate planning includes the use of an ongoing, irrevocable trust to impose controls over beneficiaries' rights to trust property. One such situation—married people who want to ensure that their property eventually goes to their children from prior marriages—is discussed in Chapter 24.

We call the types of trusts discussed here "property control trusts." Here are some of the circumstances in which you might want to consider using one:

- One of your beneficiaries is a minor. (Children's trusts are discussed in Chapter 6, Children, Section C.)

- A beneficiary is a young adult who is not yet mature enough to sensibly manage significant sums of money or property. (Also discussed in Chapter 6.)

- You want to leave money for a child's education.

- A beneficiary is disabled and will always need help managing property. These are called "special needs" trusts.

- You believe a beneficiary is improvident with money, and his rights to trust property must be restricted for his entire life. These are called "spendthrift" trusts

- You want the trustee to decide how to distribute trust income or principal among several beneficiaries. These are call "sprinkling" trusts. (For minor children, this type of trust is called a "family pot trust." See Chapter 6, Section C.)

- You want to authorize someone else to decide who will receive your property after you die. This is called a "power of appointment." While it's not technically a trust, it is used for property control purposes, and so is discussed here.

A property control trust is usually quite a complex legal animal. You are trying to impose sensible limits on what can happen with trust property in the future. But since the future cannot be foreseen, you're struggling with what is, at best, very difficult: How to create a trust document that will last for a long time and achieve what you want. Rather than worrying about coming up with a detailed plan now, you may decide to allow the trustee broad powers to decide how to use the trust property for a named group of beneficiaries.

Still, in spite of inherent uncertainties, the property control trusts discussed here have proved effective over the years for many, many people. Generally, using one of these trusts is far more desirable than not trying to arrange for the handling of a difficult beneficiary situation at all.

Most of the property control trusts discussed here become operational only after your death. In some circumstances, however, a trust can become operational either when it's initially created or on the grantor's death.

Property control trusts require a lawyer. All the types of property control trusts discussed in this chapter must be prepared by a knowledgeable estate planning attorney. These trusts inherently involve dealing with uncertainties, and can tie up property for decades. Drafting such a trust is not easy and cannot safely be done without legal help.

Although Nolo Press does not provide resources that show you how to prepare one of these trusts yourself, we hope to provide you with sufficient understanding of how these trusts work, so that you can sensibly decide whether or not to explore creating one.

A. EDUCATIONAL TRUSTS

A relatively common type of property control trust is one created to help beneficiaries pay for college or other schooling. These trusts are rarely set up by children's parents—they just pay educational costs directly, out of their own pockets. Commonly grandparents or other older relatives who want to help young relations use such trusts.

Creating an educational property control trust often involves resolving many rather difficult issues including:

When should the trust become operational? If the beneficiaries are very young, and you are unlikely to live until a child begins college, this is not a serious problem. You can arrange for the trust to become operational at your death. But if the children are older, near or at college age, you may well want the trust to become operational now, while you live.

If you create the trust now, there can be significant tax consequences. The property you give to the trust will be a taxable gift. The gift tax exemption for educational costs won't apply, because that works only for money paid directly to an educational institution. (See Chapter 16, Gifts and Gift Taxes.)

If the trust becomes operational while you're alive, do you want to be the initial trustee or appoint someone else who would continue to serve after your death?

How does a beneficiary qualify for benefits? What education levels must a child receive to get payments from the trust? For instance does a grandchild have to attend college or school full-time to receive payments? What constitutes "full-time"? What qualifies as a college or school? Your grandchild may discover another way to learn—for example, apprenticing with a metal sculptor. Would the trustee have authority to approve the payment of trust benefits? What about graduate school?

If there's more than one (potential) trust beneficiary, other issues arise. If one grandchild attends Columbia Medical School, while the other grandchild goes to a non-tuition community college, their expenses will vary greatly. Can unequal payments be made to different beneficiaries? Lawyers call a trust where a trustee can pay different amounts of principal or income to different beneficiaries based on their needs a "pot" or "sprinkling" trust—all the dough is in one pot. By contrast, if you want each child to have the same amount of money, you should set up separate trusts for each one.

What happens if new (potential) beneficiaries are born? If you're creating a trust for all your grandchildren, do you want the trustee be able to make payments to any future grandchildren born after your death? If you do, accomplishing this is largely a matter of proper legal drafting of the trust document, by an expert lawyer.

What happens if no beneficiaries attend college? Can the trust income be used for grandchildren's "emergencies?" What kinds? What do you want to happen with the trust principal if not all is spent on educational costs.

When does the trust end? What happens to any money left in the trust when no more beneficiaries are eligible for education payments? You can set out a plan or leave this up to the trustee.

If you think you want to create an educational trust, first try to tentatively resolve these questions and any others you think of. Write out your basic thoughts and resolutions of the issues. Then see an experienced estate planning attorney to have your trust prepared.

B. TRUSTS FOR PERSONS WITH SPECIAL NEEDS

Parents or others who care about someone who is disabled by serious physical or mental problems can face difficult estate planning questions. Understandably, they want to provide for the disabled person, to the extent possible, for as long as that person lives. If the disabled person cannot be expected to manage property, the property must be left in a property control trust. The trust document must be carefully drafted, so that the trustee has enough flexibility to deal with the beneficiary's medical or other special needs.

There is no standard special needs trust that can be used in all circumstances. A trust must be geared to the beneficiary's particular needs and problems, as well as how much money you place in the trust. If you're uncertain whether or not a given amount will cover all the beneficiary's expenses, you may want to prioritize the beneficiary's needs and explain your intentions in the trust document, to provide guidance for the trustee on spending trust money. At the other end of the spectrum, you can leave it up to the trustee to decide how much trust income or principal to spend for the beneficiary's needs, and when to spend it.

1. Choosing the Trustee

A primary concern with a special needs trust is making sure you select a trustee and successor trustee(s) who are willing and able to do the job. The trustee must be attentive to the disabled person's situation, discerning what is needed and providing for those needs to the extent possible. The trustee will need to be in close contact with the disabled person, so it is essential that the two get along. And finally, the trustee should have the savvy to deal with various institutions, from banks to doctors and hospitals to government agencies.

2. Eligibility for Government Assistance

Usually a major concern when preparing a special needs trust is how to prevent the trust's existence from rendering the beneficiary ineligible for government assistance, such as Supplemental Security Income (SSI) or medical or educational aid. This fear is reality based, since a disabled person who is the legal owner of any substantial amount of property usually must use up most of it before government assistance is available. In some circumstances, if a disabled person acquires property, the government may even demand reimbursement for past benefits.

Obviously, this rule can have nasty consequences. Even if the property left to the disabled person is substantial, it may be used up fairly quickly. The disabled person will then become eligible once more for governmental assistance, but no trust property is left for emergencies or the many needs governmental assistance doesn't provide for.

Technically, the beneficiary is not the legal owner of the trust property—the trustee is. But this fact alone doesn't mean that a government agency won't try to consider the trust principal (as well as, of course, any trust income the beneficiary actually receives) as part of the beneficiary's property, when it comes to determining eligibility for government aid.

If you can provide enough trust money to take care of all the beneficiary's needs, you may not need to worry about the disabled beneficiary's eligibility for government benefits. Of course, how much money must be in the trust before you reach this point is a personal, subjective decision. But few people can leave millions, or anything approaching it, in a special needs trust.

What can you do? You can, of course, elect not to give any property to the disabled beneficiary in the first place and let the person rely exclusively on government benefits. But if like most people, you are rightly skeptical of relying on public programs to provide total care for someone with special needs, this is not a solution you'll be eager to accept.

Fortunately, there is a better choice. You can establish a property control trust that allows the trust property to be used for the benefit of the disabled person without affecting eligibility for public assistance.

Under U.S. Social Security Administration (SSA) guidelines, the property in a special needs trust doesn't affect eligibility for Social Security assistance if the beneficiary cannot:

- control the amount or frequency of trust payments, or
- revoke the trust and use the property.

In other words, the beneficiary must have no rights to demand and receive money from the trust, either income or principal. Nor can the beneficiary simply revoke the trust and obtain the trust principal. All power over the trust principal, including payment of income or principal to the beneficiary, must be given to the trustee. Normally, the trustee has power to spend money for carefully defined needs of the beneficiary that are not met by government aid.

Local SSA offices have wide latitude in interpreting these SSA guidelines. For example, some SSA offices require that the trust document show that the

trust creator didn't "intend" the trust property to be used as the primary source of aid or income for the disadvantaged person.

Statutes and SSA regulations pertaining to eligibility for government programs change frequently. Further, each state has its own regulations about eligibility for government programs (many aid programs, primarily funded by the federal government, are administered through state agencies). These regulations also can change quickly.

Thus, the key to drafting a trust for a disabled person is up-to-date knowledge of:

- relevant federal law
- SSA rules and court interpretations of them
- local SSA practices, and
- state rules and regulations.

Be sure you see an expert. Because the government rules here are complex and can change suddenly, a distinct legal sub-specialty has developed: lawyers who prepare special needs trusts. The truth is that you really need not only an estate planning expert, but someone who is knowledgeable in drafting special needs trusts. (See Chapter 29, Using Lawyers, Section A, for a discussion of how to find the right lawyer for you.) Don't rely on a general practice lawyer, most of whom are not nearly knowledgeable enough to properly prepare a special needs trust.

- *Planning for the Future: Providing a Meaningful Life for a Child with a Disability After Your Death,* by Russell, Grant, Joseph and Fee (American Pub. Co.), is a thorough, readable and down-to-earth book which helps parents to be sure they've done all they can to provide a good life for a child who may always need special help. The authors emphasize the broad picture, not just the "legal" aspects of caring and planning for a disabled child. They give ample coverage to estate planning concerns, but the center-piece of the book is a document the authors call a "Letter of Intent." It's an extremely detailed document intended to give future caretakers all information they need to help the child live the best life possible.

- *The Life Planning Workbook,* by the same authors, is a companion book, full of worksheets to fill in. About half the book, almost 100 pages, is taken up with a fill-in-the-blanks Letter of Intent. These forms may prove helpful for some people, but the coverage of this topic in *Planning for the Future* is probably all the guidance most parents need.

C. SPENDTHRIFT TRUSTS

A spendthrift trust is designed to minimize an unreliable beneficiary's ability to squander trust principal. The "spendthrift" beneficiary may be someone who simply has no head for money (like some of our dearest friends—and, at times, ourselves), and could easily waste trust principal if controls weren't placed on his right to get at it. This type of trust is also used when a beneficiary might squander trust principal on drugs, alcohol, gambling or some other compulsive behavior. Creating a spendthrift trust is an attempt to balance concern for the beneficiary with a realistic appraisal of his more wasteful or destructive impulses

"Spendthrift" may sound like a harsh epithet to apply to a loved one, but sitting down to work out a sensible estate plan demands facing realities, even painful ones. If you want to help someone who is

financially irresponsible, a spendthrift trust can be a very sound idea.

With a spendthrift trust, the beneficiary is never the trustee. The trustee can spend trust money for the beneficiary's needs or make payments directly to the beneficiary, as the trust document directs or permits. The beneficiary has no right to spend trust principal. Nor does he have the legal right to pledge trust principal, or future income expected from the trust, as security for a loan.

> **Example:** Pierre wants to leave money to his son, Maurice, a charming fellow who's always spent money as if he were a millionaire. (He's not.) So Pierre creates an ongoing spendthrift trust for the benefit of Maurice, to take effect after Pierre dies. The trust will be managed by Pierre's prudent bourgeois brother Jean-Paul, who will dole out trust income to Maurice on the first of each month. If Jean-Paul predeceases Maurice, first Jean-Paul's wife, Anne-Marie (also quite prudent) and next their son Charles (a chip off the old block) will serve as trustee.
>
> Under the terms of the trust, Maurice cannot obtain the trust principal or pledge his expected trust income to obtain credit. The trust will end when Maurice becomes 50, by which point Pierre hopes he'll have learned financial prudence. If not, Pierre simply accepts the risk that he'll waste the trust principal at that age.

At the extreme, a spendthrift clause can give the trustee power to cut off benefits, temporarily or even permanently, to a beneficiary who becomes uncontrollably self-destructive. Income withheld could be accumulated in the trust or paid to another beneficiary named in the trust document.

Giving the trustee this power, however, is rarely if ever wise. It imposes a troubling burden on the trustee, who must decide what behavior by the unreliable beneficiary is so bad that income may be withheld. Even if certain offending behaviors are spelled out in the trust document, it's the trustee who must actually determine whether the beneficiary's behavior justifies withholding income payments. How is the trustee to make this determination? Must he play detective, or hire a professional to spy on the beneficiary?

Perhaps the most that you can sensibly do is to describe, in the trust document, specific, objective acts which, if undertaken by the beneficiary, would allow the trustee to withhold income payments. For example, the trust document could provide that if the beneficiary were convicted of certain types of drug offenses, payments could be withheld. But even here, is this really the wisest course? Even if the beneficiary were in prison (where access to drugs should be greatly reduced), wouldn't receiving income payments from the trust be a help? Having some personal cash could ease a prisoner's life in many ways, from purchasing canteen food to affording good legal representation.

A less draconian method is for you to direct the trustee to continue to make payments for the benefit of a beneficiary who's become obviously self-destructive (such as paying his rent, food bills or other basic needs) but withhold direct payments to that beneficiary. This still imposes on the trustee the burden of evaluating the beneficiary's behavior, with all the difficulties that involves. But sometimes imposing such a burden is necessary, particularly when the beneficiary's behavior could become (or already is) truly dangerous.

In other situations, you may decide that the trustee must make regular (monthly or quarterly) payments to the beneficiary, regardless of the beneficiary's behavior. These payments can be defined in the trust document as all of the trust income, a set amount, or a percentage of trust in-come. If you choose this option, you must accept the risk that the beneficiary won't spend the money wisely. No trust can prevent a beneficiary from squandering money once it's in his pocket.

The rigidity of some spendthrift trusts can be a problem down the road. What happens if the beneficiary needs more money than the monthly payment allowed? Does the trustee have the power to spend trust principal if the beneficiary becomes ill and lacks funds to pay medical bills? Or suppose the beneficiary sees the error of his wasteful ways and decides to settle down and go to dental school. Can the trustee use the principal to pay the beneficiary's tuition? You may decide to allow the trustee to spend trust principal for the beneficiary, either for specific needs or as the trustee determines is desirable.

D. SPRINKLING TRUSTS

Perhaps the most flexible property control trust of all is termed a "sprinkling" or "discretionary" trust. Under either lingo, this type of trust gives the trustee authority to "sprinkle" both the income and principal of the trust between named beneficiaries. (Sometimes this is called allowing "sprinkling" powers.)

A sprinkling trust differs from other trusts, including all other trusts designed to control property, in that you don't specify what property each beneficiary gets, or when. Rather, you leave money in the trust and name the group of possible beneficiaries. The trustee determines which of these beneficiaries will receive payments from trust income or principal, and how much. You can specify when the trust should end, and what happens to any money left in the trust, or you can leave these matters to the trustee.

In the trust document, however, you can give the trustee rules to follow. For instance, the trustee could be allowed to spend trust principal only for a beneficiary's educational or medical needs. Or a trustee might have the power to pay out only trust income, not principal. Or he could have the power to give no more than 20% of the trust principal to any one beneficiary in any one year.

Usually the trust document provides that if the trustee decides it's best, income may be accumulated in the trust instead of being handed out to any beneficiaries. However, the income tax rate applied to retained trust income will probably be higher than the rate applied to trust income received by beneficiaries. (See Chapter 17, Section F.) So it's unlikely that a trustee would decide to retain trust income beyond one tax year and thus effectively cost the beneficiaries money in higher taxes.

By law, you must name an independent ("disinterested") trustee—that is, a trustee who has no financial interest in how the trust money is distributed, but is dispassionate enough to hand out money as it's genuinely needed. Thus, a surviving spouse normally should not serve as trustee of a sprinkling trust. (See Section 3, below.)

1. Adding Sprinkling Powers to an AB Trust

If you create an AB trust, you may want to give your surviving spouse the power to use trust income or assets for the final beneficiaries, probably your children. A sprinkling AB trust can be appropriate for a couple with a large estate, when the surviving spouse has plenty of assets and may not need or want regular income payments. Creating "sprinkling powers" in an AB trust can accomplish several goals:

- **Helping other beneficiaries.** You can take care of possible needs of other beneficiaries, such as your children, during the surviving spouse's life. At an extreme, for example, if a wealthy surviving spouse marries someone even wealthier, the trustee can choose not to pay anything at all to that spouse, but to spend (or save) all the trust income and assets for the children or other named beneficiaries.

  More commonly, one child may need more money for education or support than another. When the beneficiaries are young, a sprinkling trust allows great flexibility over the years and makes the assets available when necessary.

- **Income tax savings.** If your surviving spouse will be well off, you can achieve income tax savings by channeling some trust income to beneficiaries in lower tax brackets, such as adult children or children over 14 with low incomes. (Income paid out to children 13 or younger is taxed at their parents' rates; see Chapter 6, Children, Section C.)

  Example: Akira and Mariko have a shared estate totaling $3 million. They have two young children, and Akira also has a teenage son by a former marriage.

  Akira drafts a sprinkling formula AB trust, directing that the maximum amount of property exempt from estate tax in the year of his death be placed in the trust. His remaining property will go into a QTIP trust, with his wife as life beneficiary and Akira's three children as the final beneficiaries. (See Chapter 19, Section A, for a discussion of QTIP trusts, which are used to defer payment of estate tax.) If he dies first, the trustee of the AB trust will have the power to sprinkle both income and principal to Mariko and to any of the children for their support for the rest of Mariko's life. Upon Mariko's death, the remaining assets will be distributed to Akira's children. The trust document specifies that this division shall take into consideration how much from the trust has been previously paid to each, with the goal of equalizing the totals.

Akira accomplishes several purposes with this trust plan. He takes advantage of his personal estate tax exemption and defers all estate tax on his remaining property until Mariko's death.

Akira also makes funds available early on for his teenage son, who will be facing college and perhaps graduate school expenses. And if Mariko doesn't want some or all of the income, she can always disclaim it (see Chapter 22, Section A), building a larger trust principal for the children to inherit later.

2. Other Uses of Sprinkling Trust Provisions

Sprinkling trust provisions can be used in a wide variety of property control trusts. For example, if you want to leave property for minor children or young adults, you may create a "family pot" trust. This is a kind of sprinkling trust, where you choose to let the trustee decide, according to the actual needs and circumstances of the children, how much money to pay to each child. (See Chapter 6, Section C.)

Similarly, a grandparent may create a sprinkling trust for grandchildren or, for that matter, for adult children. Indeed, sprinkling trust provisions can work well in any situation if you totally trust the trustee, and a number of beneficiaries may need payments from the trust for a long period of time.

3. Choosing an Independent Trustee

No matter the type of sprinkling trust, a key to making one work well is to appoint a disinterested, independent trustee, whom you trust completely. Because a sprinkling trust is intended to operate over a lengthy period, you also need to select at least one successor trustee, and often an alternate successor trustee, with similar care.

An "independent" trustee means a trustee who cannot benefit from the trust—that is, is not a beneficiary of any kind. Even someone who is named as an alternate beneficiary (or fourth alternate, for that matter) cannot serve. If the trustee has a financial interest in the trust, the IRS may consider her to be the legal owner of all the trust property and include it in her taxable estate when she dies, which is definitely not what you want.

The surviving spouse cannot be the trustee of a sprinkling AB trust. As the life beneficiary, the surviving spouse obviously has an interest in trust payments. Indeed, normally, he receives all trust income during his life. But creating a sprinkling trust means there are other possibilities. Allowing the surviving spouse to be the trustee in this situation, when there are sprinkling provisions in the trust, means the IRS will regard him as the legal owner of all trust property. That property will be included in his taxable estate when he dies, defeating the purpose of an AB trust.

You need a trustee who, although he or she has no financial interest in how the trust money is distributed, is personally interested in the welfare of the beneficiaries and will remain alert to their financial needs. A sprinkling trust, by its very nature, can create conflict among the beneficiaries. After all, they may all think they need money—and a lot of it—from the trust, so the trustee may have some serious personal as well as financial issues to handle. If you can't find a legally independent but emotionally involved person who'll do the job, and who you fully trust, a sprinkling trust isn't for you.

E. TRUSTS TO MANAGE YOUR OWN PROPERTY

If you tire of coping with your property and financial affairs, you can arrange for someone else to manage them. One method is for you to put your property in a trust, to be managed by a trustee for your benefit. The trustee would have the authority to spend any amount of trust income or principal for you. You can define as carefully as you like in the trust document what standard of living you expect. (Of course, there must be sufficient assets in the trust to pay for that standard of living.)

Unlike the other trusts discussed in this chapter, there's no need to have this type of trust be irrevocable. Indeed, there are real drawbacks to making the trust irrevocable. The trustee would have to obtain a trust taxpayer ID, maintain trust financial records, and file an annual trust income tax return. None of this would benefit you. And, obviously, if you changed your mind, you would have no legal power to end the trust and regain control of the trust assets.

If the trust is revocable, you should make yourself one of the trustees. If you don't, under IRS regulations the tax requirements applied to irrevocable trusts will apply to your revocable trust as well. One simple way to avoid this problem is for you to name yourself and some other person as co-trustees, and provide in the trust document that either trustee may act for the trust. The other person, as co-trustee, in reality becomes the sole manager of the trust property. But as long as you remain one of the official trustees, no tax reporting obligations are imposed on the trust.

You can also use other devices to allow another person to manage your property for you. One method is to give another person authority, using a document called a durable power of attorney for finances, to manage your property. It's always a good idea to create a durable power of attorney for finances as part of your estate plan. (See Chapter 26, Incapacity: Health Care and Financial Management Directives, Section B.) A durable power of attorney for finances, however, does not give authority over property in a living trust.

If you have transferred property to a living trust, there is no need to create any other device to handle that trust property in case you become incapacitated. A standard clause in a well-drafted living trust authorizes your successor trustee to take over management of your trust property, if necessary, for your benefit as long as you live. If this happens, the living trust remains revocable, if you regain the ability to manage your affairs.

F. POWERS OF APPOINTMENT

A "power of appointment" is simply the power to determine how someone's assets are distributed after his or her death.

Example: In her living trust, Anita authorizes her husband, Frederico, to distribute all her property among her children as he wishes, if he outlives her. If he doesn't outlive her, Anita grants the same authority to her brother, Marcello.

There can be a number of sensible reasons to use a power of appointment. Generally the most common reason is that you are unsure, when you prepare your estate plan, exactly who you want your beneficiaries to be. You don't want to create a sprinkling trust, because with them the trustee normally has the power to distribute trust money only among beneficiaries named in the trust document. If you trust someone—a spouse, brother or friend—completely, it may make sense to postpone the choice of beneficiaries, or what property beneficiaries will receive, until later.

Example: Malcolm, a widower, has two children: Veronica, age 24, and Jamal, age 22, who has a serious drug problem. Malcolm certainly doesn't want to leave any property outright to Jamal if he's still using drugs when Malcolm dies. On the other hand, Malcolm hopes Jamal will see the light and cease using drugs, so he surely doesn't want to cut Jamal out irrevocably. So in his living trust he creates a power of appointment in his best friend, Ted. Ted will decide, after Malcolm's death, if Jamal can be given property outright because he has been clear from drugs for a specified period of time. (Of course, determining this may not be easy.) If Ted decides Jamal still suffers from drug addiction, then the property left for Jamal will go into a trust for him, managed by Ted.

1. Kinds of Powers of Appointment

There are two kinds of powers of appointment: "general" and "special" (also called "limited"). A general power of appointment can have adverse estate tax consequences, while a limited power of appointment does not.

With a general power of appointment, you name a person to distribute your property to whomever she chooses—including herself. You can define a set time period for this decision to be made, or leave it open

Authorizing a general power of appointment is rarely a good idea. Under IRS rules, the person who has a general power of appointment will have the full value of the property subject to that power included in her taxable estate at her death. This is true even if she never gives any property to herself, had no intention of doing so, and in fact gave it all to someone else. The practical effect is that this property is subject to estate tax twice—once when you die and once when the person to whom you gave the power of appointment dies.

Example: In his living trust, Martin gives his wife Helen a general power of appointment over property worth $500,000. Martin's total estate is worth $900,000, so it is subject to federal estate tax if he dies before 2005. Ellen's estate is worth $700,000, aside from the property subject to the general power of appointment. Shortly after Martin's death in 1998, Ellen gives the entire $500,000 to their three children. Nevertheless, when Ellen dies in 2002, the entire $500,000 is included in her taxable estate, because she had the power to give all this money to herself if she had chosen to. So the $500,000 has been included in two taxable estates, which is clearly undesirable.

A special or limited power of appointment, by contrast is restricted as you see fit. Most importantly, the person who has the power cannot give the property to himself, use it to pay his creditors or leave it in his estate. This eliminates the double estate tax problem of a general power of appointment.

Typically, if you give someone a limited power of appointment, you specify which people (beneficiaries) the holder of the power can give property to. For instance, the person appointed can be given only the right to divide property among your four children. Or the person can be directed to give at least 15% of your property to each of the children, with the remaining 40% to be distributed among them as the person with the special power of appointment determines.

Example: Woody sets up an AB trust, leaving the income from the trust to his wife, Janet, and the principal to their three children upon Janet's death. He includes a limited power of appointment authorizing Janet to direct how the trust assets will pass to the children, if she so chooses. Janet lives for 20 years after Woody's death and receives the income from the trust. During that time, Sarah, one of the children, gives birth to a severely disabled child. The other children are all well-off financially and don't, in Janet's opinion, need money from the trust.

Janet considers what Woody would want if he were alive and could make the decision. Then, in her will, she exercises her limited power of appointment, by leaving 75% of the trust property outright to Sarah, with the understanding that Sarah will use the money primarily for her disabled child's needs. The other 25% of the trust property is divided between Sarah's other two children.

Watch out when using limited powers of appointment and disclaimers. With a limited power of appointment, problems can arise if the person given the power also wants to use a disclaimer at the grantor's death. If one disclaims (refuses) property that then goes into a trust, the one disclaiming cannot then direct where the disclaimed property eventually goes. So disclaiming is inconsistent with having any power of appointment, even a limited one. (See Chapter 22, Disclaimers, Section C.) See a good estate planning lawyer if you think this problem might come up.

2. Limited Power of Appointment in QTIP Trusts

Limited powers of appointment are also occasionally used in QTIP trusts. A QTIP trust is basically a device to defer estate tax until the death of a surviving spouse, while allowing the first spouse to die to name the final beneficiaries for his estate. (See Chapter 19, Other Estate Tax-Saving Marital Trusts, Section A.)

When a surviving spouse is given a limited power of appointment over QTIP trust property, the surviving spouse simply has some control over the final distribution of the assets in the QTIP trust, within the limits the grantor imposed. The grantor can choose the final group of beneficiaries, such as his children, and allow a spouse to determine the amounts received by each one. The grantor, then, still controls who the final beneficiaries are—just not how much each receives.

Example: Gert leaves $1 million in a QTIP trust with the income going to her much younger husband, Raphael, for his life. She gives him a limited power of appointment to choose at his death how much each of her four children by a previous marriage will receive of what is left. Raphael may benefit for many years from the trust, and he may adjust the final outcome according to the children's needs. But if he remarries (and Gert expects, or suspects, that he might well), the trust terms prevent him from shifting these assets to his new bride or to anyone else.

G. COMBINING A PROPERTY CONTROL TRUST WITH ESTATE TAX-SAVING TRUSTS

Sometimes one or more property control trusts is combined with one or more tax-saving trusts as the central part of the overall estate plan.

Example: Parnell, in his 60s, has an estate worth $1.8 million. He recently married Moira, who has little property of her own. He has two children from his prior marriage—a daughter, Maeve, who he worries cannot handle money, and a son, Padraic, who is severely disabled. Parnell wants to leave some property for Padraic's needs, while also ensuring, as best he can, that Padraic will remain eligible for the government medical and rehabilitation services he now receives. Parnell also wants to provide for Moira if she outlives him, and leave some property on her death to Padraic and Maeve.

After working with an expert lawyer, Parnell decides to create three trusts:

1. A special needs trust for Padraic, to be funded with the amount of the personal estate tax exemption in the year of Parnell's death

2. A QTIP trust for the remainder of his property, to provide income for Moira and postpone estate tax on the balance of his estate.

Maeve and Padraic are the final beneficiaries of this trust and will share the trust property equally when Moira dies. Parnell specifies that Padraic's share of this property will be added to his special needs trust.

3. A spendthrift trust Parnell creates for the property Maeve will eventually receive from the QTIP trust when Moira dies.

Parnell still has many matters he must resolve. For example, who should be trustee of the QTIP trust? Can Moira invade the trust principal? Who is the trustee of the spendthrift trust? How long will it last? Can the trustee decide that Maeve has become financially responsible and turn the trust principal over to her? With Padraic, Parnell faces the problems involved in creating any special needs trust.

Parnell also has to decide what he'll tell his family members about his estate plan. Moira surely needs to know about the QTIP, but how much does he want to tell his children? If he's not on good terms with Maeve, maybe he doesn't want to tell her about the spendthrift trust. But letting her discover this only after he dies could be very hurtful. Parnell decides he will write Maeve a letter, explaining his estate plan, and why he's decided it's best to leave her property in a spendthrift trust. Parnell knows Maeve has a fierce temper. He hopes that by writing her, he'll lessen the chance of a screaming fight between the two of them, Parnell being no saint himself. But if Maeve has some time to reflect on Parnell's plan, perhaps they can discuss it later, without rancor. Parnell also informs Padraic that he's created a special needs trust to try to protect him over the years. ■

26

INCAPACITY: HEALTH CARE AND FINANCIAL MANAGEMENT DIRECTIVES

A. Health Care Decisions 26/2
    1. The Importance of Putting Your Wishes in Writing 26/3
    2. Types of Medical Care Documents 26/3
    3. What You Can Cover in a Medical Care Document 26/4
    4. When a Durable Power of Attorney for Health Care
       Becomes Effective 26/5
    5. Choosing an Attorney-in-Fact or Proxy 26/6
    6. Where to Get Medical Care Forms 26/6
    7. What to Do With Your Completed Documents 26/7
    8. Changing Your Mind—and Documents 26/8
B. Financial Management Decisions 26/8
    1. Durable Powers of Attorney for Finances and Living Trusts 26/9
C. Guardianships and Conservatorships 26/9
    1. Financial Conservatorship or Guardianship 26/10
    2. Full Guardianship 26/10

We tend to think of estate planning as something we do now to arrange for handling important matters when we die. While this definition has the advantage of being concise, it's a bit too simple. As we grow older, many of us face the stern reality that before we die we may not be mentally or physically competent for some period of time, sometimes an extended period. A thorough estate plan must consider this possibility.

This chapter discusses how you can best ensure that your rights, dignity and wishes will be protected if you ever become incapable of making or communicating decisions regarding medical treatment. It also covers how your can arrange for the handling of your finances if you become incapable of handling them.

If your health deteriorates and you become unable to make financial or medical decisions, another adult must have legal authority to make these for you.

There are two ways you can deal with this possibility:

1. Do nothing, and, if you ever become incapacitated, let a judge appoint someone, called a conservator (or guardian, custodian or other name, depending on the state) to make decisions for you. Court proceedings for incapacitated persons are almost always undesirable, unless there's no other option. These proceedings are costly, time-consuming and expose to public concern what most people prefer to keep private.

If you suffer a medical emergency and are incapacitated and haven't prepared a document covering your medical care, that care will be determined according to hospital protocol or doctor's individual choices. This may be very different than what you would have wanted.

With finances, people sometimes simply ignore the requirement of court proceedings: a son signs his ill father's name to the father's retirement check, for example. Unfortunately, there's an unpleasant legal term for this act: forgery. So ignoring the law isn't wise, and often not practical either. Over an extended period of time, it's almost impossible to adequately manage another's affairs this way.

2. Complete documents called "durable powers of attorney"—the wise choice. In these documents, you give a person of your choice legal authority to act for you regarding your health care or finances in the event of your incapacity.

A related concern is financial planning for long-term medical care. These matters are discussed in *Beat the Nursing Home Trap: A Consumer's Guide to Choosing & Financing Long-Term Care,* by Joseph Matthews (Nolo Press).

A. HEALTH CARE DECISIONS

The increasing use of life-sustaining medical technology over the last decades has raised fears in many that our lives may be artificially prolonged against our wishes. The right to die with dignity, and without the tremendous agony and expense for both patient and family caused by prolonging lives artificially, has been addressed and confirmed by the U.S. Supreme Court, the federal government and the legislatures in every state.

This individual right can also provide protection in a situation where doctors might wish to provide a patient with less extensive care than he or she would like. For example, a doctor may be unwilling to try experimental treatments or maintain long-term treatments on a patient who the doctor feels has slim chances of recovering (or, worse, couldn't pay the bill).

In 1990, the United States Supreme Court held that every individual has the constitutional right to control his or her own medical treatment. The Court also stated that medical personnel must follow "clear and convincing evidence" of a person's wishes—even if those wishes are directly opposed by the patient's family. (*Cruzan v. Director, Missouri Dept. of Health,* 497 U.S. 261.)

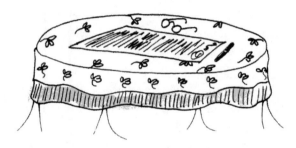

1. The Importance of Putting Your Wishes in Writing

In recognition of the legal right to control one's own medical treatment, every state now authorizes individuals to create a simple document that provides the "clear and convincing evidence" of their wishes concerning life-prolonging medical care. Depending upon the state, the document may be called by one of several different names: Durable Power of Attorney for Health Care, Living Will, Medical Directive, Directive to Physicians, Declaration Regarding Health Care, Designation of Health Care Surrogate, or Patient Advocate Designation. We'll use the term "medical care document."

The directions expressed in the document are to be followed if you are no longer capable of communicating to medical personnel your choices regarding life-prolonging and other medical care.

It is important to note that many of these documents take effect only when a patient is diagnosed to have a terminal condition or to be in a permanent coma. Such documents do not come into play when a person is able to communicate his or her wishes to doctors in any way or is only temporarily unconscious, as with general anesthesia.

Writing down your medical care instructions can help alleviate your fears, whether worries about unwanted medical treatment being administered to you or desired medical treatment being withheld. It can also help relieve family members from having to make agonizing decisions about a loved one's medical treatment. This can be particularly important when family members have different ideas about what care you should receive. Also, doctors and hospitals have their own rules and beliefs about what is proper medical treatment, and even if your family knows your wishes and tries to have them followed, medical personnel would not necessarily be bound to follow them without a valid document you have signed.

2. Types of Medical Care Documents

The two basic types of documents used to direct medical care are a Living Will and a Durable Power of Attorney for Health Care or Health Care Proxy. Some states—including Kentucky, Minnesota, Oklahoma, Oregon, South Carolina, Virginia and Wyoming—combine both documents into a single form.

A Living Will—in some states referred to as a Directive to Physicians or a Declaration—is not a conventional will at all, but a document setting forth your decision to receive or not to receive certain medical treatment. It is a statement made by you directly to medical personnel, spelling out the medical care you do or do not wish to receive if you become terminally ill and incapacitated. It acts as a contract with the treating doctor, who must either honor the wishes for medical care that you have expressed or transfer you to another doctor or facility that will honor them.

In a Durable Power of Attorney or Health Care Proxy, you appoint someone (your "attorney-in-fact") to make sure health care providers give you the kind of medical care you want You can specify in the document what types of care you want, or don't want. In a number of states, you can also give the person you appoint the broader authority to make decisions about your medical care on your behalf.

WHEN YOUR STATE FORM IS NOT DETAILED ENOUGH

When it comes to medical directives, there are many differences in the forms and formats used by different states. Some state laws say that a specific form must be followed for a directive to be valid. However, since the Supreme Court ruled in the *Cruzan* case that every individual has a constitutional right to direct his or her own medical care, the most important thing to keep in mind is that your directions should be clear and in writing.

If you feel strongly about a particular kind of care—even if your state law or the form you get does not address it—include your specific thoughts about it in your document. If you are using a state form that does not adequately address your concerns, write them in on the form with the additional request that your wishes be respected and followed. Be sure to sign the document and to be on the safe side, have it witnessed by two people if possible.

---

3. What You Can Cover in a Medical Care Document

Some people encounter difficulties when filling out a medical care document because they are not sure what's possible and what medical terms to use. Although medical technology and treatments are

evolving, filling out the forms is not as difficult as it may seem at first. In most medical care documents, you can direct:

- that all life-prolonging procedures be provided
- that all life-prolonging procedures be withheld, or
- that some be provided, while others are withheld.

The following medical procedures and treatments are usually considered to be "life-prolonging."

- Artificial breathing apparatus, such as a respirator or ventilator. Some people specify that they wish artificial breathing while they are conscious, but not if they lapse into unconsciousness.

- Artificial administration of food and water, also called nutrition and hydration. As with artificial breathing, some people want artificial food and water administered only as long as they are conscious. Others want artificially administered food and water if they are diagnosed to be in a permanent coma, but not if they become terminally ill. A few states, however, do not permit a doctor or hospital to withhold artificial food and water even if you request that it be withheld. Again, if you feel strongly that you would like artificial food and water withheld, but you are living in a state that restricts your right to direct that, include your desires in your medical care document and state that you want your desires be respected and followed, as is your constitutional right. You should also be sure to name someone to oversee your wishes, so that there will be a human being to lobby on your behalf.

- Comfort care—including relief from pain and discomfort, usually through medication. Many people specify that they do want pain medication, but do not want any other life-prolonging measures.

To make an informed decision about which procedures you do and do not want, as well as about others which might pertain to your particular medical condition, it may be a good idea to discuss your medical care document with your physician. He or she can explain medical procedures more fully and can discuss the options with you. You will also find out whether your doctor has any medical or moral objections to following your wishes. If your physician does not agree to follow your wishes, consider finding a doctor who will.

Even when you have specified your wishes in a medical care document regarding life-prolonging medical treatment and comfort care, certain decisions may still be difficult to resolve:

- when, exactly, to administer or withhold certain medical treatments

- whether or not to provide, withhold or continue antibiotic or pain medication, and

- whether to pursue complex, painful and expensive surgeries which may serve to prolong life but cannot reverse the medical condition.

To deal with these situations, in most states, the document called a Durable Power of Attorney for Health Care or Health Care Proxy allows you to appoint someone who understands your wishes and whose judgment you trust to make these decisions in accordance with your wishes and in your best interest. To provide some guidance, the power of attorney or proxy form may authorize the appointed person to:

- give, withhold or withdraw consent to medical or surgical procedures

- consent to appropriate care for the end of life, including pain relief

- hire and fire medical personnel

- visit you in the hospital or other facility even when other visiting is restricted

- have access to medical records and other personal information, and

- get any court authorization required to obtain or withhold medical treatment if, for any reason, a hospital or doctor does not honor the document.

4. When a Durable Power of Attorney for Health Care Becomes Effective

A durable power of attorney for health care can go into effect when you sign it, or only if you subsequently become unable to communicate your own health care decisions. This latter type is called a "springing" durable power of attorney. It is sensibly created as a kind of insurance against the possibility that you later need it.

A durable power of attorney for health care that becomes operational and effective when you sign it can be advisable if you have a life-threatening illness, or are facing major surgery, or know your mental powers are gravely declining.

Example: Sara is seriously ill, faces major surgery, and knows that, at a minimum, she will be unable to make all her own medical decisions. She prepares a durable power of attorney for health care, effective on signing, delegating to her sister, Kerry, the authority to make health care decisions for her. To make sure that her own wishes are complied with, she inserts several restrictions regarding Kerry's power. Specifically, Sara wants to be sure she is operated on by Dr. June Lee at Mattan Hospital. So, in defining the attorney-in-fact's authority, she includes the following clause:

"My attorney-in-fact shall comply with my stated desire that all surgery performed on me be done at Mattan Hospital, 134 Ridge Road, Linda Vista, California, by Dr. June Lee, unless Dr. Lee is unable to perform such surgery."

No matter what the state of your health, preparing a springing durable power of attorney for health care should be part of your estate plan. There is no downside to this. If you remain able to make you own medical decisions, fine—the document never becomes effective. But if you ever become unable to make those decisions, your document becomes effective and your wishes will be carried out.

5. Choosing an Attorney-in-Fact or Proxy

There are a number of things to consider in choosing a health care attorney-in-fact or proxy. Some are obvious: you should choose someone who understands your wishes and whom you trust to follow those wishes.

But there are a few other things you should also consider. Appoint someone who:

- is likely to be present when decisions need to be made—most often, this means someone who lives nearby or who is willing to travel and spend time at your side during your hospitalization

- would not easily be swayed or bullied by doctors or family members who disagree with your wishes, and

- is capable of understanding your medical condition and any proposed life-prolonging measures.

It is also a good idea to appoint a second person as a backup or replacement attorney-in-fact or proxy to act if your first choice is unable or unwilling to serve. Make it clear, however, that the second person is only a back-up. It is not wise to appoint co-proxies: having two people make decisions would only complicate the process.

Do not appoint your doctor as attorney-in-fact. Although your doctor is an important person for your attorney-in-fact or proxy to consult concerning all health care decisions, you should not appoint your doctor to act as attorney-in-fact or proxy. The laws in most states specifically forbid treating physicians from acting in this role—to avoid the appearance that they may have their own interests at heart and so may not be able to act purely according to your wishes.

6. Where to Get Medical Care Forms

Each state makes its own rules concerning medical care forms. In some states, you must use a form specifically required by state law. Some states' forms for living wills don't contain a clause allowing you to name a proxy to supervise and enforce your wishes. In these states, if you want to appoint someone to supervise your care, you must prepare a durable power of attorney for health care in addition to a living will.

Keep documents up to date. The laws on medical care forms can change frequently, so a particular form which was the right one in your state several years ago may by now have been replaced by a different, usually more complete form. In most states, documents you completed while an old law was in effect remain valid. But be warned that in some states such documents do not remain valid for an unlimited time. Review your health care documents every few years, to be sure that your documents reflect your present wishes, and that you have the current form.

You do not need to consult a lawyer to prepare a medical care form. The forms are usually simple and can be obtained, free or for a nominal fee, from a number of sources, including:

- **Senior referral and information services.** The white pages in most telephone directories have a listing for Senior Referral & Information. This number refers people to various agencies, groups and other sources of assistance for seniors. Call and ask where you can obtain your state's official medical care form.

- **Local senior center.** Many senior centers have copies of your state's forms or can obtain them for you.

• **Consumer organizations.** The national nonprofit organization Choice in Dying (formerly the Society for the Right to Die) is one of the nation's oldest patients' advocacy groups. It welcomes donations, but will provide free information on your state's current laws on medical care forms and can provide current forms. Send a stamped, self-addressed envelope and $3.50, along with your request for information on your state's medical directive law, to:

Choice in Dying
200 Varick Street
New York, NY 10014-4810

• **Computer software.** The *WillMaker* software developed by Nolo Press enables you to prepare and update a medical care form valid in your state. (*WillMaker* also lets you prepare a regular legal will, and final arrangements such as body dona-tion, cremation or burial and funeral wishes.) The program comes with a manual providing necessary background information and leads you step-by-step through the process of preparing your form.

7. What to Do With Your Completed Documents

Once you have completed the documents directing your medical care, there are several steps you should take to make them valid and binding.

Signing, witnessing, notarizing. Every state law requires that you sign your documents—or direct another person to sign them for you—as a way of verifying that you understand them and that they contain your true wishes.

Most state laws also require that you sign your documents in the presence of witnesses. The purpose of this additional formality is so that at least one other person can attest that you appeared to be of sound mind when you made the documents.

In addition, some states also require that you and the witnesses appear before a notary public and swear that the circumstances of your signing, as described on the documents, are true. In some states, you have the option of having a notary sign your document instead of having it witnessed.

Making and distributing copies. Ideally, you should make an effort to make your wishes for your future health care widely known. Keep the original of your medical care document, and give copies to:

• any physician with whom you now consult regularly

• any attorney-in-fact or health care proxy you have named

• the office of the hospital or other care facility in which you are likely to receive treatment

• the patient representative of your HMO or insur-ance plan

• close relatives, particularly immediate family members—spouse, grown children, siblings

• trusted friends, and

- clergy or lawyer, particularly if you are in regular contact with a member of the clergy or lawyer but you do not have a family member who lives nearby.

KEEPING TRACK OF COPIES

Keep a signed copy of your medical directive in an easily accessible place at home—someplace you could easily describe to someone else if they had to retrieve it for you.

Also, keep a list of all the people and places that have copies of your medical directive. Then, if you change the terms of the directive, you will be able to retrieve each of the copies or have them destroyed.

---

8. Changing Your Mind—and Documents

You can change any type of medical care document as long as you remain of sound mind. Therefore, neither your decisions about health care nor about the proxy you name are final decisions. Anytime you wish to change the terms or proxy, however, you must prepare a new document and date, sign and have it witnessed and possibly notarized again—depending on the formalities that must be followed in your state. You should also make sure that all copies of the document you made earlier are destroyed.

Review your health care documents occasionally to make sure they still accurately reflect your wishes for your medical care. Advances in technology or changes in health care attitudes are two of the kinds of changes that may cause you to revise your view about the kind of medical care you want.

In addition, you should consider making new documents if:

- you move to another state, or
- you made and finalized a document, but did so many years ago, or
- the proxy or representative you named to supervise your wishes becomes unable to do so.

B. FINANCIAL MANAGEMENT DECISIONS

To arrange for someone to manage your property if you become incapacitated, you can use a durable power of attorney for finances. This document can provide you with the peace of mind that your money and property will be managed by a trusted person, in accordance with your wishes, without the need for a court-appointed guardian or conservator.

A durable power of attorney for finances can go into effect immediately on signing, or only if you become unable to manage your financial affairs. This latter type is called a "springing" durable power of attorney for finances. Every estate plan should include one.

Durable powers of attorney can be tailored to your specific financial situation, authorizing your attorney-in-fact to take care of financial matters ranging from buying holiday gifts and maintaining garden care, to paying bills, making bank deposits, handling insurance, Social Security and other paperwork—even selling a home or other property. You can also include provisions allowing your attorney-in-fact to make tax free gifts, currently $10,000 per year per person, to continue a tax-saving gift program you've initiated. Also, your attorney-in-fact can pay for needed pain relief, comfort care or other medical treatment which may not be fully covered by Medicare and health insurance.

The success of any power of attorney arrangement depends upon the trust and understanding between you and the person you appoint to handle your affairs as your attorney-in-fact. (You should also name an alternate attorney-in-fact.) You can help make this relationship work by putting specific instructions in the document regarding particular financial actions you do and do not wish the attorney-in-fact to take. Some people also appoint a second attorney-in-fact in the same power of attorney document, with a provision that both must agree to any transaction over a certain amount.

As with durable powers of attorney for health care, you can change the attorney-in-fact or other terms of the document at any time, as long as you are legally competent.

Powers of attorney and Medicare. If you're concerned about including provisions for (or trying to) protecting your assets from the reach of a nursing facility or from Medicare, see an attorney who specializes in asset preservation. Federal law makes it a crime to transfer assets within three years of applying for Medicare. So an expert attorney is a must here.

1. Durable Powers of Attorney for Finances and Living Trusts

Many living trusts provide that the successor trustee is to manage the trust property if the grantor becomes incapacitated. Even if you use a durable power of attorney to appoint someone (your attorney-in-fact) to handle your property if you become incapacitated, property in your living trust still remains subject to your successor trustee, not the attorney-in-fact. This division is typically only one of terminology, not substance, because most people appoint the same person to handle both jobs.

Some people who plan to transfer all of their property under a living trust ask why they need

bother with a durable power of attorney for finances at all. The reason is that you're likely to receive income, even if you become incapacitated, from pensions, Social Security and other sources, and you will need an attorney-in-fact of a financial durable power of attorney to deal with this money, and maintain your personal bank account, pay bills, etc.

C. GUARDIANSHIPS AND CONSERVATORSHIPS

If you are concerned about a person who is already incapacitated and unable to make decision, most of the advice in this chapter may not apply to you. At that point, the person can no longer enter into legal documents and arrangements or delegate responsibility for decisions to others. If the person made no durable powers of attorney or living trust, financial institutions, government agencies, health care providers and bureaucrats of every variety will either refuse to take action regarding the person's affairs—or will take actions without regard for your wishes or for what you know are the person's wishes.

In this situation, you'll probably have to go to court to ask a judge to appoint you or another friend or relative to act on the person's behalf. There are procedures in every state to do this. Some states have only one legal category, usually called guardianship; others have a second category, usually called conservatorship and often limited to financial matters.

In general guardianship proceedings, the legal question is whether or not a person has become "incompetent" to handle any of his or her own affairs. In about half the states, this requires that medical evidence of incompetence be presented to the court. In more limited proceedings to establish a financial conservatorship or guardianship only (see below), the court can act if it finds that the person is unable to handle financial affairs even though not completely legally incompetent.

In conservatorship or guardianship proceedings, a person has a right to appear in court with an attorney and to consent or object to all proposed authority. In many states, if the person does not have an attorney, the court may appoint one. Similarly, any change in the conservator or guardian's authority requires an additional court order to which the person can consent or object. The conservator or guardian is held responsible for mismanagement of the person's property.

In some states, it is possible to handle conservatorship proceedings without the assistance of a lawyer if no one challenges the need for the conservatorship and its scope. More complicated guardianship procedures, however, do require the assistance of a lawyer, particularly if the person alleged to be incompetent, or anyone else, does not agree that the guardianship is needed or that the person seeking to be guardian is not the right person for the job.

1. Financial Conservatorship or Guardianship

A conservator or guardian can be appointed by a court solely to protect a person's property—savings, real estate, investments and other assets. He or she can also conduct daily financial affairs, such as paying bills, or arrange for services when the person is unable to do so. This type of limited management assistance is appropriate when the person is still capable of caring for himself or herself personally, but because of disorientation or disability is unable to carry out financial matters coherently. In this situation, the conservator or guardian does not have power over the person's personal conduct, but has authority over financial or other affairs as the court orders.

An advantage of a limited conservatorship or guardianship is that it leaves the person free to make many important decisions independently: where to live, with whom to associate, what medical care to receive. Nonetheless, it is still a court process in which a judge makes a ruling, occasionally against the person's will, that gives another person authority over some parts of his or her life. It is therefore a procedure to be used only if voluntary procedures such as making a durable power of attorney are no longer possible.

2. Full Guardianship

Full guardianship is an extreme measure that severely restricts the legal rights of a person based on a court's finding of incompetence. It reduces that person's legal status to that of a minor, with no control over her or his own money or property, decisions about medical care or institutionalization. A person under full guardianship even loses the right to vote.

If a person retains some degree of orientation and capability, a legal finding by a court that he or she is incompetent can be emotionally devastating and, in fact, self-fulfilling. The person deemed legally incompetent may well give up the will to care for himself or herself and become much less competent than before. Obviously, seeking a full guardianship is a very serious step, to be taken when a person's mental condition leaves no other choice. ■

27

BODY AND ORGAN DONATION, FUNERALS AND BURIALS

A. Making Your Own Choices 27/2

B. Leaving Written Instructions 27/3

C. Donating Your Body or Organs 27/4

D. Death Notices 27/4

E. Services and Ceremonies Following a Death 27/5

F. Funerals 27/6

        1. Commercial Funerals 27/6

        2. Funeral Societies 27/8

G. Cremation 27/8

H. Burials 27/9

People facing the grief and reality that someone they love has died face other immediate problems: disposing of the body and arranging the ceremonies desired to mark the death. It's hard to even talk directly about a body once life has left it; the word "corpse" sounds unfeeling, and "cadaver" is worse. Statutes often refer to a dead body as "the remains," a word technically accurate and almost as disturbing. Perhaps it's because many of us don't like to contemplate death that the language we have invented for it can be awkward. But, however it is described, the reality is the same: a body must, somehow, be removed from the place of death and disposed of, rapidly. And if desired, commemorative ceremonies need to be carried out.

Most people die in hospitals or nursing homes. These institutions want a dead body removed quickly. So it's nearly inevitable, if no planning has been done, for family or friends to turn to "professionals"—funeral homes. Often they do it without reflection or much knowledge of what the traditional funeral establishment offers or what it charges for its services. This passive approach often means family and friends pay far too much for a funeral they don't even like—and worst of all, for funeral goods and services that don't suit the person who has died.

Grief, guilt, sorrow, religious conviction, doubt, or whatever survivors are feeling often leave them distraught and confused. In these circumstances, expenses can seem trivial. However, we believe it's no slight to the deceased, or to the feelings of those who survive, to suggest that nothing is gained by needless costs. Funerals can be expensive. A funeral trade journal has estimated the average cost of a conventional U.S. funeral at about $7,000. It's one of the most expensive items the average American family ever purchases. To many, including these authors, this is a huge and unnecessary cost to comply with the biblical injunction: "Remember, man, thou art dust and to dust thou shall return."

A. MAKING YOUR OWN CHOICES

More and more people are reflecting on what they want to happen to their bodies when they die, and making choices that have emotional meaning for them and save their families needless expense.

Broadly viewed, there are four choices available (we don't cover some of the more esoteric options, such as cryonics/body freezing):

1. Donating the entire body to a medical school. This must be arranged beforehand. If this is done, the body is used for studies and then, usually, cremated, and the remains buried or scattered. However, family members or friends can request that the body be returned when the study is complete—usually within a year or so. Even if a person opts for whole body donation, that donation may be refused at death for any of a number of reasons, requiring survivors to make other plans.

2. Specific body organs can also be donated to an organ bank. If organs are donated, the rest of the body is normally returned to those responsible for cremation or burial, which means that you still must arrange for its disposal.

3. A traditional funeral service conducted by a commercial funeral home, with cremation or body burial.

4. A simple funeral service, without embalming of the body, either with the help of a funeral or memorial society or by independent arrangement.

How to arrange for funeral/burial problems yourself, with organizational help, is discussed in Nolo's *WillMaker*, and also in *Caring For Your Own Dead,* by Lisa Carlson (Upper Access Books).

Planning for the immediate, practical aspects of your death is essential to make sure your wishes are carried out. To take one example, if you wish to donate body parts or organs, it's almost essential to authorize it, in writing, before your death. Similarly, if you want a non-traditional funeral, such as cremation with your ashes scattered over the sea, it may not happen unless you arrange the details yourself. (Each state has rules governing how and where ashes may be scattered.) Even for a traditional commercial funeral, planning is desirable. Costs for death goods and services vary widely—for example, caskets are commonly marked up from five to ten times their wholesale costs. So comparison shopping can often result in big savings.

In our view, there's really no sensible reason to plan how to save money on probate fees or estate taxes and then toss a chunk of it away on an over-priced funeral. Equally important, there's no reason to dread thinking about what kind of death notice and ceremonial service will be fitting, if you want them. Once you've decided what is appropriate, you need to convey your intention to others, preferably in a written declaration. This kind of planning can achieve much more than saving money. It provides survivors with essential guidance, and offers you peace of mind that you've made arrangements to your liking.

B. LEAVING WRITTEN INSTRUCTIONS

Whatever decisions you make regarding the disposition of your body should be put in writing. Under most states' laws, written burial instructions left by a deceased person are binding, assuming, of course, the instructions don't violate state laws on body disposition. Even where laws do not specifically require that a deceased person's instructions be followed, they almost always are. You can also assure that your wishes are followed by joining a local funeral or memorial society. (See Section F2, below.)

Written instructions are sometimes included in a will. But relying on this exclusively is not the best choice, because it may take time to locate and read a will—and dead bodies are most often disposed of quickly. A better approach is to prepare your instructions in a separate document, and to also include them in your will.

Keep the instructions in a safe and readily accessible place, known to whomever will have the responsibility for implementing them. Or simpler yet, give a copy to the person you've chosen to be responsible for carrying out your desires. If you've joined a funeral society or chosen a mortuary make sure it has a copy of your wishes.

If you don't leave legally binding written instructions, your next of kin (the closest family relation) will have legal control over the disposition of your body. This can pose insoluble problems if a friend or lover knows you wanted a specific type of disposition that the next of kin opposes. Without legally binding written instructions, the friend or lover is powerless to prevent the next of kin from controlling the disposition.

ABOUT DEATH CERTIFICATES

Whenever a person dies, a physician must complete a death certificate shortly after the death and file it with the appropriate governmental agency, often a local registrar of health. Certified copies of the death certificate will be needed to transfer certain types of property to those legally entitled to them. For example, to collect money from a pay-on-death bank account or to end a joint tenancy of real estate, the inheritors need a certified copy of the death certificate. To wind up a probate avoidance living trust, the successor trustee will often need several copies of the death certificate.

C. DONATING YOUR BODY OR ORGANS

If you want to leave your body, or parts of it, for medical research or instruction, you have two choices:

1. You can leave your entire body to medical science, usually a medical school, or

2. You can donate certain body organs or tissues to transplant facilities.

You cannot do both. Medical schools generally won't accept a body from which any part has been removed, except sometimes for eye transplants.

The procedure for donating a body to a medical school is simple. Contact the school, see if it accepts bodies for instruction and study, and if so, what legalities and forms it requires. Medical facilities are legally prohibited from paying for bodies, but many will absorb the cost of transporting a body—at least within certain distance of the institution.

Many, but not all, medical schools won't accept bodies that are too old or too diseased, or if death occurred during surgery. So it's important to have a back-up plan if you're thinking about body donation. You can call the National Anatomical Service at 718-948-2401 or 314-726-4079 to find out more about body donation in your locale.

The other option, donating body organs, is also a generous and useful act. There is a great need for many types of organ donations. Heart transplants get the most publicity, but many more organs, tissues and bones can and are being transplanted, including middle ear, eyes, liver, lungs, pancreas, kidneys, skin tissue, bone and cartilage, pituitary glands, and even hip or knee joints. A gift of a vital organ is one of the most precious and loving acts one can make. We know this well, as we have a friend who was saved from blindness by a cornea transplant.

Every state has adopted the Uniform Anatomical Gift Act. Under this act, any mentally competent adult can promise to make after-death organ dona-tions. To authorize this, you have to sign the proper forms. In some states you can do this as part of renewing your driver's license, or simply obtain the form from your local Department of Motor Vehicles. Your doctor and local hospital should be aware of what is required in your state. Also, a person's family can agree to organ donations if the person is brain dead, but body organs have been kept alive by a life support system.

Time is truly of the essence for the successful removal of donated body parts, so if you want to have organs removed on death you should make arrangements beforehand, and discuss your intentions with family and friends. Most people put off making these arrangements, no matter how intensely they may want to donate their organs. With donation of body parts, procrastination may result in your intentions being frustrated because they cannot legally be carried out fast enough.

D. DEATH NOTICES

When someone dies, one of the first things that most families do is notify others. For close friends and relatives, phone calls normally work. But what about notifying the many other people whose lives have been touched by the deceased, such as former neighbors, golf partners, sailing or bowling friends, retired business associates and other friends? Doing this promptly is important, as many of these people will wish to attend one or more of the events which usually occur very soon after death, such as a wake, lying-in, funeral or memorial ceremony. And other people will wish to communicate with the family and extend their sympathy.

In many communities, notification is handled by a local newspaper, with either a death notice or an obituary.

Death notices generally must be paid for, and consist of small print listings of the date of death, names of survivors, and location of any services.

An obituary is a news item, usually prepared by the staff of the newspaper. It runs in standard type, contains a small headline (for example, "Former Local School Principal Dies") and is free. In small towns, many local newspapers prepare obituaries for a large percentage of people who die, giving more space to those who were locally prominent. In large metropolitan papers, however, very few people's deaths are sufficiently newsworthy to qualify for obituaries, and even fairly prominent people have their deaths recorded in the paid death notices, if at all.

Death notice information must be submitted to newspapers promptly. This can raise a real problem for survivors. Just when they are beset by difficult emotions and serious practical problems, someone has to call in to the newspaper office with details of the dead person's life and survivors. Newspapers are commonly very understanding and provide a lot of help, but it still can be difficult. Common problems involve remembering or locating dates, parents' full names, details of key events, correct spellings for clubs and other affiliations, to mention just a few.

One solution to this problem is to prepare your own death notice. This might sound a bit macabre, but it will probably only take you a little while, and those who are later spared the task will surely be appreciative. Just look at the appropriate newspaper, follow the general form it uses and write one out.

What about an obituary? At least for many local newspapers, you can help write the news story about your death in advance. The paper will have a form on which you can list all relevant biographical information, including your education and employment history, civic responsibilities, names of children, and so on. If this form is filled out in advance, it can be given to the paper immediately after death, and will be used to write the news story. In addition to completing this form, however, you may want to actually try your hand at writing your own obituary, leaving blank your date of death. Does this sound weird? Well, yes, a little, but remember, if you don't do it, someone you love may have to deal with a reporter precisely when there will be far more pressing practical and emotional concerns occasioned by your death. To get an idea of what an obituary should look like, read a few in your local paper. In our experience, if a family submits a well-written, factual obituary immediately after a person's death, a local newspaper is likely to use a good part of it, or at least echo its major themes.

E. SERVICES AND CEREMONIES FOLLOWING A DEATH

Many people wish to have input about the ceremonies held after their deaths. You may have a favorite church, synagogue or temple where you would like the service held, or a particular priest, pastor, rabbi or monk to conduct it. You may know how you want the service to be conducted. Of course, in many religious and spiritual communities, the broad outlines of rituals that accompany a death are well-established. Usually, however, when it comes to the particular prayers to be read and songs to be sung, there's room for personal choice. If the service won't be held by a religious institution, individual input becomes more urgent. It's sad to attend, as both of us have, funerals of good friends held in a commercial funeral homes where not one personal word was said.

If you have specific ideas about ceremonies you want held after your death, the best way to make sure your wishes will be carried out is to put them in writing. Simply include a brief statement as part of your final instructions. (See Section B, above.)

F. FUNERALS

For funerals, you have two basic options: use a commercial funeral home or make arrangements in advance through a non-profit funeral or memorial society.

1. Commercial Funerals

The traditional American funeral, as provided by a commercial funeral home or mortuary, normally includes the following:

- The funeral director takes care of the paperwork required for death and burial certificates.

- The funeral home removes the body from the place of death and embalms it.

- The embalmed body is shown at an open casket ceremony, or there is a closed casket. Many funeral parlors have their own chapels and encourage all services to be held there, rather than in churches.

Funerals are always products of culture. Our own culture, which has long studiously avoided contemplating death, is also made nervous by trying to decide what type of funeral is appropriate. In some ages, expensive funerals and burials were scorned as ostentatious, wasteful, and the norm was a simple, dignified and inexpensive service. In other times, as in 17th century England, expensive funerals and grand tombs were in vogue for those with status and wealth.

There is no one American cultural tradition concerning funerals and burials. Most Americans do hold ceremonies when a person dies, of course, and many ethnic and religious traditions are deeply ingrained, such as the Jewish custom of burial within 24 hours or the Irish wake. But, generally speaking, for those not close to their ethnic roots, there's still a significant cultural vacuum. As should come as no surprise, that vacuum was filled by business.

Before the Civil War, burials in America were most often simple affairs—a religious ceremony, a plain pine box, and quick burial. Undertakers did not exist until roughly the 1860s; originally they practiced some other trade, often carpentry. During the Civil War, bodies of dead soldiers were embalmed so they could be shipped home for burial. Next, undertakers emerged as a distinct trade; they later evolved into funeral directors and began to proclaim themselves professionals. The plain pine box was transformed into a luxurious coffin. Funerals became theater, and their cost rose accordingly. Embalming the dead body and showing the embalmed remains became standard funeral parlor practice—a practice which obviously adds substantially to the cost of burial, and one not used (and indeed regarded as barbaric) in most other countries. The funeral industry also developed a rationalization for embalming. It claimed that viewing the embalmed body is useful for the living, because seeing a lifelike body enables the viewers to cope with their grief. The term they invented for this is "grief therapy." Some funeral homes also offer "after care" help to a widow or widower, sometimes including support groups and professional therapists.

As many people sense, there's something odd, as well as expensive, about traditional American funerals. This shift in attitude was originally sparked by Jessica Mitford's book *The American Way of Death* (Simon & Schuster), a pioneering examination of commercial American culture in one of its more rapacious and grotesque areas. Written with wit and grace, Mitford's book (now over three decades old, but still influential) raised many questions about American funeral customs. As a result of her book and the efforts of many others, many beneficial legal changes have occurred.

Legal reform has aided the growth of funeral and memorial societies, which, in turn, have introduced real price competition into the commercial funeral business. Now some commercial funeral homes have begun to advertise less expensive funerals. So, if you do want to patronize a traditional funeral parlor, shop around for the best prices on costs and services. Mortuaries are legally required to give those who ask a detailed price list of their goods and services.

a. Embalming

One great expense of a traditional funeral is embalming the body. Generally, state law doesn't require embalming unless the body will be transported by common carrier, such as a commercial plane, or county health officials order embalming as a protection against the spread of contagious disease (a very rare event). There are those who claim that embalming is a necessary health measure, but there's little evidence to support this. If a body must be preserved for a short time, refrigeration is at least as reliable, and far cheaper.

In embalming, preservative and disinfectant fluid is injected into the arterial system and body cavities, replacing blood. Embalmed bodies aren't preserved for eternity, though medical science can do this for exceptional reasons (keeping Lenin's body on display, for example). Generally, an embalmed body begins to decompose rapidly within a few weeks.

By embalming the body, a funeral parlor can preserve it sufficiently to allow open-casket viewing of the body at a funeral service, a popular practice with some Americans. How one feels about this is, of course, a private matter. The important point is to realize that open-casket viewing—and embalming—are far from inevitable practices. The choice is up to survivors or to you, if you make plans for your own burial.

b. Costs

The major factor in the total cost of a funeral—and the item most grossly marked up—is the price of the casket. Not surprisingly, funeral directors generally urge as expensive a casket as possible. Anyone who's ever been casket shopping can tell you it's a bit like visiting a car dealership. There's always a larger, fancier model available, with more expensive options. The question all too often becomes not how much a casket costs, but how much you are willing to pay. In most facilities, rental caskets are available for a slight charge, for those who wish to be cremated or who choose not to purchase a casket.

The cost of a traditional funeral can easily add up to many thousands of dollars. In addition to the casket, there's normally a charge for each extra, and there are a lot of possible extras, including flowers, special burial clothing, additional limousines, clergyman's honorarium, music and cards. Also, watch out for fraudulently tacked-on fees, such as "handling" charges or AIDS body handling costs.

Flowers have become traditional at American funerals. A significant percentage of all flowers sold by commercial florists in America are sold for funerals. Not surprisingly, the florist industry resists any attempt to cut back on the practice of sending flowers to funerals. Some people prefer that money which would have been spent on flowers be given to a particular charity. Sometimes funeral notices or announcements state "Please Omit Flowers." Whether flowers are a beautiful and moving statement or an unnecessary expense is a choice each person can make; again, the point is to realize that there's a choice.

Finally, transporting a body from a distant place of death, or to a distant burial place, is particularly expensive. If you must arrange for the return of a body from a distant place of death, consult a customer service representative of the airlines to make sure you get the most affordable rates.

2. Funeral Societies

Funeral societies are private, nonprofit organizations, open to any who wishes to join. They are devoted to the concept of simple, dignified burial services for a reasonable cost. There's usually a small fee for joining. Members are entitled to the burial programs offered through the society. Funeral societies don't generally employ their own morticians, or own their own cemeteries; rather, they have contracts of varying types with cooperating local mortuaries and crematoriums. The societies make a price list of goods and services available, and members choose the mortuary and service they would like. After a death, the society ensures that only the services selected are performed and billed for.

Specific policies, funeral costs and options vary somewhat from organization to organization, but the basics are common to all. Dignified, simple funerals can be arranged for hundreds of dollars, not thousands. Members are concerned not only with reducing the excessive costs, but at least equally with what they believe are the excesses and lack of spiritual values inherent in many commercial funerals. As the literature of the funeral societies notes, in the traditional funeral the emphasis is on the dead body—lying in an open casket, embalmed, often painted, rouged, or otherwise altered cosmetically in the belief that the embalmer's skills will make a more lifelike body, and that viewing a lifelike dead body is a sign of respect or affection.

Funeral societies want new members and readily provide information on their programs, services and membership rules, as well as the names of all cooperating mortuaries. If you move, there's a good chance you can transfer your membership to another society; there are funeral societies in most urban areas of the United States.

There are hundreds of funeral societies throughout the U.S. To locate one near you, check the phone book or contact:

Funeral and Memorial Societies of America
800-458-5563

G. Cremation

Cremation means the burning of the body. Cremation is common in many parts of the world and is now used for roughly half the deaths in the U.S. It's opposed by certain religions, such as Muslims, and Greek and Jewish Orthodox creeds. Catholics are supposed to receive the permission of their local bishop to be cremated, but the Catholic Church no longer bans cremation outright.

Be careful if you make a direct arrangement with a profit-making cremation organization. Some have been known to rip off customers, charging for "handling," "transportation" or "disposal" fees. Regular fees commonly are $900 or more for a "basic" cremation, plus possible additional charges of $350 to $700 for scattering the ashes, and $1,500 to $20,000 for urn placement, putting the ashes in an (attractive) container.

Despite the risk of excessive costs, many people have been able to arrange for sensibly priced cremations. By law in many states, a crematory cannot require that a casket (rather than a bag) be used in cremation. This makes sense, as it seems particularly needless to pay for an expensive wood casket that is almost immediately burned. Cheaper wood caskets are often used, by custom, if no contrary directions are given.

Whether and how ashes can be scattered depends on state law. Scatterings were rare a few generations ago, but there has been a marked increase in their number as the number of cremations has grown. Cremated remains can be removed from the place of cremation or inurnment and disposed of by scattering by the person with the legal right to control the remains. Once again, leaving specific instructions regarding your wishes is a sound idea. A permit is usually required for scattering, whether at sea or over private land. The crematory or mortuary involved should be able to handle the paperwork.

H. Burials

A body must be disposed of in a lawful way. Unless it's cremated and the ashes scattered or kept in an urn or in a licensed columbarium (a building in which urns and ashes may be kept) it must be buried somewhere. Often this means the remains must be buried in a cemetery (graveyard, if you prefer the more descriptive word).

In this country, there's a wide variety of types of cemetery, including profit-making ones, large mutually owned ones, church burial grounds, small co-ops, municipal ones, and national cemeteries, in which most veterans and their spouses are entitled to free burial.

Most American cemeteries, however, are private businesses. You have to buy your way in. Private cemeteries are normally separate businesses from funeral homes, although they often have working relationships with one another. Sometimes, though, they compete, and some cemeteries sell caskets. Usually, the fact that private cemeteries are separate means only that there's one more transaction to arrange—buying a burial plot. This purchase can often be arranged through a funeral society or a funeral home. If there's a specific cemetery you desire, you should be sure the funeral home or society can arrange for that particular purchase. Also, you might save money if you select your own cemetery, as prices can vary significantly.

Probably the best known private graveyard in the world is Forest Lawn Cemetery in Los Angeles. Evelyn Waugh's justly famous satire of Forest Lawn, *The Loved One,* hasn't diminished the success of this cemetery. Many people still choose (or their relatives choose) to be buried in its "splendor." Depending on how much splendor is desired, this can be quite expensive indeed.

Cemetery costs, like everything else, are going up. The minimum cost includes:

- the plot
- the coffin enclosure, which normally consists of a vault or grave liner of concrete and steel. Cemetery owners sometimes say vaults are required to prevent the land bordering the grave from eventually collapsing. Although this danger is often nonexistent or exaggerated, yearly vault sales have recently been estimated to amount to nearly one-half billion dollars. Many vaults are bought

through a funeral director, although they are usually cheaper if bought from a cemetery.

- opening and closing the grave

- upkeep.

Many cemeteries sell "perpetual care," which they claim means that the grave will be attended "for eternity." This sounds pretty grandiose until you realize that as graves don't require much care—what this really means is that the grass will be cut. And even this task doesn't amount to much in many modern urban cemeteries, which have eliminated the use of headstones, substituting plaques that are planted flush to the ground, so as not to interfere with the power mower.

If you haven't got enough to worry about, you could worry about what will happen when we run out of cemetery land. It'll take a while, surely, although one expert suggests that in only 500 years, at the present rate of graveyard growth, all the land in the United States would be graveyards.

Finally, if there's to be a headstone or plaque, why not create your own epitaph? It's your last opportunity for self-expression.

Among our favorite epitaphs are:

Cast a cold eye, on life, on death. Horseman, pass by!

—Yeats

and the classic:

On the whole, I'd rather be in Philadelphia.

—W.C. Fields ■

28

FAMILY BUSINESS ESTATE PLANNING

A. Operation of the Business 28/2

    1. Keeping Ownership in the Family 28/2

    2. Treating Family Members Fairly 28/3

    3. Sales to Outsiders 28/4

B. Reducing Estate Taxes 28/5

    1. New Estate Tax Breaks for Family Businesses 28/5

    2. Special Rules for Valuing Business Real Estate 28/6

    3. Deferring Estate Tax Payments 28/6

    4. Gifts of Minority Interests in the Business 28/7

    5. Gifts of Stock Options 28/8

    6. Family Business Estate Tax Freezes 28/9

C. Avoiding Probate of a Family Business 28/9

    1. Individual Ownership 28/10

    2. Shared Ownership Businesses 28/10

If you own an interest in a small business, whether you're a sole proprietor, a partner in a partnership, or a shareholder in a closely held corporation or limited liability company, estate planning can get complicated fast. If a substantial part of your estate is a profit-making business of significant value, you'll need to look into three broad areas:

- operation of the business after your death

- estate tax concerns, and

- probate avoidance.

FORMING A BUSINESS TO SAVE ON TAXES

Even if you're not now a small business owner, you may wonder if you should create one to take advantage of special tax breaks applicable to family businesses. Would, say, a "family limited partnership" save your inheritors money? Be careful here. First, of course, your estate must be large enough so that estate tax will likely be paid on your death. Second, simply labeling assets a "family business" does make them so in the eyes of the IRS. A family limited partnership must have a valid business purpose. It cannot be a shell created solely to reduce or avoid estate taxes. However, in the right circumstances, establishing a family business that passes IRS muster can definitely offer estate tax savings.

Specialized legal work. Estate planning for the small business owner requires the assistance of an attorney experienced in the field. Here we can only give you a broad-brush introduction to the major concerns.

A. OPERATION OF THE BUSINESS

The death of the sole or part owner of a small business is likely to seriously disrupt that business. If no planning has been done, the disruption can be catastrophic, sometimes resulting in the failure of the business. You need to have a sound succession plan. Who will take over the business? Will family members run it? (Roughly 80% of all U.S. business are family owned, and the second generation takes over about 30% of these businesses.) If someone else will run the business, how will family members or other inheritors be paid for your interest?

1. Keeping Ownership in the Family

Obviously, to keep business ownership in the family, one or more family members must be willing and able to run the business. If they are, and you're the sole owner of your business, your main concerns are probably about dealing fairly with all your close family members. (See Section 2, below.)

But if you share ownership of a business, you must consider the rights of the other owners, even if there are capable family members who want to inherit your share. Commonly, a partnership agreement, corporate bylaws or a shareholders' agreement, or the operating agreement of a limited liability company (LLC) controls the disposition of a deceased owner's interest in the business. You need to create a business estate plan that is in harmony with the documents that restrict your options.

Agreements between owners of a shared ownership business normally cover the right of the surviving owners to buy the deceased owner's interest. One standard provision gives the surviving owners a "right of first refusal," allowing them to buy the interest for the price offered by an outside would-be purchaser. If there is no outside offer, another provision may provide a method for determining the value of the deceased owner's interest in the business. A related issue here is whether the surviving owners must buy out the deceased owners' share, or simply have the option to do so.

The agreement should also state how buy-out payments will be made. Often the agreement allows the surviving owners to pay for a deceased owner's share over months or years. Particularly if the business is a corporation, determining the most desirable pay-out process can involve sophisticated tax planning.

Arranging to buy out a deceased owner's share necessarily involves practical financial problems. Will the business really have the money to make the payments? What happens if it doesn't? If the surviving owners aren't required to buy out a deceased owner's share, what happens if they decide not to? The inheritors can try to sell that share, but, if it's a minority share they may not find an outside buyer. Then what?

In the absence of an owners' agreement, the rights of the surviving owners are determined by the laws of the state where the business is located. It is not sensible to rely on these laws, since they are highly unlikely to fit your or your family's needs. Much better to work out an agreement beforehand.

For information on how to draft a business agreement to cover sale and valuation issues, see these Nolo Press books:

The Partnership Book, by Denis Clifford and Ralph Warner

Form Your Own Limited Liability Company, by Anthony Mancuso

How to Form Your Own Corporation (California, New York, Texas or Florida edition), by Anthony Mancuso.

2. Treating Family Members Fairly

If you have more than one child, and some will run the business and some won't, you may have to resolve some difficult fairness issues. Do you want to leave all your children roughly the same amount? If so, how can you leave the business and your other assets, so that all your children are treated equally? If you don't want to leave equal shares, do you want to explain your decision to your children, in your estate planning documents or elsewhere? There certainly aren't any rules here; you have to figure out what works best for you and your family.

Example: Dante and Grace own a thriving construction business. This corporation is roughly 80% of their net worth. They have five children. After Dante and Grace die, two of the children, Steve and Patricia, will take over the business. The other three aren't interested in working in it. How can Dante and Grace achieve their goal of leaving each of their children an inheritance of roughly the same value?

One possibility is to leave the business to Steve and Patricia, and divide the remaining 20% of the estate among the other three children. The difference would be made up by the proceeds of life insurance. But the cost of life insurance turns out to be prohibitive. So Dante and Grace consider leaving the business (and the rest of their estate) equally to all five children. Only Steve and Patricia will have any voting or management powers in the business. Of course, this leaves the other three children without control over the bulk of their inheritance. Also, what if Steve and Patricia can't agree about management decisions? They've had some nasty fights in the past.

Dante and Grace strongly believe it's in all the children's best interests to keep the business going. The best hope for this is to have Steve and Patricia run it. So Dante and Grace decide to leave equal shares to all five, with only Steve and Patricia having management powers in the business. The other children will share equally in all profits from the business, including if it is sold.

Dante and Grace amend the corporation by-laws to require that if Steve and Patricia have a dispute they can't resolve themselves, they must try mediation and, if that fails, compulsory arbitration. Dante and Grace aren't thrilled with their plan, but feel it's the best they can do. They will talk with each child to explain why they've made their decision, and how they'd like the business to work.

All sorts of worries can come up when planning for a family business and more than one child. We've had people ask us what will happen if one of their children gets divorced. Others worry because their children don't get along, but each wants to run the business. All we can say is (yet another) truism—do the best you can. And remember, once you're gone, your estate planning can, at best, impose limited control over what happens to your family business. You need faith that the children you selected to manage your business will do a good and fair job. You can't control all the "what ifs."

3. Sales to Outsiders

What happens if no family member wants to carry on your business? Or there's no one you believe is capable of running it? If it's a sole proprietorship, it must be sold. If it's a shared ownership business but no co-owners are willing or able to buy your share, your inheritors would likely seek to find an outside buyer for their interest. In any case, how can you try to maximize your children's inheritance?

It's rarely desirable to simply close down or sell a business immediately on the death of its owner, unless it's a one-person service business. Even if your beneficiaries do not want to participate in running the business over the long term, you'll want them to have some flexibility in the timing of the sale—which means the business must be capable of continuing in a profitable fashion for a while. One way to achieve at least short-term continuity is for key employees, the owner and the future owners to agree in writing that these employees will stay around and continue to run the business for a period of time after the owner's death, perhaps in exchange for some portion of the eventual sale proceeds. Another way to accomplish this is to incorporate the business and make the key employees officers of the corporation and minority stockholders, perhaps through a stock option plan. Of course the officers can still quit at any time, but they are less likely to do so if they have an ownership interest in the business.

B. REDUCING ESTATE TAXES

Family business owners dread estate taxes. Will these taxes eat up the business? Will it have to be sold to raise cash to pay the estate taxes? What can be done to lower them? Happily, there are a number of legal methods owners can use to reduce or avoid estate taxes on a family business.

1. New Estate Tax Breaks for Family Businesses

Under the 1997 Taxpayer Relief Act, a family business (including farm businesses) worth up to $1.3 million can be transferred free of estate tax. This $1.3 million exemption is a combination of the personal estate tax exemption in the year of death and an additional family business tax exemption, as shown below. It became effective for people dying in 1998 or after.

SPECIAL $1.3 MILLION ESTATE TAX EXEMPTION FOR FAMILY BUSINESSES

Year	Personal Exemption	Additional Family Business Exemption
1998	$625,000	$675,000
1999	$650,000	$650,000
2000–2001	$675,000	$625,000
2002–2003	$700,000	$600,000
2004	$850,000	$450,000
2005	$950,000	$350,000
2006 and after	$1,000,000	$300,000

The family business exemption statute contains a number of requirements designed to ensure that it is not abused (IRC Section 2033A). IRS regulations that interpret this statute are sure to follow. Indeed, there are so many requirements to qualify for this exemption that it's unclear how useful it will be for many family businesses, let alone be abused (not, of course, that there won't be some clever folks trying). Here are the major requirements:

- **Ownership.** 50% of the business must be owned by one family, or 70% by two or 90% by three. If there's more than one family owner, the family seeking the business exemption must own 30% of the business.

- **Business Value.** The business's worth must exceed 50% of the value of the gross estate. (The value of business is reduced to the extent it holds passive assets or excess cash or marketable securities. Thus if 25% of the business value consists of stocks sold on the New York Stock Exchange, only 75% of the value can be used to determine if the business is more than half of the estate.)

- **Participation in Business.** The deceased or members of the deceased's family must have owned and materially participated in the business for at least five of eight years preceding the death.

- **No Public Trading.** The business cannot have been publicly traded within the past three years. This means that no business that's listed on a recognized stock exchange is eligible for this exemption.

- **Qualified Inheritors.** The special tax treatment is available only if the business is inherited by family members, or by employees who have worked for the business for at least ten years before the deceased's death.

- **Family Member.** Defined as the deceased's spouse, ancestors, lineal descendants, and lineal descendants of the spouse or the deceased's parents and spouses of any lineal descendants.

- **Participation by Qualified Inheritor.** A qualified inheritor must materially participate in the business for at least five out of any eight-year period during the ten years following the deceased's death.

- **Disposal of Interest.** If an inheritor disposes of his or her interest in the business, or ceases to materially participate in it, the estate tax that would have been due at the deceased's death but for the special business exemption must be paid to the IRS. This is called "recapture" of the tax. If the tax is recaptured in the first six years, the whole tax break must be repaid. In years seven through ten, a sliding scale applies. The sale of inventory or equipment, such as crops or vehicles, is not a disposal of an interest in the business.

If a business meets all these requirements, there can be no doubt it's genuinely a multi-generational family enterprise. Estate tax laws that encourage keeping a business in the family seem eminently sensible.

2. Special Rules for Valuing Business Real Estate

Real estate used in a family trade or business or as a family farm can be valued for estate tax purposes at its value for the present use, rather than at its "highest and best" use. For example, a family farm doesn't have to be valued for its (possibly much higher) worth as a potential location for a shopping center or subdivision, but can be valued on the basis of its worth as a farm. This valuation rule can provide a real break for family businesses. The value of the real estate can be reduced up to a maximum of $750,000 of the difference between "present use" and "best use." The $750,000 figure will be indexed to changes in the cost of living, beginning in 1999.

Several requirements must be met for the rule to apply:

- The value of the family business or farm must be at least 50% of the overall estate.
- The value of the real estate of that business must be at least 25% of the overall estate.
- The owner must leave the family business to a family member.
- The deceased or a family member must have used the real estate for the business in five of the eight years preceding the decedent's death.
- There are restrictions on the sale and use of the real estate for ten years (and in some cases 15 years) after the estate tax break. During this time, the family must agree to notify the IRS if the property is sold or no longer used for the business and may be required to repay some or all of the estate taxes if the ownership or use of the real estate changes.

3. Deferring Estate Tax Payments

If a family business, including a family farm, is part of a taxable estate, estate taxes due can be paid over a period of years, rather than within the nine months of the owner's death, as otherwise required. Do remember that if the estate qualifies for the family business/farm estate tax exemption, the estate must be worth over $1.3 million to be subject to tax.

The basic rule is that estate taxes assessed against the value of a small business or family farm can be deferred five years and then paid in ten annual installments. In other words, the final payment isn't due until 15 years after the owner's death. The principal Internal Revenue Code restriction here is that the value of the small business must exceed 35% of the total estate or 50% of the taxable estate.

Example: Andrew dies in 1999 owning Shortstop Shipping which has a net worth of $2.6 million. The total net value of his estate is $3.8 million. Under the combined family business and personal estate tax exemptions, $1.3 million can pass free from estate tax. The remaining $2.5 million is taxable. The taxes due are postponed for five years, then paid off over the next ten.

Significant income tax savings are permitted for corporate stock redeemed to pay estate taxes assessed against family businesses or farms.

4. Gifts of Minority Interests in the Business

Family business owners who may face estate tax can reduce or eliminate it by giving away minority interests in the business before death. Gifts are usually made to children or grandchildren.

The value of a minority interest in a business is reduced for gift tax purposes: whatever the interest would be worth if it were part of majority control of the business, that interest is worth significantly less as minority ownership. This is called a "valuation discount."

Two separate discounts are involved. The first is based on the fact that minority owners do not have voting control over the business. Minority owners cannot manage the business or compel its sale or liquidation, or distribution of money to owners. So outside buyers will not pay the same price for minority interests as for majority ones. This is called a "discount for minority interest." The second discount is allowed if the basic small business agreement (partnership agreement, corporate bylaws, etc.) restricts the sale of interests to family members or other narrow group, as many family businesses do. The interest cannot simply be sold to any willing buyer. This is called a "discount for lack of marketability."

The two combined discounts can range from 20% to 60%. There are no statutory rules or IRS regulations governing how valuation discounts are determined. So calculating them is not easy. This is an area where owners may benefit from "aggressive" accounting. But even without skirting the edge of legality, substantial discounts are reasonable, and significant estate tax savings can be achieved.

Example: McWilson is the sole owner of the DaaDee Corp., which has 50,000 shares of stock. By the best estimate of McWilson and his accountants, if all shares were sold, they would sell for $2 million. So, at first glance, each share seems to be worth $40. But if the shares are split between minority and majority share holders, the valuation differs. McWilson takes a 25% valuation discount for the minority shares. Each minority share is valued at $30.

In 1999, McWilson gives 10,000 shares to each of his two daughters. (In his living trust, he leaves the remaining stock to them equally.) For gift tax purposes, the minority shares are valued at $30. Realistically, each share transfers $40 worth of assets; after all, each daughter will eventually own 50% of the business, and there won't be any distinction then between majority and minority shares.

If the value of a discounted share of a family business that's given away exceeds the annual gift tax exempt amount (currently $10,000), a gift tax return must be filed. The gift tax return, IRS Form 709, now contains the question "Does the value of an item given reflect...a valuation discount?" If so, the giver must provide an explanation of the factual basis for the discounts and the amount of discount taken.

<table>
<tr><td>

PHONY BUSINESSES DON'T FOOL THE IRS

Gifts of discounted interests in a family business work only if the business is legitimate. The family enterprise must serve a real business purpose. Some wealthy folks have created family limited partnerships for their vacation homes, investment portfolios or other investments. The IRS has refused to accept valuation discounts with these kinds of alleged businesses. Currently the IRS is aggressively litigating a series of cases, claiming the family businesses are shams.

The lawsuits now in progress between the IRS and various inventive givers (and their sly estate tax advisers) should resolve the limits of a valid family business, for gift discount purposes. Some extremes are already clear. A family "business" created a few days before death, for the sole purpose of reducing estate taxes by giving away discounted minority interests, is not a valid business. Also, the enterprise must be run as an independent business. The primary owner must keep separate business records and can't mix up cash from the business with personal accounts.

With a family limited partnership, the limited partners (the children or grandchildren who receive minority interests) do not have to be actively involved in the business. But again, the basic rule is that the business itself must be real and legitimate. Some very pricey lawyers are busy right now trying to turn "real" and "legitimate" into "anything goes." It's not likely to be in your or your family's interests to be on the cutting edge of this fight.

</td></tr>
</table>

5. Gifts of Stock Options

This tax-reduction ploy is useful only for some of the financial elite, top corporate executives who receive stock options as part of their compensation. A stock option is the right to buy a certain amount stock for a set price in the future.

> **Example:** C. Hardriver receives the right to buy 2,500 shares of stock in Workamorte at $35 a share. When Hardriver gets the option, the stock is selling at $32 a share. Two years later, the stock is selling at $55 a share. Hardriver can exercise the option and buy 2,500 shares at the option price of $32 a share. If Hardriver promptly sells the stock, he makes a profit of $23 per share.

Under IRS rules, only certain types of stock options can be given to family members or family trusts. The IRS has no rules on how to value stock options for gift tax purposes. Very low values can usually be put on them. After all, if the stock never reaches the option price, the option isn't worth anything.

> **Example:** Jean-Francois, CEO of Blow-Em-Up Movie Productions, receives the right to buy 10,000 shares of company stock at $50. The stock is selling for $42 when he receives the option. American males suddenly tire of watching stuff explode on movie screens. The stock falls to between $13 and $18 and stays there. Obviously, Jean-Francois will not exercise his stock option.

Many major U.S. corporations have stock option plans which allow top employees to give options to children, grandchildren or family trusts. Because the option can be valued so low, the worth of the gift is usually under the annual gift tax exemption, and no gift tax is assessed. Even if some gift tax is assessed, it is often far below the eventual worth of the option. If the stock price rises significantly, the recipient can make a bundle.

Example: Holly, President of Cashatechnotronics, Inc., has the option to buy 2,000 shares of the corporation stock at $70 a share. The corporation is privately held, and there is no market for the stock. However, Holly is sure the company will go public soon, and then the stock will be worth much more.

She gives her option to her adult son, D.J. With the aid of a costly accountant and more costly lawyer, Holly values the option at $4 a share, or a total of $8,000. Since this is under the annual gift tax exemption, no gift tax is assessed. Three years later, the company goes public, and the market stock price is $160 a share. D.J. exercises the option, buys 2,000 shares at $70 and immediately sells them. His profit is $90 a share, for a total of $180,000.

Gifts of stock options are fancy, high-end stuff, raising many tricky problems. Complicated income tax rules govern taxation of any profits from exercise of the option and subsequent sale of the stock. The stock plan itself must meet complex IRS regulations. Obviously, an expert lawyer is needed here, which is not news to the wealthy executives who benefit from this perk.

6. Family Business Estate Tax Freezes

Some lawyers still try a sophisticated, on-the-edge (or over it) tax-saving technique called a stock "freeze" for family corporations. It was a common practice until 1987, when Congress enacted restrictive (and confusing) provisions controlling attempted estate freezes.

Estate planning lawyers no longer consider estate freezes desirable for most family businesses. However, a few small loopholes remain, which can work for family business owners if the facts are just right.

Essentially, a freeze involved the creation of two classes of stock for the company: preferred stock (with voting rights to control the business) and common stock (with no voting rights). The owners would give shares of common stock, given as low a value as possible, to their children or grandchildren. They kept all preferred voting stock. Now, for the key: all subsequent appreciation in the worth of the business (if any) was attributed to the common stock. Thus the value of the business, for the controlling owners, would be "frozen" as of the date they gave away the common stock. Because this stock was legally owned by the children, none of the appreciation (nor the worth of the common stock given away) was included in the taxable estate of the owner.

Congress attempted to eliminate this ploy. If a lawyer proposes such a freeze to you, be sure you understand exactly why he thinks it is legal. Why would the IRS accept the lawyer's scheme?

C. AVOIDING PROBATE OF A FAMILY BUSINESS

It's often disastrous for a small business to become enmeshed in probate. Not only is probate costly, but worse, it normally ties up the business under court control for a long time, often over a year. It can be burdensome, even destructive, to have to seek a probate court's approval for business decisions. Would you want a judge supervising your business for months or years? You can plan to avoid probate of your business interest by using either joint tenancy or a living trust. For a number of tax and ownership reasons discussed in detail in Chapters 9 and 10, a living trust is usually the best choice.

Although most business owners should plan to avoid probate, that's not best for everyone. If your business has many debts and creditors' claims, probate may be desirable, because it provides a convenient forum for having those claims resolved. (See Chapter 8, Section D, for more this.) These problems are unusual.

1. Individual Ownership

For most solely-owned businesses, a living trust works fine. The living trust allows the business to be transferred to its new owners promptly, without any risk of loss of control while you live.

Example 1: Sam is the sole owner of a New York restaurant. The business is not incorporated. Sam conducts the business under his name "dba [doing business as] The Manhattan Bar and Brasserie," and has filed the appropriate business and tax forms with city licensing agencies. Sam will leave the business to his son, Theodore. Sam creates a living trust and names Theodore to inherit the restaurant. Sam lists the restaurant on Schedule A of the trust: "The restaurant dba The Manhattan Bar and Brasserie...[street address]... and all assets, supplies, accounts receivable, good will or other property of the business." Of course, when Theodore inherits the business, he'll need to complete a new "dba" form.

Example 2: Natalie is sole owner of the Stay-Potted plant store. She wants to leave her interest in the store as follows:

30% to her close friend Donna;

25% to her niece Cindy;

15% to each of her three brothers (totaling 45%).

After investigating her options, she decides to incorporate and then transfer the stock of the corporation into a living trust. The trust document provides that each of the beneficiaries receives the percentage of stock she's specified. Natalie also prepares the appropriate corporate records, according to the corporation's bylaws, to approve her actions. She decides she won't worry about management and continuity of the business after she dies. It's up to her beneficiaries. If they agree to run the business and can run it—fine. If that doesn't work out, they can sell the business.

2. Shared Ownership Businesses

Living trusts also work well if you own your business together with others. The partnership agreement, corporate bylaws or shareholders' agreement, or operating agreement of an LLC should specifically permit each owner to transfer her interest to a living trust. If the document does not provide for this, it should be amended or revised so that it does. Then, each owner creates her own living trust, consistent with any requirements of the partnership agreement, bylaws or shareholders' agreement (such as the right of surviving principals to buy out the deceased's share), and transfers her interest in the business to that trust. The trust then works like any other probate avoidance living trust, as explained in Chapter 9. The business property transferred to the trust is listed on Schedule A, for example as:

"The grantor's shares in the Zeeet Corporation"

"The grantor's partnership interest in the Alphonse-Benjamin partnership"

"The grantor's interest in the "Go Giants!" Limited Liability Company."

Then, any business asset transferred to the living trust with a document of title must be re-registered in the trust's name.

Example: Vikki and Sloane each own one-half of the stock in Go-Get-'Em, Inc., which owns two apartment houses. Both Vikki and Sloane each create a living trust for their business interests. Each must do the following to transfer his or her share of the business into the living trust:

- Prepare the appropriate corporate records and resolution authorizing and approving the transfer

- Prepare new corporate shares, listing the living trust (technically, the trustee of the trust) as owner. ■

29

USING LAWYERS

A. Hiring a Lawyer 29/2
    1. What Kind of Expert Do You Need? 29/2
    2. Locating a Lawyer 29/3
    3. Checking the Lawyer Out 29/6
B. Doing Your Own Research 29/6
    1. Research Aids 29/6
    2. Legal Information Online 29/7
    3. How to Approach Research Problems 29/7
    4. Basic Research Sources 29/7

Some readers will decide that with the aid of this book and other Nolo resources, they can do all the estate planning they need themselves, without a lawyer. Others will conclude that they need the help of a lawyer to safely plan their estate. If you're in the second group, read this chapter for our views on how to find an estate planning lawyer, if you don't already know of one, and how to evaluate a lawyer and what level of expertise you'll need.

"Lawyer: one skilled in circumvention of the law."

— Ambrose Bierce, The Devil's Dictionary

We also discuss doing some legal research on your own. Even if you'll definitely need a lawyer, that doesn't prohibit doing some legal research yourself, going deeper into one or more topics than this book does. After all, the more you know about the broad legal issues involved in estate planning and the particular legal tools you are considering incorporating in your plan, the more likely you are to make good choices—and the lower your eventual legal bill should be.

Of course, you don't have to do any legal research at all. It takes effort. You may conclude that you have gone as deep into advanced estate planning as you want by reading and understanding this book. That surely is a reasonable response. After all, unless you really are ready to invest a fair number of hours climbing the estate planning learning curve, you won't acquire enough expertise to creatively challenge and debate a lawyer's technical recommendations.

A. Hiring a Lawyer

If you do determine that you want an expert's assistance, obviously you don't want to hire a lawyer at random and say "Tell me what to do." As an intelligent consumer, you not only want to gain at least as much knowledge about your problem as you conve-

niently can, but you also want to invest sufficient time to be sure the person you hire is honest, knowledgeable and provides good service for your dollar.

Your estate plan should express your intentions. No one else can know those intentions. Sometimes, when people think, or fear, that they need a lawyer, what they are really doing is longing for an authority figure (or believing one is required) to tell them what to do. Keep in mind that only you can decide who should get your property, and how and when they should get it. An estate planning expert is your paid advisor and legal technician, not your mentor.

1. What Kind of Expert Do You Need?

The first question to decide is whether you need a lawyer, or if you will be better served by a financial expert such as an accountant or financial planner. Don't just assume a lawyer is your best choice. For example, questions about federal estate taxes or how to calculate tax basis rules on the sale of appreciated property can often be better answered by an experienced CPA. Similarly, for some financial decisions, such as what type of insurance to buy to fund a small business buy-out, you may be better off talking to a financial planner. But for most estate planning concerns, you do need to see a lawyer. In the estate planning context, there are, basically, three categories of lawyers:

- general practice lawyers
- estate planning specialists, and
- highly specialized lawyers working in one very difficult aspect of estate planning.

Which type is right for you depends on your estate planning concerns and need. Let's look at each type of lawyer in more detail.

a. General Practice Lawyers

General practice lawyers handle all sorts of cases; they don't specialize in estate planning. If your needs are basic, such as a garden-variety living trust or will, or a check of some provision of your state's laws, a competent attorney in general practice should be able to do a good job at a lower cost than more specialized attorneys.

Similarly, if your small business needs to customize its partnership agreement, LLC operating agreement or corporate bylaws to allow for surviving owners to buy out the shares of a deceased owner from his or her inheritors, a general practice lawyer should do fine.

b. Estate Planning Specialists

For any type of sophisticated estate planning work, you need to see a specialist. Estate planning, as this book may have convinced you, is often a complex matter, and to do a good job, a lawyer needs to be absolutely up-to-date on estate tax law and regulations, the rules governing ongoing trusts and numerous other matters. Whether your concern is to establish an ongoing trust for estate tax savings, handle issues raised by a second marriage, set up an ongoing gift-giving program while you live, or any one of many other possible complicated matters—you need an expert.

An expert may charge relatively high fees, but a good one is worth it. Most general practice lawyers are simply not sufficiently educated in estate planning to handle complex matters.

c. Highly Specialized Lawyers

These lawyers specialize in a particularly difficult aspect of estate law. For example, to prepare a "special needs" trust for a disabled person, a lawyer must be current on complex federal and state regulations regarding trust property and eligibility for government benefits. Even most estate planning experts don't have sufficient expertise for this. Also consult a specialized estate planning lawyer if you want to try to protect your, or your spouse's, assets from the cost of medical care for catastrophic illnesses or disabilities, or if you own property in two or more countries and need an attorney who's expert at multinational estate planning.

Unfortunately, finding a lawyer with the specialized skills you need may not be easy. In some states, such as California, state bar associations certify lawyers as expert estate planners, but even this is no guarantee they are competent in one of the very specialized areas of estate planning. You simply have to seek until you find a lawyer with the experience you need.

2. Locating a Lawyer

How do you find a lawyer? Ours is such a lawyer-ridden society that it's unusual if one hasn't already found you. There is certainly a growing surplus of lawyers. The difficulty, of course, is not just finding a lawyer, but retaining one who is trustworthy and competent, and charges fairly. In addition, as noted above, many readers will need to find an estate planning expert, not just a general practitioner who says "no problem" when you ask if she can prepare, say, sophisticated tax-saving trusts. A few words of advice on how you can find a good lawyer may be helpful.

When looking for a good lawyer, especially an estate planning expert, personal routes are the traditional, and probably best, method. If a relative or good friend who has good business and financial sense has found an estate planning lawyer she recommends, chances are you'll like him too. Failing this, check with people you know in any political or social organization you're involved with, especially those with a large number of members over age 40. Assuming they themselves are savvy, they may well be able to point you to a competent lawyer who handles estate planning matters and whose attitudes are similar to yours.

Another good approach is to ask for help from a lawyer you are personally acquainted with and think well of, even if she doesn't work in the estate planning area. Very likely she can refer you to someone trustworthy who is an estate planning expert.

Also, check with people you respect who own their own small businesses. Almost anyone running a small business has a relationship with a lawyer, and chances are they've found one they like. Again, this lawyer will probably not be an estate planning expert, but he'll likely know one, or several.

If you are a member of a legal insurance plan, you may be offered sophisticated estate planning assistance from a referral panel member at a reduced fee. Some of these referrals may be to excellent lawyers. In our experience, however, too often lawyers who sign up to do cut-rate work are not the best alternative. Excellent lawyers, particularly good estate planning experts, tend to have lots of work, and don't need to cut fees to gain clients.

Also, be cautious when dealing with bar association referral panels. Never assume a listing on a referral panel is a seal of approval. Although lawyers are supposed to be screened as to their specialty to get on these panels, screening is usually perfunctory. Often the main qualification is that the lawyer needs business. (We've been there too.)

HOW MANY LAWYERS DOES A COUPLE NEED?

Sounds like a joke question, right? Unfortunately, it isn't. Most couples can safely use one lawyer for both spouses' estate planning. However, if there's a potential conflict between different spouses' desires, then perhaps each needs a separate lawyer. For example, in a second or subsequent marriage, if children from one or both spouses' prior marriage(s) don't get along with the other spouse, each spouse may want their own attorney. Or, say, where the estate lawyer is a good friend of one spouse and the other spouse's children are suspicious that somehow they'll get cheated of their inheritance or if one spouse can be extremely domineering, each spouse may sensibly decide they want independent advice regarding their estate planning. In this case, choosing two lawyers can be a sensible form of insurance against possible later claims of undue influence or unfair representation by a single attorney. Happily though, in real life few couples will decide their interests are, or could be, so in conflict that each one must pay for a separate lawyer.

As you already know, lawyers are expensive, and expert lawyers are even more expensive. Lawyer's estate planning fees usually range from $150 to $400 per hour, with experts at the higher end of the scale. While fancy office trappings, dull clothes and solemn (or aggressive) demeanor are no guarantee (or even a good indication) that a particular lawyer will provide top-notch service in a manner you will feel comfortable with, this conventional style does almost always ensure that you will be charged at the upper end of the fee range. At Nolo, our experience tells us that high fees and quality service don't necessarily go hand in hand. Indeed, many of the attorneys we think most highly of tend to charge moderate fees (for lawyers, that is), and seem to get along very nicely without most stuffy law office trappings.

Keep in mind that in any field, certainly including estate planning, there are good high-priced experts and bad ones. It's all too easy to get a mumbo-jumbo speaking lawyer who confuses you at first, and enrages you later, when you receive an exorbitant bill. Don't be afraid to keep looking until you find a lawyer you like. Many people who have had unhappy experiences with lawyers (and we all know some) wish they had done so.

HIRING A LAWYER TO REVIEW YOUR ESTATE PLANNING DOCUMENTS

Hiring a lawyer solely to review a will or living trust you've prepared from a Nolo resource sounds like a good idea. It shouldn't cost much, and seems to offer a comforting security. Sadly though, it can be difficult to find a lawyer who will accept the job. The reason is, many lawyers feel that by reviewing a document for a relatively small fee they become just as legally responsible for a client's entire estate plan situation as if they did all the work from scratch. Or, put more directly, many lawyers see every client as the author of a future malpractice claim, or at least, the source of later hassles and simply don't want to get involved for a modest fee.

To counter this mentality and help provide self-helpers with the coaching and advice they often need, Nolo Press has advocated unbundling legal services. The idea is that a customer should be able to contract with a lawyer for only the services wanted and the lawyer should have no broader liability beyond providing those services competently. With new phone law services, and lawyers who are setting up businesses to provide advice only, this approach is sure to be more common soon. But in the meantime, if you have trouble finding a lawyer who will help you help yourself, all you can do here is to keep trying to find a sympathetic lawyer. It will help if you are prepared to pay a decent fee so that the lawyer can take the time necessary to carefully review your work.

3. Checking the Lawyer Out

Personally evaluate any lawyer you've been referred to before you agree to have her handle your estate plan. Don't hesitate to question the lawyer, no matter how expert she is considered to be. To ask sensible questions, you need to have done some preparation; you should have at least a rough general idea of what you want to accomplish. Also, you need enough information (gleaned from this book or other sources) to intelligently pose good questions and evaluate the lawyer's answers.

It's important that you feel a personal rapport with your lawyer. You want one who treats you as an equal. (Interestingly, the Latin root of the word "client" translates as "to hear, to obey.") When talking with a lawyer on the phone or at a first conference, ask specific questions that concern you. If the lawyer answers them clearly and concisely—explaining, but not talking down to you—fine. If he acts wise, but says little except to ask that the problem be placed in his hands, watch out. You are either talking with someone who doesn't know the answer and won't admit it (common), or someone who finds it impossible to let go of the "me expert, you peasant" way of looking at the world (even more common). You need a lawyer who's open and sympathetic to people who want to actively participate in handling their own legal affairs.

Be sure you've settled your fee arrangement—in writing—at the start of your relationship. Depending on the area of the county where you live, generally, we feel that fees for a general practice lawyer in the range of $150 to $250 per hour are reasonable in urban areas, given the average lawyer's overhead. In rural counties and small cities, excellent general help may be available for a little less. Expert estate planning lawyers usually cost more, sometimes a lot more. In addition to the amount charged per hour, you also want a clear commitment from the lawyer concerning how many hours she expects to put in on your problem.

B. DOING YOUR OWN RESEARCH

Learning how to do your own research into estate planning law can provide real benefits. Of course, legal research isn't for everyone. You have to have the energy, patience and ability to enter new mental areas, as well as the desire to do so. But for the intrepid, not only are you likely to save money on professional fees, you'll gain at least some sense of mastery over an area of law that concerns you.

Once you understand some research techniques, some aspects of estate planning law can be fairly easy to research. For example, to answer questions concerning technical aspects of state laws affecting wills or probate avoidance, you probably need only to check the relevant statutes of your state to find the provision you need.

1. Research Aids

If you decide you want to do your own research, how do you go about it? First, you need to find a good law library.

There's often a law library in your principal county courthouse. These libraries' quality varies a lot from state to state and county to county. County law libraries are normally supported by tax dollars or by the fees paid to file court papers. In our experience, county law librarians have been sensitive and generally most helpful and courteous to non-lawyers who want to learn to do their own legal research. However, some county law libraries don't have adequate resources for many types of legal research. And, of course, we can't vouch for every law librarian in the country.

If your county library is not adequate, your best bet is a law school library. Those in state colleges and universities supported by tax dollars are almost always open to the public, at least during certain hours.

Once you've found a good law library, you need an introduction to how they work. If you can't hire your own law librarian, the best book explaining how to do your own legal work is *Legal Research: How to Find and Understand the Law,* by Steve Elias and Susan Levinkind (Nolo Press). It shows you, step-by-step, how to find answers in the law library and is, as far as we know, the only legal research book written specifically for non-professionals. Nolo also publishes an excellent two-and-one-half hour video, *Legal Research Made Easy,* in which law librarian and legal research professor Bob Berring shows you how to conduct first-class legal research step-by-step.

Even with the assistance of a sympathetic law librarian and a good research aid, digging into the law can be intimidating at first. We urge you to stay with it. After a while—perhaps sooner than you anticipate—you'll understand the materials and how you can use them.

2. Legal Information Online

Another way to approach legal research is to use a computer. If you want information about current estate planning issues, such as a recent court decision or a new statute, you'll probably be able to find it somewhere in the vast online world known as the Internet. which includes the World Wide Web. Many public libraries now offer online access, if you're not connected at home or work.

Finding legal Information on the Web. Comprehensive information on over 2,000 legal sites on the Net is presented in the book *Law on the Net,* by James Evans (Nolo Press).

3. How to Approach Research Problems

There's no one standard method for approaching a legal research question. Sometimes, it's prudent to start from the general and move towards the specific. But rather than lay out a number of possible approaches, none of which may work for you, we'll simply refer you again to *Legal Research,* which explores these matters in far greater depth and clarity than any summary could.

4. Basic Research Sources

Sometimes a good way to dive into legal research is to do some background reading in a good book about a certain aspect of estate planning. This reading can provide an overview of the law applicable to your concerns, possibly provide some initial answers, and refer you to more specific sources.

There are several categories of estate planning background books. In reading these resources, please remember that they are written by estate planning attorneys, for attorneys, and often have predictable prejudices against a do-it-yourself approach. You may need to ignore an author's attitude, or, worse, struggle through wads of legalese, to get to solid legal information.

- **Overall estate planning.** There are many books covering estate planning in general. One of the best is *The CCH Estate Planning Guide,* by Kess and Westlin (Commerce Clearing House).

- **How-to-do-it estate planning books for lawyers.** Many states have estate planning books designed to show lawyers how it's done. These books contain specific clauses and forms for wills or trusts, and many other hands-on materials. For example, in California, the Continuing Education of the Bar (CEB) publishes several useful estate planning books, including *Drafting California Irrevocable Inter Vivos Trusts, Drafting California*

Revocable Inter Vivos Trusts, and *California Will Drafting*. Comparable books in New York are published by the Practicing Law Institute (PLI) and include:

* *Estate Planning*, by Manning

* *Use of Trusts in Estate Planning*, by Moore

* *Stocker on Drawing Wills*, by Stocker

* *Income Taxation of Estates and Trusts*, by Michaelson & Blattmaehr.

In other states, the best way to locate this type of book for your state is to ask the law librarian or look up "Estate Planning," or a more specific heading, in the library catalog.

* **Treatises on one area of estate planning law.** For example, for federal estate taxes there's The CCH Federal Estate and Gift Tax Code (and IRS Regulations). For trusts there's *Inter Vivos Trusts*, by Cohan and Hemmerling (Shepard's Citations), and *Federal Taxation of Trusts; Grantors and Beneficiaries*, by Peschel and Spurgeon (Warner,

Gorham and Lamont). And there are also a number of popular self-help tax guides.

* **Legal encyclopedias.** These provide an overview of virtually every legal topic. They are so broad that they rarely provide help in resolving a particular estate planning problem. The encyclopedias are indexed by subject and can be used much the same way as a regular encyclopedia. There are two national legal encyclopedias:

* *American Jurisprudence* (Am. Jur.), generally the more up-to-date and better written, and

* *Corpus Jurum Secundum* (CJS), which contains numerous references to court decisions on any legal point.

There are also encyclopedias published for specific states (mostly the larger ones). Unless you are dealing with a clearly federal topic, like federal estate and gift taxes, it is a good idea to first check out a state encyclopedia, if one exists. The material there is likely to be more specific than is an article in a national encyclopedia. ■

30

AFTER YOUR ESTATE PLAN IS COMPLETED

A. Storing Your Estate Planning Documents 30/2
B. Revising Your Estate Plan 30/3
   1. Living Trusts 30/3
   2. Wills 30/4
   3. Joint Tenancy 30/5
   4. Pay-on-Death Accounts 30/5
   5. Insurance 30/5
   6. Ongoing Trusts 30/5

I f you are serious about planning your estate, you'll eventually get the job done. What next? Up to you. A sigh of relief? A celebration? Maybe gather those you love, break out your favorite beverage and offer a toast "To Life!"

But although your big job is complete, you've still got some more to do—storing your documents safely, and making any necessary future revisions to your plan. So this chapter discusses what you may need to do once your planning documents have been completed.

A. STORING YOUR ESTATE PLANNING DOCUMENTS

Completion of an estate plan means that you have created some important documents: a will, probably a living trust, quite possibly an ongoing trust, or even several, as well as other forms, such as a durable power of attorney for health care, and one for finances. And perhaps you've signed a joint tenancy deed, business ownership documents or written instructions for your funeral or donations of body parts. Obviously, you want to keep all these documents in a safe place, where you, and your executor/trustee, can readily find them. It's no big secret how to accomplish this. Any secure place can be used for storage: a safe in your house or office, or even a drawer in your home desk or file cabinet.

Some people use a bank safe deposit box. If you do this, you must make sure that your executor or successor trustee will have ready legal access to that box when it's needed. Check with your bank to see what it requires to allow your executor/trustee to get documents from the safe deposit box. Also check with them to make sure the safe deposit isn't sealed, under state law, when one owner dies. (Some states that have death taxes require this. See Chapter 15, Section G, for a list of states with death taxes.)

While you may want to keep at least some of your estate planning documents private while you live, you also surely want them to be promptly accessible to whoever will handle your affairs at your death. This is especially true for documents that deal with your wishes as to organ transplants and funeral or burial instructions, which must be immediately available. So once you have settled on a sensible storage place, let the person who will wind up your affairs know what you've decided, and how to obtain the documents.

What about making copies of your estate planning documents? You may have to produce copies of your living trust to financial institutions, such as a brokerage company, where you have an account you want placed in trust. Whether or not to make copies for personal reasons is up to you. Often people do want copies to give to their executor or successor trustee, family members or friends. If you do need or want copies:

- Photocopy the documents you want people to see or have. These copies are not legal originals, since they are not signed by you. A photocopy of your signature is okay.

- Never sign a copy. If you do, it could legally qualify as a "duplicate original." If you later decide to change, amend or revoke the document, you have to change each duplicate original as well.

- To be extra safe, mark "copy" in ink on each page. This isn't legally required, but it ensures that no one can claim a copy is an original.

B. REVISING YOUR ESTATE PLAN

Estate plans shouldn't be changed frequently. If impromptu changes ("I'll show her, I'll cut her out of my will") occur often, you have an underlying family or personal problem to examine. Major life events, however, call for estate planning changes. If any of the following events occur, you should review your plan:

- You sell or give away any property you've specifically mentioned in your will or living trust. Estate planning transfer devices, such as wills or living trusts, don't become binding until your death. So what happens if you dispose of property but don't change your will or trust? For example, what happens if your will leaves your son your 1988 Chevy, but by the time you die, you've already sold it and purchased a 1995 Buick?

  To summarize what can be a complicated area of law: if you leave someone a specific piece of property (say the Chevy) but you no longer own it when you die, that beneficiary is out of luck. The fact that you own a Buick doesn't help the beneficiary. Lawyers call this "ademption"; people who don't inherit the property in question are often heard to use an earthier term.

- You get married. If you don't update your will, your new spouse will have the right to inherit a share of your estate, as determined by state law.

- You get divorced. In some states, a divorce ends a former spouse's right to inherit under a will. In other states, it doesn't. Also, other property left to a divorced spouse using other estate planning devices may not be affected by a divorce.

- The birth of a child. The rule here is similar to that for marriage.

- A beneficiary dies.

- Your financial situation changes significantly.

- You move to a new state. This is particularly necessary if you are married and move from a common law property state to a community property state or vice versa. (See Chapter 3, State Property Ownership Rules for Married People, Section D, for a detailed discussion of the issues that should concern you.)

- You acquire significant property.

- You want to change the successor trustee of your living trust, or the executor of your will.

- You want to change the personal or property guardian you have named for your minor children or, if you have established a children's trust, the person or institution you have named as trustee, or custodian for a gift under the UTMA.

If you do decide to change your estate plan, you must decide whether you need, or want, to create entirely new documents or simply modify your existing ones. Which route is better depends both on how complex your changes are and the estate planning document involved.

1. Living Trusts

Living trusts can be revised fairly easily

- If you just want to transfer more property to the trust, there should be no problem. A well drafted living trust has a clause permitting additions of property to the trust after it has been created (called an "after-acquired property" clause). If your trust has such a clause, you can add property by listing it on the trust schedule and taking title to that property in the trustee's name. If you only add property to a trust schedule, you do not have to have the trust notarized again.

You don't have to name a new beneficiary for this new trust property. If you don't, it will go to the residuary beneficiary of your trust unless you've provided that "all property" on the trust schedule goes to some other beneficiary.

- You can mend the trust document (not just a property schedule). For changes that don't necessitate a new document, you can make a formal amendment to your trust. Changes by amendment can include adding or deleting beneficiaries, changing gifts, or naming new successor trustees. You must sign and date the amendment and have it notarized.

- If you're making wholesale changes to your trust, you'll need to revoke the old trust and prepare a new one, reflecting your current intentions. This is the least desirable method, but is sometimes necessary. You'll have to get the new trust document notarized. Worse, you'll have to re-register property in the trustee's name, as trustee of the new trust as of the date of creation (notarization) of this trust. That's a lot of work.

2. Wills

There are only two ways to change a formal witnessed will:

- Prepare a formal witnessed codicil to the will.
- Destroy the old will and make a new one.

    Let's briefly examine each procedure.

a. Make a Codicil

A codicil is a formal legal method for making changes to a will that has already been drafted, signed and witnessed. A codicil is a sort of legal "P.S." to the will. It must be typed or printed, with a formal heading. The text of the codicil then identifies the date of the original will and sets out the change made.

> ### SAMPLE CODICIL
>
> Codicil to Will of Beth Thoreau
>
> 1. I leave $3,000 to my friend Al Smith.
>
> 2. I leave my silver tea set to Bertha Weinstock, and revoke my gift of that tea set to Mary Warbler, now deceased.
>
> 3. In all other respects I re-affirm my will dated August 23, 1996.

A codicil must be typed, signed and witnessed just like a will. Because of this requirement, it can make more sense to prepare a new will entirely, especially if you are using a computer will program. It won't take you any longer to prepare a new computer-generated will than a codicil, and the signing and witnessing requirements for both are the same.

You must sign and dated a codicil in the presence of at least two—or even better, three—witnesses, who are told that it's a codicil to your will and then sign their names. The witnesses don't have to be the same as those for the original will, though it's a good idea to use the original witnesses if they're available. Sample codicil forms can be found in *Nolo's Will Book*, by Denis Clifford.

b. Make a New Will

If you want a major revision of your will, it's better to draft a new will and revoke the old one than to use a codicil. A will that has been substantially re-written by a codicil is an awkward document and can be confusing. It may not always be clear what the relationship of the codicil to the original will provisions means.

If you make a new will, be sure you've revoked your old will. You can do this by either:

- destroying the will itself (and all copies, if you can get your hands on them)—rip 'em up and throw 'em out; and

- stating in the new will that you revoke all previous wills you have made.

    We strongly recommend that you do both.

3. Joint Tenancy

If you've established a joint tenancy, are you stuck with it? No—in most all states, one joint tenant can transform the joint tenancy into a tenancy in common, which eliminates the right of the other co-owners to automatically inherit. (See Chapter 10, Joint Tenancy and Tenancy by the Entirety, Section G.) However, it takes agreement of all the joint tenants to allow any one to become the sole owner of the property. If all joint tenants agree to end a joint tenancy, they can sign a document (a deed, for real estate) transferring the property into whatever new form of ownership is desired.

Changing a joint tenancy. If you want to transfer your share of joint tenancy property into tenancy in common, and the other owner(s) don't consent, you'll need to see a lawyer to learn the procedures required in your state, unless you live in California. In the Golden State, *The Deeds Book*, by Mary Randolph (Nolo Press) shows you how to do this.

4. Pay-on-Death Accounts

You can amend or revoke a pay-on-death account at any time. You can change a beneficiary simply by deleting the old one and entering a new one on the financial institution's registration form; sometimes a new, separate form must be completed. You can also end the pay-on-death account simply by closing it or by spending all the money the account contains. If the account is empty when you die, obviously the beneficiary gets nothing.

You cannot safely revoke a pay-on-death account by leaving the property to some one else in your will. Under the law of the great majority of states, a beneficiary under a pay-on-death account prevails over someone who was left the same property by will.

5. Insurance

If you are the owner of an insurance policy, you can cancel the policy or change the beneficiary of that policy. If you are not the legal owner of the policy, you have no right to cancel the policy or change the beneficiary, even if the policy insures your own life.

6. Ongoing Trusts

Most ongoing trusts, whether for estate tax saving, property control or both, do not become irrevocable until the grantor's death. Some, however, such as many charitable trusts or life insurance trusts, become irrevocable upon creation. Once an ongoing trust has become irrevocable, by definition it can't be changed or revoked. Until an ongoing trust is irrevocable, it can be freely changed or revoked by the grantor. ◗

31

AFTER A DEATH OCCURS

A. Wills 31/2

B. Probate-Avoidance Living Trusts 31/2

    1. Who Serves as Trustee 31/2

    2. Winding Up a Single Person's Living Trust 31/3

    3. Winding Up a Shared Living Trust 31/3

    4. Property Left to Children 31/4

C. Ongoing Trusts for Estate Tax Savings or Property Management 31/4

D. Preparing and Filing Tax Returns 31/5

E. Trustee's Reports to Beneficiaries 31/6

F. Collecting the Proceeds of a Life Insurance Policy 31/6

G. Obtaining Title to Joint Tenancy Property 31/6

When someone who has created an estate plan dies, someone else (or several someones) must take actions to carry out the deceased person's plan. This is not a book that covers after-death work in depth. That's a subject for another big book. But this chapter offers you general summaries of basic estate transfer tasks that someone may need to do after a person dies. We also refer you to other Nolo resources that describe, in more detail, how to carry out tasks connected with a specific legal document, such a will or living trust.

A. WILLS

When the will writer dies, the person named as executor is responsible for carrying out the terms of the will. This includes handling probate—normally, by hiring a probate lawyer—and then, once probate is completed, distributing property governed by the will to the beneficiaries named in that document.

If an ongoing trust (including a child's trust or family pot trust) is created in the will, the executor is often also named as trustee of that trust, and so can have ongoing duties of managing the trust property. If property is left to a minor under the Uniform Transfers to Minors Act, the executor must turn that property over to the custodian for that gift.

Some executors have additional responsibilities. If a federal or state estate tax return must be filed, it's the executor's legal responsibility to see this is done. (See Section D, below.) Also, in wealthier estates, if a QTIP trust is part of a deceased spouse's estate plan, the executor must decide whether or not to "elect" to have estate tax on the trust property postponed until the surviving spouse dies. (See Chapter 19, Other Estate Tax-Saving Marital Trusts, Section A.)

B. PROBATE-AVOIDANCE LIVING TRUSTS

With a living trust designed solely to avoid probate, the successor trustee is responsible, after a grantor dies, for carrying out the terms of the trust. This basically means transferring the trust property to the beneficiaries named in the trust.

1. Who Serves as Trustee

With a basic shared trust made by a couple, the surviving spouse serves as trustee after one spouse's death. (AB trusts are discussed below, in Section C.) With an individual trust, or when the surviving spouse dies, the successor trustee is in charge.

If more than one person is named in the trust document as successor trustee, they all serve as co-trustees. This does not, however, mean all trustees must agree on all decisions. Whether each trustee must formally agree on any action taken with regard to the living trust property, or whether one trustee can act independently, depends on the terms of the trust document.

If more than one successor trustee is named, but cannot serve, the other(s) remain as trustee(s). The person named as alternate successor trustee does not take over unless all the people named as successor trustees cannot serve.

A trustee can resign at any time by preparing and signing a written resignation statement. The ex-trustee should deliver the notice to the person who is next in line to serve as trustee. With a well-drafted living trust, any trustee, including the last acting trustee, can appoint someone else to take over if no one named in the trust document can serve.

Usually, it's the last, or alternate, successor trustee who names someone else to act as trustee. The appointment must be in writing, signed and notarized.

2. Winding Up a Single Person's Living Trust

Normally, the job of the successor trustee of a single person's living trust is simply to transfer the trust property outright to the designated beneficiaries. Only if the successor trustee is also trustee of an ongoing trust created in the living trust are continuing duties required of her.

Unless there are explicit directions in the trust document, it is not the trustee's responsibility to sell or manage living trust property.

Example: Elliot's living trust leaves his house to his children, Clarence and Grace. After Elliot dies, Jamie, the successor trustee, deeds the house from the trust to Clarence and Grace. They can do with it what they wish— live in it, rent it or sell it. Jamie cannot sell the house and divide the proceeds between the beneficiaries—that's not his decision to make.

Normally, after the grantor dies, the living trust continues to exist only as long as it takes the successor trustee to distribute trust property to the beneficiaries. In many cases, a living trust can be wound up within a few weeks after a grantor's death. But if an ongoing business is involved, it may take longer. (See Chapter 28, Section C.)

No formal termination document is required to end a living trust. Once the trust property has been distributed, the trust ends.

3. Winding Up a Shared Living Trust

Coping with what happens when one grantor dies is more complex for a successor trustee who's in charge of a shared living trust. The successor trustee (usually the surviving spouse or mate) must divide the living trust property into two portions. Each portion goes into a new trust entity, as provided for by the original trust document.

- One new trust contains the deceased spouse's share of the living trust property. The terms of this new trust cannot be changed, and it cannot be revoked. Property is promptly distributed to its beneficiaries by the successor trustee unless the grantor provided for its ongoing management, as would be the case for property left to a minor.

- A separate trust which, as a practical matter, is usually a continuation of the original living trust, contains the surviving spouse's trust property. This trust usually includes any of the deceased spouse's share of the living trust property that is left to the surviving spouse. The surviving spouse remains free to amend the terms of this trust, or even revoke it.

Though this may sound complicated, it often isn't. If, as is common, much of the trust property is left to the surviving spouse, that spouse may have little to do beyond distributing a few items to the deceased's other beneficiaries.

When all the property in the deceased spouse's trust has been distributed to the beneficiaries, that trust ceases to exist. No formal termination document is required. In contrast, the surviving spouse's trust remains revocable

Example: Edith and Jacques create a basic shared living trust to avoid probate. They transfer their major asset, their home which they own together, to the trust, and name each other as beneficiaries. Edith names her son as alternate beneficiary.

When Jacques dies, Edith inherits his half-interest in the house. Jacques' trust then ends its existence. Edith trust remains in effect, and revocable.

Because of the way the trust document is worded, Edith doesn't have to change her trust document to name a beneficiary for the half-interest in the house that she inherited from Jacques Both halves, now consolidated, will go to her son at her death. She may, however, want to amend the trust to make her son the primary beneficiary and name someone else to be alternate beneficiary.

When the surviving spouse dies, the successor trustee named in the trust document takes over as trustee. The process of winding up the surviving spouse's living trust is the same as that for an individual trust.

4. Property Left to Children

Living trust property left for a child's benefit is normally left in a child's trust, family pot trust or through the Uniform Transfers to Minors Act. With any of these, the successor trustee must turn the child's property over to the adult manager of the child's property—the trustee of a child's trust or family pot trust, or the custodian of an UTMA gift. If the successor trustee serves in one of these capacities as well, she must manage the property until it is turned over to the child.

C. Ongoing Trusts for Estate Tax Savings or Property Management

As we've discussed, an ongoing trust is one that is irrevocable, usually becoming so on the grantor's death, and generally functioning for an extended period of time. Some ongoing trusts are created in a will, but more often an ongoing trust is combined with a living trust. First, the trust property avoids probate. Then the ongoing trust becomes operational and may well last for years or decades. As we discussed in the chapters covering ongoing trusts, the

successor's trustee's job will be much more complex here than with a simple probate-avoidance trust.

As an example, let's consider an AB trust created as part of a living trust and see what happens when one spouse dies. (See Chapter 18, Estate Tax-Saving Bypass Trusts, Section C.) The purpose of this type of trust is to save on overall estate taxes. Both spouses are the original trustees. When a spouse dies, the surviving spouse becomes sole trustee, and the living trust splits into two trusts: the irrevocable Trust A (of the deceased spouse) and the revocable Trust B (of the surviving spouse).

The surviving spouse, as trustee, must first distribute any living trust property the deceased spouse left outside of Trust A to specifically named beneficiaries. Then the trustee must establish and maintain the ongoing Trust A.

A major task here is to figure out how best to divide the couple's property (all that was in the original AB trust) between the ongoing Trust A and the surviving spouse's Trust B. Property must be clearly labeled as being owned either by Trust A or by Trust B. Any allocation of equally owned shared trust property is valid, as long as each trust gets 50% of the overall total worth of the AB trust property. Each specific item of property does not have to be split, with half going to each trust. For example, a house, worth (net) $300,000 can be placed in Trust A, as long as other property with a total worth of $300,000 is placed in Trust B.

Dividing AB trust property. Deciding how to divide AB trust property on the death of a spouse usually requires the services of a lawyer or tax accountant. These decisions have long-term tax consequences, and you can save yourself and your inheritors hassle and expense by getting good advice.

Establishing the ongoing irrevocable Trust A may require some re-registering of title of some of the deceased spouse's living trust property. For example, if the surviving spouse decides that it is wisest to put all of a shared ownership house in Trust A, a new deed should be prepared to reflect this, listing the trustee of the ongoing trust as the new owner.

Example: Moira and Joseph O'Sullivan created the Moira and Joseph O'Sullivan Living Trust. In that trust, each created an AB trust. Joseph dies. Moira, with the help of an accountant, divides the living trust property between her now separate Trust B and the newly operational Trust A for Joseph's property. Property with documents of title transferred into Trust A must be re-registered into the name of the trustee of this new trust. Thus the property would be registered as held by "Moira O'Sullivan, as trustee of the Joseph O'Sullivan Trust A."

An operational Trust A needs a federal taxpayer ID number. The surviving spouse must keep appropriate trust financial records and file a federal trust tax return every year. The IRS will want it clear which trust owns what. Annual state trust tax returns may also be required, in states with income taxes.

The spouse manages the property in Trust A and receives any income it generates. Management can include making sensible investment decisions, which may necessitate the hiring of a professional investment advisor.

The surviving spouse's Trust B goes on as before. It remains revocable and can be changed at any time. No tax return needs to be filed for this trust.

After the death of the surviving spouse, the successor trustee winds up both trusts by distributing all property of both trusts to each trust's final beneficiaries. The successor trustee must file a final tax return for Trust A. The successor trustee files a

closing tax return for the second spouse and may also manage any property left in a child's trust or a family pot trust.

D. PREPARING AND FILING TAX RETURNS

It is the responsibility of an executor to file federal estate and state death tax returns, if one or both must be filed because of the value of the deceased's estate. If most or all property is left by a living trust, however, it's the successor trustee who files any tax returns due. (Of course, the executor and successor trustee are usually the same person.)

A final federal income tax return (and state return, if there's a state income tax) must be filed for the deceased. Legally, this is the responsibility of the executor of the deceased's will. Also, a final federal trust income tax return (and state tax return, if one is required) must be filed for Trust A after both spouses die.

If a federal estate tax return must be filed (see Chapter 15), it is due nine months after the decedent's death. As we've discussed, estate tax matters can get quite sticky. For instance, for federal estate tax purposes, property can be valued as of the date of death or as of six months after death. The executor will need professional help, and is entitled to pay for it out of the deceased's assets.

The IRS publishes a helpful 20-page set of instructions for the estate tax return, "Instructions for Form 706." Another useful IRS publication is "Federal Estate and Gift Taxes" (Publication 448).

E. TRUSTEE'S REPORTS TO BENEFICIARIES

Generally, a trustee is not legally required to make any report of trust income, transactions or any other aspect of trust management to any beneficiary. There are some exceptions:

• The trustee of any ongoing trust may be required by the terms of the trust to give reports, such as copies of the trust's annual federal trust tax return, to all the trust beneficiaries.

• A few state's laws require the trustee to distribute an annual report to the beneficiaries. For example, Washington law requires distributing "a written itemization of all current receipts and disbursements made by the trustee." (Wash. Rev. Code Section 11.106.020.) In most family situations, these laws have little or no impact, since beneficiaries trust the trustee, and don't insist on these legal rights.

• In California, the trustee must notify beneficiaries when a trust becomes irrevocable. (Ca. Probate Code Section 16061.7).

F. COLLECTING THE PROCEEDS OF A LIFE INSURANCE POLICY

How to collect insurance proceeds after the insured person dies is not, strictly speaking, part of estate planning, but nevertheless people want to be sure their beneficiaries know how to collect these proceeds. Normally, this isn't a problem—they can be collected soon after the insured person's death by submitting an insurance company claim form and a certified copy of the insured person's death certificate to the company. The beneficiary may also have to file a copy of the policy, and proof of identify as the named beneficiary, if the insurance company requires it.

Although this is normally routine, there can be several flies in the ointment. In some states with state death taxes, insurance proceeds above a certain amount cannot be released until the tax officials approve. If the insured person owned the insurance policy, the insurance proceeds will be part of her taxable estate, and the state tax officials must first be satisfied that the estate has other sufficient assets to pay state death taxes before they authorize release of the proceeds to the beneficiaries.

In other instances, some companies have been known to delay payments for months, so that they can collect interest on the money for a longer time. If this happens to you, a letter to the insurance commissioner of both your state and of the one where the company is headquartered (with copies to the offending company) will normally pry the money loose pronto.

G. OBTAINING TITLE TO JOINT TENANCY PROPERTY

The major benefit of joint tenancy is the "automatic right of survivorship." But obviously, the words on a deed to real estate or certificate of title to a car don't magically change on the day one joint tenant takes that last breath. Until someone acts, the legal title will not be changed to the survivor's name. What "automatic right of survivorship" means in this context is that compared to most legal tasks it's possible to transfer title to the surviving owner fairly easily, quickly and cheaply, without probate. This is true for all joint tenancies, whether of real estate or personal property.

To get the deceased owner's name off the owner-ship document, so that the surviving joint tenants are on record as legal owners, they must:

- establish that the joint tenant has died by filing a copy of the death certificate with the appropriate government official or recorder of title; and
- file a document establishing that the surviving owners are sole owners to the property.

A lawyer can be hired to do this, but is normally unnecessary, as the procedures are routine. If a lawyer is hired, however, be sure the fee charged is a reasonable hourly one. An unfortunate practice in many states is for a lawyer to propose charging one-third of what the probate fee would be to transfer joint property to the survivors. Usually, this is far too high a fee; the work is neither complicated nor time-consuming.

For example, to terminate a joint tenancy in real estate, you need to file a certified copy of the deceased's death certificate and a form called "Affida-vit of Death of Joint Tenant," or something similar, with the county office of property records (called the "County Recorder" in many states). The affidavit is a standard legal form, available in many office supply stores. On this form, the surviving joint tenant states that a joint tenant has died. In some states, such as California, a new deed doesn't need to be completed. After the affidavit and death certificate and any deed required have been recorded, title to the property can be transferred or sold by the survivor by signing a deed as "surviving joint tenant."

Tax liens. In some states that have state death taxes, tax liens (legal claims) may be imposed on all of a deceased person's property, and title cannot be transferred until the liens are removed. Removing them may involve posting a bond, filing a final inheritance tax return, or otherwise satisfying the tax authorities that taxes will be paid. It can be a major hassle for the surviving joint tenant. You'll need to locate the governmental agency that imposes and releases these tax liens, and see what is required to release them.

Federal estate taxes. Joint tenancy property can also be liable for a proportionate share of a deceased's federal estate taxes, if the estate is large enough to be subject to them. (See Chapter 15.) The taxes due will depend on the size of the taxable estate, which probably won't be determined for some time. But if the surviving owner must wait until the full amount of estate taxes are known (or even worse, paid) before obtaining clear title to the joint tenancy property, the practical advantages of the right of survivorship are severely diminished. After all, one purpose of a right of survivorship is to obtain clear title fast. Fortunately, the IRS will usually allow prompt transfer of joint tenancy property if there's an estimate of the value of the property in the estate and clear indication that there are enough other assets to pay off all estate taxes. The proof required that all taxes due can be paid from the remaining taxable estate will vary depending on the size, complexity and liquidity of the estate. ■

32

SOME ESTATE PLANS

A. A Prosperous Couple in Their 60s and 70s 32/2

B. A Wealthy Couple in Their 70s 32/2

C. A Single Man in His 60s 32/3

D. A Younger Couple 32/4

E. A Widow in Her 80s 32/5

F. A Couple in Their 60s, in a Second Marriage 32/6

G. An Unmarried Couple in Their 40s 32/7

This chapter presents seven different estate plans, each serving the needs of a person or couple in a different situation. As we stated at the beginning of this book, we don't believe that relying on pre-set formula plans is sensible. Instead you need a personal plan. The purpose of this chapter is to illustrate how the estate planning methods discussed in this book can be assembled into a coherent plan.

A. A PROSPEROUS COUPLE IN THEIR 60S AND 70S

Robert and Teresa Casswell are a prosperous married couple. He's 68, she's 72. Both are retired and live comfortably on their savings, assets and retirement payments. They live in a non-community property state and share ownership of all their property equally. The Casswells have four children.

Their property. A house worth $650,000 (all equity; they paid off the mortgage years ago), a summer home worth $225,000 ($175,000 equity), stocks and mutual funds worth $265,000, cash savings of $160,000, art works valued at $125,000, jewelry valued at $50,000 and miscellaneous personal property worth a total of $70,000. Their current total net worth is $1.5 million, all of which is in both their names. Of course, they hope the value of their estate will increase by the time a spouse dies.

Their estate planning goals. Robert and Teresa each want to leave most of their property to the surviving spouse and then to their four children in equal shares. They also want to leave smaller gifts to friends, relatives and charities. Because their combined estate is relatively large, they also want to plan to avoid probate and reduce estate taxes to the extent feasible.

Their plan. Robert and Teresa decide to establish a living trust to avoid probate. As part of that

trust, each spouse creates a formula AB trust to reduce overall estate taxes. If there is any property of the first spouse to die which is over the amount of the personal exemption in the year of death, that property goes outright to the surviving spouse.

Each spouse names their four children as the final beneficiaries of his or her AB trust.

In their living trust, each spouse also leaves several personal gifts to friends and charities. The successor trustee for the trust, after both spouses die, will be the Casswells' eldest daughter, a stable, savvy woman who lives near them and is respected by the other children. They have discussed this with her and mentioned it to the other children; happily, none of the others objected.

The Casswells work out the basic ideas of how they want their living trust and AB trust to work. Then they see a lawyer to help draw up the necessary documents, including basic back-up wills and durable powers of attorney for health care and for finances.

B. A WEALTHY COUPLE IN THEIR 70S

Rabia and Alfonso have been married for over 35 years. Rabia is 70, Alfonso is 79. They have two grown children in their early 40s. Rabia has one child, in his late 40s, from a former marriage.

Their property. Rabia and Alfonso's shared estate has a total net worth of $8.3 million. In addition, Rabia has separate property—a rental house worth $180,000, owned free and clear—she inherited from her mother.

Their estate planning goals. Because Rabia and Alfonso have a large estate, they want to save on estate taxes, leave much of their property for the eventual use of their two children, and also make a gift to charity. Also, Rabia wants to leave a gift to her son from her prior marriage.

Their plan. Each spouse's share of their common property is $4,150,000. Rabia, of course, has an additional $180,000 of her separate property.

First, they create a living trust to avoid probate of their property.

Next, each spouse decides to leave property in an AB trust, with their two children as the final beneficiaries. This way, each spouse makes use of his or her own personal estate tax exemption.

Then, each spouse decides that they have enough money to create a generation-skipping trust of $1 million (less any portion of estate taxes due paid from this sum). For Alfonso, this trust is relatively simple. His two children will be the middle generation, and their children (his grandchildren) the final generation. But Rabia wonders if she should also include her son from her first marriage, and his children, as beneficiaries of her generation-skipping trust.

After some reflection and soul-searching, she decides not to. Her son doesn't get along very well with one of her other children, so having both be beneficiaries of the same trust could become problematic. Rabia decides, instead, that she will leave her son a substantial mount of money outright. So, as a part of her living trust, Rabia leaves an outright gift of her separate property home (worth $180,000) and $320,000 from her shared property to her son, a total gift of $600,000. In the trust document, she directs that no estate taxes be paid from this gift.

Finally, each spouse creates a QTIP trust for the balance of their estate left over after their other trusts have been funded, or gifts made. Using a QTIP trust postpones estate taxes on the property until the second spouse dies. Alfonso names his two children to divide equally all money in his QTIP trust. Rabia distributes the property held by her QTIP trust to her final beneficiaries differently: 40% to each of her children with Alfonso, and 20% to her son from the earlier marriage.

Alfonso and Rabia complete their estate plan by each preparing a simple will, a durable power of attorney for health care, and a durable power of attorney for finances.

C. A SINGLE MAN IN HIS 60s

Dick Daughterty, a bachelor, wants to leave some of his property to his sister, some to her three children, and much to many friends.

His property. Dick has personal possessions worth $75,000, jewelry worth $25,000, a limited partnership interest worth $160,000, stocks worth $47,000 and savings of $45,000. He doesn't own any real estate. His total estate is worth $352,000

His estate planning goals. Dick is most concerned with who gets his property, not how they get it. He spends considerable time evaluating exactly who gets what, making several lists and numerous revisions before he settles on a plan.

Dick definitely doesn't want his estate to have to pay probate fees. Because his estate is well below the estate tax threshold, he doesn't have to worry about federal axes.

His plan. Dick creates a probate-avoiding living trust. In his trust, he specifies the many beneficiaries he's chosen, identifying each item of property that goes to each. Then he transfers all his property, except his savings account, to the living trust. He writes the Office of the General Partner for the limited partnership and instructs it to re-register ownership of his shares in his name as trustee of his trust.

Dick changes his savings account into a pay-on-death account and names his three best friends as equal beneficiaries of the account.

Next, he prepares a basic will, although, at present, none of his property will be transferred by will. His will covers the possibility he may subsequently acquire property which he isn't able to transfer to his trust before he dies.

Then he prepares two durable powers of attorney, one for health care and the other for finances. He names his best friend, Al, to be his attorney-in-fact for both, and another friend, Jacqueline, to be alternate attorney-in-fact for both if Al can't serve. Dick is particularly concerned about health care decisions. If he's incapacitated, he wants to be treated by his personal doctors. If he needs to be hospitalized, he wants to be taken to a specific local hospital. And he does not want life support technology used to artificially extend his life if he has a fatal, irreversible disease. So he drafts a durable power of attorney that incorporates all his specific desires, making them legal and mandatory.

Finally, Dick prepares his funeral plan and instructions and gives them to Al, to insure they're carried out.

D. A YOUNGER COUPLE

Mark Ryan and Alicia Lopez are married. He's 43, she's 32. They have two young children. Mark is employed as a carpenter; Alicia works part-time as a proofreader for a publisher. They live in Texas, a community property state.

Their property. They own their house (heavily mortgaged) in joint tenancy. It's their only major asset. They also own two cars, an old Ford and an older VW station wagon, the well-used furnishings of their home, personal possessions such as clothing, books and electronic equipment, and two savings accounts—one shared with $2,000, and another with $6,000 in Mark's name, an account he had before they were married.

Their estate planning goals. Mark and Alicia's main concern is providing for their children's care, both financial and personal, if both parents die. With total assets worth less than $100,000, they don't need to worry about federal estate taxes. And because their house is owned in joint tenancy, their major asset will avoid probate, unless they die simultaneously.

Their plan. Mark and Alicia decide they don't want to create a probate avoiding living trust now, as they don't have a lot of property and, statistically, are unlikely to die for many years. They prepare a will leaving all their non-joint tenancy property, except Mark's savings account, to each other. In their wills, they name their children as alternate beneficiaries, to receive all property covered by the wills and the house, in case both parents die simultaneously.

Mark and Alicia learn, to their mutual surprise, that they disagree on what should be done with Mark's $6,000 savings account. Alicia believes it should be handled like all their other property; indeed, she points out that Mark can easily convert the account to community property by simply depositing it in their joint account. Mark states that he wants to keep exclusive control over the account, as his own separate property. Further, he wants to leave it to his brother, Herb, a struggling woodworker whom he is close to. Alicia, who has long felt Herb was a no-goodnik, becomes upset that Mark wants to hold out on his own children. After all, if Mark died, she and the kids would need every cent they could get their hands on. As Mark starts to get angry, Alicia realizes they need to slow down and talk it out.

It takes a couple of days, but finally they arrive at a compromise. Mark will transfer $3,000 of his account into their shared account. He can leave the other $3,000 to Herb in his will.

Only after they resolve this issue do Mark and Alicia approach the subject they agree is most important: providing for their two children as best they can if the unlikely occurs and they die simultaneously. They agree on who should be the children's personal guardian, named in their wills—Alicia's sister Joan, who is willing to do the job.

They also name Joan as the children's property guardian. They decide that some life insurance is necessary, at least until their savings increase and the children are older. They decide to purchase $150,000 term life policies on each of their lives, realizing that because both of them work and the family needs two incomes to get by, it's not enough just to insure Mark's life.

Each establishes a family pot trust in both their wills. If both parents die, the insurance proceeds will be paid to the trust and managed for the children's benefit until they become 18.

Finally, Mark and Alicia each prepare a durable power of attorney for health care and a separate one for finances, each naming the other to make health care or financial decisions in case he or she becomes incapacitated, with Joan as the alternate attorney-in-fact.

E. A Widow in Her 80s

Ida Grant, a widow, lives in Oregon. She wants to leave the bulk of her estate to her one child, Carla. She also has a four-year-old Irish terrier, which she loves and wants to provide care for after she dies. Finally, she wants to make a number of small gifts to friends and charities.

Her property. Mrs. Grant's estate consists of a house that she and her husband bought in 1947 for $8,000. It now has a market value of $460,000. Mrs. Grant has household furnishings worth $20,000, a car worth $5,000, and savings of $200,000. She lives primarily on interest from her savings and Social Security.

Her estate planning goals. Mrs. Grant values simplicity. She wants to transfer her property by the simplest means possible, but she also wants to avoid probate.

Her plan. Mrs. Grant considers transferring her house into joint tenancy with her daughter Carla, whom she trusts absolutely, because this seems to provide the simplest probate-avoidance transfer method. However, Mrs. Grant learns there will be serious tax disadvantages if she uses joint tenancy. The IRS will require that a gift tax return be filed because Mrs. Grant is giving a half-interest in the house to her daughter. No tax will actually be paid now because the house's worth is under the gift/estate tax threshold, but still, it's a hassle to prepare and file the tax return.

Mrs. Grant decides to use a living trust for her house. This allows the house to avoid probate. She names Carla as the trust's beneficiary and successor trustee. She then signs and records a deed transferring the house from herself to herself as trustee of her trust. When listing the house as part of the trust property on the trust schedule, Mrs. Grant includes "all household furnishings," so her daughter will receive this property outside of probate as well.

Mrs. Grant wanted to establish an ongoing trust to provide care for her dog. However, when she checked this possibility out, she learned that trusts for animals are not legal in Oregon. (This is true in almost all states. *Dog Law,* by Mary Randolph (Nolo Press), has a detailed discussion of how to provide for a dog that may survive its owner.) A better approach, she learned, is to handle the problem informally. Mrs. Grant discussed her concern with Carla, who is far from being a dog lover. Carla suggested that the dog, and a sum of money necessary to care for it, be left to Betty Planquee, a good friend who had said she would accept the responsibility.

Mrs. Grant learns that under Oregon law she can transfer property worth less than $140,000 by her will free of probate. She has her savings in two money market accounts. She divides the money in those accounts so that each contains less than $140,000. She changes one pay-on-death account, naming her daughter as beneficiary, and so avoids probate of that account. Then, using a back-up will, she leaves several cash gifts to close friends:

- "I leave the sum of $20,000 to my good friend and long-time veterinarian, Arthur Pedronnzi.
- I leave the sum of $5,000 to my good friend and faithful gardener, William Service.
- I leave the sum of $23,000 and my dog Cherry Blossom to my friend Betty Planquee.
- I leave the sum of $2,500 to my friend Mary Bale.
- I leave the sum of $2,500 to my friend Roberta Anthony."

The residuary clause of her will provides "I leave all my remaining property subject to this will to my daughter, Carla." Under this clause, all cash remain-

ing in her non-pay-on-death bank account, after the above gifts are made, goes to Carla. Because the total amount of property transferred under her will is under $140,000, no probate is required.

Mrs. Grant doesn't name any alternate beneficiaries. She wants to keep her will simple, and decides that if any of her friends die before her, she wants that money to go to Carla under the terms of the residuary clause. And she doesn't even want to consider the possibility that Carla could die before she does.

Mrs. Grant also prepares two durable powers of attorney, one for health care and one for finances, naming her daughter Carla in both as her attorney-in-fact, to act for her if she becomes incapacitated and can't make medical or financial decisions herself.

F. A COUPLE IN THEIR 60s, IN A SECOND MARRIAGE

Miriam and Ira Bloom are a married couple in their 60s. It's the second marriage for each. Miriam has one child, now 32, from her first marriage; Ira has two, who are 33 and 36, from his first marriage. The Blooms live in New York, a common law state.

Their property. Miriam and Ira share ownership of a $200,000 condominium apartment ($160,000 equity), savings of $80,000, stocks worth $55,000, and miscellaneous furnishings worth approximately $15,000. Each separately owns a car worth roughly $10,000. Ira owns, as his separate property, real estate worth $340,000 ($250,000 equity), partnership interests worth $80,000, and savings of $40,000. Miriam owns a coin collection worth $5,000 and mutual funds worth $185,000.

Their estate planning goals. Both Miriam and Ira want to provide for each other, but each also wants to ensure that their children from their prior marriages are well provided for. Ira's total estate is now worth $535,000. Miriam's is worth $355,000. Neither's estate is large enough to be subject to federal estate taxes, but they do want to avoid probate fees.

Their plan. Miriam and Ira agree that each will leave their shared ownership property outright to the other. Any New York state death taxes assessed against either's estate will be paid from this shared property. Each one's separate property will be left in an AB trust for the other spouse, with the property in the trust to ultimately go to the deceased spouse's children. Then they see a lawyer to draw up the trust document. The surviving spouse will be the trustee of whichever Trust A becomes operational (containing the separate property of the deceased spouse). Each spouse fully trusts the other to manage his or her trust property, and is confident he or she will conserve the trust principal for their children. But both spouses know that their children are somewhat mistrustful of this arrangement. So the spouses agree that the surviving spouse will send the deceased spouse's children yearly reports of the trust's financial status (a copy of the trust's annual tax return will suffice) to reassure them that the property isn't being squandered.

Because one of Ira's children still needs financial support for education, he places $20,000 of his separate savings in a pay-on-death bank account for her, so she will immediately get money, without delay, should he die before she graduates. If the daughter completes her education with Ira's help before he dies, he can then, if he wants to, revoke the informal bank account trust and place the account in his living trust.

The Blooms also each execute durable powers of attorney for health care and finances, naming the other spouse as the attorney-in-fact.

Finally, the Blooms prepare simple basic wills.

G. An Unmarried Couple in Their 40s

Pat and Mercedes have lived together for 13 years. They have no children. They have a written living-together contract, stating that they share ownership of their house and household goods. They've also recorded a deed to the house as tenants in common, with each owning half. In their agreement they've provided that all other property of each is his or her separate property.

Their estate planning goals. Each wants to leave his or her interest in the house and furnishings to the other, and other items to family and friends. Each wants to avoid probate of all their property. Neither's estate will be subject to federal estate taxes. Finally, each wants to ensure that the other can make medical and financial decisions if one becomes incapacitated.

Their plan. They decide to create three living trusts: one for their shared property and one for each one's separate property. This, they conclude, will be clearer than putting all their property into one trust.

In their shared trust, each leaves his or her interest in the house and furnishings to the other. They prepare and file a deed transferring ownership of their house into their names as trustees of their shared trust. In their individual living trusts, each leaves gifts of their separate property to the beneficiaries they've chosen. When their individual trusts are complete, they both complete all paperwork necessary to transfer documents to transfer property to the trusts.

Each also prepares a basic will and leaves all property subject to those wills (none now) to the other.

Finally, Pat and Mercedes each prepare a durable power of attorney for health care and one for finances, naming the other as their attorney-in-fact, with authority to make decisions if one becomes incapacitated. ■

GLOSSARY

Part of the hold that the legal profession has over us has to do with its use of specialized language. It is easy to be intimidated and uncomfortable when we don't know what lawyers and judges are talking about. It is only beginning to dawn on many of us that legal language is sometimes consciously, and occasionally even cynically, used to keep us intimidated, and that the concepts behind the obtuse language are often easily understandable. We'd rather use only plain English throughout this book and eliminate legalistic jargon altogether, but unfortunately we are stuck with a legal system that often creaks into motion best when "magic" (sometimes four-syllabic) words are used. (Lawyers call such words "terms of art.")

If you don't find a confusing term defined here, try a standard dictionary, but be sure to read the entire definition, as specialized legal meanings are often listed last. Or, for family matters, check *Nolo's Pocket Guide to Family Law.* As a last resort, try *Black's Law Dictionary,* available in all law libraries.

Note Definitions in quotes and with the symbol (B.) following are taken from Ambrose Bierce's *The Devil's Dictionary.*

AB trust As used in *Plan Your Estate,* a trust giving a surviving spouse (or mate) a life estate interest in property of a deceased spouse or mate. This type of trust is designed to save on eventual estate taxes by giving a surviving spouse (or member of an unmarried couple) the income from the property of the first spouse to die (not the property itself). It can also be called a "marital life estate trust," or "spousal bypass trust," or an "exemption trust."

Abatement Cutting back certain gifts under a will when it is necessary to create a fund to meet expenses, pay taxes, satisfy debts or take care of other bequests which are given a priority under law or under the will.

Abstract of Trust A condensed version of a living trust, which leaves out the key parts of what property is in the trust and who are the beneficiaries. An Abstract of Trust is used to establish, to a financial organization or other institution, that a valid living trust has been established, without revealing specifics of property or beneficiaries the person who created the trust wants to keep private and confidential.

Accumulation Trust A trust where trust income is retained, and not paid out to beneficiaries until certain conditions occur.

Acknowledgment A statement in front of a person who is qualified to administer oaths (e.g., a Notary Public) that a document bearing your signature was actually signed by you.

Ademption The failure of a specific bequest of property to take effect because the property is no longer owned by the person who made the will at the time of his death.

Administration (of an estate) The court-supervised distribution of the probate estate of a deceased person. The person who manages the distribution is called the executor if there is a will. If there is no will, this person is called the administrator. In some states, the person is called "personal representative" in either instance.

Adopted Children Any person, whether an adult or a minor, who is legally adopted as the child of another in a court proceeding.

Adult Any person over the age of 18.

Affidavit A written statement made under oath.

Annuity   Payment of a fixed sum of money to a specified person at regular intervals.

Augmented Estate   A method used in a number of states following the common law ownership of property system to measure a person's estate for the purpose of determining whether a surviving spouse has been adequately provided for. Generally, the augmented estate consists of property left by the will plus certain property transferred outside of the will by gifts, joint tenancies and living trusts. In the states using this concept, a surviving spouse is generally considered to be adequately provided for if he or she receives at least one-third of the augmented estate.

Autopsy   Examination of the body of a deceased person to determine the cause of death.

Basis   This is a tax term which has to do with the valuation of property for determining profit or loss on sale. If you buy a house (or a poodle) for $20,000, your tax basis is $20,000. If you later sell it for $35,000, your taxable profit is $15,000. A **stepped up basis** means that you have been able to raise this basic amount from which taxes are computed.

Beneficiary   A person or organization who is legally entitled to receive gifts made under a legal document such as a will or trust. Except when very small estates are involved, beneficiaries of wills only receive their benefits after the will is examined and approved by the probate court. Beneficiaries of living trusts receive their benefits outside of probate, as provided in the document establishing the trust. A primary beneficiary is a person who directly and certainly will benefit from a will or trust. A contingent beneficiary is a person who might or might not become a beneficiary, depending on the terms of the will or trust and what happens to the primary beneficiaries. For example, a contingent beneficiary might get nothing until and unless the primary beneficiary

dies, with a portion of the trust corpus still remaining.

Bequest   An old legal term for a will provision leaving personal property to a specified person or organization. In this book it is called a "gift."

Bond   A document guaranteeing that a certain amount of money will be paid to those injured if a person occupying a position of trust does not carry out his or her legal and ethical responsibilities. Thus, if an executor, trustee or guardian who is bonded (covered by a bond) wrongfully deprives a beneficiary of his or her property (say by blowing it during a trip in Las Vegas), the bonding company will replace it, up to the limits of the bond. Bonding companies, which are normally divisions of insurance companies, issue a bond in exchange for a premium, usually about 10% of the face amount of the bond.

Bypass trust   Any trust that creates a life estate for a life beneficiary, with the trust principal going to the final beneficiary when the life beneficiary dies.

Charitable trust   Any trust designed to make a substantial gift to a charity, and also achieve income and estate tax savings for the grantor.

Children   For the purposes of *Plan Your Estate,* one's children are: (1) the biological offspring of a will maker, (2) persons who were legally adopted by a will maker, (3) children born out of wedlock if the will maker is the mother, (4) children born out of wedlock if the will maker is the father and has acknowledged the child as being his as required by the law of the particular state, or (5) children born to the will maker after the will is made, but before his or her death.

Child's trust   A trust created for a minor child, or young adult.

Codicil   A separate legal document which, after it has been signed and properly witnessed, changes an existing will.

Common law marriage   In a minority of states, couples may be considered married if they live together for a certain period of time and intend to be husband and wife.

Community and separate property   Eight states follow a system of marital property ownership called "community property," and Wisconsin has a very similar "marital property" law. Very generally, all property acquired after marriage and before permanent separation is considered to belong equally to both spouses, except for gifts to and inheritances by one spouse, and, in some community property states, income from property owned by one spouse prior to marriage.

Conditional gift   A gift which passes only under certain specified conditions or upon the occurrence of a specific event. For example, if you leave property to Aunt Millie provided she is living in Cincinnati when you die, and otherwise to Uncle Fred, you have made a "conditional gift."

Conservator   Someone appointed by a court to manage the affairs of a mentally incompetent person.

Contract   An agreement between two or more people to do something. A contract is normally written, but can be oral if its terms can be carried out within one year and it doesn't involve real estate. A contract is distinguished from a gift in that each of the contracting parties pledges to do something in exchange for the promises of the other.

Creditor   As used in this book, this means a person or institution to whom money is owed. A creditor may be the person who actually lent the money, or he may be a lawyer or bill collector who is trying to collect the money for the original creditor.

Curtesy   See **Dower and curtesy.**

Custodian   A person named to care for property left to a minor under the Uniform Transfers (or Gifts) to Minors Act.

Death taxes   Taxes levied on the property of a person who died. Federal death taxes are called "Estate Taxes." State death taxes (if any) go by various names, including "inheritance tax."

Debtor   A person who owes money.

Decedent   A person who has died.

Deed   The legal document by which one person (or persons) transfers title (recorded ownership) to real estate to another person or persons. If the transfer is by a grant deed, the person transferring title makes certain guarantees or warranties as regards the title. If the transfer is by quitclaim deed, the person transferring does not make any guarantees, but simply transfers to the other persons all the interest he has in the real property.

Descendant   A person who is an offspring, however remote, of a certain person or family.

Devise   An old English term for real estate given by a will. In this book, it is called a "gift."

Disclaimer   The right to refuse to accept property left to you by trust or will.

Domicile   The state, or country, where one has his or her primary home.

Donor   One who gives a gift. A **donee** is one who receives a gift.

Dower and curtesy   The right of a surviving spouse to receive or enjoy the use of a set portion of a deceased spouse's property (usually one-third to one-half) in the event the surviving spouse is not left at least that share and chooses to take against the will. Dower refers to the title which a surviving wife gets, while curtesy refers to what a man receives. Until recently, these amounts differed in a number of states. However, since discrimination on the basis of sex is now illegal in most cases, states generally provide the same benefits regardless of sex.

Durable power of attorney A power of attorney which remains effective even if the person who created it (called the "principal") becomes incapacitated. The person authorized to act (called the "attorney-in-fact") can make health care decisions and handle financial affairs of the principal.

Encumbrances If property is used as collateral for payment of a debt or loan, the property is "encumbered." The debt must be paid off before title to the property can pass to a new owner. Generally, the value of a person's ownership in such property (called the "equity") is measured by the market value of the property less the sum of all encumbrances.

Equity The difference between the current fair market value of your real and personal property and the amount you owe on it, if any.

Escheat We put this in here because it's one of our favorite legal words; it means property that goes to a state government because there are no legal inheritors to claim it.

Estate Generally, all the property you own when you die. There are different ways to measure your estate, depending on whether you are concerned with tax reduction (the taxable estate), probate avoidance (the probate estate) or net worth (the net estate).

Estate planning What this book is about—the art of continuing to prosper when you're alive, then dying with the smallest taxable estate and probate estate possible, and passing your property to your loved ones with a minimum of fuss and expense.

Estate taxes Taxes imposed on your property as it passes from the dead to the living. The federal government exempts a set dollar amount of property (between $625,000 and $1 million, depending on the date of death). Taxes are only imposed on property actually owned by you at the time of your death. Thus, estate planning techniques designed to reduce taxes usually concentrate on the legal transfer of ownership of your property while you are living, to minimize the amount of such property you own at your death.

Executor The person named in your will to manage your estate, deal with the probate court, collect your assets and distribute them as you have specified. In some states this person is called the "personal representative." If you die without a will, the probate court will appoint such a person, who is called the "administrator" of the estate.

Exemption trust A trust funded with an amount no larger than the personal federal estate tax exemption as of the year of death.

Final beneficiaries People or institutions designated to receive life estate trust property outright upon the death of a life beneficiary.

Financial guardian See **Guardian of the Minor's Property.**

Funding a Trust Transferring ownership of property to a trust, in the name of the trustee.

Funeral "A pageant whereby we attest to our respect to the dead by enriching the undertaker, and strengthen our grief by an expenditure that deepens our groans and doubles our tears." (B.)

Future interest A right to property which cannot be enforced in the present, but at some future time.

Generation-skipping trust An estate tax-saving trust, where the principal is left in trust for one's grandchildren, with one's children receiving only the trust income.

Gifts   As used in *Plan Your Estate,* any property you give to another person or organization, either during your lifetime, or leave by will or living trust after your death.

Gift taxes   Taxes levied by governments on gifts made during a person's lifetime.

Grantor   The person who establishes a trust; also sometimes called a "settlor" or "trustor."

Grantor retained income trusts   Various types of trusts where the grantor retains some interest in the trust property during his life.

Guardian of the minor's property   Termed "property guardian" in this book, this is the person you name in your will to care for property of your minor child not supervised by some other legal method, such as a minor's trust. Also sometimes called "the guardian of the minor's estate," or "financial guardian."

Guardian of the person   An adult appointed or selected to care for a minor child in the event no biological or adoptive parent (legal parent) of the child is able to do so. If one legal parent is alive when the other dies, the child will automatically go to that parent, unless the best interests of the child require something different, or (in some states) the court finds the child would suffer detriment.

Hearse   "Death's baby carriage." (B.)

Heirs   Persons who are entitled by law to inherit your estate if you don't leave a will or other device to pass property at your death.

Holographic will   A will that is completely hand-written by the person making it. While legal in many states, it is never advised except as a last resort.

Incidents of ownership   All (or any) control over a life insurance policy.

Inherit   To receive property from one who dies.

Inheritance taxes   Taxes some states impose on property received by inheritors from a deceased's estate.

Inheritors   Persons or organizations who inherit property.

Instrument   Legalese for document; often used to refer to the document which creates a trust.

Insurance   "An ingenious modern game of chance in which the player is permitted to enjoy the comfortable conviction that he is beating the man who keeps the table." (B.)

Inter vivos trusts   See **Living Trusts.**

Intestate   To die without a will or other valid estate transfer device.

Intestate succession   The method by which property is distributed when a person fails to distribute it in a will. In such cases, the law of each state provides that the property be distributed in certain shares to the closest surviving relatives. In most states, these are a surviving spouse, children, parents, siblings, nieces and nephews, and next of kin, in that order. The intestate succession laws are also used in the event an heir is found to be pretermitted (not mentioned or otherwise provided for in the will).

Irrevocable trust   Means what it says. Once you set it up, that's it. Unlike a revocable, probate-avoidance trust, you can't later revoke it, amend it, or change it in any way.

Issue   Legalese for one's direct descendants—children, grandchildren, etc.

Joint tenancy   A way to take title to jointly owned real or personal property. When two or more people own property as joint tenants, and one of the owners dies, the other owners automatically become owners of the deceased owner's share. Because of this "right of survivorship," a joint tenancy interest in property does not go through probate.

Lawful   "Compatible with the will of a judge having jurisdiction." (B.)

Lawyer   "One skilled in circumvention of the law." (B.)

Legacy   "A gift from one who is legging it out of this vale of tears." (B.)

Letters testamentary   The term for the document issued by a probate court authorizing the executor to discharge her responsibilities.

Life beneficiary   A person who can receive use of trust property, and benefit of trust income for his or her life, but who doesn't own the trust property itself (the "principal") and has no power to dispose of the trust property upon his or her own death.

Life estate   The right to use trust property, and receive income from it, during one's lifetime.

Life insurance trust   An irrevocable trust that owns a life insurance policy to reduce the size of the original owner's taxable estate.

Liquid assets   Cash or assets that can readily be turned into cash.

Living trusts   A trust set up while a person is alive and which remains under the control of that person until death. Also referred to as an "inter vivos trust," a living trust is an excellent way to minimize the value of property passing through probate. This is because it enables people (called "grantors") to specify that money or other property will pass directly to their beneficiaries at the time of their death, free of probate, and yet also allows the grantors to continue to control the property during their lifetime and even end the trust or change the beneficiaries if they wish.

Living will   A document where you provide that you do not want to have your life artificially prolonged by technical means, but choose a natural death.

Marital deduction   A deduction allowed by the federal estate tax law for all property passed to a surviving spouse. This deduction (which really acts like an exemption) allows anyone, even a billionaire, to pass his or her entire estate to a surviving spouse without any tax at all. This might be a good idea if the surviving spouse is relatively young and in good health.

Marriage   A specific status conferred on a couple by the state. In most states, it is necessary to file papers with a county clerk and have a marriage ceremony conducted by an authorized individual in order to be married. However, in a minority of states called "common law marriage" states, you may be considered married if you have lived together for a certain period of time and intended to be husband and wife.

Mausoleum   "The final and funniest folly of the rich." (B.)

Minor   Persons under 18 years of age. A minor is not permitted to make certain types of decisions (for example, enter into most contracts). All minors are required to be under the care of a competent adult (parent or guardian) unless they qualify as emancipated minors (in the military, married or living independently with court permission). This also means that property left to a minor must be handled by a guardian or trustee until the minor becomes an adult under the laws of the state.

Mopery   Not genuine legalese, but a humorous facsimile, such as "indicted on two counts of mopery."

Mortgage   A document that makes a piece of real estate the security (collateral) for the payment of a debt. Most house buyers sign a mortgage when they buy; the bank lends money to buy the house, and the house serves as security for the debt. If the owners don't pay back the loan on time, the bank can seize the house and have it sold to pay off the loan.

Net taxable estate   The value of all your property at death less all encumbrances and your other liabilities.

Next of kin   The closest living relation.

Ongoing trust   Any trust that is designed to be irrevocable and be operational for an extended period of time.

Pay-on-death designation   A method of providing, on a property account form, who will inherit what remains of that property when you die. Most commonly used for bank accounts.

Personal property   All property other than land and buildings attached to land. Cars, bank accounts, wages, securities, a small business, furniture, insurance policies, jewelry, pets and season baseball tickets are all personal property.

Pour-over will   A will that "pours over" property into a trust. Property left through the will must go through probate before it goes into the trust.

Power of appointment   Having the legal authority to decide who shall receive someone else's property, usually property held in a trust.

Power of attorney   A legal document where you authorize someone else to act for you. *See also* **Durable Power of Attorney.**

Pretermitted heir   A child (or the child of a deceased child) who is either not named or (in some states) not provided for in a will. Most states presume that persons want their children to inherit. Accordingly, children, or the children of a child who has died, who are not mentioned or provided for in the will (even by as little as $1) are entitled to a share of the estate.

Probate   The court proceeding in which: (1) the authenticity of your will (if any) is established, (2) your executor or administrator is appointed, (3) your debts and taxes are paid, (4) your heirs are identified, and (5) your property in your probate estate is distributed according to your will (if there is a will).

Probate estate   All of your property that will pass through probate. Generally, this means all property owned by you at your death less any property that has been placed in joint tenancy, a living trust, a bank account trust or in life insurance.

Probate fees   Because probate is so laden with legal formalities, it is usually necessary to hire an attorney to handle it. The attorney will take a substantial fee from the estate before it is distributed to the heirs.

Property control trust   Any trust that imposes limits or controls over the rights of beneficiaries, for one of a number of reasons. These trusts include:

Special needs trusts designed to assist disadvantaged persons with special physical or other needs;

Spendthrift trusts designed to prevent a beneficiary from being able to waste trust principal;

Sprinkling trusts which authorize the trustee to decide how to distribute trust income or principal among different beneficiaries.

Proving a will   Getting a probate court to accept the fact after your death that your will really is your will. In many states this can be done simply by introducing a properly signed and witnessed will. In others, it is necessary to produce one or more witnesses (or their affidavits) in court, or offer some proof of the will maker's handwriting. Having the will maker and witnesses sign an affidavit before a notary public stating that all will-making formalities were complied with usually allows the will to "prove" itself without the need for the witnesses to testify, or other evidence.

QDOT trust   A trust used to postpone estate taxes, when more than the amount of the personal estate tax exemption in the year of death is left to a non-U.S. citizen spouse by the other spouse.

QTIP trust   A marital trust with property left for use of the surviving spouse as life beneficiary. No estate taxes are assessed on the trust property until the death of the life beneficiary spouse.

Quasi-community property   A rule that applies to married couples who have moved to California, Idaho or Washington. Laws in those states require all property acquired by people during their marriage in other states to be treated as community property at their death.

Real estate   A term used by *Plan Your Estate* as a synonym for the legalese "real property."

Real property   All land and items attached to the land, such as buildings, houses, stationary mobile homes, fences and trees are real property or "real estate." All property which is not real property is personal property.

Recording   The process of filing a copy of a deed with the county land records office. Recording creates a public record of all changes in ownership of property in the state.

Residual beneficiary   Can have various meanings, including: a person who receives any property left by will or trust not otherwise given away by the document; a person receiving the property of a trust after the life beneficiary dies.

Residue, residuary estate   All property given by your will or trust to your residuary beneficiary after all specific gifts of property have been made—that is, what's left.

Right of survivorship   The right of a surviving joint tenant to take ownership of a deceased joint tenant's share of the property.

Rule against perpetuities   A rule of law which limits the durations of trusts (except charitable ones). The workings of the rule are very complicated, and have baffled law students for generations. Very roughly, a trust cannot last longer than the lifetime of someone alive when the trust is created, plus 21 years.

Separate property   In states which have community property, all property which is not community property. See also **Community and separate property.**

Spouse   In *Plan Your Estate,* your spouse is the person to whom you are legally married.

Successor trustee   The person (or institution) who takes over as trustee of a trust when the original trustee(s) have died or become incapacitated.

Surviving spouse's trust   Where a couple has created an AB trust, the revocable living trust (Trust B) of the surviving spouse, after the other spouse has died.

Taking against the will   The ability of a surviving spouse to choose a statutorily allotted share of the deceased spouse's estate instead of the share specified in his or her will. In most common law property states, the law provides that a surviving spouse is entitled to receive a minimum percentage of the other spouse's estate (commonly one-third to one-half). If the deceased spouse leaves the surviving spouse less than this in, or outside of, the will, the surviving spouse may elect the statutory share instead of the will provision ("take against the will"). If the spouse chooses to accept the share specified in the will, it is called "taking under the will." See **Dower and Curtesy.**

Taxable estate   The portion of your estate that is subject to federal or state estate taxes.

Tenancy by the entirety   A form of marital property ownership, with a right of survivorship between spouses; similar to joint tenancy.

Tenancy in common   A way for co-owners to hold title to property that allows them maximum freedom to dispose of their interests by sale, gift or will. At a co-owner's death, his or her share goes to beneficiaries named in a will or trust or to the legal heirs, not to the other co-owners. Compare **Joint tenancy.**

Testamentary trust   A trust created by a will.

Testate   Someone who dies leaving a valid will, or other valid property transfer devices, dies "testate."

Testator   A person making a will.

Title   Document proving ownership of property.

Totten trust   Another term for a pay-on-death bank account.

Trust   A legal arrangement under which one person or institution (called a "trustee") controls property given by another person (called a "grantor" or "trustor") for the benefit of a third person (called a "beneficiary"). The property itself can be termed the "principal" of the trust.

Trust corpus or res   Legalese (in Latin, no less) for the property transferred to a trust. For example, if a trust is established (funded) with $250,000, that money is the corpus or res.

Trust merger   Occurs when the sole trustee and sole beneficiary are the same person. Then, there's no longer the separation between the trustee's legal ownership of trust property from the beneficiary's interest, which is the essence of a trust. So, the trust "merges" and ceases to exist.

Trustee   The people or institutions who manage a trust and trust property under the terms of the trust.

Trustee powers   The provisions in a trust document defining what the trustee may and may not do.

Uniform Transfers (or Gifts) to Minors Act   A series of state statutes that provide a method for transferring property to minors.

Usufruct   Included because it's another of our favorite legal words, meaning the right to use property, or income from it, owned by another.

Will   A legal document in which a person states various binding intentions about what he or she wants done with his or her property after death. ■

APPENDIX

STATE DEATH TAX RULES

CHART 1. INHERITANCE TAXES

Following are the rules for each state which imposes inheritance taxes:

CONNECTICUT

Class AA: Surviving spouse

Class A: Parent, grandparent, adoptive parent or natural or adopted descendant

Class B: Son- or daughter-in-law of child (natural or adopted) who has not remarried. Stepchild, brother or sister (full or half or adopted), brother or sister's children (descendants, natural or adopted)

Class C: All other persons

Taxable Amount			Tax Rate
Class AA			No Tax
Class A	50,000	to 150,000	3%
	150,000	to 250,000	4%
	250,000	to 400,000	5%
	400,000	to 600,000	6%
	600,000	to 1,000,000	7%
	1,000,000	And Over	8%
Class B	6,000	to 25,000	4%
	25,000	to 150,000	5%
	150,000	to 250,000	6%
	250,000	to 400,000	7%
	400,000	to 600,000	8%
	600,000	to 1,000,000	9%
	1,000,000	And Over	10%
Class C	1,000	to 25,000	8%
	25,000	to 150,000	9%
	150,000	to 250,000	10%
	250,000	to 400,000	11%
	400,000	to 600,000	12%
	600,000	to 1,000,000	13%
	1,000,000	And Over	14%

DELAWARE

Class A: Spouse

Class B: Parent, grandparent, child (by birth or adoption), son- or daughter-in-law, lineal descendant, or stepchild

Class C: Brother, sister, their descendants; aunt, uncle, their descendants

Class D: All others

Taxable Amount			Tax Rate
Class A	70,000	to 100,000	2%
	100,000	to 200,000	3%
	200,000	And Over	4%
Class B	25,000	to 50,000	2%
	50,000	to 75,000	3%
	75,000	to 100,000	4%
	100,000	to 200,000	5%
	200,000	And Over	6%
Class C	5,000	to 25,000	5%
	25,000	to 50,000	6%
	50,000	to 100,000	7%
	100,000	to 150,000	8%
	150,000	to 200,000	9%
	200,000	And Over	10%
Class D	1,000	to 25,000	10%
	25,000	to 50,000	12%
	50,000	to 100,000	14%
	100,000	And Over	16%

INDIANA

Class A: Spouse, parents, children, grandchildren

Class B: Sibling, nieces and nephews, son- or daughter-in-law

Class C: All others

Taxable Amount			Tax Rate		
			Base Tax	Plus %	of Amt Over
Class A					
0	to	25,000	0	+ 1%	0
25,000	to	50,000	250	+ 2%	25,000
50,000	to	200,000	750	+ 3%	50,000
200,000	to	300,000	5,250	+ 4%	200,000
300,000	to	500,000	9,250	+ 5%	300,000
500,000	to	700,000	19,250	+ 6%	500,000
700,000	to	1,000,000	31,250	+ 7%	700,000
1,000,000	to	1,500,000	52,250	+ 8%	1,000,000
1,500,000		And Over	92,250	+ 10%	1,500,000
Class B					
0	to	100,000	0	+ 7%	0
100,000	to	500,000	7,000	+ 10%	100,000
500,000	to	1,000,000	47,000	+ 12%	500,000
1,000,000		And Over	107,000	+ 15%	1,000,000
Class C					
0	to	100,000	0	+ 10%	0
100,000	to	1,000,000	10,000	+ 15%	100,000
1,000,000		And Over	45,000	+ 20%	1,000,000

Exemptions

1. Spouse: All tax

2. Child under 21 at death: $10,000

3. Child over 21 at death: $5,000

4. Parents: $5,000

5. Other Class A: $2,000

6. Class B: $500

7. Class C: $100

IOWA

Class 1:   Spouse

Class 2:   Parent, child, lineal descendant

Class 3:   Sibling, son- or daughter-in-law, stepchild

Class 4:   All others

Taxable Amount			Tax Rate
Class 1			No Tax
Class 2			
0	to	5,000	1%
5,000	to	12,000	2%
12,000	to	25,000	3%
25,000	to	50,000	4%
50,000	to	75,000	5%
75,000	to	100,000	6%
100,000	to	150,000	7%
150,000		And Over	8%
Class 3			
0	to	12,500	5%
12,500	to	25,000	6%
25,000	to	75,000	7%
75,000	to	100,000	8%
100,000	to	150,000	9%
150,000		And Over	10%
Class 4			
0	to	50,000	10%
50,000	to	100,000	12%
100,000		And Over	15%

Exemptions

1. Each son and daughter: $50,000

2. Father or mother: $15,000

3. Any other lineal descendant: $15,000

4. Any estate not exceeding $10,000

KANSAS

Class A: Lineal ancestors and descendants; stepparents,
stepchildren, adopted children, lineal descendants of
adopted child or stepchild, spouse or surviving
spouse of son or daughter, spouse or surviving
spouse of an adopted child or stepchild

Class B: Siblings

Class C: All others

	Taxable Amount			Tax Rate
Class A	0	to	25,000	1%
	25000	to	50,000	2%
	50,000	to	100,000	3%
	100,000	to	500,000	4%
	500,000	And Over		5%
Class B	0	to	25,000	3.0%
	25,000	to	50,000	5.0%
	50,000	to	100,000	7.5%
	100,000	to	500,000	10.0%
	500,000	And Over		12.5%
Class C	0	to	100,000	10%
	100,000	to	200,000	12%
	200,000	And Over		15%

Exemptions

(Taxable amount begins after taking applicable exemption)

1. Spouse: All tax

2. Class A: $30,000

3. Class B: $5,000

4. Qualified real estate: to $750,000, if left to family member
and used for family farm or business

KENTUCKY

Class A: Parent, spouse, child, stepchild, adopted child, or
grandchild

Class B: Sibling, nephew or niece, daughter- or son-in-law,
aunt or uncle

Class C: All others

	Taxable Amount			Tax Rate
Class A	0	to	20,000	2%
	20,000	to	30,000	3%
	30,000	to	45,000	4%
	45,000	to	60,000	5%
	60,000	to	100,000	6%
	100,000	to	200,000	7%
	200,000	to	500,000	8%
	500,000	And Over		10%
Class B	0	to	10,000	4%
	10,000	to	20,000	5%
	20,000	to	30,000	6%
	30,000	to	45,000	8%
	45,000	to	60,000	10%
	60,000	to	100,000	12%
	100,000	to	200,000	14%
	200,000	And Over		16%
Class C	0	to	10,000	6%
	10,000	to	20,000	8%
	20,000	to	30,000	10%
	30,000	to	45,000	12%
	45,000	to	60,000	14%
	60,000	And Over		16%

Exemptions

1. Spouse: All tax

2. Infant/child: $20,000

3. Mentally disabled child: $20,000

4. Parent: $5,000

5. Child or stepchild: $5,000

6. Grandchild: $5,000

7. Class B: $1,000

8. Class C: $500

LOUISIANA

Class 1: Spouse, descendants, lineal ancestors

Class 2: Collateral relatives (siblings, their children)

Class 3: All others

	Taxable Amount			Tax Rate
Class 1	0	to	20,000	2%
	20,000		And Over	3%
Class 2	0	to	1,000	No Tax
	1,000	to	21,000	5%
	21,000		And Over	7%
Class 3	0	to	500	No Tax
	500	to	5,500	5%
	5,500		And Over	10%

Exemptions

1. Spouse: All tax if death in 1992 or after

2. Class 1: $25,000 if death is in 1987 or after

MARYLAND

Class 1: Spouse, parent, children, grandparent, descendants, stepchild, stepparent

Class 2: All others

	Taxable Amount	Tax Rate
Class 1	All Amounts	1%
Class 2	All Amounts	10%

Exemptions

1. Spouse: First $100,000 of personal property; all real property

2. Property administered under small estates law

Special tax rates

Spouse of descendant: 1% for first $2,000 of jointly owned savings; thereafter at 10%

MICHIGAN

Class 1: Spouse, parent, grandparent, sibling, son- or daughter-in-law, children and adopted children

Class 2: All others

	Taxable Amount			Tax Rate
Class 1	0	to	50,000	2%
	50,000	to	250,000	4%
	250,000	to	500,000	7%
	500,000	to	750,000	8%
	750,000		And Over	10%
Class 2	0	to	50,000	12%
	50,000	to	500,000	14%
	500,000		And Over	17%

Exemptions

1. Spouse: $65,000

2. All other Class 1: $10,000

3. Family-owned business—no tax if transferred to qualified heir

MONTANA

Class 1: Spouse, lineal descendant or child, and lineal ancestor

Class 2: Siblings, their offspring, son- or daughter-in-law

Class 3: Uncle, aunt, or first cousins

Class 4: All others

	Taxable Amount			Tax Rate
Class 1	0	to	25,000	2%
	25,000	to	50,000	4%
	50,000	to	100,000	6%
	100,000	And Over		8%
Class 2	0	to	25,000	4%
	25,000	to	50,000	8%
	50,000	to	100,000	12%
	100,000	And Over		16%
Class 3	0	to	25,000	6%
	25,000	to	50,000	12%
	50,000	to	100,000	18%
	100,000	And Over		24%
Class 4	0	to	25,000	8%
	25,000	to	50,000	16%
	50,000	to	100,000	24%
	100,000	And Over		32%

Exemptions

1. Spouse or child or lineal descendant: All tax

2. Lineal ancestors: $7,000

3. Class 2: $1,000

4. Charitable, educational, religious gifts: All tax

NEBRASKA

Class 1: Spouse, parent, child, son- or daughter-in-law

Class 2: Uncle, aunt, niece, nephew or their descendants or spouses

Class 3: All others

	Taxable Amount			Tax Rate
Class 1	0	to	10,000	No Tax
	10,000	And Over		1%
Class 2	0	to	2,000	No Tax
	2,000	to	60,000	6%
	60,000	And Over		9%
Class 3	0	to	5,000	6%
	5,000	to	10,000	9%
	10,000	to	20,000	12%
	20,000	to	50,000	15%
	50,000	And Over		18%

Exemptions

1. Spouse: All tax

2. Class 1: $10,000

3. Class 2: $2,000

4. Class 3: $500

NEW HAMPSHIRE

Class 1: Spouse, lineal ancestors, and descendants, their spouses and all adopted children in descendant's line of succession

Class 2: All others

Taxable Amount		Tax Rate
Class 1	Any Amount	No Tax
Class 2	Any Amount	18%

Exemptions

1. Property left to care for cemetery lots

2. Contributions to charities

3. Members of household of deceased (must have lived with deceased from age 5-15): All taxes

4. Stepchildren, stepparents, descendants and their spouses: All taxes

NEW JERSEY

Class A: Spouse, parent, grandparent, children, stepchildren, direct descendants

Class B: Sibling, daughter- or son-in-law

Class C: All others

Taxable Amount				Tax Rate
Class A				No Tax
Class B	0	to	1,100,000	11%
	1,100,000	to	1,400,000	13%
	1,400,000	to	1,700,000	14%
	1,700,000	And Over		16%
Class C	0	to	700,000	15%
	700,000	And Over		16%

Exemptions

1. Class B: First $25,000

2. Life insurance proceeds: All tax

3. Pension to surviving spouse: All tax

NORTH CAROLINA

Class A: Spouse, lineal descendants, ancestor, stepchild, adopted child, or son- or daughter-in-law whose spouse is not entitled to any beneficiary interest in property of deceased

Class B: Sibling, their issue, aunt or uncle

Class C: All others

Taxable Amount				Tax Rate
Class A	0	to	10,000	1%
	10,000	to	25,000	2%
	25,000	to	50,000	3%
	50,000	to	100,000	4%
	100,000	to	200,000	5%
	200,000	to	500,000	6%
	500,000	to	1,000,000	7%
	1,000,000	to	1,500,000	8%
	1,500,000	to	2,000,000	9%
	2,000,000	to	2,500,000	10%
	2,500,000	to	3,000,000	11%
	3,000,000	And Over		12%
Class B	0	to	5,000	4%
	5,000	to	10,000	5%
	10,000	to	25,000	6%
	25,000	to	50,000	7%
	50,000	to	100,000	8%
	100,000	to	250,000	10%
	250,000	to	500,000	11%
	500,000	to	1,000,000	12%
	1,000,000	to	1,500,000	13%
	1,500,000	to	2,000,000	14%
	2,000,000	to	3,000,000	15%
	3,000,000	And Over		16%
Class C	0	to	10,000	8%
	10,000	to	25,000	9%
	25,000	to	50,000	10%
	50,000	to	100,000	11%
	100,000	to	250,000	12%
	250,000	to	500,000	13%
	500,000	to	1,000,000	14%
	1,000,000	to	1,500,000	15%
	1,500,000	to	2,500,000	16%
	2,500,000	And Over		17%

Exemptions

All Class A beneficiaries and gross estate less than $250,000

OKLAHOMA

Class 1:   Parent, child, child of spouse, descendant

Class 2:   All others

Taxable Amount			Tax Rate
Class 1	0 to	10,000	No Tax
	10,000 to	20,000	1.0%
	20,000 to	40,000	1.5%
	40,000 to	60,000	2.0%
	60,000 to	100,000	2.5%
	100,000 to	250,000	3.0%
	250,000 to	500,000	6.5%
	500,000 to	750,000	7.0%
	750,000 to	1,000,000	7.5%
	1,000,000 to	3,000,000	8.0%
	3,000,000 to	5,000,000	8.5%
	5,000,000 to	10,000,000	9.0%
	10,000,000	And Over	10.0%
Class 2	0 to	10,000	1.0%
	10,000 to	20,000	2.0%
	20,000 to	40,000	3.0%
	40,000 to	60,000	4.0%
	60,000 to	100,000	5.0%
	100,000 to	250,000	6.0%
	250,000 to	500,000	13.0%
	500,000 to	1,000,000	14.0%
	1,000,000	And Over	15.0%

Exemptions

(Taxable amount begins after taking applicable exemption)

1. Spouses: All tax

2. Other Class 1: $175,000

PENNSYLVANIA

Class A: Grandparents, parents, spouse, lineal descendants, widower or widow of child, spouse of child

Class B: All others

Taxable Amount	Tax Rate
Class A All Amounts	6%
Class B All Amounts	15%

Exemptions

1. Spouse: All property

2. Family: $2,000

3. Life insurance proceeds

4. Social Security death payments

5. Employments benefits

6. Family exemption

SOUTH DAKOTA

Class 1:   Issue, adopted child, child, stepchild

Class 2:   Ancestor of decendant

Class 3:   Sibling or their issue or son- or daughter-in-law

Class 4:   Aunt or uncle

Class 5:   All others

Class 6:   Any person if in business with decendant for ten or 15 years before death of decendant

	Taxable Amount			Tax Rate
Class 1	0	to	30,000	No Tax
	30,000	to	50,000	3.75%
	50,000	to	100,000	6.00%
	100,000		And Over	7.50%
Class 2	0	to	3,000	No Tax
	3,000	to	15,000	3.00%
	15,000	to	50,000	7.50%
	50,000	to	100,000	12.00%
	100,000		And Over	15.00%
Class 3	0	to	500	No Tax
	500	to	15,000	4.00%
	15,000	to	50,000	10.00%
	50,000	to	100,000	16.00%
	100,000		And Over	20.00%
Class 4	0	to	200	No Tax
	200	to	15,000	5.00%
	15,000	to	50,000	12.50%
	50,000	to	100,000	20.00%
	100,000		And Over	25.00%
Class 5	0	to	100	No Tax
	100	to	15,000	6.00%
	15,000	to	50,000	15.00%
	50,000	to	100,000	24.00%
	100,000		And Over	30.00%
Class 6	0	to	15,000	3.00%
	15,000	to	50,000	7.50%
	50,000	to	100,000	12.00%
	100,000		And Over	15.00%

Exemptions

1. Spouse: All tax

TENNESSEE

Class A: Spouse, child, lineal ancestor or descendant, sibling, stepchild, son- or daughter-in-law, adopted child

Class B: All other

Taxable Amount	Tax Rate		
	Base Tax	Plus %	of Amt Over
$440,000	$30,200	9.5%	$440,000

Exemptions

(Taxable amount begins after taking applicable exemption)

Classes A and B: $600,000

CHART 2. ESTATE TAXES

Following are the rules for each state which imposes estate taxes.

MASSACHUSETTS

Taxable Amount			Tax Rate		
			Base Tax	Plus %	of Amt Over
0	to	50,000	5% of the taxable estate		
50,000	to	100,000	2,500	+ 7%	50,000
100,000	to	200,000	6,000	+ 9%	100,000
200,000	to	400,000	15,000	+ 10%	200,000
400,000	to	600,000	35,000	+ 11%	400,000
600,000	to	800,000	57,000	+ 12%	600,000
800,000	to	1,000,000	81,000	+ 13%	800,000
1,000,000	to	2,000,000	107,000	+ 14%	1,000,000
2,000,000	to	4,000.000	247,000	+ 15%	2,000,000
4,000,000			547,000	+ 16%	4,000,000

Exemptions

Estates under $600,000

MISSISSIPPI

Taxable Amount			Tax Rate		
			Base Tax	Plus %	of Amt Over
0	to	60,000	0	1%	0
60,000	to	100,000	600	+ 1.6%	60,000
100,000	to	200,000	1,240	+ 2.4%	100,000
200,000	to	400,000	3,640	+ 3.2%	200,000
400,000	to	600,000	10,040	+ 4.0%	400,000
600,000	to	800,000	18,040	+ 4.8%	600,000
800,000	to	1,000,000	27,640	+ 5.6%	800,000
1,000,000	to	1,500,000	38,840	+ 6.4%	1,000,000
1,500,000	to	2,000,000	70,840	+ 7.2%	1,500,000
2,000,000	to	2,500,000	106,840	+ 8.0%	2,000,000
2,500,000	to	3,000,000	146,840	+ 8.8%	2,500,000
3,000,000	to	3,500,000	190,840	+ 9.6%	3,000,000
3,500,000	to	4,000,000	238,840	+ 10.4%	3,500,000
4,000,000	to	5,000,000	290,840	+ 11.2%	4,000,000
5,000,000	to	6,000,000	402,840	+ 12.0%	5,000,000
6,000,000	to	7,000,000	522,840	+ 12.8%	6,000,000
7,000,000	to	8,000,000	650,840	+ 13.6%	7,000,000
8,000,000	to	9,000,000	786,840	+ 14.4%	8,000,000
9,000,000	to	10,000,000	930,840	+ 15.2%	9,000,000
10,000,000	and Over		1,082,840	+ 16.0%	10,000,000

Exemption

$600,000, taxable amount begins after taking exemption

NEW YORK

Taxable Amount			Tax Rate		
			Base Tax	Plus %	of Amt Over
0	to	50,000	0 +	2%	0
50,000	to	150,000	1,000 +	3%	50,000
150,000	to	300,000	4,000 +	4%	150,000
300,000	to	500,000	10,000 +	5%	300,000
500,000	to	700,000	20,000 +	6%	500,000
700,000	to	900,000	32,000 +	7%	700,000
900,000	to	1,100,000	46,000 +	8%	900,000
1,100,000	to	1,600,000	62,000 +	9%	1,100,000
1,600,000	to	2,100,000	107,000 +	10%	1,600,000
2,100,000	to	2,600,000	157,000 +	11%	2,100,000
2,600,000	to	3,100,000	212,000 +	12%	2,600,000
3,100,000	to	3,600,000	72,000 +	13%	3,100,000
3,600,000	to	4,100,000	337,000 +	14%	3,600,000
4,100,000	to	5,100,000	407,000 +	15%	4,100,000
5,100,000	to	6,100,000	557,000 +	16%	5,100,000
6,100,000	to	7,100,000	717,000 +	17%	6,100,000
7,100,000	to	8,100,000	887,000 +	18%	7,100,000
8,100,000	to	9,100,000	1,067,000 +	19%	8,100,000
9,100,000	to	10,100,000	1,257,000 +	20%	9,100,000
10,100,000		And Over	1,457,000 +	21%	10,100,000

Tax credits

Tax			Credit
$0	to	$2,950	Full credit (No tax)
$2,950	to	$5,400	Difference between tax and $5,500
$5,400	or more		$500

OHIO

Taxable Amount			Tax Rate		
			Base Tax	Plus %	of Amt Over
0	to	40,000	0 +	2%	0
40,000	to	100,000	800 +	3%	40,000
100,000	to	200,000	2,600 +	4%	100,000
200,000	to	300,000	6,600 +	5%	200,000
300,000	to	500,000	11,600 +	6%	300,000
500,000		And Over	23,6000 +	7%	500,000

Exemption

Marital deduction for the lesser of the federal marital deduction or one-half of adjusted gross estates greater than $500,000

Tax credit

Lesser of $5,000 or amount of tax

INDEX

Abatement, 5/11

AB trust
  avoiding tax traps, 15/7, 19/4-5
  choosing trustee, 18/11
  combining with living trust, 9/6
  combining with QTIP trust, 19/3, 23/2-3
  disclaimers, 22/8-9
  formula clause, 18/13-14
  guidelines for choosing, 18/8
  overview, 1/7-8, 18/5-6
  property in, 18/12-16, 31/4
  reducing estate tax, 18/6-8
  retirement benefits, 13/9
  risks of, 18/8-10
  sprinkling powers, 25/8-9
  vs. QTIP trust, 19/4-5

Accountant, vs. lawyer, 29/2

Ademption, 30/3

Affidavit, summary transfer of property, 14/4, 14/10-13

Alternate beneficiaries, 5/3, 5/6-7

Alternate personal guardian, 6/3

Alternate property manager, 6/5-6

Alternate residuary beneficiaries, 5/7

Annuity, 12/9-10, 20/7-8, 21/12-14

Appraisal, 15/6, 18/7

Assets, 1/10, 4/3, 15/12, 17/2, 26/9

Attorney. See Lawyer

Bank, 6/6, 7/4, 9/11, 17/9

Bank account, 10/3-4, 11/3-5

Bankruptcy, tenancy by the entirety property, 10/5

Bar association referral panels, 29/4

Basis. See Tax basis

Beneficiary
  alternate, 5/6-7
  charities, 5/5
  children, 5/4
  conflict between, 24/8
  disclaimers, 22/2-4
  educational trust, 25/3
  estate as, 12/10
  5 and 5 power, 18/5
  forgiving debt, 5/4
  401(k) accounts, 13/4
  government securities, 11/5
  individual retirement plans, 13/4
  life beneficiary, 5/6, 18/2-3
  life insurance, 6/14, 12/10-11
  living trust, 9/12-13
  marital property control trust, 24/2-3

  naming alternates, 5/3
  naming in QTIP trust, 19/9-10
  pay-on-death accounts, 11/2-3
  pets, 5/5-6
  primary, 5/3-6
  residuary, 5/7
  restrictions on, 5/4-5
  retirement programs, 13/7-9
  rights under special needs trust, 25/5
  second marriages, 18/10
  shared gifts, 5/7-8
  spendthrift trust, 25/6
  sprinkling trust, 25/8
  stocks and bonds, 11/5-6
  trustee's report to, 31/6
  types, 5/3
  use of trusts for, 18/8

Boats, transfer-on-death, 11/6

Burial, 27/9-10

Business. See Small business

Bypass trust
  AB trust for couples, 18/5-16
  combining with other trusts, 21/6-7
  IRS restrictions on, 18/3-5
  overview, 1/7-8, 18/2-3
  single person, 18/17-18
  unmarried couples, 18/16-17
  See also Marital property control trust, QTIP trust

California, exemptions from probate, 14/10-12, 14/4

Capital gains tax, 20/6, 21/16-17

Car registration, transfer-on-death, 11/6

Cash, 1/6, 11/3, 12/2

Cemeteries, 27/9-10

Ceremonies, after death, 27/5

Charitable deduction/exemption, 15/3, 15/8, 16/3, 20/4-5

Charitable trust
  combining with other trusts, 23/4-5
  comparison chart, 20/14
  income tax deduction, 20/4-5
  lead trust, 20/3, 20/11-13
  naming backup charity, 20/4
  remainder trust, 20/2-3
  types, 20/2

Charity
  as beneficiary, 5/5
  importance of investigating, 20/3
  as trustee, 20/3-4, 20/20

Charity as trustee, pooled income trusts, 20/20

Children
  beneficiaries of charitable lead trust, 20/3
  beneficiaries of insurance, 12/10-11
  custodianship, 6/7-8
  disabled, providing for, I/5, 2/9-10, 5/6, 25/4-6
  disclaimers, 22/6-7
  disinheritance, 5/10
  estate plans, 6/2
  and generation-skipping trust, 21/3-4
  gifts to, 16/12-15,
  life insurance beneficiaries, 6/14
  living trust, 9/7, 31/4
  naming a personal guardian, 1/3, 2/7, 6/2-5
  pay-on-death accounts, 11/2-3
  previous marriages, 2/4
  property control trusts, 17/4
  property manager, 6/5-6
  revising plans after birth, 7/9, 30/3
  social security, 13/2-3
  taxes, 6/5, 16/15
  trusts, 6/9-11
  Uniform Transfers to Minors Act (UTMA), 6/7-8, 6/11, 6/14-15
  wills, 6/2, 6/14-15

Codicils, 30/4

Commentary, leaving with will or trust, 5/8-9

Common law marriage, 3/2

Common law property, 1/3, 3/7-9 states list, 3/3

Community property
  appreciation and tax basis rules, 16/14-15
  definition, 1/3, 3/5, 4/6
  distinguishing, 3/7
  joint tenancy, 10/5-6, 10/9-10
  pensions, 3/6
  petition, summary probate, 14/10
  right of survivorship, 4/6

Community property states, 3/3, 3/5-7, 12/10

Computer, legal information online, 29/7

Conservator, incapacity, 26/2, 26/9-10

Contracts to make a will, 7/7

Corporate shares, ownership of, 4/7

Co-trustees, naming, 17/9

Couples, unmarried. See Unmarried couples

Creditors, 8/7-9, 10/12, 14/12-13, 28/10

Cremation, 27/3, 27/8-9

Crummey trust provisions, 16/8, 21/9-10, 23/4-5

Curtesy, 3/8

Custodianship, overview, 6/7-8

Custody, disputes over, 6/4-5

Dead-hand control, 5/4

Death
claiming life insurance, 31/6
disposing of body, 1/9-10
donating body or organs, 27/4
estate transfer tasks, 31/2
mystery of, I/2
overview of what next, 1/11
sealing safe deposit boxes, 10/4
simultaneous, 5/10, 6/2, 10/2
transfers to joint tenancy, 10/13
transporting body a long distance, 27/2
winding up living trust, 31/2-4
written burial instructions, 27/2-3

Death certificates, 27/3

Death notices, 27/4-5

Death taxes
definition, 1/6
federal, 11/4
insurance, 12/2
living trust, 9/6
pick-up death tax, 15/16
probate, 8/9
reason for, 15/4-5
See also Estate tax, State death tax

Debt
forgiving, 5/4
inheriting, 8/8-9
insurance, 12/3
living trust, 9/8
and ongoing trust, 17/5
paying after death, 5/11
probate, 1/6, 8/8-9

Declaration Regarding Health Care, 26/3

Designation of Health Care Surrogate, 26/3

Directive to Physicians, 7/7, 26/3

Disclaimers
AB trust, 22/8-9
advantages of, 22/2-4
couples, 22/4-5
deadline for making, 22/6-7
including in will or living trust, 22/9-11
and limited powers of appointment, 25/12
living trusts, 11/9-11
overview, 1/8, 22/2, 22/9-10
QTIP trust, 22/8-9
retirement accounts, 13/9-10

Discount for lack of marketability, 28/7

Disinheritance, 1/3, 2/12-13, 3/8-9, 5/9-10, 7/3

Divorce, 3/2, 3/4, 7/8, 21/10, 30/3

Doctor, appointing as attorney-in-fact, 26/6

Documents, storing, 10/4, 30/2-3

Domicile. *See* Residence

Dower, 3/8

Durable Power of Attorney for Finances, 15/20, 17/4, 26/8-9

Durable Power of Attorney for Health Care, 26/3, 26/4, 26/6

Educational trust, 25/3

Elder law, I/4

Embalming, 27/7

Epitaph, 27/10

Estate
definition of, I/2
determining value of exempted property, 14/3
estimating net worth, 15/5
expenses and claims, tax deduction, 15/8
size of, and trusts, 18/8

Estate planning
avoiding family conflict, 2/2-5
care for minor children, 2/7, 6/2
children from previous marriages, 2/4
choosing and naming beneficiaries, 5/2
choosing executor, 2/3-4
combining different kinds of trusts, 25/13
disabled children, 2/9-10
discussing with family/friends, 2/13-14
grantor-retained interest trusts, 21/10-12, 21/21
heirlooms, 2/5
life insurance, 12/2
Nolo resources, I/5-6
retirement planning, 13/2
revisions, 30/3-5
setting goals, 1/2
small business, 28/2-11
state books, 29/7-8
state death taxes, 15/15
state laws, 14/2
storing documents, 30/2-3
subsequent marriages, 2/8-9
unmarried couples, 2/10
using a specialist, 29/3
wills, I/4, 7/2-4

Estate planning example
couple, second marriage, 32/6-7
couple with kids, 1/11-12
properous couple, 32/2
single 60-year old man, 32/3-4

unmarried couple, 32/7
wealthy older couple, 32/2-3
widow, elderly, 32/5-6
younger couple, 32/4-5

Estate tax
AB trusts, 18/13-15
calculating, 15/10-12
deferring payment, 28/6-7
exemptions, 15/2-4
filing return, 15/9, 31/2
generation-skipping trusts, 21/2-7
inventorying estate, 4/2
joint tenancy, 10/6-7, 31/7
miscellaneous deductions, 15/8-9
non-citizen spouse, 19/13-14
ongoing trusts, 17/2
overview, 1/6-8
ownership of life insurance policies, 12/11-14
pay-on-death accounts, 11/4-5
planning for payment of, 15/12
rates chart, 15/11
reducing, 15/12-13, 18/6-8, 21/16, 23/6-7, 24/7-8, 28/5-9
retirement programs, 13/10-11
who must pay, 15/2

Estate trust, special marital deduction trust, 19/17

Executor, 2/3-4, 7/3-4, 19/10-13, 31/2, 31/5

Family
conflict, 5/8-9, 24/2, 24/6
family business, 1/10, 16/12, 28/3-4
forming limited partnership, 1/10
pot trust, 1/9, 6/9-10, 25/9
protection against disinheritance, 3/8-9

Federal death taxes. *See* Estate tax

Fiduciary, trustee, 17/7

Final beneficiaries, 5/3, 5/6

Financial institutions as trustee, 24/7

Financial planner, *vs.* lawyer, 29/2

"First to die" life insurance, 12/9

5 and 5 power, 18/5, 19/9

Florida
exemptions from normal probate, 14/13-14
house rules, 6/15

Formula clause, AB trust, 18/13

401(k) accounts, 13/4-5

Funerals, 15/8, 27/2-3, 27/6-8

Generation-skipping transfer tax (GSTT), 19/12-13, 21/2-4

Generation-skipping trusts, 21/2-7

Gifts
    to charity, 5/5, 20/4-6
    commentary on, 5/8-9
    common kinds, 16/5-6
    definition, 1/7, 16/3-6
    determining value for GRUT, 21/15
    exemptions from tax, 16/2-3
    family business, 16/12
    grantor retained trusts, 21/11
    joint tenancy and taxes, 10/7-8
    life insurance, 16/7, 16/12
    to minors, 16/7-8, 16/12-13
    to non-citizen spouse, 15/8, 19/14
    partial, 16/6
    placing restrictions on, 5/4
    present interest, 16/7-8
    receiving benefits and disclaiming, 22/7
    reducing estate tax, 16/9-13
    shared, 5/7-8
    small businesses, 28/7
    stock options, 28/8-9
    taxable, 15/3
    tax-exempt, 15/8
    who controls, 16/4-5
    why give, 5/2
Gift tax
    annual exclusion, 16/2-3, 16/10-11
    filing return, 16/8
    insurance, 12/12-13
    joint tenancy of bank account, 10/3-4
    life insurance trust, 23/4-5
    limits on gifts, 1/7
    living trust, 9/14
    rates, 15/22, 16/6-7
    reason for, 15/4-5
    rules for, 16/6-9
    using exemption to pay life insurance
      premiums, 21/9-10
    when paid, 16/3
    who pays, 16/2
Government assistance and special needs
    trusts, 25/4-5
Grantor-Retained Annuity Trusts (GRATs),
    21/12-14, 21/16-17
Grantor-Retained Income Trusts (GRITs),
    21/17-21
Grantor-retained interest trusts
    overview of GRATs, GRUTs, and GRITs,
      21/10-12
    vs. other estate planning devices, 21/21
Grantor-Retained Unitrusts (GRUTs),
    21/15-17
Graveyard, 17/9-10
Grief therapy, 27/6

Guardianships, arranging, 26/9-10
Handwritten wills, 7/5
Health care documents, in case of
    incapacity, 26/2-8
Health Care Proxy, what to include, 26/4
Heirlooms, dividing, 2/5
Holographic wills, 7/5
Homestead property, 9/9, 14/12
House, joint tenancy, 10/12-13
Icons, definition, I/4
Illness, catastrophic, paying for, 17/2
Incapacity, 1/9-10, 10/12, 26/2-10
Income taxes
    charitable trust deduction, 20/4-7
    inherited money, 13/11
    living trust, 9/6
    lowering with a trust, 17/5
    sprinkling trust, 25/8
    using gifts to reduce, 16/15
Individual Retirement Accounts (IRAs),
    13/3-4
Inheritance, 1/6, 2/11-12, 15/4, 15/16,
    16/14. *See also* Disinheritance
Insurance
    buying, 12/4
    changing beneficiary, 30/5
    financial health of company, 12/5
    owner of, 12/2, 12/8
    paying premiums for life insurance in
      trust, 21/9-10
    probate, 12/10
    single-premium payment, 12/5
    trusting agent, 12/6
Intent, and gift tax, 16/4
Internal Revenue Code, citations, 15/2
Internet, 29/7
Intestate succession, 8/2, 8/7
Irrevocable trust, as beneficiary of
    retirement plan, 13/9
IRS
    determining gift tax on GRAT, 21/12
    determining value of GRIT, 21/18-19
    phony small business scams, 28/8
    rules for disclaimers, 22/6-9
    rules for irrevocable life insurance
      trusts, 21/8-9
Joint ownership
    with documents of title, 10/13-14
    without documents of title, 10/15
Joint tenancy
    bank account, 10/3-4
    community property and tax basis,
      10/9-10
    converting to tenancy in common, 10/2

    creating just before death, 10/13
    creditors, 10/12
    definition, 4/6, 10/2
    disadvantages, 10/11-12
    gift taxes, 10/7-8
    obtaining title to, 31/6-7
    probate avoidance, 10/2-3
    purchasing a house, 10/12-13
    revising, 30/5
    with right of Survivorship, 4/6
    safe deposit boxes, 10/4
    simultaneous death of tenants, 10/2
    special rules in community property
      states, 10/5-6
    tax consequences of, 10/6-11
    terminating upon death, 31/6-7
    unmarried joint tenants and taxes, 10/6-7
    vs. living trust, 10/12-13, 11/6
Joint wills, 7/7
Keogh plans, 13/3-4
Law library, 29/6-7
Lawsuit, avoiding over will, 7/7-8
Lawyer
    AB trust, 18/6
    combining trusts, 23/2
    Crummey trusts, 16/8
    disinheriting a spouse, 3/9
    fees, 29/4, 29/6
    generation-skipping trusts, 21/2-3
    hiring, 29/2-6
    international estate planning, 15/3
    lawsuit worries, 8/8
    life insurance trust, 12/14
    marital property contracts, 3/4
    marital property control trust, 24/8-9
    needed for ongoing trusts, 17/3
    non-citizen spouse and tax planning,
      15/8
    partial gifts, 16/6
    potential custody fights, 6/5
    preparing a QTIP trust, 19/3
    probate, 8/2-4
    property control trusts, 25/2
    retirement benefits and AB trusts, 13/9
    reviewing estate planning, I/5, 29/5
    small business estate planning, 28/2
    spousal disagreement over property, 3/10
    state law and probate exemptions, 14/3
    trusts and non-citizen spouses, 19/14
    using trusts to reduce estate taxes, 15/13
    when to use, 1/11
    widow's election trust, 19/18
Legal encyclopedias, 29/8
Legal insurance plans, 29/4

Legal research, why do, 29/2
Legal separation, 3/2
Liabilities, inventory of, 4/8
Liens, tax, 31/7
Life beneficiary
    bypass trust, 18/2-3
    control of trust, 18/12
    definition, 5/3
    marital deduction trusts, 19/16
    marital property control trust, 24/2-3
    naming, 5/6
    QTIP trust, 19/3-4
    rights of, 18/11-12
Life estate trust, 5/3, 5/6, 18/16
Life insurance
    children as beneficiaries, 6/14
    collecting, 31/6
    combining with charitable trust, 23/4-5
    evaluating needs, 11/2-4
    as gift, 16/7, 16/12
    irrevocable trusts, 21/7-10
    ownership of policy, 12/11-14
    purposes of, 11/2
    trust ownership, 12/14
    types of, 12/5-10
Limited Liability Co., ownership, 4/7
Living trust
    beneficiary of retirement program, 13/9
    children's trust, 6/9
    choosing trustees, 9/10-11
    combining with ongoing trust, 17/4-5
    death taxes, 9/6
    debt, 9/8
    disclaimers, 11/9-11
    "free" seminars, 9/4
    glossary, 9/5
    incapacity, 15/20
    income taxes, 9/6
    keeping up-to-date, 9/14-15
    overview, 9/2-6, 9/8-12
    pour-over will, 7/5-6
    preparing documents, 9/12-14
    property, 9/8-9
    residuary beneficiaries, 5/7
    revising, 30/3-4
    revoking, 9/15
    shared, 9/7-8
    using Affidavit of Right with, 14/11
    using with business or partnership,
        28/10-11
    vs. joint tenancy, 10/12-13, 11/6
    winding up after death, 31/2-4
Living will, 7/7, 26/3
Loan, as gift, 16/5

Local property taxes, 10/11
Louisiana, state laws, I/2
Marital deduction, 1/6-7, 15/3, 15/6-7,
    19/13-17, 23/2-3
Marital deduction trust, 19/2, 19/15-17
Marital property control trust
    choosing trustee, 24/5-7
    combining with living trust, 24/3
    how it works, 24/2-3
Marital status, determining, 3/2
Marriage
    debt forgiveness, 5/4
    estate planning, 2/8-9
    holding property by tenancy by the
        entirety, 10/4-5
    joint tenancy and taxes, 10/6
    revising estate plan, 30/3
    revising will, 7/9
    second, 18/9-10, 24/2
    trusts for couples, 9/7, 18/5-16, 19/2
Medical bills, 16/3, 17/2
Medical care document, 26/3-8
Medical Directive, 26/3
Medical treatment, right to control, 26/2-3
Medicare, protecting assets, 26/9
Moving and changing documents, 7/9,
    9/15, 16/9
Napoleonic Code, I/2
Net worth, 4/8, 15/5
New York, exemptions from normal
    probate, 14/12
Next of kin, body disposal, 22/3
No-contest clause, will, 5/10
Non-citizen spouse. See Spouse, non-
    citizen
Notarizing a will, 7/5
Nuncupative wills, 7/6
Obituaries, 27/4-5
Oral wills, 7/6
Organ donation, 27/4
Ownership
    clarifying, 1/2-3
    inventory of shared, 4/5-8
    marital property, 3/3-5
    shared, incapacity, 10/12
    small business, 28/2-4
    valuing, 4/8
Parental rights, 6/4-5
Partnership, ownership of, 4/7
Patient Advocate Designation, 26/3
Pay-on-death accounts, 11/2-6, 30/5
Pensions, 3/6, 13/5-7, 13/11
Personal estate tax exemption, 15/2-3,
    18/6-7, 18/12-14

Personal guardian, naming, 6/2-5, 7/3
Personal injury awards, 3/7
Pets, beneficiaries, 5/5-6
Pooled income trust, charitable remainder,
    20/10-11
Pour-over wills, 7/5-6
Powers of appointment, 1/9, 19/16-17,
    25/10-13
Prenuptial contracts, 3/4
Pretermitted heirs, 6/15
Primary beneficiaries, 5/3-6
Probate
    creditors, 8/8-9
    effect on taxes, 1/7
    executor's duties toward, 31/2
    exemptions, state law, 14/2-14
    fees, 8/3-4, 15/8
    insurance, 12/10
    overview, 1/4-6, 8/2-3
    reform, 8/9-10
    retirement programs, 13/10
    simplified procedure, 14/4-5
    summary probate, 14/5, 14/10-14
    when you want it, 8/8
    wills, 7/2
Probate avoidance
    family business, 28/9-11
    informal, 8/7
    insurance, 12/2
    lawsuits over will, 8/8
    living trust, 9/2
    ongoing trusts, 17/4-5
    overview of methods, 8/4-6
    planning, 1/5, 8/7-8
    vs. will listing, 7/7-8
    wills, 7/2
Profit-sharing plans, 13/3-4
Property
    appreciation, 3/7, 16/11-12, 16/13-15,
        20/6-7
    controlling with a trust, 1/8-9, 5/6,
        17/4, 24/2-5
    determining ownership, 3/5-10,
        10/13-15
    gifts and tax basis rules, 16/13-15
    giving away, 15/13
    holding in joint tenancy, 10/3
    inventory, instructions, 4/2-8
    inventory worksheet, 4/9-20
    leaving to children, 1/6, 2/5-6, 6/6-7,
        6/13-15
    leaving to spouse, 15/6-7, 23/3
    losing control in a trust, 21/16

naming children's property manager, 6/5-6
pay-on-death transfer, 11/2
placing in AB trust, 18/9, 18/12
placing in living trust, 9/2, 9/8-9, 9/13-15
refusing to accept, 22/2
tax basis of, 10/8, 10/10
taxes on, 15/3-4
transfer, I/2, 9/2, 9/13-14, 10/11
unequal ownership shares, 10/3
unmarried couples, ownership, 1/3
valuation, 4/3, 14/3, 14/10-11, 15/5, 15/9-10, 15/13-14
wills, 5/11, 7/2-3, 7/7-8
Property control trust
    combining with tax saving trust, 25/13
    educational trust, 25/3
    special needs, 25/4-6
    spendthrift, 25/6-7
    sprinkling trust, 25/7-9
    types, 25/2
    using a lawyer, 25/2
    See also Marital property control trusts
Property guardian, pros and cons of using, 6/11-12
Property taxes, living trust, 9/9
Qualified Domestic Trust (QDOT),
    how it works, 19/14-15
    non-citizen spouse, 15/8
    overview, 1/8, 19/2
Qualified Terminable Interest Property trust (QTIP)
    combining with AB trust, 19/3-4, 23/2-3
    disclaimers, 22/8-9
    drawbacks, 19/7
    5 and 5 power, 19/9
    and limited powers of appointment, 25/12-13
    marital deduction, 19/3
    operation of, 19/4-13
    overview, 1/8, 19/2, 19/4
    partial election of, 19/11-12
    power to spend principal, 19/8
    reverse QTIP election, 19/12-13
    special power of executor, 19/10-12
    spousal right to receive all income, 19/7
    vs. AB trust, 19/4-5
Quasi-community property, 3/10
Real estate, 4/4, 10/11, 16/5, 28/6
Research, doing your own legal, 29/6-8
Residence, 3/3-4, 15/15, 21/17-21
Residence GRIT, 21/17-21
Residuary beneficiaries, 5/3, 5/7
Retirement benefits, estate planning, 13/2

Retirement programs
    accounts and disclaimers, 13/9-10
    beneficiaries, 13/7-9
    individual, 13/3-5
    living trust as beneficiary, 13/9
    probate, 13/10
Revoking living trust, 9/15
Right of survivorship, 10/2, 14/6
Roth IRA's, 13/4
Rule against perpetuities, 17/6
Safe deposit boxes, joint tenancy, 10/4
Separate property, definition, 4/6-7
SEP-IRA's, 13/3-4
Services, *vs.* gifts, 16/3-4
Single-premium life insurance, 12/5, 12/8
Small business
    deferring estate tax payments, 28/6-7
    estate planning, 1/10
    estate tax "freeze", 28/8-9
    exemption, estate taxes, 15/3
    forming to save on taxes, 28/2
    "first to die" life insurance, 12/9
    gifts of stock options, 28/8-9
    insurance for cash on death, 12/3-4
    inventory of property, 4/4
    operation of, after death of owner, 28/2-4
    ownership determination, 3/7
    phony, 28/8
    reducing estate taxes, 28/5-9
    selling to outsider, 28/4
    types of ownership, 4/7
    using a living trust, 28/10-11
Social Security, overview, 13/2-3
Special needs trust
    government assistance, 25/4-5
    lawyer, 25/5
Spendthrift trust, 18/6, 25/6-7
Spouse, non-citizen
    gifts to, 19/14
    no marital deduction, 15/6-8
    QDOT trust, 1/8, 19/2
    tax planning, 1/7, 15/8
    trust for, 19/13-15
Spouse
    AB trust beneficiary, 18/5-6
    claiming share of estate, 11/4
    disclaimers, 22/4-5, 22/8
    disinheritance, 1/3, 5/9
    generation-skipping trusts, 21/4
    gift tax exemption, 16/3
    inheritance rights, 3/8-9
    restrictions on property in trust, 18/8-9, 24/3-5
    retirement program beneficiary, 13/7-8

rights in QTIP trust, 19/6-8
    social security, 13/2
    unequal property, 18/15-16, 22/8
    using separate lawyers, 29/4
Sprinkling trust, 1/9, 25/3, 25/7-9
State death tax, 10/4, 11/4, 15/17, 15/8, 31/6
State law
    contracts to vary it, 3/4
    cremations, 27/3, 27/8-9
    disinheritance, 6/15-16
    documents for medical care, 26/6
    gift taxes, 16/8-9
    income tax basis rules, 10/10
    joint tenancy, 4/6, 10/2
    money to minors, 11/3
    no will, 8/2
    organ donation, 27/4
    ownership, 1/3
    probate exemption chart, 14/5-9
    probate exemption chart instructions, 14/3-5
    probate exemptions overview, 14/2
    probate exemption statutes, 14/5
    property ownership, 3/2, 3/7-9
    securities transfer-on-death, 11/5
    small business ownership, 28/3
    state basis rules, 16/15
    state forms and extra detail, 26/4
    statutory wills, 7/6
    tenancy by the entirety, 10/4
    Uniform Transfers to Minors Act, 6/7-8
    written burial instructions, 27/3
Statutory wills, 7/6
Stepped-up basis. *See* Tax basis
Successor trustee, living trust, 9/5, 9/10-11, 18/11, 31/5
Supplemental Security Income (SSI) and special needs trusts, 25/4-5
Survivorship, 5/8, 5/10-11, 12/8. *See also* Right of survivorship
Taking against the will, 3/9
Taxable estate, determining estate taxes, 15/2
Tax basis
    changing in a GRAT, 21/14
    community property and joint tenancy, 10/9-10
    definition, 15/13-14
    effect on gift, 16/13-15
    property, 1/7
    stepped-up, 1/7, 10/8-10
Taxes
    on AB trust assets, 18/7

assessing generation-skipping taxes, 21/5-6

bypass trusts, 18/2-3

calculating on estate, 15/10-12

charitable exemption, 15/8

charitable trusts, 20/2

children's rates, 6/5

deduction, charitable trust, 20/4-6

double taxation with general power of appointment, 25/11

effect of disclaimers, 22/2, 22/4-5

estimating size of estate, 4/2

filing returns after death, 31/5-6

401(k) accounts), 13/5

Generation-Skipping Transfer Tax (GSST), 19/12-13

individual retirement accounts, 13/11

individual retirement plans, 13/3-4

insurance, 12/7-8

living trust, 9/6

ongoing trusts, 17/6

paying after death, 5/11

pensions, 13/6-7

QTIP trusts, 19/4-5

rates for estate tax, 15/4-5

rates for gift tax, 15/4-5

rates on ongoing trusts, 17/10

real estate in small business, 28/6

retirement program beneficiaries, 13/8-9

savings from a GRAT, 21/14

savings from a GRUT, 21/15

small business exemption, 28/5-6

tax return, 15/9, 16/8, 17/8, 31/5

trusts, 6/11

See also Estate tax, State death tax

Tenancy by the entirety, 4/6, 10/4-5

Tenancy in common, 4/7, 10/2

Term insurance, 12/6

Texas, exemptions from normal probate, 14/12-13

Title, how taken, 10/13-14

Transplants, donating for, 27/2-4

Treatises, 29/8

Trust

changing irrevocable, 21/10

changing types, 6/10

charitable, 1/8, 20/2-5, 20/11-13, 20/14

combining, 18/13-14, 21/6-7, 23/2-7

conflict, 18/10

control, 19/18

creating a life estate, 5/6

duration of, 17/6

ending, 25/3

executor as trustee, 31/2

generation-skipping, 19/12-13

and gifts, 16/5-6

grantor-retained interest trust, 21/10-21

GRATs, GRUTs, and GRITs, 21/10-12

imposing controls on beneficiary, 18/6

irrevocable life-insurance trusts, 21/7-10

life insurance, 12/14

managing your own property, 25/10

marital deduction trust, 19/2, 19/15-17

marital property control trust, 24/2-7

ongoing, 17/2, 17/4-10, 31/4-5

possible controls on property, 24/4-5

revising, 30/5

right to spend principal, 18/3-5

saving on estate taxes, 15/13

selecting age of beneficiaries, 6/9, 6/11

special needs, 17/4, 18/6, 25/4-6

spendthrift, 18/6, 25/6-7

sprinkling, 1/9, 25/3, 25/7-9

storing documents, 30/2-3

using to reduce taxes, 1/7-8

vs. annuities, 12/9-10

vs. UTMA, 6/10-11

when to use for control of property, 17/4

See also AB trust, Bypass trust, Living trust

Trustee

AB trust, 18/10

bypass trusts, 18/2

charitable trusts, 20/3-4

children's trust, 6/9

choosing, 9/10-11, 17/8-10, 25/9

duties of, 17/7-8, 25/7-8

financial institution as, 24/7

living trust, 9/5

naming co-trustees, 24/6-7

ongoing trust, 17/7

QTIP trust, 19/13

report to beneficiaries, 31/6

special needs trust, 25/4

sprinkling trust, 25/9

Tuition, gifts to pay for, 16/3

Unified credit, estate taxes, 15/10-12

Uniform Anatomical Gift Act, 27/4

Uniform Transfers to Minors Act (UTMA), 6/7-8, 6/10-11, 6/14-15

UniTrusts, charitable remainder, 20/7, 20/8-10

Universal life insurance, 12/7

Unmarried couples

bypass trust, 18/16-17

disinheritance, 5/9

estate plans, 2/10

Grantor-Retained Income Trusts, advantages, 21/20-21

no marital deduction, 15/6

ownership, 1/3

property control trusts, 24/2

Valuation discount, 28/7

Variable life insurance, 12/7

Video wills, 7/6

Whole life insurance, 12/7

Widow's election trusts, 19/2, 19/17-18

Will

back-up, 7/2-4

carrying out terms of, 31/2

challenging, 7/8

children's trust, 6/9

choosing executor, 7/3-4

disclaimers, 22/2

disinheritance, 5/9-10

estate planning, 7/2-4

fill-in-the-blanks, 7/6

funeral instructions, 27/3

keeping up-to-date, 7/8-9

legality of, 7/4-5

living trust as beneficiary, 7/5-6

minor children and disinheritance, 6/15-16

moving to another state, 3/9-10, 7/9

naming a personal guardian, 6/2-5

no-contest clause, 5/10

residuary beneficiaries, 5/7

revising, 30/4-5

spousal inheritance, 3/8-9

storing, 30/2-3

types of, 7/5-7

vs. UTMA, 6/14-15

when to use pour-over, 7/6

Wisconsin, help with informal probate, 14/4

Witness, will, 7/4-5

World Wide Web, research on, 29/7 ■

CATALOG

...more from Nolo Press

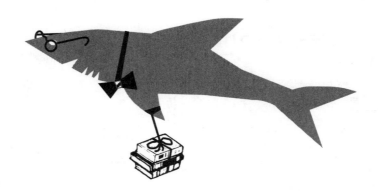

	PRICE	CODE

BUSINESS

The California Nonprofit Corporation Handbook	$29.95	NON
The California Professional Corporation Handbook	$34.95	PROF
The Employer's Legal Handbook	$29.95	EMPL
Form Your Own Limited Liability Company (Book w/Disk—PC)	$34.95	LIAB
Hiring Independent Contractors: The Employer's Legal Guide, (Book w/Disk—PC)	$29.95	HICI
How to Form a CA Nonprofit Corp.—w/Corp. Records Binder & PC Disk	$49.95	CNP
How to Form a Nonprofit Corp., Book w/Disk (PC)—National Edition	$39.95	NNP
How to Form Your Own Calif. Corp.—w/Corp. Records Binder & Disk—PC	$39.95	CACI
How to Form Your Own California Corporation (Book w/Disk—PC)	$34.95	CCOR
How to Form Your Own Florida Corporation, (Book w/Disk—PC)	$39.95	FLCO
How to Form Your Own New York Corporation, (Book w/Disk—PC)	$39.95	NYCO
How to Form Your Own Texas Corporation, (Book w/Disk—PC)	$39.95	TCOR
How to Mediate Your Dispute	$18.95	MEDI
How to Write a Business Plan	$21.95	SBS
The Independent Paralegal's Handbook	$29.95	PARA
Legal Guide for Starting & Running a Small Business, Vol. 1	$24.95	RUNS
Legal Guide for Starting & Running a Small Business, Vol. 2: Legal Forms	$29.95	RUNS2
Marketing Without Advertising	$19.00	MWAD
The Partnership Book: How to Write a Partnership Agreement, (Book w/Disk—PC)	$34.95	PART
Sexual Harassment on the Job	$18.95	HARS
Starting and Running a Successful Newsletter or Magazine	$24.95	MAG
Take Charge of Your Workers' Compensation Claim (California Edition)	$29.95	WORK
Tax Savvy for Small Business	$28.95	SAVVY
Trademark: Legal Care for Your Business and Product Name	$29.95	TRD
Wage Slave No More: Law & Taxes for the Self-Employed	$24.95	WAGE
Your Rights in the Workplace	$21.95	YRW

▣ Book with disk
● Book with CD-ROM

	PRICE	CODE

CONSUMER

	PRICE	CODE
Fed Up With the Legal System: What's Wrong & How to Fix It	$9.95	LEG
How to Win Your Personal Injury Claim	$24.95	PICL
Nolo's Everyday Law Book	$21.95	EVL
Nolo's Pocket Guide to California Law	$11.95	CLAW
Trouble-Free Travel...And What to Do When Things Go Wrong	$14.95	TRAV

ESTATE PLANNING & PROBATE

	PRICE	CODE
8 Ways to Avoid Probate (Quick & Legal Series)	$15.95	PRO8
How to Probate an Estate (California Edition)	$34.95	PAE
Make Your Own Living Trust	$24.95	LITR
Nolo's Law Form Kit: Wills	$14.95	KWL
Nolo's Will Book, (Book w/Disk—PC)	$29.95	SWIL
Plan Your Estate	$24.95	NEST
The Quick and Legal Will Book	$15.95	QUIC

FAMILY MATTERS

	PRICE	CODE
Child Custody: Building Parenting Agreements that Work	$24.95	CUST
Divorce & Money: How to Make the Best Financial Decisions During Divorce	$26.95	DIMO
Do Your Own Divorce in Oregon	$19.95	ODIV
Get a Life: You Don't Need a Million to Retire Well	$18.95	LIFE
The Guardianship Book (California Edition)	$24.95	GB
How to Adopt Your Stepchild in California	$22.95	ADOP
How to Change Child Support in California (Quick & Legal Series)	$19.95	CHLD
A Legal Guide for Lesbian and Gay Couples	$24.95	LG
The Living Together Kit	$24.95	LTK
Nolo's Pocket Guide to Family Law	$14.95	FLD

GOING TO COURT

	PRICE	CODE
Collect Your Court Judgment (California Edition)	$24.95	JUDG
The Criminal Law Handbook: Know Your Rights, Survive the System	$24.95	KYR
How to Seal Your Juvenile & Criminal Records (California Edition)	$24.95	CRIM
How to Sue For Up to 25,000...and Win!	$29.95	MUNI
Everybody's Guide to Small Claims Court in California	$18.95	CSCC
Everybody's Guide to Small Claims Court (National Edition)	$18.95	NSCC
Fight Your Ticket ... and Win! (California Edition)	$19.95	FYT
How to Change Your Name in California	$29.95	NAME
Mad at Your Lawyer	$21.95	MAD
Represent Yourself in Court: How to Prepare & Try a Winning Case	$29.95	RYC

Book with disk
Book with CD-ROM

		PRICE	CODE

HOMEOWNERS, LANDLORDS & TENANTS

	PRICE	CODE
The Deeds Book (California Edition)	$16.95	DEED
Dog Law	$14.95	DOG
▣ Every Landlord's Legal Guide (National Edition, Book w/Disk—PC)	$34.95	ELLI
Every Tenant's Legal Guide	$24.95	EVTEN
For Sale by Owner in California	$24.95	FSBO
How to Buy a House in California	$24.95	BHCA
The Landlord's Law Book, Vol. 1: Rights & Responsibilities (California Edition)	$34.95	LBRT
The Landlord's Law Book, Vol. 2: Evictions (California Edition)	$34.95	LBEV
Leases & Rental Agreements (Quick & Legal Series)	$18.95	LEAR
Neighbor Law: Fences, Trees, Boundaries & Noise	$17.95	NEI
Stop Foreclosure Now in California	$29.95	CLOS
Tenants' Rights (California Edition)	$19.95	CTEN

HUMOR

	PRICE	CODE
29 Reasons Not to Go to Law School	$9.95	29R
Poetic Justice	$9.95	PJ

IMMIGRATION

	PRICE	CODE
How to Get a Green Card: Legal Ways to Stay in the U.S.A.	$24.95	GRN
U.S. Immigration Made Easy	$39.95	IMEZ

MONEY MATTERS

	PRICE	CODE
▣ 101 Law Forms for Personal Use: (Quick and Legal Series, Book w/disk—PC)	$24.95	101LAW
Chapter 13 Bankruptcy: Repay Your Debts	$29.95	CH13
Credit Repair (Quick & Legal Series)	$15.95	CREP
▣ The Financial Power of Attorney Workbook (Book w/disk—PC)	$24.95	FINPOA
How to File for Bankruptcy	$26.95	HFB
Money Troubles: Legal Strategies to Cope With Your Debts	$19.95	MT
Nolo's Law Form Kit: Personal Bankruptcy	$14.95	KBNK
Stand Up to the IRS	$24.95	SIRS
Take Control of Your Student Loans	$19.95	SLOAN

PATENTS AND COPYRIGHTS

	PRICE	CODE
▣ The Copyright Handbook: How to Protect and Use Written Works (Book w/disk—PC)	$29.95	COHA
Copyright Your Software	$39.95	CYS
The Inventor's Notebook	$19.95	INOT
▣ License Your Invention (Book w/Disk—PC)	$39.95	LICE
The Patent Drawing Book	$29.95	DRAW
Patent, Copyright & Trademark	$24.95	PCTM
Patent It Yourself	$44.95	PAT
● Software Development: A Legal Guide (Book with CD-ROM)	$44.95	SFT

▣ Book with disk

● Book with CD-ROM

	PRICE	CODE

RESEARCH & REFERENCE

- ⬤ Government on the Net, (Book w/CD-ROM—Windows/Macintosh) .... $39.95 ... GONE
- ⬤ Law on the Net, (Book w/CD-ROM—Windows/Macintosh) .... $39.95 ... LAWN
- Legal Research: How to Find & Understand the Law .... $21.95 ... LRES
- Legal Research Made Easy (Video) .... $89.95 ... LRME

SENIORS

- Beat the Nursing Home Trap .... $18.95 ... ELD
- The Conservatorship Book (California Edition) .... $29.95 ... CNSV
- Social Security, Medicare & Pensions .... $19.95 ... SOA

SOFTWARE
Call or check our website for special discounts on Software!

- California Incorporator 2.0—DOS .... $79.95 ... INCI
- Living Trust Maker CD—Windows/Macintosh .... $79.95 ... LTM2
- Small Business Legal Pro 3 CD—Windows/Macintosh CD-ROM .... $79.95 ... SBCD3
- Nolo's Partnership Maker 1.0—DOS .... $79.95 ... PAGI1
- Personal RecordKeeper 4.0 CD—Windows/Macintosh .... $49.95 ... RKM4
- Patent It Yourself CD—Windows .... $229.95 ... PYP12
- WillMaker 6.0—Windows/Macintosh CD-ROM .... $69.95 ... WD6

Special Upgrade Offer
Get 25% off the latest edition off your Nolo book

It's important to have the most current legal information. Because laws and legal procedures change often, we update our books regularly. To help keep you up-to-date we are extending this special upgrade offer. Cut out and mail the title portion of the cover of your old Nolo book and we'll give you 25% off the retail price of the NEW EDITION of that book when you purchase directly from us. For more information call us at 1-800-992-6656. This offer is to individuals only.

- ⌑ Book with disk
- ⬤ Book with CD-ROM

ORDER FORM

Code	Quantity	Title	Unit price	Total
		Subtotal		
		California residents add Sales Tax		
		Basic Shipping ($6.00 for 1 item; $7.00 for 2 or more)		
		UPS RUSH delivery $7.50–any size order*		
		TOTAL		

Name

Address

(UPS to street address, Priority Mail to P.O. boxes)

* Delivered in 3 business days from receipt of order.
S.F. Bay Area use regular shipping.

FOR FASTER SERVICE, USE YOUR CREDIT CARD AND OUR TOLL-FREE NUMBERS

Order 24 hours a day	1-800-992-6656
Fax your order	1-800-645-0895
e-mail	cs@nolo.com
General Information	1-510-549-1976
Customer Service	1-800-728-3555, Mon.-Fri. 9am-5pm, PST

METHOD OF PAYMENT

☐ Check enclosed

☐ VISA ☐ MasterCard ☐ Discover Card ☐ American Express

Account #   Expiration Date

Authorizing Signature

Daytime Phone

PRICES SUBJECT TO CHANGE.

VISIT OUR OUTLET STORES!

You'll find our complete line of books and software, all at a discount.

BERKELEY
950 Parker Street
Berkeley, CA 94710
1-510-704-2248

SAN JOSE
111 N. Market Street, #115
San Jose, CA 95113
1-408-271-7240

VISIT US ONLINE!

on the Internet
www.nolo.com

NOLO PRESS 950 PARKER ST., BERKELEY, CA 94710

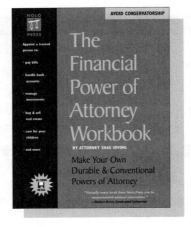

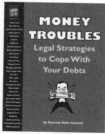

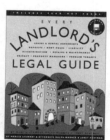

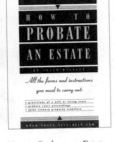
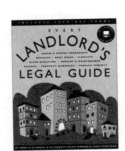
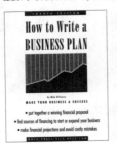

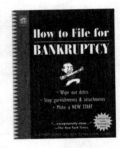

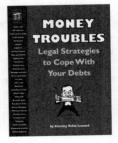

Take 1 minute &
Get a 1-year Nolo *News*
subscription free!*

With our quarterly magazine, the **NOLO** *News*, you'll

- **Learn** about important legal changes that affect you
- **Find out first** about new Nolo products
- **Keep current** with practical articles on everyday law
- **Get answers** to your legal questions in *Ask Auntie Nolo's* advice column

- **Save money** with special Subscriber Only discounts
- **Tickle your funny bone** with our famous *Lawyer Joke* column.

It only takes 1 minute to reserve your free 1-year subscription or to extend your **NOLO** *News* subscription.

CALL
1-800-992-6656

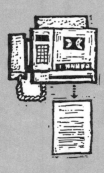

FAX
1-800-645-0895

E-MAIL
NOLOSUB@NOLOPRESS.com

OR MAIL US THIS
POSTAGE-PAID
REGISTRATION CARD

*U.S. ADDRESSES ONLY.

ONE YEAR INTERNATIONAL SUBSCRIPTIONS:
CANADA & MEXICO $10.00;
ALL OTHER FOREIGN ADDRESSES $20.00.

R E G I S T R A T I O N   C A R D

NAME _____ DATE _____

ADDRESS _____

_____

CITY _____ STATE _____ ZIP _____

PHONE _____ E-MAIL _____

WHERE DID YOU HEAR ABOUT THIS BOOK? _____

WHERE DID YOU PURCHASE THIS PRODUCT? _____

DID YOU CONSULT A LAWYER? (PLEASE CIRCLE ONE)   YES   NO   NOT APPLICABLE

DID YOU FIND THIS BOOK HELPFUL?   (VERY)   5   4   3   2   1   (NOT AT ALL)

SUGGESTIONS FOR IMPROVING THIS PRODUCT _____

_____

WAS IT EASY TO USE?   (VERY EASY)   5   4   3   2   1   (VERY DIFFICULT)

DO YOU OWN A COMPUTER? IF SO, WHICH FORMAT? (PLEASE CIRCLE ONE)   WINDOWS   DOS   MAC

We occasionally make our mailing list available to carefully selected companies whose products may be of interest to you. If you do not wish to receive mailings from these companies, please check this box ❑

NEST 4.0

NOLO IN THE NEWS

"**N**olo helps lay people perform legal tasks without the aid—or fees—of lawyers."

—**USA TODAY**

Nolo books are ..."written in plain language, free of legal mumbo jumbo, and spiced with witty personal observations."

—**ASSOCIATED PRESS**

"...Nolo publications...guide people simply through the how, when, where and why of law."

—**WASHINGTON POST**

"Increasingly, people who are not lawyers are performing tasks usually regarded as legal work... And consumers, using books like Nolo's, do routine legal work themselves."

—**NEW YORK TIMES**

"...All of [Nolo's] books are easy-to-understand, are updated regularly, provide pull-out forms...and are often quite moving in their sense of compassion for the struggles of the lay reader."

—**SAN FRANCISCO CHRONICLE**